Major Problems in American Colonial History

MAJOR PROBLEMS IN AMERICAN HISTORY SERIES

GENERAL EDITOR
THOMAS G. PATERSON

Major Problems
in American
Colonial History

DOCUMENTS AND ESSAYS

EDITED BY
KAREN ORDAHL KUPPERMAN
UNIVERSITY OF CONNECTICUT

D. C. HEATH AND COMPANY
Lexington, Massachusetts   Toronto

Address editorial correspondence to:

D. C. Heath
125 Spring Street
Lexington, MA 02173

Published simultaneously in Canada.

Printed in the United States of America.

International Standard Book Number: 0–669–19922–2

Library of Congress Catalog Number: 91–78128

10 9 8 7 6

To David and Alison Quinn

Preface

The colonial period, often seen as remote and inaccessible by Americans, has been thrust to the center of national consciousness through the issues raised by the Columbian quincentennial. Ordinary people as well as professional historians increasingly are recognizing the roots of modern problems deep in the past, and they care profoundly about how the events and assumptions of the founding years are presented and interpreted. Groups formerly not heard are demanding a role in determining what history is and how it is written. Americans no longer are satisfied with a colonial story focusing exclusively on English transplantation and conceptualizing the subject as the slow, steady movement of civilization from east to west. Teachers and scholars in this field thus face unprecedented opportunities.

Meeting the challenge is made difficult by the fragmentation plaguing colonial history. Scholars traditionally have focused their work on a single region, usually the Chesapeake, New England, or the middle colonies, implicitly endorsing the idea that each area was quite different from the others and that only the English-dominated East Coast matters. There has been little opening for comparative work or for a search for common themes. As historians increasingly have sought to weave in those formerly excluded—women, American Indians, Africans, and other Europeans—they typically have placed these peoples' experiences in the same regionally constricted framework.

This volume seeks to open the field of American colonial history to regions and peoples left out in the traditional, English-centered approach. While certainly not ignoring national, regional, and ideological differences, the essays and documents offered here also illustrate the continuities and similarities in the experience of all parties in this great confluence of peoples. A sense of coherence in the field emerges as one moves beyond the traditional categories and reads more widely in the exciting new work under way on regions and peoples previously excluded.

Scholarly work does exist to create a new, more integrated colonial history, but in widely scattered sources. Ethnohistorians are producing a substantial body of scholarship revealing Native Americans as dynamic actors in the historical drama. Other scholars emphasize the Spanish presence. They reject the traditional view of Florida and the Southwest as mere outposts of the Spanish Empire—as areas important only because of Anglo actions in the nineteenth century. Finally, a large and growing body of recent scholarship has illuminated the impact of men and women from all over Europe and Africa. This volume, by bringing together work by scholars who have studied neglected regions and topics, as well as by scholars who have followed more traditional themes, seeks to contribute to the creation of a more representative and coherent field in American colonial history and makes the material available to teachers and students.

Major Problems in American Colonial History, like other volumes in this series, features a combination of scholarly essays and primary sources. Some of the essays represent classic studies, statements that remain influential because they offer stimulating conceptions of fundamental problems that attract anew each generation of historians. Most of the essays, however, are recent publications that explore the issues and problems engaging the present generation of scholars and teachers. Noteworthy for their clarity, these recent essays relate their material to the established concerns of colonial historians and offer bridges between new and old foci.

The primary sources collected here develop or illustrate the themes of the essays and allow students to read firsthand colonial men's and women's own descriptions of fears, ambitions, and lifeways. I have tried to give voice to the largest possible range of participants: women as well as men; African-Americans as well as European-Americans; humble men and women as well as public figures. The diversity and abundance of first-person testimony that survives is the best evidence of the importance of America in European eyes. Even though the co-lonial period is farthest from the modern classroom in time, the plight of men, women, and children caught up in an unprecedented undertaking for which no reliable cultural road map existed takes on a sense of immediacy when students confront the actors speaking for themselves. In cases where archaic spelling made primary texts too difficult or remote, thus impeding this sense of immediacy, the spelling has been modernized.

Conversations and experiences with many colleagues over the years have helped shape my conception of colonial history and my approaches to teaching it. Particularly influential was the experience of co-leading an extraordinary group of teachers in 1987 in a National Endowment for the Humanities–sponsored sum-mer seminar at the University of Connecticut for college and university teachers on classic texts in early American history; these sessions highlighted the rich possibilities for incorporating primary sources into the syllabus. In addition, an NEH fellowship at the John Carter Brown Library in 1989 exposed me to scholars and staff committed to the reality of a colonial American history not bounded by anachronistic national entities. As I prepared this book, many colleagues around the country generously shared their syllabi with me. I thank them, as well as the reviewers who read and criticized the draft tables of contents for D. C. Heath: Robert A. Becker, Louisiana State University; Richard L. Haan, Hartwick College; Dan M. Hockman, Eastern Illinois University; Gregory H. Nobles, Geor-gia Institute of Technology; Alan Rogers, Boston College; Rebecca S. Shoemaker, Indiana State University; and Rosemarie Zagarri, The Catholic University of America. Charlotte Gradie aided me in locating primary sources illuminating the Spanish experience in North America, as did Robert Naeher for the English. Joel Kupperman read and discussed many essays, helping me consider their suitability for an undergraduate audience. The editorial staff at D. C. Heath was impressively professional in dealing with the project from inception to publication. Sylvia Mallory, Managing Editor in the College Division, offered important aid at all stages in developing the book. Margaret Roll handled a bewildering variety of permissions requests with aplomb, and Rosemary R. Jaffe, who supervised the final editing and production, was always prompt and constructive in dealing with objections or advice. Series editor Thomas G. Paterson helped shape the structure and content of the book with just the right degree of oversight. The Heath team provided an atmosphere of professionalism that few publishers can match.

K. O. K.

Contents

CHAPTER   5
Challenges to the New England Way: Sects and Witches
Page 158

CHAPTER   6
The Chesapeake: Bacon's Rebellion and the Creation of a Creole Society
Page 191

CHAPTER   7
New Directions in Family Life and Labor
Page 234

C H A P T E R   1 2
Settling the Backcountry
Page 442

C H A P T E R   1 3
The Impact of the European Wars for Empire on America
Page 483

C H A P T E R   1 4
The Sum of the Colonial Experience
Page 539

Two Worlds Discover

Each Other

ॐ

Five centuries have passed since Christopher Columbus's first voyage across the Atlantic and since the revelation to both hemispheres of unknown lands and peoples. European statesmen, merchants, and scholars, spurred on by the Renaissance quest for knowledge and aided by the newly invented printing press, eagerly sought information about the newfound lands across the sea. Travelers to America were urged by their friends and sponsors to write about what they saw. Thus we have accounts left by people from all walks of life, from common seafarers to highly trained scholars, as they all tried to fit America and its diverse peoples into a framework that made sense. All humanity must be descended from Noah, according to the Bible. Therefore the ancestors of the Indians must have been known to the ancient world. Many writers concluded that the Americans were the descendents of the Ten Lost Tribes of Israel.

As Christians, they believed that God had chosen their time to reveal the Western Hemisphere and had given them the task of converting the Indians. As they wrote about Native Americans' religion, marriage customs, law, inheritance, and food, partly with a view to gauging how ripe they were for conversion, the Europeans invented a kind of ethnology, a new science of humankind. Their writings give many hints that the Indians themselves were analyzing the newcomers, attempting to fit them into a framework from their own experience. Each side misunderstood much about the other.

No European involved in the encounter ever wrote from a purely scholarly or religious perspective. All the accounts are practical in focus, because expeditions were financed by merchants. Thus all reveal a constant preoccupation with the kinds of rich products to be found in America. No one believed that the land would be appreciated merely for its own sake; voyages were enormously expensive, and only the discovery of valuable commodities would make constant contact worthwhile for European backers. On their side, the Americans were interested in acquiring articles, particularly equipment and weapons of metal, that the newcomers offered in exchange for their furs and precious metals. Trade quickly became the chief medium of cultural exchange.

Scholars now accept that Norse voyagers landed in Newfoundland about A.D. 1000 and actively explored there for about a decade. Erik the Red's saga (c. 1270), excerpted in the first document, describes an encounter in northern New England that was not followed up. Christopher Columbus believed that the islands on which he landed were outliers of Asia; his calculations drastically underestimated the circumference of the earth. The findings of other explorers revealed to the European public that the islands that Columbus found lay off two vast continents. In the second document, his first letter (1493), Columbus demonstrates the mixture of Christian aspiration, feelings of wonderment, and practical considerations that motivated these ventures; his fourth letter (1503) vividly records his disappointment at the course already taken in the developing relationship. Jacques Cartier, who explored the St. Lawrence River for France in the mid-1530s, found the large city of Hochelaga at the future site of Montreal. His account, reprinted in the third selection, contains a very early description of Indian life, including the practice of smoking tobacco.

Indian interpretations of events were gathered by European reporters. The legend of Maushop and his alienation, the subject of the fourth document, was one that appeared in many forms. Thomas Harriot collected Indian reactions to the colonists and the dramatic change the newcomers brought. The account in the fifth selection by Harriot, an Oxford-educated scholar, can be compared to that in the final document of shipmaster Arthur Barlowe, who describes the same people. Both men were sent by Sir Walter Raleigh to Roanoke in the 1580s.

Erik the Red's Saga, c. 1270

Karlsefni sailed south along the land with Snorri and Bjarni and the rest of their company. They journeyed a long time till they reached a river which flowed down from the land into a lake and so to the sea. There were such extensive bars off the mouth of the estuary that they were unable to get into the river except at full flood. Karlsefni and his men sailed into the estuary, and called the place Hop, Landlock Bay. There they found self-sown fields of wheat where the ground was low-lying, and vines wherever it was hilly. Every brook there was full of fish. They dug trenches at the meeting point of land and high water, and when the tide went out there were halibut in the trenches. There were vast numbers of animals of every kind in the forest. They were there for a fortnight enjoying themselves and saw nothing and nobody. They had their cattle with them.

Then early one morning when they looked about them they saw nine skin-boats, on board which staves were being swung which sounded just like flails threshing—and their motion was sunwise.

"What can this mean?" asked Karlsefni.

"Perhaps it is a token of peace," replied Snorri. "So let us take a white shield and hold it out towards them."

They did so, and those others rowed towards them, showing their astonishment, then came ashore. They were small ill favoured men, and had ugly hair on their heads. They had big eyes and were broad in the cheeks. For a while they remained there, astonished, and afterwards rowed off south past the headland.

Karlsefni and his men built themselves dwellings up above the lake; some of their houses stood near the mainland, and some near the lake. They now spent the winter there. No snow fell, and their entire stock found its food grazing in the open. But once spring came in they chanced early one morning to see how a multitude of skin-boats came rowing from the south round the headland, so many that the bay appeared sown with coals, and even so staves were being swung on every boat. Karlsefni and his men raised their shields, and they began trading together. Above all these people wanted to buy red cloth. They also wanted to buy swords and spears, but this Karlsefni and Snorri would not allow. They had dark unblemished skins to exchange for the cloth, and were taking a span's length of cloth for a skin, and this they tied round their heads. So it continued for a while, then when the cloth began to run short they cut it up so that it was no broader than a fingerbreadth, but the Skrælings gave just as much for it, or more.

The next thing was that the bull belonging to Karlsefni and his mates ran out of the forest bellowing loudly. The Skrælings were terrified by this, raced out to their boats and rowed south past the headland, and for three weeks running there was neither sight nor sound of them. But at the end of that period they saw a great multitude of Skræling boats coming up from the south like a streaming torrent. This time all the staves were being swung anti-sun-wise, and the Skrælings were all yelling aloud, so they took red shields and held them out against them. They clashed together and fought. There was a heavy shower of missiles, for the Skrælings had warslings too. Karlsefni and Snorri could see the Skrælings hoisting up on poles a big ball-shaped object, and blue-black in colour, which they sent flying inland over Karlsefni's troop, and it made a hideous noise where it came down. Great fear now struck into Karlsefni and all his following, so that there was no other thought in their heads than to run away up along the river to some steep rocks, and there put up a strong resistance.

Freydis came out-of-doors and saw how they had taken to their heels. "Why are you running from wretches like these?" she cried. "Such gallant lads as you, I thought for sure you would have knocked them on the head like cattle. Why, if I had a weapon, I think I could put up a better fight than any of you!"

They might as well not have heard her. Freydis was anxious to keep up with them, but was rather slow because of her pregnancy. She was moving after them into the forest when the Skrælings attacked her. She found a dead man in her path, Thorbrand Snorrason—he had a flat stone sticking out of his head. His sword lay beside him; she picked it up and prepared to defend herself with it. The Skrælings were now making for her. She pulled out her breasts from under her shift and slapped the sword on them, at which the Skrælings took fright, and ran off to their boats and rowed away. Karlsefni's men came up to her, praising her courage. Two of Karlsefni's men had fallen, and four Skrælings, but even so they had been overrun by sheer numbers. They now returned to their booths, puzzling over what force it was which had attacked them from the land side. For now it looked to them as though there had been only the one host, which came from the boats, and that the rest of the host must have been a delusion.

Further, the Skrælings had found a dead man whose axe lay beside him. One of them cut at a stone, the axe broke, and then he thought it useless because it could not stand up to the stone, so threw it down.

It now seemed plain to Karlsefni and his men that though the quality of the land was admirable, there would always be fear and strife dogging them there on account of those who already inhabited it. So they made ready to leave, setting their hearts on their own country . . .

Christopher Columbus Reports to Ferdinand and Isabella

First Voyage, 1492–1493

Knowing that it will afford you pleasure to learn that I have brought my undertaking to a successful termination, I have decided upon writing you this letter to acquaint you with all the events which have occurred in my voyage, and the discoveries which have resulted from it. Thirty-three days after my departure from Cadiz I reached the Indian sea, where I discovered many islands, thickly peopled, of which I took possession without resistance in the name of our most illustrious Monarch, by public proclamation and with unfurled banners. To the first of these islands, which is called by the Indians Guanahani, I gave the name of the blessed Saviour (San Salvador), relying upon whose protection I had reached this as well as the other islands; to each of these I also gave a name, ordering that one should be called Santa Maria de la Concepcion, another Fernandina, the third Isabella, the fourth Juana, and so with all the rest respectively. As soon as we arrived at that, which as I have said was named Juana, I proceeded along its coast a short distance westward, and found it to be so large and apparently without termination, that I could not suppose it to be an island, but the continental province of Cathay. Seeing, however, no towns or populous places on the sea coast, but only a few detached houses and cottages, with whose inhabitants I was unable to communicate, because they fled as soon as they saw us, I went further on, thinking that in my progress I should certainly find some city or village. . . . I afterwards dispatched two of our men to ascertain whether there were a king or any cities in that province. These men reconnoitred the country for three days, and found a most numerous population, and great numbers of houses, though small, and built without any regard to order: with which information they returned to us. In the mean time I had learned from some Indians whom I had seized, that that country was certainly an island: and therefore I sailed towards the east, coasting to the distance of three hundred and twenty-two miles, which brought us to the extremity of it; from this point I saw lying eastwards another island, fifty-four miles distant from Juana, to which I gave the name of Española: ... In that island also which I have before said we named Española, there are mountains of very great size and beauty, vast plains, groves, and very fruitful fields, admirably adapted for tillage, pasture, and habitation. The convenience and excellence of the harbours in this island, and the abundance of the rivers, so indispensable to the health of man, surpass anything that would be believed by one who had not seen it. The trees, herbage, and fruits of Española are very different from those of Juana, and moreover it abounds in various kinds of spices, gold, and other metals. The inhabitants of both sexes in this island, and in all the others which I have seen, or of which I have received information, go always naked as they were born, with the exception of some of the women, who use the covering of a leaf, or small bough, or an apron of cotton which they prepare for that purpose. None of them, as I have already said, are possessed of any iron, neither have they weapons, being unacquainted with, and indeed incompetent to use them, not from any deformity of body (for they are well-formed), but because they are timid and full of fear. They carry however in lieu of arms, canes dried in the sun, on the ends of which they fix heads of dried wood sharpened to a point, and even these they dare not use habitually; for it has often occurred when I have sent two or three of my men to any of the villages to speak with the natives, that they have come out in a disorderly troop, and have fled in such haste at the approach of our men, that the fathers forsook their children and the children their fathers. This timidity did not arise from any loss or injury that they had received from us; for, on the contrary, I gave to all I approached whatever articles I had about me, such as cloth and many other things, taking nothing of theirs in return: but they are naturally timid and fearful. As soon however as they see that they are safe, and have laid aside all fear, they are very simple and honest, and exceedingly liberal with all they have; none of them refusing any thing he may possess when he is asked for it, but on the contrary inviting us to ask them. They exhibit great love towards all others in preference to themselves: they also give objects of great value for trifles, and content themselves with very little or nothing in return. I however forbad that these trifles and articles of no value (such as pieces of dishes, plates, and glass, keys, and leather straps) should be given to them, although if they could obtain them, they imagined themselves to be possessed of the most beautiful trinkets in the world. It even happened that a sailor received for a leather strap as much gold as was worth three golden nobles, and for things of more trifling value offered by our men, especially-newly coined blancas, or any gold coins, the Indians would give whatever the seller required; as, for instance, an ounce and a half or two ounces of gold, or thirty or forty pounds of cotton, with which commodity they were already acquainted. Thus they bartered, like idiots, cotton and gold for fragments of bows, glasses, bottles, and jars; which I forbad as being unjust, and myself gave them many beautiful and acceptable articles which I had brought with me, taking nothing from them in return; I did this in order that I might the more easily conciliate them, that they might be led to become Christians, and be inclined to entertain a regard for the King and Queen, our Princes and all Spaniards, and that I might induce them to take an interest in seeking out, and collecting, and delivering to us such things as they possessed in abundance, but which we greatly needed. They practise no kind of idolatry, but have a firm belief that all strength and power, and indeed all good things, are in heaven, and that I had descended from thence with these ships and sailors, and under this impression was I received after they had thrown aside their fears. Nor are they slow or stupid, but of very clear understanding; and those men who have crossed to the neighbouring islands give an admirable description of everything they observed; but they never saw any people clothed, nor any ships like ours. On my arrival at that sea, I had taken some Indians by force from the first island that I came to, in order that they might learn our language, and communicate to us what they knew respecting the country; which plan succeeded excellently, and was a great advantage to us, for in a short time, either by gestures and signs, or by words, we were enabled to understand each other. These men are still travelling with me, and although they have been with us now a long time, they continue to entertain the idea that I have descended from heaven; and on our arrival at any new place they published this, crying out immediately with a loud voice to the other Indians, "Come, come and look upon beings of a celestial race": upon which both women and men, children and adults, young men and old, when they got rid of the fear they at first entertained, would come out in throngs, crowding the roads to see us, some bringing food, others drink, with astonishing affection and kindness. . . . I could not clearly understand whether the people possess any private property, for I observed that one man had the charge of distributing various things to the rest, but especially meat and provisions and the like. I did not find, as some of us had expected, any cannibals amongst them, but on the contrary men of great deference and kindness. Neither are they black, like the Ethiopians: their hair is smooth and straight: for they do not dwell where the rays of the sun strike most vividly,—and the sun has intense power there, the distance from the equinoctial line being, it appears, but six-and-twenty degrees. On the tops of the mountains the cold is very great, but the effect of this upon the Indians is lessened by their being accustomed to the climate, and by their frequently indulging in the use of very hot meats and drinks. Thus, as I have already said, I saw no cannibals, nor did I hear of any, except in a certain island called Charis, which is the second from Española on the side towards India, where dwell a people who are considered by the neighbouring islanders as most ferocious: and these feed upon human flesh. The same people have many kinds of canoes, in which they cross to all the surrounding islands and rob and plunder wherever they can; they are not different from the other islanders, except that they wear their hair long, like women, and make use of the bows and javelins of cane, with sharpened spear-points fixed on the thickest end, which I have before described, and therefore they are looked upon as ferocious, and regarded by the other Indians with unbounded fear; but I think no more of them than of the rest. . . . Finally, to compress into few words the entire summary of my voyage and speedy return, and of the advantages derivable therefrom, I promise, that with a little assistance afforded me by our most invincible sovereigns, I will procure them as much gold as they need, as great a quantity of spices, of cotton, and of mastic (which is only found in Chios), and as many men for the service of the navy as their Majesties may require. I promise also rhubarb and other sorts of drugs, which I am persuaded the men whom I have left in the aforesaid fortress have found already and will continue to find; for I myself have tarried no where longer than I was compelled to do by the winds, except in the city of Navidad, while I provided for the building of the fortress, and took the necessary precautions for the perfect security of the men I left there. Although all I have related may appear to be wonderful and unheard of, yet the results of my voyage would have been more astonishing if I had had at my disposal such ships as I required. But these great and marvellous results are not to be attributed to any merit of mine, but to the holy Christian faith, and to the piety and religion of our Sovereigns; for that which the unaided intellect of men could not compass, the spirit of God has granted to human exertions, for God is wont to hear the prayers of his servants who love his precepts even to the performance of apparent impossibilities. Thus it has happened to me in the present instance, who have accomplished a task to which the powers of mortal men had never hitherto attained; for if there have been those who have anywhere written or spoken of these islands, they have done so with doubts and conjectures, and no one has ever asserted that he has seen them, on which account their writings have been looked upon as little else than fables. Therefore let the king and queen, our princes and their most happy kingdoms, and all the other provinces of Christendom, render thanks to our Lord and Saviour Jesus Christ, who has granted us so great a victory and such prosperity. Let processions be made, and sacred feasts be held, and the temples be adorned with festive boughs. Let Christ rejoice on earth, as he rejoices in heaven in the prospect of the salvation of the souls of so many nations hitherto lost. Let us also rejoice, as well on account of the exaltation of our faith, as on account of the increase of our temporal prosperity, of which not only Spain, but all Christendom will be partakers.

Such are the events which I have briefly described. Farewell.

Lisbon, the 14th of March.

CHRISTOPHER COLUMBUS,
Admiral of the Fleet of the Ocean

Fourth Voyage, 1503

. . . Who will offer himself for this work? Should any one do so, I pledge myself, in the name of God, to convey him safely thither, provided the Lord permits me to return to Spain. The people who have sailed with me have passed through incredible toil and danger, and I beseech your Highnesses, since they are poor, to pay them promptly, and to be gracious to each of them according to their respective merits; for I can safely assert, that to my belief they are the bearers of the best news that ever were carried to Spain. With respect to the gold which belongs to Quibian, the cacique of Veragua, and other chiefs in the neighbouring country, although it appears by the accounts we have received of it to be very abundant, I do not think it would be well or desirable, on the part of your Highnesses, to take possession of it in the way of plunder; by fair dealing, scandal and disrepute will be avoided, and all the gold will thus reach your Highnesses' treasury without the loss of a grain. With one month of fair weather I shall complete my voyage. As I was deficient in ships, I did not persist in delaying my course; but in everything that concerns your Highnesses' service, I trust in Him who made me, and I hope also that my health will be re-established. I think your Highnesses will remember that I had intended to build some ships in a new manner, but the shortness of the time did not permit it. I had certainly foreseen how things would be. I think more of this opening for commerce, and of the lordship over such extensive mines, than of all that has been done in the Indies. This is not a child to be left to the care of a step-mother.

I never think of Española, and Paria, and the other countries, without shedding tears. I thought that what had occurred there would have been an example for others; on the contrary, these settlements are now in a languid state, although not dead, and the malady is incurable, or at least very extensive: let him who brought the evil come now and cure it, if he knows the remedy, or how to apply it; but when a disturbance is on foot, every one is ready to take the lead. It used to be the custom to give thanks and promotion to him who placed his person in jeopardy; but there is no justice in allowing the man who opposed this undertaking, to enjoy the fruits of it with his children. Those who left the Indies, avoiding the toils consequent upon the enterprise, and speaking evil of it and me, have since returned with official appointments,—such is the case now in Veragua: it is an evil example, and profitless both as regards the business in which we are embarked, and as respects the general maintenance of justice. The fear of this, with other sufficient considerations, which I clearly foresaw, caused me to beg your Highnesses, previously to my coming to discover these islands and terra firma, to grant me permission to govern in your royal name. Your Highnesses granted my request; and it was a privilege and treaty granted under the royal seal and oath, by which I was nominated viceroy, and admiral, and governor-general of all: and your Highnesses limited the extent of my government to a hundred leagues beyond the Azores and Cape Verde islands, by a line passing from one pole to the other, and gave me ample power over all that I might discover beyond this line; all which is more fully described in the official document.

But the most important affair of all, and that which cries most loudly for redress, remains inexplicable to this moment. For seven years was I at your royal court, where every one to whom the enterprise was mentioned, treated it as ridiculous; but now there is not a man, down to the very tailors, who does not beg to be allowed to become a discoverer. There is reason to believe, that they make the voyage only for plunder, and that they are permitted to do so, to the great disparagement of my honour, and the detriment of the undertaking itself. It is right to give God His due,—and to receive that which belongs to one's self. This is a just sentiment, and proceeds from just feelings. The lands in this part of the world, which are now under your Highnesses' sway, are richer and more extensive than those of any other Christian power, and yet, after that I had, by the Divine will, placed them under your high and royal sovereignty, and was on the point of bringing your majesties into the receipt of a very great and unexpected revenue; and while I was waiting for ships, to convey me in safety, and with a heart full of joy, to your royal presence, victoriously to announce the news of the gold that I had discovered, I was arrested and thrown, with my two brothers, loaded with irons, into a ship, stripped, and very ill-treated, without being allowed any appeal to justice. Who could believe, that a poor foreigner would have risen against your Highnesses, in such a place, without any motive or argument on his side; without even the assistance of any other prince upon which to rely; but on the contrary, amongst your own vassals and natural subjects, and with my sons staying at your royal court? I was twenty-eight years old when I came into your Highnesses' service, and now I have not a hair upon me that is not grey; my body is infirm, and all that was left to me, as well as to my brothers, has been taken away and sold, even to the frock that I wore, to my great dishonour. I cannot but believe that this was done without your royal permission. The restitution of my honour, the reparation of my losses, and the punishment of those who have inflicted them, will redound to the honour of your royal character; a similar punishment also is due to those who plundered me of my pearls, and who have brought a disparagement upon the privileges of my admiralty. Great and unexampled will be the glory and fame of your Highnesses, if you do this; and the memory of your Highnesses, as just and grateful sovereigns, will survive as a bright example to Spain in future ages. The honest devotedness I have always shown to your majesties' service, and the so unmerited outrage with which it has been repaid, will not allow my soul to keep silence, however much I may wish it: I implore your Highnesses to forgive my complaints. I am indeed in as ruined a condition as I have related; hitherto I have wept over others;—may Heaven now have mercy upon me, and may the earth weep for me. With regard to temporal things, I have not even a blanca for an offering; and in spiritual things, I have ceased here in the Indies from observing the prescribed forms of religion. Solitary in my trouble, sick, and in daily expectation of death, surrounded by millions of hostile savages full of cruelty, and thus separated from the blessed sacraments of our holy Church, how will my soul be forgotten if it be separated from the body in this foreign land? Weep for me, whoever has charity, truth, and justice! I did not come out on this voyage to gain to myself honour or wealth; this is a certain fact, for at that time all hope of such a thing was dead. I do not lie when I say, that I went to your Highnesses with honest purpose of heart, and sincere zeal in your cause. I humbly beseech your Highnesses, that if it please God to rescue me from this place, you will graciously sanction my pilgrimage to Rome and other holy places. May the Holy Trinity protect your Highnesses' lives, and add to the prosperity of your exalted position.

Done in the Indies, in the island of Jamaica, on the seventh of July, in the year one thousand five hundred and three.

Jacques Cartier Observes the St. Lawrence and Its People, 1535–1536

... And we sailed on in as fine weather as one could wish until [Saturday] October 2, when we arrived at Hochelaga, which is about forty-five leagues from the spot where we had left our bark. During this interval we came across on the way many of the people of the country, who brought us fish and other provisions, at the same time dancing and showing great joy at our coming. And in order to win and keep their friendship, the Captain made them a present of some knives, beads and other small trifles, whereat they were greatly pleased. And on reaching Hochelaga, there came to meet us more than a thousand persons, both men, women and children, who gave us as good a welcome as ever father gave to his son, making great signs of joy; for the men danced in one ring, the women in another and the children also apart by themselves. After this they brought us quantities of fish, and of their bread, which is made of Indian corn, throwing so much of it into our long-boats that it seemed to rain bread. Seeing this the Captain, accompanied by several of his men, went on shore; and no sooner had he landed than they all crowded about him and about the others, giving them a wonderful reception. And the women brought their babies in their arms to have the Captain and his companions touch them, while all held a merry-making which lasted more than half an hour. Seeing their generosity and friendliness, the Captain had the women all sit down in a row and gave them some tin beads and other trifles; and to some of the men he gave knives. Then he returned on board the long-boats to sup and pass the night, throughout which the Indians remained on the bank of the river, as near the long-boats as they could get, keeping many fires burning all night, and dancing and calling out every moment *aguyase* which is their term of salutation and joy.

How the Captain and the Gentlemen, accompanied by twenty-five well-armed and marshalled sailors, went to visit the village of Hochelaga; and of the situation of the place.

At daybreak the next day, the Captain, having put on his armour, had his men marshalled for the purpose of paying a visit to the village and home of these people, and to a mountain which lies near the town. The Captain was accompanied by the gentlemen and by twenty sailors, the remainder having been left behind to guard the long-boats. And he took three Indians of the village as guides to conduct them thither. When we had got under way, we discovered that the path was as well-trodden as it is possible to see, and that the country was the finest and most excellent one could find anywhere, being everywhere full of oaks, as beautiful as in any forest in France, underneath which the ground lay covered with acorns. And after marching about a league and a half, we met on the trail one of the headmen of the village of Hochelaga, accompanied by several Indians, who made signs to us that we should rest at that spot near a fire they had lighted on the path; which we did. Thereupon this headman began to make a speech and to harangue us, which, as before mentioned, is their way of showing joy and friendliness, welcoming in this way the Captain and his company. The Captain presented him with a couple of hatchets and a couple of knives, as well as with a cross and a crucifix, which he made him kiss and then hung it about his neck. For these the headman thanked the Captain. When this was done we marched on, and about half a league thence, found that the land began to be cultivated. It was fine land with large fields covered with the corn of the country, which resembles Brazil millet, and is about as large or larger than a pea. They live on this as we do on wheat. And in the middle of these fields is situated and stands the village of Hochelaga, near and adjacent to a mountain, the slopes of which are fertile and are cultivated, and from the top of which one can see for a long distance. We named this mountain "Mount Royal" [Mont Royal]. The village is circular and is completely enclosed by a wooden palisade in three tiers like a pyramid. The top one is built crosswise, the middle one perpendicular and the lowest one of strips of wood placed lengthwise. The whole is well joined and lashed after their manner, and is some two lances in height. There is only one gate and entrance to this village, and that can be barred up. Over this gate and in many places about the enclosure are species of galleries with ladders for mounting to them, which galleries are provided with rocks and stones for the defence and protection of the place. There are some fifty houses in this village, each about fifty or more paces in length, and twelve or fifteen in width, built completely of wood and covered in and bordered up with large pieces of the bark and rind of trees, as broad as a table, which are well and cunningly lashed after their manner. . . . This whole tribe gives itself to manual labor and to fishing merely to obtain the necessities of life; for they place no value upon the goods of this world, both because they are unacquainted with them, and because they do not move from home and are not nomads like those of Canada and of the Saguenay, notwithstanding that the Canadians and some eight or nine other tribes along this river are subjects of theirs. . . .

. . . They are by no means a laborious people and work the soil with short bits of wood about half a sword in length. With these they hoe their corn which they call ozisy, in size as large as a pea. Corn of a similar kind grows in considerable quantities in Brazil. They have also a considerable quantity of melons, cucumbers, pumpkins, pease and beans of various colours and unlike our own. Furthermore they have a plant, of which a large supply is collected in summer for the winter's consumption. They hold it in high esteem, though the men alone make use of it in the following manner. After drying it in the sun, they carry it about their necks in a small skin pouch in lieu of a bag, together with a hollow bit of stone or wood. Then at frequent intervals they crumble this plant into powder, which they place in one of the openings of the hollow instrument, and laying a live coal on top, such at the other end to such an extent, that they fill their bodies so full of smoke, that it streams out of their mouths and nostrils as from a chimney. They say it keeps them warm and in good health, and never go about without these things. We made a trial of this smoke. When it is in one's mouth, one would think one had taken powdered pepper, it is so hot. The women of this country work beyond comparison more than the men, both at fishing, which is much followed, as well as at tilling the ground and other tasks. Both the men, women and children are more indifferent to the cold than beasts; for in the coldest weather we experienced, and it was extraordinary severe, they would come to our ships every day across the ice and snow, the majority of them almost stark naked, which seems incredible unless one has seen them. While the ice and snow last, they catch a great number of wild animals such as fawns, stags and bears, hares, martens, foxes, otters and others. Of these they brought us very few; for they are heavy eaters and are niggardly with their provisions. They eat their meat quite raw, merely smoking it, and the same with their fish. From what we have seen and been able to learn of these people, I am of opinion that they could easily be moulded in the way one would wish. May God in His holy mercy turn His countenance towards them. Amen.

Maushop Leaves New England: An Indian Legend About Colonization

On the west end of Martha's Vineyard, are high cliffs of variegated coloured earths, known by the name of *Gayhead*. On the top of the hill is a large cavity, which has the appearance of the crater of an extinguished volcano, and there are evident marks of former subterraneous fires. The Indians who live about this spot have a tradition that a certain deity resided there before the Europeans came into America, that his name was *Maushop*; that he used to step out on a ledge of rocks which ran into the sea, and take up a whale, which he broiled for his own eating on the coals of the aforesaid volcano, and often invited the Indians to dine with him, or gave them the relicks of his meal. That once to shew their gratitude to *Maushop* for his very great kindness to them, they made an offering to him of all the tobacco which grew upon the island in one season. This was scarcely sufficient to fill his great pipe, but he received the present very graciously, smoked his pipe, and turned out the ashes of it into the sea, which formed the island of Nantucket. Upon the coming of the Europeans into America, *Maushop* retired in disgust, and has never since been seen.

Thomas Harriot Forecasts Indian-Colonist Relationships, 1588*

Of the Nature and Manners of the People

It resteth I speak a word or two of the natural inhabitants, their natures and manners, . . . as that you may know, how that they in respect of troubling our inhabiting and planting, are not to be feared, but that they shall have cause both to fear and love us, that shall inhabit with them.

They are a people clothed with loose mantles made of Deer skins, & aprons of the same round about their middles; all else naked; of such a difference of statures only as we in England, having no edge tools or weapons of iron or steel to offend us withal, neither know they how to make any: those weapons that they have, are only bows made of Witch hazel, & arrows of reeds, flat edged truncheons also of wood about a yard long, neither have

*Some of the spelling in this document has been modernized.

they anything to defend themselves but targets made of barks, and some armours made of sticks wickered together with thread. . . .

Their manner of wars amongst themselves is either by sudden surprising one another most commonly about the dawning of the day, or moonlight, or else by ambushes, or some subtle devices. Set battles are very rare, except it fall out where there are many trees, where either part may have some hope of defence, after the delivery of every arrow, in leaping behind some or other.

If there fall out any wars between us & them, what their fight is likely to be, we having advantages against them so many manner of ways, as by our discipline, our strange weapons and devices else, especially by ordinance great and small, it may be easily imagined; by the experience we have had in some places, the turning up of their heels against us in running away was their best defence. In respect of us they are a people poor, and for want of skill and judgment in the knowledge and use of our things, do esteem our trifles before things of greater value: Notwithstanding in their proper manner considering the want of such means as we have, they seem very ingenious; For although they have no such tools, nor any such crafts, sciences and arts as we; yet in those things they do, they show excellence of wit. And by how much they upon due consideration shall find our manner of knowledges and crafts to exceed theirs in perfection, and speed for doing or execution, by so much the more is it probable that they should desire our friendships & love, and have the greater respect for pleasing and obeying us. Whereby may be hoped if means of good government be used, that they may in short time be brought to civility and the embracing of true religion.

Some religion they have already, which although it be far from the truth, yet being as it is, there is hope it may be the easier and sooner reformed.

They believe that there are many Gods which they call *Montóac,* but of different sorts and degrees; one only chief and great God, which hath been from all eternity. Who as they affirm when he purposed to make the world, made first other gods of a principal order to be as means and instruments to be used in the creation and government to follow; and after the Sun, Moon, and Stars as petty gods, and the instruments of the other order more principal. First they say were made waters, out of which by the gods was made all diversity of creatures that are visible or invisible.

For mankind they say a woman was made first, which by the working of one of the gods, conceived and brought forth children: And in such sort they say they had their beginning. But how many years or ages have passed since, they say they can make no relation, having no letters nor other such means as we to keep records of the particularities of times past, but only tradition from father to son. . . .

They believe also the immortality of the soul, that after this life as soon as the soul is departed from the body, according to the works it hath done, it is either carried to heaven the habitacle of gods, there to enjoy perpetual bliss and happiness, or else to a great pit or hole, which they think to be in the furthest parts of their part of the world toward the sunset, there to burn continually: the place they call *Popogusso.* . . .

Most things they saw with us, as Mathematical instruments, sea compasses, the virtue of the lodestone in drawing iron, a perspective glass whereby was showed many strange sights, burning glasses, wildfire works, guns, books, writing and reading, spring clocks that seem to go of themselves, and many other things that we had, were so strange unto them, and so far exceeded their capacities to comprehend the reason and means how they should be made and done, that they thought they were rather the works of gods than of men, or at the leastwise they had been given and taught us of the gods. Which made many of them to have such opinion of us, as that if they knew not the truth of god and religion already, it was rather to be had from us, whom God so specially loved than from a people that were so simple, as they found themselves to be in comparison of us. Whereupon greater credit was given unto that we spoke of concerning such matters.

Many times and in every town where I came, according as I was able, I made declaration of the contents of the Bible; that therein was set forth the true and only GOD, and his mighty works, that therein was contained the true doctrine of salvation through Christ, with many particularities of Miracles and chief points of religion, as I was able then to utter, and thought fit for the time. And although I told them the book materially & of itself was not of any such virtue, as I thought they did conceive, but only the doctrine therein contained; yet would many be glad to touch it, to embrace it, to kiss it, to hold it to their breasts and heads, and stroke over all their body with it; to show their hungry desire of that knowledge which was spoken of.

The *Wiroans* with whom we dwelt called *Wingina,* and many of his people would be glad many times to be with us at our prayers, and many times call upon us both in his own town, as also in others whither he sometimes accompanied us, to pray and sing Psalms; hoping thereby to be partaker of the same effects which we by that means also expected.

Twice this *Wiroans* was so grievously sick that he was like to die, and as he lay languishing, doubting of any help by his own priests, and thinking he was in such danger for offending us and thereby our god, sent for some of us to pray and be a means to our God that it would please him either that he might live, or after death dwell with him in bliss, so likewise were the requests of many others in the like case.

On a time also when their corn began to wither by reason of a drought which happened extraordinarily, fearing that it had come to pass by reason that in something they had displeased us, many would come to us & desire us to pray to our God of England, that he would preserve their corn, promising that when it was ripe we also should be partakers of the fruit.

There could at no time happen any strange sickness, losses, hurts, or any other cross unto them, but that they would impute to us the cause or means thereof for offending or not pleasing us.

One other rare and strange accident, leaving others, will I mention before I end, which moved the whole country that either knew or heard of us, to have us in wonderful admiration.

There was no town where we had any subtle device practiced against us, we leaving it unpunished or not revenged (because we sought by all means possible to win them by gentleness) but that within a few days after our departure from every such town, the people began to die very fast, and many in short space; in some towns about twenty, in some forty, in some sixty, & in one six score, which in truth was very many in respect of their numbers. This happened in no place that we could learn but where we had been where they used some practice against us, and after such time; The disease also was so strange, that they neither knew what it was, nor how to cure it; the like by report of the oldest men in the country never happened before, time out of mind. A thing specially observed by us, as also by the natural inhabitants themselves.

Insomuch that when some of the inhabitants which were our friends & especially the *Wiroans Wingina* had observed such effects in four or five towns to follow their wicked practices, they were persuaded that it was the work of our God through our means, and that we by him might kill and slay whom we would without weapons and not come near them.

And thereupon when it had happened that they had understanding that any of their enemies had abused us in our journeys, hearing that we had wrought no revenge with our weapons, & fearing upon some cause the matter should so rest: did come and entreat us that we would be a means to our God that they as others that had dealt ill with us might in like sort die; alleging how much it would be for our credit and profit as also theirs; and hoping furthermore that we would do so much at their requests in respect of the friendship we profess them.

Whose entreaties although we showed that they were ungodly, affirming that our God would not subject himself to any such prayers and requests of men: that indeed all things have been and were to be done according to his good pleasure as he had ordained: and that we to show ourselves his true servants ought rather to make petition for the contrary, that they with them might live together with us, be made partakers of his truth & serve him in righteousness; but notwithstanding in such sort, that we refer that as all other things, to be done according to his divine will & pleasure, and as by his wisdom he had ordained to be best.

Yet because the effect fell out so suddenly and shortly after according to their desires, they thought nevertheless it came to pass by our means, and that we in using such speeches unto them did but dissemble the matter, and therefore came unto us to give us thanks in their manner that although we satisfied them not in promise, yet in deeds and effect we had fulfilled their desires.

This marvelous accident in all the country wrought so strange opinions of us, that some people could not tell whether to think us gods or men, and the rather because that all the space of their sickness, there was no man of ours known to die, or that was especially sick: they noted also that we had no women among us, neither that we did care for any of theirs.

Some therefore were of opinion that we were not born of women, and therefore not mortal, but that we were men of an old generation many years past then risen again to immortality. . . .

Arthur Barlowe Sees America
as the Garden of Eden, 1584

The next day there came unto us divers boats, and in one of them the King's brother, accompanied with forty or fifty men, very handsome and goodly people, and in their behavior as mannerly and civil as any of Europe. His name was Granganimeo, and the king is called Wingina, the country Wingandacoa, and now by Her Majesty Virginia. The manner of his coming was in this sort: he left his boats altogether as the first man did a little from the ships by the shore, and came along to the place over against the ships, followed with forty men. When he came to the place, his servants spread a long mat upon the ground, on which he sat down, and at the other end of the mat four others of his company did the like, the rest of his men stood round about him, somewhat afar off: when we came to the shore to him with our weapons, he never moved from his place, nor any of the other four, nor never mistrusted any harm to be offered from us, but sitting still he beckoned us to come and sit by him, which we performed: and being set he made all signs of joy and welcome, striking on his head and his breast and afterwards on ours, to show we were all one, smiling and making show the best he could of all love, and familiarity. After he had made a long speech unto us, we presented him with divers things, which he received very joyfully, and thankfully. None of the company durst speak one word all the time: only the four which were at the other end, spake one in the other's ear very softly. . . .

. . . A day or two after this, we fell to trading with them, exchanging some things that we had, for Chamois, Buff, and Deer skins: when we showed him all our packet of merchandise, of all things that he saw, a bright tin dish most pleased him, which he presently took up and clapped it before his breast, and after made a hole in the brim thereof and hung it about his neck, making signs that it would defend him against his enemies' arrows: for those people maintain a deadly and terrible war, with the people and King adjoining. We exchanged our tin dish for twenty skins, worth twenty Crowns, or twenty Nobles: and a copper kettle for fifty skins worth fifty Crowns. They offered us good exchange for our hatchets, and axes, and for knives, and would have given any thing for swords: but we would not depart with any. After two or three days the King's brother came aboard the ships, and drank wine, and eat of our meat and of our bread, and liked exceedingly thereof: and after a few days overpassed, he brought his wife with him to the ships, his daughter and two or three children: his wife was very well favoured, of mean stature, and very bashful: she had on her back a long cloak of leather, with the fur side next to her body, and before her a piece of the same: about her forehead she had a band of white Coral, and so had her husband many times: in her ears she had bracelets of pearls hanging down to her middle, (whereof we delivered your worship a little bracelet) and those were of the bigness of good peas. The rest of her women of the better sort had pendants of copper hanging in

Some of the spelling in this document has been modernized.

either ear, and some of the children of the king's brother and other noble men, have five or six in either ear: he himself had upon his head a broad plate of gold, or copper, for being unpolished we knew not what metal it should be, neither would he by any means suffer us to take it off his head, but feeling it, it would bow very easily. His apparel was as his wife's, only the women wear their hair long on both sides, and the men but on one. They are of colour yellowish, and their hair black for the most part, and yet we saw children that had very fine auburn, and chestnut coloured hair. . . .

. . . And we both noted there, and you have understood since by these men, which we brought home, that no people in the world carry more respect to their King, Nobility, and Governours, then these do. . . .

The King's brother had great liking of our armour, a sword, and divers other things which we had: and offered to lay a great box of pearl in gage [pawn] for them: but we refused it for this time, because we would not make them know, that we esteemed thereof, until we had understood in what places of the country the pearl grew: which now your Worship doth very well understand.

He was very just of his promise: for many times we delivered him merchandise upon his word, but ever he came within the day and performed his promise. He sent us every day a brace or two of fat Bucks, Conies [rabbits], Hares, Fish the best of the world. He sent us divers kinds of fruits, Melons, Walnuts, Cucumbers, Gourds, Peas, and divers roots, and fruits very excellent good, and of their Country corn, which is very white, fair and well tasted, and groweth three times in five months: in May they sow, in July they reap, in June they sow, in August they reap: in July they sow, in September they reap: only they cast the corn into the ground, breaking a little of the soft turf with a wooden mattock, or pickaxe: our selves proved the soil, and put some of our Peas in the ground, and in ten days they were of fourteen inches high: they have also Beans very fair of divers colours and wonderful plenty: some growing naturally, and some in their gardens, and so have they both wheat and oats. . . .

. . . We were entertained with all love, and kindness, and with as much bounty, after their manner, as they could possibly devise. We found the people most gentle, loving, and faithful, void of all guile, and treason, and such as lived after the manner of the golden age. The earth bringeth forth all things in abundance, as in the first creation, without toil or labour. The people only care to defend themselves from the cold, in their short winter, and to feed themselves with such meat as the soil affordeth: . . .

❧ E S S A Y S

Traditionally historians have treated the events discussed here as the "discovery of the new world" by Europeans, implying passivity on the part of America's native peoples. The older view implicitly has seen the flow of culture as one way, east to west, and has assumed that the main story is the European conquest. More recently historians have emphasized that the confrontation was nothing less than a collision of biospheres, a bringing together of plants and animals from two formerly isolated worlds with enormous and entirely unforeseen consequences. Such an event could occur only once in the history of our planet. Although the participants were but dimly aware of the great drama in which they played roles, the documents they left provide evidence for environmental historians such as Alfred Crosby of the University of Texas, William Cronon of Yale University, and Richard White of the University of Utah to reshape our understanding of its consequences.

Colonization as a "Swarming"

ALFRED CROSBY

None of the major genetic groupings of humankind is as oddly distributed about the world as European, especially western European, whites. Almost all the peoples we call Mongoloids live in the single contiguous land mass of Asia. Black Africans are divided between three continents—their homeland and North and South America—but most of them are concentrated in their original latitudes, the tropics, facing each other across one ocean. European whites were all recently concentrated in Europe, but in the last few centuries have burst out, as energetically as if from a burning building, and have created vast settlements of their kind in the South Temperate Zone and North Temperate Zone (excepting Asia, a continent already thoroughly and irreversibly tenanted). In Canada and the United States together they amount to nearly 90 percent of the population; in Argentina and Uruguay together to over 95 percent; in Australia to 98 percent; and in New Zealand to 90 percent. The only nations in the Temperate Zones outside of Asia which do not have enormous majorities of European whites are Chile, with a population of two-thirds mixed Spanish and Indian stock, and South Africa, where blacks outnumber whites six to one. How odd that these two, so many thousands of miles from Europe, should be exceptions in *not* being predominantly pure European.

Europeans have conquered Canada, the United States, Argentina, Uruguay, Australia, and New Zealand not just militarily and economically and technologically—as they did India, Nigeria, Mexico, Peru, and other tropical lands, whose native people have long since expelled or interbred with and even absorbed the invaders. In the Temperate Zone lands listed above Europeans conquered and triumphed demographically. These, for the sake of convenience, we will call the Lands of the Demographic Takeover.

There is a long tradition of emphasizing the contrasts between Europeans and Americans—a tradition honored by such names as Henry James and Frederick Jackson Turner—but the vital question is really why Americans are so European. And why the Argentinians, the Uruguayans, the Australians, and the New Zealanders are so European in the obvious genetic sense.

The reasons for the relative failure of the European demographic takeover in the tropics are clear. In tropical Africa, until recently, Europeans died in

Alfred W. Crosby, "Ecological Imperialism: The Overseas Migration of Western Europeans as a Biological Phenomenon," *The Texas Quarterly*, 21(1978), 103–117. Reprinted with permission of Alfred W. Crosby.

droves of the fevers; in tropical America they died almost as fast of the same diseases, plus a few native American additions. Furthermore, in neither region did European agricultural techniques, crops, and animals prosper. Europeans did try to found colonies for settlement, rather than merely exploitation, but they failed or achieved only partial success in the hot lands. The Scots left their bones as monument to their short-lived colony at Darien at the turn of the eighteenth century. The English Puritans who skipped Massachusetts Bay Colony to go to Providence Island in the Caribbean Sea did not even achieve a permanent settlement, much less a Commonwealth of God. The Portuguese who went to northeastern Brazil created viable settlements, but only by perching themselves on top of first a population of native Indian laborers and then, when these faded away, a population of laborers imported from Africa. They did achieve a demographic takeover, but only by interbreeding with their servants. The Portuguese in Angola, who helped supply those servants, never had a breath of a chance to achieve a demographic takeover. There was much to repel and little to attract the mass of Europeans to the tropics, and so they stayed home or went to the lands where life was healthier, labor more rewarding, and where white immigrants, by their very number, encouraged more immigration.

In the cooler lands, the colonies of the Demographic Takeover, Europeans achieved very rapid population growth by means of immigration, by increased life span, and by maintaining very high birthrates. Rarely has population expanded more rapidly than it did in the eighteenth and nineteenth centuries in these lands. It is these lands, especially the United States, that enabled Europeans and their overseas offspring to expand from something like 18 percent of the human species in 1650 to well over 30 percent in 1900. Today 670 million Europeans live in Europe, and 250 million or so other Europeans—genetically as European as any left behind in the Old World—live in the Lands of the Demographic Takeover, an ocean or so from home. What the Europeans have done with unprecedented success in the past few centuries can accurately be described by a term from apiculture: They have swarmed.

They swarmed to lands which were populated at the time of European arrival by peoples as physically capable of rapid increase as the Europeans, and yet who are now small minorities in their homelands and sometimes no more than relict populations. These population explosions among colonial Europeans of the past few centuries coincided with population crashes among the aborigines. If overseas Europeans have historically been less fatalistic and grim than their relatives in Europe, it is because they have viewed the histories of their nations very selectively. When he returned from his world voyage on the *Beagle* in the 1830s, Charles Darwin, as a biologist rather than a historian, wrote, "Wherever the European has trod, death seems to pursue the aboriginal."

Any respectable theory which attempts to explain the Europeans' demographic triumphs has to provide explanations for at least two phenomena. The first is the decimation and demoralization of the aboriginal populations of Canada, the United States, Argentina, and others. The obliterating defeat of these populations was not simply due to European technological superiority.

The Europeans who settled in temperate South Africa seemingly had the same advantages as those who settled in Virginia and New South Wales, and yet how different was their fate. The Bantu-speaking peoples, who now overwhelmingly outnumber the whites in South Africa, were superior to their American, Australian, and New Zealand counterparts in that they possessed iron weapons, but how much more inferior to a musket or a rifle is a stone-pointed spear than an iron-pointed spear? The Bantu have prospered demographically not because of their numbers at the time of first contact with whites, which were probably not greater per square mile than those of the Indians east of the Mississippi River. Rather, the Bantu have prospered because they survived military conquest, avoided the conquerors, or became their indispensable servants—and in the long run because they reproduced faster than the whites. In contrast, why did so few of the natives of the Lands of the Demographic Takeover survive?

Second, we must explain the stunning, even awesome success of European agriculture, that is, the European way of manipulating the environment in the Lands of the Demographic Takeover. The difficult progress of the European frontier in the Siberian *taiga* or the Brazilian *sertão* or the South African *veldt* contrasts sharply with its easy, almost fluid advance in North America. Of course, the pioneers of North America would never have characterized their progress as easy: Their lives were filled with danger, deprivation, and unremitting labor; but as a group they always succeeded in taming whatever portion of North America they wanted within a few decades and usually a good deal less time. Many individuals among them failed—they were driven mad by blizzards and dust storms, lost their crops to locusts and their flocks to cougars and wolves, or lost their scalps to understandably inhospitable Indians—but as a group they always succeeded—and in terms of human generations, very quickly.

In attempting to explain these two phenomena, let us examine four categories of organisms deeply involved in European expansion: (1) human beings; (2) animals closely associated with human beings—both the desirable animals like horses and cattle and undesirable varmints like rats and mice; (3) pathogens or microorganisms that cause disease in humans; and (4) weeds. Is there a pattern in the histories of these groups which suggests an overall explanation for the phenomenon of the Demographic Takeover or which at least suggests fresh paths of inquiry?

Europe has exported something in excess of sixty million people in the past few hundred years. Great Britain alone exported over twenty million. The great mass of these white emigrants went to the United States, Argentina, Canada, Australia, Uruguay, and New Zealand. (Other areas to absorb comparable quantities of Europeans were Brazil and Russia east of the Urals. These would qualify as Lands of the Demographic Takeover except that large fractions of their populations are non-European.)

In stark contrast, very few aborigines of the Americas, Australia, or New Zealand ever went to Europe. Those who did often died not long after arrival. The fact that the flow of human migration was almost entirely from Europe to her colonies and not vice versa is not startling—or very enlightening. Europeans controlled overseas migration, and Europe needed to export, not import, labor. But this pattern of one-way migration is significant in that it reappears in other connections.

The vast expanses of forests, savannas, and steppes in the Lands of the Demographic Takeover were inundated by animals from the Old World, chiefly from Europe. Horses, cattle, sheep, goats, and pigs have for hundreds of years been among the most numerous of the quadrupeds of these lands, which were completely lacking in these species at the time of first contact with the Europeans. By 1600 enormous feral herds of horses and cattle surged over the pampas of the Río de la Plata (today's Argentina and Uruguay) and over the plains of northern Mexico. By the beginning of the seventeenth century packs of Old World dogs gone wild were among the predators of these herds.

In the forested country of British North America population explosions among imported animals were also spectacular, but only by European standards, not by those of Spanish America. In 1700 in Virginia feral hogs, said one witness, "swarm like vermaine upon the Earth," and young gentlemen were entertaining themselves by hunting wild horses of the inland counties. In Carolina the herds of cattle were "incredible, being from one to two thousand head in one Man's Possession." In the eighteenth and early nineteenth centuries the advancing European frontier from New England to the Gulf of Mexico was preceded into Indian territory by an avant-garde of semiwild herds of hogs and cattle tended, now and again, by semiwild herdsmen, white and black.

The first English settlers landed in Botany Bay, Australia, in January of 1788 with livestock, most of it from the Cape of Good Hope. The pigs and poultry thrived; the cattle did well enough; the sheep, the future source of the colony's good fortune, died fast. Within a few months two bulls and four cows strayed away. By 1804 the wild herds they founded numbered from three to five thousand head and were in possession of much of the best land between the settlements and the Blue Mountains. If they had ever found their way through the mountains to the grasslands beyond, the history of Australia in the first decades of the nineteenth century might have been one dominated by cattle rather than sheep. As it is, the colonial government wanted the land the wild bulls so ferociously defended, and considered the growing practice of convicts running away to live off the herds as a threat to the whole colony; so the adult cattle were shot and salted down and the calves captured and tamed. The English settlers imported wooly sheep from Europe and sought out the interior pastures for them. The animals multiplied rapidly, and when Darwin made his visit to New South Wales in 1836, there were about a million sheep there for him to see.

The arrival of Old World livestock probably affected New Zealand more radically than any other of the Lands of the Demographic Takeover. Cattle, horses, goats, pigs and—in this land of few or no large predators—even the usually timid sheep went wild. In New Zealand herds of feral farm animals were practicing the ways of their remote ancestors as late as the 1940s and no doubt still run free. Most of the sheep, though, stayed under human control, and within a decade of Great Britain's annexation of New Zealand in 1840, her new acquisition was home to a quarter million sheep. In 1974 New Zealand had over fifty-five million sheep, about twenty times more sheep than people.

In the Lands of the Demographic Takeover the European pioneers were accompanied and often preceded by their domesticated animals, walking sources of food, leather, fiber, power, and wealth, and these animals often adapted more rapidly to the new surroundings and reproduced much more rapidly than their masters. To a certain extent, the success of Europeans as colonists was automatic as soon as they put their tough, fast, fertile, and intelligent animals ashore. The latter were sources of capital that sought out their own sustenance, improvised their own protection against the weather, fought their own battles against predators and, if their masters were smart enough to allow calves, colts, and lambs to accumulate, could and often did show the world the amazing possibilities of compound interest.

The honey bee is the one insect of worldwide importance which human beings have domesticated, if we may use the word in a broad sense. Many species of bees and other insects produce honey, but the one which does so in greatest quantity and which is easiest to control is a native of the Mediterranean area and the Middle East, the honey bee (*Apis mellifera*). The European has probably taken this sweet and short-tempered servant to every colony he ever established, from Arctic to Antarctic Circle, and the honey bee has always been one of the first immigrants to set off on its own. Sometimes the advance of the bee frontier could be very rapid: The first hive in Tasmania swarmed sixteen times in the summer of 1832.

Thomas Jefferson tells us that the Indians of North America called the honey bees "English flies," and St. John de Crèvecoeur, his contemporary, wrote that "The Indians look upon them with an evil eye, and consider their progress into the interior of the continent as an omen of the white man's approach: thus, as they discover the bees, the news of the event, passing from mouth to mouth, spreads sadness and consternation on all sides."

Domesticated creatures that traveled from the Lands of the Demographic Takeover to Europe are few. Australian aborigines and New Zealand Maoris had a few tame dogs, unimpressive by Old World standards and unwanted by the whites. Europe happily accepted the American Indians' turkeys and guinea pigs, but had no need for their dogs, llamas, and alpacas. Again the explanation is simple: Europeans, who controlled the passage of large animals across the oceans, had no need to reverse the process.

It is interesting and perhaps significant, though, that the exchange was just as one-sided for varmints, the small mammals whose migrations Europeans often tried to stop. None of the American or Australian or New Zealand equivalents of rats have become established in Europe, but Old World varmints, especially rats, have colonized right alongside the Europeans in the Temperate Zones. Rats of assorted sizes, some of them almost surely European immigrants, were tormenting Spanish Americans by at least the end of the sixteenth century. European rats established a beachhead in Jamestown, Virginia, as early as 1609, when they almost starved out the colonists by eating their food stores. In Buenos Aires the increase in rats kept pace with that of cattle, according to an early nineteenth-century witness. European rats proved as aggressive as the Europeans in New Zealand, where they completely replaced the local rats in the North Islands as early as the 1840s. Those poor creatures are probably completely extinct today or exist only in tiny relict populations.

The European rabbits are not usually thought of as varmints, but where there are neither diseases nor predators to hold down their numbers they can become the worst of pests. In 1859 a few members of the species *Orytolagus cuniculus* (the scientific name for the protagonists of all the Peter Rabbits of literature) were released in southeast Australia. Despite massive efforts to stop them, they reproduced—true to their reputation—and spread rapidly all the way across Australia's southern half to the Indian Ocean. In 1950 the rabbit population of Australia was estimated at 500 million, and they were out-competing the nation's most important domesticated animals, sheep, for the grasses and herbs. They have been brought under control, but only by means of artificially fomenting an epidemic of myxomatosis, a lethal American rabbit disease. The story of rabbits and myxomatosis in New Zealand is similar.

Europe, in return for her varmints, has received muskrats and gray squirrels and little else from America, and nothing at all of significance from Australia or New Zealand, and we might well wonder if muskrats and squirrels really qualify as varmints. As with other classes of organisms, the exchange has been a one-way street.

None of Europe's emigrants were as immediately and colossally successful as its pathogens, the microorganisms that make human beings ill, cripple them, and kill them. Whenever and wherever Europeans crossed the oceans and settled, the pathogens they carried created prodigious epidemics of smallpox, measles, tuberculosis, influenza, and a number of other diseases. It was this factor, more than any other, that Darwin had in mind as he wrote of the Europeans' deadly tread.

The pathogens transmitted by the Europeans, unlike the Europeans themselves or most of their domesticated animals, did at least as well in the tropics as in the temperate Lands of the Demographic Takeover. Epidemics devastated Mexico, Peru, Brazil, Hawaii, and Tahiti soon after the Europeans made the first contact with aboriginal populations. Some of these populations were able to escape demographic defeat because their initial numbers were so large that a small fraction was still sufficient to maintain occupation of, if not title to, the land, and also because the mass of Europeans were never attracted to the tropical lands, not even if they were partially vacated. In the Lands of the Demographic Takeover the aboriginal populations were too sparse to rebound from the onslaught of disease or were inundated by European immigrants before they could recover.

The First Strike Force of the white immigrants to the Lands of the Demographic Takeover were epidemics. A few examples from scores of possible examples follow. Smallpox first arrived in the Río de la Plata region in 1558 or 1560 and killed, according to one chronicler possibly more interested in effect than accuracy, "more than a hundred thousand Indians" of the heavy riverine population there. An epidemic of plague or typhus decimated the Indians of the New England coast immediately before the founding of Plymouth. Smallpox or something similar struck the aborigines of Australia's Botany Bay in 1789, killed half, and rolled on into the interior. Some unidentified disease or diseases spread through the Maori tribes of the North Island of New Zealand in the 1790s, killing so many in a number of villages that the survivors were not able to bury the dead. After a series of such lethal and rapidly moving epidemics, then came the slow, unspectacular but thorough cripplers and killers like venereal disease and tuberculosis. In conjunction with the large numbers of white settlers these diseases were enough to smother aboriginal chances of recovery. First the blitzkrieg, then the mopping up.

The greatest of the killers in these lands was probably smallpox. The exception is New Zealand, the last of these lands to attract permanent European settlers. They came to New Zealand after the spread of vaccination in Europe, and so were poor carriers. As of the 1850s smallpox still had not come ashore, and by that time two-thirds of the Maori had been vaccinated. The tardy arrival of smallpox in these islands may have much to do with the fact that the Maori today comprise a larger percentage (9 percent) of their country's population than that of any other aboriginal people in any European colony or former European colony in either Temperate Zone, save only South Africa.

American Indians bore the full brunt of smallpox, and its mark is on their history and folklore. The Kiowa of the southern plains of the United States have a legend in which a Kiowa man meets Smallpox on the plain, riding a horse. The man asks, "Where do you come from and what do you do and why are you here?" Smallpox answers, "I am one with the white men—they are my people as the Kiowas are yours. Sometimes I travel ahead of them and sometimes behind. But I am always their companion and you will find me in their camps and their houses." "What can you do?" the Kiowa asks. "I bring death," Smallpox replies. "My breath causes children to wither like young plants in spring snow. I bring destruction. No matter how beautiful a woman is, once she has looked at me she becomes as ugly as death. And to men I bring not death alone, but the destruction of their children and the blighting of their wives. The strongest of warriors go down before me. No people who have looked on me will ever be the same."

In return for the barrage of diseases that Europeans directed overseas, they received little in return. Australia and New Zealand provided no new strains of pathogens to Europe—or none that attracted attention. And of America's native diseases none had any real influence on the Old World—with the likely exception of venereal syphilis, which almost certainly existed in the New World before 1492 and probably did not occur in its present form in the Old World.

Weeds are rarely history makers, for they are not as spectacular in their effects as pathogens. But they, too, influence our lives and migrate over the world despite human wishes. As such, like varmints and germs, they are better indicators of certain realities than human beings or domesticated animals.

The term "weed" in modern botanical usage refers to any type of plant which—because of especially large numbers of seeds produced per plant, or especially effective means of distributing those seeds, or especially tough roots and rhizomes from which new plants can grow, or especially tough seeds that survive the alimentary canals of animals to be planted with their droppings— spreads rapidly and outcompetes others on disturbed, bare soil. Weeds are plants that tempt the botanist to use such anthropomorphic words as "aggressive" and "opportunistic."

Many of the most successful weeds in the well-watered regions of the Lands of the Demographic Takeover are of European or Eurasian origin. French and Dutch and English farmers brought with them to North America their worst enemies, weeds, "to exhaust the land, hinder and damnify the Crop." By the last third of the seventeenth century at least twenty different types were widespread enough in New England to attract the attention of the English visitor, John Josselyn, who identified couch grass, dandelion, nettles, mallowes, knot grass, shepherd's purse, sow thistle, and clot burr and others. One of the most aggressive was plantain, which the Indians called "English-Man's Foot."

European weeds rolled west with the pioneers, in some cases spreading almost explosively. As of 1823 corn chamomile and maywood had spread up to but not across the Muskingum River in Ohio. Eight years later they were over the river. The most prodigiously imperialistic of the weeds in the eastern half of the United States and Canada were probably Kentucky bluegrass and white clover. They spread so fast after the entrance of Europeans into a given area that there is some suspicion that they may have been present in pre-Colombian America, although the earliest European accounts do not mention them. Probably brought to the Appalachian area by the French, these two kinds of weeds preceded the English settlers there and kept up with the movement westward until reaching the plains across the Mississippi.

Old World plants set up business on their own on the Pacific coast of North America just as soon as the Spaniards and Russians did. The climate of coastal southern California is much the same as that of the Mediterranean, and the Spaniards who came to California in the eighteenth century brought their own Mediterranean weeds with them via Mexico: wild oats, fennel, wild radishes. These plants, plus those brought in later by the Forty-niners, muscled their way to dominance in the coastal grasslands. These immigrant weeds followed Old World horses, cattle, and sheep into California's interior prairies and took over there as well.

The region of Argentina and Uruguay was almost as radically altered in its flora as in its fauna by the coming of the Europeans. The ancient Indian practice, taken up immediately by the whites, of burning off the old grass of the pampa every year, as well as the trampling and cropping to the ground of indigenous grasses and forbs by the thousands of imported quadrupeds who also changed the nature of the soil with their droppings, opened the whole countryside to European plants. In the 1780s Félix de Azara observed that the pampa, already radically altered, was changing as he watched. European weeds sprang up around every cabin, grew up along roads, and pressed into the open steppe. Today only a quarter of the plants growing wild in the pampa are native, and in the well-watered eastern portions, the "natural" ground cover consists almost entirely of Old World grasses and clovers.

The invaders were not, of course, always desirable. When Darwin visited Uruguay in 1832, he found large expanses, perhaps as much as hundreds of square miles, monopolized by the immigrant wild artichoke and transformed into a prickly wilderness fit neither for man nor his animals.

The onslaught of foreign and specifically European plants on Australia began abruptly in 1778 because the first expedition that sailed from Britain to Botany Bay carried some livestock and considerable quantities of seed. By May of 1803 over two hundred foreign plants, most of them European, had been purposely introduced and planted in New South Wales, undoubtedly along with a number of weeds. Even today so-called clean seed characteristically contains some weed seeds, and this was much more so two hundred years ago. By and large, Australia's north has been too tropical and her interior too hot and dry for European weeds and grasses, but much of her southern coasts and Tasmania have been hospitable indeed to Europe's willful flora.

Thus, many—often a majority—of the most aggressive plants in the temperate humid regions of North America, South America, Australia, and New Zealand are of European origin. It may be true that in every broad expanse of the world today where there are dense populations, with whites in the majority, there are also dense populations of European weeds. Thirty-five of eighty-nine weeds listed in 1953 as common in the state of New York are European. Approximately 60 percent of Canada's worst weeds are introductions from Europe. Most of New Zealand's weeds are from the same source, as are many, perhaps most, of the weeds of southern Australia's well-watered coasts. Most of the European plants that Josselyn listed as naturalized in New England in the seventeenth century are growing wild today in Argentina and Uruguay, and are among the most widespread and troublesome of all weeds in those countries.

In return for this largesse of pestiferous plants, the Lands of the Demographic Takeover have provided Europe with only a few equivalents. The Canadian water weed jammed Britain's nineteenth-century waterways, and North America's horseweed and burnweed have spread in Europe's empty lots, and South America's flowered galinsoga has thrived in her gardens. But the migratory flow of a whole group of organisms between Europe and the Lands of the Demographic Takeover has been almost entirely in one direction. Englishman's foot still marches in seven league jackboots across every European colony of settlement, but very few American or Australian or New Zealand invaders stride the waste lands and unkempt backyards of Europe.

European and Old World human beings, domesticated animals, varmints, pathogens, and weeds all accomplished demographic takeovers of their own in the temperate, well-watered regions of North and South America, Australia, and New Zealand. They crossed oceans and Europeanized vast territories, often in informal cooperation with each other—the farmer and his animals destroying native plant cover, making way for imported grasses and forbs, many of which proved more nourishing to domesticated animals than the native equivalents; Old World pathogens, sometimes carried by Old World varmints, wiping out vast numbers of aborigines, opening the way for the advance of the European frontier, exposing more and more native peoples to more and more pathogens. The classic example of symbiosis between European colonists, their animals, and plants comes from New Zealand. Red clover, a good forage for sheep, could not seed itself and did not spread without being annually sown until the Europeans imported the bumblebee. Then the plant and insect spread widely, the first providing the second with food, the second carrying pollen from blossom to blossom for the first, and the sheep eating the clover and compensating the human beings for their effort with mutton and wool.

There have been few such stories of the success in Europe of organisms from the Lands of the Demographic Takeover, despite the obvious fact that for every ship that went from Europe to those lands, another traveled in the opposite direction.

The demographic triumph of Europeans in the temperate colonies is one part of a biological and ecological takeover which could not have been accomplished by human beings alone, gunpowder notwithstanding. We must at least try to analyze the impact and success of all the immigrant organisms together—the European portmanteau of often mutually supportive plants, animals, and microlife which in its entirety can be accurately described as aggressive and opportunistic, an ecosystem simplified by ocean crossings and honed by thousands of years of competition in the unique environment created by the Old World Neolithic Revolution.

The human invaders and their descendants have consulted their egos, rather than ecologists, for explanations of their triumphs. But the human victims, the aborigines of the Lands of the Demographic Takeover, knew better, knew they were only one of many species being displaced and replaced; knew they were victims of something more irresistible and awesome than the spread of capitalism or Christianity. One Maori, at the nadir of the history of his race, knew these things when he said, "As the clover killed off the fern, and the European dog the Maori dog—as the Maori rat was destroyed by the Pakeha (European) rat—so our people, also, will be gradually supplanted and exterminated by the Europeans." The future was not quite so grim as he prophesied, but we must admire his grasp of the complexity and magnitude of the threat looming over his people and over the ecosystem of which they were part.

Indians, Colonists, and the Environment

WILLIAM CRONON AND RICHARD WHITE

When the historian Richard White wrote his first scholarly article about Indian environmental history in the mid-1970s, he knew he was taking a new approach to an old field, but he did not realize just how new it was. "I sent it

"Indians in the Land," a conversation between William Cronon and Richard White, pp. 18–25. Reprinted with permission from *American Heritage,* Volume 37, Number 5. Copyright 1985 by *American Heritage,* a Division of Forbes, Inc.

to a historical journal," he reports, "and I never realized the U.S. mail could move so fast. It was back in three days. The editor told me it wasn't history."

Times have changed. The history of how American Indians have lived in, used, and altered the environment of North America has emerged as one of the most exciting new fields in historical scholarship. It has changed our understanding not only of American Indians but of the American landscape itself. To learn more about what historians in the field have been discovering, *American Heritage* asked two of its leading practitioners, Richard White and William Cronon, to meet and talk about their subject.

William Cronon   If historians thought about the environment at all up until a few years ago, they thought of it in terms of an older school of American historians who are often called "environmental determinists." People like Frederick Jackson Turner argued that Europeans came to North America, settled on the frontier, and began to be changed by the environment.

Richard White   In a delayed reaction to Turner, historians in the late 1960s and early 1970s reversed this. They began to emphasize a series of horror stories when they wrote about the environment. The standard metaphor of the time was "the rape of the earth," but what they were really describing was the way Americans moving west cut down the forests, ploughed the land, destroyed the grasslands, harnessed the rivers—how they in effect transformed the whole appearance of the North American landscape.

WC   Since then, I think, we've realized that both positions are true, but incomplete. The real problem is that human beings reshape the earth as they live upon it, but as they reshape it, the new form of the earth has an influence on the way those people can live. The two reshape each other. This is as true of Indians as it is of European settlers.

RW   My first connections with Indians in the environment was very immediate. I became interested because of fishing-rights controversies in the Northwest, in which the Indians' leading opponents included several major environmental organizations. They argued that Indians were destroying the fisheries. What made this odd was that these same groups also held up Indians as sort of primal ecologists. I remember reading a Sierra Club book which claimed that Indians had moved over the face of the land and when they left you couldn't tell they'd ever been there. Actually, this idea demeans Indians. It makes them seem simply like an animal species, and thus deprives them of culture. It also demeans the environment by so simplifying it that all changes come to seem negative—as if somehow the ideal is never to have been here at all. It's a crude view of the environment, and it's a crude view of Indians.

WC   Fundamentally, it's an ahistorical view. It says not only that the land never changed—"wilderness" was always in this condition—but that the people who lived upon it had no history, and existed outside of time. They were "natural."

RW   That word *natural* is the key. Many of these concepts of Indians are quite old, and they all picture Indians as people without culture. Depending on your view of human nature, there are two versions. If human beings are inherently evil in a Calvinistic sense, then you see Indians as inherently violent and cruel. They're identified with nature, but it's the nature of the howling wilderness, which is full of Indians. But if you believe in a beneficent nature, and a basically good human nature, then you see Indians as noble savages, people at one with their environment.

WC   To understand how Indians really did view and use their environment, we have to move beyond these notions of "noble savages" and "Indians as the original ecologists." We have to look instead at how they actually lived.

RW   Well, take the case of fire. Fire transformed environments all over the continent. It was a basic tool used by Indians to reshape landscape, enabling them to clear forests to create grasslands for hunting and fields for planting. Hoe agriculture—as opposed to the plow agriculture of the Europeans—is another.

WC   There's also the Indians' use of "wild" animals—animals that were not domesticated, not owned in ways Europeans recognized. Virtually all North American Indians were intimately linked to the animals around them, but they had no cattle or pigs or horses.

RW   What's hardest for us to understand, I think, is the Indians' different way of making sense of species and the natural world in general. I'm currently writing about the Indians of the Great Lakes region. Most of them thought of animals as a species of *persons*. Until you grasp that fact, you can't really understand the way they treated animals. This is easy to romanticize—it's easy to turn it into a "my brother the buffalo" sort of thing. But it wasn't. The Indians *killed* animals. They often overhunted animals. But when they overhunted, they did so within the context of a moral universe that both they and the animals inhabited. They conceived of animals as having, not rights—that's the wrong word—but *powers*. To kill an animal was to be involved in a social relationship with the animal. One thing that has impressed me about Indians I've known is their realization that this is a harsh planet, that they survive by the deaths of other creatures. There's no attempt to gloss over that or romanticize it.

WC   There's a kind of debt implied by killing animals.

RW   Yes. You incur an obligation. And even more than the obligation is your sense that those animals have somehow surrendered themselves to you.

WC   There's a gift relationship implied . . .

RW   . . . which is also a *social* relationship. This is where it becomes almost impossible to compare Indian environmentalism and modern white environ-mentalism. You cannot take an American forester on an American wildlife manager and expect him to think that he has a special social relationship with the species he's working on.

WC   Or that he owes the forest some kind of gift in return for the gift of wood he's taking from it.

RW   Exactly. And it seems to me hopeless to try to impose that attitude onto Western culture. We distort Indian reality when we say Indians were conservationists—that's not what conservation means. We don't give them full credit for their view, and so we falsify history.

Another thing that made Indians different from modern Euro-Americans was their commitment to producing for *security* rather than for maximum yield. Indians didn't try to maximize the production of any single commodity. Most tried to attain security by diversifying their diet, by following the seasonal cycles: they ate what was most abundant. What always confused Europeans was why Indians didn't simply concentrate on the most productive part of the cycle: agriculture, say. They could have grown more crops and neglected something else. But once you've done that, you lose a certain amount of security.

WC   I like to think of Indian communities having a whole series of ecological nets under them. When one net failed, there was always another underneath it. If the corn died, they could always hunt deer or gather wild roots. In hard times—during an extended drought, for instance—those nets became crucial.

All of this was linked to seasonal cycles. For me, one of the best ways of understanding the great diversity of environmental practices among Indian peoples is to think about the different ways they moved across the seasons of the year. Because the seasons of North America differ markedly between, say, the Eastern forests and the Great Plains and the Southwestern deserts, Indian groups devised quite different ways of life to match different natural cycles.

New England is the region I know best. For Indians there, spring started with hunting groups drawing together to plant their crops after having been relatively dispersed for the winter. While women planted beans, squash, and corn, men hunted the migrating fish and birds. They dispersed for summer hunting and gathering while the crops matured, and then reassembled in the fall. The corn was harvested and great celebrations took place. Then, once the harvest was done and the corn stored in the ground, people broke up their villages and fanned out in small bands for the fall hunt, when deer and other animals were at their fattest. The hunt went on until winter faded and the season of agriculture began again. What they had was agriculture during one part of the year, gathering going on continuously, and hunting concentrated in special seasons. That was typical not just of the Indians of New England but of eastern Indians in general.

RW   For me the most dramatic example of seasonal changes among Indian peoples would be the horticulturists of the eastern Great Plains. The Pawnees are the example I know best. Depending on when you saw the Pawnees, you might not recognize them as the same people. If you came upon them in the spring or early fall, when they were planting or harvesting crops, you would have found a people living in large, semisubterranean earth lodges and surrounded by scattered fields of corn and beans and squash. They looked like horticultural people. If you encountered the Pawnees in early summer or late fall, you would have thought you were seeing Plains nomads—because then they followed the buffalo, and their whole economy revolved around the buffalo. They lived in tepees and were very similar, at least in outward appearance, to the Plains nomads who surrounded them.

For the Pawnees, these cycles of hunting and farming were intimately connected. One of my favorite examples is a conversation in the 1870s between the Pawnee Petalesharo and a Quaker Indian agent who was trying to explain to him why he should no longer hunt buffalo. Suddenly a cultural chasm opens between them, because Petalesharo is trying to explain that the corn will not grow without the buffalo hunt. Without buffalo to sacrifice at the ceremonies, corn will not come up and the Pawnee world will cease. You see them talking, but there's no communication.

WC   It's difficult for a modern American hearing this to see Petalesharo's point of view as anything other than alien and wrong. This notion of sacrificing buffalo so corn will grow is fundamental to his view of nature, even though it's utterly different from what *we* mean when we call him a conservationist.

RW   And yet, if you want to understand people's actions historically, you have to take Petalesharo seriously.

WC   Environmental historians have not only been reconstructing the ways Indians used and thought about the land, they've also been analyzing how those things changed when the Europeans invaded. A key discovery of the last couple of decades has been our radically changed sense of how important European disease was in changing Indian lives.

RW   It was appalling. Two worlds that had been largely isolated suddenly came into contact. The Europeans brought with them diseases the Indians had never experienced. The resulting death rates are almost impossible to imagine: 90 to 95 percent in some places.

WC   The ancestors of the Indians came to North America from ten to forty thousand years ago. They traveled through an Arctic environment in which many of the diseases common to temperate and tropical climates simply couldn't survive. They came in groups that were biologically too small to sustain those diseases. And they came without the domesticated animals with which we share several of our important illnesses. Those three circumstances meant that Indians shed many of the most common diseases of Europe and Asia. Measles, chicken pox, smallpox, and many of the venereal diseases vanished during migration. For over twenty thousand years, Indians lived without encountering these illnesses, and so lost the antibodies that would ordinarily have protected them.

RW   Most historians would now agree that when the Europeans arrived, the Indian population of North America was between ten and twelve million (the old estimate was about one million). By the early twentieth century it had fallen to less than five hundred thousand. At the same time, Indian populations were also under stress from warfare. Their seasonal cycles were being broken up, and they were inadequately nourished as a result. All these things contributed to the tremendous mortality they suffered.

WC   Part of the problem was biological; part of it was cultural. If a disease arrived in mid-summer, it had quite different effects from one that arrived in the middle of the winter, when people's nutrition levels were low and they were more susceptible to disease. A disease that arrived in spring, when crops had to be planted, could disrupt the food supply for the entire year. Nutrition levels would be down for the whole subsequent year, and new diseases would find readier victims as a result.

RW   The effects extended well beyond the original epidemic—a whole series of changes occurred. If Indian peoples in fact shaped the North American landscape, this enormous drop in their population changed the way the land looked. For example, as the Indians of the Southeast died in what had once been a densely populated region with a lot of farmland, cleared areas reverted to grassy woodland. Deer and other animal populations increased in response. When whites arrived, they saw the abundance of animals as somehow natural, but it was nothing of the sort.

Disease also dramatically altered relationships among Indian peoples. In the 1780s and 1790s the most powerful and prosperous peoples on the Great Plains margins were the Mandans, the Arikaras, the Hidatsas, the Pawnees, all of whom raised corn as part of their subsistence cycles. Nomadic, nonagricultural groups like the Sioux were small and poor. Smallpox changed all that. Those peoples living in large, populous farming villages were precisely those who suffered the greatest death rates. So the group that had once controlled the region went into decline, while another fairly marginal group rose to historical prominence.

WC   That's a perfect example of biological and cultural interaction, of how complex it is. A dense population is more susceptible to disease than a less dense one: that's a biological observation true of any animal species. But which Indian communities are dense and which are not, which ones are living in clustered settlements and which ones are scattered thinly on the ground—these aren't biological phenomena but *cultural* ones.

RW   Perhaps the best example of this is the way different Plains Indians responded to the horse, which, along with disease, actually preceded the arrival of significant numbers of Europeans in the region. The older conception of what happened is that when the horse arrived, it transformed the world. That may have been true for the Sioux, but not for the Pawnees. The Sioux became horse nomads; the Pawnees didn't. They were not willing to give up the security of raising crops. For them, the horse provided an ability to hunt buffalo more efficiently, but they were not about to rely solely on buffalo. If the buffalo hunt failed, and they had neglected their crops, they would be in great trouble. As far as I know, there is no agricultural group, with the exception of the Crows and perhaps the Cheyennes, that *willingly* gave up agriculture to rely solely on the buffalo. The people like the Sioux who became Plains nomads had always been hunters and gatherers, and for them horses represented a *more* secure subsistence, not a less secure one.

WC   It's the ecological safety net again. People who practiced agriculture were reluctant to abandon it, because it was one of their strongest nets.

RW   And they didn't. When given a choice, even under harsh circumstances, people tried to integrate the horse into their existing economy, not transform themselves.

The horse came to the Sioux at a time when they were in trouble. Their subsistence base had grown precarious: the buffalo and beavers they'd hunted farther east were declining, and the decline of the farming villages from disease meant the Sioux could no longer raid or trade with them for food. The horse was a godsend: buffalo hunting became more efficient, and the buffalo began to replace other food sources. Having adopted the horse, the Sioux moved farther out onto the Plains. By the time they had their famous conflicts with the United States in the 1860s and 1870s, they were the dominant people of the Great Plains. Their way of life was unimaginable without the horse and buffalo.

WC   The result was that the Sioux reduced the number of ecological nets that sustained their economy and way of life. And although the bison were present in enormous numbers when the Sioux began to adopt the horse, by the 1860s the bison were disappearing from the Plains; by the early eighties they were virtually gone. That meant the Sioux's main ecological net was gone, and there wasn't much left to replace it.

RW   To destroy the buffalo was to destroy the Sioux. Of course, given time, they might have been able to replace the buffalo with cattle and become a pastoral people. That seems well within the realm of historical possibility. But they were never allowed that option.

WC   Disease and the horse are obviously important factors in Indian history. But there's a deeper theme underlying these things. All North American Indian peoples eventually found themselves in a relationship of dependency with the dominant Euro-American culture. At some point, in various ways, they ceased to be entirely autonomous peoples, controlling their own resources and their own political and cultural life. Is environmental history fundamental to explaining how this happened?

RW   I think it's absolutely crucial. Compare the history of European settlement in North America with what happened in Asia and Africa. Colonialism in Asia and Africa was very important, but it was a passing phase. It has left a strong legacy, but Africa is nonetheless a continent inhabited by Africans, Asia a continent inhabited by Asians. American Indian peoples, on the other hand, are a small minority in North America. Part of what happened was simply the decline in population, but as we've said, that decline was not simple at all. To understand it, we have to understand environmental history.

Many Indians were never militarily conquered. They nonetheless became dependent on whites, partly because their subsistence economy was systematically undercut. Virtually every American Indian community eventually had to face the fact that it could no longer feed or shelter itself without outside aid. A key aspect of this was the arrival of a market economy in which certain resources came to be overexploited. The fur trade is the clearest example of this.

WC   No question. The traditional picture of the fur trade is that Europeans arrive, wave a few guns and kettles and blankets in the air, and Indians come rushing forward to trade. What do they have to trade? They have beaver pelts, deerskins, bison robes. As soon as the incentive is present, as soon as those European goods are there to be had, the Indians sweep across the continent, wipe out the furbearing animals, and destroy their own subsistence. That's the classic myth of the fur trade.

RW   It simply didn't happen that way. European goods often penetrated Indian communities slowly; Indian technologies held on for a long time. Indians wanted European goods, but for reasons that could be very different from why *we* think they wanted them.

WC   One of my favorite examples is the kettle trade. Indians wanted kettles partly because you can put them on a fire and boil water and they won't break. That's nice. But many of those kettles didn't stay kettles for long. They got cut up and turned into arrowheads that were then used in the hunt. Or they got turned into high-status jewelry. Indians valued kettles because they were such an extraordinarily flexible resource.

RW   The numbers of kettles that have turned up in Indian graves proves that their value was not simply utilitarian.

WC   The basic facts of the fur trade are uncontestable. Europeans sought to acquire Indian furs, food, and land; Indians sought to acquire European textiles, alcohol, guns, and other metal goods. Indians began to hunt greater numbers of furbearing animals, until finally several species, especially the beaver, were eliminated. Those are the two end points of the fur-trade story. But understanding how to get from one to the other is very complicated. Why did Indians engage in the fur trade in the first place? That's the question.

RW   We tend to assume that exchange is straightforward, that it's simply giving one thing in return for another. That is not how it appeared to Indian peoples.

WC   Think of the different ways goods are exchanged. One is how we usually perceive exchange today: we go into the local supermarket, lay down a dollar, and get a candy bar in return. Many Europeans in the fur trade thought that was what they were doing—giving a gun, or a blanket, or a kettle and receiving a number of furs in return. But for the Indians the exchange looked very different.

RW   To see how Indians perceived this, consider two things we all know, but which we don't ordinarily label as "trade." One is gifts. There's no need to romanticize the giving of gifts. Contemporary Americans exchange gifts at Christmas or at weddings, and when those gifts are exchanged, as anybody who has received one knows, you incur an obligation. You often have relatives who never let you forget the gift they've given you, and what you owe in return. There's no *price* set on the exchange, it's a *gift,* but the obligation is very real. That's one way Indians saw exchange. To exchange goods that way, the two parties at least had to pretend to be friends.
  At the other extreme, if friendship hadn't been established, goods could still change hands, but here the basis of exchange was often simple theft. If you had enemies, you could rob them. So if traders failed to establish some friendship, kinship, or alliance, Indians felt perfectly justified in attacking them and taking their goods. In the fur trade there was a fine line between people who sometimes traded with each other and sometimes stole from each other.

WC   To make that more concrete, when the Indian handed a beaver skin to the trader, who gave a gun in return, it wasn't simply two goods that were moving back and forth. There were *symbols* passing between them as well. The trader might not have been aware of all those symbols, but for the Indian the exchange represented a statement about their friendship. The Indian might expect to rely on the trader for military support, and to support him in return. Even promises about marriage, about linking two communities together, might be expressed as goods passed from hand to hand. It was almost as if a language was being spoken when goods were exchanged. It took a long time for the two sides to realize they weren't speaking the same language.

RW   Right. But for Indians the basic meanings of exchange were clear. You gave generously to friends; you stole from enemies. Indians also recognized that not everybody could be classified simply as a friend or an enemy, and this middle ground is where trade took place.
  But even in that middle ground, trade always began with an exchange of gifts. And to fail to be generous in your gifts, to push too hard on the price— Indians read that as hostility. When Europeans tried to explain the concept of a "market" to Indians, it bewildered them. The notion that demand for furs

in London could affect how many blankets they would receive for a beaver skin in Canada was quite alien to them. How on earth could events taking place an ocean away have anything to do with the relationship between two people standing right here who were supposed to act as friends and brothers toward each other?

WC   So one thing Indian peoples had trouble comprehending at certain stages in this dialogue was the concept of *price*: the price of a good fluctuating because of its abundance in the market. Indian notions were much closer to the medieval "just price." This much gunpowder is always worth this many beaver skins. If somebody tells me they want twice as many skins for the same gunpowder I bought last year at half the price, suddenly they're being treacherous. They're beginning to act as an enemy.

RW   Or in the words Algonquians often used, "This must mean my father doesn't love me any more." To Europeans that kind of language seems ludicrous. What in the world does love have to do with giving a beaver skin for gunpowder? But for Indians it's absolutely critical.

Of course, exchange became more commercial with time. Early in the fur trade, Indians had received European goods as gifts, because they were allies against other Indians or other Europeans. But increasingly they found that the only way to receive those goods was through direct economic exchange. Gift giving became less important, and trading goods for set prices became more important. As part of these commercial dealings, traders often advanced loans to Indians before they actually had furs to trade. By that mechanism, gifts were transformed into debts. Debts could in turn be used to coerce greater and greater hunting from Indians.

WC   As exchange became more commercial, the Indians' relationship to animals became more commercial as well. Hunting increased with the rise in trade, and animal populations declined in response. First the beaver, then the deer, then the bison disappeared from large stretches of North America. As that happened, Indians found themselves in the peculiar position of relying more and more on European goods but no longer having the furs they needed to acquire them. Worse, they could no longer even *make* those same goods as they once had, in the form of skin garments, wild meat, and so on. That's the trap they fell into.

RW   And that becomes dependency. That's what Thomas Jefferson correctly and cynically realized when he argued that the best way for the United States to acquire Indian lands was to encourage trade and have government storehouses assume Indian debts. Indians would have no choice but to cede their lands to pay their debts, and they couldn't even renounce those debts because they now needed the resources the United States offered them in order to survive. Not all tribes became involved in this, but most who relied on the fur trade eventually did.

Of course, the effects go both ways. As whites eliminated Indians and Indian control, they were also, without realizing it, eliminating the forces that had shaped the landscape itself. The things they took as natural—why there were trees, why there weren't trees, the species of plants that grew there— were really the results of Indian practices. As whites changed the practices, those things vanished. Trees began to reinvade the grassland, and forests that had once been open became closed.

WC   Once the wild animals that had been part of the Indians' spiritual and ecological universe began to disappear, Europeans acquired the land and began to transform it to match their assumptions about what a "civilized" landscape should look like. With native animals disappearing, other animals could be brought in to use the same food supply that the deer, the moose, and the bison had previously used. And so the cow, the horse, the pig—the animals so central to European notions of what an animal universe looks like—began to move across the continent like a kind of animal frontier. In many instances the Indians turned to these domesticated European species to replace their own decreasing food supply and so adopted a more pastoral way of life. As they lost their lands, they were then stuck with the problem of feeding their animals as well as themselves. . . .

RW   There are lessons in all this. We can't copy Indian ways of understanding nature, we're too different. But studying them throws our own assumptions into starker relief and suggests shortcomings in our relationships with nature that could cost us dearly in the long run.

WC   I think environmental history may be capable of transforming our perspective, not just on Indian history, but on all human history. The great arrogance of Western civilization in the industrial and postindustrial eras has been to imagine human beings existing somehow apart from the earth. Often the history of the industrial era has been written as if technology has liberated human beings so that the earth has become increasingly irrelevant to modern civilization—when in fact all history is a long-standing dialogue between human beings and the earth. It's as if people are constantly speaking to the earth, and the earth is speaking to them. That's a way of putting it that Indians would be far more capable of understanding than most modern Americans. But this dialogue, this conversation between earth and the inhabitants of earth, is fundamental to environmental history. With it we can try to draw together all these pieces—human population changes, cultural changes, economic changes, environmental changes—into a complicated but unified history of humanity upon the earth. That, in rather ambitious terms, is what environmental historians are seeking to do.

✤ *F U R T H E R   R E A D I N G*

K. R. Andrews, N. P. Canny, and P. E. H. Hair, *The Westward Enterprise: English Activities in Ireland, the Atlantic, and America, 1480–1650* (1978)
Carlo M. Cipolla, *Guns and Sails in the Early Period of European Expansion, 1400– 1700* (1963)

William Cronon, *Changes in the Land: Indians, Colonists, and the Ecology of New England* (1983)

Alfred Crosby, *The Columbian Exchange: Biological and Cultural Consequences of 1492* (1972)

————, *Ecological Imperialism: The Biological Expansion of Europe, 900–1900* (1986)

Alvin M. Josephy, Jr., ed., *America in 1492: The World of the Indian Peoples Before the Arrival of Columbus* (1992).

Shepard Krech III, *Indians, Animals, and the Fur Trade: A Critique of Keepers of the Game* (1981)

Calvin Martin, *The Keepers of the Game: Indian-Animal Relationships and the Fur Trade* (1978)

Samuel Eliot Morison, *The European Discovery of America:* Vol. 1, *The Northern Voyages;* Vol. 2, *The Southern Voyages* (1971–1974)

Edmundo O'Gorman, *The Invention of America: An Inquiry into the Historical Nature of the New World and the Meaning of Its History* (1961)

David Beers Quinn, *England and the Discovery of America, 1481–1620* (1974)

————, *North America from Earliest Discovery to First Settlements: The Norse Voyages to 1612* (1977)

DATE: 14/10/1999 TIME: 12:56
TILL: 0018   NO: 18189768
CASHIER: LISA G

DESCRIPTION	QTY	AMOUNT
Barcode: 9780669199222		
MAJOR PROBLE.KUPPERM 1		13.95 A
TOTAL	1	£13.95

CREDIT/DEBIT CARD   £13.95

VAT A @ 0.00% (£13.95): £0.00

CHAPTER
2

The Colonizing Impulse:
Promise and Reality

∽

The European colonization of America was undertaken by nations and supported by religious organizations. These sponsors had large goals, arguing that colonization would benefit Europeans and Americans equally. Europe would gain the goods of the newly discovered continents. In return the Americans would receive the unparalleled gift of Christianity by which to enrich their spiritual lives, and European manufactured goods with which to enhance their material lives.

This vision rested on a series of partial misperceptions. Early writers overestimated the easy wealth to be gained in America. Europe would become rich from American products, but these would require great labor and organization to produce. The welcome given early expeditions by Native Americans also misled reporters, who eagerly sought any indication that the Indians willingly and easily would relinquish their own culture and traditions for a European style of life. In reality the natives were interested in choosing from European culture the elements that would make their traditional lives fuller or more efficient. They had no desire to give up a satisfying way of life and, if pushed too hard, would resist in ways that Europeans interpreted as treachery. Disappointment at all levels fed conflict.

A further misperception concerned tribal organization. Europeans tended to see complex hierarchical structures headed by powerful leaders, where modern scholars more typically see decentralized organization, with village- or band-level leaders operating on a consensual basis. It is as misleading to speak of "the Indians" as it is to refer to "the Spanish" or "the English." Neither side was unified. Within the European empires, religious leaders argued with military officers about the paths to follow. Native Americans, with often long-standing rivalries, fought each other and vied for power in the changed situation. At the most fundamental level individuals formed friendships and families across ethnic lines and ultimately faced painful choices.

❧ D O C U M E N T S

Spanish explorer Francisco Vásquez de Coronado, lured by reports of golden cities to the north, led a two-year expedition (described in the first document by Pedro de Castañeda) through the American Southwest as far as central Kansas. Fray Alonso de Benavides, convinced of prospects for many conversions among the Pueblo and Apache Indians, in the second selection urges the Spanish authorities to concentrate efforts on the New Mexico territory. The Pueblo Revolt of 1680 so shocked the Spanish authorities that they collected testimony about its extent and causes. The reports excerpted in the third document include Indians' affirmations that proscription of their own religion drove them to rebel, as well as statements by missionaries about their suffering.

England arrived late on the colonization scene, and English promoters feared that Spain, which had grown wealthy and powerful on riches from America, would take over both continents entirely. Men such as Richard Hakluyt, whose *Discourse of Western Planting* is excerpted in the fourth document, tried to persuade Queen Elizabeth and English merchants and gentry to invest in colonization, lest England lose out in the race for international status. In the final document Ralph Lane, governor of Roanoke, the colony founded as a result of this campaign, reveals the ways in which the colonists, despite their swaggering attitude toward the Carolina Algonquians, were unprepared for the American environment and completely dependent on their Indian neighbors for food.

An Account of Coronado's Exploration of the Southwest, 1540–1542

Cibola* is seven villages. The largest is called Maçaque. The houses are ordinarily three or four stories high, but in Maçaque there are houses with four and seven stories. These people are very intelligent. They cover their privy parts and all the immodest parts with cloths made like a sort of table napkin, with fringed edges and a tassel at each corner, which they tie over the hips. They wear long robes of feathers and of the skins of hares, and cotton blankets. The women wear blankets, which they tie or knot over the left shoulder, leaving the right arm out. These serve to cover the body. They wear a neat well-shaped outer garment of skin. They gather their hair over the two ears, making a frame which looks like an old-fashioned headdress.

This country is a valley between rocky mountains. They cultivate corn, which does not grow very high. The ears start at the very foot, and each large fat stalk bears about 800 grains, something not seen before in these parts. There are large numbers of bears in this province, and lions, wild-cats, deer, and otter. There are very fine turquoises, although not so many as was reported. They collect the pine nuts each year, and store them up in advance. A man does not have more than one wife. There are estufas or hot rooms in the villages, which are the courtyards or places where they gather for con-

_____
*Coronado's Cibola is Háwikuh Pueblo.

sultation. They do not have chiefs as in New Spain, but are ruled by a council of the oldest men. They have priests who preach to them, whom they call papas. These are the elders. They go up on the highest roof of the village and preach to the village from there, like public criers, in the morning while the sun is rising, the whole village being silent and sitting in the galleries to listen. They tell them how they are to live, and I believe that they give certain commandments for them to keep, for there is no drunkenness among them nor sodomy nor sacrifices, neither do they eat human flesh nor steal, but they are usually at work. The estufas belong to the whole village. It is a sacrilege for the women to go into the estufas to sleep. They make the cross as a sign of peace. They burn their dead, and throw the implements used in their work into the fire with the bodies. . . .

Tiguex is a province with twelve villages on the banks of a large, mighty river; some villages on one side and some on the other. . . .

. . . [The villages] are governed by the opinions of the elders. They all work together to build the villages, the women being engaged in making the mixture and the walls, while the men bring the wood and put it in place. They have no lime, but they make a mixture of ashes, coals, and dirt which is almost as good as mortar, for when the house is to have four stories, they do not make the walls more than half a yard thick. They gather a great pile of twigs of thyme and sedge grass and set it afire, and when it is half coals and ashes they throw a quantity of dirt and water on it and mix it all together. They make round balls of this, which they use instead of stones after they are dry, fixing them with the same mixture, which comes to be like a stiff clay. Before they are married the young men serve the whole village in general, and fetch the wood that is needed for use, putting it in a pile in the courtyard of the villages, from which the women take it to carry to their houses.

The young men live in the estufas, which are in the yards of the village. . . . When any man wishes to marry, it has to be arranged by those who govern. The man has to spin and weave a blanket and place it before the woman, who covers herself with it and becomes his wife. The houses belong to the women, the estufas to the men. If a man repudiates his woman, he has to go to the estufa. It is forbidden for women to sleep in the estufas, or to enter these for any purpose except to give their husbands or sons something to eat. The men spin and weave. The women bring up the children and prepare the food. The country is so fertile that they do not have to break up the ground the year round, but only have to sow the seed, which is presently covered by the fall of snow, and the ears come up under the snow. In one year they gather enough for seven. A very large number of cranes and wild geese and crows and starlings live on what is sown, and for all this, when they come to sow for another year, the fields are covered with corn which they have not been able to finish gathering. . . .

. . . They keep the separate houses where they prepare the food for eating and where they grind the meal, very clean. This is a separate room or closet, where they have a trough with three stones fixed in stiff clay. Three women go in here, each one having a stone, with which one of them breaks the corn, the next grinds it, and the third grinds it again. They take off their shoes, do up their hair, shake their clothes, and cover their heads before they enter the door. A man sits at the door playing on a fife while they grind, moving the stones to the music and singing together. They grind a large quantity at one time, because they make all their bread of meal soaked in warm water, like wafers. They gather a great quantity of brushwood and dry it to use for cooking all through the year. There are no fruits good to eat in the country, except the pine nuts. They have their preachers. . . .

Cicuye* is a village of nearly five hundred warriors, who are feared throughout that country. It is square, situated on a rock, with a large court or yard in the middle, containing the estufas. The houses are all alike, four stories high. One can go over the top of the whole village without there being a street to hinder. There are corridors going all around it at the first two stories, by which one can go around the whole village. These are like outside balconies, and they are able to protect themselves under these. The houses do not have doors below, but they use ladders, which can be lifted up like a drawbridge, and so go up to the corridors which are on the inside of the village. As the doors of the houses open on the corridor of that story, the corridor serves as a street. The houses that open on the plain are right back of those that open on the court, and in time of war they go through those behind them. The village is inclosed by a low wall of stone. There is a spring of water inside which they are able to divert. The people of this village boast that no one has been able to conquer them and that they conquer whatever villages they wish. The people and their customs are like those of the other villages. . . .

Fray Alonso de Benavides Reports New Mexico Indians Eager for Conversion, 1634

On February 27 of the same year, 1632, Father Fray Martín de Arvide, who had spent many years in preaching the divine word in New Mexico [suffered martyrdom]. The great pueblo of Picuries had fallen to his lot. Here he converted more than two hundred Indians, suffering great hardships and personal dangers, as these people are the most indomitable of that kingdom. He founded a church and convent large enough to minister to all the baptized. Among the newly converted, there was a young man, a son of one of the principal sorcerers. On a certain occasion, the latter undertook to pervert his son and dissuade him from what the padre taught. When the father was informed of it, he left the convent with a crucifix in his hands and, filled with apostolic spirit, he went to the place where the infernal minister was perverting that soul and began to remonstrate with him, saying, "Is it not sufficient that you yourself want to go to hell without desiring to take your son also?" Addressing the young man, he said, "Son, I am more your father and I love you more than he, for he wants to take you with him to the suffering of hell,

---
*Cicuye is modern Pecos Indians.

while I wish you to enjoy the blessings of being a Christian." With divine zeal, he advanced these and other arguments. The old sorcerer arose, grasped a large club near by, and struck the blessed father such a blow on the head that he felled him and then he and others dragged him around the plaza and ill-treated him cruelly. Miraculously he escaped from their hands; although very eager to offer his life to its Giver, God preserved him for a later occasion.

As a result of this the Indians rebelled, so that for several years that pueblo refused to receive a friar who might preach our holy Catholic faith to them. This situation continued until the year 1628 when I stationed there Father Andrés de Zea, who converted many people. . . .

. . . All the Indians are now converted, baptized, and very well ministered to, with thirty-three convents and churches in the principal pueblos and more than one hundred and fifty churches throughout the other pueblos; here, where scarcely thirty years earlier all was idolatry and worship of the devil, without any vestige of civilization, today they all worship our true God and Lord. The whole land is dotted with churches, convents, and crosses along the roads. The people are so well taught that they now live like perfect Christians. They are skilled in all the refinements of life, especially in the singing of organ chants, with which they enhance the solemnity of the divine service.

All these nations settled in this most northerly region in order to escape the intolerable cold and to find there a milder climate, but they met with opposition and resistance from the native inhabitants of this whole land, that is, from the huge Apache nation. In fact, the Apaches surround the above-mentioned nations on all sides and have continuous wars with them.

Thus, since we had converted all these nations, we endeavored to convert the Apaches, who alone are more numerous than all the others together, and even more numerous than the people of New Spain. These Indians are very spirited and belligerent. They are a people of a clearer and more subtle understanding, and as such they laugh at the other nations because they worship idols of wood and stone. The Apaches worship only the sun and the moon. They wear clothing, and although their chief sustenance is derived from hunting, they also plant much corn. Their houses are modest, but adequate for protection against the cold spells of that region. In this nation only, the husband often has as many wives as he can support. This also depends on rank, for it is a mark of prestige to have numerous wives. They cut off the nose and ears of the woman taken in adultery. They pride themselves on never lying but on always speaking the truth. The people of this nation are countless, for they occupy the whole of New Mexico. Thus, armies of more than thirty thousand have been seen on the way to war against each other, the fields swarming with them. They have no one king who governs them, in general, but in each district or province they allow themselves to be ruled by one who is famous for some brave deed. The neighboring provinces, however, always heed and have respect for someone from a larger province. . . .

Starting, then, with that portion of this nation nearest to the Pira [Piro] nation, which is the first we meet on reaching New Mexico, there is, on the opposite

bank of the Rio del Norte to the west, the province and tribe of the Xila
Apaches. It is fourteen leagues from the pueblo of San Antonio Senecú, where
their chief captain, called Sanaba, oftentimes comes to gamble. After he had
heard me preach to the Piros several times, he became inclined to our holy
Catholic faith and confided his thoughts to me; and when I had satisfied him
in regard to certain difficulties that he had encountered, he determined to
become a Christian and said that he wanted to go and tell his people in order
that they too should become Christians. This he did, and within a few days
he returned to see me, with some of his people already converted by what
he had told them. Confirming them in their good intentions, I persuaded them,
since they were the chief lords, that, as a good beginning to their Christianity,
they should at once erect a cross in the center of the plaza of their pueblo
so that I could find and worship it when I came to visit them. They promised
me to do this and departed very happy. And, although I, because of the
demands of my office and the lack of friars, could not go there that year,
withal I learned that Captain Sanaba was an apostolic preacher and desired
that all of his tribe should be converted, and he had already prepared them
for it.

After the lapse of a few days, I returned there to ascertain the state of that
conversion. When Captain Sanaba heard that I had arrived at San Antonio
Senecú, he came those fourteen leagues to see me, accompanied by many of
his people. After I had welcomed him with honor in the presence of all, he
presented me with a folded chamois, which is a dressed deerskin. It is customary among these people, when going to visit someone, to bring a gift. I accepted it to gratify him, although I told him that I did not want anything
from him except that he and all his people should become Christians. He
asked me to unfold the chamois and see what was painted on it. This I did
and saw that it had been decorated with the sun and the moon, and above
each a cross, and although the symbolism was apparent to me, I asked him
about it. He responded in these formal words: "Father, until now we have
not known any benefactors as great as the sun and the moon, because the
sun lights us by day, warms us, and makes our plants grow; the moon lights
us by night. Thus we worship them as our gods. But, now that you have
taught us who God, the creator of all things is, and that the sun and the moon
are His creatures, in order that you might know that we now worship only
God, I had these crosses, which are the emblem of God, painted above the
sun and the moon. We have also erected one in the plaza, as you commanded."

Only one who has worked in these conversions can appreciate the joy
that such happenings bring to a friar when he sees the results of his preaching.
Recognizing this gift as the fruit of the divine word, I took the chamois and
placed it on the high altar as a banner won from the enemy and as evidence
of the high intelligence of this nation, for I do not know what more any of
the ancient philosophers could have done. With this I bade farewell to him
and his people, who were very happy. Within a few days he came more than

sixty leagues to see me, rejoicing that all of his people had decided to become Christians. In his own name and in behalf of all of them he rendered obedience to me in the name of our holy mother, the church. With this good start, I founded that conversion in their pueblo of Xila, placing it in charge of Father Fray Martín del Espíritu Santo, who administered it with great courage during the year 1628.

New Mexico's Indians Rebel Against Suppression of Their Native Religion, 1680: Four Accounts

Alonso García to Fray Francisco de Ayeta

The señor governor tells me to advise your reverence of the state in which he finds himself, which must certainly arouse great pity in every one, at seeing so many children and women on foot, naked, and dying of hunger, according to reports that have reached us, they not having been able to escape with even a shirt.

The señor governor informs me that all the rest are coming in the same plight. Let your reverence reflect upon the afflictions that the señor governor and all those of us who are present will have experienced. I am going out to meet the señor governor and to ascertain his lordship's decision, leaving all the families in this place, guarded by most of the men.

It is said that nothing remains of the temples and sacred vestments—that they have burned everything. From your reverence's report and from the necessary slowness of the señor governor, I judge that he will arrive here at about the same time as the wagons with the supplies. That which the señor governor urges me most strongly is to advise your reverence as quickly as possible, for the relief of such great suffering.

Meanwhile, may our Lord keep your reverence for the protection of so many poor people, who desire to see you with the spiritual increase which your reverence merits. In this place of Fray Cristóbal, to-day, September 4, 1680. Your reverence's humblest servant, who kisses your feet.

Alonso García

Fray Antonio de Sierra to Fray Francisco de Ayeta

... My escape from [La Isleta] was a divine dispensation, through circumstances which I will tell personally, or of which your reverence will learn from many persons. All the rest have perished. The Indians who have done the greatest harm are those who have been most favored by the religious and who are most intelligent. Many of them have already paid with their lives in the fighting in the villa, where the entire battery was, as well as a large number of Indians. The latter, terrified by the conflict, gave the Spaniards an opportunity to retire from the villa with small loss, although that of Sargento Mayor Andrés Gómez Parra and other soldiers was a great one. According to reports, few were wounded, among them the señor governor....

Statement of One of the Rebellious Christian Indians

... Having been asked his name and of what place he is a native, his condition, and age, he said that his name is Don Pedro Nanboa, that he is a native of the pueblo of Alameda, a widower, and somewhat more than eighty years of age. Asked for what reason the Indians of this kingdom have rebelled, forsaking their obedience to his Majesty and failing in their obligation as Christians, he said that for a long time, because the Spaniards punished sorcerers and idolaters, the nations of the Teguas, Taos, Pecuríes, Pecos, and Jemez had been plotting to rebel and kill the Spaniards and the religious, and that they had been planning constantly to carry it out, down to the present occasion. Asked what he learned, saw and heard in the juntas and parleys that the Indians have held, what they have plotted among themselves, and why the Indians have burned the church and profaned the images of the pueblo of Sandia, he said that he has not taken part in any junta, nor has he harmed any one; that what he has heard is that the Indians do not want religious or Spaniards. Because he is so old, he was in the cornfield when he learned from the Indian rebels who came from the sierra that they had killed the Spaniards of the jurisdiction and robbed all their haciendas, sacking their houses. Asked whether he knows about the Spaniards and religious who were gathered in the pueblo of La Isleta, he said that it is true that some days ago there assembled in the said pueblo of La Isleta the religious of Sandia, Jemez, and Zia, and that they set out to leave the kingdom with those of the said pueblo of La Isleta and the Spaniards—not one of whom remained—taking along their property. The Indians did not fight with them because all the men had gone with the other nations to fight at the villa and destroy the governor and captain-general and all the people who were with him. He declared that the resentment which all the Indians have in their hearts has been so strong, from the time this kingdom was discovered, because the religious and the Spaniards took away their idols and forbade their sorceries and idolatries; that they have inherited successively from their old men the things pertaining to their ancient customs; and that he has heard this resentment spoken of since he was of an age to understand. What he has said is the truth and what he knows, under the oath taken, and he signs and ratifies it, it being read and explained to him in his language through the interpretation of Captain Sebastián Montaño, who signed it with his lordship, as the said Indian does not know how, before me, the present secretary.

Antonio de Otermín

Statement of Pedro García

... [T]here appeared before his lordship an Indian named Pedro García, a sworn witness in these *autos,* and he stated under oath that he remembers distinctly that the captains of the Tagnos told him before the revolt that they had desired and discussed it in these parts for more than twelve years; that the said Indians wished to rebel because they resented it greatly that the religious and the Spaniards should deprive them of their idols, their dances, and their superstitions. ...

Richard Hakluyt's "Discourse of Western Planting," 1584

A brief Collection of certain reasons to induce her Majesty and the state to take in hand the western voyage and the planting there.

1. The soil yieldeth and may be made to yield all the several commodities of Europe, and of all kingdoms, dominions and Territories that England tradeth with, that by trade of merchandize cometh into this Realm.

2. The passage thither and home is neither too long nor too short, but easy and to be made twice in the year.

3. The passage cutteth not near the trade of any Prince, nor near any of their countries or Territories and is a safe passage, and not easy to be annoyed by Prince or potentate whatsoever.

4. The passage is to be performed at all times of the year. . . .

5. And where England now for certain hundred years last past by the peculiar commodities of wools, and of later years by clothing of the same, hath raised itself from meaner state to greater wealth and much higher honor, might and power than before, to the equalling of the princes of the same to the greatest potentates of this part of the world. It cometh now so to pass that by the great endeavor of the increase of the trade of wools in Spain and in the West Indies now daily more and more multiplying, That the wools of England and the cloth made of the same, will become base, and every day more base than other, which prudently weighed, it behoveth this Realm if it mean not to return to former old meanness and baseness, but to stand in present and late former honor glory and force, and not negligently and sleepingly to slide into beggary, to foresee and to plant at Norumbega [New England] or some like place. . . .

6. This enterprise may stay the Spanish king from flowing over all the face of that waste firm [mainland] of America, if we seat and plant there in time, in time I say, and we by planting shall let him from making more short and more safe returns out of the noble ports of the purposed places of our planting. . . . How easy a matter may it be to this Realm swarming at this day with valiant youths rusting and hurtful by lack of employment, and having good makers of cable and of all sorts of cordage, and the best and most cunning shipwrights of the world to be Lords of all those Seas, and to spoil Philip's [King Philip II of Spain] Indian navy, and to deprive him of yearly passage of his Treasure into Europe, and consequently to abate the pride of Spain and of the supporter of the great Antichrist of Rome, and to pull him down in equality to his neighbor princes, and consequently to cut off the common mischiefs that comes to all Europe by the peculiar abundance of his Indian Treasure, and this without difficulty.

7. . . . [T]his Realm shall have by that mean ships of great burden and of great strength for the defence of this Realm.

8. This new navy of mighty new strong ships so in trade to that Norumbega and to the coasts there, shall never be subject to arrest of any prince or potentate, as the navy of this Realm from time to time hath been in the ports of the empire.

9. The great mass of wealth of the Realm embarked in the merchants' ships

---

Some of the spelling in this document has been modernized.

carried out in this new course, shall not lightly in so far distant a course from the coast of Europe be driven by winds and Tempests into ports of any foreign prince. . . .

10. No foreign commodity that comes into England comes without payment of custom once, twice, or thrice before it come into the Realm, and so all foreign commodities become dearer [more expensive] to the subjects of this Realm, and by this course to Norumbega foreign prince's customs are avoided, and the foreign commodities cheaply purchased, they become cheap to the subjects of England to the common benefit of the people, and to the saving of great Treasure in the Realm, whereas now the Realm becometh poor by the purchasing of foreign commodities in so great a mass at so excessive prices.

11. At the first traffic [trade] with the people of those parts, the subjects of this Realm for many years shall change many cheap commodities of these parts, for things of high valor [value] there not esteemed, and this to the great enriching of the Realm, if common use fail not.

12. By the great plenty of those Regions the merchants and their factors shall lie there cheap, buy and repair their ships cheap, and shall return at pleasure without stay or restraint of foreign Prince . . . and so he shall be rich and not subject to many hazards, but shall be able to afford the commodities for cheap prices to all subjects of the Realm.

13. . . . [B]y thousands of things there to be done, infinite numbers of the English nation may be set on work to the unburdening of the Realm with many that now live chargeable to the state at home.

14. If the sea coast serve for making of salt, and the inland for wine, oils, oranges, lemons, figs, etc., and for making of iron, all which with much more is hoped, without sword drawn, we shall cut the comb of the French, of the Spanish, of the Portuguese, and of enemies, and of doubtful friends to the abating of their wealth and force, and to the greater saving of the wealth of the Realm.

15. . . . [W]e may out of those parts receive the mass of wrought wares that now we receive out of France, Flanders, Germany, etc. and so we may daunt the pride of some enemies of this Realm, or at the least in part purchase those wares, that now we buy dearly of the French and Fleming, better cheap, and in the end for the part that this Realm was wont to receive drive them out of trade to idleness for the setting of our people on work.

16. We shall by planting there enlarge the glory of the gospel and from England plant sincere religion, and provide a safe and a sure place to receive people from all parts of the world that are forced to flee for the truth of God's word.

17. If frontier wars there chance to arise, and if thereupon we shall fortify, it will occasion the training up of our youth in the discipline of war, and make a number fit for the service of the wars and for the defence of our people there and at home.

18. The Spaniards govern in the Indies with all pride and tyranny; and like as when people of contrary nature at the sea enter into Gallies, where men are tied as slaves, all yell and cry with one voice *liberta, liberta,* as desirous of liberty and freedom, so no doubt whensoever the Queen of England, a prince of such clemency, shall seat upon that firm of America, and shall be reported throughout all that tract to use the natural people there with all humanity, courtesy, and freedom, they will yield themselves to her government and revolt clean from the Spaniard.

... [A]nd if it be high policy to maintain the poor people of this Realm in work, I dare affirm that if the poor people of England were five times so many as they be, yet all might be set on work in and by working linen and such other things of merchandise as the trade in the Indies doth require.

19. The present short trades causeth the mariner to be cast off, and oft to be idle and so by poverty to fall to piracy. But this course to Norumbega being longer and a continuance of the employment of the mariner doth keep the mariner from idleness and from necessity, and so it cutteth off the principal actions of piracy, and the rather because no rich prey for them to take cometh directly in their course or any thing near their course.

20. Many men of excellent wits of divers singular gifts overthrown ... by some folly of youth, that are not able to live in England may there be raised again, and do their Country good service. . . .

21. Many soldiers and servitors in the end of the wars that might be hurtful to this Realm, may there be unladen, to the common profit and quiet of this Realm, and to our foreign benefit there as they may be employed.

22. The fry [children] of the wandering beggars of England that grow up idly and hurtful and burdenous to this Realm, may there be unladen, better bred up, and may people waste Countries to the home and foreign benefit, and to their own more happy state.

23. If England cry out and affirm that there is so many in all trades that one cannot live for another as in all places they do, This Norumbega (if it be thought so good) offereth the remedy.

Governor Ralph Lane Describes the Roanoke Colony's Attack on the Roanoke Indians, 1586

The King was advised and of himself disposed, as a ready mean to have assuredly brought us to ruin in the month of March 1586. himself also with all his Savages to have run away from us, and to have left his ground in the Island unsowed: which if he had done, there had been no possibility in common reason, (but by the immediate hand of God) that we could have been preserved from starving out of hand. For at that time we had no weirs for fish, neither could our men skill of the making of them, neither had we one grain of Corn for seed to put into the ground. . . .

... The manner of their enterprise was this.

Tarraquine and Andacon two principal men about Pemisapan, and very lusty fellows, with twenty more appointed to them had the charge of my person to see an order taken for the same, which they meant should in this sort have been executed. In the dead time of the night they would have beset my house, and put fire in the reeds that the same was covered with: meaning (as it was likely) that myself would have come running out of a sudden amazed in my shirt without arms, upon the instant whereof they would have knocked out my brains.

Some of the spelling in this document has been modernized.

The same order was given to certain of his fellows, for M. Heriots [Harriot's]: so for all the rest of our better sort, all our houses at one instant being set on fire as afore is said, and that as well for them of the fort, as for us at the town. Now to the end that we might be the fewer in number together, and so be the more easily dealt withal (for indeed ten of us with our arms prepared, were a terrour to a hundred of the best sort of them,) they agreed and did immediately put it in practise, that they should not for any copper sell us any victuals whatsoever: besides that in the night they should send to have our weirs robbed, and also to cause them to be broken, and once being broken never to be repaired again by them. By this means the King stood assured, that I must be enforced for lack of sustenance there, to disband my company into sundry places to live upon shellfish, for so the Savages themselves do, going to Hatorask, Croatoan, and other places, fishing and hunting, while their grounds be in sowing, and their corn growing: which failed not his expectation. For the famine grew so extreme among us, or weirs failing us of fish, that I was enforced to send Captaine Stafford with 20 with him to Croatoan my Lord Admiral's Island to serve two turns in one, that is to say, to feed himself and his company, and also to keep watch if any shipping came upon the coast to warn us of the same. . . .

These mischiefs being all instantly upon me and my company to be put in execution, it stood me in hand to study how to prevent them, and also to save all others, which were at that time as aforesaid so far from me: where-upon I sent to Pemisapan to put suspicion out of his head, that I meant presently to go to Croatoan, for that I had heard of the arrival of our fleet, (though I in truth had neither heard nor hoped for so good adventure,) and that I meant to come by him, to borrow of his men to fish for my company, & to hunt for me at Croatoan, as also to buy some four days' provision to serve for my voyage.

He sent me word that he would himself come over to Roanoak, but from day to day he deferred, only to bring the Weopomeioks with him & the Mandoags, whose time appointed was within eight days after. It was the last of May 1586 when all his own Savages began to make their assembly at Roanoak, at his commandment sent abroad unto them, and I resolved not to stay longer upon his coming over, since he meant to come with so good company, but thought good to go and visit him with such as I had, which I resolved to do the next day: but that night I meant by the way to give them in the Island a canvisado [a sudden attack], and at the instant to seize upon all the canoes about the Island, to keep him from advertisements. . . .

. . . The next morning with the light horseman & one Canoe taking 25 with the Colonel of the Chesepians, and the Sergeant major, I went to Dasamonquepeio: and being landed, sent Pemisapan word by one of his own Savages that met me at the shore, that I was going to Croatoan, and meant to take him in the way. . . . Here upon the king did abide my coming to him, and finding myself amidst seven or eight of his principal Weroances and followers, (not regarding any of the common sort) I gave the watch-word agreed upon, (which was, Christ our victory) and immediately those his chief men and himself had by the mercy of God for our deliverance, that which they had purposed for us. The king himself being shot through by the Colonel with a pistol, lying on the ground for dead, & I looking as watchfully for the saving of Manteo's friends, as others were busy that none of the rest should escape, suddenly he started up, and ran away as though he had not been touched, insomuch as he overran all the company, being by the way shot thwart the buttocks by mine Irish boy with my petronel. In the end an Irish man serving me, one Nugent, and the deputy provost, undertook him; and following him in the woods, overtook him: and I in some doubt lest we had lost both the king & my man by our own negligence to have been intercepted by the Savages, we met him returning out of the woods with Pemisapan's head in his hand. . . .

✑ E S S A Y S

Historians usually write American colonial history as if it were exclusively an English enterprise, with the progression of events slowly moving from footholds on the East Coast toward the West. Historian Elizabeth A. H. John of Austin, Texas, reminds us in the first essay that the West of North America was colonized at the same time as the East and that Spain was the agent there. Jamestown in Virginia and Santa Fe in New Mexico were founded within a few years of each other. In the second essay historian Karen Ordahl Kupperman of the University of Connecticut examines the first English colony, Roanoke, demonstrating the mixture of motives and expectations that fueled the venture, as well as the reasons for Sir Walter Raleigh's desertion of the famous Lost Colony. Both historians reveal how early experience misled the colonizers—who willingly placed the best possible interpretation on all signals—and how initial good relations with the Native Americans degenerated into armed conflict.

Spain and New Mexico: Conversion and Rebellion

ELIZABETH A. H. JOHN

Picture now that vast arena stretching westward from the pine-forested great bend of the Red River to the red desert mesas of the Colorado Plateau and southward from the Arkansas River to the Rio Grande. Envision it four centuries ago, homeland of countless small, diverse Indian worlds. Then consider the changes that engulfed those worlds and ponder the power of accident.

Spain made one great purposeful thrust into the Pueblo world in the sixteenth century, to claim those sober, industrious Indians as vassals of Crown and Church. A century later a chastened Spain made a second, half-hearted lunge into the Caddo world, more to balk French expansion than to advance Christendom. Frenchmen came anyway, seeking trade, their packs heavy with implications of revolution for Indian lives.

Elizabeth A. H. John, *Storms Brewed in Other Men's Worlds: The Confrontation of Indians, Spanish, and French in the Southwest, 1540–1795* (College Station: Texas A & M University Press, 1975; University of Nebraska Press, 1981). Reprinted with the permission of the author.

Thus superimposed on the multiplicity of Indian worlds were the Spanish provinces of New Mexico and Texas and the French province of Louisiana. Measured on the European scale of empire, none of the three ever amounted to much, but they unleashed forces of change that transformed the lives of Indian peoples throughout the arena, most quite remote from the initial, deliberate encounters, outside the ken as well as the intent of the invaders. The complex interplay of Indian and European cultures through two centuries molded the region before Anglo-Americans took it and called it Southwest.

The process began with a prodigious blunder. Spain's intrusion into the Pueblo world was born of a great misunderstanding, only the first of many that claimed a frightful toll of lives and property over the next two centuries. To Spanish frontiers in Mexico came rumors that far to the north lay Indian villages of great wealth, perhaps true in the eyes of people who bruited the reports southward.

Compared with camps of wandering Indians, pueblos were veritable citadels: multi-storied stone or adobe blocks of dwellings, centered upon the plazas where focused the community lives of populations ranging from four hundred to two thousand. The compact village structure lent itself not only to defense but to the cooperative way of life fundamental to Pueblo agriculture. The people of each village shared the labor of the fields and the religious observances they believed essential to their common enterprise. Together the people of the pueblos observed ceaseless rounds of inherited ceremonials to propitiate the ruling spirits of their universe. Properly done, these rituals assured the pleasant, orderly life, the fertility of crops and people, and the protection from violence and sorcery, which was the sum of the villagers' desires.

Those sober, egalitarian societies, built upon principles of harmony among themselves and with the spirits of their universe, vested principal leadership in village headmen, whose duties were primarily religious. So important were their spiritual responsibilities that no quarrels could be brought before them, lest disharmony mar rapport of village with spirit world. To be involved in conflict, even if in the right, tarnished a man's reputation. To seek leadership was considered bad form and could provoke accusations of witchcraft. Such total subordination of individual feelings to group interests cost heavy stress to some individuals, especially those of more ambitious, assertive temperaments. For all their surface harmony, Pueblo communities were gravely vulnerable in their lack of leadership in secular matters and in the absence of realistic ways to accommodate dissension within the group. Latent strife could splinter villages at times of crisis.

Although primarily peaceful Indians, Pueblos maintained efficient citizen militia in the form of war societies headed by war priests and could campaign effectively when aroused. Hostilities between pueblos were often sparked by suspicions that one pueblo had cast evil supernatural power against another. Sometimes they warred upon each other in loose alliances, usually based on linguistic or geographic affinity. Most often, however, Pueblos campaigned in reprisal for raids against their villages by such roving enemies as Apaches and Navajos. The realities of Pueblo wealth attracted nomadic Indian predators long before exaggerated rumors of that wealth lured Spaniards northward in the sixteenth century.

Pueblo wealth consisted mainly of stored foodstuffs, especially corn, hoarded over periods of three or four years against the drought cycles that brought famine to the unprepared. In good years, when Pueblo crops exceeded both storage capacity and requirements of current consumption, the villagers gladly traded for buffalo meat and hides and handsomely dressed deer skins brought from the plains by nomads.

Accumulated textiles were another Pueblo wealth, prime commodities in trade, subject to theft when one people raided another. Their fields yielded scanty crops of cotton, prized according to its scarcity and the long hours of labor required to make it into textiles for basic Pueblo dress. Men wove cloth on their looms in the kivas during winter, when harsh cold kept them below ground in the snug safety of communal chambers. Warmer than cotton, thus most valued as cloak or blanket, were fluffy textiles of turkey feathers. Flocks of turkeys were kept in most pueblos, solely for their feathers. Not only did those feathers make the warmest textiles: they also adorned important cere- monial fetishes and carried certain prayers to the spirits.

Fortunately, nomads liked to trade for Pueblo surpluses of corn and tex- tiles and occasionally for pottery in which the villagers excelled. Besides meat, hides, and tallow, the nomads sometimes bartered their war captives. Many a prosperous Pueblo householder purchased a slave to lighten his labors or expand his household's production. A captive also made a handsome present when a visiting Apache wished to honor a Pueblo friend: the donor could reasonably expect a very nice gift in return.

Thus Pueblos and roving neighbors evolved an interdependence, always wary, sometimes broken by hostilities, but generally permitting each people to specialize in its own best products and to trade for the goods of the other. Some frontier pueblos became trade centers for particular groups of nomads. Winter often found Apaches or Utes camped near the sheltering walls of a pueblo.

Because of the marked similarities of their adaptations to the land, their agricultural practices, their compact multi-storied villages, and their preoccu- pation with ceremonials, the settled Indians of New Mexico looked deceptively alike. Actually, they were diverse peoples who spoke some four or five mu- tually unintelligible languages, each with several dialects. Each of the sixty or seventy villages was autonomous. Among them were marked differences of organization and of ceremonial emphasis, although welfare of the commu- nity and fertility of its land and people were paramount concerns everywhere. Each little village society had shaped a viable balance with the difficult en- vironment, achieving orderly, purposeful existence well above survival level. No one could have guessed how fragile was the balance or how vulnerable the Pueblo world to a massive intrusion.

Misleading appearances cost the Pueblos heavily. Tales of their similari- ties to the Indians of Meso-America, in houses, textiles, and crops, led Spaniards to guess that "another Mexico" lay northward. In reality, the Pueblo Indians differed sharply from those of the Valley of Mexico in their egalitarianism, their minimization of war, and the disciplined austerity of their lives. Theirs was not a society or a land that could heap wealth upon conquerors, but misunderstandings persisted even when Spaniards came to stay in New Mexico.

Obvious similarities among Pueblos led Spaniards to miscalculate the complexity and difficulty of Hispanicizing them. Apparent simplicity, even frivolity, of Pueblo rites caused laymen and priests alike to underestimate the power and importance of native beliefs and the dangers of attacking them. Spain's decisions about New Mexico, first to undertake conquest, then to persist despite costly disappointments, derived from false assumptions that Pueblos generated considerable wealth and that they lived in a spiritual vacuum which Christianity could readily fill. Only a century of tragedy would teach Spaniards the true paucity of material resources and the tenacity of traditional beliefs in the Pueblo world.

Nothing in the Spaniards' experience prepared them to understand the Pueblo world they invaded in the sixteenth century, although years of New World experience helped to shape their New Mexican venture. Spaniards were themselves creatures of conflict. Their Hapsburg kings piously resolved to protect New Mexico's natives from such plunder and destruction as had characterized earlier conquests, but that humane royal intent clashed with the conquistadors' expectation that this New Mexico would yield wealth to rival the old. The Crown itself pursued conflicting aims in the New World: its quest for empire, prestige, and wealth required conquest and therefore war, yet its urgent commitment to win the Indians to the Roman Catholic faith could be fulfilled only in peace and conciliation. Thus, policies vacillated, while men and ideas clashed from the court in Madrid to the farthest frontier. Either aim—conquest or conversion—implied disruption of Indian cultures and values: to be caught in their conflict was perhaps cruelest of all Indian dilemmas. Nowhere was the impact greater than in New Mexico, where Spanish expectations were so ill-founded and thus so bitterly disappointed. . . .

On September 21, 1595, in the closing weeks of his term, Viceroy Velasco awarded the New Mexico contract to Don Juan de Oñate, who pledged one of the great New World mining fortunes to the venture. . . .

So Oñate headed north with a rabble too unruly to be tolerated any longer in New Spain, short of supplies, and doomed by untimely departure to reach New Mexico too late to plant crops that year. The strict inspection procedures that had consumed crucial weeks had two objectives: to ensure that the colony carry enough provisions to last until it could produce food in the new land, thus avoiding any necessity to levy supplies from the natives; and to keep careful track of persons who advanced under the Spanish flag. Official delays had undermined the first, but the official muster roll attested to the diversity of the migrants. . . .

The caravan . . . carried the tensions between Church and State that ran deep in the Spanish world. Official raison d'être of the New Mexican venture lay in a small missionary contingent—seven Franciscan friars and two lay brothers, led by Father Commissary Alonso Martínez, supported by royal benefaction, and quite independent of Governor Oñate's authority. The Franciscans feared that Oñate's settlers would undermine the conversion by abusing Indians, but the viceroy assured them that Oñate was forbidden to allot any Indians for work and that any levy of tribute would be as light as possible.

If some conflict was anticipated, there was also a moderating interdependence. The friars relied upon Oñate's force for protection and were properly concerned with the emigrants' souls. The colonists looked to the friars for their spiritual necessities, and some were piously interested in the missionary purpose. Oñate and Fray Alonso accorded each other the respectful courtesy due the ranking representatives of the king and the pope on the newest frontier of New Spain.

By April 30, 1598, Oñate had led the whole extraordinary aggregation across the Rio Grande—no mean feat with heavily laden wagons and great herds of livestock. They paused to celebrate the crossing and took formal possession of New Mexico in the name of Felipe II. Then, just as surely as the king's delays had betrayed Oñate's interests, Oñate betrayed the king's instructions. Because the supplies intended to sustain the colony until its first harvest had already dwindled alarmingly, Oñate approached the pueblos in search of food.

Lest he alarm the Indians by advancing with his whole colony unannounced, Oñate moved ahead with a few soldiers and two friars. Of course, Oñate never reported his illegal requisition, but veterans of the march later testified that Oñate loaded eighty pack animals with maize at the southernmost pueblos, to the Indians' manifest sorrow. Oñate only recorded that he renamed Teypana pueblo "Socorro" because it furnished much maize. . . .

A useful breakthrough in communications came with the discovery of two Mexican Indians, Tomás and Cristóbal, who had lived among the Pueblos since the time of Bonilla. They became Oñate's interpreters. Perhaps their command of Pueblo tongues was no better than their limited Spanish, but they translated Pueblo speeches into Mexican Indian languages that more fluent Indians of Oñate's party then translated into Spanish.

That small breach in the language barrier helped the Spanish and Pueblo leadership grope toward some means of dealing with each other. Oñate, obligated to deal with the Indians peacefully and not to harm or annoy them, needed to find authorities with whom to treat. Probably the leading men of the Pueblos held council in those early summer weeks to decide their course of action toward the intruders and to designate spokesmen to meet with them. Somehow, on July 7, 1598, Pueblo leaders met Oñate in a council in the great kiva of Santo Domingo pueblo. . . .

How fared the feudal concepts of vassalage, the complex structure of mutual obligations, of protection and tribute, in translation from Castilian to a Mexican Indian language and then to Pueblo tongues? Whatever they heard, the Pueblo leaders courteously agreed, through the interpreters, to become vassals of the Most Christian King. Oñate carefully explained the obligations of vassals: that they would be subject to the wills, orders, and laws of the king; that, if they did not obey, they would be severely punished as transgressors of the commands of their king and master. It was a commitment to be made only with the most careful thought. Again, the process of double translation; again, favorable response: the Pueblo spokesmen did indeed wish to submit to His Majesty and become his vassals.

Next serving the other Majesty, Oñate explained that the Spaniards' principal purpose was to save Indian souls. If the Pueblos should become Christians, they would go to heaven to enjoy eternal life of great bliss in the presence of God; if not, they would go to hell to suffer cruel and everlasting torment. All this, he promised, would be further explained by the friars, who represented the pope.

Surely the concepts of Christianity, of heaven and hell and pope, taxed the interpretive skills of Don Tomás and Don Cristóbal, but no one demurred. Indicating that they understood and were ready to become vassals, all the Pueblo leaders knelt to kiss the hand of the father commissary in the name of God and the hand of Oñate in the name of the king. Eminently satisfied with his council, Oñate recorded the Indians' free decision for the peace and satisfaction of the royal conscience.

With what authorities did Oñate actually deal at Santo Domingo? He could not be sure, nor can we in retrospect. . . . Perhaps they were war captains, perhaps representatives designated for this particular meeting by the councils of elders, perhaps only leaders of certain village factions that favored coexistence with the Spaniards. There did not exist in the pueblos any institution of chieftainship in the sense understood by Oñate. He had in fact achieved at Santo Domingo utter futility: a contract binding nonexistent authorities to obey totally uncomprehended authority.

Oñate had next to find a home for his colony. . . . Rather than build a new Spanish village, Oñate occupied an existing pueblo at the confluence of the Chama and Rio Grande rivers. At his request, the natives vacated Ohke, which the Spaniards dubbed San Juan de los Caballeros. Later, when San Juan proved too small, the Spaniards moved across the stream to occupy the four hundred houses of Yunque pueblo, which they named San Gabriel. Again the natives acquiesced. San Gabriel would remain the capital of New Mexico for a dozen years, until the founding of Santa Fe; San Juan would survive the ordeal of dispossession to endure to the present.

The main party of colonists arrived in mid-August. The sixty-one wagon loads of Spanish goods and domestic gear, the great herds, the families (both Spanish and Mexican Indian) obviously come to stay with their women and children must have astonished the Indians who saw them. Had the Pueblo representatives at the great kiva of Santo Domingo really anticipated intrusion on that scale? If the Indians began to have misgivings about welcoming the Spaniards, they concealed them, filling requests for food and clothing without complaint and making seasonal repairs on the adobe dwellings of San Juan as in all pueblos.

Oñate's earliest troubles were with his own people: most were sorely disappointed by the absence of wealth in the land; some adventurers resented Oñate's firm prohibition against looting or other abuse of Indians. Two days after the wagon train arrived, Oñate discovered a conspiracy of some soldiers to rebel and harshly quashed it. Discontents still simmered within the colony, latent threats to the authority of Oñate and the peace of the land, but surface calm was restored. . . .

With its minimum of truth about New Mexico, Oñate's report [to the Viceroy of New Spain] carried maximum effect as recruiting propaganda. Enlistments went well: at the end of summer 1600, seventy-three new Spanish colonists set out for New Mexico, most with wives, children, and many servants. With them traveled seven more Franciscans. Thanks to Oñate's well-publicized report and his agents' propaganda, all were enormously hopeful of success in the new land. . . .

The new colonists arrived on Christmas Eve 1600 for a brief season of joyous celebration, the new arrivals thankful to end their arduous journey safely, the first settlers heartened by reinforcements and supplies. But the newcomers soon discovered shocking discrepancies between the recruiters' stories and actual conditions. The rich resources reported by Oñate were nowhere to be seen; the colony had achieved almost no agricultural development. Worst of all was the pitiful condition of the Indians, who nevertheless remained so docile that it had been unnecessary to build any kind of fortification at San Gabriel. Oñate had not granted any *encomiendas,** much to the settlers' dismay, but he had required a great deal of labor from the Indians and had exacted so much tribute that the native economy was ruined.

The friars had urged the governor to establish extensive common fields to feed the colony, and the Indians had been willing to do the work in order to protect their own supplies, but Oñate had not come to New Mexico to farm. Instead, he instituted monthly requisitions, sending squads of soldiers to take from the pueblos enough corn to feed his colony of more than five hundred men, women, and children. Oñate also levied an annual tribute of blankets and hides, much of which he distributed to the colonists according to needs. That left the Indians in dire poverty, not only short of food but also stripped of protection against the cold. The effect of the corn levies grew even worse in 1601, a drought year, for the colony's demands had consumed the stores of corn customarily hoarded against drought. Squads of soldiers even ferreted out the Pueblos' sacred seed corn. Indians followed piteously behind to pick up kernels falling from sacks as the soldiers rode away. Often the Indians fled as the soldiers approached a pueblo, leaving behind everything but the turkeys they could carry in their arms, hiding in the highlands until the visitors left with their loot.

The colonists realized that their own hardships were as nothing compared with those of the Pueblos, and some worried intensely. Not only did the abuse of the Indians weigh heavily upon their consciences; they feared that the Indians must surely rise up one day to end their suffering by killing all the Spaniards.

The Indians' suffering also appalled the friars, who felt little hope of

---

*The *encomienda* was a grant of the fruits of Indian labor, initially collectable either in personal service or in material tribute.

converting people who fared so badly at the hands of Christians. Even with Indians who responded somewhat to their ministry, the friars proceeded very cautiously about baptism. Doubting the colony's permanence, they hesitated to baptize souls that might later be left without the sacraments and the means of fulfilling their Christian duties—better leave them unbaptized innocents than expose their souls to the worse risk of apostasy. By March 1601, only one hundred Indians were baptized, mostly San Gabriel residents closely associated with the Spaniards.

The colonists lived sharply divided among themselves that spring. Many young, single men, restive in their disappointment, wanted to abandon the province. More stable members, mostly married men burdened with family responsibilities, were willing, or at least resigned, to settle down to work for the modest living that the land would yield, and they wanted to build a proper Spanish town. For them, the best prospect that life now afforded was to make the most of the New Mexican venture on which they had gambled all they owned. A few, richer and with fewer responsibilities, wanted to concentrate on exploration, still dreaming that if only they could search far enough some great wealth would be discovered.

Oñate led seventy of the most optimistic and adventurous to Quivira in June 1601, unaware that in Mexico City the viceroy was interrogating messengers from New Mexico and beginning to doubt the colony's viability. Like Coronado before him, Oñate reached the grass villages of Wichitan bands on the Arkansas River, where the only "gold" to be seen lay in their fields of pumpkins and corn, and turned back disillusioned.

Meanwhile, drought shriveled that summer's crops at the pueblos and brought to a climax the human ordeal in the upper Rio Grande Valley. Harsh levies stripped the pueblos of food, yet did not yield enough to feed the colonists. Their corn and blankets gone, the Pueblos had nothing to trade to Apaches for meat, and in their starving condition they lacked the strength to go hunting. Emboldened by desperation, the Pueblos began killing livestock. The Spaniards guessed that they themselves would be slaughtered if they did not first starve to death.

In September the colonists convened to examine their plight. Many feared for their souls as well as their lives. Friars cited scriptures proving that mortal wrongs had been done the Indians; the settlers protested that they had been forced to do those things lest their own women and children perish and sadly admitted that they would repeat the sins if they stayed. Abandonment seemed the only remedy. A majority agreed to return at once to Mexico, lay their case before the viceroy, and trust his mercy against the possible charge of criminal desertion. They left early in October, ahead of the winter's cold and Oñate's certain wrath.

Not until he reached San Gabriel on November 24, 1601, did Oñate learn the heavy cost of his Quiviran quest. Of the colony on which he had gambled his fortune and reputation, only twenty-five Spaniards awaited him. He dispatched a hard-riding force to arrest the defectors, but they beat their pursuers to Santa Barbara and the viceroy's protection. The defectors' testimony utterly damned Oñate.... [The viceroy] judged the New Mexican venture a costly fiasco and advised disengagement, but the king's Christian obligations forbade total abandonment. As long as there existed in New Mexico a single baptized Indian, there remained the duty of protection. While Spanish officialdom wrestled with that dilemma, assuming the conditions reported in 1601, circumstances changed on the Rio Grande.

The departure of most of the Spanish population reduced the pressure on Pueblo food supplies, to the advantage of both peoples. The drought cycle ended. The dwindling of the livestock further diminished the Spaniards' ability to feed themselves, but it also minimized damages to Pueblo fields. Somehow the two peoples coexisted for eight more years, while the Spaniards wondered whether they would receive permission to leave or reinforcements to enable them to stay. Meanwhile, the pressure of Apache raiders against the Pueblos worsened until some feared that the Spaniards' departure would be an even greater calamity than their presence. . . .

Just when the Spaniards' exactions weakened the Pueblos, the goods they brought attracted raiders. Metal implements lent themselves to Apache uses, as domestic tools, as ornaments, and as weapons. Some were to be found in the pueblos, where Spaniards had once bartered them for food. The livestock also tempted Apaches, and they began to take a toll, first killing horses, cattle, and sheep indiscriminately for food, then making off with the horses and sometimes their trappings. In the Apache world, revolution began, based on horses and metal.

For Pueblos it was a new testing time: what of those protections promised them as recompense for the burdens borne as vassals of the Spanish king? Oñate, who had so zealously exacted tribute, fell woefully short on the reciprocal obligation of defense. . . . Appalled by the breakdown of responsibility to the Crown's Pueblo vassals, [Viceroy] Velasco ordered the governor to defend New Mexico and sent eight soldiers to shore up his forces.

Perhaps that gesture toward improved protection bolstered confidence in the Spanish alliance. Perhaps terror of other Indians drove the Rio Grande Pueblos to strengthen their Spanish connection. Picurís, Taos, and Pecos Pueblos leagued with Apaches to extirpate those Pueblos who had accepted Spanish dominion and who would not heed the call to throw off the invaders' yoke. The Rio Grande Pueblos responded in 1608 with a sudden surge toward Christianity. Where the friars had counted only four hundred Indians baptized in 1607, they counted seven thousand in 1608, with more clamoring for baptism when Fray Lázaro Ximénez left New Mexico to report the new situation to Viceroy Velasco.

At that point the government had nearly decided to abandon New Mexico and escort the four hundred Christian Indians to Mexico for protected, subsidized resettlement, but that would hardly be practicable for seven thousand or more. Reluctantly, the viceroy decided to maintain the worrisome province at government expense, expressly to defend the baptized Indians and provide them ministry.

While obligations to Christian Pueblos ruled out abandonment of New Mexico, the known limitations of the province forbade continuation under Oñate or any other entrepreneur. Thus, in 1609, the compromise decision:

maintain New Mexico as a royal colony with fifty married soldiers, but eschew further explorations. Twelve friars would be sent to continue teaching and ministering to the Indians; if they wished, they could peacefully and discreetly seek converts in outlying regions. A new governor, seasoned, reliable, sympathetic to friars and colonists alike, would be appointed. No Oñate would ever again be permitted any connection with New Mexico.

Don Pedro de Peralta arrived in 1609 to take charge of the colony, which had been practically leaderless and adrift since Oñate's resignation in 1607. Oñate and his lieutenants returned to Mexico in 1610, stood trial, and sustained heavy penalties for their misdeeds in New Mexico, among which the excessive punishment of the Ácomas counted heavily. Courts did not levy the grimmest penalty that Oñate paid for his New Mexican venture: in a skirmish on the way back to Mexico, *indios bárbaros* killed his only son. Oñate lived another twenty years in Mexico, bereft of realm and heir.

Apaches, on the other hand, were catching a rising tide—revolutionizing their lives with horses and metal, expanding their ranges and prowess, scoring against old enemies and new rivals on every side. Perhaps the seventeenth century was as exhilarating for Apaches as the sixteenth had been for Spaniards, though Apaches too would feel the abrupt shock of ebb tide in the next century. . . .

The Spaniards' demand for slaves intensified patterns of warfare and enslavement of captives long antedating the Spanish occupation. Taking captives, either to hold in one's own group or to trade to another, was a common feature of Indian warfare and had figured in intermittent Pueblo-Apache hostilities. Apaches had also marketed their captives, as well as meat and hides, at the pueblos. Spaniards were soon involved through their commitment to defend the Pueblos. Spanish squads sallied forth to punish raiders, usually with warriors from the injured pueblos, and successful retaliation often involved captures. Spaniards enslaved their own captives and often purchased those taken by Pueblos.

Excuses to campaign against Apaches were seldom wanting after 1601, thanks to the Spaniards' disruption of established Pueblo-Apache trade and the new lure of metal goods and livestock in the pueblos, but Spaniards sometimes went slave hunting on the plains without Apache provocation. Pueblos often served on those expeditions, sometimes to render required service to an *encomendero,* sometimes just to strike a blow at an old foe. Apache vengeance usually fell upon pueblos, which were handier targets than Santa Fe.* There evolved an endless round of Apache attacks on pueblos and any unguarded livestock, followed by Spanish-Pueblo campaigns against Apaches, which sparked yet more Apache raids.

With Apaches they captured and captives they purchased from Apaches, some Spanish entrepreneurs turned a nice profit in slave marts down south.

---

*Santa Fe, founded in 1610, was the first permanent European settlement in the southwest of the present-day United States.

Over the years, their success cost New Mexico's population, both Pueblo and Spanish, a heavy price in Apache vengeance. Apache raids particularly impaired the quality of Pueblo life. The frequent need to defend the pueblos from attack and to pursue raiders bore heavily upon Indians already oppressed by the demands of the missionary program, duties of tribute and service to their *encomenderos* [holders of *encomiendas*], and the governors' often grueling exactions.

In their suffering, most Pueblos turned increasingly to the consolations of their native religion, trusting ancient rituals to restore the shattered harmonies of their world. Outraged, uncomprehending friars blamed the governors for their neophytes' disaffection and battled them for control of Pueblo time and energies; at the same time, they invoked ever harsher methods to beat the devil in the struggle for Indian souls.

Both the fanaticism of the friars' assault on native customs and their scandalous quarrels with the governors outraged Pueblo ideals of harmony and moderation. By those standards, the Christian religion thrust upon them by the Spaniards seemed sadly deficient. Taking sanctuary underground in their kivas, most of the disillusioned Pueblos hardened their loyalties to the old ways. Some fled to the sierras to take refuge among old Athapaskan enemies, preferring those uncertain mercies to the ordeal of coercion in the pueblos. As disaffected Pueblos bore their tale of exploitation and abuse to Apache and Navajo camps, they also brought knowledge of new goods and skills, especially livestock management, thus diffusing change even as they fled it.

In the first two decades of the royal colony, many Athapaskans saw the Spanish regime at closer quarters. Despite intensified raiding, old visiting and trading relationships still flourished at the frontier pueblos, and Apaches experienced missionary contacts. Pecos, long a principal trade center for Apaches from the plains, was by 1617 the regular gateway of Spanish entrepreneurs seeking plains Apache trade. Taos and Picurís were traditional markets for more northerly Apaches, probably Jicarilla forebears. The Franciscans, who had always understood their responsibility to include conversion of "wild" Indians as well as Pueblos, welcomed Apache visitors and encouraged them to watch and ask about the interesting, often impressively colorful, rituals and paraphernalia of the mission chapels and to enjoy the hospitality of mission kitchens.

In 1626 a new leader, Fray Alonso de Benavides, brought fresh impetus to missionary interest in the Apaches. Even more strongly than most Franciscans, Benavides considered it his mission to wrestle the devil for possession of the souls of all the unfortunate natives who had been in Satan's power ever since God created them. Confident that miraculous aid would be forthcoming and that success must attend a missionary enterprise founded upon the blood of ten Franciscan martyrs, Benavides saw New Mexico as a base from which to convert all natives of North America. Assuming the Rio Grande's source to be at the North Pole and Virginia nearby, he feared that English and Dutch heretics then settling on the Atlantic coast would not only corrupt the seaboard natives but would also reach out to contaminate those of New Mexico unless the Roman Catholic faith were speedily and firmly established there. He therefore launched a vigorous expansion of the missionary program in New Mexico.

A forceful penman, Benavides let his dreams for the future override current realities in his reports. He wrote of 500,000 converts in New Mexico, firmer in the faith than Europeans who had been Catholics for generations; he also described remarkable wealth in New Mexico, especially rich mines. Published promptly, his reports not only excited the Spanish court but also aroused such interest that French, Dutch, Latin, and German editions quickly followed. In his enthusiasm, Benavides made New Mexico attractive to the very elements, Catholic and heretic, most inimical to his own pious purpose.

If Benavides' dreams were outsized, his capacity for work was real. Not content just to supervise the twenty-seven missions and numerous *visitas* already serving Pueblos, Benavides advanced the mission frontiers. . . .

Gila Apaches had long frequented Piro pueblos, for their territories on the headwaters of the Gila River lay not far west of Senecú. A sociable Gila leader, Sanaba, regularly visited Senecú to gamble. Hearing Benavides preach there, Sanaba grew receptive to missionaries for his own people. In 1628 Benavides dispatched Fray Martín del Espíritu Santo to Sanaba's territory for an extended visit. Though he did not achieve the desired mass conversion, the Gilas entertained him cordially, and he helped them plant some crops. . . .

Few of those great dreams of conversion would be realized in the Spanish centuries, but it is important to remember that in the beginning the missionaries found the *indios bábaros* approachable. Centuries of "Apache wars" have obscured the fact that once, about 1630, Franciscans in New Mexico had very real hope of converting Apaches and Navajos. There seems to be no reason to doubt the *bárbaros'* sincere willingness to listen to missionaries. It was obvious to them, as indeed to Pueblos, that the Spaniards must have very powerful gods who had given them many wonderful things. The mission churches, as richly adorned as the friars could manage, candlelit and filled with music, the solemn rituals, and the priests' earnest harangues all attested a power that merited close inquiry, and the New Mexican colony included several hundred Mexican Indians witnessing that it was not a power for Spaniards alone.

Swept by the momentum of their own compelling faith, the friars too readily assumed that their gospel, once heard, must surely be accepted. Nothing in their very differently structured universe prepared them to comprehend such enormous cultural barriers as those between Apache ways and the disciplines of Christian life that the friars expounded. Thus, Benavides could write of 500,000 converts in New Mexico because he saw in each encounter with the *bárbaros* a promise of converting all their people, whose numbers he could only guess. He tempered his claim with the admission that only 86,000 Indians were actually baptized, and, despite his optimism, he recognized that certain conditions in New Mexico impeded conversions. As soon as his tour of duty in the province ended, he hurried to Spain to advocate reforms required for the Christianization of all peoples in New Mexico.

Benavides presented the court a blunt analysis of New Mexican problems.

The most direct, persistent affront to *bárbaros* was enslavement of war captives, not only those taken in "just" war, but also many seized in deliberate slave raids. Benavides proposed instead to place all captives in convents or in exemplary Christian Spanish or Indian households, to be converted by kind example. Of course, escapes would occur, but he hoped escapees would report their good treatment to their people, perhaps paving the way for future conversions. The thrust of Benavides' argument was that disposition of captives should not be an economic matter but rather a charitable act for purposes of conversion, a wise, compassionate proposal, quite unenforceable on that remote frontier of poverty.

Benavides also denounced virtual enslavement of Pueblo children. Orphans were often taken forcibly from pueblos to serve in Spanish households, on pretext of charitable care. Benavides contended that no Pueblo child was truly orphaned, because extended-family households included grandparents and aunts who reared a child as their own in the event of parental deaths. That Spaniards preyed upon Pueblo children was a keen grievance among Pueblos and well known to their Apache visitors. With neither people did it advance the cause of Christianity.

Exactions of tribute and service from Christian Pueblos also discouraged new conversions among outlying pueblos and *bárbaros*. Households in converted pueblos paid annual tributes of one blanket or skin and two-and-a-half bushels of corn. Other Indians were naturally loath to assume such burdens. Converted pueblos were deteriorating as families consolidated in larger households to minimize tributes and let empty houses crumble. To counter that evasion, some *encomenderos* levied tributes on individuals instead of households, thus increasing tributes to levels never contemplated by the Crown.

Again, Benavides proposed reforms of substantial merit if only Crown authority could be enforced in New Mexico. Tributes should be deferred for at least five years after an entire pueblo had been baptized. Pueblos should have total freedom to move as they pleased, and only after a year's residence in a pueblo should they pay taxes to that pueblo's *encomendero*. Benavides hoped thus to spark a competition of kindness and justice among *encomenderos* vying for residents in their *encomiendas*. In no case should *encomenderos* collect tribute from individuals: they would have to accept fluctuating numbers of households in a pueblo as part of the natural order.

Benavides reminded the Crown of abuses of Indian property rights, especially encroachment on their lands and damages to their fields by livestock. But he pointed out that *encomenderos* often suffered abuses, too. Spanish law entitled settlers who served five years at their own expense in New Mexico to the dignity of *hijodalgo* [the lowest rank of nobility] and to the compensation of an *encomienda* in the pueblos. But newly arrived governors often expropriated *encomiendas* earned by bona fide settlers and conferred the income upon members of their personal retinues, who would contribute little to the province and would depart with the governor. Benavides wanted no one granted an *encomienda* before serving five years in New Mexico, and preference given native sons and daughters of the province in order to encourage more families to settle there permanently at their own expense. Clearly,

Benavides meant to foster a stable Spanish population in New Mexico, with incentives for kind, responsible treatment of Indians.

Benavides spent several years in Spain and in Rome as an eloquent propagandist for development of New Mexico. He persuaded the Crown to approve in 1635 some important reforms: exemption of all New Mexican Indians from tribute and personal service for ten years after baptism; permanent exemptions for principal Indian leaders; and exemption during term of service from both tribute and service for Pueblo aides of both civil and church administrations.

Had New Mexico been destined to progress as Benavides envisioned, or indeed as he sometimes implied had already happened, his further suggestion of a bishopric there would have followed logically. Although abortive, his proposal led the Crown to enlightening examination of its New Mexican problem.

The Crown liked the idea that New Mexico could now support a bishopric: the mission program was costly and the province yielded no revenue to the Crown. Felipe IV was perenially short of money ... Benavides' proposal implied that a province that could support a bishopric could sustain its own missionary activities. Indeed, if his reports of its wealth and population were accurate, New Mexico should even produce revenues for the Crown. The proposition merited investigation.

The inquiry revealed astonishing unanimity among Franciscan veterans of New Mexico and its most recent ex-governor. Grueling poverty gripped Pueblos and Spaniards alike in New Mexico, and there was no prospect of improvement. No one denied Benavides' reports of fertile lands and probable mineral veins, but what were New Mexico's few beleaguered inhabitants to make of them? Perhaps there had been 60,000 baptisms among Pueblos over the years, but by 1638 disease, famine, and war had reduced inhabitants of the pueblos to some 40,000. The Spanish colony amounted to fifty households at Santa Fe and another dozen on farms downstream on the Rio Grande. They could muster perhaps two hundred men-at-arms to defend the Pueblos against Apaches. All raised grain and cattle for their livelihood; *encomenderos* had also the bleak little annual tribute of a blanket and corn from each Pueblo household. All New Mexicans, Pueblo and Spanish alike, lived forever on the defensive against Apaches. It was difficult to imagine that they would ever have the energies, the time, or the heart to develop any wealth. Even Pueblo conversions were precarious, easily reversible if new demands should be imposed or other conditions worsen. Those who knew the province agreed that, if the Crown contemplated any changes of policy toward New Mexico, it had better increase its aid, not its demands.

The investigation seemed to make nonsense of all Benavides had said. Resigned to a continuing financial drain in New Mexico, the Crown turned its attention back to more pressing problems of empire. Unfortunately, the new information on New Mexico came in confidential documents and never circulated abroad to counter the effect of the Benavides *Memorials*. Thus, unseemly and largely unwarranted interest in New Mexico persisted at some foreign courts.

Perhaps the most interested observers of events in New Mexico were the

Apaches and Navajos of whose impending conversion Benavides had felt so sure. Even Fray Alonso's optimism would have been sorely tried had he served in New Mexico another decade, for the 1630's saw disaster piled upon disaster. Watching Apaches and Navajos could see little evidence that adherence to the new religion had brought the Pueblos any benefits.

Indians expected definite results from proper ceremonial obeisance to specific gods, but everything seemed to go wrong in the pueblos. The rains failed year after year, and the drought cycle brought famine. Many people died. Weakened by starvation, they suffered from repeated epidemics of smallpox and of the fever that Mexicans called *cocolitzli*. When troubled Pueblos tried to perform their old ceremonials to make things right in their world again, the friars objected, and there were dreadful times when friars broke up Pueblo meetings and destroyed sacred masks and fetishes. Some Pueblos fled to Apache and Navajo camps; some who stayed in their homes took strong measures to end their troubles. In 1632 Zuñis rid themselves of missionaries by murdering two. Toward the end of the decade, Taos and Jémez revolted, killing their priests and destroying much of the mission properties. All pueblos seethed with tension and fear. The friars did their best to feed the hungry during famines, but on the whole there was little to envy in the lives of "converted" Pueblos. . . .

Among the Pueblos, the ordeal of death and destruction evoked a resurgence of their old religion stronger than any before. The principal leaders were Tewa shamans, but the movement affected every pueblo. Spaniards, friars and settlers alike, were frightened and dismayed by the apparent surge of witchcraft. Half a dozen priests and several settlers died mysteriously, presumed victims of witchcraft; it was whispered that the priest at San Idelfonso was bewitched. Throughout the Tewa pueblos and at the outlying pueblos of Zuñi, Ácoma, and Taos, friars found "idolatry" so prevalent that they could no longer perform their ministry.

Against a foe identified as witchcraft, surely the appropriate remedy should have been exorcism, but of such response no record remains. The friars approved of the forceful reaction of Governor Juan Francisco Treviño (1675–1677), who dispatched soldiers to seize the leaders, confiscate their religious paraphernalia, and burn their kivas. They hanged three shamans of Nambé, San Felipe, and Jémez. Another despairing soul hanged himself. Forty-three more leaders of the movement were publicly whipped, then jailed at Santa Fe, and sentenced to be sold into slavery for the crime of idolatry.

To the Spaniards' amazement, the Pueblos rallied to save their shamans. A horde of warriors appeared at Santa Fe, and seventy entered the Governor's Palace, weapons in hand, to demand release of the imprisoned leaders. Quiet, courteous, but in deadly earnest, they prevailed. Governor Treviño released to them the prisoners and all went home to their pueblos, but nothing was ever the same after that. Scars on flogged backs healed, but wounds in pride and spirit did not. The strongest leaders plotted more earnestly than ever before. Many Pueblos would continue to avoid strife at nearly any price, but now they could all remember a time when they had stood together to defend the Pueblo way and had made the Spaniards bow to their will.

Spaniards would later recall that quiet, compelling confrontation in the Governor's Palace in 1675 and know that it foreshadowed the holocaust. But at that moment the overriding threat was imminent destruction of the province by *bárbaros,* and Treviño needed every able-bodied man in New Mexico to defend the frontiers. He dared not risk battle with Pueblos.

By autumn 1676, the leadership of the province united in a desperate appeal for help [w]hen Custodian and Procurator General Fray Francisco de Ayeta journeyed to Mexico for the triennial mission supply caravan . . .

Fray Ayeta sought permanent remedy, encouraged by reports that the Crown had approved the viceroy's earlier assistance and had asked to be kept informed of the New Mexican situation. Ayeta requested fifty more men to defend the frontier at once and perhaps someday to reduce the *bárbaros* to peace. . . .

With luck, a caravan could reach Santa Fe in six months, but big supply trains were vulnerable to many delays, and this proved a difficult year. The next August found the caravan marking time at El Paso, held up by unseasonal high waters in the Rio Grande. With it waited twenty-seven New Mexican soldiers under Pedro de Leiva, sent by Governor Otermín to escort the caravan up the dangerous road to Santa Fe. At eight o'clock on the morning of August 25, 1680, stunning news reached Leiva and Ayeta: general Pueblo revolt in New Mexico. . . .

Looking back from El Paso that autumn, Governor Otermín was still amazed at the revolt. No one denied that the Pueblos had had grievances in the past, but New Mexico had lately enjoyed greater tranquillity. Otermín had carefully protected the Pueblos from excessive demands, requiring them only "to assist in the cultivation of the soil in order to obtain the necessary subsistence." Spaniards had enjoyed cordially cooperative relationships with many Pueblos. Some groups had preferred their *encomenderos* to live in or near their pueblos for maximum security against *bárbaros.* Even the Apaches and Navajos had been less troublesome than usual that year, and the Utes had kept their peace pact of 1678 so faithfully that Otermín had thought their conversion imminent.

Utterly incomprehensible to Otermín was the depth of rancor rooted in old grievances, although he came to Santa Fe only two years after the crucial episode of 1675. Among the shamans rescued from Governor Treviño by the Tewa warriors had been Popé, who carried home to San Juan pueblo a grim determination to destroy the Spaniards. His persistent invocation of traditional spirits and his burning hostility to Spaniards made him suspect in San Juan, so Popé moved north to Taos. There he secluded himself in a kiva, communing with spirit messengers of the old war gods, who made Popé their envoy to all Pueblos. In the summer of 1680 he proclaimed their message throughout the Pueblo world: rise up together to destroy the Spaniards or drive them out forever, then forget all they taught you and discard all they brought. Go back to ancient ways.

Popé had negotiated many months with like-minded Pueblo leaders and perhaps with *bárbaros,* too. He brooked no resistance. When he suspected that his son-in-law, the governor of San Juan, would report him to Spanish authorities, he killed the man in his own house. When at last Popé issued the call to revolt, he threatened to have Apaches destroy any pueblo that failed to join in the rebellion.

Runners carried the message to all pueblos, as far south as Isleta. A knotted thong told the days that must pass before they would rise together on August 11, first destroying all Spaniards in their own vicinity, then converging on Santa Fe to finish off the colony.

The response was far from unanimous. Although many shared Popé's longing for liberation from the Spanish regime, there were compelling arguments against his scheme. Many Pueblos preferred peace above all else, and they dreaded a return to the old days of internecine strife. Although few practiced the exclusive devotion the Franciscans expected, some valued Christianity as they understood it and were loath to lose the sacraments or harm the friars. Some Pueblos had ties of blood or friendship in the Spanish community. The indigenous and colonial populations had mingled for eight decades; many Pueblos and Spaniards cordially acknowledged kinsmen of the other race. While Pueblo labor had often been abused, some pleasant and even close relationships had grown between employers and workers. Some *encomenderos* had won the gratitude of the Indians they protected during the years that Pueblos and Spaniards fought side by side against the *bárbaros*. Most Pueblos had become involved in the more complex economy introduced by the Spaniards: many would find it difficult to revert to the limited old economy.

Even Pueblos without personal ties to any Spaniard raised questions. Perhaps the Apaches and Navajos would indeed help them to get rid of the Spaniards, but what if they should afterward attack the Pueblos when the soldiers and their guns were gone? And what of Popé himself? Such a self-assertive, overweening man was the very antithesis of the Pueblo ideal, perhaps a dangerous sorcerer. Would they be better off at his mercy than under Spanish rule? Many doubted it, some so vehemently that they warned the Spaniards.

Leaders of five nearby pueblos rode to Santa Fe to warn Governor Otermín on August 9, the same day that he received warning messages from the two priests and the *alcalde mayor* at Taos. Meanwhile, at Pecos, Governor Don Felipe tried in vain to convince the priests and soldiers stationed there of the impending revolt. The story did confound Spanish minds: no Pueblo group totally uninvolved in the plot, Apache allies poised on the rim of the province to support the rebels. But Popé's two runners, intercepted by Spaniards, confirmed the plot.

Their arrest precipitated the rebellion a little prematurely. The Indians of Tesuque murdered their missionary, rounded up the cattle and horses, and fled to the mountains. Every pueblo north of Isleta erupted. Once the die was cast, many who had opposed the plot saw no choice but to join in the fray. Some dispersed settlers were warned in time to escape, but many Spanish families suffered devastating losses. About a thousand survivors in the northern district took refuge in the Governor's Palace at Santa Fe; those in the southern district flocked to loyal Isleta pueblo, certain that no one could have survived the bloodbath in the north.

Ácoma, Zuñi, and Hopi warriors did not trek to Santa Fe to join the siege, but no Spaniards survived at those remote pueblos or at Picurís. Even at Taos, where the plot had been discovered, only two soldiers managed to fight their way out after their families were killed. They reported at Santa Fe that the Apaches del Acho had joined the forces of Picurís and Taos.

On August 13, a sizeable body of Tano warriors formed across the river, just south of Santa Fe's main plaza. Their leader, a Spanish-speaking Tano resident of Santa Fe called Juan, parleyed with Governor Otermín in the plaza. The governor appealed to the rebels' Christian consciences, promising pardon if they would abandon the insurrection, but to no avail. Juan boasted of reinforcements coming from the other pueblos and from the Apaches, all sworn to destroy the villa, and demanded that Otermín choose between a red cross, signifying war, and a white cross, signifying abandonment of the province. The governor chose to fight that day, before those reinforcements could arrive. Battle swirled through the Barrio Analco, around the church of San Miguel. Otermín claimed victory over the Tanos, but as they fled their allies arrived: Tewas, Taoseños, and Picurís.

More followed. By August 16, 2,500 Indians surrounded Santa Fe. For nine days they besieged the Spanish community, barricaded with their livestock in the Governor's Palace. No Spanish soldiers died, but many were wounded. The Indians had seized the guns and ammunition of Spaniards slain throughout the province and they used them to good effect. The soldiers' leather armor repelled arrows but not shot. Himself wounded in a desperate, futile charge from the Palace on August 20, Otermín took stock of his situation.

Of more than a thousand persons in the Palace, less than one hundred were men who could fight. The sole hope for the lives of all those women and children was to walk to Isleta to join the other survivors. On August 21, they evacuated the Palace and marched toward Isleta. The Indians gleefully swarmed to sack the Palace, apparently content for the moment despite their heavy casualties. More vindictive rebels would have pursued Otermín's rabble of refugees to wipe them out, but those Pueblos were satisfied just to see them go: "We are at quits with the Spaniards and the persons whom we have killed; those of us whom they have killed do not matter, for they are going, and now we shall live as we like and settle in this villa and wherever we see fit."

The fleeing colonists progressed mournfully downstream from one deserted pueblo to another, past haciendas gruesome with corpses of families known to all the marchers. Mounted Indians watched from the heights, carefully herding numerous horses and cattle, more eager now to keep livestock than to kill Spaniards.

To the governor's chagrin, Isleta also lay deserted. Runners were sent ahead to order the retreating southern survivors to wait, and the group trudged on. Grimly aware now that they trod Apache country, Otermín pressed to consolidate the two groups at the earliest possible moment, but it was September 13 before he reached the southern refugees' camp at Fray Cristóbal, forty miles below Socorro.

Otermín had hoped there to muster enough soldiers to turn back and quell the rebellion, but none had any stomach for the venture. At most, 155 men could bear arms; they had only 471 horses and mules, most in bad shape. Of the estimated 2,500 persons in camp, most were women and children, suffering agonies of hunger and fatigue. With winter imminent, they had to be escorted safely to El Paso. Bowing to those arguments, Otermín led his wretched band on to El Paso.

The fugitives were a heterogeneous lot. A few Spaniards were householders of substance; most were desperately poor; many were servants attached to some household. Much of the non-Spanish population had chosen to stay on in New Mexico. Only six convicts* made the trek south: few had had time to finish their sentences since Ayeta delivered them to Santa Fe less than three years before, so the sentence to New Mexico must have proved a death sentence to most of the forty-nine.

With the retreating colonists trudged 317 Christian Indians of all ages and sexes from the pueblos of Isleta, Sevilleta, Alamillo, Socorro, and Senecú, plus one Tewa couple with their six children. Since the Isletas had not honored the call to revolt and since the Piros had not even been invited, they had every reason to fear the Pueblos upstream. Enmity between northern Pueblos and Piros long antedated the Spanish presence: apparently the old distrusts endured.

Of the 380 Spaniards killed in the uprising, 73 were men of military age, a telling blow to a colony that had rarely boasted more than two hundred men-at-arms. The Franciscans had grave shortages to repair if they were to restore their ministry, for twenty-one priests had died at the pueblos.

Many of the fleeing settlers would gladly have escaped deeper into New Spain to forget New Mexico forever. Anticipating that, and determined that these colonists would spearhead prompt reconquest, Fray Ayeta had taken steps to hold them. Although they crossed the Rio Grande into Nueva Vizcaya to establish their camp, Ayeta had arranged for Otermín's jurisdiction to cover the refugees south of the Rio Grande, too. Any deserters fleeing deeper into Nueva Vizcaya would be rounded up and returned to El Paso. No matter how sick they were of New Mexico, or how grievous their losses, or how little they had to go back for, they must camp on the Rio Grande to await reconquest. Fray Ayeta promised to support them with every resource at his command until the Crown could assume the responsibility. . . .

Leaders of the rebellion had worked hard all year to consolidate their gains. Popé and his lieutenants had promptly sought to erase every trace of the Spanish regime and restore the old ways in absolute purity. At his direction, people waded into streams to scrub themselves with yucca root, so as to purge themselves of Christian baptism. Churches were destroyed, sacred images defaced, religious accouterments put to homely uses. Building new kivas and bringing ritual paraphernalia out of hiding or fashioning it anew,

---

*Men in jail were released if they agreed to go to New Mexico.

the people celebrated an intensive round of rituals to restore the old, essential harmonies among Pueblos and the spirits of their universe.

When Popé urged Pueblos to repudiate marriages based on the Christian sacrament and choose any mates they wished for however long they wished, some gladly returned to the older, more flexible Pueblo style of marriage. But Popé's fanaticism carried him too far when he told them to relinquish everything the Spaniards had brought. Many of the innovations had enriched the Pueblos' material lives, and they had gladly expropriated the colonists' possessions. Cattle, sheep, oxen, and especially horses and mules were carefully husbanded. No one wished to quit using carts and teams, or to eschew plows and hoes in favor of pointed sticks, or to abandon the friars' better irrigation methods. Worst of all was Popé's demand that the Pueblos destroy the seeds of crops the Spaniards had introduced. Who would willingly renounce the wheat, the melons, the tomatoes, and the chiles which the Spaniards had brought to New Mexico? Who would destroy the orchards of apple and peach and apricot and pear trees, sacrificing not only their luscious fruits but their pleasant green shade about the pueblos?

Nor would people discard their new skills. Traditions of fine craftsmanship were old in the Pueblo world, but they had gained much from the Spaniards. Now Pueblo weavers turned out fine woolen textiles; some were skilled carpenters and metalworkers. Pueblo blacksmiths were competent to run the Spanish smithies and to repair and manufacture weapons and tools as long as the metal supply should last.

Nor would Pueblos go back to old ways of fighting. They had carefully salvaged the arms of slain Spaniards: swords, lances, daggers, and armor, as well as guns. Some would meet Spaniards on equal terms in any future encounter, armed like Europeans and mounted on horses that they could handle well. With that complement, those Pueblos who, by choice or necessity, battled on foot with their bows and arrows would stand all the firmer. Even if the Spaniards should never return, what rational people would cling to old-style warfare now that Apaches, Navajos, and Utes rode horses and fought with metal weapons?

Popé had been a useful leader against the Spaniards, but he was dangerous to anyone who opposed his ideas, and he was in some ways conspicuously unwise. He soon became such a nuisance that his own people killed him. Even in the early stages, while Popé stirred men's minds like a whirlwind with his nativist crusade, more practical leaders labored to assure the Pueblos' safety. . . .

The Pueblos' tragedy was that the trials of freedom had nearly outweighed the joys. Support for the revolt had never been unanimous. As troubles occurred, recriminations arose inexorably. Crops still failed, enemies still raided, and critics of the rebellion recalled that friars and soldiers had been useful in such crises. Since Pueblo society had never developed any practicable way of handling dissent within a village, major issues inevitably spawned bitter factions. The quarrels within and among pueblos, the stresses of enemy raids and warfare, the realities of hunger, and the shadowy apprehensions of Spanish vengeance led many to flee, either to the remote Hopi territory or to the Navajos.

Ironically, the principal beneficiaries of the revolt were the Apaches and Navajos who had not rallied to support it. For the far-riding Apaches, it was a time to claim vast new hunting grounds, scouring away weaker peoples, driving them to seek nearly any refuge from oblivion. Some of their victims sought alliance with other Indians; some looked southward to the Spanish frontier for protection. There the livestock herds of missions and presidios beckoned to Apache raiders, who exploited the opportunity to the hilt. Some retaliatory campaigns from Sonora and El Paso struck *rancherías* of the Gila and Siete Rios Apaches, but, for the most part, Apache raiders enjoyed in the late seventeenth century a wide choice of targets and relative safety from retaliation.

Far to the north, safely remote from Spanish forces for two valuable decades, Navajos shrewdly assimilated people and goods, ideas and skills, with which they evolved their own unique, enduring way of life. The most recent Athapaskan migrants to the region, not many centuries earlier than the Spaniards, Navajos had found the Pueblo example powerful. Their folk memory has it that they acquired corn from the Pueblos; many of the myths and rituals by which Navajos live reflect Pueblo influence. However, Navajos never wavered from their strong sense of identity as a people. Always they were selective adapters, not slavish imitators of the more advanced culture. Their work of selective adaptation continued when Spaniards intruded so many novelties upon the Pueblo world. While Pueblos suffered the traumas of imposed change, Navajos freely made important choices that transformed their own lives.

The Navajo homeland lay just northwest of the Pueblo heartland. Its well-guarded mesatop dwellings and canyon farms offered a natural refuge to Pueblos fleeing the periodic turmoils after the Spanish occupation. The flow of Pueblo refugees climaxed with the many who abandoned their homes forever during the final agonizing sequence of revolt, chaotic independence, and eventual reconquest. By virtue of their numbers, the refugees partly compensated for Navajos lost over the years to Spanish raiders. Even more significant, however, were the skills the Pueblos brought to Navajos when the Navajos were reorienting their lives around the livestock introduced by Spaniards in New Mexico.

Pueblos had learned from Spaniards how to use the fleece of the tough, wiry little sheep, and they brought that complex of skills to the Navajos: the shearing, the washing with yucca root, and the carding and spinning, which precede the weaving or knitting of finished textiles. Weaving was an old skill among Pueblo men, who had readily adapted to use of woolen yarns on the stationary looms with which they had long made cotton textiles. Woolen textile weaving rapidly became important among Navajos, too, but in their world the weavers were women, and they did not adopt either the stationary loom of the Pueblos or the treadle loom of the Spaniards. They preferred the distinctive portable loom, which they perhaps knew when they came to the Southwest. With that loom and the wool of their ever-increasing flocks, Navajo women became peerless weavers. The women owned the sheep and, with their children's help, herded, sheared, and butchered.

While ownership and management of sheep brought new focus to the lives of Navajo women, horses transformed the men's lives. They owned and herded the horses, and they used them for the hunting, raiding, and warfare that remained prime duties of men. Men also had primary responsibility for farming, although women and children helped to tend crops when their shepherd duties permitted.

Navajos proved good husbandmen: their herds grew with natural increase as well as raiding. The need for pasture, especially for the voracious sheep, dictated new patterns of Navajo life, ranging over wider expanses of grassland, yet revolving about the little farms and orchards that grew ever more important to Navajo life. New crops introduced by Spaniards and adopted by Pueblos had come also to Navajos. Some innovations, especially peach orchards, grew nearly as vital as the sacred crops of corn, beans, squash, and tobacco.

The Navajos' new riches required their geographic expansion just when the horse widened their practicable range of operations. Thus, Navajos expanded westward, establishing farmsteads in sheltered, watered canyons, settling their matrilocal extended families in little clusters of hogans from which family members ranged in accord with seasonal requirements of their livestock. The lands into which they moved had been home centuries earlier to Pueblo forebears. Navajos lived in respectful proximity to the ruined homes of the Ancient Ones, reverently grinding ancient potsherds to temper new Navajo pots made with techniques learned from contemporary Pueblo guests. . . .

Roanoke: England's Lost Colony

KAREN ORDAHL KUPPERMAN

. . . Sir Walter Raleigh was a rising young man of thirty in 1584, when he decided to found the first English colony in North America. He was a younger son of a distinguished but impoverished family, and his parents had managed to give him the education of an aristocrat. . . .

By 1581, when he was twenty-seven, Raleigh was a veteran of the kind of experiences that had prepared countless other sons of the gentry for lives as country gentlemen. But at this point he was noticed by Queen Elizabeth, and he became a member—for a while the most important member—of a charmed circle of young men who played her lovestruck suitors. Raleigh was a master at the punning word games she loved. His poetry was prized, and his exotic good looks, enhanced by flamboyant clothes, made him stand out. The queen loved him; most people found him too arrogant, "damnable proud," as John Aubrey wrote.

Becoming the queen's favorite meant wealth beyond imagining. Over the next several years Elizabeth bestowed on Raleigh land and houses all over England and Ireland. Moreover, she gave him monopoly control of the wine and woolen-cloth industries, and his agents raked off a percentage of the profits to subsidize his extravagant life.

Karen Ordahl Kupperman, "Roanoke Lost," in *American Heritage,* pp. 81–96. Reprinted with permission from *American Heritage,* Volume 36, Number 5. Copyright 1985 by *American Heritage,* a Division of Forbes, Inc.

In 1583 Sir Humphrey Gilbert died at sea, attempting to start a colony in Newfoundland, and Raleigh asked the queen to transfer to him his half brother's exclusive right to colonize in North America. In 1584, with his patent in hand, Raleigh sent two ships to reconnoiter the southern coast of North America.

That year was a turning point in Queen Elizabeth's foreign policy; it was no accident that Raleigh's colonizing activities began then, for that was when the growing animosity between Spain and England erupted into open war. The immense wealth flowing from its American possessions had helped make Spain the superpower of the sixteenth century; England was seen even by its own citizens as a scrappy underdog. Moreover, the English saw Spain . . . as the leader of an international conspiracy to crush Britain and restore it to papal control. . . .

Elizabeth conducted [the Anglo-Spanish War] as she did her other enterprises: by issuing licenses and patents to private citizens. In theory, commissions to go after Spanish ships were strictly controlled; in practice, corruption allowed wide access to privateering licenses, and legalized piracy became big business for the next decade and a half, sometimes bringing in 10 percent of the nation's imports. Gentlemen like Raleigh, joining forces with merchants to field large fleets, saw themselves as patriots, and history has celebrated their exploits.

Though all Spanish ships were vulnerable, attention focused on the treasure fleet, heavily laden cargo ships that annually carried the wealth of the Indies to Spain. By the mid-1580s Spain was so overextended that this treasure was no longer a luxury. By seizing Spanish ships, English privateers could set themselves up for life and cripple the enemy at the same time.

Roanoke initially was planned purely to make preying on the treasure fleet easier. A base near the West Indies, yet hidden away, could make privateering a year-round occupation, even during fall and winter storms. Colonization, like privateering, was licensed by the government, but since each expedition had to pay its own way, a colony at Roanoke would never have been attempted without the tie to privateering. Spanish treasure partially repaid Roanoke's investors, yet privateering also killed the plantation and led to the tragedy of the Lost Colony.

Raleigh's reconnaissance fleet, commanded by Arthur Barlowe and Philip Amadas, was sent in April 1584. They followed the route normal at the time: south along the coast of Europe to pick up the trade winds off the Canaries and then west to the Caribbean and the coastal current that helped propel them northward. After several weeks of exploration around the Outer Banks, Amadas and Barlowe were sure they had found a perfect location for the new settlement: sheltered yet providing easy access to the treasure fleet's homeward path.

Barlowe, who wrote the official account of the voyage, described the land in the most glowing terms. . . . In reality the Outer Banks are relatively infertile, and the location was a poor one for a settlement.

Even before the reconnaissance fleet returned, backers were being signed up for a full colony. Elizabeth gave the project many marks of favor. Though she declined to put government money behind it, she invested her own money and a ship and even allowed the territory to be called Virginia in her honor. She refused to let Raleigh go on such a dangerous voyage, so he chose his hotheaded cousin Sir Richard Grenville to command the expedition.

The composition of the fleet bearing the colony of 108 men, which sailed in April 1585, clearly indicated the investors' expectations: five large and two small ships carried almost three hundred sailors and as many soldiers. Such huge crews were a sure sign of an intention to go privateering: prize ships were to be boarded and conquered in hand-to-hand fighting and then sent home to England manned by the privateers. . . .

As soon as the ships arrived off the Outer Banks, it became clear that the location was a mistake. The flagship was driven repeatedly against the shore and was almost lost, and most of the colonists' food supplies were destroyed. The inlet that gave access to Roanoke Island was so shallow and treacherous that only the tiny pinnaces could be taken through, and then only with extreme care. Medium-size ships could shelter along the Banks, but the largest vessels were forced to anchor several miles out to sea, exposed to dangerous storms.

It must have been a grim council that sat down to decide what to do. There is some evidence that Grenville and his entire fleet were supposed to stay and inaugurate the colony's use as a privateering base, but that was now clearly impossible. Grenville promised that he would bring supplies in the spring, just as soon as the Atlantic was safe, so Lane and his colonists agreed to stay, spending the winter looking for a better location and learning about the territory. The colonists set to work building a fort, and Grenville and his men went exploring on the Carolina mainland.

We know a great deal about the Carolina Algonquians, on whom the colonists were intruding, because Raleigh was a true Renaissance man whose scholarly interests were as important to him as fighting Spain and making money. He had sent along Thomas Harriot, a young scientist and mathematician recently graduated from Oxford, to study the land and its resources and make a full report on Indian culture. Amadas and Barlowe had returned from their reconnaissance with two Indians, named Manteo and Wanchese, and Harriot had spent a year learning their language and teaching them English. An artist named John White accompanied Harriot to Virginia to illustrate his findings.

Together, White and Harriot created a remarkable record; their maps are said to be the most accurate done in America in the sixteenth century, and White's paintings of Indian life were not equaled before the advent of photography. They show strong, dignified Indians and a highly successful culture. Harriot's descriptions allow us to see that culture from the inside.

The coastal Carolina Algonquians were organized in tribal groupings consisting of several towns of approximately one to two hundred people each. The Roanoke Indians had their capital on the mainland opposite the island, under a werowance named Wingina. Werowance means "he who is rich," but the Indians' meaning of riches was different from the colonists'. The tribe's goods, including the novel European trade items, all flowed into the hands of the chief, but his role was redistributing, so that all shared the bounty. If he had tried to control the wealth, he would have lost his people's respect. Though he moved among his subjects in great state, the werowance lacked coercive power and led by moral authority alone.

Justice and war were also governed by a principle of balance. When an individual or a tribe sustained injury, redress was sought through compensation or the infliction of a similar injury. Warfare was therefore limited and controlled, and generosity was rewarded. Barlowe and Amadas had seen a vivid illustration of this principle in their first contact with the Roanokes. A single man approached their ships and greeted them. He was taken aboard and given a hat and shirt and a taste of wine and meat. When he left, they saw him fishing a short way off; soon he returned, divided his catch into piles, and told the colonists in sign language that one pile was to go to each ship. He would not leave until he had reciprocated their hospitality.

Harriot was particularly interested in Indian religion, and his description allows us to understand some of their theology. The priest, a man chosen for his wisdom, was responsible for overseeing his people's relationship to the deity and maintaining the round of ceremonies that helped the crops grow. Another figure, whom White called the Flyer, was a much younger man, chosen for his magical powers, which derived from a personal relationship with a supernatural being. This conjurer wore a small black bird on the side of his head and a skin with an animal's face on his front. Because disease was thought to be caused by the vengeful spirits of improperly killed animals and because the conjurer had magical relationships with animals, he was considered able to effect cures. The Flyer probably represented an older, individualistic hunting cult that was being edged out by the newer, more abstract religion of the priest.

The English were pleased to find that the Indians lived in towns organized around village greens and surrounded by cornfields just like familiar towns at home. Yield was, to Harriot's mind, almost miraculous: "at the least two hundred London bushelles ... [whereas] in England fourtie bushelles of our wheate yeelded out of such an acre is thought to be much." Corn was planted in hills, with beans growing up the stalks; the beans, with their nitrogen-fixing properties, fertilized the corn as it grew, and the two crops eaten together formed superior protein. There is incontrovertible evidence of the efficiency of Indian agriculture: the Carolina Algonquians had on hand enough surplus food to keep more than one hundred colonists alive during the winter of 1585–86.

Praise for Indian society did not imply a vision of coexistence: even Europeans like Harriot who were truly interested in the natives saw themselves as bringing the priceless gifts of Christianity and civilization. Indian sophistication simply meant that the job of conversion would be easier; the natives would see the superiority of English culture and spontaneously choose it for themselves.

The Indians showed interest in Harriot's magnet, compass, and books and in the colonists' guns and "spring clocks that seeme to goe of themselves," and according to Harriot, they assumed such technology was a divine gift. When many Indians died of European diseases to which they had no immunity while the English did not suffer, the natives saw the hand of a powerful god at work.

The Indians were not, however, ready to give up their own culture wholesale. Like Indians all over America, the Carolina Algonquians picked and chose from the Europeans those items of technology, particularly metal tools, that made tasks within their own economy easier; they wanted to enhance their way of life, not relinquish it. Moreover, it is easy for us to exaggerate the apparent superiority of European technology; what the Indians saw at Roanoke was a large party of men who were so helpless that Gov. Ralph Lane at one point accused the Indians of making war simply by cutting off all contact with the English.

While the Roanoke colonists were learning about the Indians, they were revealing a great deal about themselves. The Indians must have been deeply disturbed by what they saw. Almost as soon as the first colony arrived, in 1585, Grenville took his small boats and went exploring on the mainland. The explorers at one point discovered a silver cup missing from their baggage and returned to a village they had visited two days previously to demand its return. When they found that all the inhabitants had fled, they "burnt, and spoyled their corne, and Towne. . . ."

It is hard for us to understand why Grenville would have ordered an act so damaging to friendly relations—especially since the colonists, whose supplies had been destroyed in the accident to the flagship, would be totally dependent on the Indians until spring. His thinking rested on a view of human nature prevalent in that age: All relationships, even among Europeans, were seen as involving domination and submission. The colonists revealed again and again their assumption that anyone who showed vulnerability would be a victim of treachery and would deserve it. Grenville thought that by exacting severe vengeance on those he suspected of stealing, he was protecting the colonists, not damaging their chances. And though the backers in England had counseled the colonists to win the Indians through loving kindness, they had ensured the policy of intimidation by sending over veterans of the Irish and continental wars as colonists. We will never know if a peaceful relationship might have been possible; it was not given a chance.

The English were also obsessed with control within their own settlement. The relation between leaders and the "meaner sort" was expected to be one of iron discipline; the rank-and-file colonists, whom Gov. Ralph Lane referred to as "wild men of mine own nation," would be mutinous if given a chance. Lane believed that the low rate of disease in his colony's year in America was a direct product of his "severely executed" discipline. We have veiled hints of trouble in the colony; apparently the taverns of England rang with complaints once the soldiers returned home, and Harriot pointed out that those who complained were men who had been disciplined in America. . . .

Meanwhile, as spring came on, the Roanokes' food supply was stretched beyond endurance. Both Indians and English split up into small groups to live off the land, vastly increasing English vulnerability. At the same time, the goods traded to the Roanokes in return for their corn gave them unprecedented power to attract alliances with other tribes.

Spring brought the death of Wingina's brother Granganimeo, the man most friendly to the English in Roanoke councils; Wingina changed his name to Pemisapan, which implied a watchful, wary attitude. It may have been a war name. The colonists became convinced he was planning a conspiracy with other tribes to get rid of the settlement. Lane struck first, and Pemisapan died in an attack that began with the battle cry "Christ our victory!"

Though the immediate threat was ended, the colonists were desperate: there would be no harvest for weeks, and they could expect no Indian aid. A week after the death of Pemisapan, long after Lane had expected relief from home, his lookout sighted an English fleet; the colonists knew they were saved.

The fleet was that of Sir Francis Drake, who had been privateering in Spanish America almost as long as the settlers had been at Roanoke. He came expecting to make use of their base, but what he found was quite different: a colony in disarray and an anchorage that kept his ships two miles out to sea. He and Lane discussed the possibility of his leaving ships, men, and supplies so that Lane could continue his explorations over the summer, but a great storm so damaged Drake's fleet that he was forced to leave. The colonists all went with him. The sailor hosts were so anxious to get under way that most of the settlers' baggage, including Harriot's notes and specimens and many of White's drawings, was thrown overboard. . . .

Once the colonists were safely back home, all agreed that a new site on Chesapeake Bay should be tried. Though farsighted men such as Thomas Harriot and the great promoter Richard Hakluyt argued for the development of identified American resources, the governor and many of his colonists were contemptuous of the possibilities of the new land unless gold was found. Lane now saw the land as a barrier and wrote that the best hope was for discovery of a passage through to the East. Potential backers saw clearly that all income so far had flowed from privateering.

Nonetheless, there were those who felt strongly that with a new site and the proper backing a colony could become self-sustaining and ultimately provide a rich trade for England. John White was preeminent among them. He and Thomas Harriot hoped their findings would help attract new backing. Harriot's *A briefe and true report of the new found land of Virginia,* a careful survey of resources, was published on its own in 1588 and with woodcuts of White's paintings in 1590.

. . . By 1587 a new colonial venture had been set up, and White, the man who had worked hardest for it, was the new governor. Its promoters set out to correct all the obvious errors made in 1585, but the legacy of the first colony, particularly its connection with privateering, was to haunt the new effort and ultimately to destroy it.

Raleigh, with his estates and concerns all over England, was losing interest in running a colonial venture the future of which seemed dim. He encouraged White to organize a corporation in which the colonists themselves would take a leading role. The City of Raleigh, as the corporation was called, was to be governed by White and a board of directors known as the assistants, most of whom intended to emigrate. The leadership would be much less authoritarian than that of the earlier colony, and the settlement would be on Chesapeake Bay, on fertile land approachable by oceangoing ships—probably very near where Jamestown was to be founded in 1607.

The colonists—men, women, and children—were people with something to invest, at least to the extent of outfitting themselves for the journey. Each family was to receive five hundred acres in the new land, and they came to America planning to stay, to re-create English culture. There were seventeen women and nine children. Two of the women were so heavily pregnant that they gave birth within weeks of their arrival at Roanoke. Several of the families consisted of men and their sons; presumably mothers and other children were to join them later. In its population as well as in its corporate organization, the City of Raleigh pointed to the future: all successful colonies were built on this family-centered model.

The colony set out on three small ships in the spring of 1587. Simon Fernandes, a Portuguese navigator who was one of the corporation's assistants, was in charge of the voyage and saw no reason not to place top priority on privateering. Almost three months elapsed before the ship finally landed in America.

Shipboard life was miserable. Only the highest officers had bunks; ordinary seamen and passengers rolled up in blankets between decks. Rations were salt meat and fish and hardtack, with some oatmeal, butter, and cheese. The water and beer began to go bad after the first four weeks. During storms the passengers stayed belowdecks, where rats and cockroaches, stirred up by the ship's motion, scuttled over them. Vomit, feces, and urine mixed with the seawater leaking into the ship. The stench quickly became overpowering.

Also, the passengers' lives were in danger as long as their little fleet attacked other ships. White raged impotently at Fernandes, who gambled with the entire venture. Fernandes refused to take the colonists north to Chesapeake Bay and dumped them instead at Roanoke. According to White, the explanation from "our Simon" was that "the summer was farre spent" and he wanted to get back to privateering. But the ships stayed with the colonists for a month, until they were settled for the winter, and, in fact, Fernandes may have felt it was too late in the year to begin a wholly new settlement—the houses on Roanoke were still standing—and White may have been secretly pleased to be back on familiar ground.

Once the houses were cleaned up, the settlers began to assess their situation. From the beginning there was evidence of Indian hostility. . . . White decided to approach the Croatoans, Manteo's people, who had always been friendly. Manteo had made a second trip to England with Lane's men and had just now returned to his land with White's colonists.

The Croatoans, though fearful at first, welcomed the colonists and gave the delegation a feast. There were signs of tension, though: the Croatoans asked the colonists "not to gather or spill any of their corne, for that they had but little." They also hesitantly mentioned the fact that some of their people had been wounded when Lane's men mistook them for enemies, and they asked for some badge to indicate their friendly status.

The Croatoans confirmed what the colonists already knew—that the nearby mainland Indians were now implacably hostile. . . .

The delegation asked Manteo's people to organize a meeting between the settlers and their enemies in one week. When no word came, the English, true to their view of human nature, saw it as a challenge they could not ignore. They decided to surprise the Roanokes at their mainland capital. . . . The attack was a fiasco. The village was inhabited only by Croatoans, including women and children, who had moved in after the Roanokes had fled. The colonists thus offended their only friends while failing to prove that Indians could not kill Englishmen with impunity.

The colonists must have been heavyhearted as they observed the mariners cleaning and recaulking their ships for the return voyage. White said they kept busy writing letters and preparing "tokens" for family and friends back home. He proudly recorded the birth of his own granddaughter, Virginia Dare, the first baby born in America of English parentage, and noted that Margery Harvie was also delivered successfully. As the fleet's departure approached, the colonists grew fearful; they wanted to make sure that they were not forgotten and begged White to go along as their representative. He held out for days, fearing he would be accused of desertion, but finally agreed after getting the request in writing.

As soon as he was back in England, White rushed to Raleigh, and plans were laid for a great supply fleet of seven or eight ships to sail in the spring under Sir Richard Grenville. Raleigh arranged for the publication of Harriot's report to encourage investment. White devoted the winter to gathering the necessary supplies and more colonists. Everything was ready for an early departure.

Suddenly the connection with privateering intervened in the most fateful possible way: Spain decided to cut off harassment at the source, assembling the great Spanish Armada of one hundred and thirty ships manned by eight thousand sailors and nineteen thousand soldiers. Elizabeth and her advisers were afraid; the Privy Council announced that no ships capable of service in war were to leave England. Grenville's great fleet was diverted to defense, and throughout the summer of 1588 England focused on its own danger. . . .

Early in 1589 the corporation backing Roanoke was reorganized again, and this time Raleigh signed over most of his rights. . . . Nothing was done all year. In 1590 the Privy Council, fearing a renewed attack by Spain on the homeland, issued another general stay of shipping. White, desperately impatient, managed to get some privateers an exemption if they would promise to take him to Roanoke.

Long weeks were spent preying on ships in the West Indies. Finally, in August 1591, two of the ships moved northward to the Outer Banks. When they finally anchored off Roanoke, White was excited to see smoke rising from the settlement. After several false starts they reached the island in their rowboats just as night fell. To reassure the colonists that they were a friendly party, they sounded a trumpet call and sang folk songs.

White and his companions were astounded to find the colony deserted. The fire had apparently been kindled by lightning. They concluded, though, that the settlers had clearly not gone away in distress. Everything left behind, including all of White's books and pictures and his armor, had been neatly buried. The colonists had left a message: CROATOAN was carved on a post, and CRO was found on a nearby tree. The governor recalled that before he had left, nearly three years earlier, the settlers had decided to try to go overland to a better location, so he was not downcast. The message had been planned, moreover, and there would have been a Maltese cross added if the colonists had left in distress. White was reassured that they were safe at Croatoan, "the place where Manteo was borne, and the Savages of the Island our friends."

White's next step, obviously, was to go to Croatoan for a joyful reunion. At this point nature once more intervened and crushed the last hope of seeing the colonists alive. The two ships were battered by a gale; then, as the anchor was being raised on White's vessel, the chain broke. A second anchor was lost in an attempt to prevent the ship from being driven aground. Only one anchor remained. Plans to replenish supplies in the West Indies and return in the spring were shelved when another storm blew the vessels to the east, and the party decided to head home. John White had made his last attempt to find his colonists. Years later he wrote of his hope that God would comfort them; he could do no more.

Raleigh's days of great power were almost over. His secret marriage in 1592 so enraged Elizabeth that she first imprisoned him and then exiled him from London. He began to concentrate his American schemes on Guiana, rumored to be the site of gold mines, hoping that a rich strike would restore him to royal favor. He made his first transatlantic voyage there in 1595 but found nothing. The next year his participation in the English attack on Cádiz earned him admittance to the queen's circle once again.

In 1603 Queen Elizabeth died, and the anti-Spanish policy died with her. Her successor, James I, the Stuart king of Scotland, wanted to avoid war at all costs and quickly signed a treaty with Spain. Privateering was now the work of outlaws. Raleigh had lost most of his fortune in his various ventures; he now lost everything. James, convinced that Raleigh was plotting against him, threw him into the Tower of London.

Raleigh was allowed contact with the outside world during his imprisonment and became famous as a scientist and writer. . . .

Finally he persuaded the king, who was deeply in debt, to allow him another chance to find his Guiana gold. The expedition, plagued by tropical sickness, failed, and contrary to royal instructions, some Spanish subjects were killed. Raleigh, on his return to England, was executed on the original treason warrant. He came to be seen as a martyr by those who opposed James I and his son Charles; when Charles was beheaded in 1649 by a victorious Parliament, Raleigh's vision of England's future greatness once more ruled.

Meanwhile, once privateering was closed off as an outlet, patriotic gentry and merchants poured money into colonization in America. In 1607 Jamestown was founded near Chesapeake Bay. Whereas Roanoke had had a few investors, Jamestown had hundreds. Many mistakes were made, there was great suffering in the new Virginia colony, and investors saw little or no return; but since this was all that prevented Spain from dominating the whole of America, investment and reinvestment poured in. Both Harriot and Raleigh lived to see Jamestown established; they must have reflected on how Roanoke might have done with such support. By the time Harriot died in 1621, tobacco was firmly established as Virginia's cash crop, and he surely drew satisfaction from seeing an American product emerge triumphant. Local commodities were indeed America's gold.

The Jamestown settlers heard rumors of people who looked and dressed like them and hoped they could locate the lost colonists of Roanoke, whose twenty years' experience in the country could have been very useful. The story, as finally pieced together, was that most of White's settlers had made their way overland to Chesapeake Bay and had been taken in by the Chesapeake tribe. Powhatan, the father of Pocahontas, dominated many of the tribes in Jamestown's neighborhood but was resisted by the Chesapeakes. At about the time Jamestown was founded, he attacked and wiped out the Chesapeakes, including their English members. This reconstruction was accepted by the Virginia Company, and historians believe it is probably near the truth.

Some part of the colony must have remained with the Croatoans so it could guide White and the supply fleets; the CROATOAN legend was meant to direct White to them. This party, like the main group, was never seen again. There were persistent rumors that some English people had escaped the attack on the Chesapeakes and were with other tribes. John Smith claimed that Powhatan showed him "divers utensils of theirs," and another Virginian, George Percy, reported seeing an Indian boy whose hair was "a perfect yellow." But that was all.

❧ F U R T H E R   R E A D I N G

Nicholas P. Canny, "The Ideology of English Colonization: From Ireland to America," *William and Mary Quarterly,* 3d ser., 30 (1973), 575–598

J. H. Elliott, *The Discovery of America and the Discovery of Man* (1972)

Charles Gibson, *Spain in America* (1966)

Ramón A. Gutiérrez, *When Jesus Came, the Corn Mothers Went Away: Marriage, Sexuality, and Power in New Mexico, 1500–1846* (1991)

Lewis Hanke, *Aristotle and the American Indians: A Study of Race Prejudice in the Modern World* (1959)

Paul E. Hoffman, *A New Andalucia and a Way to the Orient: The American Southeast During the Sixteenth Century* (1990)

Elizabeth A. H. John, *Storms Brewed in Other Men's Worlds: The Confrontation of Indians, Spanish, and French in the Southwest, 1540–1795* (1975)

Karen Ordahl Kupperman, *Roanoke, the Abandoned Colony* (1984)

David Beers Quinn, *Set Fair for Roanoke: Voyages and Colonies, 1584–1606* (1985)

Edward H. Spicer, *Cycles of Conquest: The Impact of Spain, Mexico, and the United States on the Indians of the Southwest, 1533–1960* (1962)

Joan Thirsk, *Economic Policy and Projects: The Development of a Consumer Society in Early Modern England* (1978)

CHAPTER
3

The Chesapeake: England's
First Successful Colonization

☙

English colonization differed from the successful Spanish example in that it was fostered by private enterprise. The royal government issued their charters, but overseas ventures were entirely planned and financed by joint-stock companies, corporations created for the purpose. Some of these companies were very small groups of wealthy men, but the Virginia Company, sponsor of the first successful American colony, hit on the idea of setting the price of each share relatively low and opening membership to a wide variety of investors across the country.

Such innovation was necessary because founding a colony was immensely expensive. Stocking a venture with settlers and supplying them over the years until they built an infrastructure and could feed themselves meant constant outlay. And backers expected much more than mere self-sufficiency from the settlers. They had hazarded their money in the expectation of receiving a return on that investment; thus settlers were under overwhelming pressure to find or develop a product of value. Otherwise the colonists feared abandonment by the company.

The earliest returns from America came in the form of furs and fish, but neither enterprise required an expensive colony to support it. Settlers and backers quickly realized that no gold or other easy wealth existed; if colonies were to succeed, they must develop a true commodity, to be produced by their own labor. After a decade of hardship, Virginia colonists began to cultivate tobacco in earnest, and this crop became the Chesapeake's gold. Then they most needed labor to till the region's abundant land. This labor was provided by adapting an English institution, temporary servitude. In England most young men and women spent their adolescence in a series of annual contracts as servants before marrying and setting up on their own in their mid-twenties. In America they served a term of several years to pay for their overseas passage. The payoff was a grant of land of their own when the term expired—something that most could never attain in England, where inflation and population explosion squeezed opportunities.

In the course of the later seventeenth century, the temporary servitude of English men and women who were destined to become landowners and full members of society was largely replaced by permanent servitude (slavery) of African men and women who were forever excluded from membership in Chesapeake society. Historians continue to debate how and why this transition came about.

❧ D O C U M E N T S

Captain John Smith is one of the most famous names associated with early colonization. During Jamestown's first year (1607–1608) he explored Chesapeake Bay, in the course of which he was captured and brought before the region's overlord, Powhatan. The famous episode in which the chief's young daughter Pocahontas saved Smith's life was probably a symbolic death and rebirth as an Indian. It was followed by his adoption as a subchief, or werowance, under Powhatan. Smith, who wrote about himself in the third person, used his capacity to communicate by writing and examples of European technology to dazzle his captors. In the excerpts reprinted in the first document, Smith describes his accomplishments as president of the colony, especially in forcing the unwilling settlers to work and feed themselves. He comments incidentally on the introduction of destructive rats and on the colonists' learning from the Indians how to cope with the new environment. Finally he describes the terrible starving time that befell the settlers after he had been forced out of the colony.

In 1620 the Virginia Company, with tobacco established and the offer of a headright (guaranteed land), published a new call for investment and emigration, which is reprinted as the second document. In the third selection historian Walter Woodward offers up satire on this campaign, presenting it as a modern condominium offering. Richard Frethorne, who went to Virginia as a servant, wrote his parents in 1623 of the realities of his experience and his desire to return home. Frethorne penned his letter, which is excerpted in document four, in the aftermath of the concerted Indian attack of 1622. The Chesapeake encompassed the colonies of Virginia and Maryland. *A Relation of Maryland* (1635) published a blank indenture form (see the fifth document) providing for a servant to serve "according to the custom of the country"; illiterate recruits, of whom there were many, could not read what they signed. In the sixth selection, written later in the century, promoter George Alsop answers the charge that servitude in the Chesapeake was more like slavery. In the final document planter-historian Robert Beverley describes the completed transition to African slavery by the early eighteenth century, and the benefits that accrued to English servants.

Captain John Smith on Early Jamestown (1607–1610)

And now the winter approaching, the rivers became so covered with swans, geese, ducks, and cranes, that we daily feasted with good bread, Virginia peas, pumpkins, and putchamins [persimmons], fish, fowl, and diverse sorts of wild beasts as fat as we could eat them: so that none of our Tuftaffaty humorists desired to go for *England.*

But our *Comedies* never endured long without a *Tragedy*; some idle exceptions being muttered against Captain *Smith,* for not discovering the head of *Chickahamania* river, and [being] taxed by the Council, to be too slow in

---

Some of the spelling in this document has been modernized.

so worthy an attempt. The next voyage he proceeded so far that with much labour by cutting of trees insunder he made his passage; but when his Barge could pass no farther, he left her in a broad bay out of danger of shot, commanding none should go ashore til his return: himself with two English and two Savages went up higher in a Canoe; but he was not long absent, but his men went ashore, whose want of government gave both occasion and opportunity to the Savages to surprise one *George Cassen,* whom they slew, and much failed not to have cut of[f] the boat and all the rest. . . .

Six or seven weeks those Barbarians kept him prisoner, many strange triumphs and conjurations they made of him, yet he so demeaned himself amongst them, as he not only diverted them from surprising the Fort, but procured his own liberty, and got himself and his company such estimation amongst them, that those Savages admired him more than their own Quiyouckosucks. . . .

He demanding for their Captain, they showed him *Opechankanough,* King of *Pamavnkee,* to whom he gave a round Ivory double compass Dial. Much they marveled at the playing of the Fly and Needle, which they could see so plainly, and yet not touch it, because of the glass that covered them. But when he demonstrated by that Globe-like Jewel the roundness of the earth, and skies, the sphere of the Sun, Moon, and Stars, and how the Sun did chase the night round about the world continually; the greatness of the Land and Sea, the diversity of Nations, variety of complexions, and how we were to them *Antipodes,* and many other such like matters, they all stood as amazed with admiration.

Notwithstanding, within an hour after they tied him to a tree, and as many as could stand about him prepared to shoot him: but the King holding up the Compass in his hand, they all laid down their Bows and Arrows, and in a triumphant manner led him to *Orapaks,* where he was after their manner kindly feasted, and well used.

Their order in conducting him was thus; Drawing themselves all in file, the King in the middle had all their Pieces and Swords born before him. Captain *Smith* was led after him by three great Savages, holding him fast by each arm: and on each side six went in file with their Arrows nocked. But arriving at the Town [*Orapaks*] (which was but only thirty or forty hunting houses made of Mats, which they remove as they please, as we our tents) all the women and children staring to behold him, the soldiers first all in file . . . and on each flank, officers as Sergeants to see them keep their orders. A good time they continued this exercise, and then cast themselves in a ring, dancing in such several Postures, and singing and yelling out such hellish notes and screeches; being strangely painted, every one his quiver of Arrows, and at his back a club; on his arm a Fox or an Otter's skin, or some such matter for his vambrace [armor for forearm]; their heads and shoulders painted red, . . . which Scarlet-like colour made an exceeding handsome show; his Bow in his hand, and the skin of a Bird with her wings abroad dried, tied on his head, a piece of copper, a white shell, a long feather, with a small rattle growing at the tails of their snak[e]s tied to it, or some such like toy. All this while *Smith* and the King stood in the middest guarded, as before is said: and after three dances they all departed. *Smith* they conducted to a long house, where thirty or forty tall fellows did guard him; and ere long more bread and venison was brought him than would have served twenty men. I think his stomach at that time was not very good; what he left they put in baskets and tied over his head. About midnight they set the meat again before him, all this time not one of them would eat a bit with him, till the next morning they brought him as much more; and then did they eat all the old, and reserved the new as they had done the other, which made him think they would fat him to eat him. Yet in this desperate estate to defend him from the cold, one *Maocassater* brought him his gown, in requital of some beads and toys *Smith* had given him at his first arrival in *Virginia.* . . .

. . . [His captors] made all the preparations they could to assault *James* town, craving his advice; and for recompence he should have life, liberty, land, and women. In part of a Table book [tablet] he wrote his mind to them at the Fort, what was intended, how they should follow that direction to affright the messengers, and without fail send him such things as he wrote for. And an Inventory with them. The difficultie and danger, he told the Savages, of the Mines, great guns, and other Engines exceedingly affrighted them, yet according to his request they went to *James* town, in as bitter weather as could be of frost and snow, and within three days returned with an answer.

But when they came to *Jame[s]* town, seeing men sally out as he had told them they would, they fled; yet in the night they came again to the same place where he had told them they should receive an answer, and such things as he had promised them: which they found accordingly, and with which they returned with no small expedition, to the wonder of them all that heard it, that he could either divine, or the paper could speak. . . .

After this they brought him a bag of gunpowder, which they carefully preserved till the next spring, to plant as they did their corn; because they would be acquainted with the nature of that seed. . . .

At last they brought him to *Werowocomoco* where was *Powhatan* their Emperor. Here more than two hundred of those grim Courtiers stood wondering at him, as he had been a monster; till *Powhatan* and his train had put themselves in their greatest braveries. Before a fire upon a seat like a bedstead, he sat covered with a great robe, made of *Rarowcun* [raccoon] skins, and all the tails hanging by. On either hand did sit a young wench of 16 or 18 years, and along on each side the house, two rows of men, and behind them as many women, with all their heads and shoulders painted red: many of their heads bedecked with the white down of Birds; but every one with something: and a great chain of white beads about their necks.

At his entrance before the King, all the people gave a great shout. The Queen of *Appamatuck* was appointed to bring him water to wash his hands, and another brought him a bunch of feathers, instead of a Towel to dry them: having feasted him after their best barbarous manner they could, a long consultation was held, but the conclusion was, two great stones were brought before *Powhatan*: then as many as could laid hands on him, dragged him to them, and thereon laid his head, and being ready with their clubs, to beat out his brains, *Pocahontas* the King's dearest daughter, when no entreaty could prevail, got his head in her arms, and laid her own upon his to save him from death: whereat the Emperour was contented he should live to make him hatchets, and her bells, beads, and copper; for they thought him aswell of all occupations as themselves. For the King himself will make his own robes, shoes, bows, arrows, pots; plant, hunt, or do anything so well as the rest. . . .

Two days after [7 *Jan.* 1608], *Powhatan* having disguised himself in the most fearfulest manner he could, caused Captain *Smith* to be brought forth to a great house in the woods, and there upon a mat by the fire to be left alone. Not long after from behind a mat that divided the house, was made the most dolefulest noise he ever heard; then Powhatan more like a devil than a man, with some two hundred more as black as himself, came unto him and told him now they were friends, and presently he should go to *James* town, to send him two great guns, and a grindstone, for which he would give him the Country of *Capahowosick,* and forever esteem him as his son *Nantaquoud.* . . .

Now ever once in four or five days, *Pocahontas* with her attendants, brought him so much provision, that saved many of their lives, that else for all this had starved with hunger. . . .

His relation of the plenty he had seen, especially at *Werawocomoco,* and of the state and bounty of *Powhatan,* (which till that time was unknown) so revived their dead spirits (especially the love of *Pocahontas*) as all men's fear was abandoned. . . .

What was done in three months having Victuals. The Store devoured by Rats, how we lived three months of such natural fruits as the Country afforded.

Now we so quietly followed our business, that in three months we made three or four Last of Tar, Pitch, and Soap ashes; produced a trial of Glass; made a Well in the Fort of excellent sweet water, which till then was wanting; built some twenty houses; re-covered our Church: provided Nets and Weirs for fishing; and to stop the disorders of our disorderly thieves, and the Savages, built a Blockhouse in the neck of our Isle, kept by a Garrison to entertain the Savages' trade, and none to pass nor repass Savage nor Christian without the president's order. Thirty or forty Acres of ground we digged and planted. Of three sows in eighteen months, increased 60 and odd Pigs. And near 500 chickens brought up themselves without having any meat given them: but the Hogs were transported to Hog Isle: where also we built a blockhouse with a garrison to give us notice of any shipping, and for their exercise they made Clapboard and wainscot, and cut down trees.

We built also a fort for a retreat near a convenient River upon a high commanding hill, very hard to be assaulted and easy to be defended; but ere it was finished this defect caused a stay.

In searching our casked corn, we found it half rotten, and the rest so consumed with so many thousands of Rats that increased so fast, but their original was from the ships, as we knew not how to keep that little we had.

This did drive us all to our wits end, for there was nothing in the country but what nature afforded.

Until this time *Kemps* and *Tassore* were fettered prisoners, and did double task and taught us how to order and plant our fields: whom now for want of victual we set at liberty, but so well they liked our company they did not desire to go from us. . . .

And to express their loves, for 16 days continuance, the Country people brought us (when least) 100 a day, of Squirrels, Turkeys, Deer and other wild beasts.

But this want of corn occasioned the end of all our works, it being work sufficient to provide victual. . . .

Till this present, by the hazard and endeavors of some thirty or forty, this whole Colony had ever been fed. We had more Sturgeon, than could be devoured by Dog and Man, of which the industrious by drying and pounding, mingled with Caviar, Sorél and other wholesome herbs would make bread and good meat: others would gather as much *Tockwhogh* roots in a day as would make them bread a week, so that of those wild fruits, and what we caught, we lived very well in regard of such a diet.

But such was the strange condition of some 150, that had they not beene forced *nolens, volens,* perforce to gather and prepare their victual they would all have starved or have eaten one another. Of those wild fruits the Savages often brought us, and for that the president would not fulfill the unreasonable desire of those distracted Gluttonous Loiterers, to sell not only our kettles, hoes, tools, and iron, nayswords, pieces, and the very Ordnance and houses, might they have prevailed to have been but Idle: for those Savage fruits, they would have had imparted all to the Savages, especially for one basket of Corn they heard of to be at *Powhatans*, fifty miles from our Fort. . . .

. . . [H]e argued the case in this manner.

> Fellow soldiers, I did little think any so false to report, or so many to be so simple to be persuaded, that I either intend to starve you, or that *Powhatan* at this present hath corn for himself, much less for you; or that I would not have it, if I knew where it were to be had. Neither did I think any so malicious as now I see a great many; yet it shall not so passionate me, but I will do my best for my most maligner. But dream no longer of this vain hope from *Powhatan,* nor that I will longer forbear to force you from your Idleness, and punish you if you rail. But if I find any more runners for Newfoundland with the Pinnace, let him assuredly look to arrive at the Gallows. You cannot deny but that by the hazard of my life many a time I have saved yours, when (might your own wills have prevailed) you would have starved; and will do still whether I will or not; But I protest by that God that made me, since necessity hath not power to force you to gather for yourselves those fruits the earth doth yield, you shall not only gather for yourselves, but those that are sick. As yet I never had more from the store than the worst of you: and all my English extraordinary provision that I have, you shall see me divide it amongst the sick.
>
> And this Savage trash you so scornfully repine at; being put in your mouths your stomachs can digest: if you would have better, you should have brought it; and therefore I will take a course you shall provide what is to be had. The sick shall not starve, but equally share of all our labors; and he that gathereth not

every day as much as I do, the next day shall be set beyond the river, and be banished from the Fort as a drone, till he amend his conditions or starve. . . .

Now we all found the loss of Captain *Smith,* yea his greatest maligners could now curse his loss: as for corn provision and contribution from the Savages, we had nothing but mortal wounds, with clubs and arrows; as for our Hogs, Hens, Goats, Sheep, Horse, or what lived, our commanders, officers and Savages daily consumed them, some small proportions sometimes we tasted, till all was devoured; then swords, arms, pieces, or any thing, we traded with the Savages, whose cruel fingers were so oft imbrewed in our blood, that what by their cruelty, our Governours indiscretion, and the loss of our ships, of five hundred within six months after Captain *Smith's* departure, there remained not past sixty men, women and children, most miserable and poor creatures; and those were preserved for the most part, by roots, herbs, acorns, walnuts, berries, now and then a little fish: they that had starch in these extremities, made no small use of it; yea, even the very skins of our horses.

Nay, so great was our famine, that a Savage we slew and buried, the poorer sort took him up again and eat him; and so did diverse one another boiled and stewed with roots and herbs: And one amongst the rest did kill his wife, powdered [*salted*] her, and had eaten part of her before it was known; for which he was executed, as he well deserved: now whether she was better roasted, boiled or carbonado'd [grilled], I know not; but of such a dish as powdered wife I never heard of.

This was that time, which still to this day we called the starving time; it were too vile to say, and scarce to be believed, what we endured: but the occasion was our own, for want of providence industry and government, and not the barrennesse and defect of the Country, as is generally supposed; . . . Yet had we been even in Paradise itselfe with these Governours, it would not have been much better with us; yet there was amongst us, who had they had the government as Captain *Smith* appointed, but that they could not maintain it, would surely have kept us from those extremities of miseries. This in ten days more, would have supplanted us all with death. . . .

The Virginia Company's Declaration on Virginia, 1620

After the many disasters, wherewith it pleased Almighty God to suffer the great Enemy of all good Actions and his Instruments, to encounter and interrupt, to oppress and keep weak, this noble Action for the planting of *Virginia,* with Christian Religion, and English people: It having pleased him now contrarily of his especial great grace, so to bless and prosper our late careful endevours, as well for the repairing of all former breaches, as for supplying of the present defects, wherewith the Colony was kept down, that it hath as it were on a sudden grown to double that height, strength, plenty, and prosperity, which it had in former times attained: We have thought it now the

---

Some of the spelling in this document has been modernized.

peculiar duty of our place, accordingly as it hath been also ordered by a general Court, to Summon as it were by a kind of loving invitement, the whole Body of the Noble and other worthy Adventurers, as well to the consurving and perfecting of this happy work, as to the reaping of the fruit of their great expenses and travails.

And first to remove that unworthy aspersion, wherewith ill disposed minds, guiding their Actions by corrupt ends have both by Letters from thence, and by rumours here at home, sought unjustly to stain and blemish that Country, as being barren and unprofitable; We have thought it necessary for the full satisfaction of all, to make it publicly known, that by diligent examination we have assuredly found, those Letters and Rumours to have been false and malicious; procured by practice, and suborned to evil purposes: and contrarily disavowed by the testimony upon Oath of the chief Inhabitants of all the Colony; by whom we are ascertained, that the Country is rich, spacious and well watered; temperate as for the Climate; very healthful after men are a little accustomed to it; abounding with all God's natural blessings: The Land replenished with the goodliest Woods in the world, and those full of *Deer,* and other Beasts for sustenance: The Seas and Rivers (whereof many are exceeding fair and navigable,) full of excellent Fish, and of all sorts desirable; both Water and Land yielding Fowl in very great store and variety: In Sum, a Country, too good for ill people; and we hope reserved by the providence of God, for such as shall apply themselves faithfully to his service, and be a strength and honour to our King and Nation. But touching those Commodities for which that Country is proper, and which have been lately set up for the Adventurers' benefit: we refer you to a true note of them, lately delivered in a great and general Court, and hereunto annexed for your better information. By which and other approved information brought unto us, We rest in great assurance, that this Country, as it is seated near the midst of the world, between the extremities of heat and cold; So it also participateth of the benefits of both, and is capable (being assisted with skill and industry) of the richest commodities of most parts of the Earth. The rich Furs, Caviar, and Cordage, which we draw from *Russia* with so great difficulty, are to be had in *Virginia,* and the parts adjoining, with ease and plenty. The Masts, Planks, and Boards, and Pitch and Tar, the Pot-ashes and Soap-ashes, the Hempe and Flax, (being the materials of Linen,) which now we fetch from *Norway, Denmark, Poland,* and *Germany,* are there to be had in abundance and great perfection. The *Iron,* which hath so wasted our *English* Woods, that itself in short time must decay together with them, is to be had in *Virginia,* (where wasting of Woods is a benefit) for all good conditions answerable to the best in the world. The Wines, Fruit, and Salt of *France* and *Spain;* The Silks of *Persia* and *Italy,* will be found also in *Virginia,* and in no kind of worth inferior. We omit here a multitude of other natural Commodities, dispersed up and down the divers parts of the world: of Woods, Roots, and Berries, for excellent Dyes: of Plants and other Drugs, for Physical service: of sweet Woods, Oils, and Gums, for pleasure and other use: of Cotton-wool, and Sugar Canes: all which may there also be had in abundance, with an infinity of other more: And will conclude with these three, Corn, Cattle and

Fish, which are the substance of the food of man. The Grains of our Country do prosper there very well: Of Wheat they have great plenty: But their *Maize,* being the natural Grain of that Country, doth far exceed in pleasantness, strength, and fertility. The Cattle which we have transported thither, (being now grown nearer to five hundred) become much bigger of Body, than the breed from which they came: The Horses also more beautiful, and fuller of courage. And such is the extraordinary fertility of that *Soil,* that the *Does* of their *Deer* yield two Fawns at a birth, and sometimes three. The Fishings at *Cape Cod,* being within those Limits, will in plenty of Fish be equal to those of *New-found-Land,* and in goodness and greatness much superiour. To conclude, it is a Country, which nothing but ignorance can think ill of, and which no man but of a corrupt mind and ill purpose can defame. . . .

Jamestown Estates: A Contemporary Parody, 1991

JAMESTOWN ESTATES

For As Little As £10 12s. 6d., You, Too, Can Own A Share of Paradise.

*F*rom the moment the gentle, southern breezes waft your pinnace to the verdant, gardenlike shore, you'll know this is where you belong. Jamestown Estates, where only a few are living a life those in England can hardly imagine.

Jamestown Estates — another proud project of the Virginia Company — combines the best in colonial living with the excitement, adventure, and opportunity for which the Virginia Company is famous.

At Jamestown Estates, your every need is provided for in an environment that shows how caring people can live in symbiotic dominance of nature. And only Jamestown Estates offers an exclusive low cholesterol meal plan, the Sure-Fit™ exercise program, and a unique "Friends Together" living arrangement. In all details, Jamestown Estates is designed with your peace and well-being in mind. Each of our charming, thatch-roofed cottages—which you will share with congenial, adventuresome people just like yourself (specially designed to maximize both privacy and interpersonal contact)—has a spectacular river view. At Jamestown Estates, nature itself invites you to relax, reflect, converse with new-found friends, and share stories of your New World experiences, while becoming the sort of person you've always wanted to be. But it's not all play at Jamestown Estates — not by a long shot. For Jamestown Estates offers one of the most active labor markets in the New World. Whatever you do, you can do it better here.

Our employment office has many people anxious to welcome you to our growing work force.

No single ad can tell you all the remarkable things you'll want to know about Jamestown Estates. Consider, however, some of these exceptionally valuable Jamestown Pluses:
• 24-hour security, palisaded grounds.
• Hunting, fishing right on premises. Native guides teach you to hunt like a lord.
• The Sotweed Garden Center—learn how to plant like a pro. No experience necessary.
• Regularly scheduled "Trash For Treasure" excursions to the nearby Pamunkey Flea Market. Come & "Meet the Chief."
• And, as a special bonus to those who visit Jamestown Estates soon, we are introducing a new program called the Headright System*—your chance to receive 50 acres of land just for bringing yourself (or someone you know) to experience this new world of opportunity.
• Coming with a group? Ask about our Particular Plantations™ Program. Build your private world right here in our new one.

Finally, for those who appreciate the phenomenal profit potential of New World investment, there is the chance to secure shares in the Virginia Company itself, —a once in a lifetime time opportunity —starting at just £10 12s. 6d. To find out more, contact your nearest friendly, knowledgeable Virginia Company Representative.

* Headright™ and Headright System™ are registered trademarks of the Virginia Company. Offer void where prohibited.

Virginia   A WHOLE NEW WORLD

Walter Woodward, "Jamestown Estates," *William and Mary Quarterly*, 3d ser., XLVII (1991), 116–117. Reprinted by permission.

Richard Frethorne Writes to His Mother and Father, 1623

Loving and kind father and mother, my most humble duty remembered to you hoping in God of your good health, as I my self am at the making hereof, this is to let you understand that I your Child am in a most heavy Case by reason of the nature of the Country is such that it Causeth much sickness, as the scurvy and the bloody flux [dysentery], and divers other diseases, which maketh the body very poor, and Weak, and when we are sick there is nothing to Comfort us; for since I came out of the ship, I never ate any thing but peas and loblollie (that is water gruel) as for deer or venison I never saw any since I came into this land, there is indeed some fowl, but We are not allowed to go and get it, but must Work hard both early and late for a mess of water gruel, and a mouthful of bread, and beef, a mouthful of bread for a penny loaf must serve for 4 men which is most pitiful if you did know as much as I, when people cry out day, and night, Oh that they were in England without their limbs and would not care to lose any limb to be in England again, yea though they beg from door to door, for we live in fear of the Enemy every hour, yet we have had a Combat with them on the Sunday before Shrovetide, and we took two alive, and make slaves of them, but it was by policy, for we are in great danger, for our Plantation is very weak, by reason of the dearth, and sickness, of our Company, for we came but Twenty for the merchants, and they half dead Just; as we look every hour When two more should go, yet there came some for other men yet to live with us, of which there is but one alive, and our Lieutenant is dead, and his father, and his brother, and there was some 5 or 6 of the last year's 20 of which there is but 3 left, so that we are fain to get other men to plant with us, and yet we are but 32 to fight against 3000 if they should Come, and the nighest help that We have is ten miles of us, and when the rogues overcame this place last, they slew 80 persons. How then shall we doe for we lie even in their teeth, they may easily take us but that God is merciful, and can save with few as well as with many; as he showed to Gilead and like Gilead's soldiers if they lapped water, we drink water which is but Weak, and I have nothing to Comfort me, nor there is nothing to be gotten here but sickness, and death, except that one had money to lay out in some things for profit; But I have nothing at all, no not a shirt to my backe, but two Rags nor no Clothes, but one poor suit, nor but one pair of shoes, but one pair of stockings, but one Cap, but two bands, my Cloak is stolen by one of my own fellows, and to his dying hour would not tell me what he did with it but some of my fellows saw him have butter and beef out of a ship, which my Cloak I doubt [think] paid for, so that I have not a penny, nor a half penny Worth to help me to either spice, or sugar, or strong Waters, without the which one cannot live here, for as strong beer in England doth fatten and strengthen them so water here doth wash and weaken these here, only keep life and soul together. But I am not half a quarter so strong as I was in England, and all is for want

---

Some of the spelling in this document has been modernized.

of victuals, for I do protest unto you, that I have eaten more in a day at home than I have allowed me here for a Week. You have given more than my day's allowance to a beggar at the door; and if Mr. Jackson had not relieved me, I should be in a poor Case, but he like a father and she like a loving mother doth still help me, for when we go up to James Town that is 10 miles of us, there lie all the ships that Come to the land, and there they must deliver their goods, and when we went up to Town as it may be on Monday, at noon, and come there by night, then load the next day by noon, and go home in the afternoon, and unload, and then away again in the night, and be up about midnight, then if it rained, or blowed never so hard we must lie on the boat on the water, and have nothing but a little bread, for when we go into the boat we have a loaf allowed to two men, and it is all if we stayed there 2 days, which is hard, and must lie all that while in the boat, but that Goodman Jackson pitied me and made me a Cabin to lie in always when I come up, and he would give me some poor Jacks [fish] home with me which Comforted me more than peas, or water gruel. Of they be very godly folks, and love me very well, and will do any thing for me, and he much marveled that you would send me a servant to the Company. He sayeth I had been better knocked on the head, and Indeed so I find it now to my great grief and misery, and saith, that if you love me you will redeem me suddenly, for which I do entreat and beg, and if you cannot get the merchants to redeem me for some little money then for God's sake get a gathering or entreat some good folks to lay out some little sum of money, in meal, and Cheese and butter, and beef, any eating meat will yield great profit, oil and vinegar is very good, but father there is great loss in leaking, but for God's sake send beef and Cheese and butter or the more of one sort and none of another, but if you send Cheese it must be very old Cheese, and at the Cheesemonger's you may buy good Cheese for twopence farthing or half-penny that will be liked very well, but if you send Cheese you must have a Care how you pack it in barrels, and you must put Cooper's chips between every Cheese, or else the heat of the hold will rot them, and look whatsoever you send me be it never so much, look what I make of it. I will deal truly with you. I will send it over, and beg the profit to redeem me, and if I die before it Come I have entreated Goodman Jackson to send you the worth of it, who hath promised he will. If you send you must direct your letter to Goodman Jackson, at James Town, a Gunsmith. . . . Good Father do not forget me, but have mercy and pity my miserable Case. I know if you did but see me you would weep to see me, for I have but one suit, but it is a strange one, it is very well guarded, wherefore for God's sake pity me. I pray you to remember my love to all my friends, and kindred, I hope all my Brothers and sisters are in good health, and as for my part I have set down my res-olution that certainly Will be, that is, that the Answer of this letter will be life or death to me, there good Father send as soon as you can, and if you send me any thing let this be the mark.

ROT

RICHARD FRETHORNE
Martin's Hundred

Blank Servant Indenture Form, 1635

The forme of binding a servant.

This Indenture *made the   day of
in the*
yeere of our Soueraigne Lord King Charles, *&c.
betweene   of the one
party, and   on the
other party,* Witnesseth, *that the said
                    doth hereby covenant promise, and
grant, to and with the said
his Executors and Assignes, to serve him from
the day of the date hereof, vntill his first and
next arrivall in* Maryland; *and after for and
during the tearme of   yeeres, in such
service and imployment, as he the said
                    or his assignes shall there im-
ploy him, according to the custome of the Countrey
in the like kind. In consideration whereof, the said
                        doth promise
and grant, to and with the said
                    to pay for his passing, and to
find him with Meat, Drinke, Apparell and Lodging, with other necessaries during the said terme;
and at the end of the said terme, to give him one
whole yeeres provision of Corne, and fifty acres of
Land, according to the order of the countrey. In
witnesse whereof, the said
hath hereunto put his hand and seale, the day and
yeere above written.*
        Sealed and delivered in
            the presence of   H

The usuall terme of binding a servant, is for
five yeers; but for any artificer, or one that shall
deserve more then ordinary, the Adventurer
shall doe well to shorten that time, and adde
encouragements of another nature (as he shall
see cause) rather then to want such usefull men.

George Alsop on the Benefits of Servitude, 1666

*The necessariness of Servitude proved, with the common usage
of Servants in Mary-Land, together with their Priviledges.*

... There is no truer Emblem of Confusion either in Monarchy or
Domestick Governments, then when either the Subject, or the Servant, strives
for the upper hand of his Prince, or Master, and to be equal with him, from
whom he receives his present subsistance: Why then, if Servitude be so necessary that no place can be governed in order, nor people live without it, this
may serve to tell those which prick up their ears and bray against it, That
they are none but Asses, and deserve the Bridle of a strict commanding power
to rein them in: For I'me certainly confident, that there are several Thousands
in most Kingdoms of Christendom, that could not at all live and subsist,
unless they had served some prefixed time, to learn either some Trade, Art,
or Science, and by either of them to extract their present livelihood.

Then methinks this may stop the mouths of those that will undiscreetly
compassionate them that dwell under necessary Servitudes; for let but Parents
of an indifferent capacity in Estates, when their Childrens age by computation
speak them seventeen or eighteen years old, turn them loose to the wide
world, without a seven years working Apprenticeship (being just brought up
to the bare formality of a little reading and writing) and you shall immediately
see how weak and shiftless they'le be towards the maintaining and supporting
of themselves; and (without either stealing or begging) their bodies like a
Sentinel must continually wait to see when their Souls will be frighted away
by the pale Ghost of a starving want.

Then let such, where Providence hath ordained to live as Servants, either
in England or beyond Sea, endure the pre-fixed yoak of their limited time
with patience, and then in a small computation of years, by an industrious
endeavour, they may become Masters and Mistresses of Families themselves.
And let this be spoke to the deserved praise of Mary-Land, That the four
years I served there were not to me so slavish, as a two years Servitude of
a Handicraft Apprenticeship was here in London. . . . Not that I write this to
seduce or delude any, or to draw them from their native soyle, but out of a
love to my Countrymen, whom in the general I wish well to, and that the
lowest of them may live in such a capacity of Estate, as that the bare interest
of their Livelihoods might not altogether depend upon persons of the greatest
extendments. . . .

They whose abilities cannot extend to purchase their own transportation
over into Mary-Land, (and surely he that cannot command so small a sum
for so great a matter, his life must needs be mighty low and dejected) I say
they may for the debarment of a four years sordid liberty, go over into this
Province and there live plentiously well. And what's a four years Servitude
to advantage a man all the remainder of his dayes, making his predecessors
happy in his sufficient abilities, which he attained to partly by the restrainment
of so small a time?

Now those that commit themselves unto the care of the Merchant to carry them over, they need not trouble themselves with any inquisitive search touching their Voyage; for there is such an honest care and provision made for them all the time they remain aboard the Ship, and are sailing over, that they want for nothing that is necessary and convenient.

The Merchant commonly before they go aboard the Ship, or set themselves in any forwardness for their Voyage, has Conditions of Agreements drawn between him and those that by a voluntary consent become his Servants, to serve him, his Heirs or Assigns, according as they in their primitive acquaintance have made their bargain, some two, some three, some four years; and whatever the Master or Servant tyes himself up to here in England by Condition, the Laws of the Province will force a performance of when they come there: Yet here is this Priviledge in it when they arrive, If they dwell not with the Merchant they made their first agreement withall, they may choose whom they will serve their prefixed time with; and after their curiosity has pitcht on one whom they think fit for their turn, and that they may live well withall, the Merchant makes an Assignment of the Indenture over to him whom they of their free will have chosen to be their Master, in the same nature as we here in England (and no otherwise) turn over Covenant Servants or Apprentices from one Master to another. Then let those whose chaps are always breathing forth those filthy dregs of abusive exclamations, . . . against this Country of Mary-Land, saying, That those which are transported over thither, are sold in open Market for Slaves, and draw in Carts like Horses; which is so damnable an untruth, that if they should search to the very Center of Hell, and enquire for a Lye of the most antient and damned stamp, I confidently believe they could not find one to parallel this: For know, That the Servants here in Mary-Land of all Colonies, distant or remote Plantations, have the least cause to complain, either for strictness of Servitude, want of Provisions, or need of Apparel: Five dayes and a half in the Summer weeks is the alotted time that they work in; and for two months, when the Sun predominates in the highest pitch of his heat, they claim an antient and customary Priviledge, to repose themselves three hours in the day within the house, and this is undeniably granted to them that work in the Fields.

In the Winter time, which lasteth three months (*viz.*) December, January, and February, they do little or no work or imployment, save cutting of wood to make good fires to sit by, unless their Ingenuity will prompt them to hunt the Deer, or Bear, or recreate themselves in Fowling, to slaughter the Swans, Geese, and Turkeys (which this Country affords in a most plentiful manner:) For every Servant has a Gun, Powder and Shot allowed him, to sport him withall on all Holidayes and leasurable times, if he be capable of using it, or be willing to learn. . . .

. . . He that lives in the nature of a Servant in this Province, must serve but four years by the Custom of the Country; and when the expiration of his time speaks him a Freeman, there's a Law in the Province, that enjoyns his Master whom he hath served to give him Fifty Acres of Land, Corn to serve him a whole year, three Sutes of Apparel, with things necessary to them, and Tools to work withall; so that they are no sooner free, but they are ready to set up for themselves, and when once entred, they live passingly well.

The Women that go over into this Province as Servants, have the best luck here as in any place of the world besides; for they are no sooner on shoar, but they are courted into a Copulative Matrimony, which some of them (for aught I know) had they not come to such a Market with their Virginity might have kept it by them until it had been mouldy.... Men have not altogether so good luck as Women in this kind, or natural preferment, without they be good Rhetoricians, and well vers'd in the Art of perswasion, then (probably) they may ryvet themselves in the time of their Servitude into the private and reserved favour of their Mistress, if Age speak their Master deficient.

In short, touching the Servants of this Province, they live well in the time of their Service, and by their restrainment in that time, they are made capable of living much better when they come to be free; which in several other parts of the world I have observed, That after some servants have brought their indented and limited time to a just and legal period by Servitude, they have been much more incapable of supporting themselves from sinking into the Gulf of a slavish, poor, fettered, and intangled life, then all the fastness of their pre-fixed time did involve them in before....

Robert Beverley on the Servants and Slaves in Virginia, 1705

Their Servants, they distinguish by the Names of Slaves for Life, and Servants for a time.

Slaves are the Negroes, and their Posterity, following the condition of the Mother, according to the Maxim, *partus sequitur ventrem* [status proceeds from the womb]. They are call'd Slaves, in respect of the time of their Servitude, because it is for Life.

Servants, are those which serve only for a few years, according to the time of their Indenture, or the Custom of the Country. The Custom of the Country takes place upon such as have no Indentures. The Law in this case is, that if such Servants be under Nineteen years of Age, they must be brought into Court, to have their Age adjudged; and from the Age they are judg'd to be of, they must serve until they reach four and twenty: But if they be adjudged upwards of Nineteen, they are then only to be Servants for the term of five Years.

The Male-Servants, and Slaves of both Sexes, are imployed together in Tilling and Manuring the Ground, in Sowing and Planting Tobacco, Corn, &c. Some Distinction indeed is made between them in their Cloaths, and Food; but the Work of both, is no other than what the Overseers, the Freemen, and the Planters themselves do.

Sufficient Distinction is also made between the Female-Servants, and Slaves; for a White Woman is rarely or never put to work in the Ground, if she be good for any thing else: And to Discourage all Planters from using any Women so, their Law imposes the heaviest Taxes upon Female-Servants working in the Ground, while it suffers all other white Women to be absolutely exempted: Whereas on the other hand, it is a common thing to work a Woman Slave out of Doors; nor does the Law make any distinction in her Taxes, whether her Work be Abroad, or at Home.

Because I have heard how strangely cruel, and severe, the Service of this Country is represented in some parts of *England;* I can't forbear affirming, that the work of their Servants, and Slaves, is no other than what every common Freeman do's. Neither is any Servant requir'd to do more in a Day, than his Overseer. And I can assure you with a great deal of Truth, that generally their Slaves are not worked near so hard, nor so many Hours in a Day, as the Husbandmen, and Day-Labourers in *England.* An Overseer is a Man, that having served his time, has acquired the Skill and Character of an experienced Planter, and is therefore intrusted with the Direction of the Servants and Slaves.

But to compleat this account of Servants, I shall give you a short Relation of the care their Laws take, that they be used as tenderly as possible.

By the Laws of their Country.

1. All Servants whatsoever, have their Complaints heard without Fee, or Reward; but if the Master be found Faulty, the charge of the Complaint is cast upon him, otherwise the business is done *ex Officio.*
2. Any Justice of Peace may receive the Complaint of a Servant, and order every thing relating thereto, till the next County-Court, where it will be finally determin'd.
3. All Masters are under the Correction, and Censure of the County-Courts, to provide for their Servants, good and wholsome Diet, Clothing, and Lodging.
4. They are always to appear, upon the first Notice given of the Complaint of their Servants, otherwise to forfeit the Service of them, until they do appear.
5. All Servants Complaints are to be receiv'd at any time in Court, without Process, and shall not be delay'd for want of Form; but the Merits of the Complaint must be immediately inquir'd into by the Justices; and if the Master cause any delay therein, the Court may remove such Servants, if they see Cause, until the Master will come to Tryal.
6. If a Master shall at any time disobey an Order of Court, made upon any Complaint of a Servant; the Court is impower'd to remove such Servant forthwith to another Master, who will be kinder; Giving to the former Master the produce only, (after Fees deducted) of what such Servants shall be sold for by Publick Outcry.
7. If a Master should be so cruel, as to use his Servant ill, that is faln Sick, or Lame in his Service, and thereby render'd unfit for Labour, he must be remov'd by the Church-Wardens out of the way of such Cruelty, and boarded in some good Planters House, till the time of his Freedom, the charge of which must be laid before the next County-Court, which has power to levy the same from time to time, upon the Goods and Chattels of the Master; After which, the charge of such Boarding is to come upon the Parish in General.
8. All hired Servants are intituled to these Priviledges.
9. No Master of a Servant, can make a new Bargain for Service, or other Matter with his Servant, without the privity and consent of a Justice of Peace, to prevent the Master's Over-reaching, or scareing such Servant into an unreasonable Complyance.

10. The property of all Money and Goods sent over thither to Servants, or carry'd in with them; is reserv'd to themselves, and remain intirely at their disposal.

11. Each Servant at his Freedom, receives of his Master fifteen Bushels of Corn, (which is sufficient for a whole year) and two new Suits of Cloaths, both Linnen and Woollen; and then becomes as free in all respects, and as much entituled to the Liberties, and Priviledges of the Country, as any other of the Inhabitants or Natives are.

12. Each Servant has then also a Right to take up fifty Acres of Land, where he can find any unpatented: But that is no great Privilege, for any one may have as good a right for a piece of Eight.

This is what the Laws prescribe in favour of Servants, by which you may find, that the Cruelties and Severities imputed to that Country, are an unjust Reflection. For no People more abhor the thoughts of such Usage, than the *Virginians,* nor take more precaution to prevent it.

☙ E S S A Y S

During the first half of the seventeenth century, tens of thousands of young English men and women were willing to immigrate to the colonies because of the growth of poverty and constriction of opportunity at home. They continued to leave England for America even after the risks, particularly the high disease and death rates in the southern colonies, came to be known. Peopling the colonies with single young servants, many of whom would not live to complete their terms, had immense consequences. Because of imbalanced sex ratios and the postponement of marriage and childbearing until terms of indenture ended, many young servants died without reproducing, and so the colonist population was composed largely of immigrants until near the end of the century. Lois Green Carr, the historian of Maryland's St. Mary's City Commission, and Lorena S. Walsh, historical researcher at Colonial Williamsburg, in the first essay consider the consequences for the women who were recruited for the Chesapeake. They are especially interested in whether women's status was enhanced in the frontier setting. In the second essay Russell Menard, a historian at the University of Minnesota, provides an answer to the puzzle of why servitude was replaced by slavery and why this transition occurred toward the end of the century.

The Experience of White Women in the Chesapeake

LOIS GREEN CARR AND LORENA S. WALSH

Four facts were basic to all human experience in seventeenth-century Maryland. First, for most of the period the great majority of inhabitants had been born in what we now call Britain. Population increase in Maryland did not

Lois Green Carr and Lorena Walsh. "The Planter's Wife: The Experience of Women in Seventeenth-Century Maryland," *William and Mary Quarterly,* 3d ser., XXXIV (1977), 542–565. Reprinted by permission of the authors and the publisher.

result primarily from births in the colony before the late 1680s and did not produce a predominantly native population of adults before the first decade of the eighteenth century. Second, immigrant men could not expect to live beyond age forty-three, and 70 percent would die before age fifty. Women may have had even shorter lives. Third, perhaps 85 percent of the immigrants, and practically all the unmarried immigrant women, arrived as indentured servants and consequently married late. Family groups were never predominant in the immigration to Maryland and were a significant part for only a brief time at mid-century. Fourth, many more men than women immigrated during the whole period. These facts—immigrant predominance, early death, late marriage, and sexual imbalance—created circumstances of social and demographic disruption that deeply affected family and community life.

We need to assess the effects of this disruption on the experience of women in seventeenth-century Maryland. Were women degraded by the hazards of servitude in a society in which everyone had left community and kin behind and in which women were in short supply? Were traditional restraints on social conduct weakened? If so, were women more exploited or more independent and powerful than women who remained in England? Did any differences from English experience which we can observe in the experience of Maryland women survive the transformation from an immigrant to a predominantly native-born society with its own kinship networks and community traditions? The tentative argument put forward here is that the answer to all these questions is Yes. There were degrading aspects of servitude, although these probably did not characterize the lot of most women; there were fewer restraints on social conduct, especially in courtship, than in England; women were less protected but also more powerful than those who remained at home; and at least some of these changes survived the appearance in Maryland of New World creole communities. However, these issues are far from settled, and we shall offer some suggestions as to how they might be further pursued.

Maryland was settled in 1634, but in 1650 there were probably no more than six hundred persons and fewer than two hundred adult women in the province. After that time population growth was steady; in 1704 a census listed 30,437 white persons, of whom 7,163 were adult women. Thus in discussing the experience of white women in seventeenth-century Maryland we are dealing basically with the second half of the century.

Marylanders of that period did not leave letters and diaries to record their New World experience or their relationships to one another. Nevertheless, they left trails in the public records that give us clues. Immigrant lists kept in England and documents of the Maryland courts offer quantifiable evidence about the kinds of people who came and some of the problems they faced in making a new life. Especially valuable are the probate court records. Estate inventories reveal the kinds of activities carried on in the house and on the farm, and wills, which are usually the only personal statements that remain for any man or woman, show something of personal attitudes. . . .

Whatever their status, one fact about immigrant women is certain: many fewer came than men. Immigrant lists, headright lists, and itemizations of servants in inventories show severe imbalance. On a London immigrant list of 1634–1635 men outnumbered women six to one. From the 1650s at least until the 1680s most sources show a ratio of three to one. From then on, all sources show some, but not great, improvement. Among immigrants from Liverpool over the years 1697–1707 the ratio was just under two and one half to one.

Why did not more women come? Presumably, fewer wished to leave family and community to venture into a wilderness. But perhaps more important, women were not as desirable as men to merchants and planters who were making fortunes raising and marketing tobacco, a crop that requires large amounts of labor. The gradual improvement in the sex ratio among servants toward the end of the century may have been the result of a change in recruiting the needed labor. In the late 1660s the supply of young men willing to emigrate stopped increasing sufficiently to meet the labor demands of a growing Chesapeake population. Merchants who recruited servants for planters turned to other sources, and among these sources were women. They did not crowd the ships arriving in the Chesapeake, but their numbers did increase.

To ask the question another way, why did women come? Doubtless, most came to get a husband, an objective virtually certain of success in a land where women were so far outnumbered. The promotional literature, furthermore, painted bright pictures of the life that awaited men and women once out of their time; and various studies suggest that for a while, at least, the promoters were not being entirely fanciful. Until the 1660s, and to a less degree the 1680s, the expanding economy of Maryland and Virginia offered opportunities well beyond those available in England to men without capital and to the women who became their wives.

Nevertheless, the hazards were also great, and the greatest was untimely death. Newcomers promptly became ill, probably with malaria, and many died. What proportion survived is unclear; so far no one has devised a way of measuring it. Recurrent malaria made the woman who survived seasoning less able to withstand other diseases, especially dysentery and influenza. She was especially vulnerable when pregnant. Expectation of life for everyone was low in the Chesapeake, but especially so for women. A woman who had immigrated to Maryland took an extra risk, though perhaps a risk not greater than she might have suffered by moving from her village to London instead.

The majority of women who survived seasoning paid their transportation costs by working for a four- or five-year term of service. The kind of work depended on the status of the family they served. A female servant of a small planter—who through about the 1670s might have had a servant—probably worked at the hoe. Such a man could not afford to buy labor that would not help with the cash crop. In wealthy families women probably were household servants, although some are occasionally listed in inventories of well-to-do planters as living on the quarters—that is, on plantations other than the dwelling plantation. Such women saved men the jobs of preparing food and washing linen but doubtless also worked in the fields. In middling households experience must have varied. Where the number of people to feed and wash for was large, female servants would have had little time to tend the crops. . . .

An additional risk for the woman who came as a servant was the possibility of bearing a bastard. At least 20 percent of the female servants who came to Charles County between 1658 and 1705 were presented to the county court for this cause. A servant woman could not marry unless someone was willing to pay her master for the term she had left to serve. If a man made her pregnant, she could not marry him unless he could buy her time. Once a woman became free, however, marriage was clearly the usual solution. Only a handful of free women were presented in Charles County for bastardy between 1658 and 1705. Since few free women remained either single or widowed for long, not many were subject to the risk. The hazard of bearing a bastard was a hazard of being a servant.

This high rate of illegitimate pregnancies among servants raises lurid questions. Did men import women for sexual exploitation? Does John Barth's Whore of Dorset have a basis outside his fertile imagination? In our opinion, the answers are clearly No. Servants were economic investments on the part of planters who needed labor. A female servant in a household where there were unmarried men must have both provided and faced temptation, for the pressures were great in a society in which men outnumbered women by three to one. Nevertheless, the servant woman was in the household to work—to help feed and clothe the family and make tobacco. She was not primarily a concubine. . . .

A female servant paid dearly for the fault of unmarried pregnancy. She was heavily fined, and if no one would pay her fine, she was whipped. Furthermore, she served an extra twelve to twenty-four months to repay her master for the "trouble of his house" and labor lost, and the fathers often did not share in this payment of damages. On top of all, she might lose the child after weaning unless by then she had become free, for the courts bound out bastard children at very early ages. . . .

Were women sold for wives against their wills? No record says so, but nothing restricted a man from selling his servant to whomever he wished. Perhaps some women were forced into such marriages or accepted them as the least evil. But the man who could afford to purchase a wife—especially a new arrival—was usually already an established landowner. Probably most servant women saw an opportunity in such a marriage. In addition, the shortage of labor gave women some bargaining power. Many masters must have been ready to refuse to sell a woman who was unwilling to marry a would-be purchaser.

If a woman's time was not purchased by a prospective husband, she was virtually certain to find a husband once she was free. . . . In the four counties of the lower Western Shore only two of the women who left a probate inventory before the eighteenth century are known to have died single. Comely or homely, strong or weak, any young woman was too valuable to be overlooked, and most could find a man with prospects.

The woman who immigrated to Maryland, survived seasoning and service, and gained her freedom became a planter's wife. She had considerable liberty in making her choice. There were men aplenty, and no fathers or brothers were hovering to monitor her behavior or disapprove her preference. This is the modern way of looking at her situation, of course. Perhaps she missed the protection of a father, a guardian, or kinfolk, and the participation in her decision of a community to which she felt ties. There is some evidence that the absence of kin and the pressures of the sex ratio created conditions of sexual freedom in courtship that were not customary in England. A register of marriages and births for seventeenth-century Somerset County shows that about one-third of the immigrant women whose marriages are recorded were pregnant at the time of the ceremony—nearly twice the rate in English parishes. There is no indication of community objection to this freedom so long as marriage took place. No presentments for bridal pregnancy were made in any of the Maryland courts.

The planter's wife was likely to be in her mid-twenties at marriage. . . .

Because of the age at which an immigrant woman married, the number of children she would bear her husband was small. She had lost up to ten years of her childbearing life—the possibility of perhaps four or five children, given the usual rhythm of childbearing. At the same time, high mortality would reduce both the number of children she would bear over the rest of her life and the number who would live. One partner to a marriage was likely to die within seven years, and the chances were only one in three that a marriage would last ten years. In these circumstances, most women would not bear more than three or four children—not counting those stillborn—to any one husband, plus a posthumous child were she the survivor. The best estimates suggest that nearly a quarter, perhaps more, of the children born alive died during their first year and that 40 to 55 percent would not live to see age twenty. Consequently, one of her children would probably die in infancy, and another one or two would fail to reach adulthood. Wills left in St. Mary's County during the seventeenth century show the results. In 105 families over the years 1660 to 1680 only twelve parents left more than three children behind them, including those conceived but not yet born. The average number was 2.3, nearly always minors, some of whom might die before reaching adulthood.

For the immigrant woman, then, one of the major facts of life was that although she might bear a child about every two years, nearly half would not reach maturity. The social implications of this fact are far-reaching. Because she married late in her childbearing years and because so many of her children would die young, the number who would reach marriageable age might not replace, or might only barely replace, her and her husband or husbands as child-producing members of the society. Consequently, so long as immigrants were heavily predominant in the adult female population, Maryland could not grow much by natural increase. It remained a land of newcomers. . . .

A hazard of marriage for seventeenth-century women everywhere was death in childbirth, but this hazard may have been greater than usual in the Chesapeake. Whereas in most societies women tend to outlive men, in this malaria-ridden area it is probable that men outlived women. Hazards of childbirth provide the likely reason that Chesapeake women died so young. Once a woman in the Chesapeake reached forty-five, she tended to outlive men who reached the same age. Darrett and Anita Rutman have found malaria a probable cause of an exceptionally high death rate among pregnant women, who are, it appears, peculiarly vulnerable to that disease....

However long they lived, immigrant women in Maryland tended to outlive their husbands—in Charles County, for example, by a ratio of two to one. This was possible, despite the fact that women were younger than men at death, because women were also younger than men at marriage. Some women were widowed with no living children, but most were left responsible for two or three. These were often tiny, and nearly always not yet sixteen.

This fact had drastic consequences, given the physical circumstances of life. People lived at a distance from one another, not even in villages, much less towns. The widow had left her kin 3,000 miles across an ocean, and her husband's family was also there. She would have to feed her children and make her own tobacco crop. Though neighbors might help, heavy labor would be required of her if she had no servants, until—what admittedly was usually not difficult—she acquired a new husband.

In this situation dying husbands were understandably anxious about the welfare of their families. Their wills reflected their feelings and tell something of how they regarded their wives. In St. Mary's and Charles counties during the seventeenth century, little more than one-quarter of the men left their widows with no more than the dower the law required—one-third of his land for her life, plus outright ownership of one-third of his personal property. If there were no children, a man almost always left his widow his whole estate. Otherwise there were a variety of arrangements.

During the 1660s, when testators begin to appear in quantity, nearly a fifth of the men who had children left all to their wives, trusting them to see that the children received fair portions. Thus in 1663 John Shircliffe willed his whole estate to his wife "towards the maintenance of herself and my children into whose tender care I do Commend them Desireing to see them brought up in the fear of God and the Catholick Religion and Chargeing them to be Dutiful and obedient to her." As the century progressed, husbands tended instead to give the wife all or a major part of the estate for her life, and to designate how it should be distributed after her death. Either way, the husband put great trust in his widow, considering that he knew she was bound to remarry. Only a handful of men left estates to their wives only for their term of widowhood or until the children came of age. When a man did not leave his wife a life estate, he often gave her land outright or more than her dower third of his movable property. Such bequests were at the expense of his children and showed his concern that his widow should have a maintenance which young children could not supply.

A husband usually made his wife his executor and thus responsible for paying his debts and preserving the estate. Only 11 percent deprived their wives of such powers. In many instances, however, men also appointed overseers to assist their wives and to see that their children were not abused or their property embezzled. Danger lay in the fact that a second husband acquired control of all his wife's property, including her life estate in the property of his predecessor. Over half of the husbands who died in the 1650s and 1660s appointed overseers to ensure that their wills were followed. Some trusted to the overseers' "Care and good Conscience for the good of my widow and fatherless children." Others more explicitly made overseers responsible for seeing that "my said child . . . and the other [expected child] (when pleases God to send it) may have their right Proportion of my Said Estate and that the said Children may be bred up Chiefly in the fear of God." A few men—but remarkably few—authorized overseers to remove children from households of stepfathers who abused them or wasted their property. On the whole, the absence of such provisions for the protection of the children points to the husband's overriding concern for the welfare of his widow and to his confidence in her management, regardless of the certainty of her remarriage. Evidently, in the politics of family life women enjoyed great respect. . . .

What happened to widows and children if a man died without leaving a will? There was great need for some community institution that could protect children left fatherless or parentless in a society where they usually had no other kin. By the 1660s the probate court and county orphans' courts were supplying this need. If a man left a widow, the probate court—in Maryland a central government agency—usually appointed her or her new husband administrator of the estate with power to pay its creditors under court supervision. Probate procedures provided a large measure of protection. These required an inventory of the movable property and careful accounting of all disbursements, whether or not a man had left a will. William Hollis of Baltimore County, for example, had three stepfathers in seven years, and only the care of the judge of probate prevented the third stepfather from paying the debts of the second with goods that had belonged to William's father. As the judge remarked, William had "an uncareful mother." . . .

. . . Every year the county courts were expected to check on the welfare of orphans of intestate parents and remove them or their property from guardians who abused them or misused their estates. From 1681, Maryland law required that a special jury be impaneled once a year to report neighborhood knowledge of mistreatment of orphans and hear complaints.

This form of community surveillance of widows and orphans proved quite effective. In 1696 the assembly declared that orphans of intestates were often better cared for than orphans of testators. From that time forward, orphans' courts were charged with supervision of all orphans and were soon given powers to remove any guardians who were shown false to their trusts, regardless of the arrangements laid down in a will. The assumption was that the deceased parent's main concern was the welfare of the child, and that the orphans' court, as "father to us poor orphans," should implement the parent's intent. In actual fact, the courts never removed children—as opposed to their property—from a household in which the mother was living, except to apprentice them at the mother's request. These powers were mainly exercised over guardians of orphans both of whose parents were dead. The community as well as the husband believed the mother most capable of nurturing his children.

Remarriage was the usual and often the immediate solution for a woman who had lost her husband. The shortage of women made any woman eligible to marry again, and the difficulties of raising a family while running a plantation must have made remarriage necessary for widows who had no son old enough to make tobacco. One indication of the high incidence of remarriage is the fact that there were only sixty women, almost all of them widows, among the 1,735 people who left probate inventories in four southern Maryland counties over the second half of the century. Most other women must have died while married and therefore legally without property to put through probate.

One result of remarriage was the development of complex family structures. Men found themselves responsible for stepchildren as well as their own offspring, and children acquired half-sisters and half-brothers. Sometimes a woman married a second husband who himself had been previously married, and both brought children of former spouses to the new marriage. They then produced children of their own. The possibilities for conflict over the upbringing of children are evident, and crowded living conditions, found even in the households of the wealthy, must have added to family tensions. Luckily, the children of the family very often had the same mother. In Charles County, at least, widows took new husbands three times more often than widowers took new wives. The role of the mother in managing the relationships of half-brothers and half-sisters or stepfathers and stepchildren must have been critical to family harmony.

Early death in this immigrant population thus had broad effects on Maryland society in the seventeenth century. It produced what we might call a pattern of serial polyandry, which enabled more men to marry and to father families than the sex ratios otherwise would have permitted. It produced thousands of orphaned children who had no kin to maintain them or preserve their property, and thus gave rise to an institution almost unknown in England, the orphans' court, which was charged with their protection. And early death, by creating families in which the mother was the unifying element, may have increased her authority within the household. . . .

So far we have considered primarily the experience of immigrant women. What of their daughters? How were their lives affected by the demographic stresses of Chesapeake society?

One of the most important points in which the experience of daughters differed from that of their mothers was the age at which they married. In this woman-short world, the mothers had married as soon as they were eligible, but they had not usually become eligible until they were mature women in their middle twenties. Their daughters were much younger at marriage. A vital register kept in Somerset County shows that some girls married at age twelve and that the mean age at marriage for those born before 1670 was sixteen and a half years. . . .

Not only did native girls marry early, but many of them were pregnant before the ceremony. Bridal pregnancy among native-born women was not as common as among immigrants. Nevertheless, in seventeenth-century Somerset

County 20 percent of native brides bore children within eight and one half months of marriage. This was a somewhat higher percentage than has been reported from seventeenth-century English parishes.

These facts suggest considerable freedom for girls in selecting a husband. Almost any girl must have had more than one suitor, and evidently many had freedom to spend time with a suitor in a fashion that allowed her to become pregnant. . . .

Native girls married young and bore children young; hence they had more children than immigrant women. This fact ultimately changed the composition of the Maryland population. Native-born females began to have enough children to enable couples to replace themselves. These children, furthermore, were divided about evenly between males and females. By the mid-1680s, in all probability, the population thus began to grow through reproductive increase, and sexual imbalance began to decline. In 1704 the native-born preponderated in the Maryland assembly for the first time and by then were becoming predominant in the adult population as a whole. . . .

From Servitude to Slavery in the Chesapeake

RUSSELL MENARD

Why, in the decades surrounding 1700, did Chesapeake planters turn their labor force from one dominated by white servants bound for a term of years into one dominated by black slaves held for life? There would seem, on the surface at least, no compelling necessity, nothing inevitable about the transformation. Unlike sugar and rice, tobacco was not a crop that Englishmen believed themselves unsuited to cultivate. Indeed, until the end of the seventeenth century most Chesapeake tobacco was made by Englishmen; even after the rise of slavery Englishmen and their descendants continued to work in tobacco fields, sometimes as servants to substantial planters, more often as planters in their own right on small family farms. Why, then, the rise of slavery along the tobacco coast?

Briefly stated, this essay contends that the usual answer, which stresses the superior profitability of slaves, is not satisfactory. Chesapeake planters did not abandon indentured servitude because they preferred slaves; rather, a decline in the traditional labor supply forced planters to recruit workers from new sources, principally but not exclusively from Africa. . . .

I

There is a long tradition among economists that—and there is more than a touch of irony here—associates slavery with the widespread availability of free or nearly free land. . . . Under some conditions free land promotes opportunity, relative equality of condition, family farms, and political democracy;

Russell R. Menard, "From Servants to Slaves: The Transformation of the Chesapeake Labor System," *Southern Studies*, XVI (1977), 355–390. Reprinted by permission.

under others it tends toward rigid social stratification, slavery, plantation agriculture, and oligarchy. . . .

. . . A high land/man ratio creates a demand among landowners for unfree labor precisely because it drives wages up and offers widespread opportunities for workers to become landlords. In short, free land was an important precondition for both the slave-based, gentry dominated colonial South and the small farmer communities of early New England. . . .

. . . [W]hile the model highlights conditions which made unfree labor desirable, it offers little help in accounting for the switch to slaves late in the seventeenth century. For more than fifty years, Chesapeake planters met their demand for labor with indentured servants. And, although in the eyes of aspiring rentiers it perhaps had disadvantages, servitude appears to have been a largely satisfactory institution. For a time it at least permitted planters to expand the size of their labor force and therefore of their plantations without resort to slavery, despite the brevity of servants' terms. The model, then, is incomplete when applied to the Chesapeake: it simply does not tell us why slaves replaced servants along the tobacco coast.

II

Historians have offered a simple answer to the question of why slaves replaced servants: profit. In most accounts, servants and slaves are treated as competing forms of labor, vying for the planter's allegiance. In that competition, servitude suffered disadvantages that made the outcome inevitable. Servants were unruly and difficult to discipline, served for only short terms, needed replacement within a few years, and were relatively expensive. Slaves were easier to control, served for life, reproduced themselves, and, in spite of a higher initial investment, were cheaper than servants in the long run. Given the relative cost advantages of slavery, historians have argued, the demand for servants, and consequently the numbers arriving annually, declined as the availability of slaves increased. The critical event in this process was the destruction of the Royal African Company's monopoly in 1698 which led to a sharp increase in the supply of slaves to the Chesapeake.

This argument employs a series of untested assertions. There is, for example, no hard evidence that slaves were easier to discipline than servants, although the argument that blacks could be treated more severely than whites and were more readily identifiable if they attempted escape is persuasive. Nor is there evidence that planters were fully aware of the benefits of a self-perpetuating labor force in the seventeenth century. Quite the contrary, for what data exist, as limited and unsatisfactory as they may be, suggest that the first slave owners did little to encourage high fertility among their bondsmen and that blacks were unable to fully reproduce. In addition, there has as yet been no successful effort to demonstrate that slaves were a more profitable short-run investment than servants. My suspicion is—if the returns from natural increase are excluded from the equation, and seventeenth- and early eighteenth-century planters reveal little interest in slave rearing—that efficiency of management was a more important determinant of the rate of return than the type of labor employed. In fact, it would not be surprising to find that unassimilated Africans were less productive than English servants who came to the Chesapeake knowing their master's language and something of his work routines. Most important, no one has yet attempted to test the traditional argument's fundamental proposition: that planter demand for indentured labor declined as the supply of slaves increased.

The first task is to date the transition: when did black slaves replace white servants as the principal source of unfree labor in the Chesapeake colonies? Probate inventories and tax lists indicate that blacks came to predominate about 1690. On Maryland's lower Western Shore, servants outnumbered slaves by more than two and one-half to one in probate inventories taken in the middle to late 1670s. By the early 1690s, the relative position of the two groups had changed: more than twice as many slaves as servants appeared in inventories taken between 1690 and 1694. In Maryland as a whole, the change was even more striking. Between 1674 and 1679, there were nearly four servants for every slave found in inventories; in the early 1690s, there were nearly four slaves for every servant. . . .

These data are not incompatible with the traditional interpretation, although the shift in the composition of the labor force occurred roughly a decade earlier than is usually supposed. One could still contend that planter demand for servants declined as the supply of slaves increased. Were that the case the following sequence would be expected: an increase in the supply of slaves, a decline in the price of servants, and, finally, a decline in the supply of servants. The evidence describes a different pattern: a decline in the supply of servants followed by an increase in the price of indentured labor and in the supply of slaves. . . .

. . . Given the rapid growth of population in the Chesapeake colonies in the last half of the seventeenth century, this evidence suggests that the supply of servants declined relative to the number of plantation owners after the early 1660s, a decline that gained speed in the last two decades of the century.

If the decline in the supply of servants were a product of a fall in planter demand as the availability of slaves increased, evidence of substantial black immigration should appear before the mid 1660s. If such a migration occurred it has left few traces in the surviving records. Slaves did reach the Chesapeake colonies during the middle decades of the seventeenth century. By Governor Berkeley's estimate, 2000 blacks, about 5% of the population, lived in Virginia in 1671. But it was not until at least a decade after the decline in the supply of servants that the number of blacks imported each year rose above a trickle and it was the end of the century before the supply of slaves proved dependable.

Edmund Jennings, based on conversations with "some ancient Inhabitants" and his own recollection, offered a history of Virginia slave imports to the Board of Trade in 1708. After reporting the arrival of over 6600 slaves in the preceding nine years, he noted "that before the year 1680 what negros were brought to Virginia were imported generally from Barbados for it was very rare to have a Negro ship come to this County directly from Africa." "Since that time," Jennings continued, "and before the year 1698, the Trade of Negros became more frequent, tho not in proportion to what it hath been of late, during which the Affrican Company sent several Ships and others by their Licence (as I have been informed) having bought their Slaves of the Company brought them in hither for Sale." In a letter of the same year, Governor John Seymour offered a similar description of Maryland's trade: "before the year 1698, this province has been supplyd by some small Quantitys of Negro's from Barbados and other her Ma'tys Islands and Plantations, as Jamaica and New England Seaven, eight, nine or ten in a Sloope, and sometymes larger Quantitys, and sometymes, tho very seldom, whole ship Loads of Slaves have been brought here directly from Affrica by Interlopers, or such as have had Lycenses, or otherwise traded there." Since 1698, Seymour reported, nearly 3000 slaves, the large majority fresh from Africa, had arrived in Maryland. . . .

. . . [T]he major point to emerge from the letters of Jennings and Seymour stands: before 1698 and the end of the monopoly the supply of slaves to the Chesapeake was small, unreliable, and inadequate to the needs of tobacco planters for labor. An increase in the supply of slaves did not precede and thereby produce the decline in the importation of indentured servants. The sequence was the reverse: the decline in the supply of servants occurred at least a decade before blacks began to arrive in the Chesapeake from Africa in large numbers and over thirty years before the supply of slaves became dependable. . . .

It would be an error to dismiss the decade after the ending of the Royal African Company's monopoly as unimportant to the rise of slavery in the Chesapeake. At least 10,348 slaves arrived in Maryland and Virginia from 1698 to 1709, a figure that probably excludes some substantial shiploads direct from Africa and certainly does not count numerous small groups of slaves brought from the West Indies. Yet even these did not at first satisfy the demand for labor, a demand long frustrated by declining supplies of white servants and the disruptions of war and then accelerated by the return of peace and prosperity. "There were as many buyers as negros," Francis Nicholson noted in 1700 in a comment on the sale of 230 slaves in York River, "and I think that, if 2000 were imported, there would be substantial buyers for them." Blacks brought better prices than ever before and, for a time, the Chesapeake surpassed Jamaica as the most profitable slave market in British America. Nor did demand fall off with the return of war and depression in 1703. Frenzied buying continued, more blacks were imported, and prices advanced even higher, until, by the end of the decade, planters had "ruined the Credit of the Country." Still, slaves did not drive servants from the tobacco coast; servitude was already in decline for other reasons. The rise of black slavery was more a consequence than a cause of the decline of white servitude; it perhaps hastened the process, but it did not begin it.

III

. . . [T]he price of servants did not behave as the traditional argument demands. Servant prices were steady from the mid-1640s to the early 1660s, increased slowly in the mid-1670s, rose sharply to the late 1680s, peaked about 1690, and then remained stable for the next twenty years, despite fairly violent short-term fluctuations. In short, the price of servants rose as the supply declined and blacks replaced whites as the majority among bound laborers in the Chesapeake. This is a strong criticism of the traditional argument: the supply of servants did not fall in response to a decline in planter demand.

The price ratios of servants to slaves during the period of transition provide further evidence of relative demand for the two types of labor. . . . The ratio is not a pure measure of relative demand for servants and slaves: obviously, supply played a role, and the tobacco coast was only a small part of the total market for slaves. Nonetheless, it does not suggest that planters preferred slaves to servants when the labor force moved from white to black. In fact, they seem to have preferred servants, or, perhaps more accurately, they were reluctant to exchange laborers they were used to for workers who were unfamiliar and, doubtless to some, a bit frightening. If price ratios reflect relative demand, it was only after blacks had come to predominate among bound laborers that planters expressed a clear preference for slaves.

Why, then, if planters did not prefer slaves to servants, did they increase their holdings in slaves and decrease them in servants during the late seventeenth century? Further consideration of servant migration patterns provides some clues. Despite violent and distinctly cyclical fluctuations in the number of immigrants and a paucity of evidence, there is a discernible trend in the supply of servants to the Chesapeake colonies relative to the number of potential labor owners. If my reading of the limited data is correct, the supply of servants increased more rapidly than the number of households in the Chesapeake from 1640 until the early to middle 1660s. As a result, planters were able to expand their labor force, and therefore the size of their operations, without resort to slaves. The price of indentured labor seems to have remained stable across this period, although changes in mortality and limited evidence make it impossible to speak with assurance.

Opportunity soon undermined the ability of supply to keep ahead of demand. Many of the servants who came to Maryland and Virginia in the 1640s and 1650s completed their terms, accumulated capital, purchased land, and entered the market for indentured labor. The process described by Adam Smith operated in the early Chesapeake: cheap land and scarce labor forced planters to pay high wages to servants once they became free, permitting a quick transition from agricultural laborer to yeoman planter. As a result of the rapid growth in the number of farms, the number of servants arriving in the Chesapeake had to increase each year in order to keep pace with demand. If the number of new arrivals merely remained steady, or even if it increased but more slowly than the number of households, planters would face a labor shortage.

The turning point was reached in the mid-1660s. The number of servants brought to Maryland and Virginia, after growing steadily across the middle decades of the century, peaked in about 1665, and then levelled out, or at least grew at a slower rate, before registering an absolute decline in the 1680s. The rate of farm formation also declined, but much less steeply than the supply of servants: the number of plantations in the Chesapeake colonies expanded at roughly three percent per year during the last third of the seventeenth century. As a result, the ratio of servants to plantations fell and the price of indentured labor rose. . . .

. . . During the last third of the seventeenth century, when the initial thrust toward heavy investment in slaves occurred, Chesapeake planters faced a severe labor shortage, a shortage produced by the failure of white immigration to keep pace with the growth in farms.

Why did the supply of servants prove inadequate during the last third of the seventeenth century? . . . To begin with, it is important to place the process of migrating to the Chesapeake under indentures in context. A young Englishman of the seventeenth century who found life at home constricting, who sought greater opportunities or simply a change of scene had several options. He could try Maryland or Virginia of course, but there were other choices. He could go to the West Indies, New England, Pennsylvania, or the Carolinas. He could join the army or navy. If he lived in a village he could move to a town. And there was always London, the colonies' most serious competitor for immigrants. In sum, moving to the New World should be considered within a broad context of English migratory patterns in which colonies competed with each other and with places in England for new recruits.

Within this framework, three factors regulated the size of the English-Chesapeake migratory stream: the intensity of the recruiting effort; the size of the potential migrant group; and the attractiveness of the Chesapeake region relative to other possible destinations. The first, intensity of recruitment, will not submit to measurement, although it is likely, particularly over the short-run as merchants responded to changes in the price of tobacco, that this was a powerful influence. For the moment, we will hold recruitment constant in our model, an assumption soon to be relaxed. The remaining factors—size of the migrant group and relative attractiveness of the Chesapeake—can be measured, albeit indirectly and with less precision than one would like: both changed in ways that tended to reduce the number of servants willing to try their luck in tobacco.

The size of the migrant group in seventeenth-century England was a function of total population, an assertion that must be qualified by a recognition that migration was highly age, sex, and probably class specific (young men of the middling classes in their late teens and early twenties predominated) and that the propensity to migrate varied with time. Nevertheless, changes in the rate of population growth can provide a rough index to changes in the size of the migrant group. Despite disagreement over the absolute size of total population and the rates and sources of change, it is clear that England's population grew at a slower rate during the last half of the seventeenth century than during the first. . . . Other things being equal, a decline in the birth rate in the mid-1640s would lead to a reduction in the growth of potential migrants and, therefore, of the number of servants bound for the Chesapeake roughly twenty years later, in the mid-1660s.

Of course, other things were not equal but rather tended to reduce the appeal of the tobacco coast relative to other destinations. In part this was a function of the pattern of population growth. During the sixteenth and early seventeenth centuries real wages in England fell as a growing number of workers competed for a relatively constant supply of natural resources.... Relieved of the pressure of a rapidly growing work force, real wages rose across the last half of the seventeenth century. Rising real wages worked to reduce the size of the migrating population and, for those who still chose to move, to increase the attractiveness of destinations within England. In addition to the general course of real wages, several other factors limited the success of Chesapeake planters in the competition for workers. Within England, for example, the rebuilding of London in the aftermath of the great fire provided employment at good wages for thousands of potential servants. Somewhat later, the wars at the turn of the century sharply reduced the stream of immigrants, although why—whether an unwillingness of merchants to invest in the Chesapeake during depression, alternative employment in the army or navy, or a reluctance of servants to risk an Atlantic crossing in time of war—is a puzzle. Within the colonies, a decline in opportunities in Maryland and Virginia may have discouraged immigration, although it is not clear that even the most sophisticated and knowledgeable of Englishmen, let alone impoverished young workers, knew that the tobacco coast was no longer a good poor man's country. Perhaps more important, the Chesapeake was losing its position as the most attractive New World region. During the 1630s, poor Englishmen who decided to cross the Atlantic could choose among three destinations, but in the 1640s sugar and disease gave Barbados a bad reputation and the failure of New England to find a staple crop prevented the growth of a lively demand for servants. These developments narrowed the options and focused the greatest part of the English trans-Atlantic migratory stream on the tobacco coast. After 1680, the opening up of Pennsylvania and the beginning of rapid development in the Carolinas ended this near monopoly and diverted migrants away from Maryland and Virginia. In sum, changes in the size of the migrating population and in the relative attractiveness of the Chesapeake colonies combined to reduce the supply of indentured servants available to tobacco planters in the years after 1665....

... After 1665, the proportion of young men of middling origins shrank as the number of women, Irishmen, laboring poor, and, especially after 1718, convicts in the servant population grew.

This shift in the provenance of indentured servants combined with changes in the distribution of labor, in the wealth and status of masters, and in opportunities to produce a general deterioration in the status of servants. Around mid-century, the ownership of bound labor was widespread. Most small planters owned servants and most servants were owned by small planters. The servant bound to a small planter was probably not isolated from his master's family. Such men could not afford separate servant's quarters detached from their homes. Often, servants must have been fully integrated into family life, sharing meals, sleeping under the same roof, treated like a poor relation or at times like a son or daughter. Nor could small planters afford to exempt themselves or their families from the hard work of farming. Masters and servants working side by side in the field must have been a common sight in the Chesapeake in the 1650s and 1660s. Masters and servants, furthermore, often shared a common social origin in England and a common experience in moving to the New World. Most small planters, like the bound laborers they commanded, were drawn from the middling ranks of English society and had frequently arrived in the Chesapeake under indentures. In short, despite important differences in legal status, the social distance between master and servant was often narrow. Given the widespread opportunities available at mid-century, it was a gap a servant could expect to cross once out of his time.

Both the gap and the difficulty of the crossing increased as the eighteenth century approached. As the labor shortage gained intensity, small planters were forced from the ranks of labor owners and servants became concentrated on the estates of the wealthy. These new masters, most of whom had either been born in the colonies or arrived from England as free men with capital, had little in common with their bondsmen, particularly as the middling Englishmen in the servant population were gradually replaced by the Irish, the laboring poor, and convicts. Nor did such masters work in the fields or integrate bound laborers into their families except in well-defined servile roles. In addition, the chances that an ex-servant would join the ranks of Chesapeake planters fell off sharply in the last quarter of the century. Servants who completed their terms in Maryland and Virginia after 1680 found little opportunity for advancement. Most left the tobacco coast in search of better prospects elsewhere. The last decades of the seventeenth century witnessed not only the growth of black slavery, but the sharp decline of the position and prospects of white servants in Chesapeake society. . . .

The Chesapeake labor system was transformed in the decades surrounding 1700. As the supply of white workers declined, planters turned to slaves and to servants less like themselves for labor. A landscape dominated by family farms worked by a small planter, his family, and a servant or two witnessed the rise of large plantations supervised by a rich and powerful gentry and manned by black slaves. Indentured servitude did not disappear, but it did change. The composition of the immigrant group altered and the social distance between master and servant increased. Opportunities, once abundant, declined, and former servants often left the Chesapeake for more recently established colonies where material progress was still likely. In the course of a few decades, the tobacco coast moved from a labor system that promised poor men eventual integration into the society they served to one that kept a majority of its laborers in perpetual bondage and offered most of the others a choice between poverty and emigration. . . .

℘ *F U R T H E R   R E A D I N G*

T. H. Breen and Stephen Innes, *"Myne Owne Ground": Race and Freedom on Virginia's Eastern Shore, 1640–1676* (1980)
Lois Green Carr, Russell R. Menard, and Lorena S. Walsh, *Robert Cole's World: Agriculture and Society in Early Maryland* (1991)

Lois Green Carr, Philip D. Morgan, and Jean B. Russo, eds., *Colonial Chesapeake Society* (1988)

Frank Craven, *White, Red, and Black: The Seventeenth-Century Virginian* (1977)

David Galenson, *White Servitude in Colonial America: An Economic Analysis* (1981)

Ivor Noël Hume, *Martin's Hundred* (1979)

Ann Kussmaul, *Servants in Husbandry in Early Modern England* (1981)

Peter Laslett, *The World We Have Lost* (1965)

Nancy O. Lurie, "Indian Cultural Adjustment to European Civilization," in J. M. Smith, ed., *Seventeenth-Century America* (1959)

Gloria L. Main, *Tobacco Colony: Life in Early Maryland, 1650–1720* (1982)

James R. Perry, *The Formation of a Society on Virginia's Eastern Shore, 1615–1655* (1990)

David B. Quinn, ed., *Early Maryland in a Wider World* (1982)

Thad W. Tate and David L. Ammerman, eds., *The Chesapeake in the Seventeenth Century: Essays on Anglo-American Society and Politics* (1979)

Alden Vaughan, *American Genesis: Captain John Smith and the Founding of Virginia* (1975)

Keith Wrightson, *English Society, 1580–1680* (1982)

New England: The Settlement of the Puritan Colonies

❧

At first European colonizers had little interest in the area between Chesapeake Bay and the St. Lawrence River. One short-lived attempt to settle a colony in Maine at the same time as Jamestown (1607) had convinced investors that the region was both inhospitable and unlikely to yield products of value. Attention focused on the north—on Newfoundland and the great Canadian river—where the rich fishing grounds and abundance of fur-bearing animals had attracted hundreds of voyages every year since shortly after the time of the region's discovery. These expeditions came in the spring and left in the autumn. There seemed little reason to build expensive colonies on those cold, rocky shores.

New England, then called the North Part of Virginia, became attractive when a new kind of colony was planned—transfers of entire communities of English men and women who sought an environment in which they could thrive and worship God as they saw fit. Plymouth on Cape Cod was settled in 1620 by a small group of Puritan Separatists who viewed the Church of England as so corrupt that they had separated themselves entirely from it. Then in 1630 a huge exodus of Puritans founded Massachusetts Bay. These emigrants, in contrast to the Separatists, considered themselves still loyal members of the church, who merely wished to reform it by example. Thousands left England in the 1630s, partly because of the same economic distress that fed migration to the Chesapeake but also because Charles I and his archbishop of Canterbury, William Laud, increasingly were pushing the church in directions the Puritans abhorred, and requiring conformity.

The Puritans chose New England because its environment was conducive to small family farms rather than great plantations; its lack of rich crops would keep out those who might seek to pervert their godly experiment. They found the land depleted of its native population by a disastrous plague that had struck shortly before Plymouth's founding; a second wave of European disease devastated the Indians in the early 1630s. Some Puritans, whose providential outlook disposed them to look for God's will in all events, saw this as divine intervention on their behalf, clearing the land for their habitation.

♫ D O C U M E N T S

The Pilgrims, whose backers had forced them to take a large number of skilled colonists who were not Puritans, quickly sent back reports to their friends in England, which were published in 1622. These excerpts, in the first document, describe the Mayflower Compact, by which they and the non-Puritan "strangers" agreed to live, and the first Thanksgiving, celebrated in an early spirit of peace with their Wampanoag Indian neighbors. William Bradford, Plymouth's governor, kept a journal of events. In the excerpt reprinted as the second document, Bradford describes the Pilgrims' increasingly tense relationship with their Indian neighbors and their growing suspicion of even their interpreters, Squanto and Hobbomock.

John Winthrop, governor of Massachusetts Bay, gave a famous sermon on board the *Arbella,* the ship carrying the first Puritan contingent. In the excerpts featured in the third selection, he outlines the distinctive characteristics of his colony, bound together as it was by a common purpose. Winthrop's images have been reshaped many times in American history. In the fourth selection John Pond, a far humbler member of the *Arbella* fleet, writes to his father for help, as Richard Frethorne had done from Virginia (see Chapter 3), in facing the rigors of the new plantation. Both New England colonies experienced a high death rate in their first years. In the fifth document minister Thomas Welde writes to his former parishioners in England, certifying that after two years the colony was firmly established. "The Summons to New England," the sixth selection, is a ballad ridiculing the Puritans' claims of both the bounty of their land and the purity of their religious life; it affords insight into the opposition they faced. In the seventh selection William Wood offers up a "true, lively, and experimental description" of New England in which he views the colonists' Indian neighbors with sympathy and interest and analyzes the changes wrought in the native people's gender roles by the coming of the English. Miantonomo, chief of the Narragansetts, presents a much darker picture of the Indians' changed situation in the final selection.

Plymouth's Pilgrims on the Mayflower Compact and the First Thanksgiving, 1620, 1621

The Mayflower Compact, 1620

This day before we came to harbor, observing some not well affected to unity and concord, but gave some appearance of faction, it was thought good there should be an association and agreement, that we should combine together in one body, and to submit to such government and governors, as we should by common consent agree to make and choose, and set our hands to this that follows word for word.

In the name of God, Amen. We whose names are underwritten, the loyal Subjects of our dread sovereign Lord King James, by the grace of God of Great Britain, France, and Ireland King, Defender of the Faith, etc.

Having under-taken for the glory of God, and advancement of the Chris-

---

Some of the spelling in this document has been modernized.

tian Faith, and honor of our King and Country, a Voyage to plant the first Colony in the Northern parts of VIRGINIA, do by these presents solemnly and mutually in the presence of God and one of another, covenant, and combine our selves together into a civil body politic, for our better ordering and preservation, and furtherance of the ends aforesaid; and by virtue hereof to enact, constitute, and frame such just and equal Laws, Ordinances, acts, constitutions, offices from time to time, as shall be thought most meet and convenient for the general good of the Colony: unto which we promise all due submission and obedience. In witness whereof we have here-under subscribed our names. Cape Cod 11 of November, in the year of the reign of our sovereign Lord King James, of England, France, and Ireland 18 and of Scotland 54. Anno Domino 1620.

The First Thanksgiving, 1621

A Letter Sent from New-England to a friend in these parts ...

Loving, and old Friend, although I received no Letter from you by this Ship, yet foreasmuch as I know you expect the performance of my promise, which was, to write unto you truly and faithfully of all things, I have therefore at this time sent unto you accordingly. Referring you for further satisfaction to our more large Relations. You shall understand, that in this little time, that a few of us have been here, we have built seven dwelling houses, and four for the use of the Plantation, and have made preparation for divers other. We set the last Spring some twentie Acres of Indian-Corne, and sowed some six Acres of Barley and Peas, and according to the manner of the Indian, we manured our ground with Herrings or rather Shads, which we have in great abundance, and take with great ease at our doors. Our Corne did prove well, and God be praised, we had a good increase of our Indian-Corne, and our Barley indifferent good, but our Peas not worth the gathering, for we feared they were too late sown. They came up very well, and blossomed, but the Sun parched them in the blossom. Our harvest being gotten in, our Governor sent four men on fowling, that so we might after a more special manner rejoice together, after we had gathered the fruit of our labors. They four in one day killed as much fowl, as with a little help beside, served the Company almost a week, at which time amongst other Recreations, we exercised our Arms, many of the Indians coming amongst us, and amongst the rest their greatest King Massasoit, with some ninety men, whom for three days we entertained and feasted, and they went out and killed five Deer, which they brought to the Plantation and bestowed on our Governor, and upon the Captain, and others. And although it be not always so plentiful, as it was at this time with us, yet by the goodness of God, we are so far from want, that we often wish you partakers of our planty. We have found the Indians very faithful in their Covenant of Peace with us; very loving and ready to pleasure us. We often go to them, and they come to us; some of us have been fifty miles by Land in the Country with them; the occasions and Relations whereof you shall understand by our general and more full Declaration of such things as are worth the noting. Yea it hath pleased God so to possess the Indians with a fear of us, and love unto us, that not only the greatest King amongst them called Massasoit, but also all the Princes and people round about us, have either made suit unto us, or been glad of any occasion to make peace with us, so that seven of them at once have sent their messengers to us to that end ... willingly to be under the protection, and subjects to our sovereign Lord King James, so that there is now great peace amongst the Indians themselves, which was not formerly, neither would have been but for us. And we for our parts walk as peaceably and safely in the wood, as in the highways in England, we entertain them familiarly in our houses, and they as friendly bestowing their Venison on us. They are a people without any Religion, or knowledge of any God, yet very trusty, quick of apprehension, ripe witted, just.

Governor William Bradford on the Plymouth Colonists' Relations with the Indians, Early 1620s

Anno. 1621

... But about the 16. *of March* a certain Indian came boldly amongst them, and spoke to them in broken English, which they could well understand, but marvelled at it. At length they understood by discourse with him, that he was not of these parts, but belonged to the eastern parts, where some English-ships came to fish, with whom he was acquainted, & could name sundry of them by their names, amongst whom he had got his language. He became profitable to them in acquainting them with many things concerning the state of the country in the east-parts where he lived, which was afterwards profitable unto them; as also of the people hear, of their names, number, & strength; of their situation & distance from this place, and who was chief amongst them. His name was *Samaset;* he tould them also of another Indian whose name was *Squanto,* a native of this place, who had been in England & could speak better English than himself. Being, after some time of entertainment & gifts, dismissed, a while after he came again, & 5 more with him, & they brought again all the tools that were stolen away before, and made way for the coming of their great Sachem, called *Massasoyt;* who, about 4 *or* 5 *days after,* came with the chief of his friends & other attendance, with the aforesaid *Squanto.* With whom, after friendly entertainment, & some gifts given him, they made a peace with him (which hath now continued this 24 years) in these terms.

1. That neither he nor any of his, should injure or do hurt to any of their people.
2. That if any of his did any hurt to any of theirs, he should send the offender, that they might punish him.
3. That if anything were taken away from any of theirs, he should cause it to be restored; and they should do the like to his.

Some of the spelling in this document has been modernized.

4. If any did unjustly war against him, they would aid him; if any did war against them, he should aid them.

5. He should send to his neighbours confederates, to certify them of this, that they might not wrong them, but might be likewise comprised in the conditions of peace.

6. That when their men came to them, they should leave their bows & arrows behind them.

After these things he returned to his place called *Sowams,* some 40 mile from this place, but *Squanto* continued with them, and was their interpreter, and was a special instrument sent of God for their good beyond their expectation. He directed them how to set their corn, where to take fish, and to procure other commodities, and was also their pilot to bring them to unknown places for their profit, and never left them till he died. He was a *native of this place,* & scarce any left alive besides himself. He was carried away with diverse others by one *Hunt,* a master of a ship, who thought to sell them for slaves in Spain; but he got away for England, and was entertained by a merchant in London, & employed to New-found-land & other parts, & lastly brought hither into these parts by one Mr. *Dermer,* a gentle-man employed by Sir Ferdinando Gorges & others, for discovery, & other designs in these parts. . . .

. . . Then the sickness began to fall sore amongst them, and the weather so bad as they could not make much sooner any dispatch. Againe, the Govr. & chief of them, seeing so many die, and fall down sick daily, thought it no wisdom to send away the ship, their condition considered, and the danger they stood in from the Indians, till they could procure some shelter; and therefore thought it better to draw some more charge upon themselves & friends, than hazard all. . . .

Afterwards they (as many as were able) began to plant their corn, in which service Squanto stood them in great stead, showing them both the manner how to set it, and after how to dress & tend it. Also he tould them except they got fish & set with it (in these old grounds) it would come to nothing, and he showed them that in the middle of April they should have store enough come up the brook, by which they began to build, and taught them how to take it, and where to get other provisions necessary for them; all which they found true by trial & experience. Some English seed they sow, as wheat & peas, but it came not to good, either by the badness of the seed, or lateness of the season, or both, or some other defect.

In this month of *April* whilst they were busy about their seed, their Govr. (Mr. John Carver) came out of the field very sick, it being a hot day; he complained greatly of his head, and lay down, and within a few hours his senses failed, so as he never spoke more till he died, which was within a few days after. Whose death was much lamented, and caused great heaviness amongst them, as there was cause. He was buried in the best manner they could, with some volleys of shot by all that bore arms; and his wife, being a weak woman, died within 5 or 6 weeks after him.

Shortly after William Bradford was chosen Govr. in his stead, and being not yet recovered of his illness, in which he had been near the point of death, Isaak Allerton was chosen to be an Assistant unto him, who, by renewed election every year, continued sundry years together, which I hear note once for all. . . .

Having in some sort ordered their business at home, it was thought meet to send some abroad to see their new friend Massasoyet, and to bestow upon him some gratuity to bind him the faster unto them; as also that hereby they might view the country, and see in what manner he lived, what strength he had about him, and how the ways were to his place, if at any time they should have occasion. So the 2 *of July* they sent Mr. Edward Winslow & Mr. Hopkins, with the foresaid Squanto for their guide, who gave him a suit of clothes, and a horseman's coat, with some other small things, which were kindly accepted; but they found but short comons [food rations], and came both weary & hungry home. For the Indians used then to have nothing so much corn as they have since the English have stored them with their hoes, and seen their industry in breaking up new grounds therewith. *They found his place to be* 40 *miles from hence,* the soil good, & the people not many, being dead & abundantly wasted in the late great mortality which fell in all these parts about *three years* before the coming of the English, wherein thousands of them died, they not being able to bury one another; their skulls and bones were found in many places lying still above ground, where their houses & dwellings had been; a very sad spectacle to behold. But they brought word that the Narighansets lived but on the other side of that great bay, & were a strong people, & many in number, living compact together, & had not been at all touched with this wasting plague. . . .

Thus their peace & acquaintance was pretty well established with the natives about them; and there was another Indian called *Hobamack* come to live amongst them, a proper lusty man, and a man of account for his valour & parts amongst the Indians, and continued very faithful and constant to the English till he died. . . .

After this, the 18 of September: they sent out their shallop [small boat] to the Massachusetts, with 10 men, and Squanto for their guide and interpreter, to discover and view that bay, and trade with the natives; the which they performed, and found kind entertainment. The people were much afraid of the Tarentins, a people to the eastward which used to come in harvest time and take away their corn, & many times kill their persons. They returned in safety, and brought home a good quantity of beaver, and made report of the place, wishing they had been there seated; (but it seems the Lord, who assigns to all men the bounds of their habitations, had appointed it for another use). And thus they found the Lord to be with them in all their ways, and to bless their outgoings & incomings, for which let his holy name have the praise forever, to all posterity.

They began now to gather in the small harvest they had, and to fit up their houses and dwellings against winter, being all well recovered in health & strength, and had all things in good plenty; for as some were thus employed in affairs abroad, others were exercised in fishing, about cod, & bass, & other fish, of which they took good store, of which every family had their portion.

examined by the Govr., he made as if they were at hand, and would still be looking back, as if they were at his heels. At which the Govr. caused them to take arms & stand on their guard, and supposing the boat to be still within hearing (by reason it was calm) caused a warning piece or 2 to be shot of, the which they heard and came in. But no Indians appeared; watch was kept all night, but nothing was seen. Hobamak was confidente for Massasoyt, and thought all was false; yet the Govr. caused him to send his wife privately, to see what she could observe (pretending other occasions), but there was nothing found, but all was quiet. After this they proceeded on their voyage to the Massachusetts, and had good trade, and returned in safety, blessed be God.

But by the former passages, and other things of like nature, they began to see that Squanto sought his own ends, and played his own game, by putting the Indians in fear, and drawing gifts from them to enrich himself; making them believe he could stir up war against whom he would, & make peace for whom he would. Yea, he made them believe they kept the plague buried in the ground, and could send it among whom they would, which did much terrify the Indians, and made them depend more on him, and seek more to him than to Massasoyte, which procured him envy, and had like to have cost him his life. For after the discovery of his practices, Massasoyt sought it both privately and openly; which caused him to stick close to the English, & never durst go from them till he died. They also made good use of the emulation that grew between Hobamack and him, which made them carry more squarely. And the Govr. seemed to countenance the one, and the Captain the other, by which they had better intelligence, and made them both more diligent. . . .

. . . Squanto fell sick of an Indian fever, bleeding much at the nose (which the Indians take for a symptom of death), and within a few days died there; desiring the Govr. to pray for him, that he might go to the Englishmen's God in heaven, and bequeathed sundry of his things to sundry of his English friends, as remembrances of his love; of whom they had a great loss. . . .

Governor John Winthrop of Massachusetts Bay Gives a Model of Christian Charity, 1630

1. For the persons, we are a Company professing ourselves fellow members of Christ, In which respect only though we were absent from each other many miles, and had our employments as far distant, yet we ought to account ourselves knit together by this bond of love, and live in the exercise of it, if we would have comfort of our being in Christ. . . .

2. for the work we have in hand, it is by a mutual consent through a special overruling providence, and a more than an ordinary approbation of the Churches of Christ to seek out a place of Cohabitation and Consortship under a due form of Government both civil and ecclesiastical. In such cases as this the care of the public must oversway all private respects, by which not only conscience, but mere

---

Some of the spelling in this document has been modernized.

All the summer there was no want. And now began to come in store
as winter approached, of which this place did abound when they c:
(but afterward decreased by degrees). And besides water fowl, there '
store of wild Turkeys, of which they took many, besides venison, &c
they had about a peck a meal a week to a person, or now since
Indian corn to the proportion. Which made many afterwards write ;
of their plenty here to their friends in England, which were not f;
true reports. . . .

 . . . [T]he great people of the Narigansets, in a braving mann
messenger unto them with a bundle of arrows tied about with a gr(
skin; which their interpreters told them was a threatening & a challe
which the Govr., with the advice of others, sent them a round an
if they had rather have war than peace, they might begin when th
they had done them no wrong, neither did they fear them, or shoulc
them unprovided. And by another messenger sent the snake-skin
bullets in it; but they would not receive it, but sent it back again.
is like the reason was their own ambition, who, (since the death c
of the Indians,) thought to dominate & lord it over the rest, & coi
English would be a bar in their way, and saw that Massasoyt t(
already under their wings.

But this made them the more carefully to look to themselves,
agreed to enclose their dwellings with a good strong pale, and make
convenient places, with gates to shut, which were every night locked,
kept, and when need required there was also warding in the daytir
company was by the Captain's and the Govr.'s advise, divided into {
and every one had their quarter appointed them, unto which they w
upon any sudden alarme. And if there should be any cry of fire,
were appointed for a guard, with muskets, whilst others quenched
prevent Indian treachery. This was accomplished very cheerfully, {
impailed round by the beginning of March, in which every family
garden plot secured. And herewith I shall end this year. . . .

Anno 1622

At the spring of the year they had appointed the Massachusetts t(
and trade with them, and began now to prepare for that voya
later end of March. But upon some rumors heard, Hobamak, the
them upon some jealousies he had, he feared they were joined
ighansets and might betray them if they were not careful. He
some jealousy of Squanto, by what he gathered from some priva
between him and other Indians. But they resolved to proceed
their shallop with 10 of their chief men about the beginning
both Squanto & Hobamake with them, in regard of the jealousy
But they had not been gone long, but an Indian belonging to S(
came running in seeming great fear, and told them that mar
ihgansets, with Corbytant, and he thought also Massasoyte,
against them; and he got away to tell them, not without dan;

Civil policy doth bind us; for it is a true rule that particular estates cannot subsist in the ruin of the public.

3. The end is to improve our lives to do more service to the Lord the comfort and increase of the body of christ whereof we are members that ourselves and posterity may be the better preserved from the Common corruptions of this evil world to serve the Lord and work out our Salvation under the power and purity of his holy Ordinances.

4. for the means whereby this must be effected, they are 2fold, a Conformity with the work and end we aim at, these we see are extraordinary, therefore we must not content ourselves with usual ordinary means whatsoever we did or ought to have done when we lived in England, the same must we do and more also where we go: That which the most in their Churches maintain as a truth in profession only, we must bring into familiar and constant practice, as in this duty of love we must love brotherly without dissimulation, we must love one another with a pure heart fervently we must bear one another's burdens, we must not look only on our own things, but also on the things of our brethren, neither must we think that the lord will bear with such failings at our hands as he doth from those among whom we have lived. . . .

. . . Thus stands the cause between God and us, we are entered into Covenant with him for his worke, we have taken out a Commission, the Lord hath given us leave to draw our own Articles we have professed to enterprise these Actions upon these and these ends, we have hereupon besought him of favour and blessing: Now if the Lord shall please to hear us, and bring us in peace to the place we desire, then hath he ratified this Covenant and sealed our Commission, [and] will expect a strict performance of the Articles contained in it, but if we shall neglect the observation of these Articles which are the ends we have propounded, and dissembling with our God, shall fall to embrace this present world and prosecute our carnal intentions, seeking great things for ourselves and our posterity, the Lord will surely break out in wrath against us be revenged of such a perjured people and make us know the price of the breach of such a Covenant.

Now the only way to avoid this shipwreck and to provide for our posterity is to follow the Counsel of Micah, to do Justly, to love mercy, to walk humbly with our God, for this end, we must be knit together in this work as one man, we must entertain each other in brotherly Affection, we must be willing to abridge ourselves of our superfluities, for the supply of others' necessities, we must uphold a familiar Commerce together in all meekness, gentleness, patience and liberality, we must delight in each other, make others' Conditions our own, rejoice together, mourn together, labour, and suffer together, always having before our eyes our Commission and Community in the work, our Community as members of the same body, so shall we keep the unity of the spirit in the bond of peace, the Lord will be our God and delight to dwell among us, as his own people and will command a blessing upon us in all our ways, so that we shall see much more of his wisdom power goodness and truth than formerly we have been acquainted with, we shall find that the God of Israel is among us, when ten of us shall be able to resist a thousand of our enemies, when he shall make us a praise and glory, that men shall say of succeeding plantations: the lord make it like that of New England: for we must Consider that we shall be as a City upon a Hill, the eyes of all people are upon us; so that if we shall deal falsely with our god in this work we have undertaken and so cause him to withdraw his present help from us, we shall be made a story and a by-word through the world, we shall open the mouths of enemies to speak evil of the ways of god and all professors for God's sake; we shall shame the faces of many of gods worthy servants, and cause their prayers to be turned into Curses upon us till we be consumed out of the good land whether we are going. . . .

Colonist John Pond Writes to His Mother and Father for Help, 1631

Most loving and kind Father and Mother:

My humble duty remembered unto you, trusting in God you are in good health, and I pray, remember my love unto my brother Joseife, and thank him for his kindness that I found at his hand at London, which was not the value of a farthing. I know, loving Father, and do confess that I was an undutiful child unto you when I lived with you and by you, for the which I am much sorrowful and grieved for it, trusting in God that He will so guide me that I will never offend you so any more, and I trust in God that you will forgive me for it, and my writing unto you is to let you understand what a country this new Eingland is where we live.

Here are but few eingeines [Indians], and a great sort of them died this winter. It was thought it was of the plague. They are a crafty people and they will cozen and cheat, and they are a subtle people, and whereas we did expect great store of beaver, here is little or none to be had, and their Sackemor John weigheth it, and many of us truck with them and it layeth us many times in eight shillings a pound. They are proper men and clean-jointed men, and many of them go naked with a skin about their loins, but some of them get eingellische menes [Englishmen's] parell [apparel].

And the country is very rocky and hilly and some champion [open] ground, and the soil is very fleet [shallow], and here is some good ground and marsh ground, but here is no Michaelmas [autumnal] spring. Cattle thrive well here, but they give small store of milk. The best cattle for profit is swines, and a good swine is here at five pounds price and a goat is worth three pounds, a gardene [garden?] goat. Here is timber good store and acorns good store, and here is good store of fish, if we had boats to go eight or ten leagues to sea to fish in. Here are good store of wild fowl, but they are hard to come by. It is harder to get a shot than it is in ould eingland. And people here are subject to disease, for here have died of the scurvy and of the burning fever two hundred and odd, besides many layeth lame, and all Sudberey men

John Pond, letter to his father and mother, March 15, 1631, in Everett Emerson, ed., *Letters from New England* (Amherst: University of Massachusetts Press, 1976), 64–66. Reprinted Courtesy of Massachusetts Historical Society.

are dead but three and the women and some children. And provisions are here at a wonderful rate. Wheat meal is fourteen shillings a bushel and peas ten shillings and malt ten shillings and eindey seid [Indian seed] wheat is fifteen shillings and their other wheat is ten shillings, butter twelve pence a pound, and cheese is eight pence a pound, and all kinds of spices very dear and almost none to be got, and if this ship had not come when it did, we had been put to a wonderful straight, but thanks be to God for sending of it in. I received from the ship a hogshead of meal, and the governor telleth me of a hundredweight of cheese, the which I have received part of it. I humbly thank you for it. I did expect two cows, the which I had none nor I do not earnestly desire that you should send me any because the country is not so as we did expect it. Therefore, loving Father, I would entreat you that you would send me a firkin of butter and a hogshead of malt unground, for we drink nothing but water, and a coarse cloth of four-pound price, so it be thick. And for the freight, if you of your love will send them, I will pay the freight, for here is nothing to be got without we had commodities to go into the east parts amongst the eingeines [Indians] to truck, for here where we live is no beaver, and here is no cloth to be had to make no apparel, and shoes are at five shillings a pair for me, and that cloth that is worth two shillings eight pence a yard is worth here five shillings. So I pray, father, send me four or five yards of cloth to make us some apparel, and, loving Father, though I be far distant from you, yet I pray you remember me as your child, and we do not know how long we may subsist, for we cannot live here without provisions from ould eingland. Therefore, I pray, do not put away your shopstuff, for I think that in the end if I live it must be my living, for we do not know how long this plantation will stand, for some of the merchants that did uphold it have turned off their men and have given it over. Besides, God hath taken away the chiefest stud in the land, Mr. Johnson and the lady Arabella his wife, which was the chiefest man of estate in the land and one that would have done most good.

Here came over twenty-five passengers and there come back again four score and odd persons and as many more would have come if they had wherewithal to bring them home, for here are many that came over the last year, which was worth two hundred pounds afore they came out of ould eingland that between this and Michaelmas will be hardly worth thirty pounds, so here we may live if we have supplies every year from ould eingland; otherwise we cannot subsist. I may, as I will work hard, set an ackorne [acre] of eindey [Indian] wheat and if we do not set it with fish and that will cost twenty shillings, and if we set it without fish they shall have but a poor crop.

So, Father, I pray consider of my cause, for here will be but a very poor being and no being without, loving Father, your help with provisions from ould eingland. I had thought to have came home in this ship, for my provisions were almost all spent, but that I humbly thank you for your great love and kindness in sending me some provisions, or else I should and mine have been half famished, but now I will, if it please God that I have my health, I will plant what corn I can, and if provisions be no cheaper between this and Michaelmas and that I do not hear from you what I was best to do, I purpose to come home at Michaelmas.

My wife remembers her humble duty unto you and to my mother and my love to my brother Joseife and to Sarey myler. Thus I leave you to the protection of almighty God.

> from Walltur Toune [Watertown] in new eingland   [no signature]
> the 15 of March 1630[/1]

We were wonderful sick as we came at sea with the smallpox. No man thought that I and my little child would have lived, and my boy is lame and my girl too, and there died in the ship that I came in fourteen persons. To my loving father William Ponde at Etherston in Suffolcke give these.

The Reverend Thomas Welde Describes the Success of the Massachusetts Bay Colony, 1632

Most dear and well beloved in Tarling [Welde's former parish], even all that love the Lord Jesus Christ's gospel, and myself, rich and poor, weak and strong, young and old, male and female, I [write] unto you all in one letter, wanting time to mention you all in particular, you being all dear unto me, yea, most dear to my heart in Jesus Christ, for whom I bow the knee to the Father of lights, longing to hear of your great welfare and spiritual growth in his dear son. From your presence though I be placed and must see your faces no more, yet I shall after a few weary days ended and all tears wiped away, and though happily never on earth yet in the New Jerusalem. . . .

. . . Here I find three great blessings, peace, plenty, and health in a comfortable measure. The place well agreeth with our English bodies that they were never so healthy in their native country. Generally all here as never could be rid of the headache, toothache, cough, and the like are now better and freed here, and those that were weak are now well long since, and I can hear of but two weak in all the plantation. God's name be praised. And although there was wanting at the first that provision at the first glut of people that came over two years since, but blessed be God, here is plenty of corn that the poorest have enough. Corn is here at five shillings six pence a bushel. In truth you cannot imagine what comfortable diet the Indian corn doth make and what pleasant and wholesome food it makes. Our cattle of all do thrive and feed exceedingly. I suppose that such as are to come need bring no more or little or no provision except malt (but no more of these things). I would have none aim at outward matters in such an attempt as this, iest the Lord meet him in the way as he met Balaam with a drawn sword, but at things of an higher nature and more spiritual nature.

O how hath my heart been made glad with the comforts of His house and the spiritual days in the same wherein all things are done in the form and pattern showed in the mount, members provided, church officers elected and ordained, sacrament administered, scandals prevented, censured, fast days

Reprinted from *Letters from New England: The Massachusetts Bay Colony, 1629–1638,* Everett Emerson, ed., pp. 94–98 (Amherst: University of Massachusetts Press, 1976). Copyright © 1976 by The University of Massachusetts Press.

and holy feast days and all such things by authority commanded and performed according to the precise rule. Mine eyes, blessed be God, do see such administration of justice in civil government, all things so righteously, so religiously and impartially carried, I am already fully paid for my voyage who never had so much in the storms at sea as one repenting thought rested in my heart. Praised and thanked be God who moved my heart to come and made open the way to me. And I profess if I might have my wish in what part of the world to dwell I know no other place on the whole globe of the earth where I would be rather than here. We say to our friends that doubt this, Come and see and taste. Here the greater part are the better part. . . .

"The Summons to New England," n. d.

Let all the Purisidian sect,
I mean the counterfeit elect,
All zealous bankroute Punke devout,
Preachers suspended, rabble rout,—
Let them sell all, and out of hand
Prepare to go to New England,
 To build New Babel strong and sure,
 Now called a church unspotted, pure.

There milk from springs like rivers flows,
And honey upon hawthorne grows;
Hemp, wools, & flax there grows on trees;
Their mould is fat, & cut like cheese;
All fruit & herbs springs in the fields;
Tobacco in great plenty yields;
 And there shall be a church most pure,
 Where you may find salvation sure.

There's venison, of all sorts, great store;
Both stag & buck, wild goat & boar;
And yet so tame, as you with ease
May eat your fill,—take what you please.
There's beavers plenty; yea, so many,
That you may have 2 skins a penny.
 Above all this, a church most pure:
 There to be saved you may be sure.

There's flights of fowls do cloud the light;
And turkeys, threescore pounds in weight,
And big as ostriches. Their geese
Are sold with thanks for pence a-piece.
Of duck & mallard, widgeon [a duck], teal,
Twenty, for 2 pence, make a meal.
 Yea, & a church unspotted, pure,
 Within whose bosom all are sure.

Some of the spelling in this document has been modernized.

Lo, there in shoals all sorts of fish,
Of salt sea & of water fresh,—
King cod, pore John, & habberdines [a kind of cod],—
Are taken with your hooks & lines:
A painful fisher on the shore
May take of each twenty in an hour.
  But, above all, a church most pure,
  Where you may live & die secure.

There, twice a year, all sorts of grain
Do down like hail from the heavens rain.
You never need to serve or plough:
There's plenty of all things inough.
Wine, sweet & wholesome, drops from trees,
As clear as crystal, without lees.
  Yea, & a church unspotted, pure,
  From dregs of Papistry secure.

No feasts, or festival set-days,
Are here observed. The Lord we praise,
Though not in churches rich & strong,
Yet where no mass was ever sung.
The bulls of Bason war not here;
Surplice & cap dare not appear.
  Old order all they will abjure:
  This church hath all things new & pure.

No discipline shall there be used:
The law of nature they have chused.
All that the spirit seems to move,
Each man may take, & that approve.
There's government without command;
There's unity without a band;
  A synagogue unspotted, pure,
  Where lust & pleasures dwell secure.

Lo, in this church all shall be free
T' enjoy all Christian liberty.
All things made common. To void strife,
Each man may have another's wife;
And keep a handmaid too, if need,
To multiply, increase, and breed.
  And is not this foundation sure
  To raise a church unspotted, pure?

The native people, though yet wild,
Are all by nature kind & mild,
And apt already (by report)
To live in this religious sort.
Soon to conversion they'll be brought,
When Warham's miracles are wrought;
  Who, being sanctified & pure,
  May, by the Spirit, them allure.

L'envoy.

Let Amsterdam send forth her brats,
Her fugitives & runnigates;
Let Bedlam, Newgate, & the Clink
Disgorge themselves into the sink;
Let Brydewell & the Stewes be swept,—
And all sent thither to be kept:
    So may *our* church, cleans'd & made pure,
    Keep both itself & State secure.

William Wood on the Indians' Response to the English Presence, 1634

First of their [the Indians'] stature, most of them being between five or six foot high, straight bodied, strongly composed, smooth-skinned, merry countenanced, of complexion something more swarthy than Spaniards, black haired, high foreheaded, black eyed, out-nosed, broad shouldered, brawny armed, long and slender handed, out breasted, small waisted, lank bellied, well thighed, flat kneed, handsome grown legs, and small feet. In a word, take them when the blood brisks in their veins, when the flesh is on their backs and marrow in their bones, when they frolic in their antic deportments and Indian postures, and they are more amiable to behold (though only in Adam's livery) than many a compounded fantastic in the newest fashion.

It may puzzle belief to conceive how such lusty bodies should have their rise and daily supportment from so slender a fostering, their houses being mean, their lodging as homely, commons scant, their drink water, and nature their best clothing. In them the old proverb may well be verified: *Natura paucis contenta* ["Nature is satisfied with a few things"], for though this be their daily portion they still are healthful and lusty. I have been in many places, yet did I never see one that was born either in redundance or defect a monster, or any that sickness had deformed, or casualty made decrepit, saving one that had a bleared eye and another that had a wen on his cheek. The reason is rendered why they grow so proportionable and continue so long in their vigor (most of them being fifty before a wrinkled brow or gray hair bewray their age) is because they are not brought down with suppressing labor, vexed with annoying cares, or drowned in the excessive abuse of overflowing plenty, which oftentimes kills them more than want, as may appear in them. For when they change their bare Indian commons for the plenty of England's fuller diet, it is so contrary to their stomachs that death or a desperate sickness immediately accrues, which makes so few of them desirous to see England.

Their swarthiness is the sun's livery, for they are born fair. Their smooth skins proceed from the often annointing of their bodies with the oil of fishes and the fat of eagles, with the grease of raccoons, which they hold in summer the best antidote to keep their skin from blistering with the scorching sun, and it is their best armor against the mosquitoes, the surest expeller of the hairy excrement, and stops the pores of their bodies against the nipping winter's cold.

Their black hair is natural, yet it is brought to a more jetty color by oiling, dyeing, and daily dressing. Sometimes they wear it very long, hanging down in a loose, disheveled, womanish manner; otherwhile tied up hard and short like a horse tail, bound close with a fillet, which they say makes it grow the faster. They are not a little fantastical or custom-sick in this particular, their boys being not permitted to wear their hair long till sixteen years of age, and then they must come to it by degrees, some being cut with a long foretop, a long lock on the crown, one of each side of his head, the rest of his hair being cut even with the scalp. The young men and soldiers wear their hair long on the one side, the other side being cut short like a screw. Other cuts they have as their fancy befools them, which would torture the wits of a curious barber to imitate. But though they be thus wedded to the hair of their head, you cannot woo them to wear it on their chins, where it no sooner grows but it is stubbed up by the roots, for they count it as an unuseful, cumbersome, and opprobrious excrement, insomuch as they call him an Englishman's bastard that hath but the appearance of a beard, which some have growing in a staring fashion like the beard of a cat, which makes them the more out of love with them, choosing rather to have no beards than such as should make them ridiculous. . . .

To satisfy the curious eye of women readers, who otherwise might think their sex forgotten or not worthy a record, let them peruse these few lines wherein they may see their own happiness, if weighed in the woman's balance of these ruder Indians who scorn the tutorings of their wives or to admit them as their equals—though their qualities and industrious deservings may justly claim the preeminence and command better usage and more conjugal esteem, their persons and features being every way correspondent, their qualifications more excellent, being more loving, pitiful, and modest, mild, provident, and laborious than their lazy husbands.

Their employments be many: first their building of houses, whose frames are formed like our garden arbors, something more round, very strong and handsome, covered with close-wrought mats of their own weaving which deny entrance to any drop of rain, though it come both fierce and long, neither can the piercing north wind find a cranny through which he can convey his cooling breath. They be warmer than our English houses. At the top is a square hole for the smoke's evacuation, which in rainy weather is covered with a pluver [rain cover]. These be such smoky dwellings that when there is good fires they are not able to stand upright, but lie all along under the smoke, never using any stools or chairs, it being as rare to see an Indian sit on a stool at home as it is strange to see an Englishman sit on his heels abroad. Their houses are smaller in the summer when their families be dispersed by reason of heat and occasions. In winter they make some fifty or threescore foot long, forty or fifty men being inmates under one roof. And as is their husbands' occasion, these poor tectonists [builders or carpenters] are often troubled like snails to carry their houses on their backs, sometime to fishing places, other times to hunting places, after that to a planting place where it abides the longest.

Another work is their planting of corn, wherein they exceed our English husbandmen, keeping it so clear with their clamshell hoes as if it were a garden rather than a corn field, not suffering a choking weed to advance his audacious head above their infant corn or an undermining worm to spoil his spurns. Their corn being ripe they gather it, and drying it hard in the sun convey it to their barns, which be great holes digged in the ground in form of a brass pot, sealed with rinds of trees, wherein they put their corn, covering it from the inquisitive search of their gourmandizing husbands who would eat up both their allowed portion and reserved seed if they knew where to find it. But our hogs having found a way to unhinge their barn doors and rob their garners, they are glad to implore their husbands' help to roll the bodies of trees over their holes to prevent those pioneers whose thievery they as much hate as their flesh.

Another of their employments is their summer processions to get lobsters for their husbands, wherewith they bait their hooks when they go afishing for bass or codfish. This is an everyday's walk, be the weather cold or hot, the waters rough or calm. They must dive sometimes over head and ears for a lobster, which often shakes them by their hands with a churlish nip and bids them adieu. The tide being spent, they trudge home two or three miles with a hundredweight of lobsters at their backs, and if none, a hundred scowls meet them at home and a hungry belly for two days after. Their husbands having caught any fish, they bring it in their boats as far as they can by water and there leave it; as it was their care to catch it, so it must be their wives' pains to fetch it home, or fast. Which done, they must dress it and cook it, dish it, and present it, see it eaten over their shoulders; and their loggerships having filled their paunches, their sweet lullabies scramble for their scraps. In the summer these Indian women, when lobsters be in their plenty and prime, they dry them to keep for winter, erecting scaffolds in the hot sunshine, making fires likewise underneath them (by whose smoke the flies are expelled) till the substance remain hard and dry. In this manner they dry bass and other fishes without salt, cutting them very thin to dry suddenly before the flies spoil them or the rain moist them, having a special care to hang them in their smoky houses in the night and dankish weather.

In summer they gather flags [probably cattail], of which they make mats for houses, and hemp and rushes, with dyeing stuff of which they make curious baskets with intermixed colors and protractures [drawings or designs] of antic imagery. These baskets be of all sizes from a quart to a quarter [eight bushels], in which they carry their luggage. In winter they are their husbands' caterers, trudging to the clam banks for their belly timber, and their porters to lug home their venison which their laziness exposes to the wolves till they impose it upon their wives' shoulders. They likewise sew their husbands' shoes and weave coats of turkey feathers, besides all their ordinary household drudgery which daily lies upon them, so that a big belly hinders no business, nor a childbirth takes much time, but the young infant being greased and sooted, wrapped in a beaver skin, bound to his good behavior with his feet up to his bum upon a board two foot long and one foot broad, his face exposed to all nipping weather, this little papoose travels about with his barefooted mother to paddle in the icy clam banks after three or four days of age have sealed his passboard and his mother's recovery.

For their carriage it is very civil, smiles being the greatest grace of their mirth; their music is lullabies to quiet their children, who generally are as quiet as if they had neither spleen or lungs. To hear one of these Indians unseen, a good ear might easily mistake their untaught voice for the warbling of a well-tuned instrument, such command have they of their voices.

These women's modesty drives them to wear more clothes than their men, having always a coat of cloth or skins wrapped like a blanket about their loins, reaching down to their hams, which they never put off in company. If a husband have a mind to sell his wife's beaver petticoat, as sometimes he doth, she will not put it off until she have another to put on. Commendable is their mild carriage and obedience to their husbands, notwithstanding all this—their [husband's] customary churlishness and savage inhumanity—not seeming to delight in frowns or offering to word it with their lords, not presuming to proclaim their female superiority to the usurping of the least title of their husband's charter, but rest themselves content under their helpless condition, counting it the woman's portion.

Since the English arrival, comparison hath made them miserable, for seeing the kind usage of the English to their wives, they do as much condemn their husbands for unkindness and commend the English for their love, as their husbands—commending themselves for their wit in keeping their wives industrious—do condemn the English for their folly in spoiling good working creatures. These women resort often to the English houses, where *pares cum paribus congregatae* ["equals gathered with equals"], in sex I mean, they do somewhat ease their misery by complaining and seldom part without a relief. If her husband come to seek for his squaw and begin to bluster, the English woman betakes her to her arms, which are the warlike ladle and the scalding liquors, threatening blistering to the naked runaway, who is soon expelled by such liquid comminations.

In a word, to conclude this woman's history, their love to the English hath deserved no small esteem, ever presenting them something that is either rare or desired, as strawberries, hurtleberries, raspberries, gooseberries, cherries, plums, fish, and other such gifts as their poor treasury yields them. But now it may be that this relation of the churlish and inhumane behavior of these ruder Indians towards their patient wives may confirm some in the belief of an aspersion which I have often heard men cast upon the English there, as if they should learn of the Indians to use their wives in the like manner and to bring them to the same subjection—as to sit on the lower hand and to carry water and the like drudgery. But if my own experience may out-balance an ill-grounded scandalous rumor, I do assure you, upon my credit and reputation, that there is no such matter, but the women find there as much love, respect, and ease as here in old England. I will not deny but that some poor people may carry their own water. And do not the poorer sort in England do the same, witness your London tankard bearers and your country cottagers? But this may well be known to be nothing but the rancorous venom of some that bear no good will to the plantation. For what need they carry water, seeing everyone hath a spring at his door or the sea by his house?

Thus much for the satisfaction of women, touching this entrenchment upon their prerogative, as also concerning the relation of these Indian squaws.

Miantonomo's Call for Indian Unity, 1642

A while after this came Miantenomie from Block-Island to Mantacut with a troop of men . . . ; and instead of receiving presents, which they used to do in their progress, he gave them gifts, calling them brethren and friends, for so are we all Indians as the English are, and say brother to one another; so must we be one as they are, otherwise we shall be all gone shortly, for you know our fathers had plenty of deer and skins, our plains were full of deer, as also our woods, and of turkies, and our coves full of fish and fowl. But these English having gotten our land, they with scythes cut down the grass, and with axes fell the trees; their cows and horses eat the grass, and their hogs spoil our clam banks, and we shall all be starved; therefore it is best for you to do as we, for we are all the Sachems from east to west, both Moquakues and Mohauks joining with us, and we are all resolved to fall upon them all, at one appointed day; and therefore I am come to you privately first, because you can persuade the Indians and Sachem to what you will, and I will send over fifty Indians to Block-Island, and thirty to you from thence, and take an hundred of Southampton Indians with an hundred of your own here; and when you see the three fires that will be made forty days hence, in a clear night, then do as we, and the next day fall on and kill men, women, and children, but no cows, for they will serve to eat till our deer be increased again. . . .

❧ E S S A Y S

The saga of Squanto, kidnapped by the unscrupulous English ship captain Thomas Hunt and returned to Plymouth to find his village deserted, offers us a chance to see the confrontation between English and Indian cultures on a personal level. As presented in the first essay, by historian Neal Salisbury of Smith College, Squanto was a man who, faced with an unprecedented situation, elected to create a new and demanding role, that of cultural intermediary. That the Pilgrims, who settled on the site of his village, came to mistrust him is evidence that Squanto always acted as a free agent; he never submerged his own interests and those of other Indians in favor of the newcomers.

The colonization of New England differed dramatically from that of the southern plantation colonies. Whereas the Chesapeake immigrant stream was composed largely of single young men, with few women, New England was settled by families, including a wide variety of ages. Except for the very wealthy and the very poor, its society resembled that of the parent country. Moreover, a very large number, more than ten thousand, came during the single decade of the 1630s, creating the preconditions for success from the beginning. In the second essay historian Virginia DeJohn Anderson of the University of Colorado confronts the issue of these immigrants' motivation. The problem stems from the fact that although the New England migrants were Puritan, most Puritans chose not to emigrate. Therefore we must explain what drove this particular group. Some historians have argued that economic distress primarily caused them to leave at that particular time. Using extant passenger lists, Anderson re-creates the lives of migrants—their circumstances and aspirations—and concludes that religion was the chief motivating factor in their decision.

Squanto, the Last of the Patuxets

NEAL SALISBURY

. . . As befits a mythic hero, the time and circumstances of Squanto's birth are unknown. His birth date can only be inferred from what the sources say and do not say. The firsthand descriptions of him, written between 1618 and his death in 1622, do not suggest that he was strikingly young or old at that time. All we can safely conclude is that he was probably in his twenties or thirties at the time he was forcibly taken to Europe in 1614.

Though Squanto's early years are obscured by a lack of direct evidence, we know something of the cultural milieu that prepared him for his unexpected and remarkable career. Squanto and his fellow Patuxet spoke an Algonquian dialect that they shared with the other natives around Plymouth Bay and west as far as the near shore of Narragansett Bay. Moreover, its differences from other dialects in what is now southern New England were minimal, so that the Patuxet could communicate with the natives throughout this region. Like other coastal villages below the mouth of the Saco River, Patuxet was positioned to allow its inhabitants to grow crops, exploit marine resources, and have easy access to wild plants and animals. In accordance with the strict sexual division of labor maintained by virtually all eastern North American Indians, Squanto's major activities would have been to hunt game and to engage in certain kinds of fishing. He would also have fashioned a wide variety of tools and other material items and participated in the intensely ritualized world of trade, diplomacy, religious ceremonies, recreation, warfare, and political decision making that constituted a man's public life. . . .

Patuxet men such as Squanto also exercised their independence in making political judgments and decisions. As elsewhere in southern New England, the band, consisting of one or more villages, was the primary political unit. Its leader, the sachem, was drawn from one of a select group of lineages elevated in prestige above the rest. The sachems distributed garden plots to families and exercised certain judicial prerogatives. They also represented the band on diplomatic and ceremonial occasions. But a sachem's power was derived directly from the band members. To secure economic and political

Neal Salisbury, "Squanto: Last of the Patuxets," in *Struggle and Survival in Colonial America,* ed. David Sweet and Gary Nash. pp. 228–244. Copyright © 1981 The Regents of the University of California. Reprinted by permission.

support he or she needed leadership ability as well as a family name. Band members could oblige a faltering sachem to share the office with a relative or step down altogether. Moreover, major political decisions were reached through a consensus in meetings attended by all adult males. Squanto came from a world, then, where politics was a constant and integral component of a man's life.

Squanto was even better prepared for his unusual career if, as seems probable, he was a *pniese* in his band. In preparation for this position, young men were chosen in childhood and underwent unusually rigorous diets and training. The purpose of this preparation was not simply to fortify them and develop their courage but to enable them to call upon and visualize Hobbamock, a deity capable of inflicting great harm and even death on those he did not favor. Hobbamock appeared in many forms to "the chiefest and most judicious amongst them," in [Edward] Winslow's words, "though all of them strive to attain to that hellish height of honor." It is clear that those who succeeded in the vision quest had developed the mental self-discipline demanded of all Indians to an extraordinary degree. By calling on Hobbamock, the *pnieses* protected themselves and those near them in battle and frightened their opponents. They constituted an elite group within the band, serving as counselors and bodyguards to the sachems. They were universally respected not only for their access to Hobbamock and for their courage and judgment but for their moral uprightness. Because of his psychological fortitude, his particularly astute grasp of Indian politics and protocol, and his continued sense of duty to his band after its demise, it is quite likely that Squanto was a *pniese*.

The few recorded observations of Patuxet during Squanto's early years show that it was a very different place from the "wilderness" the Plymouth colonists later found there. Both Samuel de Champlain, in 1605 and 1606, and John Smith, in 1614, noted that most of the coast between Massachusetts and Plymouth bays was under cultivation. The colonists were told, probably by Squanto himself, that in Plymouth Bay "in former time hath lived about 2,000 Indians." The population of the surrounding area—that is, of the Indians with whom the Patuxet maintained the closest relations—was probably between twenty and twenty-five thousand in 1615. Most of these natives were concentrated in village communities ranging in size from five hundred to fifteen hundred individuals. Squanto was thus accustomed to a more densely settled environment than we might expect and was probably as comfortable in the European cities he later visited as in the tiny colonies.

Though no one could have known it at the time, Squanto was born at a turning point in the history of his people and his region. For a century Europeans had been trading and skirmishing with, and sometimes kidnapping, Indians along the coast. At the time of Squanto's birth, however, these activities had not been extended south of Canada on a regular basis. Infrequent visits from European explorers and traders and the natives' own well-established exchange routes brought some iron tools and glass beads to Patuxet. But these were too scattered to induce any economic or cultural changes of a substantive nature. Unlike the fur-trading Indians to the north, the Patuxet and their neighbors had not become dependent on European trade items for their survival.

The turn of the century marked an intensification of French and British interest in New England's resources. The differing economic goals of the colonizers from the two countries gave rise to differing attitudes and policies toward the natives. The French were concerned primarily with furs. Following Champlain's explorations of the New England coast in 1605 and 1606, French traders using his descriptions and maps began to visit the Indians annually and to cultivate an extensive trade as far south as Cape Cod. Their goals encouraged the maintenance of friendly relations with stable Indian bands and even the development of broad regional ties among the natives.

For the English, however, furs were at best a useful by-product of more pressing interests. Beginning with Bartholomew Gosnold's expedition in 1602, they showed a preference for resources such as fish and sassafras that did not require the cooperation of the natives. Moreover, they thought in long-range terms of making Indian land available to Englishmen for farming, a goal that virtually guaranteed eventual conflict with the natives. Indian allies were cultivated, but only for purposes of assisting the English in establishing themselves, and the methods used were generally more coercive than those of the French. Nearly every English expedition from Gosnold's to that of the *Mayflower* generated hostility with the Indians. By 1610 taking captured Indians to England had become routine. Would-be colonizers such as Sir Ferdinando Gorges hoped to impress their captives with the superiority of English culture, to learn as much as they could about the lay of the land, and to acquire mediators with the local Indians. They also displayed their captives prominently in order to attract financial and public support for their projected colonies.

John Smith, the former Virginia leader, witnessed the results of the competition between the two colonial strategies when he explored the coast from the Penobscot River to Cape Cod in 1614. Smith found that he had arrived at the end of an active trading season. Aside from one Englishman's cozy monopoly at the mouth of the Pemaquid River, all the ships were French. Though the better-endowed region north of the Pemaquid had yielded twenty-five thousand skins that year, Smith judged the south capable of producing six to seven thousand annually. He himself had retrieved thirteen hundred pelts, mostly beaver, in the wake of the French departure. He also found that all the Indians in the region he visited were friendly with one another through three loose regional alliances. Ostensibly formed to resist incursions from the Micmac in eastern Canada, the friendship chain had an economic function as well, for Smith noted that some primarily horticultural Indians in southern New England traded corn to Abenaki hunting groups farther north whose concentration on the fur trade was apparently leading to food shortages. In return the horticulturalists obtained some of the Abenaki's supply of European trade goods. Though only minimally developed by 1614, this trade was already fostering a specialized division of labor among France's clients in New England.

The extent of Patuxet's participation in the corn trade is unknown. But

Squanto and his people were producing substantial fur surpluses by the time of Smith's visit in 1614 and had gained at least some acquaintance with the Europeans. From the visits of Champlain, Smith, and the traders, Squanto had learned something of European approaches to trade, diplomacy, and military conflict and had witnessed some of their technological accomplishments. But the regularized trade was less than a decade old. And the ease with which groups of Patuxet men were manipulated by Smith and his officer, Thomas Hunt, in 1614 suggests that they had not developed the wariness toward Europeans, particularly the English, of the more experienced Indians to the north.

Squanto's life reached a sudden and dramatic turning point with Hunt's visit. Smith had returned to England, leaving Hunt in charge of his fishing crew to complete the catch and carry it to Malaga, Spain. Before departing, Hunt stopped at Patuxet. Using his association with Smith, who had left on friendly terms, he lured about twenty natives, including Squanto, aboard. Quickly rounding Cape Cod, he drew off seven more from Nauset and then turned east for Malaga. Hunt's action indelibly marked the English as an enemy of all the Indians in the Patuxet–Cape Cod region. In the words of Sir Ferdinando Gorges, Hunt's action resulted in "a warre now new begunne betweene the inhabitants of those parts and us," and John Smith condemned Hunt for moving the Indians' "hate against our Nation, as well as to cause my proceedings to be more difficult." . . .

. . . Squanto and his fellow captives reached Malaga, where Hunt tried to sell them as slaves. A few had already been sold when, according to Gorges, "the Friers of those parts took the rest from them and kept them to be instructed in the Christian faith." What happened to Squanto in the next three years is not clear. Particularly intriguing are questions about the extent and influence of his Catholic instruction and the means by which, in William Bradford's words, "he got away for England." We know only that by 1617 he was residing in the London home of John Slany, treasurer of the Newfoundland Company, where he learned or at least improved his English and his understanding of colonial goals. In the following year he went to Newfoundland itself, presumably at Slany's instigation. Here he met for the second time Thomas Dermer, an officer with Smith in 1614 who now worked for Gorges. Dermer was so impressed with Squanto's tales of Patuxet that he took him back to England to meet Gorges. Though the strategy of employing captive Indians as guides had backfired several times, Gorges was ready to try again. He saw in Squanto the key to countering the recent successes of the French and reestablishing England's reputation among the Indians. For his part Squanto knew, as had earlier captives, how to tell Gorges what he wanted to hear in order to be returned home. In March 1619 he and Dermer were bound for New England.

Moving in the circles he did, Squanto undoubtedly knew something of the epidemic that had ravaged New England, including Patuxet, during his absence. A Gorges expedition under Richard Vines had witnessed what Vines called simply "the plague" at Sagadahoc in 1616 and reported on its effects. Most notable was the immunity of the English; while most of the Indians were dying, Vines and his party "lay in the Cabins with those people, [and] not one of them ever felt their heads to ake." This immunity and the 75 to 90 percent depopulation among the Indians make it clear that a virgin soil epidemic of European origin had been planted in New England's isolated disease environment. . . .

Squanto found his own village completely vacated. Most of its inhabitants had died, but some had fled inland to other villages. He surely noticed, as did others, the undergrowth that had overtaken the formerly cultivated fields and the vast numbers of unburied dead whose "bones and skulls," in one Englishman's words, "made such a spectacle. . . . it seemed to me a new found Golgotha." The depopulation was so great that the Narragansett were able to force the weakened Pokanoket to abandon their position at the head of Narragansett Bay and to retain only the eastern shore.

The Narragansetts' avoidance of the epidemic gave them a greater advantage than that derived from numbers alone. In the view of their stricken neighbors, the Narragansetts' good health reflected their faithful sacrifices to the deity, Cautantowwit. The ritual worlds and belief systems of the stricken Indians, however, had been badly shaken by the epidemic. The usual practice of gathering with the *pow-wow* (shaman) in a sick person's wigwam could only have served to spread the disease more rapidly. With even the *pow-wows* succumbing, the Indians could only conclude that their deities had aligned against them. And being unable to observe the proper burial rituals, the survivors had to fear the retribution of the dead. The Indians' perception that they had lost touch with the sources of power and that others controlled the access to them would be a critical factor in facilitating Squanto's later political success. . . .

The Patuxet–Pokanoket–Cape Cod region was vastly different in the autumn of 1620 from a decade earlier when French traders had begun to frequent it regularly. Fewer than 10 percent of its twenty thousand or more former inhabitants were still living, and they were now consolidated into a few bands. The region was vulnerable as never before to exploitation by outsiders. The once-powerful Pokanoket and their sachem, Massasoit, had been subjected to a humiliating tributary relationship with the Narragansett, who were emerging as the most powerful aggregation in New England because of their size and their control of Indian-European trade links east of Long Island. Moreover, the decimated Indians could no longer count on the fur trade as a means of compensating for other weaknesses. Always limited in both the quality and quantity of its fur resources, the region's loss of most of its hunters now made it an unprofitable stop for traders.

. . . Squanto was able to capitalize on the Pokanokets' despair. "He told Massasoit what wonders he had seen in England," according to a future settler, "and that if he could make English his friends then Enemies that were too strong for him would be constrained to bow to him." He did not have to wait long to be proved right. In December 1620, less than six months after Dermer's departure, word reached Pokanoket that a shipload of English colonists had established a permanent settlement at Patuxet.

Like the other Puritans who later settled New England, the group at Plymouth (for so they renamed Patuxet) was motivated by a combination of religious and economic motives that shaped their attitudes toward the natives. Their experience with persecution in England and exile to the Netherlands had sharpened their desire to practice their exclusionary, intolerant separatism without external interference. Moreover, though seeking distance from English ecclesiastical authorities, the settlers were attempting to reinforce their English identities. They had abandoned their Dutch haven for fear that their children would be assimilated there. Finally, though ostensibly migrating to fish and trade for furs, the colonists sought land to improve themselves materially and, they supposed, spiritually. Though Plymouth lacked the sense of divine mission of the later nonseparatist Puritan colonies, its goals of religious and ethnic exclusivity and an abundance of land had obvious implications for its relations with the natives.

These implications were apparent in Plymouth's early policies and attitudes toward the Indians. In a major promotional pamphlet published in 1622, Robert Cushman restated what had already become a familiar justification for dispossession of native lands:

> Their land is spacious and void, and there are few and do but run over the grass, as do also the foxes and wild beasts. They are not industrious, neither have art, science, skill, or faculty to use either the land or the commodities of it, but all spoils or rots, and is marred for want of manuring, gathering, ordering, etc. As the ancient patriarchs therefore removed from straiter places into more roomy . . . so is it lawful now to take a land which none useth, and make use of it.

Cushman's statement was consistent with the emerging European doctrine of *vacuum domicilium,* by which "civil" states were entitled to the uncultivated lands of those in a "natural" state. Though Plymouth's own "civility" was formalized by the hastily contrived *Mayflower* Compact, its financial backers had anticipated its need for more than an abstract principle to press its claim— among its own people as well as among any natives they might encounter. Accordingly, they had hired Miles Standish, a soldier of fortune fresh from the Dutch wars, to organize the colony militarily. It was Standish who would shape Plymouth's Indian policy during its first generation.

Standish began to execute this policy even before the *Mayflower* arrived at Patuxet. Landing first at Cape Cod, the settlers aroused native hostilities by ransacking Indian graves, houses, and grain stores. At Patuxet they also stirred suspicions during the first four months of their stay. But their own situation grew desperate during their first New England winter. They lost half their numbers to starvation and disease, and as inexperienced farmers they were ill-prepared for the approaching planting season. In this condition they could no longer expect to alleviate their shortages through pilferage with impunity. The impasse was broken one day in March 1621 by the appearance of Samoset, a sachem of the Pemaquid River band, which had been trading with the English for more than a decade. Samoset learned the needs and intentions of the colony and returned a few days later with Squanto.

The Pokanoket had been watching the Plymouth group throughout the winter. With Samoset and the newly useful Squanto offering advice and experience, they concluded that the time was ripe to befriend the settlers instead of maintaining a hostile distance. Such an alliance would enable them to break from the hold of the Narragansetts, whose haughty demeanor stung even more than that of the English. Nevertheless, the decision was not to be taken lightly. Bradford wrote that the Indians did first "curse and execrate them with their conjurations" before approaching the settlers. But this description betrays his fear of witchcraft as it was understood by Europeans, rather than his comprehension of Indian rituals. More likely the Pokanoket were ritually purging themselves of their hostilities toward the English.

Samoset and Squanto arranged the meeting between the Pokanoket and Plymouth colony that resulted in their historic treaty. In it each side agreed to aid the other in the event of attack by a third party, to disarm during their meetings with each other, and to return any tools stolen from the other side. But in addition to these reciprocal agreements, several others were weighted against the natives. Massasoit, the Pokanoket sachem, was to see that his tributaries observed the terms; the Indians were to turn over for punishment any of their people suspected of assaulting any English (but no English had to fear being tried by Indians); and, the treaty concluded, "King James would esteem of him [Massasoit] as his friend and ally." The meaning of the last honor was made explicit by the colony's annalist, Nathaniel Morton, who wrote that by the treaty Massasoit "acknowledged himself content to become the subject of our sovereign lord the King aforesaid, his heirs and successors, and gave unto them all the lands adjacent to them and theirs forever." Morton made clear that among themselves the English did not regard the treaty as one of alliance and friendship between equals but as one of submission by one party to the domination of the other, according to the assumptions of *vacuum domicilium.*

For the Pokanoket, however, the meaning of a political relationship was conveyed in the ritual exchange of speeches and gifts, not in written clauses or unwritten understandings based on concepts such as sovereignty that were alien to one party. From their standpoint, the English were preferable to the Narragansett because they demanded less tribute and homage while offering more gifts and autonomy and better protection.

The treaty also brought a change in status for Squanto. In return for his services, the Pokanoket now freed him to become guide, interpreter, and diplomat for the colony. Thus he finally returned to his home at Patuxet, a move that had, as we shall see, more than sentimental significance. Among his first services was the securing of corn seed and instruction in its planting, including the use of fish fertilizer, which he learned from his own people or from the Newfoundland colonists.

Squanto also enabled Plymouth to strengthen its political position in the surrounding area. He helped secure peace with some bands on Cape Cod and guided an expedition to Massachusetts Bay. His kidnapping by anti-English Indians at Nemasket and subsequent rescue by a heavily armed Plymouth force speaks compellingly of his importance to the colony. Moreover, this incident led to a new treaty, engineered in part by Squanto, with all the Indian groups of Massachusetts Bay to the tip of Cape Cod. . . . By establishing a tributary system with the surrounding Indian bands, the colony was filling the political vacuum left by the epidemic and creating a dependable network of corn suppliers and buffers against overland attack. But it also incurred the resentment of the Narragansett by depriving them of tributaries just when Dutch traders were expanding their activities in the bay. The Narragansett challenged Plymouth's action in January 1622 by sending a snakeskin filled with arrows. On Squanto's advice Plymouth's leaders returned the skin filled with powder and shot. The Narragansett sachem, Canonicus, refused to accept this counterchallenge, in effect acknowledging the colony's presence and political importance.

However effective in appearance, Plymouth's system of Indian diplomacy was fraught with tensions that nearly destroyed it. A Pokanoket *pniese,* Hobbamock (named for his patron deity), became a second adviser to Plymouth in the summer of 1621. Whether the English thought that Hobbamock would merely assist Squanto or would serve to check him is unclear. In any event, Squanto was no longer the only link between the colony and the Indians; indeed, as a Pokanoket, Hobbamock had certain advantages over him. As one whose very life depended on the colony's need for him, Squanto had to act decisively to check this threat to his position. His most potent weapon was the mutual distrust and fear lingering between English and Indians; his most pressing need was for a power base so that he could extricate himself from his position of colonial dependency. Accordingly, he began maneuvering on his own.

Squanto had been acting independently for several months before being discovered by the English in March 1622. As reconstructed by Edward Winslow:

> his course was to persuade [the Indians] he could lead us to peace or war at his pleasure, and would oft threaten the Indians, sending them word in a private manner we were intended shortly to kill them, that thereby he might get gifts to himself, to work their peace; ... so that whereas divers were wont to rely on Massasoit for protection, and resort to his abode, now they began to leave him and seek after Tisquantum [Squanto].

In short, he sought to establish himself as an independent native political leader. At the same time he endeavored to weaken the Pokanoket's influence on Plymouth by provoking armed conflict between the two allies. He circulated a rumor that Massasoit was conspiring with the Narragansett and Massachusett to wipe out the colony. The English quickly verified the continued loyalty of the Pokanoket but, though angry at Squanto, were afraid to dispense with him. Instead they protected him from Massasoit's revenge, which brought tensions into the Pokanoket-Plymouth relationship that were only finally assuaged when Squanto died later in the year.

In seeking to establish his independence of Plymouth, Squanto was struggling for more than his survival. As Winslow put it, he sought "honor, which he loved as his life and preferred before his peace." What did honor mean to Squanto? For one thing, of course, it meant revenge against the Pokanoket, not only for threatening his position at Plymouth but for his earlier captivity. But it meant more than that. Squanto appears to have made substantial inroads among Indians loyal to Massasoit in a short period of time. Winslow indicated, unknowingly and in passing, the probable key to this success. The news of Massasoit's alleged treachery against Plymouth was brought, he said, by "an Indian of Tisquantum's family." Contrary to the Plymouth sources (all of which were concerned with establishing the colony's unblemished title to the land around Plymouth Bay), there were certainly a few dozen Patuxet survivors of the epidemic at Pokanoket, Nemasket, and elsewhere. Though Squanto undoubtedly sought the loyalty and tribute of others, it was to these relatives and friends that he would primarily have appealed. The honor he sought was a reconstituted Patuxet band under his own leadership, located near its traditional home.

Squanto's hopes were shattered when his plot collapsed. With Massasoit seeking his life, he had, in Bradford's words, "to stick close to the English, and never durst go from them till he dies." This isolation from other Indians and dependence on the colonists helps explain the latter's willingness to protect him. In July, Squanto again engineered an important breakthrough for Plymouth by accompanying an expedition to Monomoy, where suspicion of all Europeans persisted. The Indians here had attacked Champlain's party in 1606 and Dermer's in 1619. Standish's men had taken some of their corn during their stop at Cape Cod in November 1620. Now, as Winslow phrased it, "by Tisquantum's means better persuaded, they left their jealousy, and traded with them." The colony's take was eight hogsheads of corn and beans. But as the expedition prepared to depart, Squanto "fell sick of an Indian fever, bleeding much at the nose (which the Indians take for a symptom of death) and within a few days died there."

By the time of Squanto's death, Plymouth colony had gained the foothold it had sought for two and a half years. The expedition to Monomoy marked the establishment of firm relations with the last local band to withhold loyalty. Moreover, the trade in corn was no longer an economic necessity, remaining important primarily as a means of affirming tributary relationships. These accomplishments would have been infinitely more difficult, if not impossible, without Squanto's aid. But it is questionable whether his contributions after the summer of 1622 would have been as critical. Thereafter, the colony's principal dealings were with the hostile Massachusett and Narragansett Indians beyond Patuxet's immediate environs. Moreover, the world in which Squanto had flourished was vanishing. A rationalized wampum trade had begun to transform Indian-European relations in southern New England. And the end of the decade would bring a mighty upsurge in English colonization that would surround and dwarf Plymouth. Within the restrictions imposed by his dependence on Plymouth's protection, Squanto would have adapted to these changes. But his knowledge and skills would no longer have been unique nor his services indispensable.

It is difficult to imagine what direction the life of this politically and historically isolated man, who valued "honor" above all else, might have taken in the coming decades. It is in this light that we should read his well-known deathbed conversion wherein he requested Bradford "to pray for him that he might go to the Englishmen's God in Heaven; and bequeathed sundry of his things to sundry of his English friends as remembrances of his love." He was acknowledging that after eight years of acting with honor in alien settings, he had been cornered. Dying so ignominiously, the last Patuxet would have found it ironic that later generations of Americans celebrated him as a hero.

Religion, the Common Thread of Motivation

VIRGINIA DEJOHN ANDERSON

No man, perhaps, would seem to have been an unlikelier candidate for transatlantic migration that John Bent. He had never shown any particular interest in moving; indeed, in 1638, at the age of forty-one, Bent still lived in Weyhill, Hampshire, where both he and his father before him had been born. Having prospered in the village of his birth, John Bent held enough land to distinguish himself as one of Weyhill's wealthiest inhabitants. One might reasonably expect that Bent's substantial economic stake, combined with his growing familial responsibilities—which by 1638 included a wife and five children—would have provided him with ample incentive to stay put. By embarking on a transatlantic voyage—moving for the first time in his life and over a vast distance—Bent would exchange an economically secure present for a highly uncertain future and venture his family's lives and fortunes no less than his own. Yet in the spring of 1638, Bent returned his Weyhill land to the lord of the manor, gathered his family and possessions, and traveled twenty-five miles to the port of Southampton. There, he and his family boarded the *Confidence,* bound for Massachusetts Bay.

In doing so, the Bent family joined thousands of other men, women, and children who left for New England between 1630 and 1642. We know more about John Bent than about the vast majority of these other emigrants because certain information has fortuitously survived. Bent's name appears on one of the few extant ship passenger lists of the Great Migration, and genealogists and local historians have compiled enough additional data to sketch in the outlines of his life in Old and New England. Yet despite this rare abundance of information, John Bent's reasons for moving to Massachusetts remain obscure. In fact, the surviving biographical details render the question of motivation all the more tantalizing because they provide no identifiable economic reason for leaving but rather depict a man firmly rooted in his English homeland.

Most accounts of early New England include a general discussion of the emigrants' motivations, but none has dealt with the issue systematically. If we are ever to comprehend the nature and significance of the Great Migration, however, we must understand why men like John Bent left their homes. The Great Migration to New England, unlike the simultaneous outpouring of Englishmen to other New World colonies, was a voluntary exodus of families

Virginia DeJohn Anderson, "Migrants and Motives: Religion and the Settlement of New England," *New England Quarterly,* LVIII (1985), 339–383. Reprinted by permission of the author and the publisher. Includes 1992 updates.

and included relatively few indentured servants. The movement, which began around 1630, effectively ceased a dozen years later with the outbreak of the English Civil War, further distinguishing it from the more extended period of emigration to other colonies.

These two factors—the emigrants' voluntary departure and the movement's short duration—suggest that the Great Migration resulted from a common, reasoned response to a highly specific set of circumstances. Such circumstances must have been compelling indeed to dislodge a man like John Bent from a comfortable niche in his community. And while Bent and his fellows could not have known it, their reasons for embarking for New England would not only change their own lives but also powerfully shape the society they would create in their new home.

I

Although modern commentators have disagreed over why New England's settlers left the mother country, none of the original chroniclers ever suggested that motivation was an open question. Edward Johnson, for example, knew exactly why the Great Migration occurred. The author of *The Wonder-Working Providence of Sion's Saviour in New England* . . . announced that he and his fellow emigrants left England to escape the evils generated by "the multitude of irreligious lascivious and popish affected persons" who had spread "like Grashoppers" throughout the land. As England strayed from the paths of righteousness, the Lord had sought to preserve a saving remnant of His church by transferring it to an untainted refuge. Johnson adopted a military metaphor to describe the process: the decision to emigrate constituted a voluntary enlistment in Christ's Army, the instrument with which He would "create a new Heaven, and a new Earth in, new Churches, and a new Common-wealth together." Other writers concurred with Johnson's providentialist interpretation. Nathaniel Morton and William Hubbard, both of whom emigrated as children, likewise believed the founding of Massachusetts to be the centerpiece of a divine plan to preserve the Gospel and proper forms of worship. The most emphatic explication of the settlers' religious motivation, however, came not from a participant in the Great Migration but from a descendant of emigrants. Cotton Mather never doubted that the Lord "carried some Thousands of *Reformers* into the Retirements of an *American Desart,* on purpose," that "He might there, *To* them first, and then *By* them, give a *Specimen* of many Good Things, which He would have His Churches elsewhere aspire and arise unto."

Few modern scholars have shared the steadfast conviction of Mather and his predecessors. . . . They have instead reminded us that deciding to emigrate was a complicated and highly individualistic affair. But their conclusions are, in the end, disappointing, for they suggest that we must accept the notion that the motives for emigration were so complex as to be irrecoverable. If we examine more closely the lives of the emigrants themselves, we may yet find clues that reveal a common incentive underlying the Great Migration.

In seeking to identify emigrants and explore their motives for moving, historians have received invaluable assistance from none other than Charles I.

Not long after the exodus to Massachusetts began, the king and his archbishop of Canterbury became increasingly concerned about the departure of so many English folk for wilderness homes across the seas. On 21 July 1635, in an attempt to keep track of the movement, Charles I issued a proclamation requiring all those who wished to leave the realm to obtain a special license from the Privy Council. Customs officers were instructed to obtain certain information from prospective emigrants aboard each ship, including name, residence, occupation, age, and destination. Although the royal edict was loosely enforced and the passage of more than three centuries has inevitably reduced the amount of extant information, several of these ship passenger lists do survive, and they provide a unique opportunity to examine the lives of ordinary emigrants.

Seven ship passenger lists, which together include the names of 693 colonists, provide the information upon which this essay is based. These appear to be the only lists that have been published in their entirety from surviving documents. All the lists contain the names of emigrants; most also include occupation (for adult males), residence, age, and evidence of family structure. In other words, each list provides sufficiently specific information to permit accurate tracing of individual passengers in the New World. The lists themselves, of course, can only tell us about the emigrants at one moment in time, the date of registration for the voyage, but an astonishingly large amount of additional information can be found in genealogies and local histories. Using these materials, it has been possible to reconstruct the New England careers of 578 emigrants, or 83.4 percent of those included on the lists. . . .

Evidence from these lists suggests that although few emigrants left explicit records of their reasons for moving, the motives of the majority need not remain a mystery. Analyzing the lists in light of supporting genealogical materials enables us to construct a social profile of the emigrants, which can then be compared with that of the English population at large. This comparison in turn suggests that once we know who the emigrants were, we can begin to understand why they came.

II

The New England settlers more closely resembled the nonmigrating English population than they did other English colonists in the New World. The implications of this fact for the development of colonial societies can scarcely be overstated. While the composition of the emigrant populations in the Chesapeake and the Caribbean hindered the successful transfer of familiar patterns of social relationships, the character of the New England colonial population ensured it. The prospect of colonizing distant lands stirred the imaginations of young people all over England but most of these young adults made their way to the tobacco and sugar plantations of the South. Nearly half of a sample of Virginia residents in 1625 were between the ages of twenty and twenty-nine, and groups of emigrants to the Chesapeake in the seventeenth century consistently included a majority of people in their twenties. In contrast, only a quarter of the New England settlers belonged to this age group.

The age structure of New England's emigrant population virtually mirrored that of the country they had left. Both infancy and old age were represented: the *Rose* of Great Yarmouth carried one-year-old Thomas Baker as well as Katherine Rabey, a widow of sixty-eight. The proportion of people over the age of sixty was, not surprisingly, somewhat higher in the general English population than among the emigrants. Although Thomas Welde reported in 1632 that he traveled with "very aged" passengers, "twelve persons being all able to make well nigh one thousand years," a transatlantic voyage of three months' duration was an ordeal not easily undertaken, and the hardships involved in settling the wilderness surely daunted prospective emigrants of advanced years. On the whole, however, New England attracted people of all ages and thus preserved a normal pattern of intergenerational contact.

Similarly, the sex ratio of the New England emigrant group resembled that of England's population. If women were as scarce in the Chesapeake as good English beer, they were comparatively abundant in the northern colonies. In the second decade of Virginia's settlement, there were four or five men for each woman; by the end of the century, there were still about three men for every two women. Among the emigrants studied here, however, nearly half were women and girls. Such a high proportion of females in the population assured the young men of New England greater success than their southern counterparts in finding spouses.

These demographic characteristics derive directly from the fact that the migration to New England was primarily a transplantation of families. Fully 87.8 percent (597 out of 680) of the emigrants traveled with relatives of one sort or another. Nearly three-quarters (498 out of 680) came in nuclear family units, with or without children. Occasionally, single spouses migrated with their children, either to meet a partner already in the New World or to wait for his or her arrival on a later ship. Grandparents comprised a relatively inconspicuous part of the migration, but a few hardy elders did make the trip. In 1637, Margaret Neave sailed to Massachusetts with her granddaughter Rachel Dixson, who was probably an orphan. In the following year, Alice Stephens joined her sons William and John and their families for the voyage to New England. More frequently, emigrant family structure extended horizontally, within a generation, rather than vertically, across three generations. Several groups of brothers made the trip together, and when the three Goodenow brothers decided to leave the West Country, they convinced their unmarried sister Ursula to come with them as well.

Thus, for the majority of these New England settlers, transatlantic migration did not lead to permanent separation from close relatives. Some unscrupulous men and women apparently migrated in order to flee unhappy marriages, but most nuclear family units arrived intact. When close kin were left behind, they usually joined their families within a year or so. Samuel Lincoln, for instance, who traveled abroad the *Rose* in 1637, soon joined his brother Thomas, who had settled in Hingham in 1633. Another brother, Stephen, arrived in the following year with both his family and his mother. Edward Johnson, who had first crossed the ocean with the Winthrop fleet in 1630, returned to England in 1637 to fetch his wife and seven children.

For Thomas Starr, who left Sandwich in 1637, migration meant a reunion with his older brother Comfort, a passenger on the *Hercules* two years earlier. Although some disruption of kin ties was unavoidable, it was by no means the rule. . . .

Further exploration of demographic patterns reveals . . . subtle but significant differences between the migrating population and that of England. These differences illustrate the important fact that migration was a selective process; not all people were equally suited to or interested in the rigors of New World settlement. Since the movement to New England was a voluntary, self-selective affair, most of this winnowing-out process occurred before the hearths of English homes, as individuals and families discussed whether or not to leave.

Although family groups predominated within the emigrant population, many individuals came to New England on their own. The vast majority of these solitary travelers were male—men outnumbered women by a factor of ten to one—and together they constituted 38 percent of the emigrant households. This figure stands in sharp contrast to England's population, where only about 5 percent of all households were composed of one individual. About one in six emigrants aged twenty-one to thirty sailed independently, perhaps drawn to New England by hopes of employment or freeholdership. These men were hardly freewheeling adventurers; instead, they provided the new settlements with skilled labor. The unaccompanied travelers included shoemakers, a carpenter, butcher, tanner, hempdresser, weaver, cutler, physician, fuller, tailor, mercer, and skinner. Some were already married at the time of the voyage, and those who were single seldom remained so for more than a couple of years after their arrival. Through marriage, the men became members of family networks within their communities. Within a few years of his arrival in 1635, for instance, Henry Ewell, a young shoemaker from Sandwich in Kent, joined the church in Scituate and married the daughter of a prominent local family. William Paddy, a London skinner, managed to obtain land, find a wife, and get elected to Plymouth's first general court of deputies within four years of his voyage. . . .

Yet it is important to remember that New England primarily attracted families—and families of a special sort. . . . The westward-bound ships carried couples who were mature, who had probably been married for nearly a decade, and who had established themselves firmly within their communities. The typical migrating family was complete—composed of husband, wife, and three or four children—but was not yet completed. They were families in process, with parents who were at most halfway through their reproductive cycle and who would continue to produce children in New England. They would be responsible for the rapid population growth that New England experienced in its first decades of settlement. Moreover, the numerous children who emigrated with their parents contributed their efforts to a primitive economy sorely lacking in labor.

The task of transforming wilderness into farmland, however, demanded more labor than parents and their children alone could supply, and more than half of the emigrating families responded to this challenge by bringing servants with them to the New World. Perhaps some had read William Wood's advice in *New England's Prospect* and learned that "men of good estates may do well there, always provided that they go well accommodated with servants." In any case, servants formed an integral part, just over 17 percent, of the colonizing population and in fact were at first somewhat more commonplace in New England than in England. Most were males (80 of 114) and labored alongside their masters, clearing land, planting corn, and building houses and barns. Their presence substantially increased the ratio of producers to consumers in the newly settled towns. . . .

Before departing for New England, the emigrants had called a wide variety of English towns and villages their homes. Most lived in the lowland area of England . . . and within this expanse of territory . . . had known many different forms of social organization, agricultural practice, industrial development, and local government. At one end of the spectrum, Parnell Harris, William Paddy, and Edmund Hawes all left the burgeoning metropolis of London, which was about to overtake Paris as the largest city in Europe; at the other, the widow Emme Mason left the tiny Kentish parish of Eastwell, which was "not more than a mile across each way" and whose church in 1640 counted just 55 communicants.

A relatively large proportion of the New England settlers dwelled in urban areas prior to their emigration. . . . Among other things, town life . . . equipped future emigrants with complex and regionally distinctive experiences of local government. Most incorporated boroughs were run by an annually elected mayor, but the numbers and duties of subsidiary officeholders varied widely. . . . In addition, seventeenth-century English towns, especially the larger ones, often encompassed a multiplicity of civil and ecclesiastical jurisdictions. . . . Provincial centers such as Canterbury and Norwich were divided into several parishes; the Kentish city had at least eight in 1640, while the East Anglian capital boasted thirty-four parishes. Moreover, town-dwellers lived in the midst of a more heterogeneous population than did persons who resided in the countryside. Major textile manufacturing centers received an influx of foreign artisans in the late sixteenth and early seventeenth centuries. The newcomers, mainly Dutch and Walloon tradesmen, settled primarily in Kent and East Anglia and helped to revitalize the depressed cloth industry in those areas. . . .

In the countryside, although the contrasts were perhaps less striking, villages also differed significantly from one another. Much of seventeenth-century England was an intricate patchwork of parishes with particular local customs dating from time out of mind. Ancient practice often dictated the shape of the landscape, patterns of settlement, modes of landholding, and rituals of agrarian activity. Even within a single county, substantial variation was evident. . . . In the migration to New England, then, not only would villagers and townsfolk intermingle but farmers would also encounter other countrymen with very different experiences of rural life.

The diversity of the emigrants' English backgrounds—and their urban origins in particular—influenced the distribution of their occupations. . . . Artisans, both in the cloth trades and in other pursuits, formed a greater proportion of the emigrant population than tradesmen did in the English population as a whole. In 1696, Gregory King estimated that "freeholders" and "farmers" outnumbered "artizans and handicrafts" by a factor of more than seven to one; among the emigrants to New England, however, artisans predominated by a ratio of nearly two to one.

The occupational spectrum of future New Englanders placed them at the more prosperous end of English society.... Yet in striking contrast to Virginia, where, at least initially, the population included "about six times as large a proportion of gentlemen as England had," New England attracted very few members of the upper class. Sir Henry Vane and Sir Richard Saltonstall were unique among the leaders of the migration, and for the most part even they submitted to government by such gentle but untitled figures as John Winthrop and Thomas Dudley. On the whole, emigrants were neither very high nor very low in social and economic status. Husbandmen predominated among the farmers who came to Massachusetts; thirty of them emigrated compared to just five yeomen. By the seventeenth century, the legal distinctions between the status of yeoman and that of husbandman had largely eroded and evidence indicates that the labels generally denoted relative position on the economic and social ladder. Both groups primarily made their livings from the land, but yeomen were generally better off. New England, however, was peopled by less affluent—but not necessarily poor—husbandmen.

Emigrant clothworkers practiced trades that also placed them on the middle rungs of the economic ladder.... Among the non-clothworking artisans, shoemakers and carpenters predominated, and they too worked in trades that would bring comfort, if not riches. All in all, the New England–bound ships transported a population characterized by a greater degree of social homogeneity than existed in the mother country. Despite Winthrop's reminder to his fellow passengers on the *Arbella* that "some must be rich some poor, some highe and eminent in power and dignitie; others meane and in subieccion," New Englanders would discover that the process of migration effectively reduced the distance between the top and the bottom of their social hierarchy.

III

In a letter to England written in 1632, Richard Saltonstall commented on the social origins of New England's inhabitants. "It is strange," he wrote, "the meaner sort of people should be so backward [in migrating], having assurance that they may live plentifully by their neighbors." At the same time, he expressed the hope that more "gentlemen of ability would transplant themselves," for they too might prosper both spiritually and materially in the new land. For young Richard, the twenty-one-year-old son of Sir Richard Saltonstall, New England promised much but as yet lacked the proper balance of social groups within its population that would ensure its success. The migration of the "meaner sort" would help lower the cost of labor, while richer emigrants would "supply the want we labor under of men fitted by their estates to bear common burdens." Such wealthy men would invest in the colony's future even as they enhanced their own spiritual welfare by becoming "worthy instruments of propagating the Gospel" to New England's natives.

Saltonstall wrote early in the migration decade, but the succeeding years did little to redress the social imbalance he perceived in Massachusetts. Two years later, William Wood could still write that "none of such great estate went over yet." Throughout the decade of the 1630s, New England continued to attract colonists who were overwhelmingly ordinary. Demographically they presented a mirror image of the society they had left behind, and socially and economically they fairly represented England's relatively prosperous middle class. The question is inescapable: why did so many average English men and women pass beyond the seas to Massachusetts' shores?

Whether or not they have assigned it primary importance, most historians of the period have noted that economic distress in England in the early seventeenth century must have been causally related to the Great Migration. These were years of agricultural and industrial depression, the farmers and weavers were conspicuous passengers on the transatlantic voyages. A closer examination of the connections between economic crisis and the movement to New England, however, indicates that the links were not as close as they have been assumed to be.

Agriculture—especially in the early modern period—was a notoriously risky business. Success depended heavily upon variables beyond human control. A dry summer or an unusually wet season rendered futile the labor of even the most diligent husbandman, and English farmers in the early seventeenth century had to endure more than their share of adversity. While the decade of the 1620s began propitiously, with excellent harvests in 1619 and 1620, the farmers' luck did not hold. The next three years brought one disastrous harvest after another; improvement in 1624 was followed by dearth in 1625. The beginning of the 1630s, especially in the eastern counties, was marked by further distress; in 1630, the mayor of Norwich complained that "scarcity and dearth of corn and other victuals have so increased the number and misery of the poor in this city" that civic taxes had to be boosted to unprecedented heights and the city's stock of grain dwindled dangerously. In 1637, a severe drought spawned further hardship.

Although this period of agricultural depression undoubtedly touched the lives of many English families, it did not necessarily compel them to emigrate. The worst sustained period of scarcity occurred in the early 1620s, a decade or so before the Great Migration began; if agrarian distress was a "push" factor, it produced a curiously delayed reaction. Furthermore, annual fluctuations were endemic in early modern agriculture. Englishmen knew from experience that times would eventually improve, even if that day were unpleasantly distant; moreover, they had no reason to suppose that farmers in New England would somehow lead charmed lives, exempt from similar variations in the weather. In addition, dearth was not an unmitigated disaster for families engaged in husbandry: as supplies of grain and other products shrank, prices rose. In 1630, a year with one of the worst harvests in the first half of the seventeenth century, the price of grain was twice what it had been in the more plentiful years of 1619 and 1620. Thus for farmers involved in market agriculture, a bad year, with half the yield of a good one, could still bring the same income. As the Norwich mayor's lament amply demonstrates, the people really hurt in times of scarcity were city-dwellers dependent on the countryside for their food. That urban dwellers left for New England to assure themselves of a steady food supply, however, is highly unlikely. Emigrants would surely have anticipated the primitive state of the region's agriculture; reports of scarcity at Plymouth and the early Massachusetts Bay settlements had quickly filtered back to England. Moreover, emigrating urban artisans certainly understood that, in the New World, responsibility for feeding their families would lie in their own hands—hands more accustomed to the loom or the last than the plow.

The slump in England's textile industry has also been accounted an incentive for emigration. The industry was indeed mired in a severe depression in the early seventeenth century; it is true as well that a quarter of the adult male emigrants were employed in a trade related to cloth manufacture. . . .

Yet even if evidence did suggest that emigrant weavers were compelled by economic adversity to leave their homeland, Massachusetts would not have been a wise choice of destination if they hoped to continue in their trade. Flight to the Netherlands, a place with a well-developed textile industry, would have been a more rational choice for artisans worried about the fate of their trade in England and anxious to persist in its practice. Massachusetts lacked both the wool supply and the intricate network of auxiliary tradesmen—such as combers, carders, calenderers, fullers, dyers, etc.—upon which England's weavers depended. Several of the emigrants packed up their looms along with their other belongings, but there is little evidence that they were able to earn their livings in Massachusetts solely by weaving.

Arguments linking the Great Migration to economic hardship in England all share an important weakness. Although historians have discovered that many *places* from which emigrants came suffered from agricultural or industrial depression, they have had little success in connecting those unfavorable economic circumstances to the fortunes of individual emigrants. On the contrary, it appears that the families that went to New England had largely avoided the serious setbacks that afflicted many of their countrymen during those years. . . .

. . . If migration to New England was not a sensible economic decision for farmers or weavers hurt by hard times in England, it was even less sensible for people doing well. Most emigrants exchanged an economically viable present for a very uncertain future. . . . The emigrant groups studied here all left England five or more years after the Great Migration had begun and a decade and a half after the landing at Plymouth; they surely heard from earlier arrivals that New England was no land of milk and honey. If any had a chance to read Edward Winslow's *Good Newes from New England,* published in 1624, he or she would have learned that the "vain expectation of present profit" was the "overthrow and bane" of plantations. People might prosper through "good labor and diligence," but in the absence of a cash crop, great wealth was not to be expected. The message of William Wood's *New England's Prospect,* published a decade later, was similar. Some colonists were lured westward by descriptions of plenty, Wood acknowledged, but they soon fell to criticizing the new society, "saying a man cannot live without labor." . . . Letters as well as published reports informed would-be settlers that New England was not a particularly fertile field for profit. In 1631, one young colonist wrote to his father in Suffolk, England, that "the cuntrey is not so as we ded expecte it." Far from bringing riches, New England could not even provide essentials; the disillusioned settler begged his father to send provisions, for "we do not know how longe we may subeseiste" without supplies from home.

If prospective emigrants were not hearing that New England offered ample opportunities for economic betterment, they *were* informed that life in Massachusetts could bring betterment of another sort. When Governor Thomas Dudley provided the countess of Lincoln with an account of his first nine months in New England, he announced that "if any come hether to plant for worldly ends that canne live well at home hee comits an errour of which he will soon repent him. But if for spirituall [ends] and that noe particular obstacle hinder his removeall, he may finde here what may well content him." Dudley worried that some might be drawn to Massachusetts by exaggerations of the land's bounty and wanted to make clear who would benefit most from emigration. "If any godly men out of religious ends will come over to helpe vs in the good worke wee are about," the governor wrote, "I think they cannot dispose of themselves nor of their estates more to God's glory and the furtherance of their owne reckoninge." New England promised its settlers *spiritual* advantages only; men merely in search of wealth could go elsewhere. Emmanuel Downing, in a letter to Sir John Coke, clarified the important difference between New England and other colonial ventures. "This plantation and that of Virginia went not forth upon the same reasons nor for the same end. Those of Virginia," he explained, "went forth for profit. . . . These went upon two other designs, some to satisfy their own curiosity in point of conscience, others . . . to transport the Gospel to those heathen that never heard thereof." . . .

Prospective emigrants, then, could hardly have been unaware of the peculiar religious character of New England society. Accounts of the region's commitment to Puritanism were too numerous to be overlooked; those who made the voyage had to know what they were getting into. Adherence to Puritan principles, therefore, became the common thread that stitched individual emigrants together into a larger movement. As Rev. John White declared, "Necessitie may presse some; Noveltie draw on others; hopes of gaine in time to come may prevaile with a third sort: but that the most and most sincere and godly part have the advancement of the *Gospel* for their maine scope I am co[n]fident."

White's confidence was by no means misplaced. The roster of passengers to New England contains the names of scores of otherwise ordinary English men and women whose lives were distinguished by their steadfast commitment to nonconformity, even in the face of official harassment. . . .

. . . Those few men who recorded their own reasons for removal likewise stressed the role of religion. Roger Clap, who sailed in 1630, recalled in his memoirs that "I never so much as heard of *New-England* until I heard of many godly Persons that were going there" and firmly believed that "God put it into my Heart to incline to Live abroad" in Massachusetts. John Dane, who seems to have spent most of his youth fighting off his evil inclinations, "bent myself to cum to nu ingland, thinking that I should be more fre here then thare from temptations." Arriving in Roxbury in the mid-1630s, Dane soon discovered that relocation would not end his struggle with sinfulness; the devil sought him out as readily in the New World as in the Old.

To declare that most emigrants were prompted by radical religious sentiment to sail to the New World, however, does not mean that these settlers resembled Hawthorne's memorable "stern and black-browed Puritans" in single-minded pursuit of salvation. The decision to cross the seas indelibly marked the lives of those who made it. Even the most pious wrestled with the implications of removal from family, friends, and familiar surroundings. Parents often objected to the departure of their children; a son following the dictates of his conscience might risk the estrangement of a disappointed father. Although religious motivation is the only factor with sufficient power to explain the departure of so many otherwise ordinary families, the New England Puritans should not be seen as utopians caught up in a movement whose purpose totally transcended the concerns of daily life.

Solitary ascetics can afford to reject the things of this world in order to contemplate the glories of the next; family men cannot. Even as prospective settlers discussed the spiritual benefits that might accompany a move to New England, they worried about what they would eat, where they would sleep, and how they would make a living. In the spring of 1631, Emmanuel Downing wrote with considerable relief to John Winthrop that the governor's encouraging letters "haue much refreshed my hart and the myndes of manie others" for "yt was the Iudgement of most men here, that your Colonye would be dissolved partly by death through want of Food, howsing and rayment, and the rest to retorne or to flee for refuge to other plantacions." Other leaders and publicists of the migration continued both to recognize and to sympathize with the concerns of families struggling with the decision of whether or not to move, and they sought to reassure prospective settlers that a decision in favor of emigration would not doom their families to cold and starvation in the wilderness. At the same time, the way in which these writers composed their comforting messages to would-be emigrants underscored the settlers' understanding of the larger meaning of their mission.

Although several of the tracts and letters publicizing the migration contained favorable descriptions of the new land, they were never intended to be advertisements designed to capture the interest of profit-seekers. When John White, Thomas Dudley, and others wrote about the blessings of New England's climate, topography, and flora and fauna, they simply hoped to assure godly English men and women that a move to the New World would not engender poverty as well as piety. . . . John White repeatedly assured his readers that "all Gods directions"—including the divine imperative to settle New England—"have a double scope, mans good and Gods honour." "That this commandement of God is directed unto mans good *temporall and spirituall,*" he went on, "is as cleere as the light." The Lord, in other words, would take care of His own.

To providentialists steeped in the conviction that God intervened directly in human lives, that divine pleasure or disapproval could be perceived in the progress of daily events, White's statement made eminent sense. If emigrant families embarked on their voyages with the purpose of abandoning England's corruption in order to worship God according to biblical precepts in their new homes, and if they adhered to this purpose, they might expect as a sign of divine favor to achieve a competency, if not riches. Thus John Winthrop could assert that "such thinges as we stand in neede of are vsually supplied by Gods blessing vpon the wisdome and industry of man." The governor's firm belief in the connection between divine favor and human well-being explains why in his "Particular Considerations" concerning his own removal out of England, he admitted that "my meanes heere [in England] are so shortned (now my 3 eldest sonnes are come to age) as I shall not be able to continue in this place and imployment where I now am." If he went to Massachusetts, Winthrop anticipated an improvement in his fortunes, noting that "I [can] live with 7. or 8: servants in that place and condition where for many years I have spent 3: or 400 *li.* per an[num]." Winthrop, despite these musings on his worldly estate, did not emigrate in order to better his economic condition. Rather, he removed in order to undertake the "publike service" that God had "bestowed" on him and hoped that God might reward him if his efforts were successful. In similar fashion, thousands of other emigrants could justify their decisions to move to New England. They believed that, by emigrating, they followed the will of God and that their obedience would not escape divine notice. In return for their submission to His will, the emigrants sincerely hoped that God might allow them—through their own labor—to enjoy a competency of this world's goods.

Historians have generally agreed that early New England displayed a distinctive social character. The first colonists, after all, succeeded in creating a remarkably stable society on the edge of a vast wilderness. But stability alone does not sum up the New Englanders' achievement, for colonists who went to other parts of North America also established lasting settlements. What set New England society apart was its Puritan heritage. Religious and social ideals became inextricably intertwined as settlers applied the Puritan concept of the covenantal relationship between God and man to their temporal as well as religious affairs. When New Englanders pledged themselves to God in their churches and to each other in their towns, they imbued their society with a deeply spiritual significance. Other British colonists would also strive to create social harmony, but none would do so with the same intensity of religious purpose as New England's founding generation. . . .

At the heart of the colonists' achievement lies an apparent paradox. Settlers in Massachusetts, Plymouth, and Connecticut created a remarkably unified culture and a homogeneous society in a setting where the power of central authorities was exceedingly weak. Preachers and magistrates could have expended every effort extolling the virtues of communal and spiritual harmony and yet failed miserably had not their audience shared in their aspirations. But since the majority of emigrants responded to a common spiritual impulse in moving to New England, they readily accepted the idea of the covenant as the proper model for their social as well as spiritual relationships. Indeed, covenants, because of their voluntary nature, provided the only truly effective means of maintaining social cohesion where coercive power was limited. The social homogeneity of the emigrant population—the absence of both rich and poor folk—unintentionally reinforced covenantal ideals by reducing the differences in status among partners. In this way, social fact joined with communal ideals to create a society of comparative equals pledged to one another's support. At the same time, social and religious covenants helped settlers from diverse geographical and occupational backgrounds to come to terms with their new common enterprise. Emigrants concerned solely with their own material improvement would scarcely have acceded so readily to an ideal of mutual cooperation. It is only because most colonists (at least initially) placed the good of their souls above all else and trusted in the Lord to provide for them that the story of New England's origins occupies a unique place in American history.

✿ F U R T H E R   R E A D I N G

David Grayson Allen, *In English Ways: The Movement of Societies and the Transferal of English Local Law and Custom to Massachusetts Bay in the Seventeenth Century* (1982)

David Cressy, *Coming Over: Migration and Communication Between England and New England in the Seventeenth Century* (1987)

John Demos, *A Little Commonwealth: Family Life in Plymouth Colony* (1970)

G. D. Langdon, Jr., *Pilgrim Colony: A History of New Plymouth, 1620–1691* (1966)

Edmund S. Morgan, *The Puritan Dilemma: The Story of John Winthrop* (1958)

Howard S. Russell, *Indian New England Before the Mayflower* (1980)

Neal Salisbury, *Manitou and Providence: Indians, Europeans, and the Making of New England, 1500–1643* (1982)

Frank Shuffleton, "Indian Devils and Pilgrim Fathers: Squanto, Hobomock, and the English Conception of Indian Religion," *New England Quarterly* 49 (1976), 108–116

CHAPTER

5

Challenges to
the New England Way:
Sects and Witches

০৩০

*Puritanism was a highly individualistic creed. Its adherents approached God and
God's revelation in the Bible without the aid of the hierarchy of bishops. The Puritans held learning in the highest regard; indeed, many leaders in the New England
towns were university-educated men. The people looked to these scholars for guidance and inspiration. But there could be no abdication of responsibility; each
church member was expected to read the Bible and understand God's message.
Each went through the same process of self-examination to find the sparks of
God's grace within. Those chosen by God ultimately would receive grace—the ability to believe.*

*When Puritans created their own society, the challenge was to harness and
focus this individualistic thrust so as to keep the society from dissolving into countless sects, each with its own version of the truth. New England Puritans formed
their communities around church covenants, pledging themselves to abide by decisions of the community in the congregation. Only the "visible saints," those judged
to have received grace, were admitted to membership in the congregations, and only
church members could vote and hold office. These close ties between the political
and religious life of the colony were institutionalized as the "New England Way."*

*Protests rose from within Puritanism itself. They began as early as the Antino-
mian movement of Anne Hutchinson and the challenge of Roger Williams in the
middle of the 1630s. Often, as in the case of the Quakers, those who believed that
they had received grace argued that they need listen only to their own inner voice
to know God's will. If the leadership differed, then the leadership was wrong, its
ability to understand the reality of divine presence stifled by too much scholarly
study. As discord grew, many were prepared to believe that the dissension was the
work of the devil through the influence of people—witches—who chose to ally
themselves with him. Everything that happened reflected divine will; if God allowed*

*the devil to be active, then Puritans must both rid their society of his agents and re-
double examination of their own conduct to see what had brought God's wrath.*

◑ D O C U M E N T S

Anne Hutchinson convinced the majority of the Boston congregation that their
preachers were almost all preaching a doctrine that one could earn salvation by
good works rather than by focusing on the work of divine grace within. She was
tried and banished, and the authorities published the trial testimony, excerpted here
as the first document, to bolster their case. Quakers soon posed an equally threatening challenge, and Massachusetts Bay reacted harshly. Mary Dyer, who had begun
as a disciple of Anne Hutchinson, later, as a Quaker, defied a sentence of banishment on pain of death to preach the truth as she saw it, as the second document reveals. Ultimately the Bay Colony authorities executed her. Quakers saw her as a
martyr. When Charles II came to the English throne in 1660, his accession ended a
period of Puritan rule under Oliver Cromwell. In the third selection Massachusetts
governor John Endecott writes to the new king, attempting to justify the colonists'
prohibition of Quakers while at the same time excusing their failure to conform to
the Church of England. English traveler John Josselyn presents the same information less sympathetically in the fourth document.

Prosecutions of witches were endemic in New England as in England. Increase
Mather, one of the greatest intellectuals of the time, collected instances of bewitching in his book *Remarkable Providences* (1684), an except from which is reprinted
as the fifth document. Fear of witches as agents of the devil culminated in the massive accusations at Salem in 1692, from which the trial testimony has been preserved.
The genuine puzzlement and dismay both of one of the accused, Rebecca Nurse,
and of her neighbors come through in the testimony presented in the final selection.

Testimony from the Trial
of Anne Hutchinson, 1637

... [A] woman had been the breeder and nourisher of all these distempers,
one Mistress *Hutchison,* the wife of Mr. *William Hutchison* of *Boston* (a very
honest and peaceable man of good estate) and the daughter of Mr. *Marbury,*
sometimes a Preacher in *Lincolnshire,* after of *London,* a woman of a haughty
and fierce carriage, of a nimble wit and active spirit, and a very voluble
tongue, more bold than a man, though in understanding and judgement, in-
feriour to many women. This woman had learned her skill in *England,* and
had discovered some of her opinions in the Ship, as she came over, which
had caused some jealousy of her, which gave occasion of some delay of her
admission, when she first desired fellowship with the Church of *Boston,* but
she cunningly dissembled and coloured her opinions, as she soon got over
that block, and was admitted into the Church, then she began to go to work,
and being a woman very helpful in the times of childbirth, and other occasions

---

Some of the spelling in this document has been modernized.

of bodily infirmities, and well furnished with means for those purposes, she easily insinuated herself into the affections of many, and the rather, because she was much inquisitive of them about their spiritual estates, and in discovering to them the danger they were in, by trusting to common gifts and graces, without any such witness of the Spirit, as the Scripture holds out for a full evidence; . . . [I]ndeed it was a wonder upon what a sudden the whole Church of *Boston* (some few excepted) were become her new converts, and infected with her opinions, and many also out of the Church, and of other Churches also, yea, many profane persons became of her opinion, for it was a very easy, and acceptable way to heaven, to see nothing, to have nothing, but wait for Christ to do all; so that after she had thus prevailed, and had drawn some of eminent place and parts to her party (whereof some profited so well, as in a few moneths they outwent their teacher) then she kept open house for all comers, and set up two Lecture days in the week, when they usually met at her house, threescore or fourscore persons, the pretence was to repeat Sermons, but when that was done, she would comment upon the Doctrines, and interpret all passages at her pleasure, and expound dark places of Scripture. . . .

When she appeared, the Court spoke to her to this effect.

Mistris *Hutchison.* You are called hither as one of those who have had a great share in the causes of our public disturbances, partly by those erroneous opinions which you have broached and divulged amongst us, and maintaining them, partly by countenancing and encouraging such as have sowed seditions amongst us, partly by casting reproach upon the faithful. Ministers of this Country, and upon their Ministry, and so weakening their hands in the work of the Lord, and raising prejudice against them, in the hearts of their people, and partly by maintaining weekly and public meetings in your house, to the offence of all the Country, and the detriment of many families, and still upholding the same, since such meetings were clearly condemned in the late general Assembly.

Now the end of your sending for, is, that either upon sight of your errors, and other offences, you may be brought to acknowledge, and reform the same, or otherwise that we may take such course with you as you may trouble us no further.

We do desire therefore to know of you, whether you will Justify and maintain what is laid to your charge or not?

Mistris *Hutchison.* I am called here to answer to such things as are laid to my charge, name one of them.

Court Have you countenanced, or will you justify those seditious practises which have been censured here in this Court?

Hutch. Do you ask me upon point of conscience?

Court No, your conscience you may keep to yourself, but if in this cause you shall countenance and encourage those that thus transgress the Law, you must be called in question for it, and that is not for your conscience, but for your practise.

Hutch. What Law have they transgressed? the Law of God?

Court Yes, the fifth Commandement, which commands us to honour Father and Mother, which includes all in authority, but these seditious practices of theirs, have cast reproach and dishonour upon the Fathers of the Commonwealth.

Hutch. Do I entertain, or maintain them in their actions, wherein they stand against anything that God hath appointed?

Court Yes, you have justified Mr. *Wheelwright** his Sermon, for which you know he was convict of sedition, and you have likewise countenanced and encouraged those that had their hands to the Petition.

Hutch. I deny it, I am to obey you only in the Lord.

Court You cannot deny but you had your hand in the Petition.

Hutch. Put case, I do fear the Lord, and my Parent do not, may not I entertain one that fear the Lord, because my Father will not let me? I may put honour upon him as a child of God.

Court That's nothing to the purpose, but we cannot stand to dispute causes with you now, what say you to your weekly public meetings? can you show a warrant for them?

Hutch. I will show you how I took it up, there were such meetings in use before I came, and because I went to none of them, this was the special reason of my taking up this course, we began it but with five or six, and though it grew to more in future time, yet being tolerated at the first, I knew not why it might not continue.

Court There were private meetings indeed, and are still in many places, of some few neighbours, but not so public and frequent as yours, and are of use for increase of love, and mutual edification, but yours are of another nature, if they had been such as yours they had been evil, and therefore no good warrant to justify yours; but answer by what authority, or rule, you uphold them.

Hutch. By *Tit.* 2. where the elder women are to teach the younger.

Court So we allow you to do, as the Apostle there means, privately, and upon occasion, but that gives no warrant of such set meetings for that purpose; and besides, you take upon you to teach many that are elder than yourself, neither do you teach them that which the Apostle commands, *viz.* to keep at home.

Hutch. Will you please to give me a rule against it, and I will yield?

Court You must have a rule for it, or else you cannot do it in faith, yet you have a plain rule against it; I permit not a woman to teach.

Hutch. That is meant of teaching men.

Court If a man in distress of conscience or other temptation, &c. should come and ask your counsel in private, might you not teach him?

Hutch. Yes.

Court Then it is clear, that it is not meant of teaching men, but of teaching in public.

Hutch. It is said, I will pour my Spirit upon your Daughters, and they shall prophesie, &c. If God give me a gift of Prophecy, I may use it.

John Wheelwright, Anne Hutchinson's brother-in-law, was banished from Boston and settled with his followers at Piscataqua in Maine in 1637.

Court First, the Apostle applies that prophecy unto those extraordinary times, and the gifts of miracles and tongues were common to many as well as the gift of Prophecy. Secondly, in teaching your children, you exercise your gift of prophecy, and that within your calling.

Hutch. I teach not in a public congregation: The men of *Berea* are commended for examining *Paul's* Doctrine; we do no more but read the notes of our teachers' Sermons, and then reason of them by searching the Scriptures.

Court You are gone from the nature of your meeting, to the kind of exercise, we will follow you in this, and show you your offence in them, for you do not as the *Bereans* search the Scriptures for their confirming in the truths delivered, but you open your teachers' points, and declare his meaning, and correct wherein you think he hath failed, &c. and by this means you abase the honour and authority of the public Ministry, and advance your own gifts, as if he could not deliver his matter so clearly to the hearers' capacity as yourself.

Hutch. Prove that, that anybody doth that.

Court Yes, you are the woman of most note, and of best abilities, and if some other take upon them the like, it is by your teaching and example, but you show not in all this, by what authority you take upon you to be such a public instructor: (after she had stood a short time, the Court gave her leave to sit down, for her countenance discovered some bodily infirmity.)

Hutch. Here is my authority, *Aquila* and *Priscilla,* took upon them to instruct *Apollo,* more perfectly, yet he was a man of good parts, but they being better instructed might teach him.

Court See how your argument stands, *Priscilla* with her husband, took *Apollo* home to instruct him privately, therefore Mistris *Hutchison* without her husband may teach sixty or eighty.

Hutch. I call them not, but if they come to me, I may instruct them.

Court Yet you show us not a rule.

Hutch. I have given you two places of Scripture.

Court But neither of them will suit your practise.

Hutch. Must I show my name written therein?

Court You must show that which must be equivalent, seeing your Ministry is public, you would have them receive your instruction, as coming from such an Ordinance.

Hutch. They must not take it as it comes from me, but as it comes from the Lord Jesus Christ, and if I took upon me a public Ministry, I should break a rule, but not in exercising a gift of Prophecy, and I would see a rule to turn away them that come to me. . . .

Quaker Testimony: The Execution
of Mary Dyer, 1660

Mary Dyer, being freed as aforesaid, returned to Rhode Island, and afterwards to Long Island, and there was most part of the winter, over the Island, where she had good service for the Lord; and then came to Shelter Island, whence she thought she might pass to Rhode Island. And being there, sometime she had movings from the Lord to go to Boston, and there she came the 21st of the 3rd Month, 1660. And the 30th day was their Governor chosen, and the 31st of the 3rd Month, in the former part of the day, she was sent for to the General Court.

The Governor said, "Are ye the same Mary Dyer that was here before?" . . .

Mary Dyer: "I am the same Mary Dyer that was here the last General Court."

The Governor said, "You will own yourself a Quaker, will you not."

M.D.: "I own my self to be so reproachfully called." The bloody minded Jailer, having now opportunity to have his bloodthirsty will fulfilled, said "she is a vagabond."

The Governor said, "The sentence was passed upon her the Last General Court, and now likewise: 'you must return to the prison from whence you came, and there remain until tomorrow at nine of the clock, then from thence you must go to the gallows, and there be hanged till you are dead.'"

Mary Dyer said, "this is no more than that thou saidst before."

"Aye, aye," the Governor said, "and now it is to be executed. Therefore prepare yourself tomorrow at nine of the clock," (being the first day of the 4th Month, 1660).

Mary Dyer answered and said, "I came in obedience to the will of God, the last General Court, desiring you to repeal your unrighteous laws of banishment upon pain of death; and that same is my work now, and earnest request, because ye refused before to grant my request, although I told you that if ye refused to repeal them the Lord will send others of his servants to witness against them."

John Endicott asked her whether she was a prophet.

She said she spake the words that the Lord spake in her; "and now the thing is come to pass." She beginning to speak of her Call, J. Endicott said, "away with her, away with her."

So she was brought to the prison-house, where she was before, close shut up until the next day. About the time prefixed, the marshal Michaelson came and called hastily for her. When he came into the room, she desired him to stay a little, and speaking mildly to him she said she should be ready presently, even like a sheep prepared for the slaughter. But he in the wolvish nature said he could not wait upon her, but she should now wait upon him. Margaret Smith, her companion, hearing him speak these words with others from the Cain-like spirit, was moved to testify against their unjust laws and proceedings, being grieved to see both him and many others in such gross darkness and hardheartedness. Then he said, "you shall have your share of the same," with other violent words.

Then they brought her forth, and drums were beat before and behind her, with a band of soldiers, through the town, and so to the place of execution, which is about a mile, the drums being that none might hear her speak all the way.

Some said unto her, that if she would return she might come down and save her life. She answered and said, "Nay, I cannot. For in obedience to the will of the Lord God I came, and in his will I abide faithful to the death."

Their Captain, John Webb said, She had been here before, and had the sentence of banishment upon pain of death; and had broken this law in coming again now, as well as formerly; and therefore she was guilty of her own blood. To which M. Dyer said, "Nay, I came to keep blood-guiltiness from you, desiring you to repeal the unrighteous and unjust law of banishment upon pain of death, made against the innocent servants of the Lord. Therefore my blood will be required at your hands, who wilfully do it; but for those that do it in the simplicity of their hearts, I do desire the Lord to forgive them. I came to do the will of my Father, and in obedience to his will I stand even to the death."

John Wilson, their priest of Boston, said, "M. Dyer, O repent; O repent, and be not so deluded and carried away by the deceit of the Devil." M. Dyer answered and said, "Nay, man, I am not now to repent."

Some asked her whether she would have the Elders to pray for her. She said, "I know never an Elder here." They asked whether she would have any of the people to pray for her. She said she desired the prayers of all the People of God. Some scoffingly said, "It may be she thinks there is none here; this is a mock." M. Dyer looked about and said, "I know but few here."

Then they spake to her again, that one of the Elders might pray for her. She replied and said, "Nay, first a child, then a young man, then a strong man, before an Elder of Christ Jesus." Some charged her with something that was not understood what it was. But her answer was, "It's false; it's false; I never spoke the words."

Then one said she should say she had been in Paradise. And she answered, "Yea, I have been in Paradise several days." And more she spake of her eternal happiness, that's out of mind. And so sweetly and cheerfully in the Lord she finished her testimony and died a faithful martyr of Jesus Christ.

And still they are going on in acting their cruel laws: for the same day, in the former part of it, they sent for Joseph Nicholson and his wife Jane Nicholson, and banished them on pain of death. Then sent for three more, and whilst they were examining them, there came one to the Court spake to this purpose, and one scoffingly said "she did hang as a flag for them to take example by." (But precious in the sight of the Lord is the death of his saints). . . . These are the people that say their churches are the purest churches in the world, and that their magistrates are godly magistrates, and godly ministers. A fair show to the world! Even "another Beast coming up out of the earth; and he had two horns, like a lamb, and he spake as a dragon; and he exerciseth the power of the first Beast before him." [Rev. 13:11–12] . . .

Governor John Endecott Defends Religious Practice in Massachusetts, 1660

To the High and Mighty Prince, Charles the Second, by the Grace of God, King of Great Britain, France, and Ireland, Defender of the Faith, &c.

Most Gracious and Dread Sovereign,

. . . This, viz. our liberty to walk in the faith of the Gospel with all good conscience, according to the order of the Gospel, (unto which the former, in these ends of the earth, is but subservient,) was the cause of our transporting ourselves with our wives, our little ones, and our substance, from that pleasant land over the Atlantic Ocean into the vast [and waste] wilderness, choosing rather the pure Scripture worship, with a good conscience, in this [poor] remote wilderness amongst the heathen, than the pleasures of England, with submission to the impositions of the then so disposed and so far prevailing hierarchy, which we could not do without an evil conscience. For this cause we are [at] this day in a land which lately was not sown, wherein we have conflicted with the sufferings thereof, much longer than Jacob was in Syria. Our witness is in Heaven, that we left not our native country upon any dissatisfaction as to the constitution of the civil state. Our lot, after the example of the good old Nonconformists, hath been, only to act a passive part throughout these late vicissitudes and successive overturnings of States. . . .

Touching complaints put in against us, our humble request only is, that for the interim while we are as dumb, by reason of our absence, your Majesty would permit nothing to make an impression on your Royal Heart against us, until we have both opportunity and leave to answer for ourselves. . . .

Concerning the Quakers, open and capital blasphemers, open seducers from the glorious Trinity, the Lord Jesus Christ, our Lord Jesus Christ, the blessed Gospel, and from the holy Scriptures as the rule of life, open enemies to the government itself, as established in the hands of any but men of their own principles, malignant and assiduous promoters of doctrines directly tending to subvert both our Church and State, after all other means for a long time used in vain, we were at last constrained, for our own safety, to pass a sentence of banishment against them, upon pain of death. Such was their dangerous, and impetuous, and desperate turbulence, both to religion and [the] State, civil and ecclesiastical, as that, how unwillingly soever, (could it have been avoided,) the magistrate at last, in conscience both to God and man, judged himself called, for the defence of all, to keep the passage with the point of the sword held towards them. This could do no harm to him that would be warned thereby; their wittingly rushing themselves thereupon was their own act, [and] we with all humility conceive a crime, bringing their blood on their own head. The Quakers died not because of their other crimes, how capital soever, but upon their superadded presumptuous and incorrigible contempt of authority, breaking in upon us, notwithstanding their sentence of banishment made known to them. Had they not been restrained, so far as appeared, there was too much cause to fear that we ourselves must quickly have died, or worse; and such was their insolency, that they would not be restrained but by death; nay, had they at last but promised to depart the jurisdiction, and not to return without leave from authority, we should have been glad of such an opportunity to have said they should not die. . . .

. . . We are not seditious as to the interest of Caesar, nor schismatics as to the matters of religion. We distinguish between churches and their impurity, between a living man, though not without sickness or infirmity, and no man; irregularities, either in ourselves or others, we desire to be amended. We could not live without the public worship of God, nor [were we] permitted the [use of] public worship without such a yoke of subscription and conformities [as] we could not consent unto without sin. That we might therefore enjoy divine worship without [the] human mixtures, without offence [either] to God, man,

[or] our own consciences, we with leave, but not without tears, departed from our country, kindred, and fathers' houses, into this Pathmos; in relation whereunto we do not say our garments are become old by reason of the very long journey, but that ourselves, who came away in our strength, are by reason of [very] long absence many of us become grey-headed, and some of us stooping for age. The omission of the prementioned injunctions, together with the walking of our churches, as to the point of order, [in] the Congregational Way, is it wherein we desire our orthodox brethren would bear with us. . . .

John Josselyn Criticizes the Treatment of Dissenters, 1675

. . . Every Town sends two Burgesses to their great and solemn general Court.

For being drunk, they either whip or impose a fine of Five shillings; so for swearing and cursing, or boring through the tongue with a hot Iron.

For kissing a woman in the street, though in way of civil salute, whipping or a fine.

For Single fornication whipping or a fine.

For Adultery, put to death, and so for Witchcraft.

An *English* woman suffering an *Indian* to have carnal knowledge of her, had an *Indian* cut out exactly in red cloth sewed upon her right Arm, and injoyned to wear it twelve moneths.

Scolds they gag and set them at their doors for certain hours, for all comers and goers by to gaze at.

Stealing is punished with restoring four fould, if able; if not, they are sold for some years, and so are poor debtors.

If you desire a further inspection to their Laws, I must refer you to them being in print, too many for to be inserted into this Relation.

The Governments of their Churches are Independent and Presbyterial, every Church (for so they call their particular Congregations) have one Pastor, one Teacher, Ruling Elders and Deacons.

They that are members of their Churches have the Sacraments administered to them, the rest that are out of the pale as they phrase it, are denied it. Many hundred Souls there be amongst them grown up to men & womens estate that were never Christened.

They judge every man and woman to pay Five shillings *per* day, who comes not to their Assemblies, and impose fines of forty shillings and fifty shillings on such as meet together to worship God.

Quakers they whip, banish, and hang if they return again.

Anabaptists they imprison, fine and weary out.

The Government both Civil and Ecclesiastical is in the hands of the thorow-pac'd Independents and rigid Presbyterians. . . .

Increase Mather on Proofs of Witchcraft, 1684

Inasmuch as things which are preternatural, and not accomplished without diabolical operation, do more rarely happen, it is pity but that they should be observed. Several accidents of that kind have hapned in New England, which

I shall here faithfully relate, so far as I have been able to come unto the knowledge of them.

Very remarkable was that Providence wherein Ann Cole of Hartford in New England was concerned. She was, and is accounted, a person of real piety and integrity; nevertheless, in the year 1662, then living in her fathers house (who has likewise been esteemed a godly man), she was taken with very strange fits, wherein her tongue was improved by a dæmon to express things which she herself knew nothing of; sometimes the discourse would hold for a considerable time; the general purpose of which was, that such and such persons (who were named in the discourse which passed from her) were consulting how they might carry on mischievous designs against her and several others, mentioning sundry wayes they should take for that end, particularly that they would afflict her body, spoil her name, &c. The general answer made amongst the dæmons was, "She runs to the rock." This having continued some hours, the dæmons said, "Let us confound her language, that she may tell no more tales." She uttered matters unintelligible. And then the discourse passed into a Dutch tone (a Dutch family then lived in the town), and therein an account was given of some afflictions that had befallen divers; amongst others, what had befallen a woman that lived next neighbour to the Dutch family, whose arms had been strangely pinched in the night, declaring by whom and for what cause that course had been taken with her. The Reverend Mr. Stone (then teacher of the church in Hartford) being by, when the discourse hapned, declared, that he thought it impossible for one not familiarly acquainted with the Dutch (which Ann Cole had not in the least been) should so exactly imitate the Dutch tone in the pronunciation of English. Several worthy persons (viz., Mr. John Whiting, Mr. Samuel Hooker, and Mr. Joseph Hains) wrote the intelligible sayings expressed by Ann Cole, whilest she was thus amazingly handled. The event was, that one of the persons (whose name was Greensmith, being a lewd and ignorant woman, and then in prison on suspicion for witchcraft) mentioned in the discourse as active in the mischief done and designed, was by the magistrate sent for; Mr. Whiting and Mr. Haines read what they had written, and the woman being astonished thereat, confessed those things to be true, and that she and other persons named in this preternatural discourse, had had familiarity with the devil. Being asked whether she had made an express covenant with him, she answered, she had not, only as she promised to go with him when he called, which accordingly she had sundry times done, and that the devil told her that at Christmass they would have a merry meeting, and then the covenant between them should be subscribed. The next day she was more particularly enquired of concerning her guilt respecting the crime she was accused with. She then acknowledged, that though when Mr. Haines began to read what he had taken down in writing, her rage was such that she could have torn him in pieces, and was as resolved as might be to deny her guilt (as she had done before), yet after he had read awhile, she was (to use her own expression) as if her flesh had been pulled from her bones, and so could not deny any longer: she likewise declared, that the devil first appeared to her in the form of a deer or fawn, skipping about her, wherewith she was not much affrighted, and that by degrees he became very familiar, and at last would talk with her; moreover, she said that the devil had frequently the carnal knowledge of her body; and that the witches had meetings at a place not far from her house; and that some appeared in one shape, and others in another; and one came flying amongst them in the shape of a crow. Upon this confession, with other concurrent evidence, the woman was executed; so likewise was her husband, though he did not acknowledge himself guilty. Other persons accused in the discourse made their escape. Thus doth the devil use to serve his clients. After the suspected witches were either executed or fled, Ann Cole was restored to health, and has continued well for many years, approving herself a serious Christian.

There were some that had a mind to try whether the stories of witches not being able to sink under water were true; and accordingly a man and woman, mentioned in Ann Cole's Dutch-toned discourse, had their hands and feet tyed, and so were cast into the water, and they both apparently swam after the manner of a buoy, part under, part above the water. A by-stander, imagining that any person bound in that posture would be so born up, offered himself for trial; but being in the like matter gently laid on the water, he immediately sunk right down. This was no legal evidence against the suspected persons, nor were they proceeded against on any such account; however, doubting that an halter would choak them, though the waters would not, they very fairly took their flight, not having been seen in that part of the world since. Whether this experiment were lawful, or rather superstitious and magical, we shall enquire afterwards.

Another thing which caused a noise in the countrey, and wherein Satan had undoubtedly a great influence, was that which hapned at Groton. There was a maid in that town (one Elizabeth Knap) who in the moneth of October, anno 1671, was taken after a very strange manner, sometimes weeping, sometimes laughing, sometimes roaring hideously, with violent motions and agitations of her body, crying out "Money, money," &c. In November following, her tongue for many hours together was drawn like a semicircle up to the roof of her mouth, not to be removed, though some tried with their fingers to do it. Six men were scarce able to hold her in some of her fits, but she would skip about the house yelling and looking with a most frightful aspect. December 17: Her tongue was drawn out of her mouth to an extraordinary length; and now a dæmon began manifestly to speak in her. Many words were uttered wherein are the labial letters, without any motion of her lips, which was a clear demonstration that the voice was not her own. Sometimes words were spoken seeming to proceed out of her throat, when her mouth was shut; sometimes with her mouth wide open, without the use of any of the organs of speech. The things then uttered by the devil were chiefly railings and revilings of Mr. Willard (who was at that time a worthy and faithful pastor to the church in Groton). Also the dæmon belched forth most horrid and nefandous blasphemies, exalting himself above the Most High. After this she was taken speechless for some time. One thing more is worthy of remark concerning this miserable creature. She cried out in some of her fits, that a woman (one of her neighbours) appeared to her, and was the cause of her affliction. The person thus accused was a very sincere, holy woman, who did hereupon, with the advice of friends, visit the poor wretch; and though she was in one of her fits, having her eyes shut, when the innocent person impeached by her came in, yet could she (so powerful were Satans operations upon her) declare who was there, and could tell the touch of that woman from any ones else. But the gracious party, thus accused and abused by a malicious devil, prayed earnestly with and for the possessed creature; after which she confessed that Satan had deluded her, making her believe evil of her good neighbour without any cause. Nor did she after that complain of any apparition or disturbance from such an one. Yea, she said, that the devil had himself, in the likeness and shape of divers, tormented her, and then told her it was not he but they that did it. . . .

Testimony and Examination on Rebecca Nurse of Salem, 1692

Testimony of Ann Putnam, Junior

The deposition of Ann Putnam, junior, who testifieth and saith that on the 13th March, 1691/92, I saw the apparition of Goody Nurse, and she did immediately afflict me, but I did not know what her name was then, though I knew where she used to sit in our meetinghouse. But since that, she hath grievously afflicted by biting, pinching, and pricking me, [and] urging me to write in her book. And, also, on the 24th of March, being the day of her examination, I was grievously tortured by her during the time for her examination, and also several times since. And, also, during the time of her examination, I saw the apparition of Rebekah Nurs go and hurt the bodies of Mercy Lewis, Mary Wolcott, Elizabeth Hubbard, and Abigail Williams.

Ann Putnam, Junr, did own the oath which she hath taken: this her evidence to be truth, before us, the Jurors for Inquest, this 4 day of June, 1692.

Testimony of Ann Putnam, Senior, and Ann Putnam, Junior

The deposition of Ann Putnam, the wife of Thomas Putnam, aged about 30 years, who testifieth and saith that on the 18th March 1692, I being wearied out in helping to tend my poor afflicted child and maid, about the middle of the afternoon I lay me down on the bed to take a little rest; and immediately I was almost pressed and choked to death, that, had it not been for the mercy of a gracious God and the help of those that were with me, I could not have lived many moments; and presently I saw the apparition of Martha Corey, who did torture me so as I cannot express, ready to tear me all to pieces,

---

"Testimony of Ann Putnam, Senior and Ann Putnam, Junior Against Rebecca Nurse, May 31, 1692;" "Testimony of Israel and Elizabeth Porter, Daniel Andrew, and Peter Cloyse;" and "Examination of Rebecca Nurse," in Paul Boyer and Stephen Nissenbaum, eds., *Salem-Village Witchcraft: A Documentary Record of Local Conflict in Colonial New England* (Belmont, California: Wadsworth, 1972), 18–19, 21–22, 23–25. Reprinted by permission of Stephen Nissenbaum.

and then departed from me a little while; but before I could recover strength or well take breath, the apparition of Martha Corey fell upon me again with dreadful tortures, and hellish temptations to go along with her. And she also brought to me a little red book in her hand and a black pen, urging me vehemently to write in her book; and several times that day she did grievously torture me, almost ready to kill me.

And on the 19th March, Martha Corey again appeared to me; and also Rebecca Nurse, the wife of Francis Nurse, Sr.; and they both did torture me a great many times this day with such tortures as no tongue can express, because I would not yield to their hellish temptations, that, had I not been upheld by an Almighty arm, I could not have lived [the] night. The 20th March being sabbath-day, I had a great deal of respite between my fits. 21st March being the day of the examination of Martha Corey I had not many fits, though I was very weak, my strength being, as I thought, almost gone.

But on the 22nd March, 1692, the apparition of Rebecca Nurse did again set upon me in a most dreadful manner, very early in the morning, as soon as it was well light. And now she appeared to me only in her shift, and brought a little red book in her hand, urging me vehemently to write in her book; and because I would not yield to her hellish temptations, she threatened to tear my soul out of my body, blasphemously denying the blessed God and the power of the Lord Jesus Christ to save my soul, and denying several places of Scripture which I told her of, to repel her hellish temptations. And for near two hours together, at this time, the apparition of Rebecca Nurse did tempt and torture me, and also the greater part of this day with but very little respite. 23d March, am again afflicted by the apparitions of Rebecca Nurse and Martha Corey, but chiefly by Rebecca Nurse. 24th March being the day of the examination of Rebecca Nurse, I was several times in the morning afflicted by the apparition of Rebecca Nurse, but most dreadfully tortured by her in the time of her examination, insomuch that the honored magistrates gave my husband leave to carry me out of the meetinghouse; and as soon as I was carried out of the meetinghouse doors, it pleased Almighty God, for his free grace and mercy's sake, to deliver me out of the paws of those roaring lions, and jaws of those tearing bears [so] that ever since that time they have not had power so to afflict me, until this 31st May 1692. At the same moment that I was hearing my evidence read by the honored magistrates, to take my oath, I was again re-assaulted and tortured by my before-mentioned tormentor, Rebecca Nurse.

> Sworn Salem Villiage, May the 31st, 1692
> Before us   John Hathorne ⎫
>   Jonathan Corwin ⎭ Assistants

Ann Putnam, Senior, appeared before us, the Jurors of Inquest, and owned this her evidence this 3rd day of June, 1692.

The testimony of Ann Putnam, Jr., witnesseth and saith that being in the room when her mother was afflicted, she saw Martha Corey, Sarah Cloyse and Rebecca Nurse, or their apparition, upon her mother.

Testified to the truth thereof by
Ann Putnam, Salem, May 31st, 1692
Before us   John Hathorne   } Assistants
            Jonathan Corwin

Testimony of Israel and Elizabeth Porter, Daniel Andrew, and Peter Cloyse

We whose names are underwritten, being desired to go to Goodman Nurse's house to speak with his wife and to tell her that several of the afflicted persons mentioned her; and accordingly we went, and we found her in a weak and low condition in body as she told us, and had been sick almost a week.

And we asked her how it was, otherwise, with her. And she said she blessed God for it, she had more of his presence in this sickness than sometime she have had, but not so much as she desired. But she would, with the apostle, press forward to the mark, and many other places of Scripture to the like purpose.

And then, of her own accord, she began to speak of the affliction that was amongst them, and in particular of Mr. Parris's family, and how she was grieved for them, though she had not been to see them by reason of fits that she formerly used to have, for people said it was awful to behold. But she pitied them with all her heart, and went to God for them. But she said she heard that there was persons spoke of that were as innocent as she was, she believed.

And after much to this purpose, we told her we heard that she was spoken of also. Well, she said, if it be so, the will of the Lord be done. She sat still a while, being as it were amazed, and then she said, Well, as to this thing, I am as innocent as the child unborn. But surely, she said, what sin hath God found out in me unrepented of, that he should lay such an affliction upon me in my old age? And, according to our best observation, we could not discern that she knew what we come for before we told her.

Israel Porter
Elizabeth Porter

To the substance of what is above we, if called thereto, are ready to testify on oath.

Daniel Andrew
Peter Cloyse

Examination of Rebecca Nurse

The examination of Rebeckah Nurse at Salen Village, 24 Mar., 1691/92.

Mr. Harthorn. What do you say (speaking to one afflicted), have you seen this woman hurt you?

Yes, she beat me this morning.

Abigail, have you been hurt by this woman?

Yes.

Ann Putnam, in a grievous fit, cried out that she hurt her.

Goody Nurse, here are two—Ann Putnam the child and Abigail Williams—complains of your hurting them. What do you say to it?

N. I can say before my Eternal Father, I am innocent, and God will clear my innocency.

Here is never a one in the assembly but desires it. But if you be guilty, pray God discover you.

Then Hen: Kenney rose up to speak.

Goodman Kenney, what do you say?

Then he entered his complaint and farther said that since this Nurse came into the house he was seized twice with an amazed condition.

Here are not only these, but here is the wife of Mr. Tho Putnam who accuseth you by creditable information, and that both of tempting her to iniquity and of greatly hurting her.

N. I am innocent and clear, and have not been able to get out of doors these 8 or 9 days.

Mr. Putman, give in what you have to say.

Then Mr. Edward Putnam gave in his relate.

Is this true, Goody Nurse?

I never afflicted no child, never in my life.

You see these accuse you. Is it true?

No.

Are you an innocent person, relating to this witchcraft?

Here Tho: Putnam's wife cried out: Did you not bring the Black man with you? Did you not bid me tempt God and die? How oft have you eat and drunk your own damnation? What do you say to them?

Oh Lord, help me, and spread out her hands, and the afflicted were grievously vexed.

Do you see what a solemn condition these are in? When your hands are loose, the persons are afflicted.

Then Mary Walcott (who often heretofore said she had seen her, but never could say, or did say, that she either bit or pinched her, or hurt her) and also Elis. Hubbard, under the like circumstances, both openly accused her of hurting them.

Here are these 2 grown persons now accuse you. What say you? Do not you see these afflicted persons, and hear them accuse you?

The Lord knows. I have not hurt them. I am an innocent person.

It is very awful for all to see these agonies, and you, an old professor, thus charged with contracting with the devil by the effects of it, and yet to see you stand with dry eyes when there are so many wet.

You do not know my heart.

You would do well, if you are guilty, to confess. Give Glory to God.

I am as clear as the child unborn.

What uncertainty there may be in apparitions I know not, yet this with me strikes hard upon you, that you are, at this very present, charged with familiar spirits. This is your bodily person they speak to. They say now they see these familiar spirits come to your bodily person. Now what do you say to that?

I have none, sir.

If you have confessed, and give Glory to God, I pray God clear you, if you be innocent. And if you be guilty, discover you. And therefore give me an upright answer: have you any familiarity with these spirits?

No. I have none but with God alone.

How came you sick, for there is an odd discourse of that in the mouths of many.

I am sick at my stomach.

Have you no wounds?

I have not but old age.

You do know whether you are guilty, and have familiarity with the devil, and now when you are here present, to see such a thing as these testify: a black man whispering in your ear and birds about you. What do you say to it?

It is all false. I am clear.

Possibly you may apprehend you are no witch, but have you not been led aside by temptations that way?

I have not.

What a sad thing it is that a church member here, and now another of Salem, should be thus accused and charged.

Mrs. Pope fell into a grievous fit and cried out: a sad thing sure enough. And then many more fell into lamentable fits.

Tell us, have you had visible appearances more than what is common in nature?

I have none, nor never had in my life.

Do you think these suffer voluntary or involuntary?

I cannot tell.

That is strange: everyone can judge.

I must be silent.

They accuse you of hurting them, and if you think it is not unwilling but by design, you must look upon them as murderers.

I cannot tell what to think of it. Afterwards, when this was somewhat insisted on, she said: I do not think so. She did not understand aright what was said.

Well then, give an answer now, do you think these suffer against their wills or not?

I do not think these suffer against their wills.

Why did you never visit these afflicted persons?

Because I was afraid I should have fits, too.

Note: Upon the motion of her body, fits followed upon the complainants, abundantly and very frequently.

Is it not an unaccountable case that when you are examined these persons are afflicted?

I have got nobody to look to but God.

Again, upon stirring her hands, the afflicted persons were seized with violent fits of torture.

Do you believe these afflicted persons are bewitched?

I do think they are.

When this witchcraft came upon the stage, there was no suspicion of Tituba (Mr. Parris's Indian woman). She professed much love to that child, Betty Parris. But it was her apparition did the mischief, and why should not you also be guilty, for your apparition doth hurt also?

Would you have me belie myself?

She held her neck on one side, and accordingly so were the afflicted taken.

Then, authority requiring it, Sam: Parris read what he had in characters taken from Mr. Tho: Putman's wife in her fits.

What do you think of this?

I cannot help it, the Devil may appear in my shape.

This is a true account of the sum of her examination, but by reason of great noise, by the afflicted and many speakers, many things are pretermitted.

Memorandum

Nurse held her neck on one side and Eliz. Hubbard (one of the sufferers) had her neck set in that posture. Whereupon another patient, Abigail Williams, cried out: Set up Goody Nurse's head, the maid's neck will be broke. And when some set up Nurse's head, Aaron Wey observed that Betty Hubbard's was immediately righted. . . .

✑ E S S A Y S

In the first essay Carla Gardina Pestana, a historian at Ohio State University, takes up the question of why the Quakers, whom we are accustomed to see as tolerant pacifists, posed such a threat to the Massachusetts Bay authorities. She makes clear how dramatically early Quakerism differed from the form it took even a few decades later, after the Quakers' persecution in England, and argues that the original form was indeed menacing. Quakerism also was threatening in part because, viewed by some as the logical extension of Puritan doctrine, it therefore attracted many earnest seekers after truth. Therein lay the greatest danger.

As historian John Putnam Demos of Yale University demonstrates in the second essay, witchcraft beliefs also grew directly out of the Puritans' highly religious worldview; all events demonstrated God's will. God granted the devil some powers in order to test and chastise his people. Witchcraft beliefs allowed early modern men and women to explain mysterious occurrences and to understand and account for evil and disorder. Outbreaks called for the godly to redouble their efforts to search their own hearts and police their society, opening the way to true religious peace.

Quakerism in Massachusetts:
Threat and Response

CARLA GARDINA PESTANA

Shortly after sailing into Boston harbor aboard the ship *Swallow* in July 1656, Anne Austin and Mary Fisher found themselves in jail. The two Englishwomen had been stripped and searched for "witches teats," evidence that they suckled a demonic familiar. Recalling the ordeal later, Austin said that "she had not suffered so much in the birth of them all [her five children] as she had done under their barbarous and cruel hands." The women who had examined the matronly Austin and her companion, a former serving woman, had been thorough. Finding no strange marks or appendages between the toes or in the hair of the two women, the examiners left them alone in their cell. Having refused to work for their food, Fisher and Austin were hungry. The cell was dark, for the windows had been boarded up to prevent them from speaking to any passers-by, and their candles, along with most of their other things, had been confiscated. Over one hundred books and pamphlets found in a trunk belonging to the two women had been burned by the public executioner that day.

The authorities in Boston, having forced the shipmaster who brought the two women from Barbados to agree to take them away again at his own expense, could feel satisfied that they had done everything in their power to contain this menace to public well-being. Some were concerned because Nicholas Upshall, an elderly tavern keeper, had tried to bribe the jailer to feed the two women, but Upshall had been fined and surely saw the sinfulness of his actions. For these women were Quakers, members of that "cursed sect of heretics lately risen up in the world," and the godly magistrates of Massachusetts Bay could hardly imagine a more serious threat to their holy commonwealth than that represented by Austin and Fisher. It took the *Swallow* eight weeks to prepare to leave Boston, and just as Austin and Fisher sailed out of the harbor, eight more of the same sect arrived. The Quaker "invasion" of Massachusetts was under way.

From these tense beginnings, the conflict escalated rapidly. The unorganized but tenacious Quakers filtered into the Bay Colony to witness against Congregationalist New England. After shipmasters learned of the fate awaiting

Carla Gardina Pestana, "The City upon a Hill under Siege: The Puritan Perception of the Quaker Threat to Massachusetts Bay, 1656–1661," *New England Quarterly*, LVI (1983) 323–353. Reprinted by permission of the author.

them if they transported the sectaries to Massachusetts, the witnesses were forced to find other ways to carry their message to the colony. First, English Quaker Robert Fowler was called to build the small ship *Woodhouse,* which miraculously transported eleven Quakers across the Atlantic. Soon the missionaries were traveling overland from Rhode Island and even Virginia to preach the truth to the Puritans of New England. In the five-year period from 1656 to 1661, at least forty Quakers from England, Rhode Island, and Barbados came to witness against the New England Way. Some avoided Boston and certain imprisonment to roam around the countryside preaching; others marched straight into "the most vainest and beastliest place of all bruits" to challenge the authorities and their laws.

The Puritan reaction was no less energetic. With the arrival of the second group of Quakers, the General Court passed the first in a series of laws dealing with the invaders, and for five years the first order of business handled by each session of that body often involved the sect. After whippings, fines, imprisonments, expulsions, and mutilations failed to deter the foreign Quakers or their Massachusetts converts, the General Court resorted to banishment on pain of death to rid their colony of the fanatics. By 1661 two Englishmen, one woman from Rhode Island, and a man from Barbados had been hanged, and Boston jail was full of Quakers. Barring one Vatican-ordered Quaker execution during this period, the Massachusetts Bay authorities would stand alone as the only governing elite that found it necessary to condemn Quaker missionaries to death. Even lacking that distinction, the Puritans of the Bay Colony were known for the intensity of their reaction. Whippings were extremely severe, banishments were often ordered in the dead of the Massachusetts winter, and imprisoned Quakers were in immediate danger of starving or freezing to death. The conflict gradually tapered off after the restored Charles II admonished the colony for mistreating his subjects, and thereafter the Puritans were reduced to whipping the Quaker "vagabonds" to the borders of the colony.

Both the Puritans and the Quakers published their versions of the confrontation, and the bias of each was reflected in the historiography of the next two and one-half centuries. First, in 1659, the General Court commissioned John Norton, pastor of Boston's First Church, to write *The Heart of New England Rent* to explain its actions. In response, George Bishop collected reports brought back to England by itinerate Quakers and published them in 1661 in his invaluable *New England Judged.* Through the nineteenth century, histories of the confrontation relied heavily upon (and were almost as partisan as) these first two accounts. Quakers were presented as martyrs or lunatics, Puritans as sadists and hypocrites or righteous protectors of the common good. With the establishment of a successful and godly Quaker colony in the New World in the late seventeenth century and the growing popularity of the myth that North America was colonized as a haven for religious liberty, the Puritans' apologists have become increasingly sheepish. . . .

The reaction of the Puritan leaders to the Quakers can be fully understood only by closely examining the threat that the invaders represented to the Puritans' city upon a hill. Historians have failed to take into account the anarchistic nature of early Quakerism or the overriding concern that the Puritan elite had for order. . . .   By the end of the seventeenth century, the Society of Friends was working to minimize the radicalism of the early Quakers in order to weather the intolerance of the restored Stuarts. Subsequently most historians, regardless of their stance on the controversy in New England, have projected the characteristics of the later Society of Friends onto the early Quakers. If one assumes that the traveling witnesses were pacifistic, respectable, well educated, and contemplative, the reaction of the Massachusetts Bay leaders becomes inexplicable. In fact, the early Quaker movement was unorganized, enthusiastic, and millennial; it lacked definite leadership, a well-articulated theology, and even a name. The people who were "in scorn called Quakers" would eventually unite behind the charismatic George Fox, give up hope for the imminent end of the world, and withdraw into the disciplined, respectable, and well-organized Society of Friends. . . .

. . . The Puritan reaction to the Quakers drew on a series of associations between the sectaries and deep-seated fears that historically lay at the heart of Puritanism. In order to understand the initial confrontation between English Quakerism and New England Puritanism, these fears and associations should be examined in the context of early American culture. Not only this conflict but New England society can be better understood as a result.

Even before Austin and Fisher arrived in Boston, the colonial elite was aware of the hazards posed by these "wicked and dangerous seducers." In 1656 Quakerism was the largest and fastest growing radical sect in England. A flood of anti-Quaker pamphlets had been published, including one by a leading resident of the Bay Colony. The tracts, which described the Quaker heresy in detail, left little doubt that these lunatics were agents of the devil. . . . Well before the onslaught of the Quaker witnesses, the Puritan leaders knew that this sect represented a serious threat to everything they had labored so long so achieve.

The Quakers did nothing to quell these fears; instead, they launched an attack on Puritan religion in their efforts to bring the truth of the inner light to all humanity. There was no more potent symbol of the Quaker attack on established religion than their practice of interrupting meetings to harangue the minister and witness against the proceedings. A Puritan congregation came together three times a week to worship, in the morning and afternoon on Sunday and for a mid-week lecture. In Massachusetts the gatherings ideally included the entire community, although only the visible saints participated in the Lord's Supper and were considered full members. Once gathered, the congregation sat in rigidly defined ranks, according to their place in the spiritual and social hierarchy. For hours they would listen to a sermon, a highly logical unfolding of the meaning and application of a particular scriptural passage.

The Quakers found these services a likely arena in which to publish the truth. Usually one or more witnesses would enter a meetinghouse during the service and stand shouting at the minister that he was a hireling, a priest, or even one of Baal's priests. In the Salem meeting in 1657, Christopher Holder had a handkerchief and a glove stuffed in his mouth and was dragged out by the hair at this point. Had he been allowed to continue, he would undoubtedly have turned his attention to the congregation and warned them of the retribution awaiting them if they persisted in this false worship. Boston meeting, another favorite target, was interrupted repeatedly for two decades. Bottles were broken on the floor of the Boston meetinghouse in 1658 to illustrate the fate in store for the congregation. Quakers in New England did not adopt the more dramatic forms of witnessing, common in England by 1656, until after the most severe period of persecution had ended in 1661. On occasion, for two decades thereafter, meetings were disrupted by women who were either naked or clad in sackcloth and smeared with ashes. The former practice, referred to as "going naked for a sign," was meant to symbolize the spiritual nakedness of the unconvinced. In whatever form they took, Quaker disturbances of church services grew out of their belief that the inner light was the ultimate guide for human behavior. Their faith was universalistic and highly emotional, the direct converse of the Puritan's elitism and rationalism.

By denying the utter sinfulness of man and elevating themselves to the level of their spiritual betters, Quakers revealed that they suffered from the sin of pride. As Richard Mather reminded his flock in the midst of the controversy, "the pith and power of religion and godliness is . . . a true sight of man's own sin and vileness." When Thomas Parker, minister of the church of Newbury, wrote to his sister, Elizabeth Parker Avery, who was still in England and a recent convert to Quakerism, he returned repeatedly to the subject of her pride. She "seemed to be lifted up as if . . . a goddess," and Parker prayed for her "Seasonable Reduction." Quaker men sometimes wore their hair long; even if they were not doing so in imitation of Christ, as was rumored, long hair was considered a sign of pride. The most startling and obnoxious example of the spiritual pride of the heretics was their pretense to unique knowledge of God. For example, magistrates on the General Court were enraged by the reports that Cassandra Southwick, an elderly Massachusetts Quaker, claimed that she was "greater than Moses, for Moses had seen God but twice and his back side only, and she had seen him three times and face and face."

The fact that uneducated Quakers preached or wrote about complicated theological matters was another indication of their proud spirit. Francis Higginson, pastor to Kerby-Stevens in England, former Massachusetts resident, and son and brother to two of Salem's ministers, recorded one of the first Puritan reactions to Quaker witnessing:

> His beginning is without a text, abrupt and sudden to his hearers, his voice for the most part low, his sentences incoherent, hanging together like ropes of sand, very frequently full of impiety and horrid errors, and sometimes full of sudden pauses, his whole speech a mixed bundle of words and heap of nonsense.

The Quaker Higginson described was not well versed in the proper form and content of a godly sermon, and the university-educated Puritan was shocked that such a speaker commanded the respect of his peers. Elizabeth Avery's brother was equally shocked that she had published a book presenting her interpretations of Scriptures in a manner "beyond your gifts and sex." Later in the century, Roger Williams attacked the Quakers', and particularly George Fox's, intellectual pretensions. Williams, ridiculing Fox's grammar, pointed out that he confounded the singular and the plural. Regarding Fox's attempts to debate with Puritan divines, Williams wrote:

> I observe the loose and wild spirit of George Fox in dealing with so many heavenly champions, the leaps and skips like a wild satyre or Indian, catching and snapping at here and there a sentence, like children skipping ore hard places and chapters, picking and culling out what is common and easy.

. . . The Quaker challenge of the learned minister was also interpreted as an attack on all education. Many Puritans were convinced that Quakerism, that "chokeweed of Christianity," denied the Scriptures. For the Puritan, education was inexorably tied to religion, "it being one chief project of that old deluder, Satan, to keep men from the knowledge of the Scriptures." The great achievement of the Protestant Reformation had been to bring God's word to every Christian; the vernacular Bible, the plain style of preaching, and education were all part of a campaign to make religion accessible to everyone. . . .

The fear that Quakers sought to discredit education and the Scriptures led to rumors that the sect burned Bibles. Actually Quakers did believe that the Bible was the word of God; however, they also felt that the spirit that had guided its authors was at work again in the world as the inner light. Far from reassuring the Puritans, this argument was seen as a satanic trap that prevented the Quakers from being persuaded by the real truth. When Quakers cited the Bible to challenge the Puritans' intolerance, their practice was seen as perfectly in keeping with Satan's use of Scripture to deceive men. Sometimes Puritans maintained that the Quakers were sent by God to test the faithful; at other times, they were thought to be a punishment. In either case, the scriptural arguments presented by the "vile seducers" were to be ignored.

Without the Bible as their guide, the sect was likely to follow the inner light straight into anarchy. Some Quaker leaders recognized that this was a very real danger and institutionalized a series of curbs on the individual sectary's behavior. In 1656, however, the Quakers followed the promptings of the inner light without hesitation. In fact, they argued that a woman who was moved to go naked for a sign knew that this message was from the Lord if she was repelled by the thought. The Puritans were uncomfortably aware of what might result from such logic. A Quaker so guided could commit the most heinous of crimes and demand toleration, compliance, even cooperation from the unconvinced. The potential for anarchy in the doctrine of the inner light was not lost on leading Bay residents, who believed that God no longer spoke directly to his people. . . .

This fact, coupled with the Quaker attacks on the ministry, education, and the Bible, led the Puritans to the conclusion that the sectaries were the agents of the devil. . . . In the 1650s, the miracles the Quakers claimed to perform were considered to be either fraudulent or accomplished with the assistance of Satan.

The Quakers' tendency to quake when they received a message from the inner light was taken to be an indication that they were possessed. Roger Williams was appalled at the general disorder of a Quaker meeting and compared the quaking he had observed there to that of the Indians. Others, making the same comparison, often noted that both used fasting to induce demonic visitations. . . . To the Puritans, correspondences between the Quakers and the Indians were frightening but not really surprising; in a world divided between good and evil, the devil's emissaries would naturally have much in common, whether they were barbarous savages or heretical Englishmen. . . .

. . . Puritan divines meticulously described the sinful tradition out of which Quakerism had sprung. Delineating the heretical genealogy of the sect illustrated clearly just how threatening Quakerism was. . . .

Quakers were by far most frequently compared to the Anabaptists of Munster. The dangers of heresy were symbolized for many in the story of the sectaries who took control of the city of Munster for over a year in the 1530s; they declared free love, an end to private property, and death to all nonbelievers. All the heretics listed by Norton in *The Heart of New England Rent* shared a belief in direct revelation, a denial of Scriptures, and a propensity for lascivious behavior and communal ownership of property. Norton argued that the similarities between these heresies and Quakerism were a warning from God, for "reason teaches us . . . to expect the same fruits from the same principles." As far as he was concerned, these "dogmatick rogues" could be condemned to die strictly on the basis of the correspondence of their beliefs to those of John of Leyden, "king" of the Anabaptists of Munster.

For any orthodox Puritan not ready to condemn the Quakers on "genealogical" evidence alone, the welcome the sectaries received from all sorts of radicals and heretics offered further proof of the social dangers inherent in their evil nature. . . . Banished heretics and troublemakers living on the borders of the Bay Colony also received the Quakers enthusiastically. Rhode Island, "that cesspool of New England," refused to comply with the efforts of the United Colonies to keep New England free from Quakers, and many residents of the colony were subsequently convinced. . . . Certainly there was plenty of contemporary evidence linking Quakerism with fanaticism, radicalism, and heresy to confirm the Puritans' fears.

The colonial elite who contemplated the Quaker attack on the Congregational churches of New England were almost overwhelmed by its implications. Without a learned ministry or education, Christians would not be able to understand God's will as revealed in the Bible. They would, instead, follow their own sinful inclinations regardless of where these led. Such beliefs, aimed as they were at destroying the only spiritual guidelines God had given his people, were obviously inspired by the devil. In becoming a Quaker, a person succumbed to his pride and depravity and joined the ranks of pagans, papists, witches, and other heretics in the service of Satan. As the devil's retainer, a Quaker could be expected to fight against all that was godly in the world.

As John Norton pointed out in 1659 in his anti-Quaker tract, heretics never confined themselves to attacking religion but always went on to challenge civil authority as well. The sectaries arrived in Massachusetts with a number of peculiar mannerisms that were well calculated to defy secular authority, the second social institution erected by the Puritans to safeguard their holy commonwealth. For instance, the Quakers insisted upon using "thee" and "thou" instead of the more formal "you." "Thee" and "thou" were reserved in the dialect still spoken in the north of England for social inferiors and intimates, whereas "you" was used when speaking to a superior or a stranger. The use of the intimate address symbolized the equality of all people in Christ; the Puritans, depending as they did on social and spiritual hierarchies to order the world, rejected these gestures of equality.

A second symbolic bid for equality was the Quaker refusal to doff their hats to their social superiors. This was a powerful statement in an era when the head of a household was the only one permitted to wear his hat in his own home.... The ritual of hat honor reflected a hierarchical society; it put every man in his proper place in relation to all other men. In Massachusetts, Quaker men repeatedly had their hats forcibly removed when they were brought before the colonial elite.... The Quaker claims that they were beaten, imprisoned, and banished for wearing their hats or for saying "thou," although calculated to make the colonial elite appear unreasonable, reveal that the issue of respect for authority was at stake.

Quakers further defied the authority of the godly magistrates by refusing to remain banished. Puritan apologists have often argued that the colonial authorities were forced to execute Quakers because they completely disregarded the sentences of banishment passed upon them. Certainly the General Court, which had been banishing undesirables since the first years of settlement, had never had its authority so blatantly ignored....

The Puritan leaders believed that their authority was God-given, that they were called by God to labor in the office of magistrate, minister, or elder. In fact, every individual in colonial society was thought to have received such a call. The concept of a calling made every task, no matter how menial, crucially important and created a spiritual incentive for remaining in one's place in life. The minister who described the ideal earthly world as one in which everyone did his or her duty as an act of obedience to God was repeating a cliché to his congregation. The Quakers not only attacked the authority of the Puritan leaders and by implication the legitimacy of their callings but refused to work at their own. Quaker witnesses were labeled "itinerates, vagabonds, rogues" who abandoned their families and responsibilities to roam about publishing their beliefs....

As dedicated itinerants, Quakers aroused the fears and wrath of the saints. English Puritans, commenting on Quaker itineracy, emphasized it as one of the sect's most obnoxious traits. The travels of Mary Fisher are illustrative. She had been a servant in Selby, Yorkshire, when convinced in 1652. From that time until she arrived in Boston in 1656, she was imprisoned in York castle, flogged in Cambridge, and apparently better received in Barbados. After her stay in Boston jail, she traveled to the West Indies again and to Adrianople, where she attempted to convince the Great Sultan. Finally, Mary Fisher Bayly Cross returned to the colonies, settled in South Carolina with her second husband, and died there a widow in 1698....

The social origins of the early Quakers reinforced the belief in the susceptibility of the poor to heretical opinions. The first Quakers were largely drawn from the lower levels of English society, and it was only with the Restoration that the movement began to attract more influential friends. . . .

Quakers certainly did not possess the credentials a Puritan congregation required of its minister, and yet they claimed to preach the truth. Those who listened to their message were equally marginal. The largest community of Massachusetts Quakers, in the town of Salem, included thirteen husbandmen, twelve artisans, four mariners, and only one family of large landowners. At least twenty-six Salem women were convinced by the sect's message. One motive that has been advanced for their convincement is that they were denying the male-dominated spiritual and civil regime. Two of the male converts, the son and stepson of prominent colonists, perhaps were also using Quakerism as a vehicle for rebellion. . . .

The third important social institution that the Quakers seemed determined to destroy was the family. Unlike the migrants entering the Chesapeake region, the New England colonists came to the New World in families. Education, discipline, and spiritual guidance were the responsibility of the family, and Puritan sermons and tracts emphasized the importance of good family governance in a holy commonwealth. . . . Under normal circumstances, the father was to his family what the minister was to his flock or the magistrate was to his community: disciplinarian and teacher.

In contrast to the Puritans, who listened to sermons, passed laws, and read books outlining proper family governance, the early Quakers revealed a marked lack of concern for the family. . . . [T]he entire thrust of the early movement was away from the Puritan emphasis on education and discipline, the two most important functions of the family. . . .

. . . As perfectionists who denied original sin, [Quakers] believed that children were innocent, even godly. . . . The Quakeress who reportedly preferred to pray with "first a child, then a young man, then a strong man, before an elder" revealed as much about her belief in the godliness of children as her contempt for Puritan elders. Quaker witnesses described themselves as children following the commands of their loving Father. . . .

Since the Quakers elevated women and children to the level of the patriarch, he no longer retained his special role in the family. The inner light was the great leveler and shined as readily in an illiterate or irrational person as in an educated one. Anyone, regardless of age or sex, could witness to the truth of Christ. Women frequently published the truth; about half of the invaders were Quakeresses, and similarly high proportions of resident women were among the convinced. The conversion of these women was unfortunate, but that they presumed to preach was far worse. . . .

In the never-ending battle with evil, the Puritan leaders of Massachusetts Bay had shaped all their social institutions—the church, the state, the family—into weapons to be used in the cause of good. They expected Satan to attempt to undermine their holy commonwealth in countless ways, and they looked for his minions everywhere. In the New World these men, governing and guiding a colony initially challenged by an orgy of servants, Indians, and papists at the maypole of Merrymount, constantly surrounded by Indians, and periodically inundated with heretics, had experienced little that encouraged them to modify their world view. Four Quakers died and many others suffered horribly because they touched off a whole series of fears in the minds of the saints. Blasphemous vagabond men and women; pagan Indians; communalistic, licentious heretics; unchurched, superstitious highlanders—Quakers bore the brunt of these associations as the fear of disorder and anarchy played itself out in the New World.

The Role of Witchcraft in Social Discourse

JOHN PUTNAM DEMOS

The place is the fledgling community of Windsor, Connecticut: the time, an autumn day in the year 1651. A group of local militiamen has assembled for training exercises. They drill in their usual manner through the morning, then pause for rest and refreshment. Several of the younger recruits begin a moment's horseplay; one of these—a certain Thomas Allen—cocks his musket and inadvertently knocks it against a tree. The weapon fires, and a few yards away a bystander falls heavily to the ground. The unfortunate victim is an older man, also a trainee, Henry Stiles by name. Quickly, the group converges on Stiles, and bears him to the house of the local physician. But the bullet has fatally pierced his heart.

One month later the "particular court" of the Connecticut colony meets in regular session. On its agenda is an indictment of Thomas Allen: "that ... [thou] didst suddenly, negligently, carelessly cock thy piece, and carry the piece ... which piece being charged and going off in thine hand, slew thy neighbor, to the great dishonor of God, breach of the peace, and loss of a member of this commonwealth." Allen confesses the fact, and is found guilty of "homicide by misadventure." For his "sinful neglect and careless carriages" the court orders him to pay a fine of twenty pounds sterling. In addition he is bound to good behavior for the ensuing year, with the special proviso "that he shall not bear arms for the same term."

But this is not the end of the matter. Stiles's death remains a topic of local conversation, and three years later it yields a more drastic result. In November, 1654, the court meets in special session to try a case of witchcraft—against a woman, Lydia Gilbert, also of Windsor: "Lydia Gilbert, thou art here indicted ... that not having the fear of God before thine eyes, thou hast of late years or still dost give entertainment to Satan, the great enemy of God and mankind, and by his help hast killed the body of Henry Stiles, besides other witchcrafts, for which according to the law of God and the established law of this commonwealth thou deservest to die." The court, in effect, is considering a complicated question: did Lydia Gilbert's witchcraft

John Demos, "Entertaining Satan" in *American Heritage,* pp. 15–21. Reprinted with permission from *American Heritage,* Volume 29, Number 5. Copyright 1978 by *American Heritage,* a Division of Forbes, Inc.

cause Thomas Allen's gun to go off, so as to kill Henry Stiles? Evidence is taken on various points deemed relevant. Henry Stiles was a boarder in the Gilbert household for some while before his death. The arrangement was not a happy one; neighbors could recall the sounds of frequent quarreling. From time to time Stiles loaned money and property to his landlord, but this served only to heighten the tension. Goodwife Gilbert, in particular, violated her Christian obligation of charitable and peaceable behavior. A naturally assertive sort, she did not conceal her sense of grievance against Goodman Stiles. In fact, her local reputation has long encompassed some unfavorable elements: disapproval of her quick temper, envy of her success in besting personal antagonists, suspicion that she is not above invoking the "Devil's means." The jury weighs the evidence and reaches its verdict—guilty as charged. The magistrates hand down the prescribed sentence of death by hanging. A few days thereafter the sentence is carried out.

On the next succeeding Sabbath day, and with solemn forewarning, the pastor of the Windsor church climbs to the pulpit to deliver his sermon. Directly he faces the questions that are weighing heavily in the minds of his parishioners. Why has this terrible scourge of witchcraft been visited on their little community? What has created the opportunity which the Devil and his legions have so untimely seized? For what reason has God Almighty condoned such a tragic intrusion on the life of Windsor? The pastor's answer to these questions is neither surprising nor pleasant for his audience to hear, but it carries a purgative force. The Windsor townsfolk are themselves at least partially to blame. For too long they have strayed from the paths of virtue: overvaluing secular interests while neglecting religious ones, tippling in alehouses, "nightwalking," and—worst of all—engaging one another in repeated strife. In such circumstances the Devil always finds an opening; to such communities God brings retribution. Thus the recent witchcraft episode is a lesson to the people of Windsor, and a warning to mend their ways.

Lydia Gilbert was not the first witch to have lived at Windsor, nor would she be the last. For so-called Puritans, the happenstance of everyday life was part of a struggle of cosmic dimensions, a struggle in which witchcraft played a logical part. The ultimate triumph of Almighty God was assured. But in particular times and places Satan might achieve some temporary success—and claim important victims. Indeed he was continually adding earthly recruits to his nefarious cause. Tempted by bribes and blandishments, or frightened by threats of torture, weak-willed persons signed the "Devil's Book" and enrolled as witches. Thereafter they were armed with his power and obliged to do his bidding. God, meanwhile, opposed this onslaught of evil—and yet He also permitted it. For errant men and women there was no more effective means of "chastening."

In a sense, therefore, witchcraft was part of God's own intention. And the element of intention was absolutely central, in the minds of the human actors. When a man lay dead from a violent accident on a training field, his fellow townspeople would carefully investigate how events had proceeded to such an end. But they sought, in addition, to understand the *why* of it all—the motives, whether human or supernatural (or both), which lay behind the events. The same was true for other forms of everyday mischance. When cows took strangely ill, when a boat capsized in a sudden storm, when bread failed to rise in the oven or beer went bad in the barrel, there was cause for careful reflection. Witchcraft would not necessarily provide the best explanation, but it was always a possibility—and sometimes a most convenient one. To discover an unseen hand at work in one's life was to dispel mystery, to explain misfortune, to excuse incompetence. Belief in witchcraft was rooted in the practical experience no less than the theology of the time.

A single shocking episode—the Salem "hysteria" of 1692—has dominated the lore of this subject ever since. Yet the Salem trials were distinctive only in a quantitative sense—that is, in the sheer numbers of the accused. Between the late 1630's and 1700 dozens of New England towns supported proceedings against witchcraft; some did so on repeated occasions. The total of cases was over a hundred (and this includes only actual trials from which some record survives today). At least forty of the defendants were put to death; the rest were acquitted or convicted of a lesser charge. Numerous additional cases went unrecorded because they did not reach a court of law; nonetheless they generated much excitement—and distress. "Witches" were suspected, accused informally, and condemned in unofficial ways. Gossip and rumor about such people constituted a staple part of the local culture.

The typical witch was a woman of middle age. Like Lydia Gilbert, she was married, had children, and lived as a settled member of her community. (However, widows and childless women were also suspected, perhaps to an extent disproportionate to their numbers in the population at large.) Some of the accused were quite poor and a few were given to begging; but taken altogether they spanned the entire social spectrum. (One was the wife of a leading magistrate in the Massachusetts Bay Colony.) Most seemed conspicuous in their personal behavior: they were cantankerous, feisty, quick to take offense, and free in their expression of anger. As such they matched the prevalent stereotype of a witch, with its emphasis on strife and malice and vengeance. It was no accident, in a culture which valued "peaceableness" above all things, that suspected witches were persons much given to conflict. Like deviant figures everywhere, they served to mark the accepted boundaries between Good and Evil.

Their alleged victims, and actual accusers, are much harder to categorize. Children were sometimes centrally involved—notoriously so at Salem—but witchcraft evidence came from people of both sexes and all ages. The young had their "fits"; older witnesses had other things of which to complain. Illness, injury, and the loss of property loomed largest in such testimony; but there were reports, too, of strange sights and sounds, of portents and omens, of mutterings and curses—all attributable in some way to the supposed witch. The chances for conviction were greatest when the range of this evidence was wide and the sources numerous. In some cases whole neighborhoods joined the ranks of the accusers.

Usually a trial involved only a single witch, or perhaps two; the events at issue were purely local. A finding of guilt would remove the defendant forever from her community. An acquittal would send her back, but with a clear warning to watch her step. Either way tension was lowered.

Occasionally the situation became more complicated. In Connecticut, during the years from 1662 to 1665, the courts heard a long sequence of witch-craft cases—perhaps as many as a dozen. Some of the accused were eventually executed; others fled for their lives to neighboring colonies. Almost none of the legal evidence has survived; it is known, however, that Connecticut was then experiencing severe problems of religious factionalism. The witch trials may well have been a direct result.

The context for the other wide-scale outbreak is much clearer. Salem, in the closing decades of the seventeenth century, was a town notorious for internal contention. An old guard of village farmers was arrayed against newly prosperous merchants and townsmen. For years, indeed decades, local gover-nance was disrupted: town meetings broke up with important issues unre-solved, ministers came and left (out of favor with one side or the other), lawsuits filled the court dockets. Thus when the first sparks of witchcraft were fanned, in a small group of troubled girls, they acted like tinder on a dried-out woodpile. Suspicion led immediately to new suspicion, and accusation to ac-cusation—with results that every schoolchild knows. Soon the conflagration burst the boundaries of Salem itself; eventually it claimed victims throughout eastern Massachusetts. By the time cooler heads prevailed—especially that of the new governor, Sir William Phips—twenty witches had been executed and dozens more were languishing in local jails.

But the Salem trials—to repeat—were highly unusual in their sheer scope: witch-hunting gone wild. In the more typical case, events moved slowly, even carefully, within a limited and intensely personal framework. This dimension of the witchcraft story also deserves close attention.

October, 1688. A cart stops by the roadside in the south part of Boston. A tall man alights and hurries along a pathway toward a small house. A door opens to admit him and quickly closes again. The visitor is Rev. Cotton Mather, a young but already eminent clergyman of the town. The house is occupied by the family of a mason named John Goodwin.

Immediately upon entering, Mather becomes witness to an extraordinary scene. On the parlor floor in front of him two small human forms are thrash-ing about. A girl of thirteen (named Martha) and a boy of eleven (John, Jr.) are caught in the throes of agonizing fits. Their bodies contort into strange, distended shapes. Their eyes bulge. Their mouths snap open and shut. They shriek uncontrollably. From time to time they affect the postures of animals, and crawl about the room, barking like dogs or bellowing like frightened cows. Their father and several neighbors look on in horror, and try by turns to prevent serious damage to persons or property.

Mather waits for a moment's lull; then he opens a Bible, kneels, and begins to pray. Immediately the children stop their ears and resume their shrieking. *"They* say we must not listen," cries the girl, while hurling herself toward the fireplace. Her father manages to block the way; briefly he catches her in an awkward embrace. But she reels off and falls heavily on her brother.

Soon it is time for supper. The children quiet temporarily, and come to the table with their elders. However, when food is offered them, their teeth are set as if to lock their mouths shut. Later there are new troubles. The children need assistance in preparing for bed, and they tear their nightclothes fearfully. At last they quiet and pass into a deep sleep.

Mather sits by the fireside and reviews the history of their affliction with the distraught parents. The family is a religious one, and until the preceding summer the children were unfailingly pious and well behaved. Martha's fits had begun first, John's soon thereafter; indeed, two still younger children in the family have also been affected from time to time. A physician had been summoned, but he could discover no "natural maladies" at work.

The parents recall an episode that had directly preceded the onset of Martha's fits. The girl was sent to retrieve some family linen from a laundress who lived nearby. Several items had disappeared, and Martha complained— intimating theft. The laundress angrily denied the charges, and was joined in this by her own mother, an Irishwoman named Glover. Goodwife Glover was already a feared presence in the neighborhood; her late husband, on his death-bed, had accused her of practicing witchcraft. Now she poured out her retaliative anger on young Martha Goodwin. The girl has not been the same since.

Late in the evening, having listened with care to the entire story, Mather prepares to leave. John Goodwin explains that several neighbors have been urging the use of "tricks"—countermagic—to end his children's difficulties. But Goodwin prefers a strategy based on orthodox Christian principles.

In this Cotton Mather is eager to cooperate. He returns to the Goodwin house each day for a week, and on one particular afternoon he is joined by his fellow clergymen from all parts of Boston. Eventually he invites Martha Goodwin into his own home for a period of intensive pastoral care. (Martha's younger brother is taken, at the same time, into the home of the minister at Watertown.) Their afflictions continue, though with lessened severity.

Meanwhile the courts intervene and Goodwife Glover is put on trial for her alleged crimes. She has difficulty answering the prosecutor's questions; she can speak only in her native tongue (Gaelic), so the proceedings must involve interpreters. Her house is searched, and "poppets" are discovered— small images, made of rags, believed to be instrumental in the perpetration of witchcraft. Eventually she confesses guilt and raves wildly in court about her dealings with the Devil. The judges appoint six physicians to assess her sanity; they find her compos mentis. The court orders her execution.

On her way to the gallows Goodwife Glover declares bitterly that the children will not be cured after her death, for "others had a hand in it as well." And in fact, the fits suffered by Martha and young John increase immediately thereafter. Winter begins, and suspicion shifts to another woman of the neighborhood. However, the new suspect dies suddenly, and under strange circumstances, before she can be brought to trial. At last the children show marked improvement, and by spring they are virtually their former selves. Meanwhile a relieved, and triumphant, Cotton Mather is spending long days in his study, completing a new book that will soon be published under the title *Memorable Providences, Relating to Witchcrafts and Possessions*. A central chapter deals at length with selected "examples," and includes the events in which Mather himself has so recently participated. The Goodwin children will be leading characters in a local best seller.

Goodwife Glover was relatively rare, among those accused of witchcraft in early New England, in confessing guilt. Only at Salem did any considerable number choose to convict themselves—and there, it seemed, confession was the strategy of choice if one wished to avoid the gallows. Were Goody Glover's admissions, in effect, forced out of her? Was she perhaps seriously deranged (the opinion of the court-appointed physicians notwithstanding)? Did she truly believe herself guilty? Had she, in fact, sought to invoke the power of the Devil, by stroking poppets with her spittle—or whatever?

We have no way now to answer such questions; the evidence comes to us entirely through persons who believed—and prosecuted—the case against her. It does seem likely, in a community where virtually everyone accepted the reality of witchcraft, that at least a few would have tried to practice it. In a sense, however, it no longer matters whether specific individuals were guilty as charged. What does matter is that many of them were believed guilty—and that this belief was itself efficacious. As anthropologists have observed in cultures around the world, people who regard themselves as objects of witchcraft are vulnerable to all manner of mischance. They blunder into "accidents," they lose their effectiveness in work and social relations, they occasionally sicken and die.

No less was true in early New England. The victims of witchcraft—whatever the variety of their particular afflictions—had this in common: they believed *beforehand* that they had been marked as targets for attack. Their fearful expectation became, at some point, incapacitating—and yielded its own directly feared result. Thus the idea of witchcraft served both as the *ad hoc* cause of the victim's troubles and as the *post hoc* explanation. The process was neatly circular, for each explanation created a further cause—which, in turn, required additional explanation. In the language of modern medicine, these episodes were "symptoms," and their basis was "psychogenic."

The seizures of the afflicted children were but the extreme end of the symptomatic continuum. When Martha Goodwin had been drawn into a bitter exchange with a suspected witch, she was left deeply unsettled. She feared retaliation; she wished to retaliate herself; she felt acutely uncomfortable with the anger she had already expressed. Henceforth an anguished "victim" of witchcraft, she was, in effect, punished for her own vengeful impulse. Yet, too, she *had* her revenge, for her accusations led straight to the trial and conviction of her antagonist. The same inner processes, and a similar blend of wish and fear, served to energize fits in victims of witchcraft all across New England.

But fits could be explained in other ways—hence the requirement that all such victims be examined by medical doctors. Only when natural causes had been ruled out was a diagnosis of witchcraft clearly justified. Normally, beyond this point, clergymen would assume control of the proceedings, for they were "healers of the soul" and experts in the struggle against Evil. Long sessions of prayer, earnest conversation with the afflicted, occasional periods of fasting and humiliation—these were the preferred methods of treatment.

At least they were the *Christian* methods. For—much to the chagrin of the clergy—there were other ways of combating witchcraft. From obscure sources in the folk culture of pre-Christian times the New Englanders had inherited a rich lore of countermagic—including, for example, the tricks which John Goodwin refused to try. Thus a family might decide to lay branches of "sweet bays" under their threshold. ("It would keep a witch from coming in.") Or a woman tending a sick child would perform elaborate rituals of protection. ("She smote the back of her hands together sundry times, and spat in the fire; then she . . . rubbed [herbs] in her hand and strewed them about the hearth.") Or a man would hurl a pudding into a fire in order to draw a suspect to the scene of his alleged crimes. ("To get hay was no true cause of his coming thither, but rather the spirit that bewitched the pudding brought him.") All this was of a piece with other strands of belief and custom in seventeenth-century New England: fortunetelling, astrology, healing charms, love potions and powders—to mention a few. Witchcraft, in short, belonged to a large and complex world of interest in the supernatural.

Beyond the tricks against witches, besides the efficacy of prayer, there was always legal recourse. Witchcraft was a capital crime in every one of the New England colonies, and thus was a particularly solemn responsibility of the courts. Procedure was scrupulously observed: indictment by a grand jury, depositions from qualified witnesses, verdict by a jury of trials, sentencing by the magistrates. Some features of witchcraft trials seem highly repugnant today—for example, the elaborate and intimate body searches of defendants suspected of having "witch's teats" (nipplelike growths through which the witch or wizard was believed to give suck to Satan). But in the context of the times, such procedures were not extraordinary. Contrary to popular belief, physical torture was *not* used to obtain evidence. Testimony was taken on both sides, and character references favorable to the defendant were not uncommon. Guilt was never a foregone conclusion; most trials ended in acquittal. Perhaps *because* the crime was a capital one, many juries seemed reluctant to convict. Some returned verdicts like the following: "[We find her] not legally guilty according to indictment, but [there is] just ground of vehement suspicion of her having had familiarity with the Devil."

At Salem, to be sure, such caution was thrown to the winds. The creation of special courts, the admission of "spectral evidence" (supplied by "shapes" visible only to the afflicted victims), the strong momentum favoring conviction—all this marked a decided tilt in the legal process. But it brought, in time, its own reaction. Magistrates, clergymen, and ordinary participants eventually would see the enormity of what they had done at Salem in the name of law and religion. And they would not make the same mistakes again. . . .

✿ F U R T H E R   R E A D I N G

Emery Battis, *Saints and Sectaries: Anne Hutchinson and the Antinomian Controversy in the Massachusetts Bay Colony* (1962)

Charles Lloyd Cohen, *God's Caress: The Psychology of Puritan Religious Experience* (1986)

John Putnam Demos, *Entertaining Satan: Witchcraft and the Culture of Early New England* (1982)

Kai Erikson, *Wayward Puritans: A Study of the Sociology of Deviance* (1966)

Stephen Foster, *The Long Argument: English Puritanism and the Shaping of New England Culture, 1570–1700* (1991)

Philip F. Gura, *A Glimpse of Sion's Glory: Puritan Radicalism in New England, 1620–1660* (1984)

David D. Hall, John M. Murrin, and Thad W. Tate, eds., *Saints and Revolutionaries: Essays on Early American History* (1984)

Charles E. Hambrick-Stowe, *The Practice of Piety: Puritan Devotional Disciplines in Seventeenth-Century New England* (1982)

Carol F. Karlsen, *The Devil in the Shape of a Woman: Witchcraft in Colonial New England* (1987)

Alan Macfarlane, *Witchcraft in Tudor and Stuart England: A Regional and Comparative Study* (1970)

Marion L. Starkey, *The Devil in Massachusetts: A Modern Enquiry into the Salem Witch Trials* (1949)

Keith Thomas, *Religion and the Decline of Magic: Studies in Popular Beliefs in Sixteenth- and Seventeenth-Century England* (1973)

The Chesapeake: Bacon's Rebellion and the Creation of a Creole Society

❧

The final quarter of the seventeenth century saw dramatic changes in the colonial Chesapeake. Although these changes proceeded from different causes, they combined to reinforce each other and to produce a very different society by the beginning of the eighteenth century. Whereas the earlier period had seen a society of immigrants threatened by a high death rate—a population that thus required constant infusions of newcomers—the last quarter saw the emergence of a strong and growing group of creoles, native-born settlers of English descent. These creoles, more capable than the immigrants of coping with the Chesapeake environment, married young and bore children who lived to adulthood. Following the upheavals of Bacon's Rebellion in 1676 and the Maryland Rising of 1689, leading families were established in roles that they would play throughout the colonial period.

This period also witnessed the transition from a labor force composed primarily of temporary servants to one of permanently enslaved Africans, and the emergence of a body of laws making skin color the distinguishing mark of the slave. New colonies—the middle colonies of Pennsylvania and New York to the north and the Carolinas to the south—gave a wider choice of destination to European immigrants and opened up opportunities for those unable to acquire land in the older colonies. Chesapeake planters came to understand the problems as well as the benefits of concentration on tobacco, a crop that firmly tied their economy to the fluctuations of international trade and made them dependent to a large degree on European brokers. The pattern set in this period of change would also last throughout the colonial era.

Finally, the later seventeenth century saw the creation and elaboration of neighborhood networks and systems of local government that supplied the traditional place of kin and community at home. Thus although the Chesapeake lacked the substantial towns of colonies to the north, the region's settlers broke down the isolation of plantation life by creative adaptation.

∾ D O C U M E N T S

John Hammond's *Leah and Rachel* (Virginia and Maryland), published in 1656, sought to overturn the Chesapeake's reputation as a place where servants were exploited and life was hard and mean. Hammond's work, from which the first selection is taken, gave new colonists plentiful advice on how to plan for life in America—advice that reflected the greater sense of choice they had—and described some of the networks into which newcomers could fit. In the second document Edward Williams also seeks to ease the hardships of transplantation by listing necessities to be brought from home.

Bacon's Rebellion, which waged indiscriminate war on Indians on the frontier, produced conflicting accounts and manifestos. Nathaniel Bacon's own manifesto (see the third document) accused Virginia's governor, William Berkeley, and his associates of corruption and of ignoring the plight of settlers on the frontier while they enriched themselves. In the fourth selection Bacon's wife, Elizabeth, writes to her sister of the fear and the perceived danger under which the frontier settlers lived, demonstrating why the rebellion received such support. Similarly Mary Byrd, wife of the Bacons' neighbor, Captain William Byrd, testifies in the fifth selection to the grievances of their region. In the sixth document William Sherwood condemns Bacon and his defiance of the law. Planter William Fitzhugh's letters from the 1680s, excerpted in the final selection, testify to the new settled life of the late seventeenth century.

John Hammond on Chesapeake Development, 1656

Leah *and* Rachell, *or the two fruitfull Sisters of* Virginia *and* Mary-land; *their present condition impartially stated and related.*

It is the glory of every Nation to enlarge themselves, to encourage their own foreign attempts, and to be able to have of their own, within their own territories, as many several commodities as they can attain to, that so others may rather be beholding to them, than they to others; and to this purpose have Encouragements, Privileges and Immunities been given to any Discoveries or Adventurers into remote Colonies, by all politic Commonwealths in the world.

But alas, we Englishmen (in all things else famous, and to other Countries terrible) do not only fail in this, but vilify, scandalize and cry down such parts of the unknown world, as have been found out, settled and made flourishing, by the charge, hazard and diligence of their own brethren, as if because removed from us, we either account them people of another world or enemies.

This is too truly made good in the odiums and cruel slanders cast on

---

Some of the spelling in this document has been modernized.

those two famous Countries of *Virginia* and *Mary-land,* whereby those Countries, not only are many times at a stand, but are in danger to moulder away, and come in time to nothing; nor is there anything but the fertility and natural gratefulness of them, left a remedy to prevent it.

To let our own Nation (whose common good I covet, and whose Commonwealth's servant I am, as born to no other use) be made sensible of these injuries: I have undertaken in this Book to give the true state of those places, according to the condition they are now in; and to declare either to distressed or discontented, that they need not doubt because of any rumour detracting from their goodnesses, to remove and cast themselves and Fortunes upon those Countries, in which if I should deviate from the truth; I have at this present carping enemies in *London* enough, to contradict and cry down me and this, for Imposters. It is not long since I came from thence (God knows sore against my will) having lived there upward of one and twenty years; nor do I intend (by God's assistance) to be long out of it again: and therefore can by experience, not hearsay (as *Bullock* and other lying Writers have done, who at random or for their own private lucre have rendered their Books ridiculous and themselves infamous liars, nor will I like them, overextol the places, as if they were rather Paradises than earthly habitations; but truly let ye know, what they are, and how the people there live.) Which when impartially viewed, will undoubtedly clear up those Foggy Mists, that hath to their own ruin blinded and kept off many from going thither, whose miseries and misfortunes by staying in *England* are much to be lamented, and much to be pitied.

In respect these two Sister Countries (though distinct Governments) are much of one nature, both for produce and manner of living; I shall only at present, Treat of the elder Sister *Virginia,* and in speaking of that include both: And ere I leave off, shall in particular rehearse the unnatural usage *Mary-land* the younger Sister, hath had, not by *Virginia*; but by those Vipers she hath received and harboured with much kindness and hospitality.

The Country is reported to be an unhealthy place, a nest of Rogues, whores, desolate and rooking persons; a place of intolerable labour, bad usage and hard Diet, &c.

To Answer these several calumnies, I shall first show what it was? next, what it is?

At the first settling and many years after, it deserved most of those aspersions (nor were they then aspersions but truths) it was not settled at the public charge; but when found out, challenged, and maintained by Adventurers, whose avarice and inhumanity, brought in these inconveniences, which to this day brands *Virginia.*

Then were Jails emptied, youth seduced, infamous women drilled in, the provisions all brought out of *England,* and that embezzled by the Trustees (for they durst neither hunt fowl, nor Fish, for fear of the *Indian,* which they stood in awe of, their labour was almost perpetual, their allowance of victual small, few or no cattle, no use of horses nor oxen to draw or carry, (which labours men supplyed themselves) all which caused a mortality; no civil courts of justice but under a Marshal law, no redress of grievances, complaints were repayed with stripes, moneys with scoffs, tortures made delights, and in a word all and the worst that tyranny could inflict or act, which when complained of in *England:* (but so were they kept under that it was long ere they would suffer complaints to come home) the bondage was taken of, the people set free, and had lands assigned to each of them to live of themselves, and enjoy the benefit of their own industry; men then began to call what they laboured for their own, they fell to making themselves convenient housing to dwell in, to plant corn for their food, to range the wood for flesh, the rivers for fowl and fish, to find out somewhat staple for supply of clothing, to continue a commerce, to purchase and breed cattle, &c. but the bud of this growing happiness was again nipped by a cruel Massacre committed by the Natives, which again pull'd them back and kept them under, enforcing them to get into Forts (such as the infancy of those times afforded: they were taken off from planting; their provisions destroyed, their Cattle, Hogs, Horses, &c. kill'd up, and brought to such want and penury, that diseases grew rife, mortality exceeded; but receiving a supply of men, ammunition and victuals out of *England,* they again gathered heart, pursued their enemies, and so often worsted them, that the *Indians* were glad to sue for peace, and they desirous of a cessation) consented to it.

They again began to bud forth, to spread further, to gather wealth, which they rather profusely spent as gotten with ease then providently husbanded, or aimed at any public good; or to make a Country for posterity; but from hand to mouth, and for a present being; neglecting discoveries, planting of Orchards, providing for the Winter preservation of their stocks, or thinking of anything staple or firm; and whilst Tobacco, the only Commodity they had to subsist on bore a price, they wholly and eagerly followed that, neglecting their very planting of Corn, and much relied on *England* for the chiefest part of their provisions; so that being not always amply supplied, they were often in such want, that their case and condition being related in *England,* it hindered and kept off many from going thither, who rather cast their eyes on the Barren and freezing soil of *New-England,* than to join with such an indigent and sottish people, as were reported to be in *Virginia.*

Yet was not *Virginia* all this while without divers honest and virtuous inhabitants, who observing the general neglect and licentiousnesses there, caused Assemblies to be call'd and Laws to be made tending to the glory of God, the severe suppression of vices, and the compelling them not to neglect (upon strict punishments) planting and tending such quantities of Corn, as would not only serve themselves, their Cattle and Hogs plentifully, but to be enabled to supply *New-England* (then in want) with such proportions, as were extreme reliefs, to them in their necessities.

From this industry of theirs and great plenty of Corn, (the main staff of life) proceeded that great plenty of Cattle and Hogs, (now innumerable) and out of which not only *New-England* hath been stocked and relieved, but all other parts of the *Indies* inhabited by Englishmen.

The inhabitants now finding the benefit of their industries, began to look with delight on their increasing stocks: (as nothing more pleasurable than profit) to take pride in their plentifully furnished Tables, to grow not only civil, but great observers of the Sabbath, to stand upon their reputations, and to be ashamed of that notorious manner of life they had formerly lived and wallowed in. . . .

Then began the Gospel to flourish, civil, honourable, and men of great estates flocked in: famous buildings went forward, Orchards innumerable were planted and preserved; Tradesmen set on work and encouraged, staple Commodities, as Silk, Flax, Pot-ashes, &c. of which I shall speak further hereafter, attempted on, and with good success brought to perfection; so that this Country which had a mean beginning, many back friends, two ruinous and bloody Massacres, hath by God's grace out-grown all, and is become a place of pleasure and plenty.

And having briefly laid down the former state of *Virginia,* in its Infancy, and filth, and the occasion of its scandalous aspersions: I come to my main subject, its present Condition and Happiness . . .

I affirm the Country to be wholesome, healthy and fruitful; and a model on which industry may as much improve itself in, as in any habitable part of the World; yet not such a Lubberland as the Fiction of the land of Ease, is reported to be, nor such a *Utopian* as Sir Thomas More hath related to be found out.

In the Countries minority, and before they had well cleared the ground to let in air (which now is otherwise) many imputed the stifling of the wood to be the cause of such sickness; but I rather think the contrary; for divers new Rivers lately settled, where at their first coming upon them as woody as *James* Rivers, the first place they settled in, and yet those Rivers are as healthy as any former settled place in *Virginia* or *England* itself: I believe (and that not without reason) it was only want of such diet as best agreed with our English natures, good drinks and wholesome lodgings were the cause of so much sicknesses, as were formerly frequent, which we have now amended; and therefore enjoy better healths; to which I add, and that by experience since my coming into *England,* and many (if not all *Virginians* can do the like,) that change of air does much alter the state of our bodies: by which many travellers thither may expect some sickness, yet little danger of mortality. . . .

Let such as are so minded not rashly throw themselves upon the voyage, but observe the nature, and enquire the qualities of the persons with whom they engage to transport themselves, or if (as not acquainted with such as inhabit there, but go with Merchants and Mariners, who transport them to others,) let their covenant be such, that after their arrival they have a fortnight's time assigned them to enquire of their Master, and make choice of such as they intend to expire their time with, nor let that brand of selling of servants, be any discouragement to deter any from going, for if a time must be served, it is all one with whom it be served, provided they be people of honest repute, with which the Country is well replenished.

And be sure to have your contract in writing and under hand and seal, for if ye go over upon promise made to do this or that, or to be free or your own men, it signifies nothing, for by a law of the Country (waiving all promises) any one coming in, and not paying their own passages, must serve if men or women four years, if younger according to their years, but where an Indenture is, that is binding and observing.

The usual allowance for servants is (besides their charge of passage defrayed) at their expiration, a year's provision of corn, double apparel, tools necessary, and land according to the custom of the Country, which is an old delusion, for there is no land accustomary due to the servant, but to the Master, and therefore that servant is unwise that will not dash out that custom in his covenant, and make that due of land absolutely his own, which although at the present, not of so great consequence; yet in few years will be of much worth, as I shall hereafter make manifest.

When ye go aboard, expect the Ship somewhat troubled and in a hurly-burly, until ye clear the land's end; and that the Ship is rummaged, and things put to rights, which many times discourages the Passengers, and makes them wish the Voyage unattempted: but this is but for a short season, and washes off when at Sea, where the time is pleasantly passed away, though not with such choice plenty as the shore affords.

But when ye arrive and are settled, ye will find a strange alteration, an abused Country giving the lie in your own approbations to those that have calumniated it, and these infallible arguments may convince all incredible and obstinate opinions, concerning the goodness and delightfulness of the Country, that never any servants of late times have gone thither; but in their Letters to their Friends commend and approve of the place, and rather invite than dissuade their acquaintance from coming thither. Another is this, that seldom (if ever) any that hath continued in *Virginia* any time, will or do desire to live in *England,* but post back with what expedition they can; although many are landed men in *England,* and have good Estates here, and divers ways of preferments propounded to them, to entice and persuade their continuance.

The Country is as I said of a temperate nature, the days, in summer not so long as in *England,* in winter longer; it is somewhat hotter in *June, July* and *August* than here, but that heat sweetly allayed by a continual breeze of wind, which never fails to cool and refresh the labourer and traveller; the cold seldom approaches sensibly until about *Christmas,* (although the last winter was hard and the worst I or any living there knew) and when winter comes, (which is such and no worse than is in *England,*) it continues two months seldom longer, often not so long and in that time although here seldom hard-weather keep men from labour, yet there no work is done all winter except dressing their own victuals and making of fires.

The labour servants are put to, is not so hard nor of such continuance as Husbandmen, nor Handicraftmen are kept at in *England,* I said little or nothing is done in winter time, none ever work before sun rising nor after sun set, in the summer they rest, sleep or exercise themselves five hours in the heat of the day, Saturdays afternoon is always their own, the old Holidays are observed and the Sabbath spent in good exercises.

The Women are not (as is reported) put into the ground to work, but occupy such domestic employments and housewifery as in *England,* that is dressing victuals, righting up the house, milking, employed about dairies, washing, sowing, &c. and both men and women have times of recreations, as much or more than in any part of the world besides, yet some wenches that are nasty, beastly and not fit to be so employed are put into the ground, for reason tells us, they must not at charge be transported and then maintained for nothing, but those that prove so awkward are rather burdensome than servants desirable or useful.

The Country is fruitful, apt for all and more than *England* can or does produce, the usual diet is such as in *England,* for the rivers afford innumerable sorts of choice fish, (if they will take the pains to make weirs or hire the Natives, who for a small matter will undertake it,) winter and summer, and that in many places sufficient to serve the use of man, and to fatten hogs, water-fowl of all sorts are (with admiration to be spoken of) plentiful and easy to be killed, yet by many degrees more plentiful in some places than in othersome, Dear all over the Country, and in many places so many, that venison is accounted a tiresome meat, wild Turkeys are frequent, and so large that I have seen some weigh near threescore pounds; other beasts there are whose flesh is wholesome and savoury, such are unknown to us; and therefore I will not stuff my book with superfluous relation of their names; huge Oysters and store in all parts where the salt-water comes.

The Country is exceedingly replenished with Neat cattle, Hogs, Goats and Tame-fowl, but not many sheep; so that mutton is somewhat scarce, but that defect is supplied with store of Venison, other flesh and fowl; The Country is full of gallant Orchards, and the fruit generally more luscious and delightfull than here, witness the Peach and Quince, the latter may be eaten raw savourily, the former differs and as much exceeds ours as the best relished apple we have doth the crab, and of both most excellent and comfortable drinks are made, Grapes in infinite manners grow wild, so do Walnuts, Smallnuts, Chestnuts and abundance of excellent fruits, Plums and Berries, not growing or known in *England*; grain we have, both *English* and *Indian* for bread and Bear, and Peas besides *English* of ten several sorts, all exceeding ours in *England,* the gallant root of Potatoes are common, and so are all sorts of roots, herbs and Garden stuff.

It must needs follow then that diet cannot be scarce, since both rivers and woods affords it, and that such plenty of Cattle and Hogs are everywhere, which yield beef, veal, milk, butter, cheese and other made dishes, pork, bacon, and pigs, and that as sweet and savoury meat as the world affords, these with the help of Orchards and Gardens, Oysters, Fish, Fowl and Venison, certainly cannot but be sufficient for a good diet and wholesome accommodation, considering how plentifully they are, and how easy with industry to be had.

Beer is indeed in some place constantly drunken, in other some, nothing but Water or Milk, and Water or Beverage; & that is where the goodwives, (if I may so call them) are negligent and idle; for it is not for want of Corn to make Malt with (for the Country affords enough) but because they are slothful and careless: but I hope this Item will shame them out of those humours, that they will be adjudged by their drink, what kind of Housewives they are.

Those Servants that will be industrious may in their time of service gain a competent estate before their Freedoms, which is usually done by many, and they gain esteem and assistance that appear so industrious: There is no Master almost but will allow his Servant a parcel of clear ground to plant some Tobacco in for himself, which he may husband at those many idle times he hath allowed him and not prejudice, but rejoice his Master to see it, which in time of Shipping he may lay out for commodities, and in Summer sell them again with advantage, and get a Sow-Pig or two, which anybody almost will give him, and his Master suffer him to keep them with his own, which will be no charge to his Master, and with one year's increase of them may purchase a Cow Calf or two, and by that time he is for himself; he may have Cattle, Hogs and Tobacco of his own, and come to live gallantly; but this must be gained (as I said) by Industry and affability, not by sloth nor churlish behaviour.

And whereas it is rumoured that Servants have no lodging other than on boards, or by the Fireside, it is contrary to reason to believe it: First, as we are Christians; next as people living under a law, which compels as well the Master as the Servant to perform his duty; nor can true labour be either expected or exacted without sufficient clothing, diet, and lodging; all which both their Indentures (which must inviolably be observed) and the Justice of the Country requires.

But if any go thither, not in a condition of a Servant, but pay his or her passage, which is some six pounds: Let them not doubt but it is money well laid out (yet however let them not fail) although they carry little else to take a Bed along with them, and then few Houses but will give them entertainment, either out of courtesy, or on reasonable terms; and I think it better for any that goes over free, and but in a mean condition, to hire himself for reasonable wages of Tobacco and Provision, the first year, provided he happen in an honest house, and where the Mistress is noted for a good Housewife, of which there are very many (notwithstanding the cry to the contrary) for by that means he will live free of disbursement, have something to help him the next year, and be carefully looked to in his sickness (if he chance to fall sick) and let him so covenant that exceptions may be made, that he work not much in the hot weather, a course we always take with our new hands (as they call them) the first year they come in.

If they are women that go after this manner, that is paying their own passages; I advise them to sojourn in a house of honest repute, for by their good carriage, they may advance themselves in marriage, by their ill, over-throw their fortunes; and although loose persons seldom live long unmarried if free; yet they match with as desolate as themselves, and never live hand-somely or are ever respected.

For any that come over free, and are minded to diet and quarter in another man's house, it matters not whether they know on what term or conditions they are there; for by an excellent Decree, made by Sir *William Berkly,* when Governour; (as indeed he was the Author of many good Laws:) It was ordered, that if any inhabitant received any stranger Merchant, or boarder into their houses, and did not condition in Writing with him or them so entertained on what terms he received them, it should be supposed an invitation, and no satisfaction should be allowed or recovered in any Court of Justice; thereby giving notice that no stranger coming into the Country should be drilled in, or made a purchase of under colour of friendship: but that the Inhabitants at first coming shall let them know how they mean to deal with them, that if they like not the terms they may remove themselves at pleasure; a Law so good and commendable, that it is never like to be revoked or altered.

Now for those that carry over Families and estates with a determination to inhabit, my advice is that they neither sojourn for that will be chargeable; nor on the sudden purchase, for that may prove unfortunate; but that they for the first year hire a house (for seats are always to be hired) and by that means, they will not only find content and live at a cheap rate, but be acquainted in the Country and learn the worth and goodness of the Plantation they mean to purchase; and so not rashly entangle themselves in an ill bargain, or find where a convenient parcel of Land is for their turns to be taken up.

Yet are the Inhabitants generally affable, courteous and very assistant to strangers (for what but plenty makes hospitality and good neighbourhood) and no sooner are they settled, but they will be visiting, presenting and advising the stranger how to improve what they have, how to better their way of livelihood. . . .

Edward Williams Describes Necessaries for Planters, 1650

To the worthy Gentlemen, Adventurers and Planters in VIRGINIA.

My loving Friends:

I thought it convenient heere briefly to minde you of those Necessaries, that if wanted there, would greatly prove your prejudice, and render you obnoxious to many evils, which are these.

Necessaries for Planters.

For Aparell: Provide each man 1. Monmouth Cap, 1. Wastcoat, 1. Suit of Canvase, Bands, Shirts, Shooes, Stockings, Canvase to make sheets, with Bed and Bolster to till in Virginia, 1. Rugge, and Blankets.

For Armes: Provide 1. Suit of complete light Armour, and each man 1. Sword, 1. Musket or Fowling Peece, with Pouder and Shot convenient.

For Household stuffe: Provide one great Iron Pot, large and small Kettles, Skellets, Frying pannes, Gridiron, Spit, Platters, Dishes, Spoons, Knives, Sugar, Spice, Fruit, and Strong water at Sea for sicke men.

For Tools: Provide Howes broad and narrow, Axes broad and narrow, Handsawes, two-band-sawes, Whipsaws, Hammers, Shovels, Spades, Augors, Piercers, Gimblets, Hatchets, Handbills, Frowes to cleave pale, Pickaxes, Nayls of all sorts, 1. Grindstone, Nets, Hooks, Lines, Plowes: All which accomodation wherewith each to be well furnished, together with his Transportation, which is ordinarily 6l. a man, and 3l. a tun his goods, may amount unto 20l. a man, charges.

Nor needs the carefull Adventurer much doubt what Wares may prove his profit there. For any Commodities of this Country are good Merchandize transported thither. viz. Strong waters, Haberdashers wares, Ironmongers wares, Drapers wares, Stationers wares, and many other wares which those sterill witted Americans doe easily admire. But your judgements are sufficient. And likewise I have further discovered them in the insuing Treatise of the Incomparable VIRGINIA. So wishing you all prosperous happinesse and happy prosperity heere, and in the world to come eternall blisse, I rest

Your faithfull
Servant,

E. W.

Nathaniel Bacon's Manifesto Concerning the Troubles in Virginia, 1676

If virtue be a sin, if Piety be guilt, all the Principles of morality goodness and Justice be perverted, We must confess That those who are now called Rebels may be in danger of those high imputations, Those loud and several Bulls would affright Innocents and render the defence of our Brethren and the enquiry into our sad and heavy oppressions, Treason. But if there be as sure there is, a just God to appeal too, if Religion and Justice be a sanctuary here, If to plead the cause of the oppressed, If sincerely to aim at his Majesty's Honour and the Public good without any reservation or by Interest, If to stand in the Gap after so much blood of our dear Brethren bought and sold, If after the loss of a great part of his Majesty's Colony deserted and dispeopled, freely with our lives and estates to endeavor to save the remainders be Treason God Almighty Judge and let guilty die, But since we cannot in our hearts find one single spot of Rebellion or Treason or that we have in any manner aimed at the subverting the settled Government or attempting of the Person of any either magistrate or private man not with standing the several Reproaches and Threats of some who for sinister ends were disaffected to us and censured our ino[cent] and honest designs, and since all people in all places where we have yet been can attest our civil quiet peaceable behaviour far different from that of Rebellion and tumultuous persons let Truth be bold and all the world know the real Foundations of pretended guilt, We appeal to the Country itself what and of what nature their Oppressions have been or by what Cabal and mystery the designs of many of those whom we call great men have been transacted and carried on, but let us trace these men in Authority and Favour to whose hands the dispensation of the Countries' wealth has been committed; let us observe the sudden Rise of their Estates composed with the Quality in which they first entered this Country Or the Reputation

---

Some of the spelling in this document has been modernized.

they have held here amongst wise and discerning men, And let us see whither their extractions and Education have not been vile, And by what pretense of learning and virtue they could so soon into Employments of so great Trust and consequence, let us consider their sudden advancement and let us also consider whither any Public work for our safety and defence or for the Advancement and propagation of Trade, liberal Arts or sciences is here Extant in any [way] adaquate to our vast charge, now let us compare these things together and see what sponges have sucked up the Public Treasure and whither it hath not been privately contrived away by unworthy Favourites and juggling Parasites whose tottering Fortunes have been repaired and supported at the Public charge, now if it be so Judged what greater guilt can be than to offer to pry into these and to unriddle the mysterious wiles of a powerful Cabal let all people Judge what can be of more dangerous Import than to suspect the so long Safe proceedings of Some of our Grandees and whither People may with safety open their Eyes in so nice a Concern.

Another main article of our Guilt is our open and manifest aversion of all, not only the Foreign but the protected and Darling Indians, this we are informed is Rebellion of a deep dye For that both the Governour and Council are by Colonel Coale's Assertion bound to defend the Queen and the Appamatocks with their blood Now whereas we do declare and can prove that they have been for these Many years enemies to the King and Country, Robbers and Thieves and Invaders of his Majesty's Right and our Interest and Estates, but yet have by persons in Authority been defended and protected even against His Majesty's loyal Subjects and that in so high a Nature that even the Complaints and oaths of his Majesty's Most loyal Subjects in a lawful Manner proffered by them against those barbarous Outlaws have been by the right honourable Governour rejected and the Delinquents from his presence dismissed not only with pardon and indemnity but with all encouragement and favour, Their Fire Arms so destructful to us and by our laws prohibited, Commanded to be restored them, and open Declaration before Witness made That they must have Ammunition although directly contrary to our law, Now what greater guilt can be than to oppose and endeavour the destruction of these Honest quiet neighbours of ours.

Another main article of our Guilt is our Design not only to ruin and extirpate all Indians in General but all Manner of Trade and Commerce with them, Judge who can be innocent that strike at this tender Eve of Interest; Since the Right honourable the Governour hath been pleased by his Commission to warrant this Trade who dare oppose it, or opposing it can be innocent, Although Plantations be deserted, the blood of our dear Brethren Spilt, on all Sides our complaints, continually Murder upon Murder renewed upon us, who may or dare think of the general Subversion of all Manner of Trade and Commerce with our enemies who can or dare impeach any of . . . Traders at the Heads of the Rivers if contrary to the wholesome provision made by laws for the countries' safety, they dare continue their illegal practises and dare asperse the right honourable Governour's wisdom and Justice so highly to pretend to have his warrant to break that law which himself made, who dare say That these Men at the Heads of the Rivers buy and sell our blood, and do still notwithstanding the late Act made to the contrary, admit Indians painted and continue to Commerce, although these things can be proved yet who dare be so guilty as to do it.

Another Article of our Guilt is To Assert all those neighbour Indians as well as others to be outlawed, wholly unqualified for the benefit and Protection of the law, For that the law does reciprocally protect and punish, and that all people offending must either in person or Estate make equivalent satisfaction or Restitution according to the manner and merit of the Offences Debts or Trespasses; Now since the Indians cannot according to the tenure and form of any law to us known be prosecuted, Seized or Complained against, Their Persons being difficulty distinguished or known, Their many nations' languages, and their subterfuges such as makes them incapable to make us Restitution or satisfaction would it not be very guilty to say They have been unjustly defended and protected these many years.

If it should be said that the very foundation of all these disasters the Grant of the Beaver trade to the Right Honourable Governour was illegal and not grantable by any power here present as being a monopoly, were not this to deserve the name of Rebel and Traitor.

Judge therefore all wise and unprejudiced men who may or can faithfully or truly with an honest heart attempt the country's good, their vindication and liberty without the aspersion of Traitor and Rebel, since as so doing they must of necessity gall such tender and dear concerns, But to manifest Sincerity [*sic*] and loyalty to the World, and how much we abhor those bitter names, may all the world know that we do unanimously desire to represent our sad and heavy grievances to his most sacred Majesty as our Refuge and Sanctuary, where we do well know that all our Causes will be impartially heard and Equal Justice administered to all men.

Elizabeth Bacon Writes of Fear on the Virginia Frontier, 1676

Dear Sister,

I pray God keep the worst Enemy I have from ever being in such a sad condition as I have been in since my former to the: occasioned by the troublesome Indians, who have killed one of our Overseers at an outward plantation which we had, and we have lost a great stock of cattle, which we had upon it, and a good crop that we should have made there, such plantation Nobody durst come nigh, which is a very great loss to us.

If you had been here, it would have grieved your heart to hear the pitiful complaints of the people, The Indians killing the people daily the Govern: not taking any notice of it for to hinder them, but let them daily do all the mischief they can: I am sure if the Indians were not cowards, they might have destroyed all the upper plantations, and killed all the people upon them; the Governour so much their friend, that he would not suffer anybody to hurt

---

Some of the spelling in this document has been modernized.

one of the Indians; and the poor people came to your brother to desire him to help against the Indians, and he being very much concerned for the loss of his Overseer, and for the loss of so many men and women and children's lives every day, he was willing to do them all the good he could; so he begged of the Governour for a commission in several letters to him, that he might go out against them, but he would not grant one, so daily more mischief done by them, so your brother not able to endure any longer, he went out without a commission. The Governour being very angry with him put out high things against him, and told me that he would most certainly hang him as soon as he returned, which he would certainly have done; but what for fear of the Governour's hanging him, and what for fear of the Indians killing him brought me to this sad condition, but blessed be God he came in very well, with the loss of a very few men; never was known such a fight in Virginia with so few men's loss. The fight did continue nigh a night and a day without any intermission. They did destroy a great many of the Indians, thanks be to God, and might have killed a great many more, but the Governour were so much the Indians' friend and our enemy, that he sent the Indians word that Mr. Bacon was out against them, that they might save themselves. After Mr. Bacon was come in he was forced to keep a guard of soldiers about his house, for the Governour would certainly have had his life taken away privately, if he would have had opportunity; but the country does so really love him, that they would not leave him alone anywhere; there was not anybody against him but the Governour and a few of his great men, which have got their Estates by the Governour; surely if your brother's crime had been so great, all the country would not have been for him, you never knew any better beloved than he is. I do verily believe that rather than he should come to any hurt by the Governour or anybody else they would most of them willingly lose their lives. The Governour has sent his Lady into England with great complaints to the King against Mr. Bacon, but when Mr. Bacon's and all the people's complaints be also heard, I hope it may be very well. Since your brother came in he hath sought to the Governour for commission, but none would be granted him, so that the Indians have had a very good time, to do more mischief. They have murdered and destroyed a great many whole families since, and the men resolving not to go under any but your brother, most of the country did rise in Arms, and went down to the Governour, and would not stir till he had given a commission to your brother which he has now done. He is made General of the Virginia War, and now I live in great fear, that he should lose his life amongst them. They are come very nigh our Plantation where we live.

Mary Horsmanden Byrd on the Grievances of Frontier Settlers in Virginia, 1676

Mrs. Bird's relation, who lived nigh Mr. Bacon in Virginia, and came from there July last for fear of the Indians.

Who saith, that before ever Mr. Bacon went out against the Indians, there

---

Some of the spelling in this document has been modernized.

were said to be above two hundred of the English murdered by the barbarous Indians, and posts came in daily to the Governour, giving notice of it, and yet no course was taken to secure them, till Mr. Bacon went out against them. And that her husband had 3 men killed by the Indians before Mr. Bacon stirr'd, which was made known to the Governour, who notwithstanding was so possessed to the contrary, that he would not believe it to be any other than a mere pretence, for to make war against the Indians, and that the said 3 men were alive and well, and only shut up in a chamber to make the world believe they were murdered. She further affirmed that neither Mr. Bacon nor any with him had injured any English man in their persons or Estates, and that the country was generally well pleased with what they had done, and she believed most of the council also, so far as they durst show it.

That the most of them with Mr. Bacon were substantial housekeepers who bore their own charges in this war against the Indians. And that so soon as Mr. Bacon had receiv'd his commission from the Governour he went out to the people (as she heard) and told them that though he had no power before to restrain some of their too lavishly tongues, they should now find he would make use of his power, to punish any man severely, that should dare to speak a word against the Governour or Government.

William Sherwood Denounces Bacon and His Defiance of the Law, 1676

VIRGINIA'S DEPLOURED CONDITION:
Or an Impartial Narrative of the Murders comitted by the
Indians there, and of the Sufferings of his Majesty's Loyal
Subjects under the Rebellious outrages of Mr Nathaniel
Bacon Junior to the tenth day of August Anno Domini 1676.

. . . [E]very one endeavours to get great tracts of Land, and many turn Land lopers, some take up 2000 acres, some 3000 Acres, others ten thousand Acres, nay many men have taken up thirty thousand Acres of Land, and never cultivated any part of it, only set up a hog house to save the Laps, thereby preventing others seating, so that too many rather than to be Tenants, seat upon the remote barren Land, whereby contentions arise between them and the Indians, for by Articles of peace, bounds are set between the English and the Indians, yet people are not content, but encroach upon them, taking up the very Towns or Lands they are seated upon, turning their Cattle and hogs on them, and if by Vermin or otherwise any be lost, then they exclaim against the Indians, beat & abuse them (notwithstanding the Governour's endeavour to the contrary) And this by the most moderate people is looked upon, as one of the great causes of the Indians' breach of peace, for it is the opinion of too many there, (and especially of their General Mr. Bacon) that faith is

---

Some of the spelling in this document has been modernized.

not to be kept with heathens, this brings great scandal upon the Christian Religion, and makes so few Indian converts. . . .

. . . Mr. Bacon was forced to come to Anchor, and he & his men were taken, brought to Town by Capt. Gardner & Capt. Hubert Farrell. Now great hopes was, that those intestine troubles would be ended, and no obstruction in carrying on the Indian War, the Burgesses the next Morning met, and that all private animosities and grudges might be laid aside, upon Mr. Bacon's submission, on his knees in open Court, and faithful promises of future good behaviour, he was pardoned, and he & his soldiers discharged.

The Assembly proceeded in forming an Army of 1000 Men, to be immediately raised, and sent out against the Indians, But Mr. Bacon goes home, harbouring private discontent, and studying revenge for his late confinement, sends to the factious, discontented people of New Kent, & those points, that several affronts were offered to him in his confinement, for his vindicating them, that the Assembly were bringing a great charge by raising more forces, and that instead of reducing the 500 men now in pay, they had ordered a thousand soldiers to be raised, suggesting to them that the only way for carrying on the War would be by Volunteers, of which he would be General so that (as bad actions are usually attended with worse) he gets the discontented rabble together, and with them resolved to put himself, once more on the stage, and on the 21st day of June he entered James Towne, with 400 foot, & 120 horse, set guards at the state house, kept the Governour, Council and Burgesses prisoners, and would suffer none to pass in or out of Town, and having drawn up all his forces to the very door & windows of the state house, he demanded a Commission to be General of all the forces that should be raised during the Indian War, he and all his soldiers crying out No Levies, No Levies. The Assembly acquainted him they had taken all possible care for carrying on the Indian War at the easiest charge that could be, that they had redressed all their Complaints, and desired that for satisfaction of the people, what they had done might be publicly read, Mr. Bacon answered there should be no Laws read there, that he would not admit of any delays, that he came for a Commission, and would immediately have it, thereupon sending his soldiers into the State house, where the Governour, Council & Burgesses were sitting and threatening them with fire and sword if it was not granted, his soldiers mounting their Guns ready to fire, So that for fear all would be in a flame, the Council and Burgesses Joined in a request to the Governour to grant Mr. Bacon such a Commission as he would have, the Governour declared he would rather lose his life than consent to the granting such unreasonable things as he demanded, but for prevention of that ruin, which was then threatened upon their second request, Order was given for such a Commission as Mr. Bacon would have himself, and according to his own dictates. The next morning the (forced) Commission was delivered to him, and the Assembly judged he was fully answered, and so were in hopes they should without restraint proceed in dispatch of the public affairs, but now Mr. Bacon having a Commission, shows himself in his colours, and hangs out his flag of defiance (that is) Imprisoning several loyal Gentlemen and his rabble used reproachful words of the Governour. . . . These threatenings and compulsions being upon them, the Assembly granted whatever he demanded, so that it was imagined he & his soldiers would march out of Town, yet they continued drinking and domineering, the frontier Counties being left with very little force, and the next day came the sad news that the Indians had that morning killed Eight people within thirty Miles of town, in the families of some of them that were with Mr. Bacon, yet they hastened not away, but the next day having forced an Act of Indemnity, and the Assembly being at the Burgesses' request disolved, Mr. Bacon after four days' stay, marched out of Town. Thus Mr. Bacon having his Commission, men, Arms & provision, gave out he would go against the Indians, but that (as it now plainly appeareth) was the last of his thoughts . . .

During Mr. Bacon's thus Lording it, and seizing the estates of such as he terms Traitors to the Commonality in which & in revelling & drinking most of his forces were employed, The Indians taking advantage of these civil commotions, have committed many horrid murders, in most part of the Country, which is altogether unable to resist them, their Arms & Ammunition being seized by Mr. Bacon's rabble for fear they should be employed against him, and daily murders were committed not only in the frontier Counties, but in the inward Counties, . . .

Thus is that Country by the rashness of a perverse man exposed to ruin, and is in a most calamitious & confused condition, lying open to the cruelty of the savage Indians, who in all likelihood had before now been totally subjected had not an insulting rabble prevented, who account the Law their manacles, and like swine turn all into disorder & become insolent, abuse all in authority (as a common drunkard being lately committed to the stocks threatened the Magistrate to raise a Mutiny) throwing off all allegiance to his most sacred Majesty and the Crown of England, and daringly say they will have the dutch to trade thither, with such like expressions. God in mercy divert the Issues of War which much threateneth the Country, by the Indians & the rabbles killing up, & destroying the stocks of Cattle, pulling down the Corn field fences, turning their horses in, and such like Outrages, so that unless his sacred Majesty do speedily send a considerable supply of men, Arms, Ammunition, & provision, there is great cause to fear the loss of that once hopeful Country, which is not able long to resist the cruelty of the Indians or rebellion of the Vulgar.

Planter William Fitzhugh
on Settled Life in Virginia, 1686

To Mr. Henry Fitzhugh

Dearest Brother:

With the Same Content and Satisfaction as wearied travellers take up their In, or weather Beaten Voyagers their desired Port After a long tedious and

---

Some of the spelling in this document has been modernized.

stormy voyage, so did I the most welcome joyful and glad news of your health, welfare and prosperity, which I had from my Sister, Cousin William Fitzhugh & more particularly from Mr. Cooper. Yourself would not add to that happiness I believe doubting too great a repetition, might cause a Surfeit, or too great & Sudden a joy, a Suffocation of the Spirits.

If that hindered you from writing last year I have prepared by a composed frame, Not to fear the one or doubt the other, but am ready with all acrity and Cheerfulness to hear from yourself of your condition and Welfare. God Almighty hath been pleased to bless me with a very good wife and five pledges of our conjugal affection, three of which he has been pleased to call into the Arms of his Mercy, and lent me two, a hopeful boy and girl, and one other that will not suffer So close confinement is preparing to come into the world. And as he has been pleased to dispense these, his choicest of blessings he hath likewise added a plentiful Dispensation of his favours in giving me a competent subsistence to support myself and them comfortably and handsomely.

I hear that he has been bountiful in his favours to you, for which I am really glad, and heartily congratulate you therein.

By my Sister I understand our poor Mother and dear Sister have not only tasted but drank a large draught of the cup of affliction and waded through abundance of calamities and trouble, which I truly condole, & do think it both our duty not only to commiserate, but as far as our ability extended not to suffer one to want, who gave us our being, nor suffer her to struggle to live who (under God) gave us life here. Charity directs to help those in want and distress, but Nature, Duty, the Laws of God and man not only commands but enjoins to give the utmost help to a distressed Parent.

Therefore I have ordered Mr. Cooper to let you have what money you have occasion for, to the Assisting them, if it be the utmost farthing; & if it should not be enough should be sorry I had no more there.—I refer to your discretion how much to take and how to dispose thereof.

My Mother's age will not admit of such a voyage therefore I hope you will take care that she end her days comfortably in her native Soil. But for my Sister if she cannot otherwise better herself, I should be heartily glad of her good company, with an Assurance she shall never want as long as I have it to supply her. And if her inclination be to come I would desire and entreat you, that she come out handsomely & gently & well clothed, with a maid to wait on her & both their passage paid there, if she has it not of her own, out of my money in Mr. Cooper's hands, if so much can be spared from our Mother, and for the credit of it let her pay the money herself before. By Captain Smith who will not be long before he goes, & a third time this year by way of Liverpool, opportunity will admit me to write you & shall then endeavor to put in anything that I have now omitted, & always assure you I am

Most Dear Brother

Your WF.

To Mrs. Dorothy Fitzhugh

Dear Sister:

Your two Kind and endearing letters I have received and heartily congratulate. The afflictions and miseries therein mentioned that our poor dear mother & yourself have gone through, I as truly condole, as the one gives me true contentment in your health and lives, so the other gives me as true a sense of sorrows for your calamities & afflictions, which God in his good time I hope will alleviate if not take off. I thank your care and kindness in your large and particular account of all friends and relations there. I have taken care with my brother according to my ability to assist both my mother and you, who I suppose will be so kind as to show his letter, & in assurance of that will save me some trouble in writing, because to him I must refer you for a more particular relation. Dear Sister, I have advised him to pursuade you, & now do entreat you myself to come in here, (except your fortune be above it) which your letter does not signify, where you will be a welcome and kind guest, both to me and my wife, & as long as I live you shall be assured not to want. The method I have taken for your coming in I would advise you by all means to follow, which will give us both credit & reputation, without which its uncomfortable living, & I am assured my brother will both assist and direct you in it. I hope the money I have ordered him to dispense will fully pay you and a maid to wait on you, your passage, & have something overplus gently to set forth yourself. I am now tired with writing & business, & do intend to write very speedily again, therefore shall add no further now; than only to assure I am

Dear Sister your &c.

To Mrs. Mary Fitzhugh

Dear Mother:

My Sister gives me a sad account of your continued misfortunes & afflictions for which I heartily grieve, & am really sorry that my distance will not admit me the happiness of your company, to comfort you in your afflictions, & that my ability is not as great as my desires to aid and assist you, you must accept my letter for my company, & I have taken care with my brother, to draw the utmost penny that I have in England, to contribute to your & my Sister's relief, those necessaries that was, designed for, I had rather be without than your necessities should continue, as far as my ability permit. I thank God I live very comfortably with a good wife & two children now living, five I had in all but three are dead & my wife is now with child.

Praised be God I neither live in poverty nor pomp, but in a very good indifferency & to a full content. My brother & Sister will more fully give you a particular relation of me & my concerns; to whom I refer. God Almighty I beseech to take off those afflictions he has been pleased to chasten you with, or endue you with a christian patience to bear them.

I have at present only to add to crave your, blessing & continuall prayers for Dear Mother

Your dutifull &c.

To Mr. William Fitzhugh Stationer &c.

Most Kind Cousin

I joyfully receiv'd your kind courteous & particular letter, & therein receive the full satisfaction and contentment to hear of the healths & welfare of all friends & relations therein enumerated, & particularly your own & wife, & children, which I pray God continue. I have also to return you my hearty thanks for your courteous trouble in communicating my letter, to the several relations in your's mentioned, I can't say I'll serve you in the like kind, but can assure you in anything that lies in my power, shall think myself happy in receiving your commands, & now intend to give due obedience to your desires in my particular to let you know, that I have been twelve years happy in a good wife & still continue so, & God Almighty has been pleased to bless me with five pledges of conjugal affection, three boys & two girls, the eldest girl & two youngest boys, I hope are Saints in heaven, my eldest son named William is now living & his sister, & I hope e'er long I may have another, to add to the number.

I have this year particularly written to my Mother, Brother, & Sister, therefore shall not give you the trouble in my behalf of saluting them, but must beg the favour to give my service & due respects to all friends & relations else, and more particularly to your father & mother & my aunt.

My wife gives her due respects to your self, & your wife, & I must entreat you to accept of the same from

Sr. Your WF.

To Doctor Ralph Smith in Bristol

Doctr. Ralph Smith

In order to the Exchange you promised to make for me & I desire you to proceed therein, to say to Exchange an Estate of Inheritance in land there of two or three hundred pound a year, or in houses in any town of three or four hundred pound a year, I shall be something particular in the relation of my concerns here that is to go in return thereof. As first the Plantation where I now live contains a thousand acres, at least 700 acres of it being rich thicket, the remainder good hearty plantable land, without any waste either by marshes or great swamps the commodiousness, conveniency & pleasantness yourself well knows, upon it there is three quarters well furnished with all necessary houses; grounds and fencing, together with a choice crew of negroes at each plantation, most of them this country born, the remainder as likely as most in Virginia, there being twenty nine in all, with stocks of cattle & hogs at each quarter, upon the same land, is my own Dwelling house furnished with all accommodations for a comfortable & gentle living, as a very good dwelling house with rooms in it, four of the best of them hung & nine of them plentifully furnished with all things necessary & convenient, & all houses for use furnished with brick chimneys, four good Cellars, a Dairy, Dovecot, Stable, Barn, Henhouse, Kitchen & all other conveniences & all in a manner new, a large Orchard, of about 2500 Apple trees most grafted, well fenced with a Locust fence, which is as durable as most brick walls, a Garden, a hundred foot square, well pailed in, a Yard wherein is most of the foresaid necessary houses, pallizado'd in with locust Punchens [posts], which is as good as if it were walled in & more lasting than any of our bricks, together with a good Stock of Cattle, hogs, horses, mares, sheep, &c., & necessary servants belonging to it, for the supply and support thereof. About a mile & half distance a good water Grist mill, whose tole* I find sufficient to find my own family with wheat & Indian corn for our necessities & occasions up the River in this county three tracts of land more, one of them contains 21996 acres, another 500 acres, & one other 1000 acres, all good convenient & commodious Seats, & which in few years will yield a considerable annual Income. A stock of Tobacco with the crops and good debts lying out of about 250000 pounds besides sufficient of almost all sorts of goods, to supply the family's & the Quarter's occasion for two if not three years. Thus I have given you some particulars, which I thus deduce the yearly crops of Corn & Tobacco together with the surplusage of meat more than will serve the family's use, will amount annually to 60000 pounds of Tobacco Which at 10 shillings per hundred pounds 300 £ per annum, & the negroes increase being all young & a considerable parcel of breeders will keep that stock good forever. The stock of Tobacco managed with an inland trade will yearly yield 60000 pounds of Tobacco without hazard or risk, which will be both clear without charge of housekeeping or disbursements for servants' clothing. The Orchard in a very few years will yield a large supply to plentiful housekeeping or if better husbanded yield at least 10000 pounds of Tobacco annual income. What I have not particularly mentioned your own knowledge in my affairs is able to supply, if any are so desirous to deal for the estate without the stock of Tobacco I shall be ready & willing, but I will make no fractions of that, either all or none at all shall go. I have so fully discoursed you in the affair that I shall add no farther instructions but leave it to your prudent and careful management & would advise that if any Overtures of such a nature should happen, immediately given an account thereof to Mr. Nicholas Hayward, Notary public, near the Exchange London, both of the person treating, & the place's Situation, Quantity & quality of the Estate, who will take speedy & effectual care to give me a full & ready account thereof, which I hope you will provide all the opportunities to do.

Sr Your WF.

Tole is the percentage of grain that the miller kept in return for grinding other people's corn.

These two classic essays address the changes in the Chesapeake in the last decades of the seventeenth century and see Bacon's Rebellion as an indicator of the forces at work. The rebellion marked the end of the developmental period of instability and the beginning of consolidation of power in the hands of a true elite group. This creole elite cemented the horizontal and vertical ties with relatives and with social superiors and inferiors that made early modern society work. In the first essay Bernard Bailyn, Adams University Professor at Harvard University, sees Bacon's Rebellion as one of a series of upheavals across the colonies that marked the emergence of a mature political system. For Edmund S. Morgan, Emeritus Professor of History at Yale University and the author of the second essay, the rebellion marks the end of Virginia as a land of opportunity for the English poor and the beginning of the colony's full commitment to slavery. The paradox of Virginia's history is the germination of the idea of universal human rights in the soil of slavery. Both authors find stability within Virginia after the rebellion, although Bailyn points out that the system institutionalized conflict with England.

Politics and Social Structure in Virginia

BERNARD BAILYN

By the end of the seventeenth century the American colonists faced an array of disturbing problems in the conduct of public affairs. Settlers from England and Holland, reconstructing familiar institutions on American shores, had become participants in what would appear to have been a wave of civil disobedience. Constituted authority was confronted with repeated challenges. Indeed, a veritable anarchy seems to have prevailed at the center of colonial society, erupting in a series of insurrections that began as early as 1635 with the "thrusting out" of Governor Harvey in Virginia. Culpeper's Rebellion in Carolina, the Protestant Association in Maryland, Bacon's Rebellion in Virginia, Leisler's seizure of power in New York, the resistance to and finally the overthrow of Andros in New England—every colony was affected.

These outbursts were not merely isolated local affairs. Although their immediate causes were rooted in the particular circumstances of the separate colonies, they nevertheless had common characteristics. They were, in fact, symptomatic of a profound disorganization of European society in its American setting. Seen in a broad view, they reveal a new configuration of forces which shaped the origins of American politics.

In a letter written from Virginia in 1632, George Sandys, the resident treasurer, reported despondently on the character and condition of the leading settlers. Some of the councilors were "no more then Ciphers," he wrote; others

Reprinted with omissions by permission of the author and publisher, from *Seventeenth-Century America: Essays in Colonial History,* edited by James Morton Smith. Published for the Institute of Early American History and Culture, Williamsburg, Virginia. © 1959 The University of North Carolina Press.

were "miserablie poore"; and the few substantial planters lived apart, taking no responsibility for public concerns. There was, in fact, among all those "worthie the mencioninge" only one person deserving of full approval. Lieutenant William Peirce "refuses no labour, nor sticks at anie expences that may aduantage the publique." Indeed, Sandys added, Peirce was "of a Capacitie that is not to bee expected in a man of his breedinge."

The afterthought was penetrating. It cut below the usual complaints of the time that many of the settlers were lazy malcontents hardly to be preferred to the Italian glassworkers, than whom, Sandys wrote, "a more damned crew hell never vomited." What lay behind Sandys' remark was not so much that wretched specimens were arriving in the shipments of servants nor even that the quality of public leadership was declining but that the social foundations of political power were being strangely altered.

All of the settlers in whatever colony presumed a fundamental relationship between social structure and political authority. Drawing on a common medieval heritage, continuing to conceive of society as a hierarchical unit, its parts justly and naturally separated into inferior and superior levels, they assumed that superiority was indivisible; there was not one hierarchy for political matters, another for social purposes. John Winthrop's famous explanation of God's intent that "in all times some must be rich some poore, some highe and eminent in power and dignitie; others meane and in subieccion" could not have been more carefully worded. Riches, dignity, and power were properly placed in apposition; they pertained to the same individuals. . . .

. . . Nothing could have been more alien to the settlers than the idea that competition for political leadership should be open to all levels of society or that obscure social origins or technical skills should be considered valuable qualifications for office. . . .

In the first years of settlement no one had reason to expect that this characteristic of public life [leadership by the gentry and landed aristocracy] would fail to transfer itself to the colonies. For at least a decade and a half after its founding there had been in the Jamestown settlement a small group of leaders drawn from the higher echelons of English society. . . .

There was, in other words, during the first years of settlement a direct transference to Virginia of the upper levels of the English social hierarchy as well as of the lower. If the great majority of the settlers were recruited from the yeoman class and below, there was nevertheless a reasonable representation from those upper groups acknowledged to be the rightful rulers of society. It is a fact of some importance, however, that this governing elite did not survive a single generation, at least in its original form. By the [1630s] their number had declined to insignificance. . . .

. . . The group of gentlemen and illuminati that had dominated the scene during the Company era had been dispersed. Their disappearance created a political void which was filled soon enough, but from a different area of recruitment, from below, from the toughest and most fortunate of the surviving planters whose eminence by the end of the thirties had very little to do with the transplantation of social status.

The position of the new leaders rested on their ability to wring material gain from the wilderness. Some, like Samuel Mathews, started with large initial advantages, but more typical were George Menefie and John Utie, who began as independent landowners by right of transporting themselves and only one or two servants. Abraham Wood, famous for his explorations and like Menefie and Utie the future possessor of large estates and important offices, appears first as a servant boy on Mathews' plantation. Adam Thoroughgood, the son of a country vicar, also started in Virginia as a servant, aged fourteen. William Spencer is first recorded as a yeoman farmer without servants.

Such men as these—Spencer, Wood, Menefie, Utie, Mathews—were the most important figures in Virginia politics up to the Restoration, engrossing large tracts of land, dominating the Council, unseating Sir John Harvey from the governorship. But in no traditional sense were they a ruling class. They lacked the attributes of social authority, and their political dominance was a continuous achievement. Only with the greatest difficulty, if at all, could distinction be expressed in a genteel style of life, for existence in this generation was necessarily crude. Mathews may have created a flourishing estate and Menefie had splendid fruit gardens, but the great tracts of land such men claimed were almost entirely raw wilderness. They had risen to their positions, with few exceptions, by brute labor and shrewd manipulation; they had personally shared the burdens of settlement. They succeeded not because of, but despite, whatever gentility they may have had. William Claiborne [Claiborne built a trade empire in Chesapeake Bay] may have been educated at the Middle Temple; Peirce could not sign his name; but what counted was their common capacity to survive and flourish in frontier settlements. They were tough, unsentimental, quick-tempered, crudely ambitious men concerned with profits and increased landholdings, not the grace of life. They roared curses, drank exuberantly, and gambled . . . for their servants when other commodities were lacking. If the worst of Governor Harvey's offenses had been to knock out the teeth of an offending councilor with a cudgel, as he did on one occasion, no one would have questioned his right to the governorship. Rank had its privileges, and these men were the first to claim them, but rank itself was unstable and the lines of class or status were fluid. There was no insulation for even the most elevated from the rude impact of frontier life.

As in style of life so in politics, these leaders of the first permanently settled generation did not re-create the characteristics of a stable gentry. They had had little opportunity to acquire the sense of public responsibility that rests on deep identification with the land and its people. They performed in some manner the duties expected of leaders, but often public office was found simply burdensome. . . .

The private interests of this group, which had assumed control of public office by virtue not of inherited status but of newly achieved and strenuously maintained economic eminence, were pursued with little interference from the traditional restraints imposed on a responsible ruling class. Engaged in an effort to establish themselves in the land, they sought as specific ends: autonomous local jurisdiction, an aggressive expansion of settlement and trading enterprises, unrestricted access to land, and, at every stage, the legal endorsement of acquisitions. Most of the major public events for thirty years after the dissolution of the Company ... were incidents in the pursuit of these goals....

One might at that point have projected the situation forward into a picture of dominant county families dating from the 1620's and 1630's, growing in identification with the land and people, ruling with increasing responsibility from increasingly eminent positions. But such a projection would be false. The fact is that with a few notable exceptions like the Scarboroughs and the Wormeleys, these struggling planters of the first generation failed to perpetuate their leadership into the second generation. Such families as the Woods, the Uties, the Mathews, and the Peirces faded from dominant positions of authority after the deaths of their founders. To some extent this was the result of the general insecurity of life that created odds against the physical survival in the male line of any given family. But even if male heirs had remained in these families after the death of the first generation, undisputed eminence would not. For a new emigration had begun in the forties, continuing for close to thirty years, from which was drawn a new ruling group that had greater possibilities for permanent dominance than Harvey's opponents had had. These newcomers absorbed and subordinated the older group, forming the basis of the most celebrated oligarchy in American history.

Most of Virginia's great eighteenth-century names, such as Bland, Burwell, Byrd, Carter, Digges, Ludwell, and Mason, appear in the colony for the first time within ten years either side of 1655. These progenitors of the eighteenth-century aristocracy arrived in remarkably similar circumstances. The most important of these immigrants were younger sons of substantial families well connected in London business and governmental circles and long associated with Virginia; family claims to land in the colony or inherited shares of the original Company stock were now brought forward as a basis for establishment in the New World....

Claims on the colony such as these were only one, though the most important, of a variety of forms of capital that might provide the basis for secure family fortunes. One might simply bring over enough of a merchant family's resources to begin immediately building up an imposing estate, as, presumably, did that ambitious draper's son, William Fitzhugh. The benefits that accrued from such advantages were quickly translated into landholdings in the development of which these settlers were favored by the chronology of their arrival. For though they extended the area of cultivation in developing their landholdings, they were not obliged to initiate settlement. They fell heirs to large areas of the tidewater region that had already been brought under cultivation....

Favored thus by circumstance, a small group within the second generation migration moved toward setting itself off in a permanent way as a ruling landed gentry. That they succeeded was due not only to their material advantages but also to the force of their motivation. For these individuals were in social origins just close enough to establishment in gentility to feel the pangs of deprivation most acutely. It is not the totally but the partially dispossessed who build up the most propulsive aspirations, and behind the zestful lunging at propriety and status of a William Fitzhugh lay not the narcotic yearnings of the disinherited but the pent-up ambitions of the gentleman *manqué*. These were neither hardhanded pioneers nor dilettante romantics, but ambitious younger sons of middle-class families who knew well enough what gentility was and sought it as a specific objective.

The establishment of this group was rapid. Within a decade of their arrival they could claim, together with a fortunate few of the first generation, a marked social eminence and full political authority at the county level. But their rise was not uniform. Indeed, by the seventies a new circumstance had introduced an effective principle of social differentiation among the colony's leaders. A hierarchy of position within the newly risen gentry was created by the Restoration government's efforts to extend its control more effectively over its mercantile empire. Demanding of its colonial executives and their advisors closer supervision over the external aspects of the economy, it offered a measure of patronage necessary for enforcement. Public offices dealing with matters that profoundly affected the basis of economic life—tax collection, customs regulation, and the bestowal of land grants—fell within the gift of the governor and tended to form an inner circle of privilege. One can note in Berkeley's administration the growing importance of this barrier of offi-cialdom. Around its privileges there formed the "Green Spring" faction, named after Berkeley's plantation near Jamestown, a group bound to the governor not by royalist sympathies so much as by ties of kinship and patronage. . . .

The growing distinctiveness of provincial officialdom within the landed gentry may also be traced in the transformation of the Council. Originally, this body had been expected to comprise the entire effective government, central and local; councilors were to serve, individually or in committees, as local magistrates. But the spread of settlement upset this expectation, and at the same time as the local offices were falling into the hands of autonomous local powers representing leading county families, the Council, appointed by the governor and hence associated with official patronage, increasingly real-ized the separate, lucrative privileges available to it.

As the distinction between local and central authority became clear, the county magistrates sought their own distinct voice in the management of the colony, and they found it in developing the possibilities of burgess represen-tation. In the beginning there was no House of Burgesses; representation from the burghs and hundreds was conceived of not as a branch of government separate from the Council but as a periodic supplement to it. Until the fifties the burgesses, meeting in the Assemblies with the councilors, felt little need to form themselves into a separate house, for until that decade there was little evidence of a conflict of interests between the two groups. But when, after the Restoration, the privileged status of the Council became unmistakable and the county magnates found control of the increasingly important provincial administration preempted by this body, the burgess part of the Assembly took on a new meaning in contrast to that of the Council. Burgess representation now became vital to the county leaders if they were to share in any consistent way in affairs larger than those of the counties. They looked to the franchise, hitherto broad not by design but by neglect, introducing qualifications that would ensure their control of the Assembly. Their interest in provincial government could no longer be expressed in the conglomerate Assembly, and at least by 1663 the House of Burgesses began to meet separately as a distinct body voicing interests potentially in conflict with those of the Council.

Thus by the eighth decade the ruling class in Virginia was broadly based on leading county families and dominated at the provincial level by a privileged officialdom. But this social and political structure was too new, too lacking in the sanctions of time and custom, its leaders too close to humbler origins and as yet too undistinguished in style of life, to be accepted without a struggle. A period of adjustment was necessary, of which Bacon's Rebellion was the climactic episode.

Bacon's Rebellion began as an unauthorized frontier war against the Indians and ended as an upheaval that threatened the entire basis of social and political authority. Its immediate causes have to do with race relations and settlement policy, but behind these issues lay deeper elements related to resistance against the maturing shape of a new social order. These elements explain the dimensions the conflict reached.

There was, first, resistance by the substantial planters to the privileges and policies of the inner provincial clique led by Berkeley and composed of those directly dependent on his patronage. These dissidents, among whom were the leaders of the Rebellion, represented neither the downtrodden masses nor a principle of opposition to privilege as such. Their discontent stemmed to a large extent from their own exclusion from privileges they sought. Most often their grievances were based on personal rebuffs they had received as they reached for entry into provincial officialdom. Thus—to speak of the leaders of the Rebellion—Giles Bland arrived in Virginia in 1671 to take over the agency of his late uncle in the management of his father's extensive landholdings, assuming at the same time the lucrative position of customs collector which he had obtained in London. But, amid angry cries of "*pittyfull fellow, puppy* and *Sonn of a Whore,*" he fell out first with Berkeley's cousin and favorite, Thomas Ludwell, and finally with the governor himself; for his "Barbarous and Insolent Behaviors" Bland was fined, arrested, and finally removed from the collectorship. Of the two "chiefe Incendiarys," William Drummond and Richard Lawrence, the former had been quarreling with Berkeley since 1664, first over land claims in Carolina, then over a contract for building a fort near James City, and repeatedly over lesser issues in the General Court; Lawrence "some Years before . . . had been partially treated at Law, for a considerable Estate on behalfe of a Corrupt favorite." Giles Brent, for his depredations against the Indians in violation of official policy, had not only been severely fined but barred from public office. Bacon himself could not have appeared under more favorable circumstances. A cousin both of Lady Berkeley and of the councilor Nathaniel Bacon, Sr., and by general agreement "a Gent:man of a Liberall education" if of a somewhat tarnished reputation, he had quickly staked out land for himself and had been elevated, for reasons "best known to the Governour," to the Council. But being "of a most imperious and dangerous hidden Pride of heart . . . very ambitious and arrogant," he wanted more, and quickly. His alienation from and violent opposition to Berkeley were wound in among the animosities created by the

Indian problem and were further complicated by his own unstable personality; they were related also to the fact that Berkeley finally turned down the secret offer Bacon and Byrd made in 1675 for the purchase from the governor of a monopoly of the Indian trade.

These specific disputes have a more general aspect. It was three decades since Berkeley had assumed the governorship and begun rallying a favored group, and it was over a decade since the Restoration had given this group unconfined sway over the provincial government. In those years much of the choice tidewater land as well as the choice offices had been spoken for, and the tendency of the highly placed was to hold firm. Berkeley's Indian policy—one of stabilizing the borders between Indians and whites and protecting the natives from depredation by land-hungry settlers—although a sincere attempt to deal with an extremely difficult problem, was also conservative, favoring the established. Newcomers like Bacon and Bland and particularly landholders on the frontiers felt victimized by a stabilization of the situation or by a controlled expansion that maintained on an extended basis the existing power structure. They were logically drawn to aggressive positions. In an atmosphere charged with violence, their interests constituted a challenge to provincial authority. Bacon's primary appeal in his "Manifesto" played up the threat of this challenge:

> Let us trace these men in Authority and Favour to those hands the dispensation of the Countries wealth had been commited; let us observe the sudden Rise of their Estates [compared] with the Quality in wch they first entered this Country. . . . And lett us see wither their extractions and Education have not bin vile, And by what pretence of learning and vertue they could [enter] soe soon into Imployments of so great Trust and consequence, let us . . . see what spounges have suckt up the Publique Treasure and wither it hath not bin privately contrived away by unworthy Favourites and juggling Parasites whose tottering Fortunes have bin repaired and supported at the Publique chardg.

Such a threat to the basis of authority was not lost on Berkeley or his followers. Bacon's merits, a contemporary wrote, "thretned an eclips to their riseing gloryes. . . . (if he should continue in the Governours favour) of Seniours they might becom juniours, while there younger Brother . . . might steale away that blessing, which they accounted there owne by birthright."

But these challengers were themselves challenged, for another main element in the upheaval was the discontent among the ordinary settlers at the local privileges of the same newly risen county magnates who assailed the privileges of the Green Spring faction. The specific Charles City County grievances were directed as much at the locally dominant family, the Hills, as they were at Berkeley and his clique. Similarly, Surry County complained of its county court's highhanded and secretive manner of levying taxes on "the poore people" and of setting the sheriffs' and clerks' fees; they petitioned for the removal of these abuses and for the right to elect the vestry and to limit the tenure of the sheriffs. At all levels the Rebellion challenged the stability of newly secured authority.

It is this double aspect of discontent behind the violence of the Rebellion that explains the legislation passed in June, 1676, by the so-called "Bacon's Assembly." At first glance these laws seem difficult to interpret because they express disparate if not contradictory interests. But they yield readily to analysis if they are seen not as the reforms of a single group but as efforts to express the desires of two levels of discontent with the way the political and social hierarchy was becoming stabilized. On the one hand, the laws include measures designed by the numerically predominant ordinary settlers throughout the colony as protests against the recently acquired superiority of the leading county families. These were popular protests and they relate not to provincial affairs but to the situation within the local areas of jurisdiction. Thus the statute restricting the franchise to freeholders was repealed; freemen were given the right to elect the parish vestrymen; and the county courts were supplemented by elected freemen to serve with the regularly appointed county magistrates.

On the other hand, there was a large number of measures expressing the dissatisfactions not so much of the ordinary planter but of the local leaders against the prerogatives recently acquired by the provincial elite, prerogatives linked to officialdom and centered in the Council. Thus the law barring office-holding to newcomers of less than three years' residence struck at the arbitrary elevation of the governor's favorites, including Bacon; and the acts forbidding councilors to join the county courts, outlawing the governor's appointment of sheriffs and tax collectors, and nullifying tax exemption for councilors all voiced objectives of the local chieftains to privileges enjoyed by others. From both levels there was objection to profiteering in public office.

Thus the wave of rebellion broke and spread. But why did it subside? One might have expected that the momentary flood would have become a steady tide, its rhythms governed by a fixed political constellation. But in fact it did not; stable political alignments did not result. The conclusion to this controversy was characteristic of all the insurrections. The attempted purges and counterpurges by the leaders of the two sides were followed by a rapid submerging of factional identity. Occasional references were later made to the episode, and there were individuals who found an interest in keeping its memory alive. Also, the specific grievances behind certain of the attempted legal reforms of 1676 were later revived. But of stable parties or factions around these issues there were none.

It was not merely that in the late years of the century no more than in the early was there to be found a justification for permanently organized political opposition or party machinery, that persistent, organized dissent was still indistinguishable from sedition; more important was the fact that at the end of the century as in 1630 there was agreement that some must be "highe and eminent in power and dignitie; others meane and in subieccion." Protests and upheaval had resulted from the discomforts of discovering who was, in fact, which, and what the particular consequences of "power and dignitie" were.

But by the end of the century the most difficult period of adjustment had passed and there was an acceptance of the fact that certain families were distinguished from others in riches, in dignity, and in access to political authority. The establishment of these families marks the emergence of Virginia's colonial aristocracy.

It was a remarkable governing group. Its members were soberly responsible, alive to the implications of power; they performed their public obligations with notable skill. Indeed, the glare of their accomplishments is so bright as occasionally to blind us to the conditions that limited them. As a ruling class the Virginian aristocracy of the eighteenth century was unlike other contemporary nobilities or aristocracies, including the English. The differences, bound up with the special characteristics of the society it ruled, had become clear at the turn of the seventeenth century.

Certain of these characteristics are elusive, difficult to grasp and analyze. The leaders of early eighteenth-century Virginia were, for example, in a particular sense, cultural provincials. They were provincial not in the way of Polish *szlachta* isolated on their estate by poverty and impassable roads, nor in the way of sunken *seigneurs* grown rustic and oldfashioned in lonely Norman chateaux. The Virginians were far from uninformed or unaware of the greater world; they were in fact deeply and continuously involved in the cultural life of the Atlantic community. But they knew themselves to be provincials in the sense that their culture was not self-contained; its sources and superior expressions were to be found elsewhere than in their own land. They must seek it from afar; it must be acquired, and once acquired be maintained according to standards externally imposed, in the creation of which they had not participated. The most cultivated of them read much, purposefully, with a diligence the opposite of that essential requisite of aristocracy, uncontending ease. William Byrd's diary with its daily records of stints of study is a stolid testimonial to the virtues of regularity and effort in maintaining standards of civilization set abroad.

In more evident ways also the Virginia planters were denied an uncontending ease of life. They were not *rentiers*. Tenancy, when it appeared late in the colonial period, was useful to the landowners mainly as a cheap way of improving lands held in reserve for future development. The Virginia aristocrat was an active manager of his estate, drawn continuously into the most intimate contacts with the soil and its cultivation. This circumstance limited his ease, one might even say bound him to the soil, but it also strengthened his identity with the land and its problems and saved him from the temptation to create of his privileges an artificial world of self-indulgence.

But more important in distinguishing the emerging aristocracy of Virginia from other contemporary social and political elites were two very specific circumstances. The first concerns the relationship between the integrity of the family unit and the descent of real property. . . . The descent of landed estates in eighteenth-century England was controlled by the complicated device known as the strict settlement, which provided that the heir at his marriage received the estate as a life tenant, entailing its descent to his unborn eldest son and specifying the limitations of the encumbrances upon the land that might be made in behalf of his daughters and younger sons.

It was the strict settlement, in which in the eighteenth century perhaps half the land of England was bound, that provided continuity over generations for the landed aristocracy. This permanent identification of the family with a specific estate and with the status and offices that pertained to it was achieved at the cost of sacrificing the young sons. It was a single stem of the family only that retained its superiority; it alone controlled the material basis for political dominance.

This basic condition of aristocratic governance in England was never present in the American colonies, and not for lack of familiarity with legal forms. The economic necessity that had prompted the widespread adoption of the strict settlement in England was absent in the colonies. Land was cheap and easily available, the more so as one rose on the social and political ladder. There was no need to deprive the younger sons or even daughters of landed inheritances in order to keep the original family estate intact. Provision could be made for endowing each of them with plantations, and they in turn could provide similarly for their children. Moreover, to confine the stem family's fortune to a single plot of land, however extensive, was in the Virginia economy to condemn it to swift decline. Since the land was quickly worn out and since it was cheaper to acquire new land than to rejuvenate the worked soil by careful husbandry, geographical mobility, not stability, was the key to prosperity. Finally, since land was only as valuable as the labor available to work it, a great estate was worth passing intact from generation to generation only if it had annexed to it a sufficient population of slaves. Yet this condition imposed severe rigidities in a plantation's economy—for a labor force bound to a particular plot was immobilized—besides creating bewildering confusions in law.

The result, evident before the end of the seventeenth century, was a particular relationship between the family and the descent of property. There was in the beginning no intent on the part of the Virginians to alter the traditional forms; the continued vitality of the ancient statutes specifying primogeniture in certain cases was assumed. The first clear indication of a new trend came in the third quarter of the century, when the leading gentry, rapidly accumulating large estates, faced for the first time the problem of the transfer of property. The result was the subdivision of the great holdings and the multiplication of smaller plots while the net amount of land held by the leading families continued to rise.

This trend continued. Primogeniture neither at the end of the seventeenth century nor after prevailed in Virginia. It was never popular even among the most heavily endowed of the tidewater families. The most common form of bequest was a grant to the eldest son of the undivided home plantation and gifts of other tracts outside the home county to the younger sons and daughters. . . .

Entail* proved no more popular than primogeniture. Only a small minority of estates, even in the tidewater region, were ever entailed. In fact, despite the extension of developed land in the course of the eighteenth century, more tidewater estates were docked of entails than were newly entailed. . . .

Entail: to settle an estate on a number of persons in succession so that the estate must pass on intact to a specified sucession of heirs.

A mobile labor force free from legal entanglements and a rapid turnover of lands, not a permanent hereditary estate, were prerequisites of family prosperity. This condition greatly influenced social and political life. Since younger sons and even daughters inherited extensive landed properties, equal often to those of the eldest son, concentration of authority in the stem family was precluded. Third generation collateral descendants of the original immigrant were as important in their own right as the eldest son's eldest son. Great clans like the Carters and the Lees, though they may have acknowledged a central family seat, were scattered throughout the province on estates of equal influence. The four male Carters of the third generation were identified by contemporaries by the names of their separate estates, and, indistinguishable in style of life, they had an equal access to political power.

Since material wealth was the basis of the status which made one eligible for public office, there was a notable diffusion of political influence throughout a broadening group of leading families. No one son was predestined to represent the family interest in politics, but as many as birth and temperament might provide. In the 1750's there were no fewer than seven Lees of the same generation sitting together in the Virginia Assembly; in the Burgesses they spoke for five separate counties. To the eldest, Philip Ludwell Lee, they conceded a certain social superiority that made it natural for him to sit in the Council. But he did not speak alone for the family; by virtue of inheritance he had no unique authority over his brothers and cousins.

The leveling at the top of the social and political hierarchy, creating an evenness of status and influence, was intensified by continuous intermarriage within the group. The unpruned branches of these flourishing family trees, growing freely, met and intertwined until by the Revolution the aristocracy appeared to be one great tangled cousinry.

As political power became increasingly diffused throughout the upper stratum of society, the Council, still at the end of the seventeenth century a repository of unique privileges, lost its effective superiority. Increasingly through the successive decades its authority had to be exerted through alignments with the Burgesses—alignments made easier as well as more necessary by the criss-crossing network of kinship that united the two houses. Increasingly the Council's distinctions became social and ceremonial.

The contours of Virginia's political hierarchy were also affected by a second main conditioning element, besides the manner of descent of family property. Not only was the structure unusually level and broad at the top, but it was incomplete in itself. Its apex, the ultimate source of legal decision and control, lay in the quite different society of England, amid the distant embroilments of London, the court, and Parliament. The levers of control in that realm were for the most part hidden from the planters; yet the powers that ruled this remote region could impose an arbitrary authority directly into the midst of Virginia's affairs.

One consequence was the introduction of instabilities in the tenure and transfer of the highest offices. Tenure could be arbitrarily interrupted, and the transfer to kin of such positions at death or resignation—uncertain in any case because of the diffusion of family authority—could be quite difficult or even impossible. . . . There was family continuity in public office, but at the highest level it was uncertain, the result of place-hunting rather than of the absolute prerogative of birth.

Instability resulted not only from the difficulty of securing and transferring high appointive positions but also and more immediately from the presence in Virginia of total strangers to the scene, particularly governors and their deputies, armed with extensive jurisdiction and powers of enforcement. The dangers of this element in public life became clear only after Berkeley's return to England in 1677, for after thirty-five years of residence in the colony Sir William had become a leader in the land independent of his royal authority. But Howard, Andros, and Nicholson were governors with full legal powers but with at best only slight connections with local society. In them, social leadership and political leadership had ceased to be identical.

In the generation that followed Berkeley's departure, this separation between the two spheres created the bitterest of political controversies. Firmly entrenched behind their control of the colony's government, the leading families battled with every weapon available to reduce the power of the executives and thus to eliminate what appeared to be an external and arbitrary authority. Repeated complaints by the governors of the intractable opposition of a league of local oligarchs marked the Virginians' success. Efforts by the executives to discipline the indigenous leaders could only be mildy successful. Patronage was a useful weapon, but its effectiveness diminished steadily, ground down between a resistant Assembly and an office-hungry bureaucracy in England. The possibility of exploiting divisions among the resident powers also declined as kinship lines bound the leading families closer together and as group interests became clearer with the passage of time. . . .

In all of the colonies the original transference of an ordered European society was succeeded by the rise to authority of resident settlers whose influence was rooted in their ability to deal with the problems of life in wilderness settlements. These individuals attempted to stabilize their positions, but in each case they were challenged by others arriving after the initial settlements, seeking to exploit certain advantages of position, wealth, or influence. These newcomers, securing after the Restoration governmental appointments in the colonies and drawn together by personal ties, especially those of kinship and patronage, came to constitute colonial officialdom. This group introduced a new principle of social organization; it also gave rise to new instabilities in a society in which the traditional forms of authority were already being subjected to severe pressures. By the eighth decade of the seventeenth century the social basis of public life had become uncertain and insecure, its stability delicate and sensitive to disturbance. Indian warfare, personal quarrels, and particularly the temporary confusion in external control caused by the Glorious Revolution became the occasions for violent challenges to constituted authority.

By the end of the century a degree of harmony had been achieved, but the divergence between political and social leadership at the topmost level created an area of permanent conflict. The political and social structures that emerged were by European standards strangely shaped. Everywhere as the bonds of empire drew tighter the meaning of the state was changing. Herein lay the origins of a new political system.

Slavery and Freedom: The American Paradox

EDMUND S. MORGAN

American historians interested in tracing the rise of liberty, democracy, and the common man have been challenged in the past two decades by other historians, interested in tracing the history of oppression, exploitation, and racism. The challenge has been salutary, because it has made us examine more directly than historians have hitherto been willing to do, the role of slavery in our early history. . . . We owe a debt of gratitude to those who have insisted that slavery was something more than an exception, that one fifth of the American population at the time of the Revolution is too many people to be treated as an exception.

We shall not have met the challenge simply by studying the history of that one fifth, fruitful as such studies may be, urgent as they may be. Nor shall we have met the challenge if we merely execute the familiar maneuver of turning our old interpretations on their heads. The temptation is already apparent to argue that slavery and oppression were the dominant features of American history and that efforts to advance liberty and equality were the exception, indeed no more than a device to divert the masses while their chains were being fastened. To dismiss the rise of liberty and equality in American history as a mere sham is not only to ignore hard facts, it is also to evade the problem presented by those facts. The rise of liberty and equality in this country was accompanied by the rise of slavery. That two such contradictory developments were taking place simultaneously over a long period of our history, from the seventeenth century to the nineteenth, is the central paradox of American history. . . .

The story properly begins in England with the burst of population growth there that sent the number of Englishmen from perhaps three million in 1500 to four-and-one-half million by 1650. The increase did not occur in response to any corresponding growth in the capacity of the island's economy to support its people. And the result was precisely that misery which Madison pointed out to Jefferson as the consequence of "a high degree of populousness." Sixteenth-century England knew the same kind of unemployment and poverty that Jefferson witnessed in eighteenth-century France and Fletcher in seventeenth-century Scotland. Alarming numbers of idle and hungry men drifted about the country looking for work or plunder. The government did what it could to make men of means hire them, but it also adopted increasingly severe measures against their wandering, their thieving, their roistering, and indeed their very existence. Whom the workhouses and prisons could not swallow the gallows would have to, or perhaps the army. When England had

Edmund Morgan, "Slavery and Freedom: The American Paradox," *Journal of American History,* 59 (June 1972), 5–29. Reprinted by permission of the publisher.

military expeditions to conduct abroad, every parish packed off its most unwanted inhabitants to the almost certain death that awaited them from the
diseases of the camp.

As the mass of idle rogues and beggars grew and increasingly threatened
the peace of England, the efforts to cope with them increasingly threatened
the liberties of Englishmen. Englishmen prided themselves on a "gentle government," a government that had been releasing its subjects from old forms
of bondage and endowing them with new liberties, making the "rights of
Englishmen" a phrase to conjure with. But there was nothing gentle about
the government's treatment of the poor; and as more Englishmen became
poor, other Englishmen had less to be proud of. Thoughtful men could see
an obvious solution: get the surplus Englishmen out of England. Send them
to the New World, where there were limitless opportunities for work. There
they would redeem themselves, enrich the mother country, and spread English
liberty abroad.

The great publicist for this program was Richard Hakluyt. His *Principall
Navigations, Voiages and Discoveries of the English nation* was not merely
the narrative of voyages by Englishmen around the globe, but a powerful
suggestion that the world ought to be English or at least ought to be ruled
by Englishmen. Hakluyt's was a dream of empire, but of benevolent empire,
in which England would confer the blessings of her own free government on
the less fortunate peoples of the world. It is doubtless true that Englishmen,
along with other Europeans, were already imbued with prejudice against men
of darker complexions than their own. And it is also true that the principal
beneficiaries of Hakluyt's empire would be Englishmen. But Hakluyt's dream
cannot be dismissed as mere hypocrisy any more than Jefferson's affirmation
of human equality can be so dismissed. Hakluyt's compassion for the poor
and oppressed was not confined to the English poor, and in Francis Drake's
exploits in the Caribbean Hakluyt saw, not a thinly disguised form of piracy,
but a model for English liberation of men of all colors who labored under
the tyranny of the Spaniard. . . .

. . . Hakluyt's vision endured, of liberated natives and surplus Englishmen,
courteously governed in English colonies around the world. Sir Walter Raleigh
caught the vision. He dreamt of wresting the treasure of the Incas from the
Spaniard by allying with the Indians of Guiana and sending Englishmen to
live with them, lead them in rebellion against Spain, and govern them in the
English manner. Raleigh also dreamt of a similar colony in the country he
named Virginia. Hakluyt helped him plan it. And Drake stood ready to supply
Negroes and Indians, liberated from Spanish tyranny in the Caribbean, to help
the enterprise.

Virginia from the beginning was conceived not only as a haven for
England's suffering poor, but as a spearhead of English liberty in an oppressed
world. That was the dream; but when it began to materialize at Roanoke
Island in 1585, something went wrong. Drake did his part by liberating Spanish Caribbean slaves, and carrying to Roanoke those who wished to join him.
But the English settlers whom Raleigh sent there proved unworthy of the role
assigned them. By the time Drake arrived they had shown themselves less

than courteous to the Indians on whose assistance they depended. The first group of settlers murdered the chief who befriended them, and then gave up and ran for home aboard Drake's returning ships. The second group simply disappeared, presumably killed by the Indians.

What was lost in this famous lost colony was more than the band of colonists who have never been traced. What was also lost and never quite recovered in subsequent ventures was the dream of Englishman and Indian living side by side in peace and liberty. When the English finally planted a permanent colony at Jamestown they came as conquerors, and their government was far from gentle. The Indians willing to endure it were too few in numbers and too broken in spirit to play a significant part in the settlement.

Without their help, Virginia offered a bleak alternative to the workhouse or the gallows for the first English poor who were transported there. During the first two decades of the colony's existence, most of the arriving immigrants found precious little English liberty in Virginia. But by the 1630s the colony seemed to be working out, at least in part, as its first planners had hoped. Impoverished Englishmen were arriving every year in large numbers, engaged to serve the existing planters for a term of years, with the prospect of setting up their own households a few years later. The settlers were spreading up Virginia's great rivers, carving out plantations, living comfortably from their corn fields and from the cattle they ranged in the forests, and at the same time earning perhaps ten or twelve pounds a year per man from the tobacco they planted. A representative legislative assembly secured the traditional liberties of Englishmen and enabled a larger proportion of the population to participate in their own government than had ever been the case in England. The colony even began to look a little like the cosmopolitan haven of liberty that Hakluyt had first envisaged. Men of all countries appeared there: French, Spanish, Dutch, Turkish, Portuguese, and African. Virginia took them in and began to make Englishmen out of them.

It seems clear that most of the Africans, perhaps all of them, came as slaves, a status that had become obsolete in England, while it was becoming the expected condition of Africans outside Africa and of a good many inside. It is equally clear that a substantial number of Virginia's Negroes were free or became free. And all of them, whether servant, slave, or free, enjoyed most of the same rights and duties as other Virginians. There is no evidence during the period before 1660 that they were subjected to a more severe discipline than other servants. They could sue and be sued in court. They did penance in the parish church for having illegitimate children. They earned money of their own, bought and sold and raised cattle of their own. Sometimes they bought their own freedom. In other cases, masters bequeathed them not only freedom but land, cattle, and houses. Northampton, the only county for which full records exist, had at least ten free Negro households by 1668.

As Negroes took their place in the community, they learned English ways, including even the truculence toward authority that has always been associated with the rights of Englishmen. Tony Longo, a free Negro of Northampton, when served a warrant to appear as a witness in court, responded with a scatological opinion of warrants, called the man who served it an idle rascal, and told him to go about his business. The man offered to go with him at any time before a justice of the peace so that his evidence could be recorded. He would go with him at night, tomorrow, the next day, next week, any time. But Longo was busy getting in his corn. He dismissed all pleas with a "Well, well, Ile goe when my Corne is in," and refused to receive the warrant.

The judges understandably found this to be contempt of court; but it was the kind of contempt that free Englishmen often showed to authority, and it was combined with a devotion to work that English moralists were doing their best to inculcate more widely in England. As England had absorbed people of every nationality over the centuries and turned them into Englishmen, Virginia's Englishmen were absorbing their own share of foreigners, including Negroes, and seemed to be successfully moulding a New World community on the English model.

But a closer look will show that the situation was not quite so promising as at first it seems. It is well known that Virginia in its first fifteen or twenty years killed off most of the men who went there. It is less well known that it continued to do so. If my estimate of the volume of immigration is anywhere near correct, Virginia must have been a death trap for at least another fifteen years and probably for twenty or twenty-five. In 1625 the population stood at 1,300 or 1,400; in 1640 it was about 8,000. In the fifteen years between those dates at least 15,000 persons must have come to the colony. If so, 15,000 immigrants increased the population by less than 7,000. There is no evidence of a large return migration. It seems probable that the death rate throughout this period was comparable only to that found in Europe during the peak years of a plague. Virginia, in other words, was absorbing England's surplus laborers mainly by killing them. The success of those who survived and rose from servant to planter must be attributed partly to the fact that so few did survive.

After 1640, when the diseases responsible for the high death rate began to decline and the population began a quick rise, it became increasingly difficult for an indigent immigrant to pull himself up in the world. The population probably passed 25,000 by 1662, hardly what Madison would have called a high degree of populousness. Yet the rapid rise brought serious trouble for Virginia. It brought the engrossment of tidewater land in thousands and tens of thousands of acres by speculators, who recognized that the demand would rise. It brought a huge expansion of tobacco production, which helped to depress the price of tobacco and the earnings of the men who planted it. It brought efforts by planters to prolong the terms of servants, since they were now living longer and therefore had a longer expectancy of usefulness.

It would, in fact, be difficult to assess all the consequences of the increased longevity; but for our purposes one development was crucial, and that was the appearance in Virginia of a growing number of freemen who had served their terms but who were now unable to afford land of their own except on the frontiers or in the interior. In years when tobacco prices were especially low or crops especially poor, men who had been just scraping by were obliged to go back to work for their larger neighbors simply in order to stay alive. By 1676 it was estimated that one fourth of Virginia's freemen were without land of their own. And in the same year Francis Moryson, a member of the governor's council, explained the term "freedmen" as used in Virginia to mean "persons without house and land," implying that this was now the normal condition of servants who had attained freedom.

Some of them resigned themselves to working for wages; others preferred a meager living on dangerous frontier land or a hand-to-mouth existence, roaming from one county to another, renting a bit of land here, squatting on some there, dodging the tax collector, drinking, quarreling, stealing hogs, and enticing servants to run away with them.

The presence of this growing class of poverty-stricken Virginians was not a little frightening to the planters who had made it to the top or who had arrived in the colony already at the top, with ample supplies of servants and capital. They were caught in a dilemma. They wanted the immigrants who kept pouring in every year. Indeed they needed them and prized them the more as they lived longer. But as more and more turned free each year, Virginia seemed to have inherited the problem that she was helping England to solve. Virginia, complained Nicholas Spencer, secretary of the colony, was "a sinke to drayen England of her filth and scum."

The men who worried the uppercrust looked even more dangerous in Virginia than they had in England. They were, to begin with, young, because it was young persons that the planters wanted for work in the fields; and the young have always seemed impatient of control by their elders and superiors, if not downright rebellious. They were also predominantly single men. Because the planters did not think women, or at least English women, fit for work in the fields, men outnumbered women among immigrants by three or four to one throughout the century. Consequently most of the freedmen had no wife or family to tame their wilder impulses and serve as hostages to the respectable world.

Finally, what made these wild young men particularly dangerous was that they were armed and had to be armed. Life in Virginia required guns. The plantations were exposed to attack from Indians by land and from privateers and petty-thieving pirates by sea. Whenever England was at war with the French or the Dutch, the settlers had to be ready to defend themselves. In 1667 the Dutch in a single raid captured twenty merchant ships in the James River, together with the English warship that was supposed to be defending them; and in 1673 they captured eleven more. On these occasions Governor William Berkeley gathered the planters in arms and at least prevented the enemy from making a landing. But while he stood off the Dutch he worried about the ragged crew at his back. Of the able-bodied men in the colony he estimated that "at least one third are Single freedmen (whose Labour will hardly maintaine them) or men much in debt, both which wee may reasonably expect upon any Small advantage the Enemy may gaine upon us, wold revolt to them in hopes of bettering their Condicion by Shareing the Plunder of the Country with them."

Berkeley's fears were justified. Three years later, sparked not by a Dutch invasion but by an Indian attack, rebellion swept Virginia. It began almost as Berkeley had predicted, when a group of volunteer Indian fighters turned from a fruitless expedition against the Indians to attack their rulers. Bacon's Rebellion was the largest popular rising in the colonies before the American Revolution. Sooner or later nearly everyone in Virginia got in on it, but it began in the frontier counties of Henrico and New Kent, among men whom the governor and his friends consistently characterized as rabble. As it spread eastward, it turned out that there were rabble everywhere, and Berkeley understandably raised his estimate of their numbers. "How miserable that man is," he exclaimed, "that Governes a People wher six parts of seaven at least are Poore Endebted Discontented and Armed."

Virginia's poor had reason to be envious and angry against the men who owned the land and imported the servants and ran the government. But the rebellion produced no real program of reform, no ideology, not even any revolutionary slogans. It was a search for plunder, not for principles. And when the rebels had redistributed whatever wealth they could lay their hands on, the rebellion subsided almost as quickly as it had begun.

It had been a shattering experience, however, for Virginia's first families. They had seen each other fall in with the rebels in order to save their skins or their possessions or even to share in the plunder. When it was over, they eyed one another distrustfully, on the lookout for any new Bacons in their midst, who might be tempted to lead the still restive rabble on more plundering expeditions. When William Byrd and Laurence Smith proposed to solve the problems of defense against the Indians by establishing semi-independent buffer settlements on the upper reaches of the rivers, in each of which they would engage to keep fifty men in arms, the assembly at first reacted favorably. But it quickly occurred to the governor and council that this would in fact mean gathering a crowd of Virginia's wild bachelors and furnishing them with an abundant supply of arms and ammunition. Byrd had himself led such a crowd in at least one plundering foray during the rebellion. To put him or anyone else in charge of a large and permanent gang of armed men was to invite them to descend again on the people whom they were supposed to be protecting.

The nervousness of those who had property worth plundering continued thoughout the century, spurred in 1682 by the tobacco-cutting riots in which men roved about destroying crops in the fields, in the desperate hope of producing a shortage that would raise the price of the leaf. And periodically in nearby Maryland and North Carolina, where the same conditions existed as in Virginia, there were tumults that threatened to spread to Virginia.

As Virginia thus acquired a social problem analogous to England's own, the colony began to deal with it as England had done, by restricting the liberties of those who did not have the proper badge of freedom, namely the property that government was supposed to protect. One way was to extend the terms of service for servants entering the colony without indentures. Formerly they had served until twenty-one; now the age was advanced to twenty-four. There had always been laws requiring them to serve extra time for running away; now the laws added corporal punishment and, in order to make habitual offenders more readily recognizable, specified that their hair be cropped. New laws restricted the movement of servants on the highways and also increased the amount of extra time to be served for running away. In addition to serving two days for every day's absence, the captured runaway was now frequently required to compensate by labor for the loss to the crop that he had failed to tend and for the cost of his apprehension, including rewards paid for his capture. A three week's holiday might result in a year's extra service. If a servant struck his master, he was to serve another year. For killing a hog he had to serve the owner a year and the informer another year. Since the owner of the hog, and the owner of the servant, and the informer were frequently the same man, and since a hog was worth at best less than one tenth the hire of a servant for a year, the law was very profitable to masters. One Lancaster master was awarded six years' extra service from a servant who killed three of his hogs, worth about thirty shillings.

The effect of these measures was to keep servants for as long as possible from gaining their freedom, especially the kind of servants who were most likely to cause trouble. At the same time the engrossment of land was driving many back to servitude after a brief taste of freedom. Freedmen who engaged to work for wages by so doing became servants again, subject to most of the same restrictions as other servants.

Nevertheless, in spite of all the legal and economic pressures to keep men in service, the ranks of the freedmen grew, and so did poverty and discontent. To prevent the wild bachelors from gaining an influence in the government, the assembly in 1670 limited voting to landholders and householders. But to disfranchise the growing mass of single freemen was not to deprive them of the weapons they had wielded so effectively under Nathaniel Bacon. It is questionable how far Virginia could safely have continued along this course, meeting discontent with repression and manning her plantations with annual importations of servants who would later add to the unruly ranks of the free. To be sure, the men at the bottom might have had both land and liberty, as the settlers of some other colonies did, if Virginia's frontier had been safe from Indians, or if the men at the top had been willing to forego some of their profits and to give up some of the lands they had engrossed. The English government itself made efforts to break up the great holdings that had helped to create the problem. But it is unlikely that the policy makers in Whitehall would have contended long against the successful.

In any case they did not have to. There was another solution, which allowed Virginia's magnates to keep their lands, yet arrested the discontent and the repression of other Englishmen, a solution which strengthened the rights of Englishmen and nourished that attachment to liberty which came to fruition in the Revolutionary generation of Virginia statesmen. But the solution put an end to the process of turning Africans into Englishmen. The rights of Englishmen were preserved by destroying the rights of Africans.

I do not mean to argue that Virginians deliberately turned to African Negro slavery as a means of preserving and extending the rights of Englishmen. Winthrop Jordan has suggested that slavery came to Virginia as an unthinking decision. We might go further and say that it came without a decision. It came automatically as Virginians bought the cheapest labor they could get. Once Virginia's heavy mortality ceased, an investment in slave labor was much more profitable than an investment in free labor; and the planters bought slaves as rapidly as traders made them available. In the last years of the seventeenth century they bought them in such numbers that slaves probably already constituted a majority or nearly a majority of the labor force by 1700. The demand was so great that traders for a time found a better market in Virginia than in Jamaica or Barbados. But the social benefits of an enslaved labor force, even if not consciously sought or recognized at the time by the men who bought the slaves, were larger than the economic benefits. The increase in the importation of slaves was matched by a decrease in the importation of indentured servants and consequently a decrease in the dangerous number of new freedmen who annually emerged seeking a place in society that they would be unable to achieve.

If Africans had been unavailable, it would probably have proved impossible to devise a way to keep a continuing supply of English immigrants in their place. There was a limit beyond which the abridgment of English liberties would have resulted not merely in rebellion but in protests from England and in the cutting off of the supply of further servants. At the time of Bacon's Rebellion the English commission of investigation had shown more sympathy with the rebels than with the well-to-do planters who had engrossed Virginia's lands. To have attempted the enslavement of English-born laborers would have caused more disorder than it cured. But to keep as slaves black men who arrived in that condition *was* possible and apparently regarded as plain common sense.

The attitude of English officials was well expressed by the attorney who reviewed for the Privy Council the slave codes established in Barbados in 1679. He found the laws of Barbados to be well designed for the good of his majesty's subjects there, for, he said, "although Negroes in that Island are punishable in a different and more severe manner than other Subjects are for Offences of the like nature; yet I humbly conceive that the Laws there concerning Negroes are reasonable Laws, for by reason of their numbers they become dangerous, and being a brutish sort of People and reckoned as goods and chattels in that Island, it is of necessity or at least convenient to have Laws for the Government of them different from the Laws of England, to prevent the great mischief that otherwise may happen to the Planters and Inhabitants in that Island." In Virginia too it seemed convenient and reasonable to have different laws for black and white. As the number of slaves increased, the assembly passed laws that carried forward with much greater severity the trend already under way in the colony's labor laws. But the new severity was reserved for people without white skin. The laws specifically exonerated the master who accidentally beat his slave to death, but they placed new limitations on his punishment of "Christian white servants."

Virginians worried about the risk of having in their midst a body of men who had every reason to hate them. The fear of a slave insurrection hung over them for nearly two centuries. But the danger from slaves actually proved to be less than that which the colony had faced from its restive and armed freedmen. Slaves had none of the rising expectations that so often produce human discontent. No one had told them that they had rights. They had been nurtured in heathen societies where they had lost their freedom; their children would be nurtured in a Christian society and never know freedom.

Moreover, slaves were less troubled by the sexual imbalance that helped to make Virginia's free laborers so restless. In an enslaved labor force women could be required to make tobacco just as the men did; and they also made children, who in a few years would be an asset to their master. From the beginning, therefore, traders imported women in a much higher ratio to men than was the case among English servants, and the level of discontent was correspondingly reduced. Virginians did not doubt that discontent would remain, but it could be repressed by methods that would not have been considered reasonable, convenient, or even safe, if applied to Englishmen. Slaves could be deprived of opportunities for association and rebellion. They could be kept unarmed and unorganized. They could be subjected to savage punishments by their owners without fear of legal reprisals. And since their color disclosed their probable status, the rest of society could keep close watch on them. It is scarcely surprising that no slave insurrection in American history approached Bacon's Rebellion in its extent or in its success.

Nor is it surprising that Virginia's freedmen never again posed a threat to society. Though in later years slavery was condemned because it was thought to compete with free labor, in the beginning it reduced by so much the number of freedmen who would otherwise have competed with each other. When the annual increment of freedmen fell off, the number that remained could more easily find an independent place in society, especially as the danger of Indian attack diminished and made settlement safer at the heads of the rivers or on the Carolina frontier. There might still remain a number of irredeemable, idle, and unruly freedmen, particularly among the convicts whom England exported to the colonies. But the numbers were small enough, so that they could be dealt with by the old expedient of drafting them for military expeditions. The way was thus made easier for the remaining freedmen to acquire property, maybe acquire a slave or two of their own, and join with their superiors in the enjoyment of those English liberties that differentiated them from their black laborers.

A free society divided between large landholders and small was much less riven by antagonisms than one divided between landholders and landless, masterless men. With the freedman's expectations, sobriety, and status restored, he was no longer a man to be feared. That fact, together with the presence of a growing mass of alien slaves, tended to draw the white settlers closer together and to reduce the importance of the class difference between yeoman farmer and large plantation owner.

The seventeenth century has sometimes been thought of as the day of the yeoman farmer in Virginia; but in many ways a stronger case can be made for the eighteenth century as the time when the yeoman farmer came into his own, because slavery relieved the small man of the pressures that had been reducing him to continued servitude. Such an interpretation conforms to the political development of the colony. During the seventeenth century the royally appointed governor's council, composed of the largest property-owners in the colony, had been the most powerful governing body. But as the tide of slavery rose between 1680 and 1720 Virginia moved toward a government in which the yeoman farmer had a larger share. In spite of the rise of Virginia's great families on the black tide, the power of the council declined;

and the elective House of Burgesses became the dominant organ of government. Its members nurtured a closer relationship with their yeoman constituency than had earlier been the case. And in its chambers Virginians developed the ideas they so fervently asserted in the Revolution: ideas about taxation, representation, and the rights of Englishmen, and ideas about the prerogatives and powers and sacred calling of the independent, property-holding yeoman farmer—commonwealth ideas.

In the eighteenth century, because they were no longer threatened by a dangerous free laboring class, Virginians could afford these ideas, whereas in Berkeley's time they could not. Berkeley himself was obsessed with the experience of the English civil wars and the danger of rebellion. He despised and feared the New Englanders for their association with the Puritans who had made England, however briefly, a commonwealth. He was proud that Virginia, unlike New England, had no free schools and no printing press, because books and schools bred heresy and sedition. He must have taken satisfaction in the fact that when his people did rebel against him under Bacon, they generated no republican ideas, no philosophy of rebellion or of human rights. Yet a century later, without benefit of rebellions, Virginians had learned republican lessons, had introduced schools and printing presses, and were as ready as New Englanders to recite the aphorisms of the commonwealthmen.

It was slavery, I suggest, more than any other single factor, that had made the difference, slavery that enabled Virginia to nourish representative government in a plantation society, slavery that transformed the Virginia of Governor Berkeley to the Virginia of Jefferson, slavery that made the Virginians dare to speak a political language that magnified the rights of freemen, and slavery, therefore, that brought Virginians into the same commonwealth political tradition with New Englanders. The very institution that was to divide North and South after the Revolution may have made possible their union in a republican government.

Thus began the American paradox of slavery and freedom, intertwined and interdependent, the rights of Englishmen supported on the wrongs of Africans. The American Revolution only made the contradictions more glaring, as the slaveholding colonists proclaimed to a candid world the rights not simply of Englishmen but of all men. To explain the origin of the contradictions, if the explanation I have suggested is valid, does not eliminate them or make them less ugly. But it may enable us to understand a little better the strength of the ties that bound freedom to slavery, even in so noble a mind as Jefferson's. And it may perhaps make us wonder about the ties that bind more devious tyrannies to our own freedoms and give us still today our own American paradox.

❧ F U R T H E R   R E A D I N G

Lois Green Carr and David William Jordan, *Maryland's Revolution of Government, 1689–1692* (1974)

Paul G. E. Clemens, *The Atlantic Economy and Colonial Maryland's Eastern Shore: From Tobacco to Grain* (1980)

Richard Beale Davis, ed., *William Fitzhugh and His Chesapeake World* (1963)

Edmund S. Morgan, *American Slavery, American Freedom: The Ordeal of Colonial Virginia* (1975)

Darrett B. Rutman and Anita H. Rutman, *A Place in Time: Middlesex County, Virginia, 1650–1750* (1984)

Jack M. Sosin, *English America and the Restoration Monarchy of Charles II: Transatlantic Politics, Commerce, and Kinship* (1980)

————, *English America and the Revolution of 1688: Royal Administration and the Structure of Provincial Government* (1982)

Wilcomb E. Washburn, *The Governor and the Rebel: A History of Bacon's Rebellion in Virginia* (1957)

Stephen Saunders Webb, *1676: The End of American Independence* (1985)

Thomas Jefferson Wertenbaker, *Torchbearer of the Revolution: The Story of Bacon's Rebellion and Its Leader* (1940)

New Directions
in Family Life and Labor

❧

*The colonists who immigrated to America from Europe had left countries where
land was scarce and was often engrossed in the hands of great landlords but
where—especially after the population expansion of the sixteenth and seventeenth
centuries—labor was plentiful. Thus most had come in the knowledge that they
never could have looked forward to owning land in Europe. Children in England
commonly left home in early adolescence to work as servants in the shops and
farms of other families. Probably the most dramatic impact of colonization on individuals lay in the complete reversal of the land-labor equation. In America land
was widely available but the labor to develop it scarce.*

*Historians debate whether the American situation led to a redefinition of the
role of the family, not only as the center of emotional life on isolated plantations
but also, through the manipulation of inheritance systems, as the main provider of
labor and security. Because of the fluidity of life on the frontier, inherited roles were
adapted as wives, husbands, and children played unaccustomed parts. The demands
of the new environment reinforced the special reasons for the emigration of groups
such as the Puritans and the Quakers and called forth a high degree of concentration on the family as the arena in which goals would be accomplished and achieve-
ments maintained.*

*Much of the contemporary commentary on family life came from people who
were offended by what they saw, particularly the abandonment of traditional roles.
Departure from these roles was perceived as disorderliness and lack of regard; thus
historians must read documents of the times on two levels to understand what the
commentators really witnessed.*

❧ D O C U M E N T S

In the first selection Edward Johnson describes the founding of the New England
towns. Detailing the way in which the land was divided up among families within
the town, Johnson displays his pride in the development of Massachusetts. Anne

Bradstreet, New England's first poet, portrays the different roles of godly men and women in the epitaphs (see the second selection) on her mother and father. Her father, Thomas Dudley, had served as governor of Massachusetts Bay. Thomas Minor's diary, excerpted in the third document, depicts the agricultural year and the way in which labor was performed cooperatively among family members and neighbors in Stonington, Connecticut, as well as the ease with which a farmer like Minor traveled. The English calendar began the year on March 21 until the middle of the eighteenth century.

In the fourth selection William Penn offers a sober yet enthusiastic prospectus of the gains available to English families who chose to immigrate to his newly granted province of Pennsylvania. When he embarked for America, fearing that he might never see his family again, he wrote formal letters to his pregnant wife and children telling them how they should live their lives. His excerpted letters in the fifth document show the centrality of the family to the realization of Quaker goals in life. The formal letter contrasts dramatically with the short informal letters to his young children: Springett, who was seven, Laetitia, four, and Billy, just a year old.

Edward Johnson on the Founding of New England Towns, 1654

[T]his remote, rocky, barren, bushy, wild-woody wilderness, a receptacle for Lions, Wolves, Bears, Foxes, Raccoons, Bags, Beavers, Otters, and all kind of wild creatures, a place that never afforded the Natives better than the flesh of a few wild creatures and parched Indian corn inched out with Chestnuts and bitter Acorns, now through the mercy of Christ become a second England for fertileness in so short a space, that it is indeed the wonder of the world; but being already forgotten of the very persons that taste of it at present, although some there be that keep in memory his mercies' multitude, and declare it to their children's children. . . .

. . . [T]here are not many Towns in the Country, but the poorest person in them hath a house and land of his own, and bread of his own growing, if not some cattle: beside, flesh is now no rare food, beef, pork, and mutton being frequent in many houses, so that this poor Wilderness hath not only equalized England in food, but goes beyond it in some places for the great plenty of wine and sugar, which is ordinarily spent, apples, pears, and quince tarts instead of their former Pumpkin Pies. Poultry they have plenty, and great rarity, and in their feasts have not forgotten the English fashion of stirring up their appetites with variety of cooking their food; and notwithstanding all this great and almost miraculous work of the Lord, in providing for his people in this barren desert, yet are there here (as in other places) some that use these good creatures of God to excess, and others, to hoard up in a wretched and miserable manner, pinch themselves and their children with food, and will not taste of the good creatures God hath given for that end, but cut Church and Commonwealth as short also: Let not such think to escape the Lord's hand with as little a stroke, as the like do in other places.

Some of the spelling in this document has been modernized.

Secondly, For raiment, our cloth hath not been cut short, as but of late years the traders that way have increased to such a number, that their shops have continued full all the year long, all one [the same as in] England; besides the Lord hath been pleased to increase sheep extraordinarily of late, hemp and flax here is great plenty, hides here are more for the number of persons than in England; and for cloth, here is and would be materials enough to make it; but the Farmers deem it better for their profit to put away their cattle and corn for clothing, than to set upon making of cloth; if the Merchants' trade be not kept on foot, they fear greatly their corn and cattle will lie in their hands: assuredly the plenty of clothing hath caused much excess of late in those persons, who have clambered with excess in wages for their work. . . .

Further, the Lord hath been pleased to turn all the wigwams, huts, and hovels the English dwelt in at their first coming, into orderly, fair, and well-built houses, well furnished many of them, together with Orchards filled with goodly fruit trees, and gardens with variety of flowers: There are supposed to be in the Massachusetts Government at this day, near a thousand acres of land planted for Orchards and Gardens, besides their fields are filled with garden fruit, there being, as is supposed in this Colony, about fifteen thousand acres in tillage, and of cattle about twelve thousand neat, and about three thousand sheep. Thus hath the Lord encouraged his people with the increase of the general, although many particulars are outed, hundreds of pounds, and some thousands, yet are there many hundreds of labouring men, who had not enough to bring them over, yet now worth scores, and some hundreds of pounds; to be sure the Lord takes notice of all his talents, and will call to account in time: This brief survey of things will be of good use when time serves, in meantime you shall understand.

. . . There was a Town and Church erected called Wooburn, this present year, but because all the action of this wandering people meet with great variety of censures, the Author will in this Town and Church set down the manner how this people have populated their Towns, and gathered their Churches . . . [T]his Town, as all others, had its bounds fixed by the General Court, to the contenese [contents] of four miles square, (beginning at the end of Charles Town bounds). The grant is to seven men of good and honest report, upon condition, that within two years they erect houses for habitation thereon, and so go on to make a Town thereof, upon the Act of Court; these seven men have power to give and grant out lands unto any persons who are willing to take up their dwellings within the said precinct, and to be admitted to all common priviledges of the said Town, giving them such an ample portion, both of Meadow and Upland, as their present and future stock of cattle and hands were like to improve, with eye had to others that might after come to populate the said Town; this they did without any respect of persons, yet such as were exorbitant, and of a turbulent spirit, unfit for a civil society, they would reject, till they come to mend their manners; such came not to enjoy any freehold. These seven men ordered and disposed of the streets of the Town, as might be best for improvement of the Land, and yet civil and religious society maintained; to which end those that had land nearest the place for Sabbath Assembly, had a lesser quantity at home, and more farther off to improve for corn, of all kinds; they refused not men for their poverty, but according to their ability were helpful to the poorest sort, in building their houses, and distributed to them land accordingly; the poorest had six or seven acres of Meadow, and twenty five of Upland, or thereabouts. Thus was this Town populated, to the number of sixty families, or thereabout, and after this manner are the Towns of New England peopled. The situation of this Town is in the highest part of the yet peopled land, near upon the head-springs of many considerable rivers, or their branches, as the first rise of Ipswitch river, and the rise of Shashin river, one of the most considerable branches of Merrimeck, as also the first rise of Mistick river and ponds, it is very full of pleasant springs, and great variety of very good water, which the Summer's heat causeth to be more cooler, and the Winter's cold maketh more warmer; their Meadows are not large, but lie in divers places to particular dwellings, the like doth their Springs; their Land is very fruitful in many places, although they have no great quantity of plain land in any one place, yet doth their Rocks and Swamps yield very good food for cattle; as also they have Mast and Tar for shipping, but the distance of place by land causeth them as yet to be unprofitable; they have great store of iron ore; their meeting-house stands in a small Plain, where four streets meet; the people are very laborious, if not exceeding some of them. . . .

Anne Bradstreet on Parents and Children, c. 1635–1670

To the Memory of my dear and ever honoured Father
Thomas Dudley Esq;
Who deceased, July 31. 1653. and of his Age, 77.

> By duty bound, and not by custom led
> To celebrate the praises of the dead,
> My mournful mind, sore prest, in trembling verse
> Presents my Lamentations at his Hearse,
> Who was my Father, Guide, Instructer too,
> To whom I ought whatever I could do:
> Nor is't Relation near my hand shall tie;
> For who more cause to boast his worth than I?
> Who heard or saw, observ'd or knew him better?
> Or who alive then I, a greater debtor?
> Let malice bite, and envy gnaw its fill,
> He was my Father, and I'll praise him still.
> Nor was his name, or life led so obscure
> That pity might some Trumpeters procure.
> Who after death might make him falsly seem
> Such as in life, no man could justly deem.

Some of the spelling in this document has been modernized.

Well known and lov'd, where ere he liv'd, by most
Both in his native, and in foreign coast,
These to the world his merits could make known,
So needs no Testimonial from his own;
But now or never I must pay my Sum;
While others tell his worth, I'll not be dumb:
One of thy Founders, him *New-England* know,
Who stayed thy feeble sides when thou wast low,
Who spent his state, his strength, & years with care
That After-comers in them might have share.
True Patriot of this little Commonweal,
Who is't can tax thee ought, but for thy zeal?
Truth's friend thou wert, to errors still a foe,
Which caus'd Apostates to malign so.
Thy love to true Religion e're shall shine,
My Father's God, be God of me and mine.
Upon the earth he did not build his nest,
But as a Pilgrim, what he had, possessed.
High thoughts he gave no harbour in his heart,
Nor honours puffed him up, when he had part:
Those titles loath'd, which some too much do love
For truly his ambition lay above.
His humble mind so lov'd humility,
He left it to his race for Legacy:
And oft and oft, with speeches mild and wise,
Gave his in charge, that Jewel rich to prize.
No ostentation seen in all his ways,
As in the mean ones, of our foolish days,
Which all they have, and more still set to view,
Their greatness may be judg'd by what they shew.
His thoughts were more sublime, his actions wise,
Such vanities he justly did despise.
Nor wonder 'twas, low things ne'r much did move
For he a Mansion had, prepar'd above,
For which he sigh'd and pray'd & long'd full sore
He might be cloth'd upon, for evermore.
Oft spake of death, and with a smiling cheer,
He did exult his end was drawing near,
Now fully ripe, as shock of wheat that's grown,
Death as a Sickle hath him timely mown,
And in celestial Barn hath hous'd him high,
Where storms, nor showers, nor ought can damnify.
His Generation serv'd, his labours cease;
And to his Fathers gathered is in peace.
Ah happy Soul, 'mongst Saints and Angels blest,
Who after all his toil, is now at rest:
His hoary head in righteousness was found:
As joy in heaven on earth let praise resound.
Forgotten never be his memory,
His blessing rest on his posterity:

His pious Footsteps followed by his race,
At last will bring us to that happy place
Where we with joy each other's face shall see,
And parted more by death shall never be.

His Epitaph.

Within this Tomb a Patriot lies
That was both pious, just and wise,
To Truth a shield, to right a Wall,
To Sectaryes a whip and Maul,
A Magazine of History,
A Prizer of good Company
In manners pleasant and severe
The Good him lov'd, the bad did fear,
And when his time with years was spent
If some rejoyc'd, more did lament.

An Epitaph
On my dear and ever honoured Mother
Mrs. Dorothy Dudley,
who deceased Decemb. 27. 1643. and of her age, 61:

Here lies,

A Worthy Matron of unspotted life,
A loving Mother and obedient wife,
A friendly Neighbor, pitiful to poor,
Whom oft she fed, and clothed with her store;
To Servants wisely aweful, but yet kind,
And as they did, so they reward did find:
A true instructor of her Family,
The which she ordered with dexterity.
The public meetings ever did frequent,
And in her Closet constant hours she spent;
Religious in all her words and ways,
Preparing still for death, till end of days:
Of all her Children, Children, liv'd to see,
Then dying, left a blessed memory.

Thomas Minor's Diary: A Farmer's Year, 1660

The first month is March 31 days & is the first year after the leap year being the year 1660 & Thursday the first & Thursday the 8. John Russell ran away the same time our frame was raised Wednesday the 14. We ended the court Thursday the 15. I was threshing of wheat for Ralph Perker. We had our 3

Note: Thomas Minor used almost no punctuation, so it is often difficult to determine where to place periods and commas.
Some of the spelling in this document has been modernized.

pigs from Father's & Thursday the 22 I paid the last wheat. Our goats began to kid. Thomas Huet vessel was tached [?] & Tuesday the 27 John [Thomas Minor's son] carried all aboard Thursday the 29. Saturday 31 we had built our back & oven.

The second month is April 30 days & Sabbath day the first and Sabbath day the 8. We had begun the last week Monday the 9. Clement [Thomas Minor's son] went to New London to work Sabbath day the 15. Monday the 16 we made an end of sowing the wheat and peas and Tuesday the 17 we were to set forth for the day & Sabbath day the 22. The 20th of April we received a letter of John's safe arrival. Monday 23 we began to plant & Wednesday 25 I made an end of all our plowing & Sabbath day 29. Monday the 30 we had made an end of planting of our Indian corn.

The third month is May 31 days & Tuesday the first. The seventh day I was at the Town the London ship was at New London Tuesday the 8. I made the hedge at the stand & Wednesday the 9. I made an end of that work the 10th & 11th. I shingled the north side of the house & Tuesday the 15 & Tuesday the 22 we had kept a day of humiliation. The day before the 24 being Thursday we were to set forth for the Bay. We came to Boston the 30th and Thursday the 31 Ms Dyer [Quaker Mary Dyer] was Executed.

The fourth month is June 30 days & Friday the first. I was at Boston Friday the 8th. I was at Boston & Friday was 15. I lay at the trading house. I set my hand to the agreement between Major Allerton & the other English & the 3 Narraganset sachems about the land. Isaac Willy was married that day sometime before & that day promised Amos Richerson 3 cattle, one black Cow, one bull with a white face 3 years old, one red steer of 2 years old. The 21 day the court. A day of humiliation Friday the 22 & Friday 29 I paid Pepeions ten shillings for killing of two wolves & Saturday the 30.

The fifth month is July 31 days & Sabbath day the first. This week I agreed with Rogers about John's 2 Cows & a calf & Sabbath day the 8. The 7th of this month I sowed turnips. The 13 there was a town meeting & Sabbath day the 15. I pulled hemp. Ephraim & Joseph [Thomas Minor's sons] mowed in the orchard Friday & Saturday 20 and 21. We had a court at Captain Denison's Sabbath day 22. 23 I looked horses fetched one load of hay & Saturday the 28 I cut peas & Sabbath day 29 & Tuesday the 31.

The sixth month is August 31 days and Wednesday the first. I cut fence & carried them Wednesday the 8. I carried my wheat Thursday the 9. I carried the Ram to the Island & Wednesday the 15. Friday 17 Thomas & Ephraim [Thomas Minor's sons] was at Samuel Cheesbrough's. The 13 day I had the gelding at Captain Denison's. The 20th day John Tower came here & Wednesday the 22 we Carried 5 loads of hay & made a rick next to the barn. Wednesday 29 I was at town & took up things for John. I was at Prentice to show the horse Friday 31.

The seventh month is September 30 days & Saturday the first. Mr. Winthrop [John Winthrop, Jr., son of the Massachusetts Bay leader and a governor of Connecticut] was at New London. The 4th day the horses were at Culver's. John Moore began to work for me Saturday the 8. The 12 I reckoned with

Mr. Picket and made all even being Wednesday & Saturday the 15 Clement & John Moore went to New London. I & Joseph was at Borden's & the 2 horses were gone. The 12th day also I paid Toung his silver before Josias Willkins and quite freed the horse & Saturday the 22 I clove Clapboards. Sabbath day 23 we first did see Carrie's cow to spring udder. John was here. The last of September we came home from Narraganset & Master Brigden first taught here.

The eight month is October 31 days & Monday the first. This day Hannah her child [possibly Grace Minor's sister Hannah] died before day & Monday the 8 the moon was Eclipsed. I was to go with Mr. Bridgen toward Mohegan & Monday the 29 I carried the firkin of butter to Mr. Smith for Amos. I marked the Colt a bay mare without any white. The mare have a white face, a slit in the right ear, 3 white feet part of the 42, a white ring about each ear, a halfpenny on each ear Wednesday the 31.

The ninth [month] is November 30 days & Thursday the first. Friday the 2 I weighed Amos his firkin of butter at Mr. Smith's. It was 70 pounds & there is 13 pounds to pay. The 8 day being Thursday we had Carried 45 loads of muck out of the yards. There was a meeting to be at Smith's of the whole Town & Thursday the 15. This week we killed the steer. I was at New London & had the axes & guns mended. The steer came to six pounds. The 20 we began the little house. Thursday 22 it snowed the second time. Thursday the 29 we appointed a meeting to be at Cheesbrough's. That day fortnight I began to clean clapboards. Friday the 30 we had home all the timber for the little house.

The tenth month is December 31 days & Saturday is the first & Saturday the 8. I came from Connecticut the 13 day. The Towns men met at Cheesbrough's & Saturday the 15. The 11th of this month we raised the little house. Tuesday the 18 there is a court at Captain Denison's & Saturday the 22 we got stones for the Chimney. Monday 24 the Town men met at Mr. Stanton's. Tuesday the 25 called Christmas Day [Puritans did not celebrate Christmas, which they considered a pagan survival] & Saturday the 29. Monday the 31. Sabbath day the 30 I received a letter from Cambridge. Christmas day I received a letter from my Cousin in England.

The eleventh month is January 31 days and Tuesday the first. Thursday the 3 we killed the sow. Tuesday the 8 I made an end of Threshing of the wheat in the north end of the barn. The same day it snowed. I had 20 Bushels of wheat. Marie was sick & Tuesday the 15 Marie continued very sick & I fetched honey at starts & Tuesday the 22. Thursday 24 Marie died about six o'clock. [Minor and his wife, Grace Palmer Minor, lost two daughters in infancy.] We had 40 bushels of wheat. We fetched in the peas & Tuesday the 29 I Reckoned with my Father Palmer. There was all paid & 17 shillings due to me. Thursday the 31 we had 10 bushels of white peas.

The twelfth month is February and hath 28 days. Friday the first and is the first year after the leap year & is the year 1660 [1661 had begun January 1 by the modern calendar]. This week Clement & Thomas went to Stratford. The white heifer Calved. We finished the fence to the Rocks by the swamp

Friday the 8. There fell a great snow & Friday the 15 I made an end of Coming of hemp & Friday the 22 it hailed.

William Penn on the Attractions of Pennsylvania, 1681

Since (by the good providence of God) a Country in America is fallen to my lot, I thought it not less my Duty than my honest Interest to give some publick notice of it to the World, that those of our own, or other Nations, that are inclin'd to Transport themselves or Families beyond the Seas, may find another Country added to their choice, that if they shall happen to like the Place, Conditions and Constitutions, (so far as the present Infancy of things will allow us any prospect) they may, if they please, fix with me in the Province hereafter describ'd. But before I come to treat of my particular Concernment, I shall take leave to say something of the benefit of Plantations or Colonies in general, to obviate a common Objection.

Colonies then are the Seeds of Nations begun and nourished by the care of wise and populous Countries; as conceiving them best for the increase of Humane Stock, and beneficial for Commerce.

Some of the wisest men in History have justly taken their Fame from this Design and Service: . . .

Nor did any of these ever dream it was the way of decreasing their People or Wealth: For the cause of the decay of any of those States or Empires was not their Plantations, but their Luxury and corruption of Manners: For when they grew to neglect their ancient Discipline, that maintained and rewarded Virtue and Industry, and addicted themselves to Pleasure and Effeminacy, they debas'd their Spirits and debauch'd their Morals, from whence Ruine did never fail to follow to any People: With Justice therefore I deny the vulgar Opinion against Plantations, That They weaken England; they have manifestly inrich'd, and so strengthened her; Which I briefly evidence thus.

1st. Those that go into a Foreign Plantation, their Industry there is worth more than if they stay'd at home, the Product of their Labour being in Commodities of a superiour Nature to those of this Country. For Instance; What is an improved Acre in Jamaica or Barbadoes worth to an improved Acre in England? We know 'tis threetimes the value, and the product of it comes for England, and is usually paid for in English Growth and Manufacture. Nay, Virginia shews that an ordinary Industry in one man produces Three thousand pound weight of Tobacco and Twenty Barrels of Corn yearly: He feeds himself, and brings as much of Commodity into England besides as being return'd in the Growth and Workmanship of this Countrey, is much more than he could have spent here: Let it also be remembred, that the Three thousand weight of Tobacco brings in Three thousand Two-pences by way of Custom to the King, which makes Twenty five Pounds; An extraordinary Profit.

2dly. More being produc'd and imported than we can spend here, we Export it to other Countries in Europe, which brings in Money, or the Growth of those Countries, which is the same thing; And this is the Advantage of the English-Merchants and Seamen.

3dly. Such as could not only not marry here, but hardly live and allow themselves Cloaths, do marry there, and bestow thrice more in all Necessaries and Conveniencies (and not a little in Ornamental things too) for themselves, their Wives and Children, both as to Apparel and Household-stuff; which coming out of England, I say 'tis impossible that England should not be a considerable Gainer. . . .

The Journey and it's Appurtenances, and what is to be done there at first coming.

Next let us see, What is fit for the Journey and Place, when there, and also what may be the Charge of the Voyage, and what is to be expected and done there at first. That such as incline to go, may not be to seek here, or brought under any disappointments there. The Goods fit to take with them for use, or sell for profit, are all sorts of Apparel and Utensils for Husbandry and Building and Household Stuff. And because I know how much People are apt to fancy things beyond what they are, and that Immaginations are great flatterers of the minds of Men; To the end that none may delude themselves, with an expectation of an Immediate Amendment of their Conditions, so soon as it shall please God they Arrive there; I would have them understand, That they must look for a Winter before a Summer comes; and they must be willing to be two or three years without some of the conveniences they enjoy at home; And yet I must needs say that America is another thing then it was at the first Plantation of Virginia and New England: For there is better Accommodation, and English Provisions are to be had at easier rates: However, I am inclin'd to set down particulars, as near as those inform me, that know the Place, and have been Planters both in that and in the Neighbouring Colonys.

1st. The passage will come for Masters and Mistresses at most to 6 Pounds a Head, for Servants Five Pounds a Head, and for Children under Seven years of Age Fifty Shillings, except they Suck, then nothing.

Next being by the mercy of God, safely Arrived in September or October, two Men may clear as much Ground by Spring (when they set the Corn of that Country) as will bring in that time twelve month Forty Barrels, which amounts to two Hundred Bushels, which makes Twenty Five quarters of Corn. So that the first year they must buy Corn, which is usually very plentiful. They may so soon as they come, buy Cows, more or less, as they want, or are able, which are to be had at easy rates. For Swine, they are plentiful and cheap; these will quickly Increase to a Stock. So that after the first year, what with the Poorer sort, sometimes labouring to others, and the more able Fishing, Fowling, and sometime Buying; They may do very well, till their own Stocks are sufficient to supply them, and their Families, which will quickly be and to spare, if they follow the English Husbandry, as they do in New-England, and New-York; and get Winter Fodder for their Stock.

William Penn's Advice on Parting
from His Family, 1682

Warminghurst, 4 August 1682

My dear Wife and Children.

My love, that sea, nor land, nor death itself can extinguish or lessen toward you, most endearedly visits you with eternal embraces and will abide with you forever. And may the God of my life watch over you and bless you and do you good in this world and forever. Some things are upon my spirit to leave with you, in your respective capacities, as I am to one a husband, and to the rest a father, if I should never see you more in this world.

My dear wife, remember thou was the love of my youth, and much the joy of my life, the most beloved, as well as most worthy, of all my earthly comforts. And the reason of that love was more thy inward than thy outward excellences (which yet were many). God knows, and thou knows it. I can say it was a match of providence's making, and God's image in us both was the first thing and the most amiable and engaging ornament in our eyes. Now I am to leave thee, and that without knowing whether I shall ever see thee more in this world. Take my counsel into thy bosom and let it dwell with thee in my stead while thou lives.

1st. Let the fear of the Lord, and a zeal and love to His glory, dwell richly in thy heart, and thou will watch for good over thyself and thy dear children and family, that no rude, light, or bad thing be committed, else God will be offended, and He will repent Himself of the good He intends thee and thine.

2dly. Be diligent in meetings of worship and business; stir up thyself and others herein; it is thy day and place. And let meetings be kept once a day in the family to wait upon the Lord, who has given us much time for ourselves. And my dearest, to make thy family matters easy to thee, divide thy time, and be regular. It is easy and sweet. Thy retirement will afford thee to do it, as in the morning to view the business of the house and fix it as thou desire, seeing all be in order, that by thy counsel all may move, and to thee render an account every evening. The time for work, for walking, for meals, may be certain, at least as near as may be. And grieve not thyself with careless servants. They will disorder thee. Rather pay them and let them go if they will not be better by admonitions. This is best, to avoid many words, which I know wound the soul and offend the Lord.

3dly. Cast up thy income and see what it daily amounts to, by which thou may be sure to have it in thy sight and power to keep within compass. And I beseech thee to live low and sparingly till my debts are paid, and then

William Penn to his wife Guliema and their children on his departure for America, August 4, 1682, giving advice on how to live their lives. In Jean Soderlund, ed., *William Penn and the Founding of Pennsylvania, 1680–1684: A Documentary History* (Philadelphia: University of Pennsylvania Press and Pennsylvania Historical Society, 1983), 165–170, 171–172. Reprinted by permission of University of Pennsylvania Press.

enlarge as thou see it convenient. Remember thy mother's example when thy father's public-spiritedness had worsted his estate (which is my case). I know thou loves plain things and are averse to the pomp of the world, a nobility natural to thee. I write not as doubtful, but to quicken thee, for my sake, to be more vigilant herein, knowing that God will bless thy care, and thy poor children and thee for it. My mind is wrapped up in a saying of thy father's. "I desire not riches, but to owe nothing." And truly that is wealth; and more than enough to live is a snare attended with many sorrows.

I need not bid thee be humble, for thou are so; nor meek and patient, for it is much of thy natural disposition. But I pray thee, be often in retirement with the Lord and guard against encroaching friendships. Keep them at arm's end; for it is giving away our power, aye, and self too, into the possession of another. And that which might seem engaging in the beginning, may prove a yoke and burden too hard and heavy in the end. Wherefore keep dominion over thyself, and let thy children, good meetings, and Friends be the pleasure of thy life.

4thly. And now, my dearest, let me recommend to thy care my dear children, abundantly beloved of me as the Lord's blessings and the sweet pledges of our mutual and endeared affection. Above all things, endeavor to breed them up in the love of virtue and that holy plain way of it which we have lived in, that the world, in no part of it, get into my family. I had rather they were homely than finely bred, as to outward behavior; yet I love sweetness mixed with gravity, and cheerfulness tempered with sobriety. Religion in the heart leads into this true civility, teaching men and women to be mild and courteous in their behavior, an accomplishment worthy indeed of praise.

5thly. Next, breed them up in a love one of another. Tell them, it is the charge I left behind me, and that it is the way to have the love and blessing of God upon them; also what his portion is who hates, or calls his brother fool. Sometimes separate them, but not long; and allow them to send and give each other small things, to endear one another with once more. I say, tell them it was my counsel, they should be tender and affectionate one to another.

For their learning, be liberal. Spare no cost, for by such parsimony all is lost that is saved; but let it be useful knowledge, such as is consistent with truth and godliness, not cherishing a vain conversation or idle mind, but ingenuity mixed with industry is good for the body and mind too. I recommend the useful parts of mathematics, as building houses or ships, measuring, surveying, dialing, navigation, etc.; but agriculture is especially in my eye. Let my children be husbandmen and housewives. It is industrious, healthy, honest, and of good example, like Abraham and the holy ancients who pleased God and obtained a good report. This leads to consider the works of God and nature, of things that are good and divert the mind from being taken up with the vain arts and inventions of a luxurious world. It is commendable in the princes of Germany, and [the] nobles of that empire, that they have all their children instructed in some useful occupation. Rather keep an ingenious person in the house to teach them than send them to schools, too many evil impressions being commonly received there. Be sure to observe their genius and don't cross it as to learning. Let them not dwell too long on one thing, but let their change be agreeable, and all their diversions have some little bodily labor in them.

When grown big, have most care for them; for then there are more snares both within and without. When marriageable, see that they have worthy persons in their eye, of good life and good fame for piety and understanding. I need no wealth but sufficiency; and be sure their love be dear, fervent, and mutual, that it may be happy for them. I choose not they should be married into earthly covetous kindred. And of cities and towns of concourse beware. The world is apt to stick close to those who have lived and got wealth there. A country life and estate I like best for my children. I prefer a decent mansion of a hundred pounds per annum before ten thousand pounds in London, or suchlike place, in a way of trade.

In fine, my dear, endeavor to breed them dutiful to the Lord, and His blessed light, truth, and grace in their hearts, who is their Creator, and His fear will grow up with them. Teach a child (says the wise man) the way thou will have him to walk; and when he is old, he will not forget it. Next, obedience to thee their dear mother; and that not for wrath, but for conscience sake. [Be] liberal to the poor, pitiful to the miserable, humble and kind to all. And may my God make thee a blessing and give thee comfort in our dear children; and in age, gather thee to the joy and blessedness of the just (where no death shall separate us) forever.

And now, my dear children that are the gifts and mercies of the God of your tender father, hear my counsel and lay it up in your hearts. Love it more than treasure and follow it, and you shall be blessed here and happy hereafter.

In the first place, remember your Creator in the days of your youth. It was the glory of Israel in the 2d of Jeremiah: and how did God bless Josiah, because he feared him in his youth! And so He did Jacob, Joseph, and Moses. Oh! my dear children, remember and fear and serve Him who made you, and gave you to me and your dear mother, that you may live to Him and glorify Him in your generations. To do this, in your youthful days seek after the Lord, that you may find Him, remembering His great love in creating you; that you are not beasts, plants, or stones, but that He has kept you and given you His grace within, and substance without, and provided plentifully for you. This remember in your youth, that you may be kept from the evil of the world; for, in age, it will be harder to overcome the temptations of it.

Wherefore, my dear children, eschew the appearance of evil, and love and cleave to that in your hearts that shows you evil from good, and tells you when you do amiss, and reproves you for it. It is the light of Christ, that He has given you for your salvation. If you do this, and follow my counsel, God will bless you in this world and give you an inheritance in that which shall never have an end. For the light of Jesus is of a purifying nature; it seasons those who love it and take heed to it, and never leaves such till it has brought them to the city of God that has foundations. Oh! that ye may be seasoned with the gracious nature of it; hide it in your hearts, and flee, my dear children, from all youthful lusts, the vain sports, pastimes and pleasures of the world, redeeming the time, because the days are evil. You are now beginning to live—what would some give for your time? Oh! I could have lived better, were I as you, in the flower of youth. Therefore, love and fear the Lord, keep close to meetings; and delight to wait upon the Lord God of your father and mother, among his despised people, as we have done. And count it your honor to be members of that society, and heirs of that living fellowship, which is enjoyed among them—for the experience of which your father's soul blesses the Lord forever.

Next, be obedient to your dear mother, a woman whose virtue and good name is an honor to you; for she has been exceeded by none in her time for her plainness, integrity, industry, humanity, virtue, and good understanding, qualities not usual among women of her worldly condition and quality. Therefore, honor and obey her, my dear children, as your mother, and your father's love and delight; nay, love her too, for she loved your father with a deep and upright love, choosing him before all her many suitors. And though she be of a delicate constitution and noble spirit, yet she descended to the utmost tenderness and care for you, performing in painfulness acts of service to you in your infancy, as a mother and a nurse too. I charge you before the Lord, honor and obey, love and cherish, your dear mother.

Next betake yourselves to some honest, industrious course of life; and that not of sordid covetousness, but for example and to avoid idleness. And if you change your condition and marry, choose with the knowledge and consent of your mother, if living, guardians, or those that have the charge of you. Mind neither beauty nor riches, but the fear of the Lord and a sweet and amiable disposition, such as you can love above all this world and that may make your habitations pleasant and desirable to you. And being married, be tender, affectionate, and patient, and meek. Live in the fear of the Lord, and He will bless you and your offspring. Be sure to live within compass; borrow not, neither be beholden to any. Ruin not yourselves by kindness to others, for that exceeds the due bounds of friendship; neither will a true friend expect it. Small matters I heed not.

Let your industry and parsimony go no farther than for a sufficiency for life, and to make a provision for your children (and that in moderation, if the Lord gives you any). I charge you to help the poor and needy. Let the Lord have a voluntary share of your income, for the good of the poor, both in our Society and others; for we are all His creatures, remembering that he that gives to the poor, lends to the Lord. Know well your incomings, and your outgoings may be the better regulated. Love not money, nor the world. Use them only and they will serve you; but if you love them, you serve them, which will debase your spirits as well as offend the Lord. Pity the distressed, and hold out a hand of help to them; it may be your case, and as you mete to others, God will mete to you again.

Be humble and gentle in your conversation; of few words, I charge you; but always pertinent when you speak, hearing out before you attempt to answer, and then speaking as if you would persuade, not impose.

Affront none, neither revenge the affronts that are done to you; but forgive, and you shall be forgiven of your Heavenly Father.

In making friends, consider well, first; and when you are fixed, be true, not wavering by reports nor deserting in affliction, for that becomes not the good and virtuous.

Watch against anger; neither speak nor act in it, for like drunkenness, it makes a man a beast and throws people into desperate inconveniences.

Avoid flatterers; for they are thieves in disguise. Their praise is costly, designing to get by those they bespeak. They are the worst of creatures; they lie to flatter and flatter to cheat, and, which is worse, if you believe them, you cheat yourselves most dangerously. But the virtuous—though poor—love, cherish, and prefer. Remember David, who asking the Lord, "Who shall abide in Thy tabernacle; who shall dwell in Thy holy hill?" answers, "He that walks uprightly, works righteousness, and speaks the truth in his heart; in whose eyes the vile person is condemned, but honors them who fears the Lord."

Next, my children, be temperate in all things: in your diet, for that is physic by prevention; it keeps, nay, it makes people healthy and their generation sound. This is exclusive of the spiritual advantage it brings. Be also plain in your apparel; keep out that lust which reigns too much over some. Let your virtues be your ornaments; remembering, life is more than food, and the body than raiment. Let your furniture be simple and cheap. Avoid pride, avarice, and luxury. Read my *No Cross, No Crown;* there is instruction. Make your conversation with the most eminent for wisdom and piety; and shun all wicked men, as you hope for the blessing of God, and the comfort of your father's living and dying prayers. Be sure you speak no evil of any; no, not of the meanest, much less of your superiors, as magistrates, guardians, tutors, teachers, and elders in Christ.

Be no busybodies; meddle not with other folks' matters but when in conscience and duly pressed, for it procures trouble, and is ill-mannered, and very unseemly to wise men.

In your families, remember Abraham, Moses, and Joshua, their integrity to the Lord; and do as [if] you have them for your examples. Let the fear and service of the living God be encouraged in your houses, and that plainness, sobriety, and moderation in all things, as becomes God's chosen people. And, as I advise you, my beloved children, do you counsel yours, if God should give you any. Yea, I counsel and command them, as my posterity, that they love and serve the Lord God with an upright heart, that He may bless you and yours, from generation to generation.

And as for you who are likely to be concerned in the government of Pennsylvania and my parts of East Jersey, especially the first, I do charge you before the Lord God and his only angels that you be lowly, diligent, and tender; fearing God, loving the people, and hating covetousness. Let justice have its impartial course, and the law free passage. Though to your loss, protect no man against it, for you are not above the law, but the law above you. Live therefore the lives yourselves you would have the people live; and then you have right and boldness to punish the transgressor. Keep upon the square, for God sees you; therefore do your duty; and be sure you see with your own eyes, and hear with your own ears. Entertain no lurchers; cherish no informers for gain or revenge; use no tricks, fly to no devices to support or cover injustice, but let your hearts be upright before the Lord, trusting in Him above the contrivances of men, and none shall be able to hurt or supplant.

Oh! the Lord is a strong God; and He can do whatsover He pleases. And though men consider it not, it is the Lord that rules and overrules in the kingdoms of men; and He builds up and pulls down. I, your father, am the man that can say, he that trusts in the Lord shall not be confounded. But God, in due time, will make His enemies be at peace with Him.

If you thus behave yourselves, and so become a terror to evildoers and a praise to them that do well, God, my God, will be with you, in wisdom and a sound mind, and make you blessed instruments in His hand for the settlement of some of those desolate parts of the world—which my soul desires above all worldly honors and riches, both for you that go and you that stay, you that govern and you that are governed—that in the end you may be gathered with me to the rest of God.

Finally, my children, love one another with a true and endeared love, and your dear relations on both sides; and take care to preserve tender affection in your children to each other, often marrying within themselves, so [long] as it be without the bounds forbidden in God's law. That so they may not, like the forgetting and unnatural world, grow out of kindred and as cold as strangers; but, as becomes a truly natural and Christian stock, you and yours after you may live in the pure and fervent love of God toward one another, as becomes brethren in the spiritual and natural relation.

So my God, that has blessed me with His abundant mercies, both of this and the other and better life, be with you all, guide you by His counsel, bless you, and bring you to His eternal glory, that you may shine, my dear children, in the firmament of God's power, with the blessed spirits of the just, that celestial family, praising and admiring Him, the God and Father of it, forever and ever. For there is no God like unto Him: the God of Abraham, of Isaac, and of Jacob; the God of the Prophets, the Apostles, and Martyrs of Jesus; in whom I live forever.

So farewell to my thrice dearly beloved wife and children. Yours, as God pleases, in that which no waters can quench, no time forget, nor distance wear away, but remains forever.

William Penn

19 August 1682

My Dear Springett,

Be good, learn to fear God, avoid evil, love thy book, be kind to thy brother and sister, and God will bless thee and I will exceedingly love thee. Farewell dear child.

Thy dear father,
Wm Penn

My love to all the family and to Friends.

Dear Laetitia,

I dearly love thee, and would have thee sober. Learn thy book, and love thy brothers. I will send thee a pretty book to learn in. The Lord bless thee and make a good woman of thee. Farewell.

Thy dear father,
Wm Penn

My love to the family.

Dear Billy,

I love thee much, therefore be sober and quiet, and learn his book. I will send him one. So the Lord bless thee. Amen.

Thy dear father,
Wm Penn

My love to all the family.

❧ E S S A Y S

Daniel Vickers of the Memorial University of Newfoundland writes in the first essay of the way in which families solved the labor problem in New England. Initially New Englanders, like their Chesapeake counterparts, experimented with servitude; but lacking a crop or a commodity of great economic power such as tobacco, they could not sustain such a labor system. Sons then provided families with a continuing supply of labor, drawing kin together in their interdependence. Laurel Thatcher Ulrich, a professor of history at the University of New Hampshire, argues in the second essay that wives in New England took up roles not seen in traditional sources that set them apart from their English counterparts. Husbands relied on their wives to act for them in their absence, and wives shared responsibility for the family business.

Finally Barry Levy, a historian at the University of Massachusetts, argues that the word *modern* best describes the "disorderly" Quaker family life of the middle colonies. He describes a highly structured system but one that, because it was simplified from European forms, was criticized by non-Quakers. The later Quakers, reacting to persecution in England, had dropped many of the aggressive practices described by Carla Pestana in Chapter 5 and devoted themselves to building a stable life. They focused on the family as the most important institution for realization of their goals and, Levy argues, achieved a higher level of success than their neighbors.

Family Labor in New England

DANIEL VICKERS

In the middle of the seventeenth century, an unknown Englishman observed: "Virginia thrives by keeping many servants and these in strict obedience. New

Daniel Vickers, "Working the Fields in a Developing Economy: Essex County, Massachusetts, 1630–75," pp. 49–69. Reprinted from *Work and Labor in Early America,* edited by Stephen Innes. Published for the Institute of Early American History and Culture, Williamsburg, Virginia. © 1988 The University of North Carolina Press.

England conceit they and their Children can doe enough, and soe have rarely above one Servant." Here, stated for the first time, was a basic truth about early America: that free families were to the northern colonies what bound servants were to the South—the human foundation of the dominant mode of production. That planters in the Chesapeake exporting tobacco for profit adopted indentured servitude while New Englanders producing for home consumption and local markets did not made perfect sense: one economy required such help, and the other could not afford it. New Englanders lacked a bonanza crop that would generate both the rapid growth of capital and a pressing need for large amounts of labor. These contrasts, however, tell only half of the story, for settlers in both regions did share one basic challenge—developing a new country. If the Massachusetts colony never experienced the acute scarcities of capital and labor that prevailed in Virginia and Maryland, it was still a growing settlement; and relative to the abundance of unexploited land and the work required to bring it under the plow, productive equipment and manpower were in short supply. The difficulty that these northerners faced was a milder though similar version of what troubled the first settlers to the Chesapeake: how did one go about accumulating capital in a labor-scarce environment?

Although New Englanders had intended to construct a society out of households transplanted intact and unchanged from the Old Country, the exigencies of farming the wilderness would not permit this. The division of labor by gender, which in the English rural tradition meant that women worked in and around the house and yard while men toiled in the fields beyond, was preserved in Massachusetts. Several historians have portrayed the female domain within the family economy with considerable sensitivity. But what about the work relationships that connected male New Englanders: fathers with sons, masters with servants, landlords with tenants, and employers with casual help? Historians have studied most of these separately in some detail but rarely together and with little attempt to assess the relative importance of each. And this last is an important omission, for Massachusetts farmers and their sons had to adjust the rural traditions of Old England when they encountered the American frontier.

But what exactly did the English inheritance amount to? Although it is difficult to do justice to the amazing variety, both by region and class, of seventeenth-century English farm work experiences, some broad truths stand out. First, we know that agricultural labor was generally carried out in household units. Farmers usually worked the land that they occupied with the consistent help only of their children and servants. Times of special activity, such as harvest (mowing, reaping, carting, threshing, and a variety of other tasks), might necessitate the employment of some outside hands, but few farms depended on such individuals the year round. True, over the course of the early modern period, rising numbers of men and women, displaced by enclosures or by the pressure of population growth upon the land, did attempt to make a living from different forms of short-term employment, especially in the southern and eastern portions of the country which produced most of the Puritan migration. Some of these dispossessed individuals rented cottages on the fringes of the large consolidated farms that offered them daily work; others dwelt on small holdings in the forest and migrated seasonally to regions where help was in demand; still others simply drifted up and down the countryside, selling their services on a casual basis. Yet, even if contemporary Englishmen voiced growing alarm at the rising number of masterless men, it would still be a mistake to make too much of day labor in this period, for its advance was gradual and intermittent. In the years when the Puritan emigrants were departing for America, the bulk of England's agricultural output was still the product of household endeavor, even in the regions they had left behind.

Second, we know that the exchange of goods and services between households was given its primary shape by the division of property. Rural Englishmen everywhere understood that the position each occupied in the hierarchy of wealth implied power over some and submission to others. "There is nothing more plain nor certain," as one writer put it, "than that God Almighty hath ordained and appointed different degrees of Authority and Subjection." In the world of everyday work, subjection meant harking to the commands of others, and freedom from such commands stemmed only from control over land and capital. The more that one owned, the fewer days in the year that one spent in the employ of one's neighbors. Through the long procession of working days that constituted life for ordinary people, the only sure source of independence—and status—was the possession of property.

Another major factor that gave shape to the organization of work in early modern England was age. From the time when they first began to help out with minor chores until, at marriage, they established households of their own, farm boys toiled under the direction of their elders. Through their early teens, they served mainly as agents of their fathers' will, learning the arts of husbandry under continual supervision. Then, about the age of thirteen or fourteen, almost two-thirds of them departed from their parents' quarters to enter the homes of other families short of help. Thenceforth, on a series of yearly contracts, they labored as servants in husbandry and saved what they could toward launching households of their own. Even after marriage, the majority of young Englishmen continued, for a few years at least, to seek daily employment at the farms of older and wealthier neighbors. There was a dimension to economic power, therefore, that was generational.

Finally, as E. L. Jones put it, "farming proper was something done by tenants." Although the dauntingly complicated history of tenancy and other forms of dual ownership is only beginning to attract the attention it deserves, we do know that most of England's land area was held, not by outright owners, but by occupiers who paid for its use in a variety of ways. Some tenants satisfied their landlords with rents in cash or kind; most were also liable for tithes, heriot, or entry fines; others owed labor services. With growing frequency, the obligation to repair property also fell onto the shoulders of the occupier, who might even be expected to make improvements, although, in other instances, the landlord still assumed this responsibility himself. Nowhere was tenancy simple, nor did it escape enormous regional variation, but for most English farmers of the period it framed the work experience. A hierarchy of tenant householders, therefore, assisted by sons, servants, and an increasing array of hired hands, operated the greatest part of the English rural economy in the seventeenth century.

Those families who left in the 1630s to colonize Massachusetts Bay intended to build there a "New England"—a purified re-creation in the New World of that to which they were accustomed in the Old. In their letters home, they stressed time and again the ways in which Massachusetts seemed to resemble or even improve upon their relinquished homeland. Francis Higginson believed that the countryside around Salem contained as "much good ground for corn and for grass as any is under the heavens." Thomas Graves celebrated the "goodly woods," the "open lands" where "grass and weeds grow up to a man's face," and the meadows "without any tree or shrub to hinder the scythe." Furthermore, New England was good for one. Wrote Higginson: "There is hardly a more hea[l]thful place to be found in the world that agreeth better with our English bodies." Those writers emphasized, moreover, that in New England there were enough lands, rivers, and forests for everyone to partake of these advantages. With hard work, any settler could procure, if not riches, at least a fair share of this natural bounty—in brief, a comfortable and independent subsistence. Those who planned to enrich themselves were mistaken, observed Thomas Dudley in 1630, but those who had removed for spiritual ends would find ample building materials, fuel, soil, seas and rivers full of fish, pure air, and "good water to drink till wine or beer can be made." "Howsoever they are accounted poore," concluded William Wood in *New England's Prospect,* "they are well contented, and looke not so much at abundance as a competencie."

One can distinguish here two separate aspirations. First, the settlers hoped to reproduce the level of material comfort which people of their condition had known at home; and, second, they intended to go about it in an English manner. At first glance, given the natural abundance that surrounded them in the new land, the reconciliation of these two purposes might seem to be a simple affair. But between them, as events were to prove, there existed a fundamental tension. It was difficult to build farms on New England's first frontier that could guarantee their owners the level of prosperity and civilization to which, in the Old World, they had been accustomed. Land had to be cleared, barns erected, fences built, and mills constructed—all from scratch and demanding more manpower, equipment, and skill on each piece of land than most early settlers could readily obtain. So "much labour and servise was to be done aboute building and planting," complained William Bradford in 1642, that "such as wanted help in that respecte, when they could not have such as they would, were glad to take such as they could." In a thinly settled country, where most family heads could acquire an independent freehold, the means to avoid working for others, help was simply too scarce and too expensive. Servants whose times were out, declared John Winthrop with obvious annoyance in 1645, "could not be hired . . . but upon unreasonable terms." This, indeed, was a problem: how could the rural economy of old England be reestablished in an environment where workmen were so difficult to procure? How, in other words, were the twin scarcities of capital and labor to be overcome? Such a dilemma, in truth, could not be resolved within the customary rules of labor organization familiar to the resident of a seventeenth-century English village. Paradoxically, the very urge to re-create what was familiar led the Bay colonists to order their working lives in a manner that was decidedly new.

Most free colonists in the Great Migration belonged to households prosperous enough to keep servants. Indeed, the surviving passenger lists from the 1630s indicate that servants were almost half again as common among the arriving settlers as in the towns and villages left behind. Nor should this surprise us, since the poorest English households—the only ones certain not to keep servants—were scarcely represented in the planting process. Those families who departed in the 1630s to establish themselves on the far side of the Atlantic were not a wealthy group, but their landholdings in the Old Country had normally been extensive enough to support some live-in help. And since they harbored no illusions about the task ahead of them, they took their servants along. Founding new settlements, warned Edward Johnson, required "every one that can lift a hawe."

The Puritan migrants expected, therefore, that service in husbandry could be reestablished in New England; and, indeed, there were individual towns where the institution took root. In Springfield, Massachusetts, for example, John Pynchon employed servants to raise wheat, cattle, and timber for shipment abroad; and in Bristol, Rhode Island, a commercial town whose gentry bred horses and sheep for the market, such live-in help clearly was as important as in the villages of the Old Country. In Essex County, however, the English pattern did not persist. Once those servants accompanying the original migrants of the 1630s had dispersed, the system of service in husbandry swiftly collapsed. Male servants had accounted for at least 8 percent of the population of most English villages back home, and the rate was even greater if one included farming households alone. It was certainly so among those families as prosperous as those who joined in the Puritan migration. Indeed, it has been calculated that in early modern England 72 percent of yeomen, 47 percent of husbandmen, and 23 percent of tradesmen, the dominant occupational groups among New England's settlers, customarily kept at least one servant (male or female) under their roofs at any given time, and more frequently men than maids. In Essex County during the first half-century, by comparison, we can be confident that the proportion of male farm servants to the farming population as a whole did not exceed 4 percent. The owners of the large estates—the Bradstreets, Appletons, Gardners, and others—who generally scorned physical labor themselves, did employ menservants on some of their property, but rarely more than two or three. Samuel Symonds, for example, one of the wealthiest landholders in the colony, who died in possession of seventeen hundred acres, told the Essex County court in 1661 that he kept only two such men in his home. Indeed, four-fifths or more of the county farmers kept no male servants at all. By comparison to rural households of equal estate in England, about half of which included menservants, Essex families did largely without. . . .

Given the scarcity of servants, could the yeomen and husbandmen of Essex County turn easily to the employment of neighbors by the day? . . .

... The first New Englanders, fresh from their experience with the mature economy of the mother country, had few doubts on the matter. Daily help, they complained, was both expensive and difficult to find. Ecclesiastical synods, sessions of court, town meetings, and private individuals alike took account of labor's cost, though they viewed it as a product less of market forces than of moral failings. "Extortion" and "Oppression" were the terms they preferred, echoing one another repeatedly through the end of the seventeenth century. And on one level they were right: the twenty to thirty pence per day (if one converts local currency into sterling) that common agricultural labor obtained in Essex County before 1675 was an unusually healthy wage. By the English standard of twelve to fifteen pence per day, such earnings quite understandably provoked attention, and they bespoke the favorable bargaining position that scarce labor commanded. For a while, the General Court attempted to regulate these wages, but by 1641 it had given up. ... Of course, there were artisans—house carpenters, blacksmiths, and millers, for example— whom farmers might employ periodically to perform some specialized work, particularly in the early years of farm building. And no farm, of course, was entirely free of the need to ask neighbors for occasional assistance. Still, in the regular round of field chores and property maintenance, it was the rare husbandman who placed much reliance on neighbors or strangers employed by the day. ...

... On the Essex County stretch of New England's first frontier, day labor, like farm service, withered. The two forms of help which husbandmen in the mother country had employed to supplement the efforts of their own offspring could not be recreated on this side of the Atlantic in quantities or at prices that made economic sense. ... Even more than historians have realized, therefore, it must have been the family—not the English household of parents, children, and servants with the occasional hired hand, but the nuclear family alone—that dominated the rural economy of the region.

A farm boy was first likely to appear in depositions taken before the county court, working under his father's eye, about the age of ten. At the beginning, though he might be expected to help on occasion at any of the classic field chores, most of his hours were spent caring for livestock. By his thirteenth birthday, young Stephen Cross of Ipswich already had been helping his older brother for several years, tending their father's sheep; and Abraham Adams of Newbury knew the family cattle well enough at eleven years that he could describe a missing steer to the court down to its hastily cut earmark. As his teens advanced, the young New England male gradually took on a wider variety of tasks, such as fencing, carting, mowing, and breaking sod— shouldering in every respect a man's workload. Always, however, he toiled under his father's orders. William Story, aged seventeen, like most others at his age of whom we have record, went off to mow in his family's meadows, we learn from court testimony, because he had been ordered to.

Once the age of majority had been passed, the instances of direct parental supervision began to ebb. Sons continued to work on the father's lands. But less often, in their testimony before the courts, did they remember being "ordered" or "sent" to their tasks or laboring by his side. Yet, significantly enough, no real evidence of true independence normally surfaced in the economic endeavors of these young colonists until the age of twenty-five or thirty. Neither in the ownership of land and livestock nor in dealings in farm produce did men in their twenties play a part even remotely approximating their importance in the population. True, the maturing son exercised considerable control over his daily routine. Having learned what farming was about, he could be trusted, as his father discovered, to work by himself, to assume direction of the property in his parents' absence, and even to contribute his own ideas to the running of the farm. A neighbor of Peter Tappen testified in 1673 that, since the age of nineteen, young Tappen had "bin vary dutiful too his father and vary carfull of his bisnis when the old man was in Ingland . . . and late willing to Improv all sesons for his fathers good." At marriage, moreover, when the new householder first erected a dwelling elsewhere on family land and began working fields apart from his father, he came to manage even more of his own affairs.

Nevertheless, it was not until, either by deed or inheritance, he had assumed full legal control over his portion of the parental estate that a son became an independent man in his own right. And although this might happen when he formed a household of his own, it might also be delayed by years or even decades until his father's death. He was not encouraged, therefore, as in England to strike out on his own. In the new colony, where there was work to be done and few alternative sources of labor, parents preferred that their sons spend their young adulthood, even beyond the age of marriage, developing the family estate. These young householders may no longer have been living under daily parental direction, and they surely understood that they were contributing to the improvement of land that could one day be theirs. But, in the degree of their commitment to property that was still under their fathers' authority, at a time in life when they were beginning to raise children of their own, they were still accepting, albeit hesitantly, limitations on their freedom of action that were foreign to English tradition.

It was, therefore, at a measured pace, even a tardy one by the standards of the Old Country, that the male offspring of Essex County moved out from under parental control. Several centuries later, this tale possesses a familiar ring, for it is the story of the American family farm. To these English emigrants of the seventeenth century, however, it was new; the exigencies of farming in the New World had forced them to alter their habits of household production.

Emphasizing the nuclear family at the expense of larger working units that took in outside help, however, is not to argue for economic equality. Early New Englanders had grown up in a class society, and their leaders took pains to recreate those different "Condicion[s] of mankinde" with which they were familiar, especially through their distribution of land. At the foundation of most Essex County towns, close to half of the apportioned property was assigned to the wealthiest 10 percent of the population who controlled community affairs. These were the county elite: personages, like the Endecotts and the Downings, who could devote their time to public service, since the extent of their granted lands had freed them from the mundane rounds of daily work. They served as magistrates or militia captains, involved themselves in international commerce, and represented their towns at the General Court, but rarely did they ever handle livestock or wield a sickle. Virgin land, however, did not translate itself into income automatically. Owners of such estates, who considered manual labor demeaning, had to arrange for others to do the work of development. Rejecting the direct operation of their farms through the employment of servants and hired help, most of them turned, instead, to the granting of leaseholds.

Tenancy was one feature of the English countryside that Americans successfully carried with them into those portions of the new continent—notably Maryland, Pennsylvania, New Jersey, and the valleys of the Hudson and Connecticut rivers—where mixed husbandry aimed at the market was important. Estate owners discovered that their lands were most profitably managed when they rented them out to single farming families. Often obliged by their agreements to make capital improvements, in addition to rental payments, these tenant families proved to be the most effective agents for the transfer of English agricultural custom to the larger landholdings of the northern colonies.

Leaseholding flourished in those parts of Essex County where adequate land that was close to the sea made commercial agriculture possible. . . . The appropriate natural conditions, therefore, could attract men of sufficient wealth and status to acquire land and engineer its development by parceling it out to those with little property, but willing backs.

The form assumed by leaseholding in Essex County reflected the most modern of English practice. The actual agreements, for one thing, aimed foremost at a simple specificity, . . . by written agreements that spelled out the obligations of both parties in specific contractual terms. . . . Furthermore, Essex County leases, like those in other colonial regions, were often developmental. Some induced tenants to undertake capital improvements by offering them credit for work accomplished. . . . Other agreements, assumedly in return for a reduction in rent, required the leaseholder to develop the property in a specified way. . . . Such contractualism was characteristic of leaseholding in most portions of early America.

Farm tenants in Essex County were more likely than their neighbors to be recent immigrants, part of that minority of settlers whose families had come to America after the Great Migration. . . . From the larger estate owners in the county, they rented farms on relatively short terms—usually less than ten years—with the intent of eventually establishing themselves on an independent freehold. Few of them ever achieved real prosperity, but most found a living sufficient to maintain them in the county for several decades, often until the end of their lives.

It was chiefly by dint of the tenants' labor and the labor of their families that the greater landholdings of Essex County were first brought into production. Estate owners in the seventeenth century preferred to hand over the direct operation of their farms to tenant households, rather than seek out the servants and hired help needed to conduct it themselves. . . . And whereas it is certain that male servants numbered less than 4 percent of those who actually farmed the soil of Essex County before 1675, tenants and their families may have accounted for as much as 25 percent. Householders who rented undoubtedly were less numerous than those who owned their farms outright, but, throughout the period in question, tenancy was the active force in the development of large estates.

Tenants, however, shared this with landowning farmers: they followed their annual round of toil free from direct supervision. Fathers and sons, therefore, on rented farms as on those that were owned, performed the field work that generated the raw materials of agriculture. Even in those regions where commercial agriculture and inequality held sway, the dominant unit of production in which daily tasks actually were organized was the nuclear family operating without help. Despite all their intentions to recreate the Old Country in which they had grown up, these emigrants ended up scuttling the freer portion of the labor system on which the English rural economy had relied. On this particular segment of the early American frontier, and at least among men, work relationships collapsed in upon the family.

To show that, by contemporary standards, these New England households were singularly dedicated to the management of their own economies is not to argue for their economic autonomy. The web of local exchange was a part of life in New England from its foundation. Most of what rural householders exchanged, however—and this was true of the entire colonial period as even a cursory examination of contemporary account books will show—was not labor, but produce, and rented capital equipment. It was through a local trade in cider, barley malt, footwear, and oxen by the day rather than by "changing works" that New Englanders made good most specific shortcomings on their individual farms.

This brings us to a further question: whether the picture sketched here for the male portion of these families has any relevance for the female half. It has been argued, in reaction to the older and inaccurate understanding of colonial women as isolated home producers, that seventeenth-century housewives traded commodities *and* labor equally within a highly integrated community economy. Granting that the social context of female work did extend far beyond the household, it would still be interesting to know whether women, like men, saw the labor system with which they had grown up in England reorganized in the Great Migration. I suspect that it was, and in the same direction (toward family production) and for the same basic reason— because the task of farm-building in this empty land was as demanding on wives and daughters as on husbands and sons. All this remains conjectural, of course, but the issue of transatlantic comparison is clearly one that matters as much for women as for men.

Farm labor in Essex County assumed its new configuration in response to two problems common to frontier life everywhere: the dual and interrelated scarcities of capital and labor relative to land. Where there was work to be done, as there had to be in unusual quantity during a period of farm formation, and where the alternative sources of help were few, rural landowners were loath to part with the labor of their sons. So long as there was country to be cleared, farms and fences to be built, and the hungry mouths of numerous younger children to be fed, the inexpensive labor of offspring was essential to family welfare. Furthermore, in a rural economy with few large and well-equipped estates that could have generated employment opportunities, farm boys had little choice but to remain at home.... Both generations were committed to the provision of economic independence for themselves and their descendants that never could be achieved if the family scattered its scarce labor resources in pursuit of scarce capital across the county map. This exaggeration in parental authority and filial duty—beyond anything that had been known in England—stemmed primarily from the problem of developing the wilderness. Our unknown observer, with whose intuitive remarks this essay began, was absolutely right: children served the same economic function in New England that indentured servants did in the Chesapeake....

Agricultural development on the northern frontier of seventeenth-century America demanded restrictions on the mobility of labor that the family could provide, but never did the lure of bonanza profits prompt the widespread recourse to the harsher forms of coercion that were typical of the Chesapeake. As matters stood, the family farm, with its heightened interdependency of father and son, furnished sanctions on the organization of work that were entirely appropriate to the frontier economy of early New England.

Wives as Deputy Husbands

LAUREL THATCHER ULRICH

Many historians have assumed, with Page Smith, that "it was not until the end of the colonial era that the idea of a 'suitable' or 'proper' sphere of feminine activities began to emerge." For fifty years historians have relied upon the work of Elizabeth A. Dexter, who claimed that there were more "women of affairs" proportionally in eighteenth-century America than in 1900. Colonial newspapers yield evidence of female blacksmiths, silversmiths, tinworkers, shoemakers, shipwrights, tanners, gunsmiths, barbers, printers, and butchers, as well as a great many teachers and shopkeepers. Partly on the basis of such evidence, Richard Morris concluded in his pioneering study of female legal rights that American women in the colonial period attained "a measure of individuality and independence in excess of that of their English sisters."

Recently, however, a few historians have begun to question these assumptions. Mary Beth Norton has carefully studied the claims of 468 loyalist women who were refugees in Great Britain after the American Revolution. Only forty-three of these women mentioned earning money on their own or even assisting directly in their husbands' business. As a group, the loyalist women were unable to describe their family assets, other than household possessions, and they repeatedly described themselves as "helpless" to manage the business thrust upon them. She has concluded that these women were

---

"Deputy Husbands," excerpted from Chapter 2 of *Good Wives: Image and Reality in the Lives of Women in Northern New England, 1650–1750*, by Laurel Thatcher Ulrich, pp. 35–50. Copyright © 1980, 1982 by Laurel Thatcher Ulrich. Reprinted by permission of Alfred A. Knopf, Inc.

"almost wholly domestic, in the sense that that word would be used in the nineteenth-century United States." In a study of widowhood in eighteenth-century Massachusetts, Alexander Keyssar came to similar conclusions. Economic dependency, first upon husbands, then upon grown sons, characterized the lives of women in the agricultural village of Woburn.

Both groups of historians are right. The premodern world did allow for greater fluidity of role behavior than in nineteenth-century America, but colonial women were by definition basically domestic. We can account for these apparently contradictory conclusions by focusing more closely upon the economic relationship of husband and wife. There is a revealing little anecdote in a deposition recorded in Essex County in 1672. Jacob Barney of Salem had gone to Phillip Cromwell's house to negotiate a marriage. Although both Cromwell and his wife were present, Barney had turned to the husband, expecting, as he said, "to have their minds from him." But because Cromwell had a severe cold which had impaired his hearing, he simply pointed to his wife and said that whatever she agreed upon, "he would make it good." This incident dramatizes three assumptions basic to family government in the traditional world:

1. The husband was supreme in the external affairs of the family. As its titular head, he had both the right and the responsibility to represent it in its dealings with the outside world.
2. A husband's decisions would, however, incorporate his wife's opinions and interest. (Barney expected to hear *their* minds from *him*.)
3. Should fate or circumstance prevent the husband from fulfilling his role, the wife could appropriately stand in his place. As one seventeenth-century Englishman explained it, a woman "in her husband's absence, is wife and deputy-husband, which makes her double the files of her diligence. At his return he finds all things so well he wonders to see himself at home when he was abroad."

To put it simply, Dexter's evidence points to what was permissible in colonial society, Norton's to what was probable. As deputy husbands a few women, like Mistress Cromwell, might emerge from anonymity; most women did not. Yet both sets of evidence must be analyzed apart from modern assumptions about the importance of access to jobs in expanding female opportunity. The significance of the role of deputy husband cannot be determined by counting the number of women who used it to achieve independence. To talk about the independence of colonial wives is not only an anachronism but a contradiction in logic. A woman became a wife by virtue of her dependence, her solemnly vowed commitment to her husband. No matter how colorful the exceptions, land and livelihood in this society were normally transmitted from father to son, as studies like Keyssar's have shown.

One can be dependent, however, without being either servile or helpless. To use an imperfect but nonetheless suggestive analogy, colonial wives were dependent upon patriarchal families in somewhat the same way seventeenth-century ministers were dependent upon their congregations or twentieth-century engineers are dependent upon their companies. That is, they owned neither their place of employment nor even the tools of their trade. No matter how diligently they worked, they did not expect to inherit the land upon which they lived any more than a minister expected to inherit his meetinghouse or an engineer his factory. Skilled service was their major contribution, secure support their primary compensation. Unlike professionals in either century, they could not resign their position, but then neither could they be fired. Upon the death of a husband they were entitled to maintenance for life—or until they transferred their allegiance (symbolized by their name) from one domestic establishment to another.

The skilled service of a wife included . . . specialized housekeeping skills, . . . but it also embraced the responsibilities of a deputy husband. Since most productive work was based within the family, there were many opportunities for a wife to "double the files of her diligence." A weaver's wife, like Beatrice Plummer, might wind quills. A merchant's wife, like Hannah Grafton, might keep shop. A farmer's wife, like Magdalen Wear, might plant corn.

Looking backward to the colonial period from the nineteenth century, when "true womanhood" precluded either business enterprise or hard physical labor, historians may miss the significance of such work, which tells us less about economic opportunity (which for most women was limited) than about female responsibility (which was often very broad). Most occupations were indeed gender-linked, yet colonial Englishmen were far less concerned with abstract notions like "femininity" than with concrete roles like "wife" or "neighbor." Almost any task was suitable for a woman as long as it furthered the good of her family and was acceptable to her husband. This approach was both fluid and fixed. It allowed for varied behavior without really challenging the patriarchal order of society. There was no proscription against female farming, for example, but there were strong prescriptions toward dutiful wifehood and motherhood. Context was everything.

In discussing the ability of colonial women to take on male duties, most historians have assumed a restrictive ideology in Anglo-American society, an essentially negative valuation of female capacity. Some historians have argued that this negative ideology was offset by the realities of colonial life; others have concluded it was not. This [essay] reverses the base of the argument, suggesting that even in America ideology was more permissive than reality. Under the right conditions any wife not only *could* double as a husband, she had the responsibility to do so. In the probate courts, for example, widows who did not have grown sons were routinely granted administration of their husbands' estates. Gender restrictions were structural rather than psychological. Although there was no female line of inheritance, wives were presumed capable of husbanding property which male heirs would eventually inherit.

To explain fully the contradictions in such a system, we must return to the day-to-day behavior of individual husbands and wives, first examining the factors which enhanced the role of deputy husband and then exploring conditions which muted its significance for colonial women.

Historians can read wills, account books, and tax records, documents in which males clearly predominate, but they cannot so easily explore the complex decision-making behind these records. Scattered glimpses of daily interaction suggest that there was as much variation in seventeenth- and eighteenth-century families as there is today. Some wives were servile, some were shrews, others were respected companions who shared the authority of their spouses in the management of family affairs. Important conditions, however, separated the colonial world from our own. The most basic of these was spatial. . . . Male and female space intersected and overlapped. Nor was there the sharp division between home and work that later generations experienced. Because servants and apprentices lived within the household, a family occasion—mealtime or nightly prayer—could become a business occasion as well.

In June of 1661 a young maid named Naomi Hull described a discussion which took place in the parlor of the Samuel Symonds' home in Ipswich, Massachusetts, early in that year. The case concerned the length of indenture of two Irish servants. According to the maid, all of the family had gathered for prayer when one of the Irishmen asked if a neighbor's son was coming the next day to plow. *Mistress* Symonds said she thought so. One of the men asked who would plow with him. *Mistress* Symonds said, "One of you." When the two men announced that their indenture was up and that they would work no longer, both the master and the mistress questioned the servants. At one point Mistress Symonds interrupted her husband. "Let them alone," she said. "Now they are speaking let them speak their own minds." Because the involvement of Mistress Symonds was not at issue, this casual description of her participation is all the more impressive. Such an anecdote shows the way in which boundaries between male and female domains might blur in a common household setting.

Ambitious men in early America were often involved in many things at once—farming and running a gristmill, for example, or cutting timber and fishing. Because wives remained close to the house, they were often at the communications center of these diverse operations, given responsibility for conveying directions, pacifying creditors, and perhaps even making some decisions about the disposition of labor. On a day-to-day basis this might be a rather simple matter: remembering to send a servant to repair a breach in the dam after he finished in the field, for example, or knowing when to relinquish an ox to a neighbor. But during a prolonged absence of her husband a woman might become involved in more weighty matters.

Sometime in the 1670s Moses Gilman of Exeter, New Hampshire, wrote to his wife from Boston:

> Loving wife Elisabeth Gillman these are to desire you to speake to John Gillman & James Perkins and so order the matter thatt Mr. Tho. Woodbridge may have Twelve thousand fott of merchantable boards Rafted by thirsday night or sooner if poseble they Can for I have Absolutly sould them to him & if John Clough sen or any other doe deliver bords to make up the sum Give Receits of whatt you Receive of him or any other man and lett no bote bee prest or other ways disposed of untill I Returne being from Him who is yos till death

> Moses Gilman

If Gilman had doubted his wife's ability to "order the matter," he could have written a number of separate letters—to John Gilman, James Perkins,

John Clough, and perhaps others. But securing a shipment of twelve thousand feet of merchantable boards entirely by letter would have been complicated and time-consuming. Instead, Gilman relied on the good sense of his wife, who would be respected as his surrogate, and who probably had acquired some expertise in making out receipts for forest products and in conveying instructions to lumbering and shipping crews. A "loving wife" who considered herself his "till Death" was more trustworthy than a hired servant or business associate. As a true consort, she would know that by furthering her husband's interest she furthered her own.

Thus, a wife with talent for business might become a kind of double for her husband, greatly extending his ability to handle affairs. This is beautifully illustrated in a document filed with the New Hampshire court papers. In February of 1674 Peter Lidget of Boston signed a paper giving Henry Dering of Piscataqua full power of attorney "to collect all debts due to him in that place and thereabout." On the reverse side of the document Dering wrote: "I Henry Dering have, and do hereby Constitute, ordaine, and appoint my loveing wife, Anne Dering my Lawful Attourney" to collect and sue for Peter Lidget's debts "by virtue of the Letter of Attourney on the other side." (Anne Dering was the widow of Ralph Benning of Boston. She left her married name—and perhaps some of her business acumen—to her great-grandson, Governor Benning Wentworth of New Hampshire.)

Court cases involving fishermen give some glimpses of the kinds of responsibility assumed by their wives, who often appear in the foreground as well as the background of the documents. Depositions in an action of 1660 reveal Anne Devorix working alongside her husband, "taking account" as a servant culled fish from a spring voyage. She herself delivered a receipt from the master of the ship to the shop where the final "reckoning" was made. When her husband was at sea, she supervised spring planting on the family corn land as well as protecting the hogsheads, barrels, and flakes at the shore from the incursions of a quarrelsome neighbor. Even more visible in the records is Edith Creford of Salem, who frequently acted as an attorney for her husband, at one point signing a promissory note for £33 in "merchantable cod fish at price current." Like the fishwives of Nantucket whom Crèvecoeur described a hundred years later, these women were "necessarily obliged to transact business, to settle accounts, and in short, to rule and provide for their families."

At a different social level the wives of merchant sea captains played a similar role. Sometime in the year 1710 Elizabeth Holmes of Boston sat down with Patience Marston of Salem and settled accounts accumulated during a voyage to Newfoundland. Neither woman had been on the ship. They were simply acting as attorneys for their husbands, Captain Robert Holmes, who had commanded the brigantine, and Mr. Benjamin Marston, who owned it. Family letters give a more detailed picture of Mistress Marston's involvement in her husband's business.

In the summer of 1719 Benjamin Marston took command of one of his own ships, taking his twenty-two-year-old son Benjamin with him. Young Benjamin wrote his mother complete details of the first stage of the journey, which ended at Casco Bay in Maine. He included the length of the journey, the state of the family enterprises in Maine, and the price of lumber and staves, adding that he was "Sorry you should sett so long in ye house for no Adv[ance] but perhaps to ye prejudice of your health." Patience was obviously "keeping shop." A week later Benjamin wrote again, assuring his mother that he was looking after the business in Maine. "My father w[oul]d have been imposed upon by m—c had I not interposed and stood stiffly to him," he explained. Was the son acting out some Oedipal fantasy here, or was he perhaps performing as his *mother's* surrogate, strengthening the resolve of the presumably more easygoing father? The next day he wrote still another letter, asking for chocolate, complaining boyishly that "ye Musketo's bitt me so prodigiously as I was writing that I can hardly tell what it was I wrote," and conveying what must by then have been a common request from the absent husband. Mrs. Marston was to get a witnessed statement regarding a piece of family business and send it by "the first Oppertunity."

Because the business activities of wives were under the "wing, protection, and cover" of a husband (to repeat Blackstone's phrase), they are difficult to measure by standard methods. Patience Marston was a custodian of messages, guardian of errands, preserver of property, and keeper of accounts. Yet without the accidental survival of a few family papers there would be no way of knowing about her involvement in her husband's business. In Benjamin's will she received the standard "thirds." She may have become impatient with her chores or anxious about her husband's business acumen, but there is no indication of this in the only writings preserved in her hand. She served as "deputy husband" as circumstances demanded, and when her husband perished from smallpox soon after arriving in Ireland, she declared herself grateful for the dear son who returned "as one from the dead" to take over his father's business.

The role of deputy husband deserves more careful and systematic study. But two cautions are in order. First, the biases of the twentieth century may tempt historians to give undue significance to what were really rather peripheral enterprises. Acting as attorney to one's husband is not equivalent to practicing law. To colonial women, it may even have been less desirable than keeping house. This leads to the second point. The value of any activity is determined by its meaning to the participant, not to the observer. In early America position was always more important than task. Colonial women might appear to be independent, even aggressive, by modern standards, yet still have derived their status primarily from their relationship to their husbands.

This is well illustrated in a New Hampshire court record of 1671. A carpenter named John Barsham testified about an argument he had heard between Henry Sherburne and his second wife, Sarah, who was the widow of Walter Abbott. Barsham had come to the house to get some nails he needed for repairing a dwelling he had rented from them. According to Barsham, Sarah became so angry at her husband's opposition that she "rose off from the seat where she was setting & came up to him with her arms akimbo saying we should have nayles & he had nothing to [do] in it." As if to add the final authority to her demand, she asked him "why he trode upon Walter Abbotts floor & bid him get out of doors, & said that he had nothing to do there." Sarah Sherburne was an experienced and assertive woman. She had kept tavern "with two husbands and none." The house in which she and Sherburne lived had been part of her inheritance from her first husband. But in the heat of the argument she did not say, "Get out of *my* house" or "Get out of the house *I* provided." She said, "Get out of Walter Abbott's house." Her identity was not as property owner, but as wife. To assert her authority over her husband, she invoked the memory of his predecessor.

. . . The economic roles of married women were based upon two potentially conflicting values—gender specialization and identity of interest. A wife was expected to become expert in the management of a household and the care of children, but she was also asked to assist in the economic affairs of her husband, becoming his representative and even his surrogate if circumstances demanded it. These two roles were compatible in the premodern world because the home was the communication center of family enterprise if not always the actual place of work. As long as business transactions remained personal and a woman had the support of a familiar environment, she could move rather easily from the role of housewife to the role of deputy husband, though few women were prepared either by education or by experience to become "independent women of affairs."

The role of deputy husband reinforced a certain elasticity in premodern notions of gender. No mystique of feminine behavior prevented a woman from driving a hard bargain or chasing a pig from the field, and under ideal conditions day-to-day experience in assisting with a husband's work might prepare her to function competently in a male world—should she lose her husband, should she find herself without a grown son, should she choose not to remarry or find it impossible to do so. But in the immediate world such activities could have a far different meaning. The chores assigned might be menial, even onerous, and, whatever their nature, they competed for attention with the specialized housekeeping responsibilities which every woman shared.

"Modern" Quaker Families in Pennsylvania

BARRY LEVY

The career of the modern family in America began early in the Delaware Valley, at least by the late seventeenth century. From their first settlement, Quaker farmers and artisans lived in families featuring the basic elements that historians and sociologists have used to define the "modern" family: purified household environments, voluntary love marriages, financially independent

Barry Levy, "The Birth of the 'Modern Family' in Early America: Quaker and Anglican Families in the Delaware Valley, Pennsylvania, 1681–1750," in Michael Zuckerman, ed., *Friends and Neighbors: Group Life in America's First Plural Society*, pp. 26–56. © 1982 by Temple University. Reprinted by permission of Temple University Press.

conjugal households, and tender child rearing. Quaker families also adapted well to the premodern Pennsylvania setting. Many historians insist, however, that the modern American family began in New England in the late eighteenth and early nineteenth centuries in response to significant economic, political, and social changes coinciding with early industrialization. Such interpretations rely on modernization theory and the centrality of New England to explain the transformation of the "traditional" American family into its modern, domestic form. Social events in colonial Pennsylvania clearly challenge such interpretations.

There will be disagreements about whether the Delaware Valley Quaker families were totally modern or slightly less than modern (typologies are always inexact). The basic emotions, commitments, and forms were there, however. And what is essential is that a group using modern strategies—love and voluntarism instead of shame and coercion—was successful in a premodern American setting. In fact, the seventeenth-century Quaker family system mastered the Delaware Valley far better than did traditional English and Welsh families. In 1715 some 204 Quaker households, 60 Anglican households, and 43 Baptist or unchurched households lived in the fertile Chester and Welsh Tract countryside near Philadelphia. These families lived differently according to their religious affiliation, and they were not equally adapted to life in colonial Pennsylvania. In the early Delaware Valley—hardly a "modern" place—the radical Quaker families thrived between 1681 and 1740. The middling Anglican families, although equipped with seemingly appropriate traditional habits, floundered economically, lost much of their previous religious identity, and gave less to the valley's social and economic development.

The Quakers' triumph was the first of many passages from public to domestic orderings in American life. Pennsylvania's thin social structure and miles of uncut farmland suited the Quakers' radical, privatistic strategy. The Anglicans struggled manfully to erect a public social order, but the Delaware Valley Quakers conquered this empty and wealthy environment by concentrating people's attention on the intricacies, feelings, and responsibilities of modern, noncoercive, domestic control. They seemed to have an effective antidote to the silence of early America: a devotion to silence itself. They introduced impressively a social form that in the nineteenth century would spread to other lonely American countrysides and cities.

The seventy-five Welsh Quaker and seventy-eight Cheshire Quaker families who settled between 1681 and 1690 along the Schuylkill and Delaware rivers near Philadelphia fashioned their family system from radical religious ideas and experiences and from the opportunities offered by Pennsylvania itself. During an awakening in the northwest of England in the late 1650s, they had become religious radicals—Quakers. Experiencing a new revelation, they believed that the "light" or "grace" was born into every person (along with original sin), that it could be experienced in silent worship meetings, that it could be uttered when a "minister" spoke spontaneously from "Truth," and that it could be spread from one person to the next as one hot coal ignites another (a favorite metaphor). Quakers therefore rejected the authority of learned ministers, traditional ceremonies, and even the final authority of Scriptural text. Their consequent emphasis on introspection, noncoercion, and love greatly influenced their thinking and feelings about family life. During the 1660s and 1670s these settlers had lived as a beleaguered and despised community in the Cheshire hills and Welsh mountains. In the 1680s and 1690s they came to Pennsylvania, as their records show, in order to realize frustrated communal and religious goals, to be organized most tellingly in their radical, involving families.

Their new familial thinking helped impel them to emigrate. Being, typically, uneducated men and women, accustomed to an aural culture, their beliefs were simple and personal, based on direct religious experience, knowledge of Scriptures, and sharp judgments of people. They thought human relations sacred. Like many other seventeenth-century people, they often joined personality, religious faith, and social relations into one concept, "conversation." What kind of "conversation" a person had, how "conversation" was developed, and how one person related to another through "conversation" were the vital issues of their communities and families. Quakers believed that people who owned the "Light" wholly or partly destroyed pride and sin and lived by the word of God or "Truth." Such people, they believed, had infectiously honest speech, gestures, and conduct, "holy conversation," which answered the "Light" in others. The settlers described themselves accordingly as having peculiarly selfless, tender, and "savory" "conversations." Thirty-six adjectives or adjectival phrases described the "conversation" of adults in sixty-two removal certificates from Wales to the Welsh Tract between 1681 and 1690. The adjectives most often used were "honest" (thirty-three), "blameless" (fourteen), "loving" (thirteen), and "tender" (nine). They wanted simply to enjoy and to glorify God by maintaining families and communities in which "holy conversation" would be constantly shared and developed.

However, they also believed that people who suppressed the "Light" by worshiping their own prideful selves or other worldly idols brought confusion and conflict to human society and tended to corrupt others. They thought it necessary therefore to protect themselves and particularly their children from such worldly "carnal talkers." The settlers required their children, whose fragility they sensitively appreciated, to live within networks of holy human influence. The sixty-two removal certificates frequently described the settlers' children as being "loving," "modest," and "affectionate," while being also "poor," "innocent," and "weak." Such recognition of children's loving dependence and fragility revealed a perception of children far removed from the traditional conception of children as resilient "little adults." Such fragile children were particularly vulnerable to "carnal talkers" and particularly in need of parental concern. . . .

Acquiring an environment for protective child rearing largely justified emigration. Keeping children in networks of "holy conversation" in Great Britain was usually too costly. Middling children were expected to provide much of the labor England required, at the least expense, and most children left home for service or apprenticeships at age ten. Most Cheshire and Welsh Quaker emigrants were also middling or poor families from among the most economically colonized and poorest areas of Great Britain, where houses were small, land ownership rare, and farms small and pastoral. And though Quaker children required an independent and secure economic future, even the paltry economic power Quaker families had individually and collectively accumulated was drained away by severe persecution from 1660 to 1688, when heavy fines fell upon Quaker patrons. William Penn, the Quaker proprietor of Pennsylvania, thus wisely promoted his colony in terms of the relief it promised from such insufficiencies of estate. He told Pennsylvanians to form townships of 5,000 acres, with each farmer having lavish, contiguous holdings of 100 to 500 acres. He advertised that cheap land would permit a "more convenient bringing up of youth" and would end English parents' addiction "to put their children into Gentlemen's service or send them to towns to learn trades." And the colonists shared his concern. When Thomas Ellis, a leader in the Welsh Tract, was challenged by George Fox in 1684 about the spiritual courage of migrating Quaker families, Ellis answered, "I wish that those that have estates of their own and to leave fullness in their posterity may not be offended at the Lord's opening a door of mercy to thousands in England especially in Wales who have not estates either for themselves or children." It was a request that George Fox and other Quaker critics of Pennsylvania migration, who shared Ellis's childrearing ideas, could only answer charitably.

During the 1670s monthly meetings in Cheshire and Wales had worked diligently to place many poor parents' children in service with other Quakers. This had been the only option available. But abundant Pennsylvania real estate inspired Friends to think of rearing virtually all children at home with parents. William Penn's settlement projections and the settlers' own practice answered this purpose. The Welsh Tract and Chester settlers chose a settlement pattern that supported community without restricting families' freedom to expand economically and geographically. Their plans also intelligently conformed to the traditions of Wales, Cheshire, and other highland areas, where dispersed farmsteads were the rule from the late Middle Ages. Quaker Pennsylvanians lived on contiguous farmsteads with their meeting houses placed near the center of each sprawling township. These highland Quaker practices, to be sure, appeared individualistic from the perspective of the lowland Massachusetts settlers' famed nucleated villages. . . . Local Quaker planning was keenly communal. But highland tolerance of distance also allowed Friends to encourage families to be economically self-sufficient, to buy land for children with little worry about expanding outside the spatial limits of the community.

The men's and women's monthly meetings to which Thomas Ellis referred maintained "helpful" and "loving" care but also gave considerable freedom to individual families to manage their own affairs. Monthly meetings were composed of Friends in good standing from all the local worship meetings under their jurisdiction. The purpose of monthly meetings was, as George Fox said, "that all order their conversation aright, that they may see the salvation of God, they may all see and know, possess and partake of, the government of Christ, of the increase of which there is no end." Their aim was to construct an ideal speech community where the word of God would be constantly and infectiously exchanged in human relations, particularly those within households. Thus newcomers were not recognized as community members unless they presented a removal certificate, an informed discussion of their spiritual personality, vouching for the high quality of their "conversations." When Friends got married in Chester and the Welsh Tract, they had their "clearness and conversation" inspected, and when disowned, they were denounced for "scandalous," "disorderly," "indecent," or "worldly" "conversation."

But highlighting the central importance within this scheme of unsupervised, spontaneous familial relations, most of the business that came before the Welsh Tract and Chester men's meetings directly concerned the question of family formation. For example, in Chester, the men's and women's meetings sat together until 1705. Between 1681 and 1705, 43 percent of the business concerned marriages. The next largest category, discipline, accounted for 14 percent of the business, and marriage infractions composed the majority of the discipline cases.

Marriage was vital to the Quaker settlers because it involved the reproduction of intimate familial environments of "holy conversation" and therefore the rearing of the Quaker faithful. It was a time-consuming and delicate business, designed to combine a maximum of personal freedom with a dose of community control. Emerging landholders who emphasized parental character in child rearing particularly desired some control in marriage. But these settlers also regarded love and marriage as spiritual matters to be dictated by the "Light," which itself was too fragile and sacred to be bullied. The Welsh Tract and Chester Quakers' marriage procedures were therefore unusually complex, voluntaristic, and generous. Entirely reversing relatively progressive Puritan marriage procedures, in which children were allowed a veto over marriages arranged by their parents, Quaker parents retained only a veto over marriages arranged by their children. And even that veto was shaky. In cases when a couple sincerely fell in love, yet faced parental objections, they could ask the monthly meeting to persuade their parents to surrender, or even to give them sanction to marry in spite of parental opinion. . . .

Thus, the final advantage in these procedures usually fell to the independent judgments of youth. Youth alone announced their marriage intentions to the local monthly meetings, and youth alone said their vows before God and witnesses. Such rituals and the doctrine of the "Light" provoked youthful assertion in matters of love. To help things along, young Welsh Tract women lobbied for their choices, filling the meeting house with supportive peers when they announced their intentions to marry. . . . And though a young woman freely selected her spouse from the first to the final stages of courtship, if at the last minute her inner testimony demurred, she simply changed her mind, no matter the inconvenience to the monthly meetings, the banished groom, or the expectant parents. . . .

Their assertiveness was also fostered by a deeper permissiveness. Traditional sanctions such as economic penalties and shaming were used lightly and sparingly. Meetings did ask couples to submit themselves before marriage to month-long inspections of their "conversations" by committees of the women's and men's monthly meetings in order to reassure the community about the fitness of youth in parenting and maintaining a proper household. But few couples were denied the privilege of marrying in meeting once they had announced their intentions. Youth with problems were warned off before the formal process began or had long been subject to the meeting's care. The meetings did seek to halt marriages between Quakers and non-Quakers and between youth who sought to marry without parental consent to assure peace and proper environments for children. But if such youth persisted, the meetings merely demanded that they come to meeting and condemn their waywardness. Only if they refused to "clear the Truth" were they disowned, and though many youth had to acknowledge their sins, few were actually disowned before 1740.

Condemnations and disownments were posted publicly and doubtless caused shame and embarrassment. Nevertheless, the Quakers' use of shaming was remarkably mild compared to the methods traditionally used in English communities—a repertoire that included dunking, placing in stocks, cropping ears, branding with letters, dressing people in white gowns, hanging in effigy, and tarring and feathering. By their own account, the meetings acted tenderly in "love" and "concern" to give "care" to Friends. Personal "honor," though a tolerated psychological fact, was less emphasized than the "honor of Truth." The approved sign of contrition was not red-faced humiliation or even embarrassment, but renewed love and deep sorrow for love's past absence. . . .

Nor did Quakers use property heavy handedly to ensure compliance. Probate and meeting records reveal that young men and women who married out of the meeting were rarely disinherited. Radnor and Chester parents only delayed portioning wayward youth until their wills. . . . In this, too, they punished "bad" Quaker children—that is, Quaker children who married non-Quakers, not Quaker children who married Quakers outside the meeting—much as parents in puritan Massachusetts favored good children who, no matter how obedient, received land usually when their fathers died. On the other hand, thanks to generosity, wealth, and perhaps religious motives, Radnor and Chester Quaker parents gave land easily to good children. Among 139 second-generation sons in Chester and the Welsh Tract who married in the early eighteenth century, 71 percent received land—often by deed—before, at, or within two years of marriage. Most nuclear families in Radnor and Chester were thereby economically autonomous at their conception. . . .

The major method of knotting such ties was tender and careful child rearing. Even the local Anglican minister in 1714 observed that the "fatal weed of Quakerism" was "cultivated with the utmost skill and tenderness." These Quakers' earnestness in child rearing cannot be overestimated. The Radnor and Chester Meetings helped support families with loans, charity, and child rearing advice. Traveling ministers reinforced the advice of the meeting. And that advice virtually never mentioned physical correction. Instead, it emphasized the impact of parental examples on children, the need to keep children from corrupting influences, and the need to recognize and encourage signs of the "Light" within the child. After 1690 Quaker couples in Radnor and Chester could also expect meeting elders to visit them four times a year.

The elders inspected the household's furnishings, sensed its spiritual atmosphere, questioned the parents, prayed with the family, and issued a report to the monthly meeting. Such reports helped scotch child rearing problems before they became uncontrollable. . . .

And Radnor and Chester men often allowed tender child rearing to direct their lives. John Bevan of Treverigg, Glamorganshire, wrote that he emigrated to Merion, Pennsylvania, only because he was convinced by his wife that his four children were likely to be corrupted in Wales. "Some time before the year 1683," he wrote, "I heard that our esteemed Friend William Penn had a patent from King Charles the Second for the Province in America called Pennsylvania and my wife had a great inclination to go thither and thought it might be a good place to train up children amongst a sober people and to prevent the corruption of them here by the loose behavior of youths and the bad example of too many of riper years." Bevan loved Wales almost as much as his children and religion, "but as I was sensible her aim was an upright one, on account of our children, I was willing to weigh the matter in a true balance." In 1683, in his prime, Bevan went to Pennsylvania. In 1704, an old man, he returned to Wales, where he later wrote, "We stayed there [Pennsylvania] many years, and had four of our children married with our consent, and they had several children, and the aim intended by my wife was in good measure answered." . . . But no matter how much Quaker men sacrificed or worried about child rearing, the major burden, as these examples also suggest, fell upon women.

Believing in women's centrality to child rearing, Quaker men gave them unusual authority in the Welsh Tract and in Chester. Uniquely in early America, Quaker women exercised some formal authority within their communities in the women's monthly meetings. The existence of those meetings sprang partly from a belief in the spiritual equality of Quaker men and women, but more profoundly from an appreciation of the importance of mothering to the Quakers' social strategies. Social equality was generally not practiced. Quaker women as individuals were not expected to be independent of familial responsibility or patriarchal power. Bequests to daughters rarely included land. And as Marylynn Salmon has shown, although Quaker men had control of the government in Pennsylvania from 1681 through the 1750s, Pennsylvania government held to the common law rule of *feme covert* whereby women lost all their property at marriage, and Pennsylvania courts interpreted this rule as strictly as English courts. . . .

More than through the sometimes honored doctrine of spiritual equality, Quaker women gained some communal authority through motherhood. Inasmuch as Quakers' ideas about child rearing emphasized human relations and children's observations of parental behavior, Quakers had to save a place within their monthly meeting structure for maintaining holy female character and guiding the social reproduction of mothering. Thus the inclusion of women into the meeting structure and their separation into their own meetings developed partly from recognition of female spiritual equality but chiefly from a traditional understanding of women's natural talents (in the household) and an untraditional insight into the essential nature of early child rearing and domestic organization in maintaining and reproducing the religiously faithful. Accordingly, the women's meetings were not to be equal to or an imitation of the men's meetings; they were to have their own sphere. . . .

The distribution of tasks and authority between the men's and women's monthly meetings reflected, acknowledged, and asserted women's roles as mothers. While the Chester and Radnor Men's Meetings established worship meetings, collected and allocated money, judged the validity of old and new testimonies, and monopolized the power to disown men and women, the women's meetings dispensed small amounts of charity, visited families, disciplined women Quakers, and inspected the characters of young women who intended to marry. Demonstrating kindness, love, and charity, they were to define, enforce, and reproduce the standards of Quaker womanhood and motherhood. Women's meetings had to be separate. Frank discussions about the dark mysteries of female bodies, sexuality, and character frightened and embarrassed Quaker men. . . .

Despite early resistance in Chester, the Radnor and Chester mothers, meeting in closet, gained control over vital aspects of their communities. Given their role in marriage inspections, they were able to limit the males of the meeting to choices among women whose characters they approved. And their authority often extended beyond marriage and the meeting house. . . .

Viewed from the inside, these families lived quietly, keeping faith with the "Light" and "holy conversation" by trying to maintain peace and love and by rearing their "tender plants" into a new generation of faithful Quakers. But muting their own vocabulary for a moment and viewing them along a sociological scale of family types, they must be judged as being basically modern. Quaker marriages were formed voluntarily on love; conjugal households were economically autonomous early in their careers; men and especially women were devoted to child rearing; and the scheme of child rearing was noncoercive and based on ideas of intimate spiritual communication in a nurturing environment. . . . [T]he Radnor and Chester Quaker families were clearly more modern than traditional, and therefore an ugly sight to local, traditional families and to Anglican authorities.

Conventional historical wisdom holds that the Quakers' family system would flounder in a premodern setting, where the family's primary responsibility was the production of wealth, not the provision of expert socialization of children and emotional support. Quaker emphasis on motherhood, on this logic, would overburden women with too many jobs; Quaker willingness to bankroll children's marriages would squander available resources; and Quaker emphasis on noncoercive schemes of child rearing would produce a feeble and unruly labor force. Nevertheless, analysis of seventy-two Welsh Tract and Chester Quaker families—their wills, inventories, tax assessments, deeds, and related court records—shows that middling Quakers sought to, and generally did, protect their children from the "world" and did maintain nurturing familial love and peace by effectively accumulating wealth. To John Woolman's later worry, Quaker parents bought vast amounts of land, built large and comfortable houses, and distributed their wealth carefully and shrewdly to their children. A similar study of fifty-five Welsh Tract and Chester Anglican families shows that middling Anglican parents, unburdened by concern for delicate nurturance and protecting environments, were actually less economically aggressive and able. They accumulated less land, built smaller houses, and distributed their wealth carelessly and unwisely, occasionally in efforts to establish gentlemanly lines in Chester County. Modern strategies had their use in an unusual premodern setting such as Pennsylvania.

The Quakers clearly used the valley's chief economic resource, land, with more skill than did the Anglican families. For the protection of future generations and as a balm for family relations, Quaker settlers seized William Penn's generous terms for land. They bought an average of over 300 acres per family before 1690 and then continued to buy more land after prices began to rise. Quaker farmers purchased over 300 acres apiece, on average, after 1700, and 45 percent of all their land purchases occurred after 1690. Typical Quaker immigrant fathers in the Welsh Tract and Chester collected over 700 acres by the time of their death; more than 70 percent accumulated over 400 acres. Such accumulations represented, in all probability, the highest average acreage per family of any religious group in early America.

Quaker land use was consistent with Quaker religious goals. Friends did not plant much of their land. Analysis of crop and livestock listings in their inventories shows that the average Quaker family used about eighty acres of land for farming and grazing. The remaining 620 acres lay fallow and often uncut, awaiting children's marriages. Land purchasing was clearly child-centered, correlating closely with the number of sons in a family. . . .

The Welsh Tract and Chester Quaker families also distributed this land to their sons with care, generosity, and general profit. They gave over two-thirds of their sons over 200 acres of land. . . .

The Anglican farmers and artisans had a less involving relationship to land. Although they bought more land than they might have in England and Wales, Anglican parents saw no need to bankroll every son's love story or to insure them all dignified and protected situations. Scattered returns have shown that the Quakers' and Anglicans' desire for land appeared similar in the early 1690s. However, by the end of this settling generation, the Quakers accumulated almost three times the land per family that the local Anglicans did. . . .

Many historians have told, of course, how the Quakers led the Delaware Valley settlers in the making of a successful province, which enjoyed almost spectacular economic growth, illustrated by the rise of Philadelphia, the largest city in North America by 1765. But with other things, the Quakers were clearly benefited by their radical, "modern" family system, which despite (really, because of) its emphasis on love and noncoercive controls, used the Delaware Valley's ample resources effectively, while maintaining adequate social discipline. In this way, the Quakers made the valley into a basic source of American culture: the first scene of a major, widespread, obviously successful assertion of the child-centered, fond-fostering, nuclear family in early America and most likely in the Anglo-American world. Granted, the strategies of the modern family would prove influential elsewhere—in nineteenth-century cities, countrysides, even in New England. But despite the damage to prevailing interpretations, this family form was actually never more clearly workable, more visibly productive, nor more palpably triumphant than it was in the early, formative decades of William Penn's colony.

ॐ *F U R T H E R   R E A D I N G*

Richard L. Bushman, *From Puritan to Yankee: Character and the Social Order in Connecticut, 1690–1765* (1967)

Philip J. Greven, Jr., *Four Generations: Population, Land, and Family in Colonial Andover, Massachusetts* (1970)

James A. Henretta, "Families and Farms: *Mentalité* in Pre-Industrial America," *William and Mary Quarterly,* 3d ser., 30 (1978), 3–32

Stephen Innes, *Labor in a New Land: Economy and Society in Seventeenth-Century Springfield* (1983)

James T. Lemon, *The Best Poor Man's Country: A Geographical Study of Early Southeastern Pennsylvania* (1972)

Barry M. Levy, *Quakers and the American Family: British Settlement in the Delaware Valley* (1988)

Kenneth A. Lockridge, "Land, Population, and the Evolution of New England Society, 1630–1790," *Past and Present* 34 (1968), 62–80

——, *A New England Town, the First Hundred Years: Dedham, Massachusetts, 1636–1736* (1970)

Sumner Chilton Powell, *Puritan Village: The Formation of a New England Town* (1963)

Daniel Blake Smith, "The Study of the Family in Early America: Trends, Problems, and Prospects," *William and Mary Quarterly,* 3d ser., 34 (1982), 3–28

Roger Thompson, *Women in Stuart England and America* (1974)

John J. Waters, "Family, Inheritance, and Migration in Colonial New England: The Evidence from Guildford, Connecticut," *William and Mary Quarterly,* 3d ser., 34 (1982), 64–86

Robert V. Wells, "Quaker Marriage Patterns in a Colonial Perspective," *William and Mary Quarterly,* 3d ser., 24 (1972), 415–442

CHAPTER
8

The Middle Colonies:
Ethnicity, Competition,
and Economic Success

꙰

The middle colonies—Delaware, New Jersey, Pennsylvania, and New York—differed radically from the Chesapeake and New England colonies from the beginning. Whereas the latter regions were settled by English companies and continued predominantly English in their free populations, the middle colonies were the true melting pot, ethnically and religiously mixed from the time of their foundation. New York was founded as New Netherland in 1624; Delaware was settled as New Sweden with a mixed population of Swedes and Finns in 1638. Both colonies held a mixture of people from all over Europe; New Sweden was incorporated into New Netherland in 1655.

New Netherland and New Sweden plunged immediately into the complex trade activity along the coast. Delaware Bay and the Hudson River were major trade centers; the Susquehannocks and the Iroquois League were powerful and highly organized Indian entities eager for trade and prepared to link the colonies with the resources of the interior. These trade opportunities, when combined with the region's rich farmland, poised the middle colonies for economic success.

England and Holland fought a series of wars in the later seventeenth century whose results included the English conquest of New Netherland (which was renamed New York) in 1664. Settlers of continental European origin, now facing a new imperial government, responded in different ways to the dominant English. Pennsylvania was settled in the early 1680s as a proprietary colony of Quaker leader William Penn. Because of the falling-off of English interest in emigration, promoters of the middle colonies sought colonists among economically deprived groups within Britain, such as the Scots-Irish, and victims of religious persecution in Europe, particularly French Huguenots and German pietists, who, like Quakers, stressed the inner experience of religion. Thus the middle colonies' tradition of ethnic and religious diversity continued. Historians today debate whether these colonies were a melting pot or rather a series of islands of self-isolated ethnic enclaves.

❧ D O C U M E N T S

As they remarked on the communities through which they passed, colonial men and women categorized people in terms of ethnic stereotypes. Many travelers commented on Dutch culture in New York and New Jersey, incidentally revealing the success with which colonists of Dutch descent protected their heritage. In the first document Jasper Dankaerts describes his 1680 visit with Maria van Rensselaer, who ran her plantation, Rensselaerswyck on the Hudson River, after the death of her husband. In the mid-eighteenth century Swedish scientist Per Kalm found settlers of Dutch descent living in a recognizably Dutch way and keeping separate from their neighbors; in the second document he transmits some of the prejudice against them. Traveler Andrew Burnaby in the third selection similarly perceives the inhabitants of New York as Dutch in 1759–1760.

George Fox, founder of the Society of Friends (Quakers) in England, traveled through the American plantations in the early 1670s, before the creation of the Quaker colony of Pennsylvania. His journal, excerpted in the fourth document, describes the difficulties of travel and the response to his preaching. He directed his message to American Indians as well as Europeans. In the fifth document William Penn invites merchants to settle in Pennsylvania, describing the advantages they would have there. Next Francis Daniel Pastorius records his founding in 1685 of the settlement of Germantown in Pennsylvania, "situated in the Farthest Limits of America, in the Western World." In the final document Gabriel Thomas, who resided in the colony from its beginning, describes the high wages that labor commanded and the opportunities for both men and women.

Traveler Jasper Dankaerts Calls on New York Planter Maria van Rensselaer, 1680

27th, Saturday. We went to call upon a certain Madam Rentselaer, widow of the Heer Rentselaer, son of the Heer Rentselaer of the colony named the colony of Rentselaerswyck, comprising twelve miles square from Fort Orange, that is, twenty-four miles square in all. She is still in possession of the place, and still administers it as *patroonesse,* until one Richard van Rentselaer, residing at Amsterdam, shall arrive in the country, whom she expected in the summer, when he would assume the management of it himself. This lady was polite, quite well informed, and of good life and disposition. She had experienced several proofs of the Lord. The breaking up of the ice had once carried away her entire mansion, and every thing connected with it, of which place she had made too much account. Also, in some visitations of her husband, death, and others before. In her last child-bed, she became lame or weak in both of her sides, so that she had to walk with two canes or crutches. In all these trials, she had borne herself well, and God left not Himself without witness in her. She treated us kindly, and we ate here exceedingly good pike, perch, and other fish, which now began to come and be caught in great numbers. We had several conversations with her about the truth, and practical religion, mutually satisfactory. We went to look at several of her mills at work, which she had there on an ever-running stream, grist-mills, saw-mills, and others. One of the grist-mills can grind 120 schepels [90 bushels] of meal in twenty-four hours, that is, five an hour. Returning to the house, we politely took our leave. Her residence is about a quarter of an hour from Albany up the river. . . .

Per Kalm Offers Impressions
of New Jersey and New York, 1750

[New Jersey]

Trenton is a long narrow town, situated at some distance from the Delaware River, on a sandy plain; it belongs to New Jersey, and they reckon it thirty miles from Philadelphia. . . . [F]rom Trenton to New Brunswick, the travellers go in wagons which set out every day for that place. Several of the inhabitants however subsist on the transportation of all sorts of goods, which are sent every day in great quantities, either from Philadelphia to New York, or from there to the former place. Between Philadelphia and Trenton all goods are transported by water, but between Trenton and New Brunswick they are carried by land, and both these means of transportation belong to people of this town. . . .

We continued our journey in the morning; the country through which we passed was for the greatest part level, though sometimes there were some long hills; some parts were covered with trees, but by far the greater part of the country was without woods; on the other hand I never saw any place in America, the city excepted, so well peopled. An old man, who lived in the neighborhood and accompanied us a short distance, assured me however that he could well remember the time when between Trenton and New Brunswick there were not above three farms, and he reckoned it was about fifty and some odd years ago. During the greater part of the day we saw very extensive cultivated fields on both sides of the road, and we observed that the country generally had a noticeable declivity towards the south. Near almost every farm was a spacious orchard full of peaches and apple trees, and in some of them the fruit had fallen from the trees in such quantities as to cover nearly the whole surface of the ground. Part of it they left to rot, since they could not take care of it all or consume it. Wherever we passed by we were welcome to go into the fine orchards and gather our hats and pockets full of the choicest fruit, without the owner so much as looking at us. Cherry trees were planted near the farms, on the roads, etc.

The *barns* had a peculiar kind of construction in this locality, of which I shall give a concise description. The main building was very large almost the size of a small church; the roof was high, covered with wooden shingles, sloping on both sides, but not steep. The walls which supported it were not much higher than a full grown man; but on the other hand the breadth of the building was all the greater. In the middle was the threshing floor and above it, or in the loft or garret, they put the unthrashed grain, the straw, or anything else, according to the season. On one side were stables for the horses, and on the other for the cows. The young stock had also their particular stables or stalls, and in both ends of the building were large doors, so that one could drive in with a cart and horses through one of them, and go out at the other. Here under one roof therefore were the thrashing floor, the barn, the stables, the hay loft, the coach house, etc. This kind of building is used chiefly by the Dutch and Germans, for it is to be observed that the country between Trenton and New York is not inhabited by many Englishmen, but mostly by Germans or Dutch, the latter of which are especially numerous.

Indians. Before I proceed I must mention one thing about the Indians or old Americans; for this account may find readers, who, like many people of my acquaintance, have the opinion that North America is almost wholly inhabited by savage or heathen nations; and they may be astonished that I do not mention them more frequently in my account. Others may perhaps imagine that when I state in my journal that the country is widely cultivated, that in several places houses of stone or wood are built, round which are grain fields, gardens and orchards, that I am speaking of the property of the Indians. To undeceive them I shall here give the following explanation. The country, especially that along the coasts in the English colonies, is inhabited by Europeans, who in some places are already so numerous that few parts of Europe are more populous. The Indians have sold the land to the Europeans, and have retired further inland. In most parts you may travel twenty Swedish miles, or about a hundred and twenty English miles, from the coast, before you reach the first habitation of the Indians. And it is very possible for a person to have been at Philadelphia and other towns on the seashore for half a year without so much as seeing an Indian. . . .

About noon we arrived at *New Brunswick,* (situated about thirty miles from Trenton and sixty from Philadelphia), a pretty little town in the province of New Jersey, in a valley on the west side of the river Raritan. On account of its low location, it cannot be seen (coming from Pennsylvania) before you get to the top of the hill, which is quite close to it. The town extends north and south along the river. The German inhabitants have two churches, one of stone and the other of wood. The English church is likewise of the latter material, but the Presbyterians are building one of stone. The Town Hall makes a good appearance. Some of the other houses are built of brick, but most of them are made either wholly of wood, or of brick and wood. The wooden buildings are not made of strong timber, but merely of boards or planks, which are within joined by laths. Houses built of both wood and brick have only the wall towards the street made of the latter, all the other sides being boards. This peculiar kind of ostentation would easily lead a traveller who passes through the town in haste to believe that most of the houses are built of brick. The houses are covered with shingles. Before each door is a veranda to which you ascend by steps from the street; it resembles a small balcony, and has benches on both sides on which the people sit in the evening to enjoy the fresh air and to watch the passers-by. The town has only one street lengthways, and at its northern extremity there is a cross street: both of these are of a considerable length.

The river Raritan passes close by the town, and is deep enough for large sailing vessels. Its breadth near the town is about the distance of a common gun shot. The tide comes up several miles beyond the town, which contributes not a little to the ease and convenience of securing vessels which dock along the bridge. The river has generally very high and steep banks on both sides, but near the town there are no such banks, because it is situated in a low valley. One of the streets is almost entirely inhabited by Dutchmen who came hither from Albany, and for that reason it is called Albany Street. These Dutch people keep company only with themselves, and seldom or never go amongst the other inhabitants, living as it were quite separate from them. . . .

[New York]

The Jews. Besides the different sects of Christians, many Jews have settled in New York, who possess great privileges. They have a synagogue, own their dwelling-houses, possess large country-seats and are allowed to keep shops in town. They have likewise several ships, which they load and send out with their own goods. In fine, they enjoy all the privileges common to the other inhabitants of this town and province. . . .

During my residence in New York, both at this time and for the next two years, I was frequently in company with Jews. I was informed among other things that these people never boiled any meat for themselves on Saturday, but that they always did it the day before, and that in winter they kept a fire during the whole Saturday. They commonly eat no pork; yet I have been told by several trustworthy men that many of them (especially the young Jews) when travelling, did not hesitate the least about eating this or any other meat that was put before them, even though they were in company with Christians. I was in their synagogue last evening for the first time, and to-day at noon I visited it again, and each time I was put in a special seat which was set apart for strangers or Christians. A young rabbi read the divine service, which was partly in Hebrew and partly in the Rabbinical dialect. Both men and women were dressed entirely in the English fashion; the former had their hats on, and did not once take them off during the service. The galleries, I observed, were reserved for the ladies, while the men sat below. During prayers the men spread a white cloth over their heads, which perhaps is to represent sackcloth. But I observed that the wealthier sort of people had a much richer cloth than the poorer ones. Many of the men had Hebrew books, in which they sang and read alternately. The rabbi stood in the middle of the synagogue and read with his face turned towards the east; he spoke however so fast as to make it almost impossible for any one to understand what he said. . . .

The *first colonists* in New York were Dutchmen. When the town and its territories were taken by the English and left to them by the next peace in exchange for Surinam, the old inhabitants were allowed either to remain at New York, and enjoy all the privileges and immunities which they were possessed of before, or to leave the place with all their goods. Most of them chose the former; and therefore the inhabitants both of the town and of the province belonging to it are still for the greatest part Dutch, who still, and especially the old people, speak their mother tongue.

They were beginning however by degrees to change their manners and opinions, chiefly indeed in the town and in its neighborhood; for most of the young people now speak principally English, go only to the English church, and would even take it amiss if they were called Dutchmen and not Englishmen. . . .

The Dutch Settlers. But the lack of people in this province may likewise be accounted for in a different manner. As the Dutch, who first cultivated this section, obtained the liberty of staying here by the treaty with England, and of enjoying all their privileges and advantages without the least limitation, each of them took a very large piece of ground for himself, and many of the more powerful heads of families made themselves the possessors and masters of a country of as great territory as would be sufficient to form one of our moderately-sized, and even one of our large, parishes. Most of them being very rich, their envy of the English led them not to sell them any land, but at an excessive rate, a practice which is still punctually observed among their descendants. The English therefore, as well as people of other nations, have but little encouragement to settle here. On the other hand, they have sufficient opportunity in the other provinces to purchase land at a more moderate price, and with more security to themselves. It is not to be wondered then, that so many parts of New York are still uncultivated, and that it has entirely the appearance of a frontier-land. This instance may teach us how much a small mistake in a government can hamper the settling of a country. . . .

Trade. . . . Albany carries on a considerable commerce with New York, chiefly in furs, boards, wheat, flour, peas, several kinds of timber, etc. There is not a place in all the British colonies, the Hudson's Bay settlements excepted, where such quantities of furs and skins are bought of the Indians as at Albany. Most of the merchants in this town send a clerk or agent to Oswego, an English trading town on Lake Ontario, to which the Indians come with their furs. I intend to give a more minute account of this place in my Journal for the year 1750. The merchants from Albany spend the whole summer at Oswego, and trade with many tribes of Indians who come with their goods. Many people have assured me that the Indians are frequently cheated in disposing of their goods, especially when they are drunk, and that sometimes they do not get one half or even one tenth of the value of their goods. I have been a witness to several transactions of this kind. The merchants of Albany glory in these tricks, and are highly pleased when they have given a poor Indian, a greater portion of brandy than he can stand, and when they can, after that, get all his goods for mere trifles. The Indians often find when they are sober again, that they have for once drunk as much as they are able of a liquor which they value beyond anything else in the whole world, and they are quite insensible to their loss if they again get a draught of this nectar. Besides this trade at Oswego, a number of Indians come to Albany from several places especially from Canada; but from this latter place, they hardly bring anything but beaver skins. . . .

The Dutch in Albany. The inhabitants of Albany and its environs are almost all Dutchmen. They speak Dutch, have Dutch preachers, and the divine service is performed in that language. Their manners are likewise quite Dutch; their dress is however like that of the English. It is well known that the first

Europeans who settled in the province of New York were Dutchmen. During the time that they were the masters of this province, they seized New Sweden of which they were jealous. However, the pleasure of possessing this conquered land and their own was but of short duration, for towards the end of 1664 Sir Robert Carr, by order of King Charles the second, went to New York, then New Amsterdam, and took it. Soon after Colonel Nicolls went to Albany, which then bore the name of Fort Orange, and upon taking it, named it Albany, from the Duke of York's Scotch title. The Dutch inhabitants were allowed either to continue where they were, and under the protection of the English to enjoy all their former privileges, or to leave the country. The greater part of them chose to stay and from them the Dutchmen are descended who now live in the province of New York, and who possess the greatest and best estates in that province.

The avarice, selfishness and immeasurable love of money of the inhabitants of Albany are very well know throughout all North America, by the French and even by the Dutch, in the lower part of New York province. If anyone ever intends to go to Albany it is said in jest that he is about to go to the land of Canaan, since Canaan and the land of the Jews mean one and the same thing, and that Albany is a fatherland and proper home for arch-Jews, since the inhabitants of Albany are even worse. If a real Jew, who understands the art of getting forward perfectly well, should settle amongst them, they would not fail to ruin him. For this reason nobody comes to this place without the most pressing necessity; and therefore I was asked in several places, both this and the following year, what induced me to make the pilgrimage to this New Canaan. I likewise found that the judgment which people formed of them was not without foundation. For though they seldom see any strangers, (except those who go from the British colonies to Canada and back again) and one might therefore expect to find victuals and accommodation for travellers cheaper than in places where they always resort, yet I experienced the contrary. I was here obliged to pay for everything twice, thrice and four times as much as in any part of North America which I have passed through. If I wanted their assistance, I was obliged to pay them very well for it, and when I wanted to purchase anything or be helped in some case or other, I could at once see what kind of blood ran in their veins, for they either fixed exorbitant prices for their services or were very reluctant to assist me. Such was this people in general. However, there were some among them who equalled any in North America or anywhere else, in politeness, equity, goodness, and readiness to serve and to oblige; but their number fell far short of that of the former. If I may be allowed to declare my conjectures, the origin of the inhabitants of Albany and its neighborhood seems to me to be as follows. While the Dutch possessed this country, and intended to people it, the government sent a pack of vagabonds of which they intended to clear their native country, and sent them along with a number of other settlers to this province. The vagabonds were sent far from the other colonists, upon the borders towards the Indians and other enemies, and a few honest families were persuaded to go with them, in order to keep them in bounds. I cannot in any other way account for the difference between the inhabitants of Albany and the other descendants of so respectable a nation as the Dutch, who are settled in the lower part of New York province. The latter are civil, obliging, just in prices, and sincere; and though they are not ceremonious, yet they are well meaning and honest and their promises may be relied on. . . .

Dutch Food. The whole region about the Hudson River above Albany is inhabited by the Dutch: this is true of Saratoga as well as other places. During my stay with them I had an opportunity of observing their way of living, so far as food is concerned, and wherein they differ from other Europeans. Their breakfast here in the country was as follows: they drank tea in the customary way by putting brown sugar into the cup of tea. With the tea they ate bread and butter and radishes; they would take a bite of the bread and butter and would cut off a piece of the radish as they ate. They spread the butter upon the bread and it was each one's duty to do this for himself. They sometimes had small round cheeses (not especially fine tasting) on the table, which they cut into thin slices and spread upon the buttered bread. At noon they had a regular meal and I observed nothing unusual about it. In the evening they made a porridge of corn, poured it as customary into a dish, made a large hole in the center into which they poured fresh milk, but more often buttermilk. They ate it taking half a spoonful of porridge and half of milk. As they ordinarily took more milk than porridge, the milk in the dish was soon consumed. Then more milk was poured in. This was their supper nearly every evening. After that they would eat some meat left over from the noonday meal, or bread and butter with cheese. If any of the porridge remained from the evening, it was boiled with buttermilk in the morning so that it became almost like a gruel. In order to make the buttermilk more tasty, they added either syrup or sugar, after it had been poured into the dish. Then they stirred it so that all of it should be equally sweet. Pudding or pie, the Englishman's perpetual dish, one seldom saw among the Dutch, neither here nor in Albany. But they were indeed fond of meat. . . .

Reverend Andrew Burnaby's Thumbnail Sketch of New York, 1759–1760

. . . The inhabitants of New York, in their character, very much resemble the Pennsylvanians: more than half of them are Dutch, and almost all traders: they are, therefore, habitually frugal, industrious, and parsimonious. Being, however, of different nations, different languages, and different religions, it is almost impossible to give them any precise or determinate character. The women are handsome and agreeable; though rather more reserved than the Philadelphian ladies. Their amusements are much the same as in Pennsylvania; viz. balls, and sleighing expeditions in the winter; and, in the summer, going in parties upon the water, and fishing; or making excursions into the country. There are several houses pleasantly situated upon East river, near New York, where it is common to have turtle feasts: these happen once or twice in a week. Thirty or forty gentlemen and ladies meet and dine together, drink tea in the afternoon, fish and amuse themselves till evening, and then return home in Italian chaises, (the fashionable carriage in this and most parts of America, Virginia excepted, where they chiefly make use of coaches, and these commonly drawn by six horses), a gentleman and lady in each chaise. In the way there is a bridge, about three miles distant from New York, which you always pass over as you return, called the Kissing Bridge; where it is a part of the etiquette to salute the lady who has put herself under your protection. . . .

Quaker George Fox Describes His Travels Through America, 1672

. . . The 17th of 6th month [August] we had a very large meeting at Flushing with many hundreds of the people of the world, some came about thirty miles. And a justice of the peace was there and his family, and many considerable persons were there. A glorious and heavenly meeting it was, praised be the Lord God, and the people much satisfied.

At Flushing as soon as the meeting was done, there stood up a priest's son and laid down three things that he would dispute, the first was the ordination of ministers, the second women's speaking, and the third that we held a new way of worship. And I spoke to him and demanded what he had against what I had spoken and he could say nothing. Then I said it was like Christ's way of worship which he set up above 1,600 years ago, and was a new way of worship to him and his priests, it being in the spirit and in the truth. And as for women's speaking, such as the apostles did own I owned, and such as they did deny I did deny. . . .

And when the wind served we came to the sloop, and many Friends came with us, where we took water for the new country, Jersey, down the great bay twenty-one miles and we were much toiled to get in our horses; and the 27th day of the 6th month [August], we landed in the morning by break of the day, in the new country at Middletown Harbour. As we passed down the bay we passed by Coney Island, and by Naton Island, and by Staten Island, and we came to Richard Hartshorne's. And on the 28th day we passed about thirty miles in the new country through the woods, very bad bogs, one worse than all, where we and our horses were fain to slither down a steep place, and then let them lie and pant, and breathe themselves, and they call this place Purgatory. And so we came to Shrewsbury in East Jersey, and on the first day of the week, the 1st day of the 7th month [September], we had a very large and a precious meeting; and the blessed presence of the Lord was with us. And in that place a Friend is made a justice. Friends and other people came far to this meeting. And on the 2nd day of the 7th month [September], we had a men's and women's meeting, out of most parts of the new country Jersey, which will be of great service in keeping the gospel order and government of Christ Jesus (the increase of which hath no end) and for them to see that all do live in the pure religion and to walk as becometh the Gospel; and there is a Monthly and a General Meeting set up, and they are building a meeting-place in the midst of them. I passed about six miles to Porback a mile by water to visit a Friend, and came back again to Shrewsbury.

And there a Friend, John Jay of Barbados, that was with me went to try a horse, and got on his back. And the horse ran and cast him on his head and broke his neck as they called it, and the people took him up dead, and carried him a good way, and laid him on a tree. And I came to him and felt on him, and saw that he was dead, and as I was pitying his family and him, for he was one that was to pass with me through the woods to Maryland that land journey, I took him by the hair of his head, and his head turned like a cloth it was so loose. I threw away my stick and gloves, and took his head in both my hands, and set my knees against the tree and wrested his head and I did perceive it was not broken out that way. And I put my hand under his chin, and behind his head, and wrested his head two or three times with all my strength, and brought it in, and I did perceive his neck began to be stiff, and then he began to rattle, and after to breathe, and the people were amazed, and I bid them have a good heart and be of good faith, and carry him into the house, and then they set him by the fire, and I bid them get him some warm thing to drink and get him to bed. So after he had been in the house awhile, he began to speak, and did not know where he had been. So we bound up his neck warm with a napkin, and the next day we passed on and he with us, pretty well, about sixteen miles to a meeting at Middletown, and many hundreds of miles afterwards, through the woods and bogs. And we swam our horses over a river, and went over on a tree ourselves. And at the meeting was most of the town. And Friends were and are very well, blessed be the Lord, and a glorious meeting we had and the Truth was over all, blessed be the great Lord God for ever. And after the meeting we passed to Middletown harbour about five miles, on the 9th day of the 7th month [September], to take our long journey through the woods towards Maryland. So we hired Indians, for it was upon me to pass through the woods on the other side Delaware Bay, to head the creeks and rivers if it were possible. So the 9th of the 7th month [September], we set forward, and passed through many Indian towns, and rivers, and bogs, and at night made us a fire, and lay by it. When we had passed about forty miles among the Indians, we declared the day of the Lord to them, and the next day we passed fifty miles and found an old house, which the Indians had forced the people to desert, and got us some fire, at the head of Delaware Bay. And the next day we swam our horses over a river about a mile, at twice, first to an island called Upper Tineconk and then to the mainland, and hired Indians to help us over in their canoes, and our horses.

The 12th day of the 7th month [September], this day we passed about thirty miles and came at night to a Swede's house, and got a little straw, and lay there all night. And there we hired another guide; and next day we travelled about forty miles through the woods and rivers, and made us a fire at night and lay in the woods. And we were continually wet on our feet in our travels by day, but we dried us by our fires at night. On the 14th day of the 7th month [September], we passed over a desperate river of rocks and broad stones, very dangerous to us and our horses; and from thence we came to Christian River and swam over our horses, and it was bad and miry, some were like to have lain bogged there. We came over in canoes.

From thence we came to New Castle, called Delaware or New Amsterdam, sixteen miles, and being very weary in the streets and enquiring to buy some corn for our horses, the governor came in to the street and invited me to his house and to lodge there, and said that he had a bed for me and I was welcome. I went to his house on the Seventh-day of the week, and he proffered his house for a meeting, and so I had a meeting at his house the First-day, a precious one, blessed be the Lord, and pretty large. The heads of the town were there and most of the town, the governor and his wife, and the sheriff, and the scout, who is a man of great esteem amongst them. Many men and women were tender and confessed to the Truth and received it, blessed be the Lord for ever, Amen. Here had never been a meeting before, not within a great way of it till now, by any of our Friends.

The Indians at Delaware lay in wait to cut off some of our company as they passed that way, but their design was discovered, one being hanged at Delaware two or three days before we came thither. The Lord gave us power over all, blessed me his name for ever.

On the 16th day of the 7th month [September], we travelled about fifty miles in the woods and through the bogs, and headed Bohemia River and Sassafras River, and some of the branches of the above said rivers, and at night made us a fire and lay all night in the woods. And in the night it rained but we got under trees, and after dried us. On the 17th day we waded through Chester River, a great river. And this day we passed through many bad bogs, and made us a fire and lay in the woods, and went above thirty miles.

On the 18th day we passed through many tedious bogs, and travelled hard about fifty miles, and came well through the woods to Maryland, to Robert Harwood's at Miles River, very weary. The next day, the 19th of 7th month [September], all being weary and dirty through the bogs, yet we went this day to a meeting about a mile or half by water. From thence we passed about three miles by land and one mile by water to John Edmondson's, and from thence on the 22nd day, three or four miles by water to the First-day's meeting. And a judge's wife was there who was never at our meeting before, and many others there who were well satisfied, and the power of the Lord was over all, blessed be his name for ever. And she said after the meeting she had rather hear this man once than the priests a thousand times, and she is convinced. Then I passed about twenty-two miles, and had a meeting upon the Kentish shore and one of the burgesses was there at it. A Friend went to invite him to the meeting, and he said that he would go to hear Mr. Fox, as far as any of them that desired him, for he was a grounded man. And a good meeting we had at Henry Wilcock's house on the 26th day of 7th month [September].

And on the 27th day we passed by water twenty miles to a meeting, very large, some hundreds of the world, and an establishing meeting it was, and there were four justices of the peace and an Indian emperor, and one of his great men, and another great man of another nation of Indians, and they stayed all the meeting. And I had a good speech with them the night before; and I spoke by an interpreter, and they received the Truth, and were very loving; and the emperor said he did believe that I was a very honest man.

Blessed be the Lord, his Truth doth spread.

And after the meeting was done, the wife of a judge of that side of the country, one of the Assembly, being at the meeting that day sent to speak with me and desired me to go with her, home to her house, for her husband was sick and not like to live; and it was three miles. And after the meeting I was hot, but I got a horse and went with her; and he was finely raised up and after came to our meetings. And then I came three miles back to the house, the man being much refreshed when I left him. And the high sheriff of Delaware and some others from thence were at the meeting that day; and a blessed one it was beyond words.

On the 30th we passed five miles by water and then about fourteen miles by land through the woods to John Edmondson's at Tred Avon Creek. And on the 3rd day of the 8th month [October], we came to the General Meeting of all Maryland Friends; and it held from the Sixth-day to the Third-day of the next week, which was five days, that is three days were the General Meetings for public worship, and two days the men's and women's meetings. And many of the world were at the public meetings, some Papists, clerks of their courts, and there were eight justices of the peace, and one of the judges and his wife, and another judge's wife, and many considerable persons of quality. And they judged that there was a thousand people; and one of the justices said, that he never saw so many people together in the country, though it was rainy weather. And Friends and people were generally satisfied and convinced, and the blessed power of the Lord was over all, and a great convincement there is, and a great inquiring after the Truth among all sorts of people, and the Truth is of a good report and Friends are much established, and the world convinced. They said they had never heard the Scriptures so clearly opened before, for said they, 'He hath them at his fingers' ends, and as a man should read them in a book and hold it open before him.' And the people were satisfied beyond words, and a glorious powerful meeting there was, blessed be the Lord for ever. And when the General Meeting was done, we had some of all the choice of the men and women to meet together for I had something to inform them concerning the glory of God, and the order of the Gospel and the government of Christ Jesus and concerning the great meeting. I went every day by boat to the meeting, about four or five miles. And there was never seen there so many boats together. (And one of the justices said) it was almost like the Thames. There was one whose place is above a justice of the peace, a great man, he was much taken with the Truth, was at most of the meetings, and many others would have been there, but there was a general court that did prevent, and take up their time, and some of them sent a man to me, to know where they might come to hear me. Some of them were judges and justices. And there was never such a meeting the people said in Maryland, they had of late made the meeting place as big again as heretofore, and yet it would not hold them. . . .

William Penn's Prospectus for Merchants, 1683

. . . Your Provincial Settlements both within and without the Town, for Scituation and Soil, are without Exception; Your City-Lot is an whole Street, and one side of a Street, from River to River, containing near one hundred Acers, not easily valued, which is besides your four hundred Acers in the City Liberties, part of your twenty thousand Acers in the Countery. Your Tannery hath such plenty of Bark, the Saw-Mill for Timber, the place of the Glasshouse so conveniently posted for Water-carriage, the City-Lot for a Dock, and the Whalery for a sound and fruitful Bank, and the Town Lewis by it to help your People, that by Gods blessing the Affairs of the Society will naturally grow in their Reputation and Profit. I am sure I have not turned my back upon any Offer that tended to its Prosperity; and though I am ill at Projects, I have sometimes put in for a Share with her Officers, to countenance and advance her Interest. You are already informed what is fit for you further to do, whatsoever tends to the Promotion of Wine, and to the Manufacture of Linnen in these parts, I cannot but wish you to promote it; and the French People are most likely in both respects to answer that design: To that end, I would advise you to send for some Thousands of Plants out of France, with some able Vinerons, and People of the other Vocation: But because I believe you have been entertained with this and some other profitable Subjects by your President, I shall add no more, but to assure you, that I am heartily inclined to advance your just Interest, and that you will always find me

Your Kind Cordial Friend,
WILLIAM PENN.

Philadelphia, the 16th of the 6th Moneth, call'd August, 1683.

A Short Advertisement upon the Scituation and Extent of the City of Philadelphia and the Ensuing Plat-form thereof, by the Surveyor General.

The City of Philadelphia, now extends in Length, from River to River, two Miles, and in Breadth near a Mile; and the Governour, as a further manifestation of his Kindness to the Purchasers, hath freely given them their respective Lots in the City, without defalcation of any their Quantities of purchased Lands; and as its now placed and modelled between two Navigable Rivers upon a Neck of Land, and that Ships may ride in good Anchorage, in six or eight Fathom Water in both Rivers, close to the City, and the Land of the City level, dry and wholsom: such a Scituation is scarce to be parallel'd.

The Model of the City appears by a small Draught now made, and may hereafter, when time permits, be augmented; and because there is not room to express the Purchasers Names in the Draught, I have therefore drawn Directions of Reference, by way of Numbers, whereby may be known each mans Lot and Place in the City.

The City is so ordered now, by the Governour's Care and Prudence, that it hath a Front to each River, one half at Delaware, the other at Skulkill; and though all this cannot make way for small Purchasers to be in the Fronts, yet they are placed in the next Streets, contiguous to each Front, *viz.* all Purchasers of One Thousand Acres, and upwards, have the Fronts, (and the High-street) and to every five Thousand Acres Purchase, in the Front about an Acre, and the smaller Purchasers about half an Acre in the backward Streets; by which means the least hath room enough for House, Garden and small Orchard, to the great Content and Satisfaction of all here concerned.

The City, (as the Model shews) consists of a large Front-street to each River, and a High-street (near the middle) from Front (or River) to Front, of one hundred Foot broad, and a Broad-street in the middle of the City, from side to side, of the like breadth. In the Center of the City is a Square of ten Acres; at each Angle are to be Houses for publick Affairs, as a Meeting-House, Assembly or State-House, Market-House, School-House, and several other Buildings for Publick Concerns. There are also in each Quarter of the City a Square of eight Acres, to be for the like Uses, as the Moore-fields in London; and eight Streets, (besides the High-street), that run from Front to Front, and twenty Streets, (besides the Broad-street) that run cross the City, from side to side; all these Streets are of fifty Foot breadth.

In each Number in the Draught, in the Fronts and High-street, are placed the Purchasers of One Thousand Acres, and upwards, to make up five Thousand Acres Lot, (both in the said Fronts and High-street) and the Numbers direct to each Lot, and where in the City; so that thereby they may know where their Concerns are therein.

The Front Lots begin at the South-ends of the Fronts, by the Numbers, and so reach to the North-ends, and end at Number 43.

The High-street Lots begin towards the Fronts, at Number 44, and so reach to the Center.

The lesser Purchasers begin at Number 1, in the second Streets, and so proceed by the Numbers, as in the Draught; the biggest of them being first placed, nearest to the Fronts.

Francis Daniel Pastorius Recalls the Founding of Germantown, 1685

On October 24, 1683, I, Francis Daniel Pastorius, with the good will of the governor, laid out another new city, of the name of Germanton, or Germanopolis, at a distance of two hours' walk from Philadelphia, where there are a good black fertile soil, and many fresh wholesome springs of water, many oak, walnut, and chestnut trees, and also good pasturage for cattle. The first settlement consisted of only twelve families of forty-one persons, the greater part High German mechanics and weavers, because I had ascertained that linen cloth would be indispensable.

I made the main street of this city sixty feet wide, and the side streets forty; the space, or ground-plot, for each house and garden was as much as three acres of land, but for my own dwelling twice as much. Before this, I had also built a little house in Philadelphia, thirty feet long and fifteen wide. Because of the scarcity of glass the windows were of oiled paper. Over the house-door I had written: *Parva Domus, sed amica Bonis, procul este profani* [A little house, but a friend to the good; remain at a distance, ye profane.], Whereat our Governor, when he visited me, burst into laughter, and encouraged me to keep on building.

I have also acquired for my High-German Company fifteen thousand acres of land in one piece, upon the condition that, within a year, they shall actually place thirty households thereon; and for this reason, that we High-Germans may maintain a separate little province, and thus feel more secure from all oppression.

It would, therefore, be a very good thing if the European associates should at once send more persons over here, for the common advantage of the Company; for only the day before yesterday, the Governor said to me that the zeal of the High-Germans in building pleased him very much, and that he preferred them to the English, and would grant them special privileges. . . .

Concerning the Inhabitants of this Province

Of these, three sorts may be found: 1. The natives, the so-called savages. 2. The Christians who have come here from Europe, the so-called Old Settlers. 3. The newly-arrived Associations and Companies.

So far as concerns the first, the savages, they are, in general, strong, agile, and supple people, with blackish bodies; they went about naked at first and wore only a cloth about the loins. Now they are beginning to wear shirts. They have, usually, coal-black hair, shave the head, smear the same with grease, and allow a long lock to grow on the right side. They also besmear the children with grease, and let them creep about in the heat of the sun, so that they become the color of a nut, although they were at first white enough by Nature.

They strive after a sincere honesty, hold strictly to their promises, cheat and injure no one. They willingly give shelter to others, and are both useful and loyal to their guests.

Their huts are made of young trees, twined, or bent, together, which they know how to roof over with bark. They use neither table nor bench, nor any other household stuff, unless perchance a single pot in which they boil their food.

I once saw four of them take a meal together in hearty contentment, and eat a pumpkin cooked in clear water, without butter and spice. Their table and bench was the bare earth, their spoons were mussel-shells, with which they dipped up the warm water, their plates were the leaves of the nearest tree, which they do not need to wash with painstaking after the meal, nor to keep with care for future use. I thought to myself, these savages have never in their lives heard the teaching of Jesus concerning temperance and contentment, yet they far excel the Christians in carrying it out.

They are, furthermore, serious and of few words, and are amazed when they perceive so much unnecessary chatter, as well as other foolish behavior, on the part of the Christians.

Each man has his own wife, and they detest harlotry, kissing, and lying. They know of no idols, but they worship a single all-powerful and merciful God, who limits the power of the Devil. They also believe in the immortality of the soul, which, after the course of life is finished, has a suitable recompense from the all-powerful hand of God awaiting it.

They accompany their own worship of God with songs, during which they make strange gestures and motions with the hands and feet, and when they recall the death of their parents and friends, they begin to wail and weep most pitifully.

They listen very willingly, and not without perceptible emotion, to discourse concerning the Creator of Heaven and earth, and His divine Light, which enlightens all men who have come into the world, and who are yet to be born, and concerning the wisdom and love of God, because of which he gave his only-begotten and most dearly-beloved Son to die for us. It is only to be regretted that we can not yet speak their language readily, and therefore cannot set forth to them the thoughts and intent of our own hearts, namely, how great a power and salvation lies concealed in Christ Jesus. They are very quiet and thoughtful in our gatherings, so that I fully believe that in the future, at the great day of judgment, they will come forth with those of Tyre and Sidon, and put to shame many thousands of false nominal and canting Christians.

As for their economy and housekeeping, the men attend to their hunting and fishing. The women bring up their children honestly, under careful oversight and dissuade them from sin. They plant Indian corn and beans round about their huts, but they take no thought for any more extensive farming and cattle-raising; they are rather astonished that we Christians take so much trouble and thought concerning eating and drinking and also for comfortable clothing and dwellings, as if we doubted that God were able to care for and nourish us.

Their native language is very dignified, and in its pronunciation much resembles the Italian, although the words are entirely different and strange. They are accustomed to paint their faces with colors; both men and women use tobacco with pleasure; they divert themselves with fifes, or trumpets, in unbroken idleness.

The second sort of inhabitants in the province are the old Christians, who came here from Europe.

These have never had the upright intention to give these needy native creatures instruction in the true living Christianity, but instead they have sought only their own worldly interests, and have cheated the simple inhabitants in trade and intercourse, so that at length those savages who dealt with these Christians, proved themselves to be also for the most part, crafty, lying, and deceitful, so that I can not say much that is creditable of either. These misguided people are wont to exchange the skins and peltry which they obtain for strong drink, and to drink so much that they can neither walk nor stand; also they are wont to commit all sorts of thievery, as the occasion may arise.

Owing to this, their kings and rulers have frequently complained of the sins of falsehood, deceit, thieving, and drunkenness, introduced here by the Christians, and which were formerly entirely unknown in these parts.

If one of these savages allows himself to be persuaded by a Christian to work, he does it with complaining, shame, and fear, as an unaccustomed act; he looks about him all the while on all sides, lest any of his people may find him working, just as if work were a disgrace, and idleness were an especial inborn privilege of the nobility, which should not be soiled by the sweat of toil.

The third sort of inhabitants of this province are the Christian Societies.

We, the latest arrivals, being Christians included in honorable associations and companies, after obtaining royal permission from England, in the year 1681, bought certain portions of the country for ourselves from the governor, William Penn, with the intention to erect new cities and colonies, and not only to gain thereby our own temporal advantage and support, but also to make the savages gentle and docile, and to instruct them in the true knowledge of God, insomuch that I live in the hope of being able to announce more good news of their conversion to Christianity within a short time.

Colonist Gabriel Thomas on High Wages and Great Opportunities in Pennsylvania, 1698

. . . I must needs say, even the present Encouragements are very great and inviting, for Poor People (both Men and Women) of all kinds, can here get three times the Wages for their Labour they can in England or Wales.

I shall instance in a few, which may serve; nay, and will hold in all the rest. The first was a Black-Smith (my next Neighbour), who himself and one Negro Man he had, got Fifty Shillings in one Day, by working up a Hundred Pound Weight of Iron, which at Six Pence per Pound (and that is the common Price in that Countrey) amounts to that Summ.

And for Carpenters, both House and Ship, Brick-layers, Masons, either of these Trades-Men, will get between Five and Six Shillings every Day constantly. As to Journey-Men Shooe-Makers, they have Two Shillings per Pair both for Men and Womens Shooes: And Journey-Men Taylors have Twelve Shillings per Week and their Diet. Sawyers get between Six and Seven Shillings the Hundred for Cutting of Pine-Boards. And for Weavers, they have Ten or Twelve Pence the Yard for Weaving of that which is little more than half a Yard in breadth. Wooll-Combers, have for combing Twelve Pence per Pound. Potters have Sixteen Pence for an Earthen Pot which may be bought in England for Four Pence. Tanners may buy their Hides green for Three Half Pence per Pound, and sell their Leather for Twelve Pence per Pound. And Curriers have Three Shillings and Four Pence per Hide for Dressing it; they buy their Oyl at Twenty Pence per Gallon. Brick-Makers have Twenty Shillings per Thousand for their Bricks at the Kiln. Felt-Makers will have for their Hats Seven Shillings a piece, such as may be bought in England for Two Shillings a piece; yet they buy their Wooll commonly for Twelve or Fifteen Pence per Pound. And as to the Glaziers, they will have Five Pence a Quarry for their Glass. The Rule for the Coopers I have almost forgot; but this I can affirm of some who went from Bristol (as their Neighbours report), that could hardly get their Livelihoods there, are now reckon'd in Pensilvania, by a modest Computation to be worth some Hundreds (if not Thousands) of Pounds. The Bakers make as White Bread as any in London, and as for their Rule, it is the same in all Parts of the World that I have been in. The Butchers for killing a Beast, have Five Shillings and their Diet; and they may buy a good fat large Cow for Three Pounds, or thereabouts. The Brewers sell such Beer as is equal in Strength to that in London, half Ale and half Stout for Fifteen Shillings per Barrel; and their Beer hath a better Name, that is, is in more esteem than English Beer in Barbadoes, and is sold for a higher Price there. And for Silver-Smiths, they have between Half a Crown and Three Shillings an Ounce for working their Silver, and for Gold equivalent. Plasterers have commonly Eighteen Pence per Yard for Plastering. Last-Makers have Sixteen Shillings per dozen for their Lasts. And Heel-Makers have Two Shillings a dozen for their Heels. Wheel and Mill-Wrights, Joyners, Brasiers, Pewterers, Dyers, Fullers, Comb-Makers, Wyer-Drawers, Cage-Makers, Card-Makers, Painters, Cutlers, Rope-Makers, Carvers, Block-Makers, Turners, Button-Makers, Hair and Wood Sieve-Makers, Bodies-Makers [corset-makers], Gun-Smiths, Lock-Smiths, Nailers, File-Cuters, Skinners, Furriers, Glovers, Patten-Makers, Watch-Makers, Clock-Makers, Sadlers, Coller-Makers, Barbers, Printers, Book-Binders, and all other Trades-Men, their Gains and Wages are about the same proportion as the forementioned Trades in their Advancements, as to what they have in England.

Of Lawyers and Physicians I shall say nothing, because this Countrey is very Peaceable and Healthy; long may it so continue and never have occasion for the Tongue of the one, nor the Pen of the other, both equally destructive to Mens Estates and Lives; besides forsooth, they, Hang-Man like, have a License to Murder and make Mischief. Labouring-Men have commonly here, between 14 and 15 Pounds a Year, and their Meat, Drink, Washing and Lodging; and by the Day their Wages is generally between Eighteen Pence and a Half a Crown, and Diet also; But in Harvest they have usually between Three and Four Shillings each Day, and Diet. The Maid Servants Wages is commonly betwixt Six and Ten Pounds per Annum, with very good Accommodation. And for the Women who get their Livelihood by their own Industry, their Labour is very dear, for I can buy in London a Cheese-Cake for Two Pence, bigger than theirs at that price when at the same time their Milk is as cheap as we can buy it in London, and their Flour cheaper by one half.

Corn and Flesh, and what else serves Man for Drink, Food and Rayment, is much cheaper here than in England, or elsewhere; but the chief reason why Wages of Servants of all sorts is much higher here than there, arises from the great Fertility and Produce of the Place; besides, if these large Stipends were refused them, they would quickly set up for themselves, for they can have Provision very cheap, and Land for a very small matter, or next to nothing in comparison of the Purchase of Lands in England; and the Farmers there, can better afford to give that great Wages than the Farmers in England can, for several Reasons very obvious.

As First, their Land costs them (as I said but just now) little or nothing in comparison, of which the Farmers commonly will get twice the encrease of Corn for every Bushel they sow, that the Farmers in England can from the richest Land they have.

In the Second place, they have constantly good price for their Corn, by reason of the great and quick vent [sale] into Barbadoes and other Islands; through which means Silver is become more plentiful than here in England, considering the Number of People, and that causes a quick Trade for both Corn and Cattle; and that is the reason that Corn differs now from the Price formerly, else it would be at half the Price it was at then; for a Brother of mine (to my own particular knowledge) sold within the compass of one Week, about One Hundred and Twenty fat Beasts, most of them good handsom large Oxen.

Thirdly, They pay no Tithes, and their Taxes are inconsiderable; the Place is free for all Persuasions, in a Sober and Civil way; for the Church of England and the Quakers bear equal Share in the Government. They live Friendly and Well together; there is no Persecution for Religion, nor ever like to be; 'tis this that knocks all Commerce on the Head, together with high Imposts, strict Laws, and cramping Orders. Before I end this Paragraph, I shall add another Reason why Womens Wages are so exorbitant; they are not yet very numerous, which makes them stand upon high Terms for their several Services, in Sempstering, Washing, Spinning, Knitting, Sewing, and in all the other parts of their Imployments; for they have for Spinning either Worsted or Linen, Two Shillings a Pound, and commonly for Knitting a very Course pair of Yarn Stockings, they have half a Crown a pair; moreover they are usually Marry'd before they are Twenty Years of Age, and when once in that Noose, are for the most part a little uneasie, and make their Husbands so too, till they procure them a Maid Servant to bear the burden of the Work, as also in some measure to wait on them too. . . .

Reader, what I have here written, is not a Fiction, Flam, Whim, or any sinister Design, either to impose upon the Ignorant, or Credulous, or to curry Favour with the Rich and Mighty, but in meer Pity and pure Compassion to the Numbers of Poor Labouring Men, Women, and Children in England, half starv'd, visible in their meagre looks, that are continually wandering up and down looking for Employment without finding any, who here need not lie idle a moment, nor want due Encouragement or Reward for their Work, much less Vagabond or Drone it about. Here are no Beggars to be seen (it is a Shame and Disgrace to the State that there are so many in England) nor indeed have any here the least Occasion or Temptation to take up that Scandalous Lazy Life.

Jealousie among Men is here very rare, and Barrenness among Women hardly to be heard of, nor are old Maids to be met with; for all commonly Marry before they are Twenty Years of Age, and seldom any young Married Women but hath a Child in her Belly, or one upon her Lap.

What I have deliver'd concerning this Province, is indisputably true, I was an Eye-Witness to it all, for I went in the first Ship that was bound from England for that Countrey, since it received the Name of Pensilvania, which was in the Year 1681. The Ship's Name was the *John and Sarah* of London,

Henry Smith Commander. I have declin'd giving any Account of several things which I have only heard others speak of, because I did not see them my self, for I never held that way infallible, to make Reports from Hear-say. I saw the first Cellar when it was digging for the use of our Governour Will. Penn. . . .

❧ E S S A Y S

A. G. Roeber, a historian at the University of Illinois, Chicago Circle, in the first essay looks at Dutch colonists before and after the English conquest of New Netherland, comparing the immigrant stream from the Netherlands to the contemporary English migration. Examining attempts to maintain Dutch culture after 1664, he seeks to explain why these efforts varied from region to region, as well as why some aspects of culture continued strong in Dutch ways even as other, more public, parts of life quickly anglicized. In the second essay Gary B. Nash, a professor of history at the University of California, Los Angeles, treats the first generation of English merchants in Pennsylvania and their failure (or unwillingness), despite economic success, to pass their businesses on to sons who would follow in their footsteps. The answers cast light both on the esteem in which mercantile activities were held and the ways in which the careers of these men seem to replicate the earlier pattern of Chesapeake planters as delineated by Bernard Bailyn in Chapter 6.

Dutch Colonists Cope with English Control

A. G. ROEBER

Migration to New Netherland was an option considered by people on the margins of the spectacular Dutch culture and economy of the seventeenth century. The first colonists were Walloon refugees from the southern part of the Spanish Netherlands, and they mingled with West Frieslanders and others with a minimal stake in the mainstream of Netherlands society. Most came from economically depressed areas such as Utrecht, whose earlier glory had been eclipsed by the rise of Gouda, Delft, and Haarlem. Amsterdam, the cultural center of the Dutch Republic, and its northern environs contributed few settlers to New Netherland.

By 1673, when perhaps six thousand persons inhabited the colony, relatively few were Dutch. Nearly 40 percent came from High Germany—most from Aachen, Cleves, East Friesland, Westphalia, Bremen, Hamburg, and Oldenburg. From an early list of German immigrants to New Amsterdam and New York between 1630 and 1674, 125 of the 180 families can be traced from the Hanseatic cities or extreme northern Germany and not further south than Cologne, Braunschweig, and Berlin. The earliest recorded emigration

A. G. Roeber from *Strangers Within the Realm: Cultural Margins of the First British Empire,* edited by Bernard Bailyn and Philip D. Morgan, 222–236. Reprinted by permission of the author and publisher. Published for the Institute of Early American History and Culture, Williamsburg, Virginia. © 1991 The University of North Carolina Press.

among the Frieslanders—a cryptic petition cited by the chronicler Peter Sax in 1639–1640—probably refers to the migration via Amsterdam to North America. Danes and Norwegians were attracted to the colony, and European Jews also trickled into the colony's main town. Together, these European arrivals mingled with the dwindling native Americans and growing numbers of African-American slaves in contributing to the heterogeneity of the settlements.

Before the English conquest, but more notably after, Dutch-speakers further diluted their culture by scattering widely. Thus, by 1663, Horekill, a Mennonite colony on the Delaware, numbered only forty-one Dutch Mennonites from Zwaanendael, under Pieter Cornelius Plockhoy's leadership. Jasper Danckaerts and Peter Sluyter, both radical Dutch pietist followers of Jean de Labadie, secured Bohemia Manor on the Delaware from Ephrahim Hermann in 1683, but the experiment in communitarian farming never exceeded one hundred persons and by 1698 faltered, having attracted no migrants from the Netherlands, only displaced Dutch from New York.

The diversity of the original New Netherland population, together with the scattered, isolated locations of later Dutch-speakers, effectively prevented creation of support networks linking the settlements to each other and back to the Netherlands. Settlements were virtual islands, interested only in the territory immediately surrounding them. The New Jersey Dutch or those on the Delaware cared little about Manhattan's life or what went on in Schenectady or Albany. In 1741 the Swedish traveler Peter Kalm pointed out that in New Brunswick, New Jersey, a supposedly Dutch town, immigrants from Albany lived on one lane in utter isolation from the other Dutch "and seldom or never go amongst the other inhabitants."

Leadership was also a long-standing problem among the Dutch. From the beginning of New Netherland, private merchant-traders were at odds with the Dutch West Indies Company. Private, successful merchant-traders, not initially a part of the vision of the West Indies Company for the colony, smuggled, traded in furs, and in 1639 finally got the company to abandon monopoly for regulation. Even as the Schuyler and Cuyler merchant families emerged into prominence in the 1660s, they married on the basis of religious disputes and business alliances brought from the Netherlands that divided rather than united the merchant cadre. Clerical leaders, too, failed to emerge as symbols of unity and concord. In the 1630s Walloons refused to attend the simple services conducted in a mill loft by Jonas Michaëlius. The liberal Amsterdam classis, which favored an episcopal governance, often supplied ministers to a population drawn from more orthodox parts of the United Provinces favoring a presbyterian polity. . . .

In the late 1650s Governor Peter Stuyvesant attempted to cement a social network of patrons and officers for the colony, much like his contemporary in Virginia, Sir William Berkeley. Through this patronage network, the governor apparently intended to create a self-conscious governing cadre to whom he formally gave *burgerrecht* (city privileges). Composed of clergy, militia officers, and the members of the government appointed by him, the coalition never came together. The wealthier merchants and younger family migrants failed to share a common vision for the scattered Dutch communities stretching along the Hudson to the Delaware.

This failure is nowhere better evident than in the manner of the English conquest. The dominies and merchants, seemingly possessing a large stake in Dutch culture, urged capitulation. Those living closest to the symbol of Dutch authority, Fort Amsterdam, persuaded Stuyvesant to surrender. There is reason to believe that young people of modest means might have resisted, if given a lead by their superiors. Some excoriated "those devilish traders who have so long salted us," and the West Indies Company itself praised those who had not been "moved by the flattering tongues of Preachers and others who were troubled about their private property, without regarding the interest of the State and Company." Nor did a "charter group" of self-conscious leaders emerge after the Dutch recaptured New York in 1673. Anthony Colve, the interim authority in the reconstituted New Netherland, spent much of his time settling conflicts among fractious communities. Poorer Dutch Lutherans in Albany later in the 1670s mocked their new English rulers, the clash between supposed leaders and commoners an inherited fragmentation now intensified by final English conquest.

The rift between merchants and clerics on the one hand and the commonality on the other surfaced even more dramatically during Jacob Leisler's Rebellion. Leisler's Rebellion in 1689 nonetheless seems to undercut a simple story of assimilation of the Dutch by the conquering English. The rebellion occurred within six years of the Naturalization Act of 1683 and the adoption of an English-style Charter of Liberties that underscored the determination of English leaders to complete the political and cultural transformation of New Netherland into New York. The failure of eminent Dutch merchants and clerics to protest these developments completed their estrangement from commoners. Bitter Leislerians complained that "most of the magistrates . . . were also elders and deacons and therefore heads of our church." Following Leisler's execution, his unrepentant followers "began to feel more bitter hatred against those who had instigated this murder," especially clerical leaders like Dominie Henricus Selyns who reciprocated their hostility. Attendance at Dutch Reformed churches plummeted during the 1690s in the aftermath of Leisler's execution. Ministerial salaries went unpaid. Voting no confidence in spiritual and secular leaders with their feet, large numbers of poorer Dutch farmers left the colony for New Jersey.

Orthodox, conservative, liturgical Dutch Reformed leaders had long faced problems in building networks of support for their people. True, the number of people attending the Dutch Reformed church in New York City increased during the last third of the seventeenth century, so that by 1698 the congregation comprised 57 percent of Dutch adults in the city. True, the loyalty of Dutch women to the church was deep; they represented more than 60 percent of the communicants. Yet this was a church of the eminent: the elders and deacons were exclusively merchants or skilled artisans. Wealthy Dutch women married to English men brought their spouses into the Dutch church. Most members were of more than ten years' standing by the 1680s, and newcomers from other towns like Albany, with an occasional newcomer from the Dutch West Indies or the Netherlands, were generally also merchants, silversmiths, or traders. Defections that began with the outmigration to New Jersey in the 1690s afflicted the town congregations in New York by the 1740s. In 1756 William Smith reported that Trinity Church, the seat of New York Anglicanism, was growing from "proselytes from the Dutch churches." In contrast to the defectors of the 1690s who left to preserve their Dutch religion, the eminent who later abandoned the Reformed church were numbered among the economic and social elite of New York.

The thinness of Dutch high culture in North America had other sources. In the highly rural world of seventeenth-century America, the cosmopolitan, urban quality of Dutch culture could not survive transport beyond New Amsterdam. In urban New York, portraiture, silverware, and finely crafted furniture certainly flourished for a time among wealthy Dutch merchants. But, before long, Dutch high culture became indistinguishable from English. Mannerist portraiture, painted furniture, and mourning rings and seals reflected bonds that William and Mary, one of whom was chief magistrate and captain general in the United Provinces, enjoyed with their wealthy English and Dutch subjects alike. Colonial Dutch paintings reveal no particular Dutch use of color, background, or technique; rather, English mezzotint engravings were their models.

On the other hand, Dutch vernacular culture, particularly evident in the domestic and religious spheres, architectural styles, dietary habits, and testamentary patterns, was quite vibrant until at least the middle of the eighteenth century. "The tie that binds: church and language," in one scholar's words, accurately described the core of surviving Dutch colonial identity. The defense of the Dutch language, particularly by women in the Reformed church, was critical to its maintenance, especially when support for Dutch schooling was curtailed at the conquest. Dutch Bibles were present in many late-seventeenth-century New York homes. As late as 1769, when a catalog of more than seven hundred "mostly German" books was offered for sale in Philadelphia, the seventy-one titles in Dutch consisted mainly of Bibles, hymnals, and pietist tracts. Secular titles were limited to the occasional atlas, a description of the "old and new East Indies," a city directory of Amsterdam. But there was no Dutch press in North America, no newspaper circulating in that language, and by the 1760s only one Dutch almanac still published, by German or English printers. The arrival of the Dutch pietist pastors between the 1690s and the 1730s, however, reinforced the sense that the spoken, formal language was tied to the church. In the 1720s, with the arrival of these preachers, controversialist literature pushed the total of items published in Dutch in British North America to perhaps five a year from 1725 to 1750, as opposed to the normal single issue of the almanac. Indeed, this connection was so pronounced that in the nineteenth century, when one Dutch-American returned to the Netherlands, no one could understand his dialect any longer except an old man who said that it reminded him of the archaic form of "church Dutch" that had fallen out of use since his youth.

The domestic area of Dutch life increasingly became the focus of a separate Dutch culture that in small ways influenced the broader American culture. Foods like beets, endive, spinach, dill, parsley, and chervil were added by Dutch farmers to North American diets. The onion-potato-carrot stew *hutspot* and oil cakes (*olykoek, koekje:* cookies) enriched colonial cuisine. Dutch celebrations of Christmas, particularly the children's figure of Sinter Claes and the practice of putting out the wooden shoe by the door in anticipation of gifts, found imitators in North America from other cultures. The Dutch homes that spread these cultural practices also taught other colonials to speak of "stoops" (*stoep*) on their houses and to appreciate the bulbous Dutch clay pipes exchanged in trade with native Americans from Long Island and Connecticut to the Mohawk Valley and with other Europeans as well.

This domestically oriented culture was unquestionably a hybrid adaptation to North American conditions. If Peter Kalm's observations can be trusted, most rural Dutch were frugal eaters and contented themselves with *sapaan* every night for supper—a porridge of cornmeal in which, Kalm said, "a large hole is made in its center, into which milk is poured, and then one proceeds to help himself." German settlers from Swabia knew the identical dish as *Stöpper* or *brennts Mus*; their descendants would also adapt native American maize to the traditional dish. Like Dutch barns, so-called Dutch houses, with their gambrel roofs and flared bell eaves, were in fact composite structures, reflecting many influences of Friesian and Danish origin. They were not simple transfers from the Netherlands. From upstate New York, a painting hung in the Van Bergen home details house and barn with hay barracks in 1735, all reflecting this North American rural architecture one would not have found in the Netherlands. Black slaves, visiting Indians, and whites, presumably conversing in the dialect of the upper Hudson (itself an archaic form of Dutch by the mid-eighteenth century), complete the panorama.

The protection of family and hearth among the Dutch took a practical and serious form in property settlements. Dutch-Roman law provided that, unless a marriage contract had been entered into, a common property system prevailed, with the husband acting as the agent for his wife. Yet both partners held common property equally as well as all property acquired during the duration of marriage. Unlike English common law, Roman law provided for the woman's right to make a will jointly with her husband in disposing of both real and chattel property. The right to perpetuate this practice was guaranteed under the Articles of Capitulation of September 1664. Until the eighteenth century, the Dutch in New York continued to write mutual wills, and most gave the widow life use of the *boedel,* or estate. Moreover, Dutch women continued to use their maiden name in these documents until the early eighteenth century. Even when English practices crept in and husbands wrote wills by themselves, Dutch wives through the 1720s continued to receive the same rights of inheritance as women had who jointly prepared wills in the seventeenth century. The widow continued as before to be the administratrix of the property. Until the 1730s, wills generally gave half the estate to the widow, half to the children, in the event of a second marriage.

Unlike the English, who attempted to establish sons on the land and so excluded daughters from realty, Dutch rural testators until about 1770 either gave daughters land or stipulated that they be compensated in cash equaling the value of land given their brothers. The collapse of Dutch tendencies to provide widows with an equal proportion of the estate enjoyed by children occurred by the 1730s in urban New York; rural Dutch continued this practice for another generation. The most obvious question becomes, then, What accounts for the changed status of Dutch women and the rise of the children's interest and their capacity to inherit a larger estate upon the death of the father, and not at the mother's decease or remarriage?

Economic and social developments provide clues to the gradual erosion of distinctive testamentary patterns. If the Dutch area around Acquackamonk and Totowa is any indication, the practice of equal partition began to produce insufficient estate to sustain all heirs by the second decade of the eighteenth century. Concerned fathers naturally shifted control over diminishing resources to children earlier in their lives, even at the expense of widowed wives. Yet the continuation of control over half the estate exercised by rural Dutch women belies a simple economic explanation. Perhaps the rise of Dutch members of the urban bar in New York by the first decade of the eighteenth century is also significant. Dominie Boel's lawyer brother Tobias in New York was but one of a number of eminent Dutchmen to practice at this, one of the colonial bars where technical pleading and correct procedure were increasingly important. Successful Dutch lawyers penetrated the mysteries of the common law to demonstrate sufficiently their prosperous families' adaptation to the public British legal and political world. With Dutch-speaking legal advisers who could intervene to protect at least some of their interests, Dutch urban women may have felt less threatened by the alien legal system than did their rural cousins. Increasingly, prominent Dutch families intermarried with the English and their legal advisers, further accelerating the decline in distinct Dutch testation customs. It is not coincidental that the peculiar testamentary practices in urban New York began to falter in the same decade that the Dutch Reformed church bewailed the collapse of the language among younger people and noticed the first signs of drift away from the Dutch church by the elite in favor of the Anglican. In rural areas, the decline seems tied less to rational, intentional economic planning than to a withering away of a tradition that was also no longer sustained by the perpetuation of either a separate language or a separate religious culture.

This separate religious culture was closely bound up with a radical separatist ideology of Dutch pietism. Not that all Dutch settlements were affected by this new religious sentiment. Rather, the Dutch farmers who fled into New Jersey after 1700 to escape political, social, and religious ostracism at the hands of a prosperous Dutch-English leadership found in separatist Labadist* pietism a congenial religious sentiment and self-concept. This radical pietist tradition had its origins in Dutch Labadist attacks on ungodliness, interpreted to mean the rather laconic, tolerant style of Dutch Christianity that had

---

*Labadists were followers of the mystical quietistic sect founded by Jean de Labadie (1610–1674).

accompanied the commercial success of the Republic. Such radicalism enjoyed relatively little success in the Netherlands; it had limited appeal in New York; it would characterize the Jersey Dutch.

The arrival of Theodorus Jacobus Frelinghuysen in New Jersey in 1720 signaled a revival in Dutch Reformed Christianity heretofore unknown in North America. Born in 1692 into a Westphalian Calvinist pastor's family, Frelinghuysen studied at Hamm and Lingen. Ordained in 1715, Frelinghuysen arrived from Friesland to accept a call in 1719 from the Raritan Valley Dutch. His arrival was matched by the emergence in the same year in New York of a second pietist leader, the Lutheran tailor Johann Bernhard van Dieren, born in Königsberg, but probably of Dutch or Huguenot ancestry. Removing to Hackensack by 1725, van Dieren preached in Dutch and German to Lutherans and Reformed alike. These two leaders were joined in 1735 by the Swiss-born pietist leader Johan Hendricus Goetschius, who also preached in both continental languages. It was around these popular, charismatic figures that Dutch religious revivals centered for a generation before the English experienced the so-called First Great Awakening of the 1740s.

Pietist groups gathered by these leaders worshiped informally, as had separatist Labadist groups on the Continent. Religious services in this version of Dutch pietism emphasized emotive hymnody in simple meter and a psalmody that eventually gave way to English hymns. The tendency toward spontaneous prayer and a minimum of ritual was intended to unsettle worship in the congregations that pietists found filled with insincerity and rote prayer.

Using a formal liturgy that employed traditional Genevan hymnody in complex meter, the mainstream Dutch Reformed celebrated a high church Dutch liturgy of preaching and sacrament and observed a strict segregation of the sexes in their churches, with preferential seats going to married males, females, and church leaders. A small increase in church attendance occurred in some traditional Reformed churches in the 1720s. But the decade was marked more by a mixing of Dutch and English styles in architecture. Typically, the interior furniture, pulpit, altar, pews, and baptismal font of Dutch churches remained largely unchanged in style. But windows and exteriors that connected worshipers with the English world took on eighteenth-century British forms, with more double-hung sash windows. Fewer churches assumed the octagonal shape traceable to the rural Netherlands. The inclusion of English architectural forms in the very institution that had protected Dutch linguistic and religious distinctiveness accompanied the lament that many of the young were abandoning this semianglicized institution and its Dutch language for worship in Anglican churches, where architecture and language both spoke as one for the dominant culture.

Against this genteel, anglicized New World apostasy, Frelinghuysen mounted an assault using the separatist Labadist radicalism of his youth. Upon his own personal and immediate judgment, he claimed, he could recognize "unregenerate" people wanting baptism or access to the Lord's Supper. The public embarrassment visited upon members barred from taking communion earned him their undying enmity. Pietist children were forbidden to learn the Lord's Prayer by heart, since only a "regenerate" and "awakened" person could say these words and mean them. Prosperous Dutch bristled when told that the saved undoubtedly were to be found almost wholly among the poor and outcast of society. Despite fierce assaults directed at him by clergy and laity in North America and the Netherlands, Frelinghuysen's congregants remained fiercely loyal to him. Frelinghuysen, Goetschius, and van Dieren reached for simple values, preached a biblical loyalty to kin and family, viewed the outside world with suspicion and contempt, and enjoyed, as a result, a devoted following. Gilbert Tennent's friendship for Frelinghuysen was matched by George Whitefield's public admiration for the revivals conducted by the Dutch radical.

The appeal of these charismatic figures to Dutch women and the private sphere they defended against English incursions is suggested by the language of their sermons. When Goetschius's sermon "The Unknown God" was reprinted by John Peter Zenger in New York in 1743, the pastor's introduction immediately presented his own image as the embattled son of a persecuted mother: "Woe is me, my mother, that thou hast borne me a man of strife and a man of contention to the whole earth." Goetschius peppered his text with references to the "daughter of my people," the anguish of women in childbirth, and threats to the "daughter of my people," whose children and sucklings begged in vain for corn and wine from their mothers. These harrowing images drawn from Lamentations and Jeremiah could not have failed to touch the beleaguered Dutch, at whose center Dutch women defended both home and altar. Goetschius urged them to be patient, resisting the wealthy and the hypocrite who thinks "he does God a favor when he oppresses the true believers and usurps God's inheritance." The imagery that tied threats to family and meager property was delivered in a fiery Dutch. Observers who found both message and medium harsh and unbending, Frelinghuysen chastised. Dutch was decisively preferable to English, he retorted, the language of the seductive tempter in the garden. Even Frelinghuysen's exclusion of unworthy, unregenerate Dutch worshipers from the Lord's table smacked of the defense of home and religion against those who had cast their lot with the larger worldly, profane society. Such people would only endanger the entire congregation of the saved by their behavior.

Dominie Goetschius's ministry—a Swiss German-speaker finally ordained in Pennsylvania to minister among the Dutch by the German Reformed Peter Dorsius, the Labadist Frelinghuysen, and Presbyterian Gilbert Tennent—personified radical pietism's weakness as a system of cultural support. This was an international movement largely uninterested in ethnic, national, or cultural issues as such. By its very nature it was antagonistic to elaborate institutions and programs, and once the charismatic leadership of the prophetic first generation dissipated, the movement found affinities with English-speaking Presbyterians but failed to perpetuate uniquenesses of a Dutch religious culture.

The preservation of Dutch dialect within the walls of church and home, however, was already in trouble as the Dutch pietist renewal movement got underway, reinforced by the belated English awakening of the 1740s. The Dutch contributed to the common continental legacy of religious renewal that Scots and Irish shared with them, but even the creation of an indigenous North American clerical association dominated by the pietists, the Coetus ("assembly" or "uniting"), did not preserve the separate quality of Dutch culture for long. The classis at Amsterdam finally agreed, after much pietist lobbying from North America, to create this body in 1747. This organization, coming into being when the Dutch language was already disappearing among younger worshipers, provided a clerical network of exchange and cooperation. But by 1753 "the Dutch spoken by ministers educated in the Netherlands could no longer be understood by the Dutch of the Middle Colonies," according to one contemporary observer. The "common barbarous Dutch spoken in our families" was wholly different from the "studied and ornamented Style of the Pulpit." Preaching in the Dutch churches shifted finally to English, precisely a century after the political conquest of New Netherland. Dutch pietism was tamed, finding an institutional home in Queen's College in 1766, where its peculiarly Dutch qualities swiftly vanished. Van Dieren had dropped his ministry to become a prosperous miller by the 1740s; Goetschius also figured in the founding of Queen's and by the time of his death in 1774 was advertising his services as a tutor in the secular press.

The rural, religious, family-centered Dutch culture of the eighteenth century had enjoyed an extension on life partly because Dutch families perpetuated for a time culturally distinct notions about marital property and faith, at least until midcentury. Yet, lacking a systematic, institutionalized support for educating the young, bereft of the charismatic personalities of the pietist revivalists of the 1720s and 1730s, further isolated by more prosperous Dutch families who adapted to English legal ways, this rural culture too began to fade, though still evident in remote hamlets in New Jersey and New York in the early nineteenth century. Despite earlier seventeenth-century differences in agricultural practices, by the mid-1700s no compelling economic or political grounds existed to perpetuate even a separate domestic culture upon a younger generation.

By the 1730s, local Dutchmen in rural New York and New Jersey were functioning as justices of the peace, and their homespun notions of rough justice fitted the domestic-religious sphere they cherished. But whether the Dutch actually understood the laws they were sworn to administer is unclear. Pastor Heinrich Melchior Mühlenberg met Dutch justices of the peace in New York befriended by his father-in-law Conrad Weiser. One of these Dutch justices, Mühlenberg wrote, "had not been very well versed in English law, and ... lived rather remote from the higher and more learned authorities. Hence, when a quarrel was brought before him, he was not always able to help, and at times he could do nothing but advise both parties to go out in the courtyard and settle the matter with their fists. Whenever this happened, they had to become reconciled and go home in peace. This finally led to his resigning his office." Among the Hackensack Dutch, Mühlenberg reported, the older people were possessed of "a certain natural honesty and artlessness. They did not use documents, seals, signatures, bonds, and other such contracts. A man's word and handshake were his bond. . . . Like all other nationalities, they have a special love for their mother tongue." By 1750, when Mühlenberg wrote, these Dutch in both New York and New Jersey preserved this mother tongue only among themselves at home. Those who had appeared to function in the public arena without comprehending English laws were vanishing from the scene. In their places, Dutch-speakers entered politics or the bar, even from rural New Jersey, working in the public arena in English for their own people and the Germans, who together may have composed one-quarter of New Jersey's population.

The Revolutionary war in the Hackensack Valley proved to be a genuine civil war, pitting poorer Dutch and English settlers against rivals, reflecting bitter religious and cultural quarrels bequeathed to that area by the displaced radical pietist Dutch of the early 1700s. Dominie Goetschius had laid the groundwork for an ethic of resistance that Frelinghuysen also pioneered on the Raritan: both areas became virulently anti-British by the 1760s. The violent response of the Dutch in New Jersey to English political authority seems to have been linked to the intensity of religious renewal that did less to perpetuate an institutionalized form of Dutch life than it did to reawaken and draw upon a heritage of oppression and embattled self-definition that evoked memories of 1664, 1689, and the religious fervor of brave, embattled, charismatic pietist leaders.

Significantly, the Dutch by the 1770s seemed little threatened by Anglo-American political culture. The Dutch had made that culture their own in great measure both at home and in church organizations. They supported the Revolution in proportion to their affinity for separatist religion and a willingness to make their own way, without oversight by or connection to Amsterdam's classis.

That decision, however, worked for Dutch-Americans only when language, a peculiar domestic culture (reflected in property use and inheritance), and religious doctrine and practice watched over from Europe were no longer broadly valued within the Dutch community. The Dutch had long prospered in commerce, politics, and law. By the 1750s their religious and linguistic particularism had waned. Perhaps in rural areas, churches and homes still operated as cultural havens necessary for emotional sustenance. But the gradual disappearance of the language, the peculiar inheritance customs, and the religious identity provoked little comment from Dutch-American communities. Since more than half the Dutch-speakers on the British North American mainland lived in New York and another fifth in New Jersey's Bergen and Somerset counties, what had occurred there comprehended the experience of most Dutch in British North America. The remaining third—scattered along the Delaware in New Castle County, Delaware, in Pennsylvania, in Virginia, and in small groups from New York to Charleston and Savannah—had anglicized even faster.

The First Merchants of Pennsylvania: Generational Failure?

GARY B. NASH

When William Penn organized the Quaker migration to Pennsylvania in 1681 and drafted plans for the founding of its capital city, he demonstrated a keen

Gary Nash, "The Early Merchants of Philadelphia: The Formation and Disintegration of a Founding Elite," in *The World of William Penn*, ed. Richard Dunn and Mary Maples Dunn, 337–351. Copyright © 1986 by University of Pennsylvania Press. Reprinted by permission.

eye for the realities of colony building and the unromantic work of making a government function. No colony could prosper without a port city facing the Atlantic, and no maritime center could function without a merchant elite. Furthermore, that elite, coordinating the economic life of the colony, would necessarily play a pivotal role in government. Hence, it is not surprising that Penn, who claimed to abhor cities and dislike mercantile pursuits, took pains to recruit a nucleus of merchants to the shores of the Delaware and gave them heavy responsibilities in matters of government.

This essay is concerned with the gathering of this founding mercantile elite in Philadelphia in the years between 1681 and 1710, the failure of these merchants to perpetuate themselves into the second generation, and the emergence in the years from 1711 to 1740 of a quite different merchant community, for the most part not descended from the initial merchant families. Because this pattern bears resemblance to what Bernard Bailyn and David Jordan have described in early Virginia and Maryland and what Richard Dunn has revealed about early Barbados, we may suspect that, while the circumstances differed from colony to colony, founding elites in colonial America were fragile and short-lived—and nowhere more so than in the cities. . . .

The publicity surrounding Penn's grant in 1681 and the proprietor's skillful promotion work drew merchants from all over the English-speaking world to the "Holy Experiment." Between 1682 and 1689 at least fifty-six merchants took up residence in Philadelphia. Many were old friends and Quaker colleagues of Penn, men such as James Claypoole, an established West Indian trader living in London; Robert Turner, a Dublin cloth merchant; and Griffith Jones, who had entered the counting house by marrying the widow of a London merchant. The largest number in this first wave came from England, but others flocked in from the West Indies, Ireland, New York, and New Jersey. Many of them were First Purchasers of Pennsylvania land, especially those from England, Ireland, and Wales, and hence were entitled to large city lots in the capital city. Befitting their occupation (and consistent with the sizeable investment they were making in his colony), Penn allocated to them the Delaware River waterfront lots from Dock Creek north to Pegg's Run. Here they built their wharves, warehouses, and crude early dwellings.

Even if we take the absence of the names of five of these founding merchants from the early records of the Philadelphia Monthly Meeting to indicate no affiliation with the Society of Friends, only eight of these fifty-six early traders (14 percent) were not Quaker. They had come to Philadelphia because economic opportunity beckoned and Penn's policy of religious toleration promised freedom for all to compete for advantages in the new colony.

Many merchants in England and elsewhere, including a number of First Purchasers of land, cautiously waited before making the decision to uproot themselves and journey to the Delaware. Not all was peace and prosperity in the early years, and the outbreak of war in 1689 provided a test of whether a pacifist government could function in the militaristic world of the late seventeenth century. But at least twelve merchants did cast their lot with Penn's colony between 1690 and 1695. The most notable were Quakers Isaac Norris of Port Royal, Jamaica; Joseph Pidgeon and Charles Saunders from Bristol; Edward Shippen and Nathan Stansbury from Boston; and Pentacost Teague from Cornwall. A somewhat greater reinforcement of the merchant community occurred when Penn returned in 1699 for a second sojourn in his colony. Of the seventeen merchants who are known to have arrived in Phildelphia between 1696 and 1700, about half came with Penn or as a result of his announced intention to return to Pennsylvania to put an end to political squabbling and usher in a period of maturation and growth. They included a group of men upon whom Penn conferred important offices and upon whom he relied after his return to England in 1701: James Logan and Samuel Finney from Ireland, James Steel from Sussex, John Cadwalader from Wales, William Fishbourne and Richard Hill from Maryland, and Richard Clymer from Bristol.

This turn-of-the-century influx of merchants did not much enlarge the counting house circle; instead, the newcomers replaced traders in the founding group who had succumbed to difficult conditions in the early years and then an epidemical fever that swept through Philadelphia in 1699. No fewer than twenty-three of the fifty-six merchants who arrived between 1682 and 1689 were dead by the turn of the century, including some of Penn's principal officeholders—William Frampton, Christopher Taylor, James Claypoole, John Delaval, George Hutcheson, Thomas Budd, Arthur Cooke, and Robert Turner. The merchant community, though augmented by seventeen arrivals between 1696 and 1700, had seen an almost equal number of its members buried in those five years alone.

About seventeen merchants arrived in Philadelphia between 1701 and 1710, two of them sons of Edward Shippen, who had migrated from Boston in 1694. During the same decade another fifteen merchants died. Thus, from about 1690 to 1710 the merchant community was nearly static in number. But during these same twenty years ... the religious composition of Philadelphia's merchants changed dramatically. In the founding period, from 1682 to 1689, about six of every seven arriving merchants were Quaker; in the two decades beginning in 1690 Quaker merchant arrivals represented exactly half of the merchants establishing themselves in the city.

One further characteristic of this early group should be noted. Nearly one-fourth of them had entered the mercantile ranks from artisan status merely by emigrating to Pennsylvania. Samuel Richardson from Jamaica is the classic example. A Quaker bricklayer who had abandoned England for the Caribbean in the 1670s, he arrived in Philadelphia in 1683 and by the beginning of the eighteenth century was reputed to be the second wealthiest merchant in Philadelphia. Many others duplicated this kind of shipboard mobility in the early years. Among important merchants in the founding period, Humphrey Morrey had been a distiller, Philip James a wine cooper, Griffith Jones a glover, Benjamin Chambers a turner, John Day and Thomas Masters carpenters, Anthony Morris, Gabriel Wilkinson, and Francis Rawle bakers, Thomas Budd a cooper, and William Hudson a bricklayer. Arriving early and purchasing land at a time when £20 would buy a thousand acres of fertile farmland plus a bonus of capacious lots in the budding commercial center of the capital city, these men rose into the economic elite at a dizzying pace probably unparalleled anywhere else in the Atlantic world at this time.

Despite their success in establishing Pennsylvania's trade connections with other mainland colonies, the West Indies, England, and Ireland, Philadelphia's founding merchant elite was not very successful in passing on the mantle of commercial leadership to their sons. Of 143 merchants identified in the period from 1711 to 1740, only 31, or about 20 percent, were the sons of men in the founding merchant group. Some of these sons became important merchant leaders in Philadelphia in the age of Franklin—men such as William Allen, son of a merchant from Ireland who had married the daughter of another first-generation merchant, Thomas Budd; Samuel Coates, son of the prominent early merchant Thomas Coates; William Logan, son of James Logan, Penn's main factotum after 1700; Thomas Masters, Jr.; Isaac Norris, Jr. (as well as two of his brothers); Edward Shippen II and his cousin Joseph; Samuel Carpenter, Jr., and Joseph Wharton, son of First Purchaser Thomas Wharton. But only twenty-four first-generation merchant families produced sons who succeeded their fathers along the Delaware River wharves. Mercantile activity within all of the other seventy-eight families of first-generation merchants ended with the deaths of their founders. During the second generation of the city's history, when Philadelphia experienced rapid growth and economic development, these families played no role in the arena of commerce.

The failure of sons to succeed fathers left vacant a large number of positions in the period after 1710. By that year, in fact, at least 43 of the founding group of 102 were dead and another 28 succumbed in the following decade. To fill their places, and to add to them in a period of growth, came new men whose names cannot be found in the early records of the city. Some of them founded trading houses that would be known throughout the Atlantic world in the decades that followed. In fact, tracing backward from the American Revolution, one finds many more important merchant families that were launched in the second period than in the first. Among them were the Biddles, Bringhursts, Griffits, Inglises, Lawrences, Levys, McCalls, Merediths, Reynells, Stampers, Strettels, Willings, and Wistars—all of whom emigrated to Philadelphia after 1710 and replenished the circle of merchants so depleted by the failure of the first-generation male heirs to succeed their fathers.

Of the 111 merchants in the second generation who were not related by birth to the founding merchant elite, the origins of 71 have been traced. Two-thirds of them (46) were new immigrants to the seaport capital. Several came from Ireland, when trade connections made in the early period facilitated emigration. They included Jonathan Bennett, Thomas Griffits (who came by way of Jamaica and achieved immediate success by marrying the daughter of Isaac Norris), Benjamin Mayne, Richard Nixon, and Robert Strettel. A few came from Scotland, such as George Chalmers and George McCall. But many more arrived from Bristol and London, Philadelphia's important trading partners. They included William Dowell, Thomas Flexney, Peter and Thomas Lloyd, Abraham Taylor, John White, and Charles Willing. As in the early period, New York furnished a few new merchants, notably the founders of the city's Jewish merchant group, Isaac and Nathan Levy and David Franks, who arrived in the late 1730s. The West Indies, especially Barbados and Jamaica, continued to supply Philadelphia with merchants, with at least eight arriving from the islands in this period.

A second group of merchants who established themselves in Philadelphia after 1710 were sons of First Purchasers or others who had come to Pennsylvania in the early years, had taken up land in or near Philadelphia, and had prospered sufficiently to give their heirs a secure base from which to launch a mercantile career. Eleven of the second-generation merchants were sons of yeoman farmers. Peter Baynton, the founder of a famous merchant house, for example, was the son of Benjamin Baynton, a First Purchaser who had settled in Chester County about 1686. Robert Ellis, one of Philadelphia's largest slave traders by the 1730s, was the son of the Welshman Thomas Ellis, an early register general of Pennsylvania and a member of the Welsh community in Merion. Quakers John and George Mifflin were fathered by an early yeoman settler in the Northern Liberties, and an even more famous eighteenth-century Quaker merchant, Israel Pemberton, grew up on his father's rolling acres in Bucks County.

Successful artisans of the founding generation also contributed eleven sons to Philadelphia's second generation of merchants. John Warder, a Quaker hatter and feltmaker, trained his son Jeremiah in his trade in Philadelphia, but the son later became a considerable merchant. One of the sons of malster Thomas Paschall, himself the son of a pewterer and First Purchaser who arrived in 1683, had become an important Philadelphia merchant by the 1730s, as had the sons of carpenter Samuel Powel (Samuel Powel, Jr.), bricklayer John Redman (Joseph and Thomas Redman), and Germantown turner Isaac Shoemaker (Benjamin Shoemaker). However, in light of the rapid turnover in the merchant community in the eighteenth century, it is surprising to find that of the 102 merchants whose origins are known, only 11 were drawn from the artisan class. Although the commercial elite of the city disintegrated rapidly, it was mainly horizontal movement from the outside world that replenished the mercantile ranks rather than internal vertical movement from below.

The failure of most pioneer artisans to propel their sons upward into mercantile circles cannot be satisfactorily accounted for by an absence of opportunity since so many positions were filled from outside. Nor does it seem possible that the low incidence of artisan-to-merchant mobility was caused by pinched inheritance. A large number of Philadelphia's early artisans, in fact, acquired substantial property in the city, which by the time they passed it on to their sons, had multiplied in value. Instead, it appears that most sons of successful first-generation artisans eschewed the commercial life, preferring to follow their father's footsteps as carpenters, silversmiths, bakers, and shipbuilders, while continuing to invest in Philadelphia property. The Emlens, Elfreths, Duffields, and Penroses are only a few of the prominent examples of founding-generation artisans who accumulated considerable wealth, much of it in land, and raised sons who preferred the craftsman's existence to a life in the counting house. A pride of craft seems to have been operating here; it resulted in a tradition of passing on artisan skills to those who might, if they had wished, have entered mercantile pursuits. The numerous examples of unsuccessful merchants in Philadelphia—or successful merchants who had been badly battered during periodic downturns in commerce such as in the 1720s—may also have convinced the sons of successful artisans that the merchant's life was not the best of all worlds.

While it is clear that the mercantile elite was reconstituted in the decades after 1710, the process by which the new group assumed power remains to be analyzed. Other studies of fragile founding elites speak in terms of new men shouldering aside the older group or climbing over their backs on the way to the top. This might be inferred for Philadelphia from the fact that so many new faces appeared while old ones faded. But only by examining the sons of the founding merchant elite—by inquiring into what they did if they did *not* follow their fathers into the counting house—can we know with certainty the causes of elite disintegration.

Of the 102 merchants in the founding group, only 24 produced sons who followed in their fathers' footsteps. Seventy-eight merchants sired no sons who succeeded them. In just over half of these cases (forty) this is explained by the fact that the families either had no sons or lost their sons before they reached adulthood. Far more than we have realized, early Philadelphians did not marry, were sterile, or saw one-third, one-half, or even all of their children die in infancy. A few examples make the point. Four of Philadelphia's most prominent founding merchants—William Frampton, Richard Hill, Samuel Preston, and Robert Turner—produced among them not a single son who lived to maturity. Frampton had no children. Hill's wife bore five, all of whom died in infancy; when she died, he married again without issue. Preston, who married the daughter of Thomas Lloyd, had one son, who died in infancy, and three daughters, one of whom died early. Turner saw his only two sons die as infants. William Hudson's wife, one of those fabled "fruitful vines," presented him with fourteen children, six sons and eight daughters. But of the sons, four died in infancy, one at twenty-six, and the other at twenty-nine.

Among merchants who did produce merchant sons this fearful mortality rate also prevailed. Clement Plumstead had five sons, one of whom succeeded him as a Philadelphia merchant. But the other four died in infancy. Samuel Carpenter produced one merchant son and another who became a minister. His other two sons were buried as babies. Abraham Bickley, who had come first to East Jersey in 1681 and then moved to West Jersey in the 1690s, wore out two wives and spent his life calling for the gravedigger. Elizabeth Gardiner Bickley bore him three children in the five years they spent together before she died; of these two died in infancy. Within a year of his wife's death, Abraham married again, this time to Elizabeth Richardson in Philadelphia. She presented him with nine children, four of whom failed to survive childhood. She died seven days after giving birth to her ninth child in twelve years, and that baby followed her to the grave at two months of age. Only one son by Bickley's second marriage reached adulthood. Of William Fishbourne's four sons, one died at nine months, one at ten years, one at eighteen. Thomas Coates had six sons; four died before adolescence, one died a wastrel at twenty-three, and one, Samuel, became a successful merchant.

Edward Shippen had mid-wives coming to his door all his adult life. He sired eleven children by three wives, celebrating fatherhood for the last time when he was sixty-nine years old. Only four of the eleven children lived to maturity; three were sons of whom one died at twenty-three. The examples could be multiplied but the point is clear: the merchants who arrived in Philadelphia after 1710 did not have to push aside the sons of established merchants but had merely to fill places vacated by the plentiful deaths of founding merchants who themselves had buried scores of sons before they reached adulthood.

Among another group of first-generation merchant families it was not reproductive failure but economic achievement that accounts for the absence of merchant sons. At least a dozen of the seventy-eight merchants whose sons did not succeed them in business were successful enough in acquiring land that their male offspring retired to a gentleman farmer's life on country plantations. Some of the successful early Quaker merchants had themselves withdrawn to the countryside. Samuel Carpenter, one of the most active traders on the Delaware after arriving from Barbados in 1683, quit the city for his Bucks County plantation by 1704. The building of Fairhill and Stenton, the country mansions of Isaac Norris and James Logan, were even grander attempts, shortly after the end of Queen Anne's War, to imitate the life of the rural English gentry. For many sons of the founding commercial elite the preference for country life and the size of their inheritance apparently led to decisions to forego the trials of city merchants. Samuel Finney's sons are good examples. An Irishman, Finney had emigrated in the 1670s to Barbados where he established himself as a merchant. He returned to England in 1681 and fought for the prince of Orange at the end of that decade. Penn induced him to come to Philadelphia in 1699 as part of a corps of officeholders whom he hoped would restore leadership and stability to the colony. A purchaser of large tracts of land from Penn, Finney became captain of the Philadelphia militia, a justice of the peace, and a judge of the provincial court. He pursued mercantile affairs after marrying the widow of another founding merchant, Henry Tregany. But his sons preferred the country life: Joseph took up his father's estate at Tacony, and Charles inherited a plantation in Frankford. . . .

This avoidance of mercantile careers by so many of the sons of the first-generation merchants—perhaps as much as a fourth of the entire cohort—was made possible not so much by their fathers' amassing of personal wealth as by their acquisition of large tracts of land outside Philadelphia and extensive property within the city, which they gained as First Purchasers in England in 1681–82 or thereafter by purchase after arriving in Philadelphia. Land was very cheap in the early years. With £100 an early settler could buy five thousand acres of land outside Philadelphia and, by the terms of the Conditions and Concessions of July 1681, each such purchaser received a bonus of property in the capital city amounting to 2 percent of the country purchase. These terms proved too liberal, but under Penn's revised plan of December 1682 each First Purchaser received twenty feet of Delaware River frontage for every thousand acres of land purchased in the country and, in addition, a High Street lot twenty-six feet wide and half a block deep. As little as £20 laid out in 1682 was therefore sufficient to guarantee the sons of a first-generation merchant an income for life. Favored by the chronology of their arrival, the merchants of the first generation were supremely situated to make country gentlemen of their sons, if those sons so desired. Years later, Samuel Fothergill, the English Quaker leader, wrote of the sons of the founders: "Their fathers came into the country, and bought large tracts of land for a trifle; their sons found large estates come into their possession, and . . . they settled in ease and affluence."

A corollary of this phenomenon was that second-generation merchants arriving after 1710 found it far more difficult to become large property-holders. A simple comparison makes the point. Laying out £100, London merchant James Claypoole acquired 5,000 acres of country land in Pennsylvania and the Lower Counties, 100 acres in the Northern Liberties, 102 feet of Delaware River frontage in the heart of what became the commercial center of Philadelphia, and a lot, 132 feet broad and 306 feet deep, on High Street, the east-west axis of the town. Samuel Hassell, arriving from Barbados in 1716 with £100 to invest in property, would not have been able to purchase a single Front Street lot, no matter how small, at that price and would have had no country acreage to go with it. To purchase what Claypoole acquired for £100 in 1682, a merchant of the second generation would have laid out a minor fortune.

While early death claimed the sons of many first-generation merchants and country life lured others from the city, a few chose artisan careers. In most of the eight cases I have found this was not forced downward mobility but a preference expressed by the sons. . . .

The remarkable discontinuity in the merchant community during the first and second generations resulted from fearsome mortality in the early decades of the city's history, which carried away scores of sons who might have perpetuated their father's names along the Philadelphia waterfront, and the unusual opportunity for sons who did survive to live off land inherited from a founding group that literally got in on the ground floor. To add emphasis to this analysis we can examine the wealthiest merchants on the tax lists of 1693 and 1709, those assessed for estates of at least £250. Among this commercial elite of thirty-two founders, seven sired no children at all and only eight reared sons who became merchants. Sixty-four sons were born to the group as a whole. Sixteen died before reaching adulthood, fifteen became merchants, eleven became gentleman landowners, five pursued artisan careers, one became a minister, three remained in the West Indies where they had been born, and thirteen followed unknown careers. Thus were the ranks of Philadelphia's commercial elite open to newcomers of the second generation.

What were the economic and political experiences of merchants in the first and second periods of Philadelphia's history, and what do they tell us about the nature of early Pennsylvania society?

In entrepreneurial performance, the second generation seems to have outdone the first. The inventories of estate inscribed after the deaths of individual merchants reveal a sharp increase in accumulated personal wealth by the second-generation merchants. Among fifty-one merchant decedents in the first group for whom inventories have survived, the mean personal wealth was £1,267. Among sixty-five second-generation merchants whose inventories are extant, personal wealth averaged £2,646, more than twice as much. This may indicate primarily the growing mercantile opportunities in the period after 1729, when the business slump of that decade receded and an extended period of commercial prosperity began. Only one of every ten merchants with inventories in the first generation left personal wealth in excess of £2,500, and four of these five importers were long-lived men who survived until 1725 or later. In the second generation, more than one of every four merchants accumulated personal wealth in excess of £2,500. . . . [L]arge fortunes were uncommon among first-generation merchants. . . .

The economic performance of the first generation may be disguised by the fact that the inventories of estate only occasionally list real property, where the assets of the founding elite were probably concentrated. This propensity for investing in land can be explained by its cheapness in the early decades, but it may also owe a good deal to the uncertainties of trade during the wartime era of 1689–1713. The wars fought during the reigns of William and Anne spanned most of the years during which the founding merchants were active. Wartime commercial disruption, along with piratical activity, which was at its height in this period, undoubtedly dampened the spirits of many for risk-taking on the Atlantic sea lanes.

Second-generation merchants, by contrast, operated during a period of uninterrupted peace from the signing of the Peace of Utrecht in 1713 to the outbreak of the Anglo-Spanish War in 1739. To be sure, these later merchants had to endure a protracted dampening of trade in the mid-1720s, but their appetite for entrepreneurial activity must have been whetted by the return of peace in Europe and the colonies, the crackdown on piracy after 1715, the heavy immigration of Scots-Irish and Germans after 1714, the expanding agricultural surpluses that Pennsylvania farmers were producing, and the growing demands of a West Indian market swelled by a rapid increase in the number of slaves involved in sugar production.

Religious values also affected the economic careers of the two generations of merchants. Among the founding group, mostly Quakers before 1700, the commitment to developing the inner life reverberated powerfully. This curbed the appetite for continuous risk-taking, at least among the Quaker merchants, and may have pushed many of their sons toward different career choices. In the second generation, when circumstances encouraged entrepreneurial activity and the price of land soared, the Quaker domination of the merchant community had been broken. A more ambitious business ethic, influenced by changes in religious orientation, energized the Delaware waterfront. Three of every five merchants were Anglicans, Presbyterians, or Jews, men whose religious ethic provided no brake on economic ambition. Even among the Quaker merchants by this time the earlier spirit of equalitarianism, meekness, and self-denying attachment to following the Inward Light had atrophied. The advancing bourgeois ethic also manifested itself among Quaker merchants arriving in the colony. "Birthright" Friends such as Thomas Griffits, Peter and Thomas Lloyd, John Reynell, and Robert Strettel, men who had been reared in a far less visionary milieu than "convinced" Quakers of the founding period, proved to be more aggressive and outward looking than their predecessors in the Quaker capital. Combined with the greater opportunities that came with expansion and an era of peace, this cognitive reorientation among merchants in the second group led to many notable business successes.

In politics we can also note some sharp differences in the experience of the two groups. The failure of most of the founding merchants to rear sons to the mercantile life was paralleled by their inability to transfer political power to their male heirs. This can be seen most directly in analyzing the membership of the Council and Assembly.

The first-generation merchants were intensely involved in politics. Seventeen of them served in Council between 1682 and 1700, and twelve others received councilorships after the turn of the century. Thirty-one founding merchants served in the Assembly, nineteen of whom also occupied Council seats at some time during their careers. In all, two of every five early merchants (42 of 102) served at the highest level of provincial politics. Merchants were not the only political leaders in early Pennsylvania, but they were instrumental in governing the colony during Penn's lifetime.

Despite their crucial governing role in the early years, the merchant founders were not very successful in passing political leadership on to their progeny. The entire founding cohort produced only three sons who served in Council and not more than twelve who were elected to the Assembly. Furthermore, not a single one of the sixty early merchants who had not served in Council or Assembly reared a son who did so.

As a group, the second generation of merchants proved far less active in politics than the first. Twenty-nine of the founding merchants served in Council at some point in their careers and thirty-one sat in the Assembly. But in the second group, which was 40 percent larger than the first, only seven merchants served in Council and eleven in the Assembly, a rate of participation about one-third of that among founding merchants. Partly this may be explained by the fact that a number of early merchants died within a dozen years of reaching Philadelphia, which increased the turnover rate in high political offices. Partly it is explained by the longevity of a handful of early merchants, men such as James Logan, Clement Plumstead, William Fishbourne, and George Roche, who sat in Council for many years and thereby insured that new places were not often available to merchants arriving after 1710. Second-generation voters tended to return the same man to the Assembly year after year, whereas in the early decades continuity of service was apparently much less prized by the electors. Whatever the combination of reasons, political leadership in Philadelphia after 1710 was exercised more by men who were not merchants, such as Andrew Hamilton, Evan Morgan, John Kearsley, and John Kinsey. Commercially more distinguished, the second generation of merchants was politically undistinguished. Many of the leading business figures of the second quarter of the eighteenth century—men such as Samuel Coates, Peter Baynton, John and George Mifflin, John Bringhurst, George McCall, John Stamper, Caspar Wistar, John Reynell, and Charles Willing—played virtually no role in politics at the provincial level. . . .

Rather than promoting political instability or anarchic egalitarianism, the avoidance of political office by so many sons of founding merchants had little effect at all. It did not even hasten the gradual concentration of Quaker political power in the legislative Assembly or the eventual takeover of the Council, courts, and corporation of Philadelphia by Anglican merchants. These changes came only slowly. Quakers clung to political power with surprising tenacity in the eighteenth century in spite of the fact that sons did not often replace fathers in the Council and Assembly. This was possible because some Quaker merchants who arrived in Philadelphia after 1710, such as Thomas Griffits and Robert Strettel, assumed political leadership roles and because the sons of some first-generation country Quakers, such as Israel Pemberton and John Kinsey, also did so. By the late 1730s Anglicans (bolstered by a few prominent defecting Quakers) had eclipsed Friends in the executive branch, on the bench, and in the city corporation. But this change of power within the corps of appointed officeholders followed naturally from the shift within the proprietary family itself from Quakerism to Anglicanism. In any case, the large immigration of Scotch-Irish Presbyterians in the half-century bracketing 1750 would have eventually eroded Quaker political control in Penn's colony, and the crisis that war presented to Quaker politicians in the 1750s would have independently assured their demise.

In sum we may conclude that the building of economic dynasties—and political dynasties flowing from them—proved to be unusually difficult in the seaport towns of colonial America. Commercial centers were growth centers, always characterized by the arrival of new men on the make. Commercial fortunes were precarious; money amassed in a hurry was often lost in a hurry. And for those who did succeed on the slippery slopes of mercantile endeavour, whether they were Quaker, Anglican, or otherwise, retirement to the country was often the great goal, not the governing of cities or colonies. Paradoxically, it was in the cities, where social differentiation proceeded fastest and truly impressive wealth was most often accumulated, that economic and political dynasties least often formed. It was the countryside that provided a better rooting bed for lineally descended oligarchies, for it was there that fortunes, while amassed less quickly, were more stable and where the orientation to land rather than water nurtured the tradition of political responsibility within leading families.

❧ F U R T H E R   R E A D I N G

Thomas Archdeacon, *New York City, 1664–1710: Conquest and Change* (1975)

Randall H. Balmer, *A Perfect Babel of Confusion: Dutch Religion and English Culture in the Middle Colonies* (1989)

Richard Bauman, *For the Reputation of Truth: Politics, Religion, and Conflict Among the Pennsylvania Quakers, 1750–1800* (1971)

Linda Briggs Biemer, *Women and Property in Colonial New York: The Transition from Dutch to English Law, 1643–1727* (1983)

Richard S. Dunn and Mary Maples Dunn, eds., *The World of William Penn* (1986)

Firth Haring Habend, *A Dutch Family in the Middle Colonies, 1660–1800* (1991)

Amandus Johnson, *Swedish Settlements on the Delaware* (1911)

Michael Kammen, *Colonial New York: A History* (1975)

Sung Bok Kim, *Landlord and Tenant in Colonial New York: Manorial Society, 1664–1775* (1978)

Ned Landsman, *Scotland and Its First American Colony, 1683–1765* (1985)

Donna Merwick, *Possessing Albany, 1630–1710: The Dutch and English Experiences* (1990)

Gary B. Nash, *Quakers and Politics: Pennsylvania, 1681–1726* (1968)

Oliver A. Rink, *Holland on the Hudson: An Economic and Social History of Dutch New York* (1986)

Robert C. Ritchie, *The Duke's Province: A Study of New York Politics and Society* (1977)

Frederick B. Tolles, *Meeting House and Counting House: The Quaker Merchants of Colonial Philadelphia, 1682–1763* (1948)

Stephanie Grauman Wolf, *Urban Village: Population, Community, and Family Structure in Germantown, Pennsylvania, 1683–1800* (1976)

The Proprietary Colonies
of the Lower South

❧

Carolina, the site of Roanoke, the first English colony, was recolonized in a new wave of settlements occurring after two decades of political upheaval in England that ended with Charles II's accession in 1660. Like the contemporaneous migration to the middle colonies, the settlement of the Carolinas was carried out by an ethnically mixed population from the European continent, as well as Britain. Many of the colony's leaders were the younger sons of Barbadian planters. These men brought with them the attitudes typical of the West Indies. Thus as crops suited to plantation agriculture were quickly developed, the Lower South plunged into large-scale reliance on slavery without the long period of experimentation that the Chesapeake had seen.

The Carolinas differed from earlier English colonies because of their location in an international arena. St. Augustine in Florida had been an outpost of the Spanish Empire even before the establishment of the first English colony, and French, Spanish, and English traders had long plied their business throughout the Southeast. Large and powerful Indian confederations—Cherokees, Creeks, and Tuscaroras—participated in the trade. This multifaceted and shifting international scene gave Indians and slaves room to maneuver. On the other hand, English traders armed Indians who acted for them and made the trade, particularly in deerskins, more exploitive than formerly.

Because of its proximity to well-established French and Spanish interests, the Lower South was vulnerable to the effects of the long series of wars between France and England that began with the conflict known in America as King William's War in 1689 and continued through the American Revolution. Fears for the rich colony of South Carolina led the English government to detach a portion of its territory, forming Georgia in 1730 to serve as a buffer between South Carolina and Spanish Florida.

❧ D O C U M E N T S

In the first document, excerpted from his journal of a thousand-mile journey through the Southeast published under the title of *A New Voyage to Carolina* (1709), Indian trader John Lawson describes the Native Americans and the land.

Lawson clearly showed the close relationships between traders and Indians, as well as the devastating effect of colonization on native life. The second selection is an anonymous letter from the new Swiss settlement led by Christoph Von Graffenried near New Bern in North Carolina. The writer expresses both the great promise of the land and the colonists' intense homesickness. Eliza Lucas Pinckney, left in charge of her soldier-father's South Carolina plantation at the age of seventeen, worked to develop indigo, the subject of her letter reprinted in the third document. The crop became a major component in the colony's phenomenal economic success.

In the fourth selection Edward Randolph, sent by the Board of Trade to inspect the colonies, reports on the South Carolinians' fear of depredations from Spanish St. Augustine; rice and indigo, the two great cash crops, were not yet established when he wrote in 1699. James Oglethorpe presents in the fifth document the original benevolent picture of the founding of Georgia as a refuge for the English laboring poor, while suggesting these settlers' usefulness against the French and Spanish. In the next document William Byrd of Virginia writes to Lord Egmont, one of the Georgia Trustees, of the harm done in Virginia by large-scale reliance on slaves and praises Georgia's plan of prohibiting slavery and rum.

Slaves who could escape to Florida often found sanctuary there. William Dunlop's 1688 mission to recover eleven runaway slaves, the subject of the seventh document, resulted in the promise of a cash payment from the governor, who refused to surrender the slaves. James Oglethorpe led an expedition into Spanish Florida attempting to end the region's role as a refuge for runaway slaves. The final selection, the expedition's report to the South Carolina Assembly, blames unrest, including the Stono slave rebellion of 1739, on the Spanish.

Indian Trader John Lawson's Journal of Carolina, 1709

Next Morning very early, we waded thro' the Savanna, the Path lying there; and about ten a Clock came to a hunting Quarter, of a great many *Santees*; they made us all welcome; shewing a great deal of Joy at our coming, giving us barbacu'd Turkeys, Bear's Oil, and Venison.

Here we hir'd *Santee Jack* (a good Hunter, and a well-humour'd Fellow) to be our Pilot to the *Congeree Indians*; we gave him a Stroud-water-Blew, to make his Wife an *Indian* Petticoat, who went with her Husband. After two Hours Refreshment, we went on, and got that Day about twenty Miles.... The Weather was very cold, the Winds holding *Northerly*. We made our selves as merry as we could, having a good Supper with the Scraps of the Venison we had given us by the *Indians,* having kill'd 3 Teal and a Possum, which Medly all together made a curious Ragoo.

This Day all of us had a Mind to have rested, but the *Indian* was much against it, alledging, That the Place we lay at, was not good to hunt in; telling us, if we would go on, by Noon, he would bring us to a more convenient Place; so we mov'd forwards, and about twelve a Clock came to the most amazing Prospect I had seen since I had been in *Carolina*; we travell'd by a Swamp-side, which Swamp I believe to be no less than twenty Miles over, the other Side being as far as I could well discern, there appearing great Ridges of Mountains, bearing from us *W.N.W.* One Alp with a Top like a Sugar-loaf, advanc'd its Head above all the rest very considerably; the Day was very serene, which gave us the Advantage of seeing a long Way; these

Mountains were cloth'd all over with Trees, which seem'd to us to be very large Timbers.

At the Sight of this fair Prospect, we stay'd all Night; our *Indian* going about half an Hour before us, had provided three fat Turkeys e'er we got up to him.

The Swamp I now spoke of, is not a miry Bog, as others generally are, but you go down to it thro' a steep Bank, at the Foot of which, begins this Valley, where you may go dry for perhaps 200 Yards, then you meet with a small Brook or Run of Water, about 2 or 3 Foot deep, then dry Land for such another Space, so another Brook, thus continuing. The Land in this Per-coarson, or Valley, being extraordinary rich, and the Runs of Water well stor'd with Fowl. It is the Head of one of the Branches of *Santee*-River; but a farther Discovery Time would not permit; only one Thing is very remarkable, there growing all over this Swamp, a tall, lofty Bay-tree, but is not the fame as in *England,* these being in their Verdure all the Winter long; which appears here, when you stand on the Ridge, (where our Path lay) as if it were one pleasant, green Field, and as even as a Bowling-green to the Eye of the Beholder; being hemm'd in on one Side with these Ledges of vast high Mountains.

Viewing the Land here, we found an extraordinary rich, black Mould, and some of a Copper-colour, both Sorts very good; the Land in some Places is much burthen'd with Iron, Stone, here being great Store of it, seemingly very good: ... When we were all asleep, in the Beginning of the Night, we were awaken'd with the dismall'st and most hideous Noise that ever pierc'd my Ears: This sudden Surprizal incapacitated us of guessing what this threat-ning Noise might proceed from; but our *Indian* Pilot (who knew these Parts very well) acquainted us, that it was customary to hear such Musick along that Swamp-side, there being endless Numbers of Panthers, Tygers, Wolves, and other Beasts of Prey, which take this Swamp for their Abode in the Day, coming in whole Droves to hunt the Deer in the Night, making this frightful Ditty 'till Day appears, then all is still as in other Places.

The next Day it prov'd a small drisly Rain, which is rare, there happening not the tenth Part of Foggy falling Weather towards these Mountains, as visits those Parts. Near the Sea-board, the *Indian* kill'd 15 Turkeys this Day; there coming out of the Swamp, (about Sun-rising) Flocks of these Fowl, containing several hundreds in a Gang, who feed upon the Acorns, it being most Oak that grow in these Woods. These are but very few Pines in those Quarters.

Early the next Morning, we set forward for the *Congeree-Indians,* parting with that delicious Prospect. By the Way, our Guide kill'd more Turkeys, and two Polcats, which he eat, esteeming them before fat Turkeys. Some of the Turkeys which we eat, whilst we stay'd there, I believe, weigh'd no less than 40 Pounds.

The Land we pass'd over this Day, was most of it good, and the worst passable. At Night we kill'd a Possum, being cloy'd with Turkeys, made a Dish of that, which tasted much between young Pork and Veal; their Fat being as white as any I ever saw.

Our *Indian* having this Day kill'd good Store of Provision with his Gun, he always shot with a single Ball, missing but two Shoots in above forty;

they being curious Artists in managing a Gun, to make it carry either Ball, or Shot, true. When they have bought a Piece, and find it to shoot any Ways crooked, they take the Barrel out of the Stock, cutting a Notch in a Tree, wherein they set it streight, sometimes shooting away above 100 Loads of Ammunition, before they bring the Gun to shoot according to their Mind. We took up our Quarters by a Fish-pond-side; the Pits in the Woods that stand full of Water, naturally breed Fish in them, in great Quantities. We cook'd our Supper, but having neither Bread, or Salt, our fat Turkeys began to be loathsome to us, altho' we were never wanting of a good Appetite, yet a Continuance of one Diet, made us weary.

The next Morning, *Santee Jack* told us, we should reach the *Indian* Settlement betimes that Day; about Noon, we pass'd by several fair Savanna's, very rich and dry; seeing great Copses of many Acres that bore nothing but Bushes, about the Bigness of Box-trees; which (in the Season) afford great Quantities of small Black-berries, very pleasant Fruit, and much like to our Blues, or Huckle-berries, that grow on Heaths in *England*. Hard by the Savanna's we found the Town, where we halted; there was not above one Man left with the Women, the rest being gone a Hunting for a Feast. The Women were very busily engag'd in Gaming: The Name or Grounds of it, I could not learn, tho' I look'd on above two Hours. Their Arithmetick was kept with a Heap of *Indian* Grain. When their Play was ended, the King, or *Cassetta's* Wife, invited us into her Cabin. The *Indian* Kings always entertaining Travellers, either *English,* or *Indian*; taking it as a great Affront, if they pass by their Cabins, and take up their Quarters at any other *Indian*'s House. The Queen set Victuals before us, which good Compliment they use generally as soon as you come under their Roof.

The Town consists not of above a dozen Houses, they having other stragling Plantations up and down the Country, and are seated upon a small Branch of *Santee* River. Their Place hath curious dry Marshes, and Savanna's adjoining to it, and would prove an exceeding thriving Range for Cattle, and Hogs, provided the *English* were seated thereon. Besides, the Land is good for Plantations.

These *Indians* are a small People, having lost much of their former Numbers, by intestine Broils; but most by the Small-pox, which hath often visited them, sweeping away whole Towns; occasion'd by the immoderate Government of themselves in their Sickness; . . . treating of the *Sewees*. Neither do I know any Savages that have traded with the *English,* but what have been great Losers by this Distemper. . . .

An Anonymous Letter from the Swiss Settlement Near New Bern, 1711

With a thousandfold greeting, I wish all true friends, neighbors, and acquaintances God's grace and blessing. I an my wife, two children, and my old father have, the Lord be praised, arrived safe and sound in Carolina, and live twenty English miles from New Bern. I hope to plant corn enough this year.

The land is good, but the beginning is hard, the journey dangerous. My two children, Maria and Hansli died at Rotterdam in Holland and were buried in the common burial place.

This country is praised too lightly in Europe and condemned too much. I hope also in a few years to have cows and swine as much as I desire. Mr. Graffenried is our landgrave. Of vermin, snakes, and such like, there is not so much as they tell of in Europe. I have seen crocodiles by the water, but they soon fled. One should not trust to supporting himself with game, for there are no wild oxen or swine. Stags and deer, ducks and geese and turkeys are numerous.

I wish that I had my child with me, which I left with my father-in-law, together with forty-five pounds which I left behind me in the parish of Tofen. And if my father-in-law wishes to come to me I will give to him from my land. One can have as much swine and cattle as he wants without labor and expense. I am very sorry that Christian Balsiger took away his Uhli from me again at Bern.

Eliza Lucas Pinckney on the Perfection of Indigo, 1785

My Dear Child

You wish me to inform you what I recollect of the introducing and culture of indigo in this country. You have heard me say I was very early fond of the vegetable world, my father was pleased with it and encouraged it, he told me the turn I had for those amusements might produce something of real and public utility, if I could bring to perfection the plants of other countries which he would procure me. Accordingly when he went to the West Indies he sent me a variety of seeds, among them the indigo. I was ignorant both of the proper season for sowing it, and the soil best adapted to it. To the best of my recollection I first try'd it in March 1741, or 1742; it was destroyed (I think by a frost). The next time in April, and it was cut down by a worm; I persevered to a third planting and succeeded, and when I informed my father it bore seed and the seed ripened, he sent a man from the Island of Monserat by the name of Cromwell who had been accustomed to making indigo there, and gave him high wages; he made some brick vats on my fathers plantation on Wappo Creek and then made the first indigo; it was very indifferent, and he made a great mistery of it, said he repented coming as he should ruin his own country by it, for my father had engaged him to let me see the whole process. I observed him as carefully as I could and informed Mr. Deveaux an old gentleman a neighbour of ours of the little knowledge I had gain'd and gave him notice when the indigo was to be beat; he saw and afterwards improved upon it, not withstanding the churlishness of Cromwell, who wished

From *The Colonial South Carolina Scene: Contemporary Views, 1697–1774*, ed. H. Roy Merrens, Tricentennial Edition No. 7, 145–146. Reprinted by permission of University of South Carolina Press.

to deceive him, and threw in so large a quantity of lime water as to spoil the colour. In the year 1744 I married, and my father made Mr. Pinckney a present of all the indigo then upon the ground as the fruit of my industry. The whole was saved for seed, and your father gave part of it away in small quantities to a great number of people that year, the rest he planted the next year at Ashipo for seed, which he sold, as did some of the gentlemen to whom he had given it the year before; by this means there soon became plenty in the country. Your father gained all the information he could from the French prisoners brought in here, and used every other means of information, which he published in the Gazette for the information of the people at large.

The next year Mr. Cattle sent me a present of a couple of large plants of the wild indigo which he had just discovered. Experiments were afterwards made upon this sort, which proved to be good indigo, but it did not produce so large a quantity as the cultivated sort. I am

> Your truly affectionate mother,
> Eliza Pinckney

Edward Randolph Reports to the Board of Trade on Economic Prospects and the Spanish Threat, 1699

May it please your Lordships,

After a dangerous voyage at Sea, I landed at Charles Town, in the Province of So. Carolina. . . .

There are but few settled Inhabitants in this Province, the Lords have taken up vast tracts of land for their own use, as in Colleton County and other places, where the land is most commodious for settlement, which prevents peopling the place, and makes them less capable to preserve themselves. As to their civil Governt., 'tis different from what I have met with in the other Proprieties. Their Militia is not above 1500 Soldiers White men, but have thro' the Province generally 4 Negroes to 1 White man, and not above 1100 families, English and French.

Their Chief Town is Charles Town, and the seat of Govt. in this Province, where the Governor, Council and Triennial Parliamt. set, and their Courts are holden, being above a league distance from the entrance to their harbour mouth, which is barred, and not above 17 foot water at the highest tide, but very difficult to come in. The Harbour is called by the Spaniards, St. George; it lies 75 leagues to the Northward of St. Augustine, belonging to the Spaniards. . . . In the year 1686, one hundred Spaniards, with Negroes and Indians, landed at Edistoe, (50 miles to the southward of Charles Town,) and broke open the house of Mr. Joseph Moreton, then Governor of the Province, and carried away Mr. Bowell, his Brother-in-law, prisoner, who was found murdered 2 or 3 days after; they carried away all his money and plate, and

---

Some of the spelling in this document has been modernized.

13 slaves, to the value of £1500 sterling, and their plunder to St. Augustine. Two of the Slaves made their escape from thence, and returned to their master. Some time after, Govr. Moreton sent to demand his slaves, but the Govr. of St. Augustine answered it was done without his orders, but to this day keeps them, and says he can't deliver them up without an order from the King of Spain. About the same time they robbed Mr. Grimball's House, the Sec. of the Province, whilst he attended the Council at Charles Town, and carried away to the value of over £1500 sterling. They also fell upon a settlement of Scotchmen at Port Royal, where there was not above 25 men in health to oppose them. The Spaniards burnt down their houses, destroyed and carried away all that they had, because (as the Spaniards pretended) they were settled upon their land, and had they at any time a superior force, they would also destroy this town built upon Ashley and Cooper Rivers. . . .

I find the Inhabitants greatly alarmed upon the news that the French continue their resolution to make a settling at Messasipi River, from [whence] they may come over land to the head of Ashley River without opposition, 'tis not yet known what care the Lords Proprietors intend to take for their preservation. . . . I heard one of the Council (a great Indian Trader, and has been 600 miles up in the Country west from Charles Town) discourse that the only way to discover the Meschasipi is from this Province by land. He is willing to undertake it if His Majesty will please to pay the charge which will not be above £400 or £500 at most; he intends to take with him 50 white men of this Province and 100 Indians, who live 2 days journey east from the Meschasipi, and questions not but in 5 or 6 months time after he has His Majesty's commands and instructions to find out the mouth of it and the true latitude thereof.

The great improvement made in this Province is wholly owing to the industry and labour of the Inhabitants. They have applied themselves to make such commodities as might increase the revenue of the Crown, as Cotton, Wool, Ginger, Indigo, etc. But finding them not to answer the end, they are set upon making Pitch, Tar and Turpentine, and planting rice, and can send over great quantities yearly, if they had encouragement from England to make it, having about 5,000 Slaves to be employed in that service, upon occasion, but they have lost most of their vessels, which were but small, last war by the French, and some lately by the Spaniards, so that they are not able to send those Commodities to England for a market, neither are sailors here to be had to man their vessels.

I humbly propose that if His Majesty will for a time suspend the Duties upon Commodities, and that upon rice also, it will encourage the Planter to fall vigilantly upon making Pitch and Tar, etc., which the Lords Proprietors ought to make their principal care to obtain from His Majesty, being the only way to draw people to settle in their Province, a place of greatest encouragement to the English Navy in these parts of the world. Charles Town Bay is the safest port for all vessels coming thro' the gulf of Florida in distress, bound from the West Indies to the Northern Plantations; . . .

I have by the extreme of cold last Winter in Maryland and Pennsylvania, and by my tedious passage in the Winter time from New York to this place, got a great numbness in my right leg and foot. I am in hopes this warm climate will restore me to my health. I have formerly wrote to your Board and the Commissioners of H. M. Customs, the necessity of having a Vessel to transport me from one Plantation to another.

I humbly pray Your Lordships favour to direct that the little residence I am to make in these parts of the World, may be in this Province, and that a Vessel well manned may be sent me hither, which may answer all occasion, my intentions being not to lie idle, for when the Hurricane times come in these parts of the World, I can go securely to Virginia, Maryland and Pennsylvania and New England, without fear of being driven from those Plantations by North West Winds, and when they come I can pass from one Plantation to another without difficulty.

James Oglethorpe, "Persons Reduc'd to Poverty May Be Happy in Georgia," 1732

... Let us ... cast our Eyes on the Multitude of unfortunate People in the Kingdom of reputable Families, and of liberal, or at least, easy Education: Some undone by Guardians, some by Law-Suits, some by Accidents in Commerce, some by Stocks and Bubbles, and some by Suretyship. But all agree in this one Circumstance, that they must either be Burthensome to their Relations, or betake themselves to little Shifts for Sustenance, which ('tis ten to one) do not answer their Purposes, and to which a well-educated Mind descends with the utmost Constraint. What various Misfortunes may reduce the Rich, the Industrious, to the Danger of a Prison, to a moral Certainty of Starving! These are the People that may relieve themselves and strengthen *Georgia*, by resorting thither, and Great *Britain* by their Departure. . . .

Having thus described (I fear, too truly) the pityable Condition of the better Sort of the Indigent, an Objection rises against their Removal upon what is stated of their Imbecility for Drudgery. It may be asked, if they can't get Bread here for their Labour, how will their Condition be mended in *Georgia?* The Answer is easy; Part of it is well attested, and Part self-evident. They have Land there for nothing, and that Land is so fertile that ... they receive an Hundred Fold increase for taking very little Pains. Give here in *England* Ten Acres of good Land to One of these helpless Persons, and I doubt not his Ability to make it sustain him, and this by his own Culture, without letting it to another: But the Difference between no Rent, and Rack-Rent, is the Difference between eating and starving. If I make but Twenty Pound of the Produce of a Field, and am to pay Twenty Pound Rent for it; 'tis plain I must perish if I have not another Fund to support me: But if I pay no Rent, the Produce of that Field will supply the mere Necessities of Life.

With a View to the Relief of People in the Condition I have described, His Majesty has this present Year incorporated a considerable Number of Persons of Quality and Distinction, and vested a large Tract of *South-Carolina* in them, by the Name of *Georgia,* in Trust to be distributed among the

Necessitous. These Trustees not only give Land to the Unhappy who go thither, but are also impower'd to receive the voluntary Contributions of charitable Persons to enable them to furnish the poor Adventurers with all Necessaries for the Expence of the Voyage, occupying the Land, and supporting them 'till they find themselves comfortably settled. So that now the Unfortunate will not be obliged to bind themselves to a long Servitude, to pay for their Passage, for they may be carried *gratis* into a Land of Liberty and Plenty; where they immediately find themselves in Possession of a competent Estate, in an happier Climate than they knew before, and they are Unfortunate indeed if here they can't forget their Sorrows. . . .

It is also highly for the Honour and Advancement of our holy Religion to assign a new Country to the poor *Germans,* who have left their own for the Sake of Truth. It will be a powerful Encouragement to Martyrs and Confessors of this Kind to hold fast their Integrity, when they know their Case not to be desperate in this World. Nor need we fear that the King of *Prussia* will be able to engross them all, we shall have a Share of them if we contribute chearfully to their Removal. The Society for the Propagation of the Gospel in foreign Parts have gloriously exerted themselves on this Occasion: They have resolv'd to advance such a Sum of Money to the Trustees for the Colony of *Georgia,* as will enable them to provide for Seven Hundred poor *Salzburghers.* This is laying a Foundation for the Conversion of the Heathen, at the same Time, that they snatch a great Number of poor Christians out of the Danger of Apostacy. 'Tis to be hoped this laudable Example will be followed by private Persons, who may thus at once do much for the Glory of God, and for the Wealth and Trade of *Great Britain.* Subjects thus acquir'd by the impolitick Persecutions, by the superstitious Barbarities of neighbouring Princes, are a noble Addition to the capital Stock of the *British* Empire. . . .

The Encrease of our People, on this fruitful Continent, will probably, in due Time, have a good Effect on the Natives, if we do not shamefully neglect their Conversion: If we were moderately attentive to our Duty on this Head, we have no Reason to doubt of Success. The *Spaniard* has at this Day as many Christians, as he has Subjects in *America,* Negroes excepted. We may more reasonably hope to make Converts and good Subjects of the *Indians* in Amity with us, by using them well, when we grow numerous in their Neighbourhood, than the *Spaniards* could have expected to have done by their inexpressible Cruelties, which raised the utmost Aversion in the Minds of the poor *Indians* against them and their Religion together. One of their own Friers who had not relinquish'd his Humanity, tells us of an *Indian* Prince, who just as the *Spaniards* were about to murder him, was importuned by one of their Religious to become a Christian; the Priest told him much of Heaven and Hell, of Joy and Misery eternal; the Prince desired to be informed which of the two Places was allotted for the *Spaniards?* Heaven, quoth the Priest; says the Prince, I'm resolved not to go there. How different from this was the Reflection of an *Indian* Chief in *Pensilvania: What is the Matter, says he, with us that we are thus sick in our own Air, and these Strangers well? 'Tis as if they were sent hither to inherit our Land in our steads; but the Reason is plain, they love the Great God and we do not.* Was not this *Indian* almost become a Christian? *New-England* has many Convert-*Indians,* who are very good Subjects, tho' no other Colony had such long and cruel Wars with its *Indian* Neighbours. . . .

But this is not all, that Sum which settles one poor Family in the Colony does not end there; it in Truth purchases an Estate to be applied to like Uses, in all future Times. The Author of these Pages is credibly inform'd that the Trustees will reserve to themselves square Lots of Ground interspers'd at proper Distances among the Lands, which shall be given away: As the Country fills with People, these Lots will become valuable, and at moderate Rents will be a growing Fund to provide for those whose melancholy Cases may require Assistance hereafter: Thus the Settlement of Five Hundred Persons will open the Way to settle a Thousand more afterwards with equal Facility. Nor is this Advance of the Value of these Lots of Land a chimerical Notion; it will happen certainly and suddenly. All the Lands within Fifty Miles of *Charlestown* have within these Seven Years encreas'd near Four-Fold in their Value, so that you must pay Three or Four Hundred Pounds for a Plantation, which Seven Years ago you could have bought for a Hundred Pounds, and 'tis certain that Fifty Years ago you might have purchas'd at *Charlestown* for Five Shillings a Spot of Land which the Owner would not sell at this Day for Two Hundred Pounds Sterling.

The Legislature is only able to take a proper Course for the Transportation of small Offenders, if it shall seem best, when the Wisdom of the Nation is assembled; I mean only those who are but Novices in Iniquity. Prevention is better than the Punishment of Crimes, it may reform such to make them Servants to such Planters were reduc'd from a good Condition. The Manners and Habits of very young Offenders would meliorate in a Country not populous enough to encourage a profligate Course of Life, but a Country where Discipline will easily be preserv'd. These might supply the Place of Negroes, and yet (because their Servitude is only to be temporary) they might upon Occasion be found useful against the *French,* or *Spaniards*; indeed, as the Proportion of Negroes now stands, that Country would be in great Danger of being lost, in Case of a War with either of those Powers. The present Wealth of the Planters in their Slaves too probably threatens their future Ruin, if proper Measures be not taken to strengthen their Neighbourhood with large Supplies of Free-men. I would not here be understood to advance that our common Run of *Old-Baily* Transports wou'd be a proper Beginning in the Infancy of *Georgia.* No, they would be too hard for our young Planters, they ought never to be sent any where but to the Sugar Islands, unless we had Mines to employ them. . . .

William Byrd Praises the Plan for Georgia, 1736

. . . Your Lordship's opinion concerning Rum & negroes is certainly very just & your excluding both of them from your colony of Georgia will be very Happy: tho' with Respect to Rum, the Saints of New England, I fear will find out some trick, to evade your Act of Parliament. They have a great dexterity at palliating a perjury so well, as to leave no tast of it in the mouth, nor can any People like them slip through a Penal Statute. They will give some other name to their Rum which they may safely do, because it gos by that of Kill Devil in this Country, from its baneful qualitys. A watchfull eye, must be kept on these foul Traders, or all the precautions of the Trustees will be vain. I wish we coud be blessed with the same Prohibition. They import so many negro's hither, that I fear this Colony will sometime or other be confounded by the name of New Guinea. I am sensible of many bad consequences of multiplying these Ethiopians amongst us. They blow up the pride, & ruin the Industry of our White People, who Seeing a Rank of poor Creatures below them, detest work for fear it should make them look like Slaves. Then that poverty which will ever attend upon Idleness, disposed them, as much to pilfer as it dos the Portuguise, who account it much more like a gentleman to steal, than to dirty their hands with Labour of any kind. Another unhappy Effect of many Negroes is, the necessity of being severe. Numbers make them insolent & then foul Means must do what fair will not. We have however nothing like the Inhumanity here, that is practiced in the Islands & God forbid we ever shou'd. But these base Tempers require to be rid with a tort rein, or they will be apt to throw their Rider. Yet even this is terrible to a good natured Man, who must submit to be either a Fool or a Fury. And this will be more our unhappy case, the more the Negros are increast amongst us. But these private mischeifs are nothing, if compared to the publick danger. We have already at least 10,000 men of these descendants of Ham, fit to bear Arms, & these numbers increase every day, as well by birth, as by Importation. And in case there should arise a Man of desperate courage amongst us, exasperated by a desperate fortune, he might with more advantage than Cataline kindle a Servile War. Such a man might be dreadfully mischeivous before any opposition coud be formed against him, & tinge our Rivers as wide as they are with blood, besides the Calamitys which wou'd be brought upon us by such an attempt, it wou'd cost our Mother Country many a fair Million, to make us as profitable, as we are at present. It were there-fore, worth the consideration, of a British Parliament, My Lord, to put an end, to this unchristian Traffick, of makeing Merchandise of our Fellow Creatures. At Least, the farther importation of them, into our Colonys, should be prohibited, lest they prove as troublesome, & dangerous every where, as they have been lately in Jamaica, where besides a vast expence of money, they have cost the lives of many of his Majesty's Subjects. We have mountains in Virginia too, to which they may retire, as Safely, & do as much mischief, as they do in Jamaica. All these matters, duly considered, I wonder the Legislature will Indulge a few ravenous Traders, to the danger of the Publick safety, & such Traders as woud freely sell their Fathers, their Elder Brothers, & even the Wives of their bosomes if they cou'd black their Faces & get anything for them. In intirely agree with your Lordship in the Detestation you seem to feel for that Diabolical Liquor Rum, which dos more mischief to Peoples Industry & morals, than any thing except Gin & the Pope. And if it were not a little too Poetical, I shoud fancy, as the Gods of old are said to quaff Nector, so the Devils are fobb'd off with Rumm. Tho my Dear Country-men, woud think this unsavory Spirit, much too good for Devils, because they are fonder of it, than Wives or Children, for they often sell the Bread, out of their mouths, to buy Rumm to put in their own. Thrice happy Georgia, if it be in the power of any Law to keep out so great an enimy to Health, Industry & Virtue! The new Settlers there had much better plant vinyards like Noah & get drunk with their own wine. I wish Mr. Oglethorp after he has put his generous Scheme in Execution in that favourite Colony, would make the Tour of the Continent & then I should hope for the pleasure of seeing Him in some of his Planetary motions, I was acquainted with Him formerly, when I cou'd see he had the Seeds of Virtue in Him, which have since grown up into Fruit. Heaven give both your Lordship & him-self success in your disinterested endeavours, for makeing Georgia, a very flourishing & happy place: . . .

William Dunlop's Effort to Recover Runaway Slaves in St. Augustine, 1688

Instructions for Major William Dunlop

1. You are hereby required to repair to the most Noble Governor of fflorida and City of St. Agustine In order to which you are to provide yourselfe with a Convenient Vessell.

2. You are to congratulate in my name the Arrivall of so Noble and Excellent a person to that Government and to Let him understand on my pairt that since there is in that station a man of his worth who hath served his most Catholick Majesty in so eminent Imployments I no wayes doubt of a most perfect and good Correspondence. . . .

3. You are to let the Governor of fflorida know that since I came to the Government there have been no pirats nor other Sea Robbers admitted nor had any reception in this province without being brought to condigne punishment and that I have severall at this time in prison who are speedily to be brought to their tryalls And that I will at all times vigorously endeavour in my station and Government to extirpate abolish and destroy that sort of people who are so much enemies and destructive to all mankind.

4. You are cheifly to lay open and make evident the great damages his Majestie's subjects in this province here sustained by the two Invasions of this Country by persons who came from the City of St. Agustine (as I have been Informed) during the Government of the Last Governor. And you are to demand satisfaction for the same and to give a particular Account of the sume of the said damages; and you are the same to receave; and to demand and receave those eleven Negroes which were taken from Landgrave Mortoun who are there still

5. You are likewise to demand the delivery up to you of those English fugitive Negroes and others who have fled from this province. . . .

James Colleton

Draught of an Indenture Betwixt
the Govr. of St. Agustine and Wm. Dunlop

Be it known to all Christian people to whom these presents may come and concern that whereas diverse negroe slaves belonging to the subjects of the most serene King of England my Master Inhabitants of the province of Carolina In America did run away and desert their Masters service contrare to their duty and to Law and Eleven of the said Negroes did come into the City of St. Agustine In the province of fflorida; and whereas the Honorable Landgrave James Colleton Governor & Generall of the province of Carolina ... did Comand me to demand these fugitive negroes to be restored to their propper masters; And whereas the Most Noble Governor of fflorida in consideration that these negroes are turned Roman Catholick Christians hath desired that these negroes doe stay still in this province of fflorida and hath offered in the name and for the use of the most serene K. of Spain his master to pay their Value to me in satisfaction to the true owners And whereas I am very willing to give a clear demonstration of the firme Intentions of the Noble Governor of Carolina to keep firme the happie peace wch is betwixt the two most Serene Kings E. & S.: and to encrease the good correspondence betwixt the two provinces of Carolina and fflorida And whereas that the most Noble Governor of fflorida hath given me ample and full assurance that after this time all fugitives (if any shall be) who shall run away from Carolina to this province shall be from time to time faithfully restored in their own propper persons to the Governor of Carolina or any sent by him; As I have in the behalfe of the most Noble Governor of Carolina given the like mutuall assurance. Therefore I William Dunlop Sergeant Major of the fforces of the most serene King of England my Master In the County of Berkly and province of Carolina And Agent to the most noble the Governor of Carolina ... In consideration of ... obligations and Bonds to pay to me or my order the sume of Two Thousand peeces of eight of Mexico or Sevill coigne at or before the ffirst day of ffebruary In the year of our Lord God 1689 alias 1690: Sell ... all those eleven Negroe slaves vizt: Mingo etc. Hereby giveing and granting to the sd. most serene King or his assignes ffull Liberty power and Authority to use and dispose of the forsaid slaves as his own peculiar propper goods and as his Most serene Majesty of Spain shall think fit and doe with the delivery of these presents actually deliver the bodies of the sd. slaves here present to the Noble Govr of fflorida in the names for the propper account and use of his sd. most serene Ma: of Spain: providing always that whereas one of these negroes called Mingo is suspected to have murthered one of the subjects of the most serene King of E: my master and that the most Noble Govr. of fflorida hath given assurance that if the sd. murther shall be proved and the said Mingo Legally convicted of the same that than the sd. Most Noble Governor will cause some capitall punishment to be inflicted for the same in that caise whereby the sd. negroe will be Lost to his most serene Majesty of Spain then I oblidge myselfe that his price shall be deducted out of the above sume of 2000 p of eight or otherwise repayed whereby the damage shall be satisfied

In Testimony whereof I have syned and sealled these presents att the city of St. Agustine and 23rd of July alias 2 of Agust 1688. . . .

Report to the South Carolina General Assembly on the Failed St. Augustine Expedition of 1740

Your Committee have hitherto been prevented from making a Report to the House of the Result of their Enquiry into so unfortunate an Event to this Province, by the great Difficulties which they have met with in collecting proper Information and Vouchers from Persons living in different and remote Parts of the Province. Ungrateful also your Committee found it to lay open a Scene which hath already produced so much Concern. Those Difficulties being at Length got over, and your Committee having maturely weighed every Thing that occurred in the Course of their Enquiry, are of Opinion, that they cannot better acquit themselves of their Charge, nor more fully answer the Expectations of the House than by making a just and faithful Narrative (so far as Things have reached their Knowledge) of the Measures with which the Enterprize formed against the Town and Castle of St. Augustine was conducted in the Field from the Time General Oglethorpe first landed in Florida. This they propose to do; and therein nothing shall be contained but incontestable Facts, collected from attested Extracts of Journals kept by the Secretary of the Colonel, and by the Lieutenant Colonel, of the Carolina Regiment, from Examinations on Oath, and from original Letters laid before your Committee. They will afterwards, pursuant to the Obligation they are under, point out to the House the principal and most apparent Causes of the ill Success which attended the Expedition, and make such other Remarks and Observations upon the Whole, as shall appear to your Committee to be necessary. . . .

. . . Hitherto the Government of St. Augustine had not dared to acknowledge, much less to justify, the little Villainies and Violences offered to our Properties; but now an Edict of his Catholic Majesty himself, bearing Date in November 1733, was published by Beat of Drum round the Town of St. Augustine (where many Negroes belonging to English Vessels that carried thither Supplies of Provisions &c. had the Opportunity of hearing it) promising Liberty and Protection to all Slaves that should desert thither from any of the English Colonies but more especially from this. And, lest that should not prove sufficient of itself, secret Measures were taken to make it known to our Slaves in general. In Consequence of which Numbers of Slaves did from Time to Time by Land and Water desert to St. Augustine; and the better to facilitate their Escape carried off their Master's Horses, Boats &c., some of them first committing Murder; and were accordingly received and declared free. Our present Lieutenant Governour by Deputies sent from hence on that Occasion to Seignior Don Manuel de Montiano, the present Governour of St. Augustine, set forth the Manner in which those Slaves had escaped and redemanded them pursuant to the Stipulation between the two Governments, and to the Peace subsisting between the Crowns. Notwithstanding which, though that Governour acknowledged those Slaves to be there, yet producing the King of Spain's said Edict he declared that he could not deliver them up without a positive Order for that Purpose from the King, and that he should continue to receive all others that should resort thither, it having been an Article of Complaint against his Predecessor that he had not put the said Edict in Force sooner. The Success of those Deputies being too well known at their Return, Conspiracies were formed and Attempts made by more Slaves to desert to St. Augustine, but as every one was by that Time alarmed with Apprehensions of that Nature, by great Vigilance they were prevented from succeeding. However,

In September 1739, our Slaves made an Insurrection at Stono in the Heart of our Settlements not twenty miles from Charles Town, in which they massacred twenty-three Whites after the most cruel and barbarous Manner to be conceived and having got Arms and Ammunition out of a Store they bent their Course to the southward burning all the Houses on the Road. But they marched so slow, in full Confidence of their own Strength from the first Success, that they gave Time to a Party of our Militia to come up with them. The Number was in a Manner equal on both Sides and an Engagement ensued such as may be supposed in such a Case wherein one fought for Liberty and Life, the other for their Country and every Thing that was dear to them. But by the Blessing of God the Negroes were defeated, the greatest Part being killed on the Spot or taken, and those that then escaped were so closely pursued and hunted Day after Day that in the End all but two or three were [killed or] taken and executed. That the Negroes would not have made this Insurrection had they not depended on St. Augustine for a Place of Reception afterwards was very certain; and that the Spaniards had a Hand in prompting them to this particular Action there was but little Room to doubt. . . .

On this Occasion every Breast was filled with Concern. Evil brought Home to us within our very Doors awakened the Attention of the most Unthinking. Every one that had any Relation, any Tie of Nature; every one that had a Life to lose were in the most sensible Manner shocked at such Danger daily hanging over their Heads. With Regret we bewailed our peculiar Case, that we could not enjoy the Benefits of Peace like the rest of Mankind and that our own Industry should be the Means of taking from us all the Sweets of Life and of rendering us liable to the Loss of our Lives and Fortunes. With Indignation we looked at St. Augustine (like another Sallee) that Den of Thieves and Ruffians! Receptacle of Debtors, Servants and Slaves! Bane of Industry and Society! And revolved in our Minds all the Injuries this Province had received from thence ever since its first Settlement, that they had from first to last, in Times of profoundest Peace, both publickly and privately, by themselves and Indians and Negroes, in every Shape molested us not without some Instances of uncommon Cruelty. . . .

❧ E S S A Y S

Early accounts portrayed Carolina as a lush environment capable of growing the products of all the richest regions of the world. In reality, the environment required adjustment on the part of immigrants. In the first essay H. Roy Merrens, a geographer at York University in Canada, and George D. Terry, a historian at the University of South Carolina, assess the dialogue between reality and perception in colonial South Carolina and consider the ways in which the latter lagged behind the lessons of experience in the popular consciousness. Jane Landers, a historian at the University of Florida and former director of the History Teaching Alliance, in the second essay presents a rounded picture of a free black community in Florida and contrasts Spanish and English policies. Her essay vividly reminds us of the Spanish presence in the colonial Southeast.

Georgia, founded as a buffer between Florida and South Carolina, was originally built on a philanthropic scheme in which deserving poor families would emigrate with the promise of fifty-acre freehold estates. The colony's planners forbade planters to sell their land without permission and prohibited slaves and rum. The colonists were to be citizen-soldiers spread over the country and ready to defend their own colony and their neighbors. This original plan was amended within a few years, and Georgia came under the sway of Carolina planters. In the final essay historian Alan Gallay of Western Washington University, through examination of the career of planter Jonathan Bryan, shows how immense plantations and great power were acquired in Georgia.

Dying in Paradise: Perception and Reality in Colonial South Carolina

H. ROY MERRENS AND GEORGE D. TERRY

. . . During its initial period of settlement, South Carolina's environment was perceived and portrayed as a terrestrial paradise. Soon, however, some residents began expressing concern over the debilitating effects of the tropical climate and the ravages of disease. Early death became widespread. Most white inhabitants were dead before their fortieth birthday, and malaria in particular took a heavy toll, either directly or indirectly, by lowering resistance to the inroads of other illnesses and infectious diseases. There is some evidence that suggests that the mortality rate in South Carolina was higher than that in any other British colony on the North American continent. Ironically, the initial perceptions settlers had about their environment and the causes of diseases, such as malaria, tended to discourage actions that probably would have reduced the death rate. The colonists' perceptions of their environment, and their behavior in response to those perceptions, rather than the environment per se, played a crucial role.

In 1670 the planting of a tiny settlement on a few acres on the western bank of the Ashley River laid the foundations for the colony that eventually came to be known as South Carolina. During the subsequent decade settlers began establishing plantations adjacent to the Ashley and Cooper rivers and to low-lying swamps near the coast. Part and parcel of the planting process was a major promotional campaign mounted by the proprietors of Carolina.

H. Roy Merrens and George D. Terry, "Dying in Paradise: Perception and Reality in Colonial South Carolina," *Journal of Southern History*, L (1986), 533–550. Copyright 1986 by the Southern Historical Association. Reprinted by permission of the Managing Editor; text abridged, footnotes deleted.

Their sustained and vigorous efforts to proclaim the virtues of the region in which the colony was being planted resulted in a spate of promotional literature. The proprietors of some other colonies had also turned to promotion and the production of promotional literature. What was distinctive about the South Carolina effort was the emphasis upon the physical environment.

The dominant theme conveyed by promotional tracts was the felicitous quality of South Carolina's physical environment. The scene was presented with varying degrees of subtlety and some of the representations of it were much more plausible than others. Common to all of them, however, was the motif of the colony as something akin to a terrestrial paradise. The climate was said to be delightful, the land inviting, the soil promising, and the native plants and animals singularly useful to man. Implicit in all accounts and explicit in many was a message that must have reassured most prospective settlers, whether they read the accounts for themselves or, more likely, learned about their contents only fragmentarily and indirectly: the colony was a salubrious place and possessed a potentially productive environment. A large audience of prospective immigrants was being told that if they came to South Carolina they at last could expect to live healthfully and to labor profitably.

That the environment was healthy was a refrain sounded from the outset. An account by William Hilton printed in 1664 was moderate in tone and even offered proofs of the claims made. Hilton wrote that "the Land we suppose is healthful; for the English that were cast away on that Coast in July last, were there most part of that time of year that is sickly in Virginia; and notwithstanding hard usage, and lying on the ground naked, yet had their perfect healths all the time." Hilton continued that "The Natives are very healthful; we saw many very Aged amongst them." A couple of years later Robert Horne adopted a different tack in making the same point. He stated that when "Air comes to be considered, which is not the least considerable to the well being of a Plantation, for without a wholsom Air all other considerations avail nothing; and this is it which makes this Place so desireable, being seated in the most temperate Clime. . . ." Horne also noted that "The Summer is not too hot, and the Winter is very short and moderate, best agreeing with English Constitutions." . . .

A second environmental asset that writers addressed themselves to was the potential for producing a variety of marketable crops, forest products, and livestock, which was their reason for assuring would-be settlers that their labors would lead to substantial and rapid profits. Samuel Wilson's 1682 pamphlet, for example, devoted several pages to an inventory of plant and animal products that could be raised in South Carolina. In summing up his account of the productive promise of the colony, Wilson drew the reader's attention to the following form of proof: "In short, This Country being of the same Clymate and Temperature of Aleppo, Smyrna, Antioch, Judea, and the Province of Nanking, the richest in China, will (I conceive) produce any thing which those Countrys do, were the Seeds brought into it." . . .

Only rarely do prospective settlers seem to have concerned themselves with ascertaining whether the legendary appeal of South Carolina's environment was substantiated by the fate of contemporary colonists, and the few who did attempt to make careful inquiries on this point were not typical of the average prospective settler. One French Huguenot emigrant in London was sufficiently skeptical of the promotion tracts that he attempted to make "careful inquiry in order to ascertain whether they told the truth." There are also at least two recorded instances of companies of would-be settlers pursuing this kind of inquiry. One group was the German Thuringia Company, whose list of 228 "Points of Inquiry Concerning Carolina" included the following question: "What is the Reason that Carolina is not yet fully improved in Building, whereas it is reported to be the most wholesome and the most healthful and fruitful part of all the American Colonies?" The other company was a group of New Englanders who gave equally specific instructions to a small band of adventurers who were to investigate conditions in South Carolina before the company emigrated thence. In their instructions to the advance party the New Englanders noted that they and "all men must be very full of humane distrust if we or they should not believe Carolina to be a rich and plentifull countrie by what we have heard of it; yet you being on this errant to satisfie your selves and us more fully in the matter. . . ." Attempts to launch this kind of pointed and thorough investigation of actual conditions in the colony were exceptional rather than typical. The analysis of such matters was beyond both the inclination and the means of most migrants.

The first settlers' impressions of their environment seem to have been entirely favorable, almost as unqualified and as enthusiastic as the claims made by the promotional writers. During the initial months the contrast between the protracted unpleasantness of their sea voyage and the delights of terra firma in spring must have been impressive, and the colonists' response to the qualities of the place was unreservedly positive. Governor William Sayle, writing to the Proprietors on behalf of the new Council, reported in glowing terms that "I have been in severall places, yet never was in a sweater clymate then this is. Wee have discovered abundance of good land as a man would desire to looke on, wee doe Judge and I doe believe there is good land enough for millions of people to live & worke on. There is nothing that wee plant but it thrives very well." The favorable initial impression was apparently almost unanimous. After John Locke had analyzed all of the reports in hand from leading figures in the colony, he grouped their remarks into a number of categories. Under the heading of "country" he collected germane comments from eight different sources, none of whom had anything but praise for the qualities and the potential of the place in which they were settling.

In subsequent decades the physical environment inevitably became less of a novelty and more an unremarkable fact of life than an object of wonder. Extant comments on it typically originated with visitors rather than with residents. As a result the record of how colonists regarded their environment during the century that followed the pioneers' first encounter with it is a meager one. Enough survives, however, to indicate that they were much less enamored of it than were the initial colonists and found some features of the physical setting in the coastal region to be disagreeable.

The heat of lowcountry summers was found to be excessive, counterbalancing the initial delight accorded the mild winters and the exotic subtropical fauna and flora. Eliza Lucas Pinckney, after noting that she found the winters "very fine and pleasant," felt obliged to add that the excessive heat experienced for four months of the year was "extremely disagreeable." A physician and natural historian, Alexander Garden, complained that "Our long & hot summers enervate & unbrace the whole System. . . ." He regularly used the alleged debilitating effects of the lowcountry summer to explain and excuse his waning attention to the study of natural history. Another physician, a resident of Charleston, compiled data indicating, among other things, that average summer temperatures in Charleston were 78°F and that during one particularly hot summer the temperature in the shade for 20 successive days varied between 90°F and 101°F. He noted also that south and southwest winds in summer brought "sultry and suffocating" conditions during which "an excessive Dejection of Spirits, and Debility of Body" were "universal Complaints."

Another problem associated with summertime conditions was the presence of mosquitoes. The low-lying marshes and swamps, along with great amounts of rainfall and high temperatures, provided the perfect breeding ground for malaria-carrying mosquitoes. According to one observer, the mosquitoes' "Venom . . . is as baleful as that of a Rattle Snake. . . ." Mosquitoes were obviously not exclusively a summertime phenomenon. They were more in evidence in some parts of the settled area than in others and their incidence as an affliction no doubt varied during the colonial period as surface drainage conditions were drastically altered and population origins and numbers changed. Notwithstanding the lack of evidence about these likely variations, however, mosquitoes were apparently more of a problem in the settled area of colonial South Carolina than elsewhere in the colonies. There was as yet no inkling of the relationship between mosquitoes and malaria, but they were so numerous and bothersome enough that by 1725 at least wealthier settlers resorted to the use of mosquito netting and "Pavilions Made of Catgut Gause" to escape from the venomous biting attacks.

Despite complaints about the high summer temperatures and the annoying mosquitoes, there seems to have been no thought that the colonists could anticipate anything less than normal health. By 1680, however, as new arrivals began to push their settlement up to the headwaters of the Ashley and Cooper rivers, inhabitants began to encounter health problems. According to Maurice Mathews, in that year the inhabitants were "generally verry healthful" but "some years about July and August wee have the fevar and ague among us, but it is not mortall." The same year a promotional writer advertising the charms of the colony felt obliged to admit that "In July and August they have sometimes Touches of Agues and Fevers. . . ." He assured his readers, however, that they were "not violent, of short continuance, and never Fatal." But the agues and fevers were violent and very often fatal. In some parts of the colony the mortality rate was so high that a number of parishes did not experience a natural increase in population until the American Revolution.

That many of these deaths resulted from malaria is illustrated by the large proportion that occurred between the months of August and November. In those months the numbers of malaria-related deaths reached the highest levels.

For example, in Christ Church Parish, which was situated on the Wando River, 43 percent of all deaths recorded in the Parish register between 1700 and 1750 were during this four-month period. In St. Andrews Parish, adjacent to Charleston, 44 percent of the deaths recorded in the period between 1700 and 1750 occurred in the same four-month period.

An indication of the heavy toll malaria took on the white population can be gained through the correspondence of the ministers of the Society for the Propagation of the Gospel who served in the lowcountry. The first minister for St. Johns Parish, Robert Maule, was stricken during late summer in 1709 "with a very severe fit of Sickness; being held for three Months together of a fever and Ague which at length concluded in a most Violent Belly Ach; so violent indeed that I veryly believed it wu'd have ended my days. . . ." Seven years later, he did die of a "Consumption and Lingering feaver." . . .

. . . [Malaria] is often fatal to women during their fertile years and particularly during pregnancy. Moreover, it is not only fatal in itself but also tends to lower resistance to other diseases. Because of this, infants and young children were also frequent victims. According to the Reverend William Tredwell Bull of St. Paul's Parish in 1716, during a particularly bad outbreak of malaria "not many Children [have] been born this year and most that were are already deceased."

Infant and childhood mortality was high in all the lowcountry parishes before the Revolution. In Christ Church Parish 86 percent of all those whose births and deaths are recorded in the parish register died before the age of twenty. Thirty-three percent of all females in this group had died before reaching their fifth birthday. Among the males for whom birth and death rates are recorded, 12 percent had died before their first birthday. Another 57 percent of the males died between the ages of one and five. Most of these infant and early childhood deaths occurred between the months of August and November. Ninety percent of all children in Christ Church who died between birth and their first birthday did so during this four-month period. Eighty-five percent of the females who died between the ages of one and five did so between August and November. Fifty percent of the males who died in this age group did so during this peak period. In all, 77 percent of the persons who died before reaching the age of twenty in this parish did so between the months of August and November.

In St. Johns, because of the lack of a parish register, a composite picture of the effect of malaria upon infant and childhood mortality in the parish cannot be obtained. Information has been accumulated, however, on a number of the families in the parish that allows personal insight into the ravages that malaria and related diseases had upon inhabitants under the age of twenty. The family of Henry Ravenel and Mary De St. Julien is a good example of high mortality among infants and children. The union in 1750 between Henry and Mary of Hanover Plantation ended with the death of Mary in 1779. During this twenty-nine-year period they had sixteen children. Although their first child, Henry, lived to be seventy-four, only five others lived to see their twenty-first birthday. Rene and Daniel both lived to be sixty while Paul died at age fifty-five. Although the Ravenels had seven daughters, not one lived to be twenty. Half of the sixteen children died by the age of five. Moreover, five of those dying before age twenty did so between the months of August and November. Thus, despite the fact that the Ravenels married early, he being twenty-one and she sixteen, and despite the union's length and fertility, only six children lived to adulthood. . . .

High mortality rates were not limited to infants and young children. Few persons lucky enough to survive their childhood could expect to live to be sixty or more. This situation was particularly true of the first and second generations of native-born residents. . . . During the second generation of births between 1721 and 1760, life expectancy increased only slightly for the thirty-five males who lived beyond twenty. . . .

During the last forty years of the eighteenth century, life expectancy for males born in St. Johns and reaching adulthood increased significantly. . . .

The mortality rate among females who lived beyond twenty was also high. As would be expected in a malarial environment, the rate was even higher among females than it was among males. This situation was particularly true during the childbearing years among the females born between 1680 and 1720. . . .

As with the males, the life expectancy of females increased significantly during the last forty years of the eighteenth century. Females born in that period and surviving to adulthood could expect a much longer life than those born before 1760. . . .

The major reason for this great improvement in life expectancy in both males and females was probably the change in the perception of the inhabitants as to what conditions were fostering malaria and other related diseases. In the period before 1760 the belief was widely held that the swampy areas were healthier than the area around Charleston and on the coast. As one visitor related, Charleston and the surrounding environs were unhealthy in the "middle of summer" because of the "dangerous contagious fevers which occasionally bring many people to the grave." This visitor went on to point out that this condition was due to the arrival of numerous ships from all parts of the world, transmitting a variety of diseases. . . .

Other planters lived in the lowcountry the year round for other reasons. According to one resident, planters built their homes on the "Edge of Swamps, in a damp moist Situation" because they wanted "to view from their Rooms, their Negroes at Work in the Rice Fields." Because most planters in the colony built their homes in this manner before 1760, the majority were within the flight range of disease-carrying mosquitoes and were much more exposed to the disease than were similar populations in other areas such as the Chesapeake. As a result, the malarial environment identified by Darrett and Anita Rutman and others as producing such high rates of mortality in certain parts of the Chesapeake was not nearly so severe as that present in the South Carolina lowcountry. Whereas in Virginia only those inhabitants living within the regions of the breeding swamps were in danger of contracting malaria, in St. Johns almost everyone in the parish was in reach of the disease.

During the middle of the eighteenth century South Carolinians' perception of the wholesome environment of the lowcountry swamps began to change.

People no longer preferred these areas on the score of health as a place of summer residence. Instead, residents began to view the lowcountry as fostering both mosquitoes and death. As one visitor perceived it, "The sudden changes in the air contribute much to the unhealthiness of this climate. So do the rice lands (on which stagnant water is necessary) the culture of indico, and the swamps." Edward Rutledge, writing to Arthur Middleton in August 1782, wrote that he and his family were unhappily staying "on the Banks of the Ashley," and already three members of his family were ill.

At the same time that the planters began seeing a connection between malaria and the low-lying swamps in their neighborhood, they began noticing also that health conditions were better in other areas of the colony. Charleston came to be regarded as a haven from the ravages of the sickly season. The city served as a retreat to many during the late summer and fall months. Joseph Manigault, writing to a member of his family in 1784, complained "how unfortunate it is that the vile fall-fevers should keep one pent up in Charleston the most agreeable season of the year." Whereas it was believed earlier that the air blowing in from the seas was unhealthy, by the end of the eighteenth century it was found that "a summer residence on the sea bays, connected with a moderate attention to regularity and exposure, secures the inhabitants from the autumnal fevers incident to the climate."

Other lowcountry residents saw the advantages of higher elevations further inland. . . . Thus, local summer resorts such as Eutawville, Cordesville, Pinopolis, and Summerville began to become popular during the late eighteenth century with planters wishing to remove their families from the reach of mosquitoes. . . . Yearly trips by some members of the upper class to resorts such as Newport in the northern colonies also reduced the number of malaria-related deaths among lowcountry families. Such trips, however, were possible only for the wealthiest inhabitants. Most planters in the lowcountry preferred to spend their summers at the local resorts where they could still keep in touch with the work done on their plantations and remain close to their families.

By the second half of the eighteenth century South Carolinians had thus begun to reappraise their environment, to identify important local and regional variations within it, and to find a way to diminish their exposure to malaria. Not surprisingly, there was no immediate recognition in Europe of the lessened threat to life in the colony. A proverb allegedly current in England was "They who want to die quickly, go to Carolina." And a German observer told his readers that "Carolina is in the spring a paradise, in the summer a hell, and in the autumn a hospital." Glorious images of South Carolina's environment as a paradise had been displaced by equally picturesque depictions of the place as a purgatory, and the new longevity went unheralded. . . .

. . . The unhealthiness in early South Carolina was man-induced and not environmentally determined. Nor is a hedging reference to environmental "influences" appropriate to explain it. Indeed, the unhealthiness was as much a product of man's goals and behavior as was the paradisiacal image of South Carolina produced by imaginative writers. The livability of the new environment was drastically altered when malaria was introduced to the colony by the first generation of settlers, and the perceptions and practices of succeeding generations led to the spread of the disease and aggravated its intensity. The point warrants emphasis because the physical environment in general and climatic conditions in particular have long been invoked to explain this or that facet of settlement and development, or nondevelopment, in the colonial and antebellum South. But neither malaria nor high mortality rates were caused by environmental conditions. And conversely, the diminished virulence of malaria and the declining mortality rates of the later eighteenth century cannot be attributed to any climatic changes (or to the discovery of some quick technological fix designed to subordinate the environment). What had changed were the settlers' perceptions of their environment and their behavior toward it.

A Free Black Community in Spanish Florida

JANE LANDERS

For too long, historians have paid little attention to Spain's lengthy tenure in the South. As a result, important spatial and temporal components of the American past have been overlooked. Recent historical and archaeological research on the free black town of Gracia Real de Santa Teresa de Mose, located in northeast Spanish Florida, suggests ways in which Spanish colonial records might illuminate these neglected aspects of the Southern past. Because of this black town's unusual origins and political and military significance, Spanish bureaucrats documented its history with much care.

Gracia Real de Santa Teresa de Mose, hereafter referred to as Mose, was born of the initiative and determination of blacks who, at great risk, manipulated the Anglo-Spanish contest for control of the Southeast to their advantage and thereby won their freedom. The settlement was composed of former slaves, many of West African origin, who had escaped from British plantations and received religious sanctuary in Spanish Florida. Although relatively few in number (the community maintained a fairly stable size of about 100 people during the quarter-century between 1738 and 1763, while St. Augustine's population grew from approximately 1,500 people in the 1730s to approximately 3,000 by 1763), these freedmen and women were of great contemporary significance. By their "theft of self," they were a financial loss to their former owners, often a serious one. Moreover, their flight was a political action, sometimes effected through violence, that offered an example to other bondsmen and challenged the precarious political and social order of the British colonies. The runaways were also important to the Spanish colony for the valuable knowledge and skills they brought with them and for the labor and military services they performed. These free blacks are also historiographically significant; an exploration of their lives sheds light on questions long debated by scholars, such as the relative severity of slave systems, the varieties of

Jane Landers, "Gracia Real de Santa Teresa de Mose: A Free Black Town in Spanish Colonial Florida," *American Historical Review*, 95 (1990), 9–30, abridged. Reprinted by permission of the author and The American Historical Review.

slave experiences, slave resistance, the formation of a Creole culture, the nature of black family structures, the impact of Christianity and religious syncretism on African-American societies, and African-American influences in the "New World."

Although a number of historians have alluded to the lure of Spanish Florida for runaway slaves from the British colonies of South Carolina and Georgia, few have examined what became of the fugitives in their new lives or the implications of their presence in the Spanish province. The Spanish policy regarding fugitive slaves in Florida developed in an ad hoc fashion and changed over time to suit the shifting military, economic, and diplomatic interests of the colony as well as the metropolis. Although the Spanish crown preferred to emphasize religious and humane considerations for freeing slaves of the British, the political and military motives were equally, if not more, important. In harboring the runaways and eventually settling them in their own town, Spanish governors were following Caribbean precedents and helping the crown to populate and hold territory threatened by foreign encroachment. The ex-slaves were also served by this policy. It offered them a refuge within which they could maintain family ties. In the highly politicized context of Spanish Florida, they struggled to maximize their leverage with the Spanish community and improve the conditions of their freedom. They made creative use of Spanish institutions to support their corporate identity and concomitant privileges. They adapted to Spanish values where it served them to do so and thereby gained autonomy. They also reinforced ties within their original community through intermarriage and use of the Spanish mechanism of godparenthood (*compadrazgo*). Finally, they formed intricate new kin and friendship networks with slaves, free blacks, Indians, "new" Africans, and whites in nearby St. Augustine that served to stabilize their population and strengthen their connections to that Hispanic community.

That runaways became free in Spanish Florida was not in itself unusual. Frank Tannenbaum's early comparative work shows that freedom had been a possibility for slaves in the Spanish world since the thirteenth century. Spanish law granted slaves a moral and juridical personality, as well as certain rights and protections not found in other slave systems. Among the most important were the right to own property, which in the Caribbean evolved into the right of self-purchase, the right to personal security, prohibitions against separating family members, and access to the courts. Moreover, slaves were incorporated into the Spanish church and received its sacraments, including marriage. Slaves in the Hispanic colonies were subject to codes based on this earlier body of law. Eugene Genovese and others have persuasively argued that the ideals expressed in these slave codes should not be accepted as social realities, and it seems obvious that colonials observed these laws in their own fashion—some in the spirit in which they were written and others not at all. Nevertheless, the acknowledgement of a slave's humanity and rights, and the lenient attitude toward manumission embodied in Spanish law and social practices, made it possible for a significant free black class to exist in the Spanish world.

Although the Spanish legal system permitted freedom, the crown assumed that its beneficiaries would live among the Spaniards, under the supervision of white townspeople (*vecinos*). While the crown detailed its instructions regarding the physical layout, location, and function of white and Indian towns, it made no formal provisions for free black towns. But Spanish colonizers throughout the Americas were guided by an urban model. They depicted theirs as a civilizing mission and sought to create public order and righteous living by creating towns. . . . Royal legislation reflected a continuing interest in reforming and settling so-called vagabonds of all races within the empire. The primary focus of reduction efforts was the Indians, but, as the black and mixed populations grew, so too did Spanish concerns about how these elements would be assimilated into "civilized" society. The "two republics" of Spaniards and Indians gave way to a society of castes, which increasingly viewed the unforeseen and unregulated groups with hostility. Spanish bureaucrats attempted to count these people and to limit their physical mobility through increasingly restrictive racial legislation. Officials prohibited blacks from living unsupervised or, worse, among the Indians. Curfews and pass systems developed, as did proposals to force unemployed blacks into fixed labor situations. The crown also recognized with alarm the increased incidence of *cimmaronage,* slaves fleeing Spanish control. Communities of runaway blacks, mulattos, Indians, and their offspring were common to all slaveholding societies, but they challenged the Spanish concept of civilized living, as well as the hierarchical racial and social order the Spaniards were trying to impose. Despite repeated military efforts, the Spaniards were no more successful than other European powers at eradicating such settlements.

Paradoxically, it was in this context of increasing racial animosity that Spanish officials legitimized free black towns. . . . Faced with insurmountable problems and lacking the resources to "correct" them, the Spanish bureaucracy proved flexible and adaptable. . . . Mose was established as a buffer against foreign encroachment. . . .

Florida held great strategic significance for the Spanish: initially, for its location guarding the route of the treasure fleets, later, to safeguard the mines of Mexico from the French and British. The colony was a critical component in Spain's Caribbean defense, and, when British colonists established Charles Town in 1670, it represented a serious challenge to Spanish sovereignty. No major response by the weakened Spanish empire was feasible, but, when the British incited their Indian allies to attack Spanish Indian missions along the Atlantic coast, the Spaniards initiated a campaign of harassment against the new British colony. In 1686, a Spanish raiding party including a force of fifty-three Indians and blacks attacked Port Royal and Edisto. From the plantation of Governor Joseph Morton, they carried away "money and plate and thirteen slaves to the value of [£]1500." In subsequent negotiations, the new governor of Carolina, James Colleton, demanded the return of the stolen slaves as well as those "who run dayly into your towns," but the Spaniards refused. These contacts may have suggested the possibility of a refuge among the enemy and directed slaves to St. Augustine, for, the following year, the first recorded fugitive slaves from Carolina arrived there. Governor Diego de

Quiroga dutifully reported to Spain that eight men, two women, and a three-year-old nursing child had escaped to his province in a boat. According to the governor, they requested baptism into the "True Faith," and on that basis he refused to return them to the British delegation that came to St. Augustine to reclaim them. The Carolinians claimed that one of Samuel de Bordieu's runaways, Mingo, who escaped with his wife and daughter (the nursing child), had committed murder in the process. Governor Quiroga promised to make monetary restitution for the slaves he retained and to prosecute Mingo, should the charges be proven. Quiroga housed these first runaways in the homes of Spanish townspeople and saw to it that they were instructed in Catholic doctrine, baptized and married in the church. He put the men to work as ironsmiths and laborers on the new stone fort, the Castillo de San Marcos, and employed the women in his own household. All were reportedly paid wages: the men earned a peso a day, the wage paid to male Indian laborers, and the women half as much. . . .

. . . [A]s fugitives continued to filter into the province, the governors and treasury officials repeatedly solicited the king's guidance. Eventually, the Council of the Indies reviewed the matter and recommended approving the sanctuary policy shaped by the governors. On November 7, 1693, Charles II issued the first official position on the runaways, "giving liberty to all . . . the men as well as the women . . . so that by their example and by my liberality others will do the same."

The provocation inherent in this order increasingly threatened the white Carolinians. At least four other groups of runaways reached St. Augustine in the following decade, and, despite an early ambiguity about their legal status, the refugees were returned to their British masters only in one known example. Carolina's changing racial balance further intensified the planters' concerns. By 1708, blacks outnumbered whites in the colony, and slave revolts erupted in 1711 and 1714. The following year, when many slaves joined the Yamassee Indian war against the British, they almost succeeded in exterminating the badly outnumbered whites. Indians loyal to the British helped defeat the Yamassee, who with their black allies headed for St. Augustine. Although the Carolina Assembly passed harsh legislation designed to prevent further insurrections and control the slaves, these actions and subsequent negotiations with St. Augustine failed to deter the escapes or effect the reciprocal return of slaves. British planters claimed that the Spanish policy, by drawing away their slaves, would ruin their plantation economy. Arthur Middleton, Carolina's acting governor, complained to London that the Spaniards not only harbored their runaways but sent them back in the company of Indians to plunder British plantations. The Carolinians set up patrol systems and placed scout boats on water routes to St. Augustine, but slaves still made good their escapes on stolen horses and in canoes and piraguas.

In 1724, ten more runaway slaves reached St. Augustine, assisted by English-speaking Yamassee Indians. According to their statements, they were aware that the Spanish king had offered freedom to those seeking baptism and conversion. The royal edict of 1693 was still in force, and Governor Antonio de Benavides initially seems to have honored it. In 1729, however,

Benavides sold these newcomers at public auction to reimburse their owners, alleging that he feared the British might act on their threats to recover their losses by force....

Several of the reenslaved men were veterans of the Yamassee war in Carolina, and one of these, Francisco Menéndez, was appointed by Governor Benavides to command a slave militia in 1726. This black militia helped defend St. Augustine against the British invasion led by Colonel John Palmer in 1728, but, despite their loyal service, the Carolina refugees still remained enslaved....

... Led by Captain Menéndez of the slave militia, the blacks persisted in attempts to secure complete freedom. They presented petitions to the governor and to the auxiliary bishop of Cuba, who toured the province in 1735, but to no avail. When Manuel de Montiano became governor in 1737, their fortunes changed.... On March 15, 1738, he granted unconditional freedom to the petitioners. Montiano also wrote the governor and captain general of Cuba, attempting to retrieve eight Carolinians who had been taken to Havana during the Benavides regime. At least one, Antonio Caravallo, was returned to St. Augustine, against all odds.

Governor Montiano established the freedmen in a new town, about two miles north of St. Augustine, which he called Gracia Real de Santa Teresa de Mose.* The freedmen built the settlement, a walled fort and shelters described by the Spaniards as resembling thatched Indian huts. Little more is known about it from Spanish sources, but later British reports add that the fort was constructed of stone, "four square with a flanker at each corner, banked with earth, having a ditch without on all sides lined round with prickly royal and had a well and house within, and a look-out." They also confirm Spanish reports that the freedmen planted fields nearby. The town site was said to be surrounded by fertile lands and nearby woods that would yield building materials. A river of salt water "running through it" contained an abundance of shellfish and all types of fish. Montiano hoped the people of Mose could cultivate the land to grow food for St. Augustine, but, until crops could be harvested, he provided the people with corn, biscuits, and beef from government stores.

Mose was located at the head of Mose Creek, a tributary of the North River with access to St. Augustine, and lay directly north of St. Augustine, near trails north to San Nicholas and west to Apalache. For all these reasons, it was strategically significant. Governor Montiano surely considered the benefits of a northern outpost against anticipated British attacks. And who better to serve as an advanced warning system than grateful ex-slaves carrying Spanish arms? The freedmen understood their expected role, for, in a declaration to the king, they vowed to be "the most cruel enemies of the English" and

---

*The name is a composite of an existing Indian place name, Mose, the phrase that indicated that the new town was established by the king, Gracia Real, and the name of the town's patron saint, Teresa of Avilés, who was the patron saint of Spain.

to risk their lives and spill their "last drop of blood in defense of the Great Crown of Spain and the Holy Faith." If the new homesteaders were diplomats, they were also pragmatists, and their own interests were clearly served by fighting those who would seek to return them to chattel slavery. Mose also served a vital objective of Spanish imperial policy, and, once Governor Montiano justified its establishment, the Council of the Indies and the king supported his actions.

Since Spanish town settlement implied the extension of *justicia,* the governor assigned a white military officer and royal official to supervise the establishment of Mose. Mose was considered a village of new converts comparable to those of the Christian Indians, so Montiano also posted a student priest at the settlement to instruct the inhabitants in doctrine and "good customs." Although the Franciscan lived at Mose, there is no evidence that the white officer did. It seems rather that Captain Menéndez was responsible for governing the settlement, for, in one document, Governor Montiano referred to the others as the "subjects" of Menéndez. The Spaniards regarded Menéndez as a sort of natural lord, and, like Indian caciques, he probably exercised considerable autonomy over his village. Spanish titles and support may have also reinforced Menéndez's status and authority. Whatever the nature of his authority, Menéndez commanded the Mose militia for over forty years. . . .

As new fugitives arrived, the governor placed these in Menéndez's charge as well. A group of twenty-three men, women, and children arrived from Port Royal on November 21, 1738, and were sent to join the others at the new town. Among the newcomers were the runaway slaves of Captain Caleb Davis of Port Royal. Davis was an English merchant who had been supplying St. Augustine for many years, and it is possible that some of the runaways had even traveled to St. Augustine in the course of Davis's business. Davis went to the Spanish city in December 1738 and spotted his former slaves, whom he reported laughed at his fruitless efforts to recover them. The frustrated Davis eventually submitted a claim against the Spanish. . . . There is no evidence Davis ever recouped his losses.

In March 1739, envoys from Carolina arrived in St. Augustine to press for the return of their runaway slaves. Governor Montiano treated them with hospitality but referred to the royal edict of 1733, which required that he grant religious sanctuary. . . . The following month, a group of Angola slaves revolted near Stono, South Carolina, and killed more than twenty whites before heading for St. Augustine. They were apprehended before reaching their objective, and retribution was swift and bloody. But officials of South Carolina and Georgia blamed the sanctuary available in nearby St. Augustine for the rebellion, and relations between the colonies reached a breaking point. With the outbreak of the War of Jenkins' Ear, international and local grievances merged. In January 1740, Governor James Oglethorpe of Georgia raided Florida and captured Forts Pupo and Picolata on the St. John's River west of St. Augustine. These initial victories enabled Oglethorpe to mount a major expeditionary force, including Georgia and South Carolina regiments, a vast Indian army, and seven warships for a major offensive against the Spaniards.

The free black militia of Mose worked alongside the other citizenry to fortify provincial defenses. They also provided the Spaniards with critical intelligence reports. In May, one of Oglethorpe's lieutenants happened across five houses occupied by the freedmen and was able to capture two of them. Unable to protect the residents of Mose, Governor Montiano was forced to evacuate "all the Negroes who composed that town" to the safety of St. Augustine. Thereafter, the Mose militia continued to conduct dangerous sorties against the enemy and assisted in the surprise attack and recapture of their town in June. The success at Mose was one of the few enjoyed by the Spaniards. It is generally acknowledged to have demoralized the combined British forces and to have been a significant factor in Oglethorpe's withdrawal. . . .

. . . Governor Montiano commended all his troops to the king but made the rather unusual gesture of writing a special recommendation for Francisco Menéndez. Montiano extolled the exactitude with which Menéndez had carried out royal service and the valor he had displayed in the battle at Mose. He added that, on another occasion, Menéndez and his men had fired on the enemy until they withdrew from the castle walls and that Menéndez had displayed great zeal during the dangerous reconnaissance missions he undertook against the British and their Indians. Moreover, he acknowledged that Menéndez had "distinguished himself in the establishment, and cultivation of Mose, to improve that settlement, doing all he could so that the rest of his subjects, following his example, would apply themselves to work and learn good customs." Shortly thereafter, Menéndez twice petitioned for remuneration from his king, signing his petitions with a flourish. . . .

. . . [T]he runaways from Carolina had been successful in their most important appeal to Spanish justice—their quest for liberty. Over the many years, they persevered, and their leaders learned to use Spanish legal channels and social systems to advantage. They accurately assessed Spain's intensifying competition with England and exploited the political leverage it offered them. Once free, they understood and adapted Spanish expectations of their new status. They vowed fealty and armed service, establishing themselves as vassals of the king and deserving of royal protection. Governor Montiano commended their bravery in battle and their industry as they worked to establish and cultivate Mose. They were clearly not the lazy vagabonds feared by Spanish administrators, and the adaptive behavior of Menéndez and his "subjects" gained them at least a limited autonomy. . . .

Corsairing was practiced by both the British and the Spanish during the 1740s and 1750s, and St. Augustine became a convenient base of operations for privateers commissioned by Spain. The capture and sale of prizes provided badly needed species and supplies for war-torn Florida, which had not received government subsidies in 1739, 1740, 1741, and 1745 and which struggled under the additional burden of maintaining the large number of Cuban reinforcements that had arrived in 1740. Corsairing ships were manned by volunteers, some of whom were drawn from the free black community, for, as Governor García noted, "without those of 'broken' color, blacks, and Indians, which abound in our towns in America, I do not know if we could arm a single corsair solely with Spaniards." Unfortunately, when these men were captured, the British presupposed them by their color to be slaves and sold them for profit.

When the British ship *Revenge* captured a Spanish prize in July 1741, found aboard was a black named "Signior Capitano Francisco," who was "Capt. of a Comp'y of Indians, Mollattos, and Negroes that was att the Retaking of the Fort [Mose] att St. Augus'ne formerly taken Under the Command of that worthless G——— O———pe who by his treachory suffered so many brave fellows to be mangled by those barbarians." His captors tied Francisco Menéndez to a gun and ordered the ship's doctor to pretend to castrate him (as Englishmen at Mose had been castrated), but while Menéndez "frankly owned" that he was Captain of the company that retook Mose, he denied ordering any atrocities, which he said the Florida Indians had committed. Menéndez stated that he had taken the commission as privateer in hopes of getting to Havana, and from there to Spain, to collect a reward for his bravery. Several other mulattoes on board were also interrogated and substantiated Menéndez's account, as did several of the whites, but "to make Sure and to make him remember that he bore such a Commission," the British gave him 200 lashes and then "pickled him and left him to the Doctor to take Care of his Sore A—se." The following month, the *Revenge* landed at New Providence, in the Bahamas, and her commander, Benjamin Norton, who was due the largest share of the prize, vehemently argued before the Admiralty Court that the blacks should be condemned as slaves. "Does not their Complexion and features tell all the world that they are of the blood of Negroes and have suckt Slavery and Cruelty from their Infancy?" He went on to describe Menéndez as "this Francisco that Cursed Seed of Cain, Curst from the foundation of the world, who has the Impudence to Come into this Court and plead that he is free. Slavery is too Good for such a Savage, nay all the Cruelty invented by man . . . the torments of the World to Come will not suffice." No record of Francisco's testimony appears in this account, but the Court ordered him sold as a slave, "according to the Laws of the plantation." However, as we have seen, Menéndez was a man of unusual abilities. Whether he successfully appealed for his freedom in British courts as he had in the Spanish, was ransomed back by the Spanish in Florida, or escaped is unknown, but, by at least 1752, he was once again in command at Mose. This incident illustrates the extreme racial hatred some British felt for Spain's black allies, as well as the grave dangers the freedmen faced in taking up Spanish arms. Other blacks captured as privateers in the same period were never returned.

Although unsuccessful, Governor Oglethorpe's invasion in 1740 had wreaked havoc in Spanish Florida. Mose and the other outlying forts had been destroyed, along with many of the crops and animals on which the community subsisted. For the next twelve years, the townspeople of Mose lived among the Spanish in St. Augustine. This interlude was critical to the integration of the Carolina group into the larger and more diverse society in the city. Wage lists in treasury accounts and military reports from this period show that they performed a variety of valuable functions for the community. Free blacks labored on government projects, were sailors and privateers, tracked escaped prisoners, and helped forage food for the city. In the spring, they rounded up wild cattle for slaughter and wild horses for cavalry mounts. They probably led lives much like those of free blacks in other Spanish colonial ports and may have engaged in craft production, artisanry, and the provision of services. Although certain racial restrictions existed, they were rarely enforced in a small frontier settlement such as St. Augustine, where more relaxed personal relations were the norm. Everyone knew everyone else, and this familiarity could be a source of assistance and protection for the free blacks of Mose, who had acquired at least a measure of acceptability.

Parish registers reflect the great ethnic and racial diversity in Spanish Florida in these years. Because there were always fewer female runaways, the males of that group were forced to look to the local possibilities for marriage partners—either Indian women from the two outlying villages of Nuestra Señora de la Leche and Nuestra Señora de Tholomato, or free and slave women from St. Augustine. Interracial relationships were common, and families were restructured frequently when death struck and widowed men and women remarried. The core group of Carolina fugitives formed intricate ties among themselves for at least two generations. They married from within their group and served as witnesses at each other's weddings and as godparents for each other's children, sometimes many times over. They also entered into the same relationships with Indians, free blacks, and slaves from other locations. Some of these slaves eventually became free, which might suggest mutual assistance efforts by the black community. The people of Mose also formed ties of reciprocal obligation with important members of both the white and black communities through the mechanism of ritual brotherhood (*compadrazgo*). A few examples should serve to illustrate the complex nature of these frontier relationships.

Francisco Garzía and his wife, Ana, fled together from Carolina and were among the original group freed by Governor Montiano. Francisco was black, and Ana, Indian. As slaves in St. Augustine, they had belonged to the royal treasurer, Don Salvador Garzía. Garzía observed the church requirement to have his slaves baptized and properly married, for the couple's children are listed as legitimate. Francisco and Ana's daughter, Francisca Xaviera, was born and baptized in St. Augustine in 1736, before her parents were freed by the governor. Her godfather was a free mulatto, Francisco Rexidor. This man also served as godfather for Francisco and Ana's son, Calisto, born free two years later. Garzía died sometime before 1759, for in that year his widow, Ana, married a black slave named Diego. Calisto disappeared from the record and presumably died, while Francisca Xaviera married Francisco Díaz, a free black from Carolina. Their two children, Miguel Francisco and María, were born at Mose, and Francisco Díaz served in the Mose militia.

Juan Jacinto Rodríguez and his wife, Ana María Menéndez, were also among the first Carolina homesteaders at Mose. Shortly after the town was founded, their son Juan married Cecilia, a Mandingo from Carolina who was the slave of Juan's former owner, cavalry Captain Don Pedro Lamberto

Horruytiner. Cecilia's sister-in-law, María Francisca, had served as godmother at Cecilia's baptism two years earlier. María Francisca married Marcos de Torres, a free and legitimate black from Cartagena, Colombia, during the time the Mose homesteaders lived in St. Augustine. Marcos de Torres and María Francisca had three children born while they lived in town, and María Francisca's brother, Juan, and his wife, Cecilia, served as the children's godparents. After Marcos de Torres died, María Francisca and her three orphaned children lived with her parents at Mose. In 1760, the widowed María Francisca married the widower, Thomas Chrisostomo.

Thomas and his first wife were Congo slaves. Thomas belonged to Don Francisco Chrisostomo, and his wife, Ana María Ronquillo, to Juan Nicolás Ronquillo. The couple married in St. Augustine in 1745. Pedro Graxales, a Congo slave and his legitimate wife, María de la Concepción Hita, a Caravalí slave, were the godparents at the wedding. By 1759, Thomas was a free widower living alone at Mose. The next year, he and María Francisca were wed. By that time, Thomas's godfather, Pedro Graxales, was also living at Mose as a free man, but Pedro's wife and at least four children remained slaves in St. Augustine. . . .

Despite the relationships that developed between people of St. Augustine and the Mose settlers, there were objections to their presence in the Spanish city. Some complaints may have stemmed from racial prejudice or ethnocentrism. To some of the poorer Spanish, the free blacks represented competition in a ravaged economy. Indians allied to the British remained hostile to the Spaniards and raided the countryside with regularity. Plantations were neither safe nor productive. Havana could not provide its dependency with sufficient goods, and the few food shipments that reached St. Augustine were usually ruined. British goods were cheaper and better, and the governor was forced to depend on enemy suppliers for his needs. War and corsair raids on supplies shipped from Havana further strained the colony's ability to sustain its urban population. As new runaways continued to arrive, they only exacerbated the problem. Finally, Melchor de Navarrete, who succeeded Montiano in 1749, decided to reestablish Mose. . . .

. . . The . . . freedmen built new structures at Mose, including a church and a house for the Franciscan priest within the enclosed fort, as well as twenty-two shelters outside the fort for their own households. A diagram of the new fort, which had one side open on Mose Creek, shows the interior buildings described by Father Juan Joseph de Solana but not the houses of the villagers. The only known census of Mose, from 1759, recorded twenty-two households with a population of sixty-seven individuals. Mose had almost twice as many male as female occupants, and almost a quarter of its population consisted of children under the age of fifteen. . . . Father Solana reported that some members of the Mose community were permitted to live in St. Augustine even though they continued to serve in the Mose militia. Several of those men appear on 1763 evacuation lists for Mose.

The people of Mose were remarkably adaptable. They spoke several European and Indian languages, in addition to their own, and were exposed to a variety of subsistence techniques, craft and artistic traditions, labor patterns, and food ways. We know that the freedmen and women of Mose adopted certain elements of Spanish culture. For example, since their sanctuary was based on religious conversion, it was incumbent on them to exhibit their Catholicism. Their baptisms, marriages, and deaths were faithfully recorded in parish registers. But studies of other Hispanic colonies show that religious syncretism was widespread and tolerated by the church. Following centuries-old patterns set in Spain, Cuba's blacks organized religious brotherhoods by nations. They celebrated Catholic feast days dressed in traditional African costumes and with African music and instruments. Because St. Augustine had such intimate contact with Cuba and blacks circulated between the two locations, it would not be surprising to find that Africans in Florida also observed some of their former religious practices.

Kathleen Deagan, of the Florida Museum of Natural History, currently directs an interdisciplinary team investigating Mose. In addition to locating and excavating the site, this group is exploring the process of cultural adaptation at Mose to determine what mixture of customs and material culture its residents adopted and what in their own traditions might have influenced Spanish culture. One suggestive find is a hand-made pewter medal that depicts St. Christopher on one side and a pattern resembling a Kongo star on the other. Other recovered artifacts include military objects such as gunflints, a striker, and musket balls; and domestic articles such as metal buckles, a thimble, and pins, clay pipe bowls—of both local and European design—metal buttons, bone buttons—including one still in the process of manufacture—amber beads (perhaps from a rosary); and a variety of glass bottles and ceramic wares. Many of the latter are of English types, verifying documentary evidence of illicit, but necessary, trade with the enemy. . . .

Although noted for its poverty and the misery of its people, Mose survived as a free town and military outpost for St. Augustine until 1763, when, through the fortunes of war, Spain lost the province to the British. The Spanish evacuated St. Augustine and its dependent black and Indian towns, and the occupants were resettled in Cuba. The people of Mose left behind their meager homes and belongings and followed their hosts into exile to become homesteaders in Matanzas, Cuba—consigned once more to a rough frontier. The crown granted them new lands, a few tools, and a minimal subsidy, as well as an African slave to each of the leaders of the community; however, Spanish support was never sufficient, and the people from Mose suffered terrible privations at Matanzas. Some of them, including Francisco Menéndez, eventually relocated in Havana, which offered at least the possibility of a better life, and this last diaspora scattered the black community of Mose.

Located on the periphery of St. Augustine, between the Spanish settlement and its aggressive neighbors, Mose's interstitial location paralleled the social position of its inhabitants—people who straddled cultures, pursued their own advantage, and in the process helped shape the colonial history of the Caribbean as well as an African-American culture. In 1784, Spain recovered Florida, and many Floridanos, or first-period colonists, returned from Cuba. It is possible that among these were some of the residents of Mose. During its second regime, however, the weakened Spanish government made no effort to reestablish either Indian missions or the free black town of Mose. Free blacks took pivotal roles on interethnic frontiers of Spanish America such as Florida, serving as interpreters, craftsmen, traders, scouts, cowboys, pilots, and militiamen. The towns they established made important contributions to Spanish settlement. They populated areas the Spaniards found too difficult or unpleasant, thereby extending or maintaining Spanish dominion. They buffered Spanish towns from the attacks of their enemies and provided them with effective military reserves.

Although there were other towns like Mose in Latin America, it was the only example of a free black town in the colonial South. It provides an important, and heretofore unstudied, variant in the experience of African-born peoples in what was to become the United States. Mose's inhabitants were able to parlay their initiative, determination, and military and economic skills into free status, an autonomy at least equivalent to that of Spain's Indian allies in Florida, and a town of their own. These gains were partially offset by the constant danger and deprivation to which the townspeople of Mose were subjected, but they remained in Mose, perhaps believing it their best possible option. Despite the adversities of slavery, flight, wars, and repeated displacements, the freedmen and women of Mose managed to maintain intricate family relationships over time and shape a viable community under extremely difficult conditions. They became an example and possibly a source of assistance to unfree blacks from neighboring British colonies, as well as those within Spanish Florida. The Spanish subsequently extended the religious sanctuary policy confirmed at Mose to other areas of the Caribbean and applied it to the disadvantage of Dutch and French slaveholders, as well as the British. The lives and efforts of the people of Mose thus took on international significance. Moreover, their accomplishments outlived them. The second Spanish government recognized religious sanctuary from 1784 until it bowed to the pressures of the new U.S. government and its persuasive secretary of state, Thomas Jefferson, and abrogated the policy in 1790. Before that escape hatch closed, several hundred slaves belonging to British Loyalists followed the example of the people of Mose to achieve emancipation in Florida. Thus the determined fugitives who struggled so hard to win their own freedom inadvertently furthered the cause of freedom for others whom they never knew.

Jonathan Bryan's Plantation Empire in Georgia

ALAN GALLAY

From 1736 until his death in 1788 Jonathan Bryan acquired lands by grant and purchase in Georgia and South Carolina in excess of 32,000 acres, on which he employed, at one time or another, over 250 slaves. These

Alan Gallay, "Jonathan Bryan's Plantation Empire: Land Politics and the Formation of a Ruling Class in Colonial Georgia," *William and Mary Quarterly,* 3rd ser. XLV (1988), 253–279. Reprinted with permission of Alan Gallay.

possessions placed him at the very top of the small group of men who ruled Georgia during the quarter century before the American Revolution. Bryan became one of the colony's richest and most powerful men because he understood every aspect of landownership, from accumulation to development and sale. Aggressive and astute, he built an estate that can truly be termed a plantation empire. This essay shows how Bryan used political influence and economic calculation to create that empire. His example illustrates the process by which the ruling class of colonial Georgia was formed.

Bryan was born in the vicinity of Port Royal, South Carolina, in 1708. The few whites who inhabited this frontier region engaged in trade with the neighboring Yamassee. On several occasions Bryan's father, Joseph, a trader, was rebuked by the South Carolina government for abusing the Indians and illegally settling on their land, which the colony's governor described as "the best part of this province." In 1715 Port Royal traders provoked the Yamassee to a war that left the region virtually stripped of people of all races for fifteen years. Only a few traders and their families, including the Bryans, remained on the southern frontier, awaiting the day when the government would permit them to take possession of the Yamassees' land. In the meantime, they engaged in a variety of economic enterprises: farming, soldiering, and filling government contracts. In the late 1720s Jonathan Bryan reached adulthood and found employment as a scout. This gave him opportunities to explore the territory between South Carolina and Spanish Florida. From this experience he gained direct knowledge of the topography and ecology of the southeast, which he later applied in the management of his vast estate.

Bryan's elder brother Hugh played an active role in preparing for white settlement the so-called "Indian Land," in what became first St. Helena's and later Prince William's Parish. After this land was opened to public sale in 1731, Hugh surveyed approximately half of the tracts. His expertise, coupled with the family's political connections, provided the Bryan clan with choice parcels along the Pocotaligo River and Stoney Creek. As did many of their neighbors, the Bryans thus became wealthy in less than a decade. Using slave labor, they transformed the region from a frontier to a commercial economy. The multitalented Hugh accumulated great riches by investing in numerous capitalistic enterprises: rice production, cattle ranching, manufacture of shingles for the West Indian market, shipping, buying and selling of land, and fulfillment of government contracts for defense and internal improvements. Jonathan followed in his brother's footsteps. Hugh sold him a prime piece of land in 1736, and Jonathan began building his plantation estate. Like Hugh, Jonathan diversified investments and cultivated government contacts. Within five years, he became one of St. Helena's most prominent citizens.

The Bryans' elevated social status was reflected in their selection to ecclesiastical and political offices. Joseph Bryan was elected to the South Carolina House of Commons in 1728, and Hugh served from 1733 to 1736; Jonathan became church warden for St. Helena's Parish in 1738, while Hugh served as vestryman from 1738 to 1740. In addition, the brothers received appointments to the local militia, Hugh as major and Jonathan as lieutenant. Related by marriage to many of the leading families of their parish, the Bryans enjoyed a secure position among the social, economic, and political elite of southern South Carolina.

Concern for their region's defense led the Bryans to take an active interest in the establishment of Georgia. Quite possibly, Jonathan or his elder brother Joseph led James Oglethorpe to the site that was chosen for Savannah. All three Bryan brothers devoted time and effort to helping the new colony. They provided advice, laborers, goods, arms, and soldiers—sometimes for profit and sometimes gratis—over a twenty-year period. Although the Bryans established strong ties to the new colony, they remained in South Carolina through the 1730s and 1740s. They had no economic motive for moving south of the Savannah River, for the Georgia Trustees, intending to create a society of small landowners, sought to prevent the rise of a wealthy aristocratic class by prohibiting slavery and limiting landownership. These measures effectively deterred the Bryans and other South Carolina slaveholders from migrating to Georgia.

In the mid-1740s the prosperity of the Bryans and their neighbors began to wane. Economic depression struck South Carolina and proved especially severe in the southern parishes. . . .

. . . French privateering, rising freight and insurance rates, and declining rice prices forced many planters to sell or mortgage their lands and to contract heavy debts. . . .

Southern parish representatives submitted petitions to the assembly from their constituents begging for debtor relief. The petitioners claimed that currency was short in South Carolina "in Proportion to the Trade and Number of Inhabitants" and that "many industrious and well disposed Persons and their Families are and must be reduced to extream Poverty and Want." . . . Alienated by the government's failure to provide substantial aid, a number of planters moved their operations to Georgia when the Trustees legalized slavery in 1750. One of them was Jonathan Bryan.

The promise of free land in Georgia attracted slaveowners from South Carolina and the West Indies, who immigrated with their laborers. The influx of slaves, the lifting of restrictions on land tenure and accumulation, and the privatization of public lands resulted in a new class system in Georgia. The smallholders' utopia was replaced by a slave society modeled in important ways upon that of South Carolina. Free white men were entitled to parcels from the public domain, but their tracts were distant from market or unsuitable for cash crops. These men usually became subsistence farmers or laborers. A minority of Georgians had both capital and land that could be used to produce modest surpluses. Their standard of living placed them above the colony's majority but far below the much smaller group of men who possessed the very best land and the largest amounts of capital.

The great planters towered above the rest of society not only by the size of their estates but also by their prominence in politics. Wealthy slaveholders filled almost all official positions. In 1754, after acquiring the colony from the Trustees, the king selected from the ranks of the new slaveholding immigrants a few rich men who joined a handful of the Trustees' former assistants and several royal administrators to form the colony's Executive Council.

Officially empowered in 1755, the council served as the organizational basis of Georgia's ruling class until the American Revolution.

Jonathan Bryan was an original appointee to the council. Twenty years of social, business, and political connections with important Georgia figures had earned him a reputation as a man of great skill, and his ownership of a large labor force—he moved to Georgia with forty to fifty slaves—entitled him to extensive tracts of land, social prestige, and consideration for membership among the colony's political elite. When he petitioned for 500 acres of "Marsh and Swamp Land" in 1750, Georgia magistrates "readily granted" his request because "this piece of Land cannot be cultivated without great Strength, which they know He is capable of performing." Bryan's talents were especially valued because politically experienced men were few in the young province. Legal skills were in great demand—Georgia had no lawyers in 1755—so councillors filled multiple positions. In addition to his council seat, Bryan served on the General Court and the Court of Oyer and Terminer, as justice of the peace, and as the colony's treasurer. . . .

Bryan served on the council from 1755 until 1770, when he was expelled for patriot activities. Turnover during that period was slight: governors were replaced more frequently than councillors. Power rested in the hands of an active core of just eleven men. Bryan, James Habersham, Noble Jones, Francis Harris, James McKay, James Edward Powell, William Clifton, and Patrick Houstoun were appointed in the 1750s and were joined by William Knox, Grey Elliot, and John Graham in the early 1760s. All eleven were men of substance, though three—Jones, Harris, and Habersham—had arrived in Georgia nearly penniless. Composing the council's inner circle, this entrenched group formed a ring of prestige and power around the office of the governor.

Bryan pursued his interests on the council and in the upper house in many ways. He served as commissioner for an array of public works projects such as repairing and refurbishing the lighthouse of Tybee Island, constructing and maintaining roads in the northwest district, and erecting of sundry forts, magazines, and blockhouses. These appointments enhanced his prestige while providing numerous opportunities to dispense patronage. The activity that most attracted his attention was the distributing of the public lands.

Control over the public lands was the major source of the council's economic and political power. Although the rules governing the land-granting system appeared to be equitable (all free white males were entitled to receive a portion of the public domain), the formal entitlement to land was of negligible importance in obtaining a valuable parcel. The council held final say over who got which tracts. Since the Trustees had severely restricted land-ownership and little land had been ceded by the Indians, much of Georgia's chartered domain had yet to be granted when royal government was established. Thus it fell to the council to distribute most of the land that came under cultivation in the late colonial period.

Under the system established by royal officials, each head of household was entitled to one hundred acres for himself and fifty acres for every member of his household, including slaves. Among the slaveholders themselves, those who possessed influence on the council were most likely to receive the best land—freshwater swamp located along transportation routes and cultivatable by the tidal-flow method. Although rice could be produced inland, planters who obtained land affected by the Atlantic tides, whereby fields could be easily flooded and drained, enjoyed a distinct advantage. This land lay above the saltwater line in an area ten to twenty miles wide along the coast. Eighteenth-century maps reveal the result of the colony 's land-granting system: a small group of land barons monopolized Georgia's premier rice lands, while the rest of the population became dispersed throughout the colony.

Before examining how Bryan used his political offices and his varied skills in building his estate, we should trace the development of his plantation empire. We have seen that he began by petitioning the Trustees for 500 rice land acres in 1750. He settled the tract on New Year's Day, 1751, with forty to fifty slaves and moved his family there in August 1752. The plantation, Walnut Hill, was located on the Savannah River, several miles below the capital. Almost immediately after he received this grant, Bryan began selling parcels of his land in Prince William's Parish, though he retained the most valuable portion until 1757. Although he valued Walnut Hill, he considered establishing his base plantation in several other areas. In 1752 he received from the Trustees 500 acres on the Little Ogeechee River, several miles south of Savannah. He named this plantation Dean Forrest. An additional 500 were granted contiguous to this land in 1754.

In 1755 Bryan began petitioning for land on the Great Ogeechee, a freshwater river that many Georgians believed would replace the Savannah as the colony's major waterway. When the town of Hardwicke was laid out by Georgia's first royal governor, who tried unsuccessfully to make it the capital, Bryan petitioned for and received 500 acres and a town lot. But his gaze continued to drift southward. In August 1755 he petitioned the council: "having Seventy eight Persons in Family, he was desirous of improving another Tract; and therefore pray[ed] for eighteen hundred Acres of Land on the Fort Swamp at the Head of Sapola [Sapelo] River. Thus by 1755 Bryan had become engaged in establishing rice plantations on four Georgia rivers.

Bryan's tracts were too distant from one another for him to maintain effective control over them. Roads were few and rough; transportation from one plantation to another by water meant travel along the sometimes difficult coastal waterways. When it became apparent that the Atlantic trade would continue to flow through Savannah, Bryan began selling off or resigning lands that were not along the Savannah River. . . . Bryan determined to concentrate his holdings along the Savannah. In 1757 he began requesting land adjacent to his Walnut Hill plantation, which he supplemented with numerous tracts of "garden" and "farm" acreage on the east side of Savannah town. He also claimed 1,000 acres on Augustine's Creek, just below the town near Walnut Hill, and he sold his remaining acreage in Prince William's Parish. It was probably at this time that Bryan increased his purchases and development of tracts on the South Carolina side of the Savannah River. He had begun settling land in 1752 at Monmouth Point in the township of Purrysburg, about seventeen miles northwest of Savannah. By the mid-1760s he owned from four to seven thousand acres on the South Carolina side of the river. The £864 he made from selling land in 1756–1757 may have provided some of the capital for the purchase of those acres. . . .

. . . All together, his holdings in South Carolina probably amounted to between six and seven thousand acres, all selected because of their riverfront location. They were convenient to Savannah town and to each other, and their crops could be shipped downriver. Not all land along the Savannah was of good quality or easily reached. Much of it was worthless swamp. But Bryan selected parcels with good harbors and ones that his large labor force could turn to rice, indigo, and corn. . . .

Why Bryan established a plantation between the North Newport and South Newport rivers in 1758 is unknown. It may have been experimental, for he raised a variety of crops and animals there. In an advertisement for the plantation's sale in 1763, he described it as good for corn, rice, and indigo, and able to maintain horses, cattle, and other stock. He had built there "a good new framed barn, overseer's house, and negro houses." One hundred acres had been cleared and fenced, and he stated that the marsh land for the animals could be easily enclosed. Apparently, however, the local planters had difficulty attracting oceangoing vessels, with the result that the cost of transporting goods to market was raised. Bryan, at any rate, gave up: the result of his five-year development of land along the Newport rivers was a determination to leave the region to others.

Bryan continued to develop Walnut Hill during the 1750s and 1760s. By grant he added 600 acres of rice land and 300 acres of garden and farm lots in 1758 and 1762. He referred to himself in legal documents as Jonathan Bryan of Walnut Hill, and he used the plantation as headquarters for his other operations. In 1758 he added to his holdings Cockspur Island, east of Walnut Hill, in the Savannah River. He also requested and received a wharf in Savannah and 300 acres above the town at Pipemaker's Creek. . . .

After fifteen years in the colony Bryan finally had arranged his plantations to allow easy access from one to another. In 1762 he began to consolidate his holdings by selling all of his land below the capital on the Savannah River. He resigned his tract at Augustine's Creek and in 1763 sold his Walnut Hill plantation. Bryan determined to build a new homestead west of the city at Brampton, where Pipemaker's Creek flowed into the Savannah. This locale was considered one of the best rice-producing areas of the colony. Fields were easily flooded by both the creek and the river, and goods could be readily conveyed downriver for export abroad. Bryan's original grant on the creek was 600 acres in 1759. He added 250 acres in 1765 and 350 more in 1770. Brampton's location was excellent for both business and politics. It enabled Bryan to attend to his affairs in Savannah and gave him easy access to his Carolina holdings along the Savannah. He need travel only a few miles by piragua to reach the road to his Union and Little Yemassee plantations; both were also approachable by water. (Reaching these same plantations from Walnut Hill meant an additional ten miles of travel upstream.) Furthermore, Brampton lay close to the terminus of the Newmarket road at Pipemaker's Creek. Cattle could be run directly there from his cowpen, whereas they could not have been run to Walnut Hill. Though Bryan continued to consider establishing plantations in other areas of the colony, for the remainder of his life Brampton and his plantations along the Savannah formed the central component of his economic empire.

The sources of Bryan's extraordinary land hunger are obscure, but an important motivation may well have been a desire to leave each of his many children an estate large enough to secure a place among the ruling elite. If this was his goal, he achieved it remarkably well. His son James became a member of Georgia's Executive Council, filling Jonathan's seat when the latter retired from politics at the end of the Revolution. Bryan's daughter Hannah married John Houstoun, the son of a baronet and an original member of the council. Houstoun held many important political offices in Georgia, including the governorship in 1778 and 1784. Two other sons, Hugh and William, served in the state's Revolutionary government; daughter Mary twice married leading Georgia patriots; grandson Joseph became a United States congressman.

Bryan was able to build his empire largely because of his position on the Executive Council, which regulated Georgia's land system through legislation and control of the distribution of land in the public domain. Bryan took an active part in this advantageous business. For instance, he sponsored legislation against absentee owners who showed no intention of cultivating their land. He also initiated an act for the "quieting of men's estates." This law stipulated that those who retained twenty years' "quiet possession" of a parcel of land had legal right over past and future claimants to purchase that land from the crown. These measures probably pleased Georgia landowners of all classes who opposed outside speculators and also helped bring order to the land-granting system by resolving the problem of multiple grants made under the Trustees' careless practices. Georgia's slaveowners required order in the land system if they were going to build large estates.

The most important aspect of council control over the public domain was the consideration of petitions for land. Anyone wishing a grant presented his or her petition in person to the governor and council. This gave the council direct contact with virtually every landowner in Georgia and provided occasions for it to display its "apartness" and majesty to the populace. . . .

Over the whole colonial period perhaps one million acres were handed out by the council. The percentage of petitions granted was high. In the most competitive period, 1755–1760, 1,406 of 1,785 petitions, or 79 percent, were accepted at least in part. From 1761 to 1769 the yearly figure was over 80 percent. These statistics appear to illustrate the ease with which Georgians acquired land, but they can be misleading. What they do not show is that sponsors often were needed for the granting of land and that many who hoped to obtain a portion, particularly of valuable lowcountry swamp or marsh, had little chance of success without a friend on the council. The case of Mark Noble illustrates the importance of council patronage.

Noble's case does not enter our statistics because his petition was never officially adjudged by the council in session. He was the overseer of Henry Laurens's Broughton Island plantation. Laurens became furious when Noble, without his approval and "under the sanction of Jonathan Bryan, Esquire . . . petitioned for a Warrant to Survey a parcel of that Marsh Land adjoining to the College Land and pretending that he had eight or ten Negroes." Laurens made his displeasure known to James Habersham and other council members. In behind-the-scenes maneuvering Laurens was able to prevent his overseer from receiving the desired land. From the particulars of the case it is evident that Noble and Laurens realized that council patronage was necessary for the overseer to receive the desired land and that politicking members of the council could promote or hinder a claim. . . .

Bryan followed the granting of land with great interest. His attendance on land days was below 75 percent only one year during the period 1755–1764, and in six of those nine years was above 85 percent. One reason for this regularity was the steady stream of petitions he submitted on his own behalf, thirty-eight in all, over two-thirds of which were submitted between 1755 and 1764. The thirty-eight were for over 18,000 acres plus wharfage and town and garden lots. Only two of his petitions were postponed; only one was rejected. His completed grants totaled upwards of 10,000 acres. This land formed the basis for several of his plantations, though he used a substantial portion for speculative purposes.

Bryan's council seat enabled him to obtain not only land of best quality but more than he was entitled to by freehold. Some Georgians were permitted to obtain public land by purchase. This allowed a privileged few to receive such land at minimal cost, once their freehold was completed. To purchase public land, planters had to swear that tracts would be developed and not used for speculation. The council was the final arbiter of who could buy and who could not; thus Bryan was in an excellent position to have his purchase requests approved. . . .

Bryan had made intermittent purchases from private individuals in the 1750s, but it was not until 1764 that he began buying large tracts in Georgia. Extant evidence indicates that he bought approximately 22,000 acres in both Georgia and South Carolina. . . .

Bryan's selection of land was based upon familiarity with Georgia topography acquired through years of travel and experience. He was expert in the native plants of the southeast and an excellent assessor of soil for crop production. James Habersham recommended Bryan to naturalist John Ellis as one who possessed "a general knowledge of this Province and South Carolina, and of its many unnoticed, tho' usefull Plants—both medicinal, and ornamental." The naturalist William Bartram also testified to Bryan's horticultural talents. Bartram visited Bryan at his Brampton plantation in 1776, where he found a beautiful "villa" in "a very delightful situation." He was impressed by Bryan's "spacious gardens, furnished with a variety of fruit trees and flowering shrubs." Benjamin Franklin learned of Bryan's talents and from England sent to him for experimentation some "Upland Rice, brought from Cochin China." This experiment failed but another succeeded: Franklin sent seeds of the Chinese tallow tree, which Bryan and a few others germinated so successfully that the tree soon spread through the southeast. . . .

... His purchases and grants were often distant from Savannah and required travel over difficult terrain. But Bryan was among the most physically fit of men, with the stamina not only to visit the far reaches of Georgia but to develop much of his land into plantations. . . .

Sales of land, both developed and undeveloped, assisted Bryan in capitalizing other enterprises. The thirty-three slaves he received from the sale of Walnut Hill probably were used at his new homestead, Brampton plantation, where he built the villa admired by Bartram. He operated so many plantations that he required constant influxes of new labor. At any given moment in the 1750s, 1760s, and 1770s he had five or more plantations in production. The total number of slaves employed is unknown but may be estimated at about 250 in 1763. In Georgia alone, Bryan held 66 slaves in 1755, 94 in 1760, and 125 in 1763. In South Carolina he possessed numerous plantations, totaling about 7,000 acres in the 1760s and 1770s; Union plantation in particular comprised 2,000 acres, was highly developed, and may have employed 100 or more slaves.

Access to capital was the key factor in obtaining slave labor. Because there were few shortages of black labor in Georgia and South Carolina between 1755 and the Revolution, men who possessed credit or cash could easily buy blacks, especially when, like Bryan, they had close business contacts with Bristol and Charleston merchants. Bryan had no difficulty stocking his plantations with laborers; he was able to provide ten slaves to each of his children when they came of age.

Establishing a plantation took large amounts of capital. The cartographer William Gerhard De Brahm, who immigrated to Georgia in 1751, estimated the cost of creating a rice plantation at £2,476. This sum purchased 200 acres, a barn, slaves, oxen and horses, two carts, tools, provisions for one year, and clothes and medicine for the work force; it also paid an overseer's wages. The greatest single expense De Brahm calculated was £1,800 for the purchase of forty seasoned slaves. He estimated return on the first year of investment at £700. This would pay a quarter of the planter's debt with interest. An overseer or tradesman who earned £50 per year could hardly expect to procure a £2,500 loan. Even a plantation of ten slaves was beyond the means of most men, given the scarcity of capital. Thus most white Georgians did not own slaves. The most recent estimate, by Betty Wood, suggests that "by the early 1760s at least 5 percent of all white Georgians, and probably not less than a quarter of all households, held at least one slave." Most of these were concentrated in the tidewater area.

The value of rice plantations varied greatly. It is noteworthy that when De Brahm calculated the costs of planting he did not mention the 2,000 acres a slaveholder was entitled to by purchase of forty slaves. That was because most of the good rice land was taken by 1760 and De Brahm made his estimate sometime after 1765. He also greatly underestimated the cost of improved rice land. On the Savannah and the freshwater creeks that fed the river, good land sold for much more than the ten shillings per acre he calculated. On Hutchinson Island in the Savannah, Bryan bought and sold land in 1773 valued from £2 10s. to £6 per acre, or 500 to 1,200 percent higher than De Brahm had figured. The value of acreage on the island rose greatly in the next decade. Across from Hutchinson Island Bryan added a 250-acre tract to his holdings at Pipemaker's Creek. He paid close to £1 5s. per acre for this land. In 1768 he sold the 450-acre Little Yemassee plantation on the South Carolina side of the Savannah for £450. Only 50 acres were cleared for rice, while on another 50–60 were knolls of corn; the plantation also had an overseer's house. The Little Yemassee was not a major plantation, at least not to Bryan. He had purchased the tract five years earlier for about £150. But the few improvements he made and the value of the rice land, which was excellently located, increased the plantation's value by 200 percent, despite the fact that 300 acres of the tract were uncleared. De Brahm, though expert in topography, was not a great planter and did not understand how to use slavery and land to gain riches as Bryan did. Thus we must revise his estimate of the cost for establishing a plantation of forty slaves from £2,476 to between £3,000 and £3,600, with the latter the closer figure when prime rice land was purchased.

There are few records of how Bryan operated his plantations. We do not know whether he used his sons, slave drivers, or overseers to direct his work force. He recognized the family unit among his slaves, twice directing in his will that, if at all possible, families should not be broken up in the settlement of his estate. John Martin Boltzius asserted that Bryan's plantations were run in an orderly manner. Boltzius reported in 1742 that the slaves were well treated and, as a result, were contented and worked efficiently. Unlike most slaveholders, who denied their bondsmen the privilege of reading and of practicing Christianity, Bryan actively promoted the education and Christianization of his slaves in both South Carolina and Georgia. Cornelius Winter, an evangelical who attempted to instruct Georgia blacks in the precepts of Christianity, testified in 1771 that many of Bryan's laborers knew Christian prayers by heart. Later in the decade Bryan took the unusual step of permitting one of his slaves, Andrew Bryan, to preach. His treatment of slaves with a respect ordinarily denied them may have contributed to the great success of his plantations.

Bryan's laborers performed a variety of tasks. They were cowboys, field hands, carpenters, sawyers, and house servants. Those skilled in woodwork produced lumber and shingles for market and built barns and slave quarters. Thus with great speed Bryan cleared tracts and erected the buildings necessary to begin plantation operations; he then developed the land or sold it as a fully functioning plantation. It appears that the latter was his intention or at least the result of his efforts in the sale of Little Yemassee, Dean Forrest, his plantation on the North Newport River, and possibly those on Wereat Island and Camber's Island in the Altamaha River.

Bryan's plantations were largely self-sufficient. Not only did they produce their own food, but the skills of his laborers made him less dependent upon hired labor than most planters, thus minimizing cash expenditures. When cash was needed, he could sell slaves, plantations, or undeveloped land, but his credit was always good and we may conclude that his notes were taken everywhere. . . . By the mid-1760s he had built no less than a plantation empire.

The building of that empire illustrates the sophisticated way in which a wealthy southern planter used political office, scientific knowledge, and business acumen in the conduct of his affairs. Bryan's ability to adapt his financial interests to the environment in which he lived displays a logic that was highly rational and practical. In combining his political and personal interests, Bryan was typical of Georgia's slaveholding elite. They were men of talent who understood the importance of patronage, political preferment, and public works projects, as well as the marketing of crops and the intricacies of English law. . . .

On the eve of the Revolution, Jonathan Bryan's plantation empire contained some 10,000 acres and 300 slaves. Fueled by his aggressive quest for power, prestige, and affluence—for himself and for his offspring—it had grown over the years into a network of prosperous estates that complemented one another, and Bryan himself had grown so great, as a planter, that he could stand for Independence almost alone among the colony's ruling elite. He can thus be said to exemplify the possessive individualism of his class—a class of planter-capitalists who mastered the economic and political arts of creating, on the southern frontier, a society shaped in their image and geared to their interest.

❧ FURTHER READING

David Leroy Coon, "Eliza Lucas Pinckney and the Reintroduction of Indigo Culture in South Carolina," *Journal of Southern History* 42 (1976), 61–76

Verner W. Crane, *The Southern Frontier, 1670–1732* (1928; repr. with new introduction by Peter H. Wood, 1981)

Harold E. Davis, *The Fledgling Province: Social and Cultural Life in Colonial Georgia, 1733–1776* (1976)

A. Roger Ekirch, *"Poor Carolina": Politics and Society in Colonial North Carolina, 1729–1762* (1981)

Michael G. Hall, *Edward Randolph and the American Colonies, 1676–1703* (1960)

Daniel C. Littlefield, *Rice and Slaves: Ethnicity and the Slave Trade in Colonial South Carolina* (1981)

Robert L. Meriwether, *The Expansion of South Carolina, 1729–1765* (1940)

James H. Merrell, *The Indians' New World: Catawbas and Their Neighbors from European Contact Through the Era of Removal* (1989)

H. Roy Merrens, *Colonial North Carolina in the Eighteenth Century: A Study in Historical Geography* (1964)

M. Eugene Sirmans, *Colonial South Carolina: A Political History, 1663–1763* (1966)

Clarence L. Ver Steeg, *Origins of a Southern Mosaic: Studies of Early Carolina and Georgia* (1975)

Richard Waterhouse, "England, the Caribbean, and the Settlement of Carolina," *Journal of American Studies* 9 (1975), 259–281

Betty Wood, *Slavery in Colonial Georgia, 1730–1775* (1984)

Peter H. Wood, *Black Majority: Negroes in Colonial South Carolina from 1670 Through the Stono Rebellion* (1974)

——, Gregory A. Waselkov, and M. Thomas Hatley, eds., *Powhatan's Mantle: Indians in the Colonial Southeast* (1989)

CHAPTER
10

The Great Awakening: Religious Upheaval Across the Colonies

The Great Awakening was a series of religious revivals that affected every part of English America in the first half of the eighteenth century. Although some historians have argued that the experience was too diffuse and spread over too long a time to be considered a movement, others point out that the revivals, wherever and however they happened, had aspects in common.

The revivals stressed interior experience of salvation, emphasizing emotion rather than great learning. Many caught up in the experience characterized themselves as having been spiritually dead, merely going through the motions of worship, before being touched by the hand of God. Although the awakeners' theology stressed the Calvinist doctrine of human depravity, saying that sinful men and women could do nothing to lift themselves out of sin without divine help, the effect was energizing. Congregations left revival meetings feeling that salvation was available to them if only they reached out and wanted badly enough to achieve it.

In some cases the awakenings began with small local revivals; others were spread by itinerants, preachers who, like the famous George Whitefield, traveled throughout the colonies carrying their message. Ministers initially welcomed the itinerants and the enthusiasm they generated, but eventually many clergymen found themselves threatened. They suffered by comparison with the dramatic and gifted itinerants, and they feared that the emotional conversions were surface phenomena that would not last. Moreover, they disliked the Awakeners' denigration of learning and the implication that the experience of the lowborn and unlearned might be more genuine than theirs. Ultimately the movement divided many communities into Old Light or Old Side and New Light; some congregations split permanently, and these alignments persisted into the American Revolution.

❧ D O C U M E N T S

Benjamin Franklin, though a friend of George Whitefield, never was converted by him. Franklin listened with an analytical ear to Whitefield's preaching. At the same time, as the first document reveals, Franklin demonstrated that his analytical stance did not prevent him from being affected by the man's words. Connecticut farmer Nathan Cole writes in the second selection of his excitement at hearing that Whitefield would preach nearby; he dropped his tools and went off with his wife immediately, as did a huge throng, all attracted by word-of-mouth advertisement.

Gilbert Tennent, leader of the Great Awakening in the middle colonies, preached a famous sermon, reprinted in the third document, on the danger to congregations led by ministers who had not experienced a true spiritual rebirth. He argued that such ministers could never be good guides to their flocks. Jonathan Edwards, a sophisticated philosopher and minister, was a leader of the Great Awakening in New England. His "Sinners in the Hands of an Angry God," excerpted in the fourth document, attempted to make the congregation understand emotionally as well as intellectually that they were powerless to save themselves and that, for those who had not experienced saving grace, no attempt to lead a good life could render them less odious to God.

Many became critical of the revivals and their effects. Reverend Joseph Fish of Connecticut in the fifth reading describes the illiterate native preacher whom he found among the Narragansett Indians of Rhode Island, and recommends help. Eventually Fish became a part-time preacher to the Narragansetts. An anonymous opponent, who signed himself Anti-Enthusiasticus, wrote a letter, excerpted in the sixth selection, to the *Boston Weekly News-Letter* describing the trial and expulsion of Connecticut New Light activist James Davenport in 1742 under the newly passed laws against itinerancy. Davenport was famous for the extreme actions he and his followers undertook. In Virginia, Reverend William Dawson, representative of the bishop of London, also found the activities of the New Lights distasteful. Ministers throughout the colony sent him letters, some of which are reprinted in the final selection, warning him of the danger of tolerating such men as Samuel Davies and John Todd.

Benjamin Franklin on His Friend George Whitefield, 1739

In 1739 arrived among us from Ireland the Reverend Mr. Whitefield, who had made himself remarkable there as an itinerant preacher. He was at first permitted to preach in some of our churches; but the clergy, taking a dislike to him, soon refused him their pulpits, and he was obliged to preach in the fields. The multitudes of all sects and denominations that attended his sermons were enormous, and it was a matter of speculation to me, who was one of the number, to observe the extraordinary influence of his oratory on his hearers, and how much they admired and respected him, notwithstanding his common abuse of them, by assuring them, they were naturally *half beasts and half devils.* It was wonderful to see the change soon made in the manners of our inhabitants. From being thoughtless or indifferent about religion, it seemed as if all the world were growing religious, so that one could not walk through the town in an evening without hearing psalms sung in different families of every street.

And it being found inconvenient to assemble in the open air, subject to its inclemencies, the building of a house to meet in was no sooner proposed, and persons appointed to receive contributions, than sufficient sums were soon received to procure the ground, and erect the building, which was one hundred feet long and seventy broad; and the work was carried on with such spirit as to be finished in a much shorter time than could have been expected. Both house and ground were vested in trustees, expressly for the use of *any preacher of any religious persuasion* who might desire to say something to the people at Philadelphia; the design in building being not to accommodate any particular sect, but the inhabitants in general; so that even if the Mufti of Constantinople were to send a missionary to preach Mahometanism to us, he would find a pulpit at his service.

Mr. Whitefield, on leaving us, went preaching all the way through the colonies to Georgia. The settlement of that province had been lately begun, but, instead of being made with hardy, industrious husbandmen, accustomed to labour, the only people fit for such an enterprise, it was with families of broken shopkeepers and other insolvent debtors; many of indolent and idle habits, taken out of the jails, who, being set down in the woods, unqualified for clearing land, and unable to endure the hardships of a new settlement, perished in numbers, leaving many helpless children unprovided for. The sight of their miserable situation inspired the benevolent heart of Mr. Whitefield with the idea of building an Orphan House there, in which they might be supported and educated. Returning northward, he preached up this charity, and made large collections; for his eloquence had a wonderful power over the hearts and purses of his hearers, of which I myself was an instance.

I did not disapprove of the design, but, as Georgia was then destitute of materials and workmen, and it was proposed to send them from Philadelphia at a great expense, I thought it would have been better to have built the house at Philadelphia, and brought the children to it. This I advised; but he was resolute in his first project, rejected my counsel, and I therefore refused to contribute. I happened soon after to attend one of his sermons, in the course of which I perceived he intended to finish with a collection, and I silently resolved he should get nothing from me. I had in my pocket a handful of copper money, three or four silver dollars, and five pistoles in gold. As he proceeded I began to soften, and concluded to give the copper. Another stroke of his oratory made me ashamed of that, and determined me to give the silver; and he finished so admirably that I emptied my pocket wholly into the collector's dish, gold and all. At this sermon there was also one of our club, who, being of my sentiments respecting the building in Georgia, and suspecting a collection might be intended, had by precaution emptied his pockets before he came from home. Towards the conclusion of the discourse, however, he felt a strong inclination to give, and applied to a neighbour, who stood near him, to lend him some money for the purpose. The request was fortunately made to perhaps the only man in the company who had the firmness not to be affected by the preacher. His answer was, "At any other time, friend Hopkinson, I would lend to thee freely; but not now; for thee seems to be out of thy right senses."

Some of Mr. Whitefield's enemies affected to suppose that he would apply these collections to his own private emolument; but I, who was intimately acquainted with him, being employed in printing his Sermons and Journals, never had the least suspicion of his integrity; but am to this day decidedly of opinion that he was in all his conduct a perfectly *honest man*; and methinks my testimony in his favour ought to have the more weight, as we had no religious connexion. He used, indeed, sometimes, to pray for my conversion, but never had the satisfaction of believing that his prayers were heard. Ours was a mere civil friendship, sincere on both sides, and lasted to his death.

The following instance will show the terms on which we stood. Upon one of his arrivals from England at Boston, he wrote to me that he should come soon to Philadelphia, but knew not where he could lodge when there, as he understood his old friend and host, Mr. Benezet, was removed to Germantown. My answer was, "You know my house; if you can make shift with its scanty accommodations, you will be most heartily welcome." He replied, that if I made that kind offer for *Christ's* sake, I should not miss of a reward. And I returned, "Don't let me be mistaken; it was not for *Christ's* sake, but for *your* sake." One of our common acquaintance jocosely remarked that, knowing it to be the custom of the saints, when they received any favour, to shift the burden of the obligation from off their own shoulders, and place it in heaven, I had contrived to fix it on earth.

The last time I saw Mr. Whitefield was in London, when he consulted me about his Orphan-House concern, and his purpose of appropriating it to the establishment of a college.

He had a loud and clear voice, and articulated his words so perfectly that he might be heard and understood at a great distance; especially as his auditors observed the most perfect silence. He preached one evening from the top of the Court-House steps, which are in the middle of Market Street, and on the west side of Second Street, which crosses it at right angles. Both streets were filled with his hearers to a considerable distance. Being among the hindmost in Market Street, I had the curiosity to learn how far he could be heard, by retiring backwards down the street towards the river; and I found his voice distinct till I came near Front Street, when some noise in that street obscured it. Imagining then a semicircle, of which my distance should be the radius, and that it was filled with auditors, to each of whom I allowed two square feet, I computed that he might well be heard by more than thirty thousand. This reconciled me to the newspaper accounts of his having preached to twenty-five thousand people in the fields, and to the history of generals haranguing whole armies, of which I had sometimes doubted.

By hearing him often, I came to distinguish easily between sermons newly composed, and those which he had often preached in the course of his travels. His delivery of the latter was so improved by frequent repetition that every accent, every emphasis, every modulation of voice, was so perfectly well turned and well placed that, without being interested in the subject, one could not help being pleased with the discourse; a pleasure of much the same kind with that received from an excellent piece of music. This is an advantage itinerant preachers have over those who are stationary, as the latter cannot well improve their delivery of a sermon by so many rehearsals. . . .

Nathan Cole on Going to Hear Whitefield at Middletown, 1740

Now it pleased God to send Mr. Whitefield into this land; and my hearing of his preaching at Philadelphia, like one of the old apostles, and many thousands flocking to hear him preach the Gospel, and great numbers were converted to Christ, I felt the Spirit of God drawing me by conviction; I longed to see and hear him and wished he would come this way. I heard he was come to New York and the Jerseys and great multitudes flocking after him under great concern for their souls which brought on my concern more and more, hoping soon to see him; but next I heard he was at Long Island, then at Boston, and next at Northampton. Then on a sudden, in the morning about 8 or 9 of the clock there came a messenger and said Mr. Whitefield preached at Hartford and Wethersfield yesterday and is to preach at Middletown this morning at ten of the clock. I was in my field at work. I dropped my tool that I had in my hand and ran home to my wife, telling her to make ready quickly to go and hear Mr. Whitefield preach at Middletown, then ran to my pasture for my horse with all my might, fearing that I should be too late. Having my horse, I with my wife soon mounted the horse and went forward as fast as I thought the horse could bear; and when my horse got much out of breath, I would get down and put my wife on the saddle and bid her ride as fast as she could and not stop or slack for me except I bade her, and so I would run until I was much out of breath and then mount my horse again, and so I did several times to favour my horse. We improved every moment to get along as if we were fleeing for our lives, all the while fearing we should be too late to hear the sermon, for we had twelve miles to ride double in little more than an hour and we went round by the upper housen parish. And when we came within about half a mile or a mile of the road that comes down from Hartford, Wethersfield, and Stepney to Middletown, on high land I saw before me a cloud of fog arising. I first thought it came from the great river, but as I came nearer the road I heard a noise of horses' feet coming down the road, and this cloud was a cloud of dust made by the horses' feet. It arose some rods into the air over the tops of hills and trees; and when I came within about 20 rods of the road, I could see men and horses slipping along in the cloud like shadows, and as I drew nearer it seemed like a steady stream of horses and their riders, scarcely a horse more than his length behind another, all of a lather and foam with sweat, their breath rolling out of their nostrils every jump. Every horse seemed to go with all his might to carry his rider to hear news from heaven for the saving of souls. It made me tremble to see the sight, how the world was in a struggle. I found a vacancy between two horses to slip in mine and my wife said "Law, our clothes will be all spoiled, see how they look," for they were so covered with dust that they looked almost all of a colour, coats, hats, shirts, and horse. We went down in the stream but heard no man speak a word all the way for 3 miles but every one pressing forward in great haste; and when we got to Middletown old meeting house, there was a great multitude, it was said to be 3 or 4,000 of people, assembled together. We dismounted and shook off our dust, and the ministers were then coming to the meeting house. I turned and looked towards the Great River and saw the ferry boats running swift backward and forward bringing over loads of people, and the oars rowed nimble and quick. Everything, men, horses, and boats seemed to be struggling for life. The land and banks over the river looked black with people and horses; all along the 12 miles I saw no man at work in his field, but all seemed to be gone. When I saw Mr. Whitefield come upon the scaffold, he looked almost angelical; a young, slim, slender youth, before some thousands of people with a bold undaunted countenance. And my hearing how God was with him everywhere as he came along, it solemnized my mind and put me into a trembling fear before he began to preach; for he looked as if he was clothed with authority from the Great God, and a sweet solemn solemnity sat upon his brow, and my hearing him preach gave me a heart wound. By God's blessing, my old foundation was broken up, and I saw that my righteousness would not save me.

Gilbert Tennent on the Danger of an Unconverted Ministry, 1740

... And Pharisee-Teachers, having no Experience of a special Work of the Holy Ghost, upon their own Souls, are therefore neither inclined to, nor fitted for, Discoursing, frequently, clearly, and pathetically, upon such important Subjects. The Application of their Discourses, is either short, or indistinct and general. They difference not the Precious from the Vile, and divide not to every Man his Portion, according to the Apostolical Direction to *Timothy*. No! they carelessly offer a common Mess to their People, and leave it to them, to divide it among themselves, as they see fit. This is indeed their general Practice, which is bad enough: But sometimes they do worse, by misapplying the Word, through Ignorance, or Anger. They often strengthen the Hands of the Wicked, by promising him Life. They comfort People, before they convince them; sow before they plow; and are busy in raising a Fabrick, before they lay a Foundation. These fooling Builders do but strengthen Men's carnal Security, by their soft, selfish, cowardly Discourses. They have not the Courage, or Honesty, to thrust the Nail of Terror into sleeping Souls; nay, sometimes they strive with all their Might, to fasten Terror into the Hearts of the Righteous, and so to make those sad, whom GOD would not have made sad! And this happens, when pious People begin to suspect their Hypocrisy, for which they have good Reason. I may add, That inasmuch as Pharisee-Teachers seek after Righteousness as it were by the Works of the Law themselves, they therefore do not distinguish, as they ought, between *Law* and *Gospel* in their Discourses to others. They keep Driving, Driving, to Duty, Duty, under this Notion, That it will recommend natural Men to the

Favour of GOD, or entitle them to the Promises of Grace and Salvation: And thus those blind Guides fix a deluded World upon the false Foundation of their own Righteousness; and so exclude them from the dear Redeemer. All the Doings of unconverted Men, not proceeding from the Principles of Faith, Love, and a new Nature, nor being directed to the divine Glory as their highest End, but flowing from, and tending to Self, as their Principle and End; are doubtless damnably Wicked in their Manner of Performance, and do deserve the Wrath and Curse of a Sin-avenging GOD; neither can any other Encouragement be justly given them, but this, That in the Way of Duty, there is a Peradventure or Probability of obtaining Mercy. . . .

I may add, That sad Experience verifies what has been now observed, concerning the Unprofitableness of the Ministry of unconverted Men. Look into the Congregations of unconverted Ministers, and see what a sad Security reigns there; not a Soul convinced that can be heard of, for many Years together; and yet the Ministers are easy; for they say they do their Duty! Ay, a small Matter will satisfy us in the Want of that, which we have no great Desire after. But when Persons have their Eyes opened, and their Hearts set upon the Work of God; they are not so soon satisfied with their Doings, and with Want of Success for a Time. . . .

Third general Head was to shew, *How Pity should be expressed upon this mournful Occasion?*

My Brethren, We should mourn over those, that are destitute of faithful Ministers, and sympathize with them. Our Bowels should be moved with the most compassionate Tenderness, over those dear fainting Souls, that are *as Sheep having no Shepherd;* and that after the Example of our blessed LORD.

Dear Sirs! we should also most *earnestly pray* for them, that the compassionate Saviour may preserve them, by his *mighty* Power, thro' Faith unto Salvation; support their sinking Spirits, under the *melancholy Uneasinesses of a dead Ministry;* sanctify and sweeten to them the *dry* Morsels they get under such blind Men, when they have none better to repair to.

And more especially, *my Brethren,* we should pray to the LORD of the Harvest, to send forth faithful Labourers into his Harvest; seeing that the Harvest truly is plenteous, but the Labourers are few. And O Sirs! how humble, believing, and importunate should we be in this Petition! O! let us follow the LORD, Day and Night, with Cries, Tears, Pleadings and Groanings upon this Account! For GOD knows there is great *Necessity* of it. *O! thou Fountain of Mercy, and Father of Pity, pour forth upon thy poor Children a Spirit of Prayer, for the Obtaining this important Mercy! Help, help, O Eternal GOD and Father, for Christ's sake!*

And indeed, *my Brethren,* we should join our Endeavours to our *Prayers.* The most likely Method to stock the Church with a faithful *Ministry,* in the present Situation of Things, the publick Academies being so much corrupted and abused generally, is, To encourage private Schools, or Seminaries of Learning, which are under the Care of skilful and experienced Christians; in which those only should be admitted, who upon strict Examination, have in the Judgment of a reasonable *Charity,* the plain Evidences of experimental Religion. Pious and experienced Youths, who have a good natural Capacity, and great Desires after the Ministerial Work, from good Motives, might be sought for, and found up and down in the *Country,* and put to Private Schools of the Prophets; especially in such Places, where the Publick ones are not. This Method, in my Opinion, has a *noble Tendency,* to build up the Church of God. And those who have any Love to Christ, or Desire after the Coming of his Kingdom, should be *ready,* according to their Ability, to give somewhat, from time to time, for the Support of such poor Youths, who have nothing of their own. . . .

Jonathan Edwards's Sermon "Sinners in the Hands of an Angry God," 1741

. . . "There is nothing that keeps wicked men at any one moment out of hell, but the mere pleasure of God"—By the *mere* pleasure of God, I mean his *sovereign* pleasure, his arbitrary will, restrained by no obligation, hindered by no manner of difficulty, any more than if nothing else but God's mere will had in the least degree, or in any respect whatsoever, any hand in the preservation of wicked men one moment.—The truth of this observation may appear by the following considerations.

1. There is no want of *power* in God to cast wicked men into hell at any moment. Men's hands cannot be strong when God rises up. The strongest have no power to resist him, nor can any deliver out of his hands.—He is not only able to cast wicked men into hell, but he can most easily do it. Sometimes an earthly prince meets with a great deal of difficulty to subdue a rebel, who has found means to fortify himself, and has made himself strong by the numbers of his followers. But it is not so with God. There is no fortress that is any defence from the power of God. Though hand join in hand, and vast multitudes of God's enemies combine and associate themselves, they are easily broken in pieces. They are as great heaps of light chaff before the whirlwind; or large quantities of dry stubble before devouring flames. We find it easy to tread on and crush a worm that we see crawling on the earth; so it is easy for us to cut or singe a slender thread that any thing hangs by: thus easy is it for God, when he pleases, to cast his enemies down to hell. What are we, that we should think to stand before him, at whose rebuke the earth trembles, and before whom the rocks are thrown down?

2. They *deserve* to be cast into hell; so that divine justice never stands in the way, it makes no objection against God's using his power at any moment to destroy them. Yea, on the contrary, justice calls aloud for an infinite punishment of their sins. Divine justice says of the tree that brings forth such grapes of Sodom, "Cut it down, why cumbereth it the ground?" Luke xiii. 7. The sword of divine justice is every moment brandished over their heads, and it is nothing but the hand of arbitrary mercy, and God's mere will, that holds it back.

3. They are already under a sentence of *condemnation* to hell. They do not only justly deserve to be cast down thither, but the sentence of the law of God, that eternal and immutable rule of righteousness that God has fixed between him and mankind, is gone out against them, and stands against them; so that they are bound over already to hell. John iii. 18. "He that believeth not is condemned

already." So that every unconverted man properly belongs to hell; that is his place; from thence he is, John viii. 23. "Ye are from beneath:" And thither he is bound; it is the place that justice, and God's word, and the sentence of his unchangeable law assign to him.

4. They are now the objects of that very same *anger* and wrath of God, that is expressed in the torments of hell. And the reason why they do not go down to hell at each moment, is not because God, in whose power they are, is not then very angry with them; as he is with many miserable creatures now tormented in hell, who there feel and bear the fierceness of his wrath. Yea, God is a great deal more angry with great numbers that are now on earth: yea, doubtless, with many that are now in this congregation, who it may be are at ease, than he is with many of those who are now in the flames of hell.

So that it is not because God is unmindful of their wickedness, and does not resent it, that he does not let loose his hand and cut them off. God is not altogether such an one as themselves, though they may imagine him to be so. The wrath of God burns against them, their damnation does not slumber; the pit is prepared, the fire is made ready, the furnace is now hot, ready to receive them; the flames do now rage and glow. The glittering sword is whet, and held over them, and the pit hath opened its mouth under them.

5. The *devil* stands ready to fall upon them, and seize them as his own, at what moment God shall permit him. They belong to him; he has their souls in his possession, and under his dominion. The scripture represents them as his goods, Luke xi. 12. The devils watch them; they are ever by them at their right hand; they stand waiting for them, like greedy hungry lions that see their prey, and expect to have it, but are for the present kept back. If God should withdraw his hand, by which they are restrained, they would in one moment fly upon their poor souls. The old serpent is gaping for them; hell opens its mouth wide to receive them; and if God should permit it, they would be hastily swallowed up and lost. . . .

7. . . . Unconverted men walk over the pit of hell on a rotten covering, and there are innumerable places in this covering so weak that they will not bear their weight, and these places are not seen. The arrows of death fly unseen at noonday; the sharpest sight cannot discern them. God has so many different unsearchable ways of taking wicked men out of the world and sending them to hell, that there is nothing to make it appear, that God had need to be at the expence of a miracle, or go out of the ordinary course of his providence, to destroy any wicked man, at any moment. All the means that there are of sinners going out of the world, are so in God's hands, and so universally and absolutely subject to his power and determination, that it does not depend at all the less on the mere will of God, whether sinners shall at any moment go to hell, than if means were never made use of, or at all concerned in the case.

8. Natural men's prudence and care to preserve their own lives, or the care of others to preserve them, do not secure them a moment. To this, divine providence and universal experience do also bear testimony. . . .

9. . . . But the foolish children of men miserably delude themselves in their own schemes, and in confidence in their own strength and wisdom; they trust to nothing but a shadow. The greater part of those who heretofore have lived under the same means of grace, and are now dead, are undoubtedly gone to hell; and it was

not because they were not as wise as those who are now alive: it is not because they did not lay out matters as well for themselves to secure their own escape. If we could speak with them, and inquire of them, one by one, whether they expected, when alive, and when they used to hear about hell, ever to be the subjects of that misery: we doubtless, should hear one and another reply, "No, I never intended to come here: I had laid out matters otherwise in my mind; I thought I should contrive well for myself: I thought my scheme good. I intended to take effectual care; but it came upon me unexpected; I did not look for it at that time, and in that manner; it came as a thief: Death outwitted me: God's wrath was too quick for me. Oh, my cursed foolishness! I was flattering myself, and pleasing myself with vain dreams of what I would do hereafter; and when I was saying, Peace and safety, then suddenly destruction came upon me." . . .

10. . . . So that, thus it is that natural men are held in the hand of God, over the pit of hell; they have deserved the fiery pit, and are already sentenced to it; and God is dreadfully provoked, his anger is as great towards them as to those that are actually suffering the executions of the fierceness of his wrath in hell, and they have done nothing in the least to appease or abate that anger, neither is God in the least bound by any promise to hold them up one moment; the devil is waiting for them, hell is gaping for them, the flames gather and flash about them, and would fain lay hold on them, and swallow them up; the fire bent up in their own hearts is struggling to break out: and they have no interest in any Mediator, there are no means within reach that can be any security to them. In short, they have no refuge, nothing to take hold of; all that preserves them every moment is the mere arbitrary will, and uncovenanted, unobliged forbearance of an incensed God.

The use of this awful subject may be for awakening unconverted persons in this congregation. This that you have heard is the case of every one of you that are out of Christ.—That world of misery, that lake of burning brimstone, is extended abroad under you. There is the dreadful pit of the glowing flames of the wrath of God; there is hell's wide gaping mouth open; and you have nothing to stand upon, nor any thing to take hold of; there is nothing between you and hell but the air; it is only the power and mere pleasure of God that holds you up. . . .

The God that holds you over the pit of hell, much as one holds a spider, or some loathsome insect over the fire, abhors you, and is dreadfully provoked: his wrath towards you burns like fire; he looks upon you as worthy of nothing else, but to be cast into the fire; he is of purer eyes than to bear to have you in his sight; you are ten thousand times more abominable in his eyes, than the most hateful venomous serpent is in ours. You have offended him infinitely more than ever a stubborn rebel did his prince; and yet it is nothing but his hand that holds you from falling into the fire every moment. It is to be ascribed to nothing else, that you did not go to hell the last night; that you was suffered to awake again in this world, after you closed your eyes to sleep. And there is no other reason to be given, why you have not dropped into hell since you arose in the morning, but that God's hand has held you up. There is no other reason to be given why you have not gone to hell, since you have sat here in the house of God, provoking his pure eyes by your sinful wicked manner of attending his solemn worship. Yea, there is nothing else that is to be given as a reason why you do not this very moment drop down into hell.

O sinner! Consider the fearful danger you are in: it is a great furnace of wrath, a wide and bottomless pit, full of the fire of wrath, that you are held over in the hand of that God, whose wrath is provoked and incensed as much against you, as against many of the damned in hell. You hang by a slender thread, with the flames of divine wrath flashing about it, and ready every moment to singe it, and burn it asunder; and you have no interest in any Mediator, and nothing to lay hold of to save yourself, nothing to keep off the flames of wrath, nothing of your own, nothing that you ever have done, nothing that you can do, to induce God to spare you one moment. . . .

The Reverend Joseph Fish on Samuel Niles, Narragansett New Light Preacher, 1765

. . . Some of the Indian Brethren (as Im informd) not in any Office, took and ordaind one Samel. *Niles* their Pastor, And he has been their Minister ever Since, for a Number of years: preaching, Administing the Supper, Baptism, and Marriage.

This Niles, (Who I have known Some Years,) is a Sober Religious Man, of Good Sense and great Fluency of Speech; and know not but a very honest Man. Has a good deal of the Scriptures by heart, and professes a Regard for the Bible. But his unhappiness is this, He *cannot read a Word,* and So is wholly dependant Upon the (too Seldom) Reading of others: Which exposes him, (doubtless) to a great deal of Inacuracy in useing Texts of Scripture, if not to gross Mistakes in the Application of them. And as hereby, (I conclude,) very Much upon the *Spirit* to teach him *Doctrine* and *Conduct,* he is in imminent danger of leaving *The Word,* for the Guidance of *Feelings, Impressions, Visions, Appearances* and *Directions* of Angels and of Christ himself in a Visionary Way. An Instance, of which I have heard of in his ordaining one Indian.

I dont learn that They Are Visited and Instructed by Any english Ministers; Unless it be now and then *One* of the Seperate Stamp. I have not heard of any One of our regular Standing Ministers, being among them for Many Years: which perhaps is a Faulty omission, if they Woud be Willing to *hear* us. Which Indeed I thought they would *not,* till their Freedom to hear *Me* the Other Day, Attended with Expressions of Approbation, and Requests from Some that I'd Visit and *preach* to them Again, Convincd Me that the Door is open, much Wider than I imagind.

Im inclind to think that they are within the reach of Instruction and capable of being corrected in their religious notions, and Set right (at least greatly Mended,) in their Gospel Order, if due pains were usd, and proper Measures taken.

This woud doubtless be the most easily and effectually done, by a faithfull and prudent Missionary Sent among them, Who Should be to their liking. But

I apprehend the present Times wont admit of any Such Attempt: as it might look like, (at least be taken for,) a Superceding of their Minister *Niles,* or Some way Lessening his Influence and authority—which, I Suppose Neither *He* nor *They* would relish the Thought of.

Another Method to help them, might hopefully be, by Some Neighbouring Minister, or Ministers (who Shoud be to their good Acceptance, if Such coud be found, Visiting of them and preaching to them, frequently, Taking a little time and pains by Way of free Conversation, on Religious Matters.

Or if the Honourable Commissioners Shoud think proper to Desire their Teacher *Niles,* to come and make them a Visit at Boston, They Might, by free Conversation, hopefully, assist him greatly, in Religious Matters.

The *Report* of the Indian Committee, Who Went down with a Petition for a Schoolmaster, (containing accounts of the favourable Acceptance and kind Treatment they met with,) has raisd the Commissioners So high in the Esteem of the Indians that their Influence over them must needs be Very Considerable; and, I imagine, that They have now in hand a Singular Advantage, in Some Way that their Wisdom may direct, to Serve their best Intrest to good purpose.

The poor people are not fit to be left alone, Not being Equal to the Important affair of Conducting their Religious and ecclesiastical Matters, agreable to Gospel Order. They Want Instruction, Guidance, Counsell. But the most difficult Undertaking to administer it.

I apprehend they cant bear to be told their Errors, and Mistakes in Any *direct* way of Speech. Father Sam, (as they Call him—Their Teacher Niles,) I suppose cant endure to be told, off hand, that his Ordination twas not According to Gospel Order, though ordaind, not by the Church, (for I dont learn there was Any Formed), nor by the Presbytery, As the Gospel Directs, But only by a few Individual Professing Christian Indians. Nor will Any of them, (I imagine,) bear to be told, that the Spirit (which They think they have,) is a Safe and Sufficient Guide, Without the Scriptures, And So of *many* Enthusiastic Notions which I Suppose they have. They cant bear to be told, *Directly* that These are *Errors.* This would be too Strong meat. I apprehend They must be told, What is *Truth—Truth* opposite to their Errors, not mentioning *them. Be shown* the *right Way;* passing by the *wrong* at least for a While,) Unnoticd. So that Turning their *Eyes,* and keeping them fixd for a While, Upon *Right Objects,* they May, of themselves take up a good liking to them; and either lose Sight of the *False,* or Gradually See that they were forreign to Truth. And So with respect to all their Errors, Say little or nothing about their wrong ways, but take them by the Hand, put them into and lead them in Right *paths,* till they get a good liking to *these,* and they'll of Course leave the old, and by and by See the Danger of them. These Candi[d] Sentiments I submit to your Correction. The Indians will know that Ive writ you. And they may likely be Jealous (Jealousy being deeply rooted in their Nature,) Jealous, that I've writ Something to their Disadvantage, though I mean Nothing but their best good. If you See it needfull to tell them any thing of the Contents of Mine to you, tell them (as you may truely,) that I have writ you with the highest Friendship to their best Intrest.

A Newspaper Account of the Expulsion
of James Davenport, 1742

Extract of a Letter from Hartford, *dated* June 15th 1742.

Sir,

Inclos'd is a faithful Account of the Trial of Mr. Davenport, *which I have been desired to transmit to some Friend in order to make it publick in the News-Papers: The Gentleman that drew it up, has, I believe, been desired to do it by the most considerable in the Government. Yours, etc.*

Hartford, *June* 10, 1742.

... And now *Sir,* As the matters complain'd of and the grounds of these proceedings are in but general terms exprest, and to gratify your curiosity as to the circumstances, etc. of the above affair, I shall proceed to give you in substance from minutes taken at the time; 1. The *principal* and more *particular things* either evidenced or conceded to. And, 2 His *behaviour* and treatment during, and sundry *circumstances* attending, the agitation of these things.

I. The *particular and principal things* either evidenced or conceded to, were,

1. That speaking of his, and his adherents *conduct* and *doctrines* and the effects thereof in the land, and under the general character of, This good work; and speaking also of the *laws of the government* made, or about to be made, to regulate or restrain the same, he declared and insisted, that *all such laws ought to be disregarded,* and were *against the laws of GOD.*

2. That he earnestly inculcated it upon the minds of children and youth, that this work was the work of God, which they also were engaged in carrying on; and that all *prohibitions* and *commands* of *parents and masters* not to adhere to them, and attend their religious exercises, meetings, etc. were in *no wise to be obeyed.*

3. That he declared that *people ought not to regard or attend the preaching of unconverted ministers;* and that *he was well-assured the greater part of the ministers in the country* were such.

And. 4. That he endeavoured by *unwarrantable means* to *terrify* and *affect* his hearers. And that,

(1.) By pretending some *extraordinary discovery and assurance* of the very near approach of the *end of the world;* and that tho' he didn't assign the *very day,* yet that he then lately had it *clearly open'd to him,* and *strongly imprest upon his mind,* that in a very *short time* all these things will be involv'd in devouring flames. And also that on supposition and pretence of *extraordinary intercourse with heaven,* he frequently pray'd for direction and acted in his undertakings.

(2.) By an *indecent and affected imitation* of the agony and passion of our blessed SAVIOUR; and also, by *voice* and *gesture,* of the surprize, horror and amazement of persons suppos'd to be sentenc'd to eternal misery. And,

(3.) By a *too peremptory and unconditioned* denouncing damnation against such of his auditory he look'd upon as opposers; vehemently crying out, That *he saw hell-flames slashing in their faces;* and that *they were now! now! dropping down to hell;* and also added, *Lord! Thou knowest that there are many in that gallery and in these seats, that are now dropping down to Hell!* etc.

5. It appeared also, That sundry of these things happened *unseasonably* and *late at night.*

II. Touching his *behaviour* and *treatment* during, and the *circumstances* attending, the agitation of these things, take as follows, *viz*—On notice first given him by the sheriff of the will of the assembly, he shew'd himself thereto resign'd, tho' just before, it seems had been determined to a different course by the special guidance of a superior authority.

On his arrival at *Hartford,* by the indulgence of the sheriff (who from first to last, treated and entertain'd at his own house, him and Mr. *Pomroy,* with unexceptionable tenderness and civility) he spent the first night, and the greater part of the next day, among his special friends [and] followers, uninterrupted in religious Devotions; in his way: by no means therein forgetting to vent the most virulent invectives against both ministers and magistrates, especially the general assembly, representing them as opposers of the work of God, and doing the work of the devil, etc.

Nextly, view him at the barr of the assembly: his approach to which, his air and posture there; that inflexibility of body, that affectatious oblique reclining of the head, that elevation, or rather inversion of the eyes, that forced negligence and retirement of soul, and that uncouth shew, that motly mixture of pride and gravity wrought up to sullenness, is not easily to be described. ... With vehement stentorian voice, and wild distortions of body, said *Davenport* began an exhortation; on which the sheriff, by speaking and gently taking him by the sleeve, endeavouring to silence and remove him, he instantly fell a praying, crying out, *Lord! thou knowest somebody's got hold of my sleeve, strike them! Lord, strike them*—which said *Pumroy* also observing cry'd out to the sheriff and his assistants, *Take heed how you do that heaven daring action! 'tis heaven-daring presumption, to take him away! and the God of Heaven will assuredly avenge it on you! strike them, Lord, strike them!* many of the concourse beginning to sigh, groan, beat their breasts, cry out, and to be put into strange agitations of body. Others of their adherents rushing in violently interposed to prevent and resist the sheriff; while others refused their assistance when commanded, saying, *they were serving the devil,* etc. . . .

In the mean time, almost all night, in other parts of the town, were such shocking scenes of horror and confusion, under the name and pretext of religious devotion, as language can't describe. Which wild ungovernable efforts of enthusiastic zeal and fury, being regarded as a bold and threatening insult upon the whole legislative body of the government, then on the spot; orders were forthwith given out to one of the commanding officers of the town, with about forty men in arms the next morning to wait upon the assembly; and so 'til the conclusion of these affairs: to prevent further insolencies, which seem'd to be threatening. Which orders were accordingly observed 'til the rising of the assembly.

But to return: Next morning being again bro't before the assembly, and seeming more on a level with his fellow-mortals, and to act something in resemblance of a man, being put on his defence, he on motion, had the witnesses which the night before had given in their evidence, interrogated anew: The import of which interrogation was, Whether when they had heard him express himself as abovesaid, touching obedience to laws, etc. and the end of the world, etc. he didn't thereto annex some qualifying words from whence different construction might be put upon what he delivered? To which they all answer'd in the negative. Nextly, His own witnesses being sworn and interrogated, and especially touching such qualifications, answered generally, affirmatively, that he did so qualify such of said expressions as they heard, full to their satisfaction and understanding; but on more particular inquiry what any of those qualifying expressions were, were not able to tell one word.

Then on his defence proceeding with a demeanour wholly his own, in-sisted, That the apparent effects of his ministry might well authenticate his conduct—That the greater part of the ministers in the land were undoubtedly unconverted; and that four or five of them had lately own'd to him *they* were such—That he had lately had clear discoveries and strong impressions made on his mind touching these things, etc.—And in a word, in the face of the assembly spake and acted so like himself, as to render in a measure useless all other evidence of his extravagancies. . . .

I am Sir, Yours, etc.
Anti-Enthusiasticus.

Letters Against Virginia New Lights, 1740s–1750s

Hanover June 8th 1747.

Reverend Sir

Mr. Davies whom the Govnour was pleasd to indulge in preching about six weeks in Hanover, is to leave it to day or tomorrow: And as I still sus-pected that all of his Fraternity were disturbers of the Societies of Christians of all Denominations, by declining to settle in any place, So I am now con-firmed in that opinion of 'em by Mr. Davies's conduct. This Man (who was with me last Friday & Saturday) told us that he did not intend to return hither till next Spring & perhaps not then; and after he took his leave of me, I was inform'd by a Gentleman in Amelia That Mr. Davies is to preach at Gooch-land Court-house next Thursday, from whence he is to travel as far as Roanoke, preaching at certain appointed places in his way, and that circular Letters and Advertisements are dispersd all over the upper parts of this Col-ony, that the People may have notice of the times & places of meeting. My Informer has one of the circular Letters, and the Advertisement at Goochland Court-house has, I believe, been seen by hundreds.

I persuaded my self that the Govinor & Council never intended to encourage Itinerant Preachers, and therefore think it my duty to acquaint you with this Man's behaviour. I think also that the Govinour, by his Indulgence, did not allow Mr. Davies to administer the Sacrament of the Lords Supper, which notwithstanding he did celebrate at the meeting-house in St. Pauls parish, on Sunday the last of May, and had a great many Communicants.

I need not inform you of the present distracted condition of my Parish nor of the future disturbances I justly apprehend from these Itinerants, who make it their Study to screw up the People to the greatest heights of religious Phrenzy, and then leave them in that wild state, for perhaps ten or twelve months, till another Enthusiast comes among them, to repeat the same thing over again, and this hath been the case here for above these two years past. I purpose (God willing) to wait on you as soon as I am fit to appear in Town: and am, with my wife's and Jenny's tender of respects to you & good family.

Revd Sir your most obedient & obliged
humble Servant
Pat. Henry.

Reverend & honorable Sir,

Not doubting but, as You represent our pious & learned Diocesan, tis your great Study to preserve, as far as may be, Purity of Faith, as well as sound Morals & good order in this remote corner of his Lordship's Diocese; it seems not improper to inform You that the revd Messrs Davies & Todd have lately been guilty of what I think Intrusions upon me, in having preached each of them a Sermon at a Tavern in my Parish; within the Bounds of which I have never heard, that either of these Gentlemen, or any of their Communion, have obtained any properly authenticated License to exercise their Function. What was their real Motive to this Conduct, I dont undertake to determine: but an apparent one was, the Request of Capt Overton to Mr. Davies, & of Capt. Fox to Mr. Todd, to preach an occasional Sermon to their respective Companies, at the Time of their Departure to range upon our Frontiers. But, as few, if any, of the former Company reside in this Parish, it might perhaps, have been equally prudent & regular in the former of those Teachers to have preached in one of his own Meeting-houses in Hanover. And, tho the other Company consisted chiefly of Inhabitants of this County yet tis Matter of Question with me, whether their Request alone sufficiently justifies Mr. Todd in acting as he has done; which however is humbly submitted to your better judgment.—If these Gentlemens Conduct be warrantable in this Particular; the inconveniences, resulting thence, must be patiently acquiesced in; but, if not, every stanch Friend of the Church of England will be pleased to see those Evils obviated in Time & guarded against for the future. What they are, tis needless to mention to You, Sir, who for some years past have had frequent opportunity of remarking, what Heats & Dissentions, what Breaches of Charity, what Ruin & Decay in the Families of many well meaning but deluded People, what Confusion & Disorder, what Disaffection in the People to regular Pastors, of unblemished Morals & unquestionable Abilities, together with many other unhappy Effects, have usually attended the Ministry of Itinerants & Enthusiasts in this Colony, whenever they have either boldly intruded, or been legally licensed.—Tis a Doubt, I am told, with some worthy Members of your honorable Bench, whether the Act of Toleration extends to the Plantations. I wish that Doubt were indisputably solved, which, perhaps, it would be, on proper Application to proper persons. Not that I would be fond of seeing these or any other nonconforming Teachers molested purely for their religious tenets; but of seeing the Privileges of both Churchmen & Dissenters so precisely ascertained, as to leave no Room for Controversy in the Case. I trust I am far from the inhuman & uncharitable Spirit of Persecution. No Man either professes or thinks himself a warmer Advocate for Liberty of Conscience, that natural Right of Mankind. But when Men under Pretence of asserting & exercising this Right, sow the Seeds of Discord & Confusion: when they so industriously propagate heterodox opinions in a Manner, inconsistent with & repugnant to, the formal Sanctions of Government & Law; none, surely, not their most zealous adherents, nor even themselves, can justly complain, should they be laid under just & equitable Restraints. Such, as dissent from the established Church, & are indulged by the Government publicly to teach those of their own Communion under certain wise & moderate Restrictions, would, one would think, if influenced either by Modesty or Prudence be cautious of transgressing the Bounds, markt out to them by such wholsome & tolerating Laws; which, as they, on one Hand grant them all reasonable Indulgences, in Condescension to their scrupulous Consciences, so, on the other, must be thought just in wisely providing for the Peace, Unity & Order of the national Church, for the Security of which they have been chiefly calculated. These Gentlemens Intentions may, peradventure, have been pious. I wont assert the Negative. But this, I believe, may be safely affirmed, That if, to effectuate their Intentions, however pious, the Laws of the Community must be violated, & if the Violation of such Laws be an Evil; they have, if not intentionally, yet eventually, acted upon that unsound Principle, which St Paul disclaims with so much Abhorence, Doing Evil that Good may come. Do me the Justice, Sir, to believe, that a pure Zeal for the established Church, a sincere Desire to guard that Part of it which is intrusted to my Care from Errors in Doctrine as well as Practice, & a compassionate Concern for many honest but ignorant People who by being unhappily seduced from the Church to the Coventicle have been involved in inexplicable Difficulties, have been my only Motives in troubling You with this Complaint. To which if you find it expedient & practicable to give effectual Redress, you'll greatly oblige all, in general, who wish to see Purity in Faith & Manners flourish in this Part of the Christian Church; and, amongst the rest, in a very particular Manner,

> Reverend
> & Honorable Sir,
> > Your obliged Friend
> > & affectionate Brother
> > > James Maury

Lancaster March 3d 1758

Reverend Sir

I expect the Gentlemen of the Clergy, from these Parts, will Let your Hon. know the Evil Consequences of a Dissenter's Preaching among us.

Inclosed is a Short Representation to be laid before the Next Assembly, which I Humbly offer to your Care, till the Assembly meets, hoping the Honourable Council will then Send it to the House of Burgesses for their Consideration. Pray Excuse this Presumption in,

> Most Reverend Sir,
> Your Honrs. most Humble
> and very Obedient Servant
> Edwin Conway.

Reverend Sir

Mr. Davies hath sent among our Negroes a Small Pamphlet, I Expect one will be Sent to your Honr. wherein you may Perceive Mr. Davies hath much Reproached Virginia. And informs the Negroes they are Stronger than the Whites, being Equal in Number then, & having an Annual addition of thousands. I Can't See any Advantage to the Country, to give this account to the Negroes. . . .

ESSAYS

Patricia U. Bonomi, a historian at New York University, in the opening essay treats the Great Awakening in the middle colonies, where ethnic and generational tension sharpened divisions. The Presbyterian church, governed by synods, or assemblies of ministers and elders, was split by these conflicts. Professor Bonomi illuminates the way in which the Old Sides denigrated their opponents as unlearned and catering to the vulgar mob but demonstrates that the New Sides actually promoted learning. In the second essay Harry S. Stout of Yale University assesses the impact of the new kind of preaching in New England. He argues that to understand, we must go beyond analyzing the content of what the Awakeners said and investigate what the *listeners* heard and felt. For men and women used to an academic style of sermon delivered in a meetinghouse where every member of the community sat in a seat assigned on the basis of status, the experience of going in a jostling crowd, all jumbled together, to hear one of the itinerants deliver an emotional appeal outdoors as Nathan Cole did would have been revolutionary. The urgency of the preachers' emotionalism conveyed to the hearers that God himself was reaching out, demanding that they take their salvation seriously, and, at least by implication, rebuking the dry, academic preachers.

Rhys Isaac takes a different approach in the closing essay, his treatment of the Baptist challenge in Virginia, set in a slightly later period. Critics portrayed the Baptists as dismal people who rejected society, a characterization that makes their attraction inexplicable. Isaac, a historian at LaTrobe University in Australia, probes beyond these descriptions to show how the Baptists represented a different concept of order and social responsibility. In the process he explains why the sect drew people of all social classes.

The Middle Colonies' Awakening

PATRICIA U. BONOMI

The Great Awakening split the Presbyterian Church apart, and through the cracks long-suppressed steam hissed forth in clouds of acrimony and vituperation that would change the face of authority in Pennsylvania and elsewhere. As the passions of the Awakening reached their height in the early 1740s, evangelical "New Side" Presbyterians turned on the more orthodox "Old Sides" with the ferocity peculiar to zealots, charging them with extravagant doctrinal and moral enormities. The internecine spectacle that ensued, the loss of proportion and professional decorum, contributed to the demystification of the clergy, forced parishioners to choose between competing factions, and overset traditional attitudes about deference and leadership in colonial America.

The division that surfaced in 1740–1741 had been developing for more than a decade. Presbyterian ministers had no sooner organized their central association, the Synod of Philadelphia, in 1715 than the first lines of stress appeared, though it was not until a cohesive evangelical faction emerged in the 1730s that an open split was threatened. Most members of the synod hoped to model American Presbyterianism along orderly lines, and in 1729 an act requiring all ministers and ministerial candidates to subscribe publicly to the Westminster Confession had been approved. In 1738 the synod had further ruled that no minister would be licensed unless he could display a degree from a British or European university, or from one of the New England colleges (Harvard or Yale). New candidates were to submit to an examination by a commission of the synod on the soundness of their theological training and spiritual condition. The emergent evangelical faction rightly saw these restrictions as an effort to control their own activities. They had reluctantly accepted subscription to the Westminster Confession, but synodical screening of new candidates struck them as an intolerable invasion of the local presbyteries' right of ordination.

The insurgents were led by the Scotsman William Tennent, Sr., and his sons, William, Jr., Charles, John, and Gilbert. William, Sr. had been educated at the University of Edinburgh, receiving a bachelor's degree in 1693 and an M.A. in 1695. He may have been exposed to European pietism at Edinburgh, where new ideas of every sort were brewing in the last quarter of the seventeenth century. Though ordained a minister of the Anglican church in 1706, Tennent did not gain a parish of his own, and in 1718 he departed the Old World for the New. . . . Having a strong interest in scholarship and pedagogy,

---

From *Under the Cope of Heaven: Religion, Society, and Politics in Colonial America* by Patricia U. Bonomi. Copyright © 1986 by Patricia U. Bonomi. Reprinted by permission of Oxford University Press, Inc.

Tennent built a one-room schoolhouse in about 1730 in Neshaminy, Bucks County—the Log College, as it was later derisively called—where he set about training young men for the ministry. Exactly when Tennent began to pull away from the regular synod leadership is unclear, but by 1736 his church at Neshaminy was split down the middle and the anti-evangelical members were attempting to expel him as minister.

In 1739 the synod was confronted with a question on professional standards that brought the two factions closer to a complete break. When the previous year's synod had erected commissions to examine the education of all ministerial candidates not holding degrees from approved universities, Gilbert Tennent had charged that the qualification was designed "to prevent his father's school from training gracious men for the Ministry." Overriding the synod's rule in 1739, the radical New Brunswick Presbytery licensed one John Rowland without reference to any committee, though Rowland had received "a private education"—the synod's euphemism for the Log College. Sharply criticizing the presbytery for its disorderly and divisive action, the synod refused to approve Rowland until he agreed to submit himself for examination, which he in turn refused to do.

Since education was central to the dispute, it is unfortunate that no Log College records have survived to describe the training given the remarkable group of men that came under William Tennent, Sr.'s tutelage. We do know that they emerged to become leaders of the revivalist movement, and would in turn prepare other religious and educational leaders of the middle and southern colonies. The little existing evidence casts doubt on the synod's charge that Tennent and his followers were "destroyers of good learning" who persisted in foisting unlettered Log College students upon an undiscriminating public. As Gilbert Tennent insisted, the insurgents "desired and designed a well-qualified Ministry as much as our Brethren." To be sure, their theological emphasis was at variance with that of the Old Side clergy, and there may have been parts of the traditional curriculum they did not value as highly, as had been true· with the innovative dissenting academies in Britain. But as competition between the two factions intensified, restrained criticism gave way to enmity. Thus, when the synod charged that Gilbert Tennent had called "Physicks, Ethicks, Metophysicks and Pnuematicks [the rubric under which Aristotelian philosophy was taught in medieval universities] meer Criticks, and consequently useless," its members could not resist adding that he did so "because his Father cannot or doth not teach them."

Yet there is much that attests to both William Tennent, Sr.'s learning and his pedagogical talents. That he was a polished scholar of the classics, spoke Latin and English with equal fluency, and was a master of Greek was confirmed by many who knew him. He also "had some acquaintance with the . . . Sciences." A hint of the training Tennent offered comes from the licensing examination given his youngest son Charles in 1736 by the Philadelphia Presbytery, among whose members were several who would later emerge as chief critics of the Tennents. Young Charles was tested on his "ability in prayer [and] in the Languages," in the delivery of a sermon and exegesis, and on his answers to "various suitable questions on the arts and sciences, especially

Theology and out of Scripture." He was also examined on the state of his soul. Charles Tennent was apparently approved without question.

The strongest evidence of the quality of a Log College education comes, however, from the subsequent careers and accomplishments of its eighteen to twenty-one "alumni." Their deep commitment to formal education is demonstrated by the number of academies they themselves founded, including Samuel Blair's "classical school" at Faggs Manor in Pennsylvania, Samuel Finley's academy at Nottingham, and several others. Two early presidents of the College of New Jersey (Princeton) were Samuel Finley and Samuel Davies (the latter having been educated by Blair at Faggs Manor). Moreover, the published sermons and essays of Samuel Finley, Samuel Blair, and Gilbert Tennent not only pulse with evangelical passion but also display wide learning. In the opinion of a leading Presbyterian historian the intellectual accomplishments of the Log College revivalists far outshone those of the Old Side opposers, among whom only the scholarly Francis Alison produced significant writings. As George Whitefield observed when he visited Neshaminy in 1739 and saw the rough structure of logs that housed the school: "All that we can say of most universities is, that they are glorious without."

But the distinction that the Log College men would achieve was still unknown in 1739, when the New Brunswick Presbytery defied the synod by licensing John Rowland. It was at this juncture, moreover, that the twenty-six-year-old English evangelist, George Whitefield, made his sensational appearance. Whitefield's visits to New Jersey and Pennsylvania in the winter of 1739–1740 provided tremendous support for the Presbyterian insurgents, as thousands of provincials flocked to hear him and realized, perhaps for the first time, something of what the American evangelists had been up to. The public support that now flowed to Tennent and his sympathizers exhilarated its members, inciting them to ever bolder assaults on the synod.

The revivalists had to this point preached only in their own churches or in temporarily vacant pulpits, but that winter they began to invade the territory of the regular clergy. This action raised the issue of itinerant preaching, perhaps the thorniest of the entire conflict, for it brought the parties face to face on the question of who was better qualified to interpret the word of God. It was in this setting that Gilbert Tennent was moved on March 8, 1740 to deliver his celebrated sermon, *The Danger of an Unconverted Ministry,* to a Nottingham congregation engaged in choosing a new preacher. It was an audacious, not to say reckless, attack on the Old Side clergy, and Tennent would later qualify some of his strongest language. But the sermon starkly reveals the gulf that separated the two factions by 1740. It also demonstrates the revivalists' supreme disregard for the traditional limits on public discussion of what amounted to professional questions.

Tennent began by drawing an analogy between the opposers in the Philadelphia Synod who rejected experiential religion, and the legalistic Pharisees of old who had rejected the radical teachings of Jesus. The Pharisees, he declared, were bloated with intellectual conceit, letter-learned but blind to the truths of the Saviour. They "loved the uppermost Seats in the Synagogues, and to be called Rabbi, Rabbi." They were masterly and positive in their sayings, "as if forsooth Knowledge must die with them." Worst of all, they "had their Eyes, with Judas, fixed upon the Bag. Why, they came into the Priest's Office for a Piece of Bread; they took it up as a Trade ... O Shame!" For all these worldly conceits Jesus had denounced them as hypocrites and a generation of vipers. Tennent went on to pronounce a similar judgment on the Pharisees of his own time—"unconverted [and] wicked Men" who as nearly resembled the old Pharisees "as one Crow's Egg does another." If men are not called to the ministry by a "New Birth ... their Discourses are cold and sapless, and as it were freeze between their lips."

Tennent's solution to the problem of unconverted ministers, in addition to prayer for their "dear fainting Souls," was "to encourage private Schools, or Seminaries of Learning, which are under the Care of skilful and experienced Christians." As for itinerant preachers, Tennent assured his Nottingham auditors that it was no sin but a right well within their Christian liberty to desert their parish minister for a converted preacher. "Birds of the Air fly to warmer Climates in order to shun the Winter-cold, and also doubtless to get better Food"; should humankind do less? In the only light moment of the sermon, Tennent exclaimed: "*Faith* is said to come by *Hearing* ... But the Apostle doesn't add, *Your Parish-Minister*." Thus Tennent concluded: "Let those who live under the Ministry of dead Men ... repair to the Living, where they may be edified."

In this influential and widely disseminated sermon Tennent set forth the three principal issues over which Presbyterians would divide: the conversion experience, education of the clergy, and itinerant preaching. While his tone may have owed something to Whitefield's recent influence—humility was never a strong point with the evangelists—it also reflected the growing self-confidence of the insurgents, as a wave of public support lifted them to popular heights. During the synod of 1740 the anti-revivalist clergy, in a demonstration of their reasonableness, agreed to certain compromises on the issues of itinerancy and licensing, but when the revivalists continued to denounce them publicly as carnal and unconverted, their patience came to an end.

The break between Old Side and New Side Presbyterians came during the synod of 1741 when a protest signed by twelve ministers and eight elders demanded that the revivalists be expelled from the synod. In a preemptive move, the New Side clergy voluntarily withdrew from the Philadelphia Synod to their presbyteries, where their work continued with great zeal and met with success that would outshine that of their rivals. In 1745 the evangelical party, joined by other friends of the revival from the Middle Colonies, formed the Synod of New York, which would sustain a lively existence until 1758 when the Presbyterian schism was finally repaired.

Disagreements over theological emphasis, professional standards, and centralized authority were the most immediate causes of the Presbyterian schism, but other differences between Old and New Sides had the effect of making the conflict sharper. Disparities in education, age (and therefore career expectations), and cultural bias are of special interest.

The twelve Old Sides who moved to expel the revivalist radicals in 1741 have sometimes been labeled the "Scotch-Irish" party for good reason. Nine were born in Northern Ireland, and two in Scotland (the birthplace of the twelfth is unknown). All were educated abroad, mainly in Scotland, and especially at the University of Glasgow. Most came to the colonies between the ages of twenty-eight and thirty-two, after having completed their education. The typical Old Side clergyman was about forty-two at the time of the schism. The New Side ministers who formed the Synod of New York in 1745 numbered twenty-two. Of the twenty-one whose places of birth can be ascertained, ten were born in New England or on eastern Long Island, one in Newark, New Jersey, eight in Northern Ireland (including Gilbert, William, Jr., and Charles Tennent), one in Scotland, and one in England. Most of those born abroad emigrated to the colonies during their middle teens; Charles Tennent was but seven, and the oldest was William Robinson, the son of an English Quaker doctor, who emigrated at about twenty-eight after an ill-spent youth. The educational profile of the New Side preachers is in striking contrast to that of the Old. Of the twenty-two, nine received degrees from Yale College, two were Harvard men, and ten were educated at the Log College. One had probably gone to a Scottish university. The typical New Side minister was about thirty-two at the time of the schism, or a decade younger than his Old Side counterpart.

Several tendencies suggest themselves. The Old Sides, more mature than their adversaries, were also more settled in their professional careers; further, their Scottish education and early professional experiences in Ulster may have instilled a respect for discipline and ecclesiastical order that could not easily be cast aside. They knew it was difficult to keep up standards in provincial societies, especially the heterodox Middle Colonies where competition in religion, as in everything else, was a constant challenge to good order. Still, it was irritating to be treated as intruders by the resident notables, or by such as the Anglicans, who pretended to look down on the Presbyterians as "men of small talents and mean education." There was security in knowing that the first generation of Presbyterian leaders had been educated and licensed in accordance with the most exacting Old World criteria. But the tradition must be continued, for succeeding generations would gain respect only if the ministry were settled on a firm professional base. Though Harvard and Yale were not Edinburgh and Glasgow, they did pattern their curricula after the British universities and to that extent could serve until the Presbyterian Church was able to establish a college of its own. And only if Presbyterian leaders could control the education and admission of candidates to the ministry might they hold their heads high among rival religious groups. A professional ministry was thus crucial to the "Scotch-Irish" party's pride and sense of place.

The New Side party, on the other hand, cared less about professional niceties than about converting sinners. Its members were at the beginning of their careers, and most, being native-born or coming to the colonies in their youth, were not so likely to be imbued with an Old World sense of prerogative and order. They never doubted that an educated clergy was essential, but education had to be of the right sort. By the 1730s Harvard and Yale were being guided, in their view, by men of rationalist leanings who simply did not provide the type of training wanted by the revivalists. Thus the New Sides chafed against the controls favored by their more conservative elders, controls that restricted their freedom of action, slowed their careers, and were in their opinion out of touch with New World ways.

The anti-institutionalism of the revivalists caused some critics to portray them as social levellers, though there were no significant distinctions in social outlook or family background between Old and New Sides. But as with any insurgent group that relies in part on public support for its momentum, the New Sides tended to clothe their appeals in popular dress. At every opportunity they pictured the opposers as "the Noble & Mighty" elders of the church, and identified themselves with the poor and "common People"—images reinforced by the Old Sides' references to the evangelists' followers as an ignorant and "wild Rabble."

The revivalists may not have been deliberate social levellers, but their words and actions had the effect of emphasizing individual values over hierarchical ones. Everything they did, from disrupting orderly processes and encouraging greater lay participation in church government, to promoting mass assemblies and the physical closeness that went with them, raised popular emotions. Most important, they insisted that there were choices, and that the individual himself was free to make them.

The people, it might be suspected, had been waiting for this. The long years of imposed consensus and oversight by the Kirk [church] had taken their toll, and undercurrents of restlessness had strengthened as communities stabilized and Old World values receded. Still, the habit of deferring to the clergy was deeply rooted in Presbyterian culture, making inertia an accomplice of church authority. By 1740, however, with the clergy themselves, or a part of them, openly promoting rebellion, many Presbyterians "in imitation of their example," as it was said, joined the fray. The result was turbulence, shattered and divided congregations, and a rash of slanderous reports against Old Side clergymen. Most such charges were either proved false or are deeply suspect, owing to their connection with the factional conflict. But aspersions against the ministerial character had now become a subject of public debate, suggesting that the schisms of the Awakening were effectively challenging the old structures of authority. . . .

Preaching and Revival in New England

HARRY S. STOUT

. . . I saw before me a Cloud or fogg rising; I first thought it came from the great River, but as I came nearer the Road, I heard a noise something like a low rumbling thunder and presently found it was the noise of Horses feet coming down the Road and this Cloud was a Cloud of dust made by the Horses feet; it

Harry S. Stout, "Religion, Communications, and the Ideological Origins of the American Revolution," *William and Mary Quarterly,* 3d ser. XXXIV (1977), 519–533, 540–541. Reprinted by permission of Harry S. Stout.

arose some Rods into the air over the tops of Hills and trees and when I came within about 20 rods of the Road, I could see men and horses Sliping along in the Cloud like shadows and as I drew nearer it seemed like a steady Stream of horses and their riders, scarcely a horse more than his length behind another, all of a Lather and foam with sweat, their breath rolling out of their nostrils every Jump; every horse seemed to go with all his might to carry his rider to hear news from heaven for the saving of Souls, it made me tremble to see the Sight . . .

Nathan Cole's description of George Whitefield's appearance before four thousand avid listeners in Middletown, Connecticut, in 1740 captures our attention at least partly because Cole's voice is one that is rare in early American literature. The crude spelling and syntax signal a vernacular prose composed by an ordinary man, whose purpose is less to analyze the theological issues of the revival than to describe an exhilarating event. Lacking the literary refinements of a classical education, Cole portrayed his experience in the form of a "realistic narrative" framed against a concrete social background. Although common in setting, the passage is hardly trivial, for it brings to life the impassioned world of the common people and conveys, in their own words, a sense of the irrepressible spontaneity that marked the revivals throughout the colonies. Thunderous noise, clouds of dust, horses in a lather, and unrecognizable shadowy figures dominate a vocabulary that manages to express, as no official account could possibly do, the powerful emotions evoked by the Great Awakening.

With Whitefield's celebrated speaking tours of the colonies there appeared an innovative style of communications that redefined the social context in which public address took place. The sheer size and heterogeneity of the audience exceeded anything in the annals of colonial popular assembly. To organize the mass meetings, both speaker and audience altered the roles and language they customarily adopted in public worship. In the process, a new model of social organization and public address developed—a model which could be applied to a broad range of social, political, and religious contexts.

Contemporary and historical accounts agree that the Awakening was the most momentous intercolonial popular movement before the Revolution. Indeed, the parallel between the popular engagement and "enthusiasm" evidenced alike in the revivals and the rebellion merits close attention. Unfortunately, however, attempts to explain the meaning those two movements had for their participants must confront the fact that the documentary evidence originates overwhelmingly from an elitist "rhetorical world" that excluded the common people from the presumed audience. Although the informed writings of the Founding Fathers provide the official revolutionary vocabulary, they do not render in a realistic narrative form the ideological arousal of the common people, who, by the very rhetoric of those documents, were excluded from the message. How were revolutionary sentiments communicated with ideological force to an audience unversed in the rhetorical forms of the literature? And, conversely, how did the active popular self-consciousness manifested in the popular movements energize a republican vocabulary and push it in egalitarian directions the leaders had never intended? The documents are of little help here. More to the point, they actually create the problem of interpretation.

Cole's description of the popular enthusiasm of the revival suggests a different approach to the problem of popular culture and republican ideology. If *what* was communicated is qualified by the restrictive rhetoric through which the ideas were intended to be transmitted, it may help to ask instead *how* communications were conducted and how they changed during the second half of the eighteenth century. There could be no egalitarian culture as we know it today without an ideological predisposition toward the idea that the vulgar masses ought to be reached directly. By examining the changing style of communications in the revivals it is possible to gain insights into the nature of an egalitarian rhetoric through which, and only through which, republican ideas could be conveyed to an unlettered audience.

David Ramsay, a noted participant in and historian of the Revolution, recognized that, to understand the meaning of the Revolution, "forms and habits" must be regarded. Before a republican vocabulary could communicate radical social meanings, a new rhetoric had to appear in which familiar terms were used to express unfamiliar thoughts. And this, it is argued here, is precisely what happened in the mass assemblies inaugurated by preachers like Whitefield. Despite the differences in intellectual substance between the revivals and the rebellion, those movements exhibited a close rhetorical affinity that infused religious and political ideas with powerful social significance and ideological urgency. . . .

. . . Despite differences in style and substance between Puritanism and southern Anglicanism, all churchmen believed traditionally with Samuel Willard that God did "Ordain Orders of Superiority and inferiority among men." This hierarchical world-view presupposed a society of face-to-face personal relationships in which people identified themselves with reference to those around them and acted according to their rank in the community. Forms of attire, the "seating" of public meetings, and patterns of speech were among the more conspicuous indications of a pervasive social stratification that separated the leaders from the rank and file. . . .

The social institutions of colonial America were designed to sustain this prevailing perception of proper social organization. In this traditional social ethic, itinerancy was inconceivable because, in Increase Mather's words, "to say that a Wandering Levite who has no flock is a Pastor, is as good sense as to say, that he that has no children is a Father." What made a pastor was not simply the preaching of the Word but also a direct, authoritarian identification with a specific flock. To ignore the personal and deferential relationships of a minister with his congregation would be to threaten the organic, hierarchical principles upon which both family and social order rested.

That ministers be "settled" was no idle proposition but rather an insistence carrying with it responsibility for the whole social order. An institution as critically important as the church could deny the forms of social hierarchy only at the peril of undermining the entire organization of social authority. In terms of communications this meant that speaker and audience were steadily reminded of their *personal* place in the community; in no context were they strangers to one another, for no public gatherings took place outside of traditional associations based upon personal acquaintance and social rank.

Within this world of public address Liberals and Evangelicals alike realized that something dramatically different was appearing in the revivalists' preaching performances. The problem raised by the revivals was not their message of the new birth. Indeed, it was the familiar message of regeneration that lulled leaders into an early acceptance and even endorsement of the revivals. The problem, it soon became clear, was the revolutionary setting in which the good news was proclaimed. The secret of Whitefield's success and that of other evangelists (no less than of Patrick Henry in the 1770s) was not simply a booming voice or a charismatic presence. It was a new style: a rhetoric of persuasion that was strange to the American ear. The revivalists sought to transcend both the rational manner of polite Liberal preaching and the plain style of orthodox preaching in order to speak directly to the people-at-large.... Their technique of mass address to a voluntary audience forced a dialogue between speaker and hearer that disregarded social position and local setting.

Immensely significant were the separation of the revivalists from local ministerial rule and their unfamiliarity with the audience. Until then, preachers, like political leaders, had to know whom they were addressing. Because the very act of public speaking signified social authority, they were expected to communicate through the existing institutional forms. When public speakers in positions of authority communicated outside of the customary forms, they set themselves, by that act itself, in opposition to the established social order. The eighteenth-century leaders' obsession with demagogy and "enthusiasm" can only be understood in the context of a deferential world-view in which public speakers who were not attached to the local hierarchy created alternative settings that represented a threat to social stability. The frenzy raised by the itinerants was not born of madness but was derived from the self-initiated associations of the people meeting outside of regularly constituted religious or political meetings and, in so doing, creating new models of organization and authority. As the Harvard faculty clearly recognized in their censure of Whitefield, the "natural effect" of his preaching was that "the People have been thence ready to despise their own Ministers."

In gathering their large and unfamiliar audiences the revivalists utilized the only form of address that could be sure to impress all hearers: the spoken word proclaimed extemporaneously in everyday language. As historians immersed in printed documents, we scarcely recognize the dominance of speech and oratory in aural cultures—an orality that, by definition, never survives in the written record.... Unlike print, which is essentially passive, reflective, and learned, sound is active, immediate, and spontaneously compelling in its demand for a response. Speech remains in the deepest sense an event or psychological encounter rather than an inert record—an event that is neither detached from personal presence nor analyzed, but is intrinsically engaged and calculated to persuade. Print cannot match the persuasive power of the spoken word whose potential audience includes everyone who can understand the language. It is no wonder that literate elites have feared persuasive orators from Plato condemning the sophists to Charles Chauncy damning the demagogues of the revival. Once orators are allowed the opportunity to address the people, there is, in Chauncy's words, "no knowing how high it [their influence] may rise, nor what it may end in." . . .

Returning not only to the social doctrine of the gospel but to its rhetoric as well, the evangelists excited the people to action by "calling them out" and exhorting them to experimental Christianity. Radical attacks on an "unconverted ministry" that acted more like "Letter-learned . . . Pharisees" than preachers of the Word take on additional meaning in the social context of eighteenth-century established religion. The danger that the Liberals sensed in the revivals was rhetorical as well as doctrinal. The Anglican commissary Alexander Garden correctly, and sarcastically, identified this threat: "*What went you out,* my Brethren, *to see,* or rather to *hear?* Any *new* Gospel, or message from Heaven? Why, no? but the *old* one explained and taught in a *new* and better Manner." Pointing to the spirit of this new manner, one opponent of the revivals observed that "it abhors Reason, and is always for putting out her Eyes; but loves to reign Tyrant over the Passions, which it manages by Sounds and Nonsense." The identification of sight with reason, and of sound with the passions, is here obvious and comes very near to the center of the raging controversy surrounding the itinerants. At stake was nothing less than the rules and conventions governing public address and social authority.

The revivalists' repudiation of polite style and their preference for extemporaneous mass address cut to the very core of colonial culture by attacking the habit of deference to the written word and to the gentlemen who mastered it. Evangelical rhetoric performed a dual function: it proclaimed the power of the spoken word directly to every individual who would hear, and it confirmed a shift in authority by organizing voluntary popular meetings and justifying them in the religious vocabulary of the day. Partly through doctrine, but even more through the rhetorical strategy necessitated by that doctrine, the popular style of the revivals challenged the assumption of hierarchy and pointed to a substitute basis for authority and order in an open voluntary system.

The popular rhetoric of the evangelists contrasted sharply with the much more formal modes of address preferred by upholders of established authority. Nowhere were the social divisions of American society more clearly reflected than in the leaders' utilization of a printed form of discourse that separated the literati from the common people. . . .

Linguistic uniformity conspired with classical education to establish a learned discourse that effectively separated the literate elite from the common folk. Hugh Blair, whose handbook, *Lectures on Rhetoric and Belles Lettres,* came to epitomize the style for aspiring gentlemen, averred that the educated class "is now so much accustomed to a correct and ornamental style, that no writer can, with safety, neglect the study of it." To encourage such a style Blair pointed to the patrician cultures of classical Greece and Rome, and urged his fellow literati "to render ourselves well acquainted with the style of the best authors. This is requisite, both in order to form a just taste in style, and to supply us with a full stock of words on every subject." The classical heritage provided a vocabulary and mode of discourse which leaders had to learn if they were to communicate through the proper forms. . . .

Attached to the elitist typographic culture were social imperatives. As long as social identities depended on a traditional social order for context and location within a finely graded hierarchy, communications had to be transacted through an elitist rhetoric. Power became so closely tied to print that advanced literacy and a classical education were virtually prerequisite to authority, and a college education guaranteed rapid advance in the social hierarchy. By 1776 there were nearly three thousand college graduates in the colonies who, through the remarkable improvements in post and press, were able to communicate with one another on a scale and with a frequency unimaginable in the seventeenth century. The cosmopolitan "better sort" formed a close-knit community that provided both authors and audience for the wave of printed literature that began to surge in the late eighteenth century. Pamphlets written by educated gentlemen, primarily lawyers, merchants, ministers, and planters, were addressed to their peers. The common people were not included in the audience, but it was assumed that they would continue to defer to the leaders. There was no recognition that the pamphleteers' impassioned celebration of republicanism would require a new rhetoric of communications reflecting a profound shift in the nature of social authority—a rhetoric, in brief, that threatened to undermine the exclusive world in which the pamphlets were originally conceived. . . .

. . . The rhetorical division resulting from the revivals played a major role in generating subsequent tensions and conflicts in American society. These tensions, moreover, reflected not so much opposing ideas with conflicting literary traditions as entirely different social outlooks and attitudes toward social authority, all deriving legitimacy from the individualism implicit in a mass democratic society. Evangelical attacks on a settled and educated ministry may have expressed a pristine "anti-intellectualism" in the colonies, but it was an anti-intellectualism that was positive and creative—indeed, revolutionary. Without it there would have been no creation of an egalitarian American republic.

The oral explosion and egalitarian style evidenced in the revivals were not limited to religion, nor was the articulation of a radical ideology the conscious objective of itinerant evangelists. The primary concern of the revivals was the saving of souls, and the rhetorical innovations that lent force to the movement were not fully perceived or verbalized for what they could come to represent: a revolutionary shift in world-view. As a movement initiated from below, the social experience of the revivals existed in fact before the emergence of a literate rationale. This does not mean that the experience proceeded from irrational impulses but, rather, that the terms necessary for rational comprehension and formal legitimation had to be invented. What opponents of the revivals termed a "spirit of superstition" was, for Jonathan Edwards, a new "sense" that could not easily be rendered into the existing forms of speech: "Some Things that they are sensible of are altogether new to them, their Ideas and inward Sensations are new, and what they therefore knew not how to accommodate Language to, or to find Words to express." Edwards's concern was to fit the new social experience of the revivals to its proper spiritual vocabulary, while acknowledging that no language could fully express the essence of religious faith.

What Edwards and other churchmen failed to recognize was that the "spirit of liberty" manifest in the revivals would not be contained in religious categories. In the movement for independence both leaders and followers adopted a political vocabulary that expressed the egalitarian impulse in the secular language of republicanism. . . .

The Baptists' Challenge in Virginia

RHYS ISAAC

An intense struggle for allegiance had developed in the Virginia countryside during the decade before the Revolution. Two eye-witness accounts may open to us the nature of the conflict.

First, a scene vividly remembered and described by the Reverend James Ireland etches in sharp profile the postures of the forces in contest. As a young man Ireland, who was a propertyless schoolmaster of genteel origin, had cut a considerable figure in Frederick County society. His success had arisen largely from his prowess at dancing and his gay facility as a satiric wit. Then, like many other young men at this time (ca. 1768), he came deeply "under conviction of sin" and withdrew from the convivialities of gentry society. When an older friend and patron of Ireland heard that his young protégé could not be expected at a forthcoming assembly, this gentleman, a leader in county society, sensed the challenge to his way of life that was implicit in Ireland's withdrawal. He swore instantly that "there could not be a dance in the settlement without [Ireland] being there, and if they would leave it to him, he would convert [him], and that to the dance, on Monday; and they would see [Ireland] lead the ball that day." Frederick County, for all its geographical spread, was a close community. Young James learned that his patron would call, and dreaded the coming test of strength:

> When I viewed him riding up, I never beheld such a display of pride arising from his deportment, attitude and jesture; he rode a lofty elegant horse, . . . his countenance appeared to me as bold and daring as satan himself, and with a commanding authority [he] called upon me, if I were there to come out, which I accordingly did, with a fearful and timorous heart. But O! how quickly can God level pride. . . . For no sooner did he behold my disconsolate looks, emaciated countenance and solemn aspect, then he . . . was riveted to the beast he rode on. . . . As soon as he could articulate a little his eyes fixed upon me, and his first address was this; "In the name of the Lord, what is the matter with you?"

Rhys Isaac, "Evangelical Revolt: The Nature of the Baptists' Challenge to the Traditional Order in Virginia, 1765 to 1775," *William and Mary Quarterly,* 3d ser. XXXI (1974), 345–366. Reprinted with permission of the author.

The evident overdramatization in this account is its most revealing feature for it is eloquent concerning the tormented convert's heightened awareness of the contrast between the social world he was leaving and the one he was entering.

The struggle for allegiance between these social worlds had begun with the Great Awakening in the 1740s, but entered into its most fierce and bitter phase with the incursions of the "New Light" Separate Baptists into the older parts of Virginia in the years after 1765. The social conflict was not over the distribution of political power or of economic wealth, but over the ways of men and the ways of God. By the figures in the encounter described we may begin to know the sides drawn: on the one hand, a mounted gentleman of the world with "commanding authority" responding to challenge; on the other, a guilt-humbled, God-possessed youth with "disconsolate looks ... and solemn aspect."

A second scene—this time in the Tidewater—reveals through actions some characteristic responses of the forces arrayed. From a diary entry of 1771 we have a description of the disruption of a Baptist meeting by some gentlemen and their followers, intent on upholding the cause of the established Church:

> Brother Waller informed us ... [that] about two weeks ago on the Sabbath Day down in Caroline County he introduced the worship of God by singing. ... The Parson of the Parish [who had ridden up with his clerk, the sheriff, and some others] would keep running the end of his horsewhip in [Waller's] mouth, laying his whip across the hymn book, etc. When done singing [Waller] proceeded to prayer. In it he was violently jerked off the stage; they caught him by the back part of his neck, beat his head against the ground, sometimes up, sometimes down, they carried him through a gate that stood some considerable distance, where a gentleman [the sheriff] gave him ... twenty lashes with his horsewhip. ... Then Bro. Waller was released, went back singing praise to God, mounted the stage and preached with a great deal of liberty.

Violence of this kind had become a recurrent feature of social-religious life in Tidewater and Piedmont. We must ask: What kind of conflict was this? What was it that aroused such antagonism? What manner of man, what manner of movement, was it that found liberty in endurance under the lash?

The continuation of the account gives fuller understanding of the meaning of this "liberty" and of the true character of this encounter. Asked "if his nature did not interfere in the time of violent persecution, when whipped, etc.," Waller "answered that the Lord stood by him ... and poured his love into his soul without measure, and the brethren and sisters about him singing praises ... so that he could scarcely feel the stripes ... rejoicing ... that he was worthy to suffer for his dear Lord and Master."

Again we see contrasted postures: on the one hand, a forceful, indeed brutal, response to the implicit challenge of religious dissidence; on the other, an acceptance of suffering sustained by shared emotions that gave release— "liberty." Both sides were, of course, engaged in combat, yet their modes of conducting themselves were diametrically opposite. If we are to understand the struggle that had developed, we must look as deeply as possible into the divergent styles of life, at the conflicting visions of what life should be like, that are reflected in this episode. . . .

The gentry style, of which we have seen glimpses in the confrontation with Baptists, is best understood in relation to the concept of honor—the proving of prowess. A formality of manners barely concealed adversary relationships; the essence of social exchange was overt self-assertion.

Display and bearing were important aspects of this system. We can best get a sense of the self-images that underlay it from the symbolic importance of horses. The figure of the gentleman who came to call Ireland back to society was etched on his memory as mounted on a "lofty . . . elegant horse." It was noted repeatedly in the eighteenth century that Virginians would "go five miles to catch a horse, to ride only one mile upon afterwards." This apparent absurdity had its logic in the necessity of being mounted when making an entrance on the social scene. The role of the steed as a valuable part of proud self-presentation is suggested by the intimate identification of the gentry with their horses that was constantly manifested through their conversation. Philip Fithian, the New Jersey tutor, sometimes felt that he heard nothing but "Loud disputes concerning the Excellence of each others Colts . . . their Fathers, Mothers (for so they call the Dams) Brothers, Sisters, Uncles, Aunts, Nephews, Nieces, and Cousins to the fourth Degree!"

Where did the essential display and self-assertion take place? There were few towns in Virginia; the outstanding characteristic of settlement was its diffuseness. Population was rather thinly scattered in very small groupings throughout a forested, river-dissected landscape. If there is to be larger community in such circumstances, there must be centers of action and communication. . . .

The most frequently held public gatherings at generally distributed centers were those for Sunday worship in the Anglican churches and chapels. . . .

Philip Fithian has left us a number of vivid sketches of the typical Sunday scene at a parish church, sketches that illuminate the social nature and function of this institution. It was an important center of communication, especially among the elite, for it was "a general custom on Sundays here, with Gentlemen to invite one another home to dine, after Church; and to consult about, determine their common business, either before or after Service," when they would engage in discussing "the price of Tobacco, Grain etc. and settling either the lineage, Age, or qualities of favourite Horses." The occasion also served to demonstrate to the community, by visual representation, the rank structure of society. Fithian's further description evokes a dramatic image of haughty squires trampling past seated hoi polloi to their pews in the front. He noted that it was "not the Custom for Gentlemen to go into Church til Service is beginning, when they enter in a Body, in the same manner as they come out." . . .

The ruling gentry, who set the tone in this society, lived scattered across broad counties in the midst of concentrations of slaves that often amounted to black villages. Clearly the great houses that they erected in these settings were important statements: they expressed a style, they asserted a claim to dominance. The lavish entertainments, often lasting days, which were held in these houses performed equally important social functions in maintaining this claim, and in establishing communication and control within the elite itself. Here the convivial contests that were so essential to traditional Virginia social culture would issue in their most elaborate and stylish performances. . . .

Discussion so far has focused on the gentry, for *there* was established in dominant form the way of life the Baptists appeared to challenge. Yet this way was diffused throughout the society. All the forms of communication and exchange noted already had their popular acceptances with variations appropriate to the context. . . .

The importance of pastime as a channel of communication, and even as a bond, between the ranks of a society such as this can hardly be too much stressed. People were drawn together by occasions such as horse races, cockfights, and dancing as by no other, because here men would become "known" to each other—"known" in the ways which the culture defined as "real." Skill and daring in that violent duel, the "quarter race"; coolness in the "deep play" of the betting that necessarily went with racing, cockfighting, and cards—these were means whereby Virginia males could prove themselves. Conviviality was an essential part of the social exchange, but through its soft coating pressed a harder structure of contest, or "emulation" as the contemporary phrase had it. Even in dancing this was so. Observers noted not only the passion for dancing—"*Virginians* are of genuine Blood—They will dance or die!"—but also the marked preference for the jig—in effect solo performances by partners of each sex, which were closely watched and were evidently competitive. In such activities, in social contexts high or low, enhanced eligibility for marriage was established by young persons who emerged as virtuosos of the dominant style. Situations where so much could happen presented powerful images of the "good life" to traditional Virginians, especially young ones. It was probably true, as alleged, that religious piety was generally considered appropriate only for the aged.

When one turns to the social world of the Baptists, the picture that emerges is so striking a negative of the one that has just been sketched that it must be considered to have been structured to an important extent by processes of reaction to the dominant culture.

Contemporaries were struck by the contrast between the challenging gaiety of traditional Virginia formal exchange and the solemn fellowship of the Baptists, who addressed each other as "Brother" and "Sister" and were perceived as "the most melancholy people in the world"—people who "cannot meet a man upon the road, but they must ram a text of Scripture down his throat." The finery of a gentleman who might ride forth in a gold-laced hat, sporting a gleaming Masonic medal, must be contrasted with the strict dress of the Separate Baptist, his hair "cut off" and such "superfluous forms and Modes of Dressing . . . as cock't hatts" explicitly renounced.

Their appearance was austere, to be sure, but we shall not understand the deep appeal of the evangelical movement, or the nature and full extent of its challenging contrast to the style and vision of the gentry-oriented social world, unless we look into the rich offerings beneath this somber exterior. The converts were proffered some escape from the harsh realities of disease, debt, overindulgence and deprivation, violence and sudden death, which were the common lot of small farmers. They could seek refuge in a close, supportive, orderly community, "a congregation of faithful persons, called out of the world by divine grace, who mutually agree to live together, and execute gospel discipline among them." Entrance into this community was attained by the relation of a personal experience of profound importance to the candidates, who would certainly be heard with respect, however humble their station. There was a community resonance for deep feelings, since, despite their sober face to the outside world, the Baptists encouraged in their religious practice a sharing of emotion to an extent far beyond that which would elicit crushing ridicule in gentry-oriented society. Personal testimonies of the experiences of simple folk have not come down to us from that time, but the central importance of the ritual of admission and its role in renewing the common experience of ecstatic conversion is powerfully evoked by such recurrent phrases in the church books as "and a dore was opened to experience." This search for deep fellow-feeling must be set in contrast to the formal distance and rivalry in the social exchanges of the traditional system. . . .

A concomitant of fellowship in deep emotions was comparative equality. Democracy is an ideal, and there are no indications that the pre-Revolutionary Baptists espoused it as such, yet there can be no doubt that these men, calling each other brothers, who believe that the only authority in their church was the meeting of those in fellowship together, conducted their affairs on a footing of equality in sharp contrast to the explicit preoccupation with rank and precedence that characterized the world from which they had been called. Important Baptist church elections generally required unanimity and might be held up by the doubts of a few. The number of preachers who were raised from obscurity to play an epic role in the Virginia of their day is a clear indication of the opportunities for fulfillment that the movement opened up to men who would have found no other avenue for public achievement. There is no reason to doubt the contemporary reputation of the early Virginia Baptist movement as one of the poor and unlearned. Only isolated converts were made among the gentry, but many among the slaves.

The tight cohesive brotherhood of the Baptists must be understood as an explicit rejection of the formalism of traditional community organization. . . .

The popular style and appeal of the Baptist Church found its most powerful and visible expression in the richness of its rituals, again a total contrast to the "prayrs read over in haste" of the colonial Church of England, where even congregational singing appears to have been a rarity. The most prominent and moving rite practiced by the sect was adult baptism, in which the candidates were publicly sealed into fellowship. A scrap of Daniel Fristoe's journal for June 15–16, 1771, survives as a unique contemporary description by a participant:

(Being sunday) about 2000 people came together; after preaching [I] heard others that proposed to be baptized. . . . Then went to the water where I preached and baptized 29 persons. . . . When I had finished we went to a field and making a circle in the center, there laid hands on the persons baptized. The multitude stood round weeping, but when we sang *Come we that love the lord* and they were so affected that they lifted up their hands and faces towards heaven and discovered such chearful countenances in the midst of flowing tears as I had never seen before.

The warm emotional appeal at a popular level can even now be felt in that account, but it must be noted that the scene was also a vivid enactment of *a* community within and apart from *the* community. We must try to see that closed circle for the laying on of hands through the eyes of those who had been raised in Tidewater or Piedmont Virginia with the expectation that they would always have a monistic parish community encompassing all the inhabitants within its measured liturgical celebrations. The antagonism and violence that the Baptists aroused then also become intelligible. . . .

Virginia Baptist sermons from the 1770s have not survived, perhaps another indication that their purely verbal content was not considered of the first importance. Ireland's account of his early ministry (he was ordained in 1769) reveals the ritual recurrence of the dominant themes expected to lead into repentance those who were not hardened: "I began first to preach . . . our awful apostacy by the fall; the necessity of repentance unto life, and of faith in the Lord Jesus Christ . . . our helpless incapacity to extricate ourselves therefrom I stated and urged."

As "seriousness" spread, with fear of hell-fire and concern for salvation, it was small wonder that a gentleman of Loudoun County should find to his alarm "that the *Anabaptists* . . . growing very numerous . . . seem to be increasing in afluence [influence?]; and . . . quite destroying pleasure in the Country; for they encourage ardent Pray'r; strong and constant faith, and an intire Banishment of *Gaming, Dancing,* and Sabbath-Day Diversions." That the Baptists were drawing away increasing numbers from the dominant to the insurgent culture was radical enough, but the implications of solemnity, austerity, and stern sobriety were more radical still, for they called into question the validity—indeed the propriety—of the occasions and modes of display and association so important in maintaining the bonds of Virginia's geographically diffuse society. Against the system in which proud men were joined in rivalry and convivial excess was set a reproachful model of an order in which God-humbled men would seek a deep sharing of emotion while repudiating indulgence of the flesh. Yet the Baptist movement, although it must be understood as a revolt against the traditional system, was not primarily negative. Behind it can be discerned an impulse toward a tighter, more effective system of values and of exemplary conduct to be established and maintained within the ranks of the common folk.

In this aspect evangelicalism must be seen as a popular response to mounting social disorder. It would be difficult—perhaps even impossible—to establish an objective scale for measuring disorder in Virginia. What can be established is that during the 1760s and 1770s disorder was perceived by many as increasing. . . . [T]he gentry's growing perception of disorder was focused on those forms of activity which the Baptists denounced and which provided the main arenas for the challenge and response essential to the traditional "good life." It was coming to be felt that horse racing, cockfighting, and card play, with their concomitants of gambling and drinking, rather than serving to maintain the gentry's prowess, were destructive of it and of social order generally. Display might now be negatively perceived as "luxury." . . .

. . . The hypothesis here advanced is that the social process was one in which popular perceptions of disorder in society—and hence by individuals in themselves—came to be expressed in the metaphor of "sin." It is clear that the movement was largely spread by revolt from within, not by "agitators" from without. Commonly the first visit of itinerant preachers to a neighborhood was made by invitation of a group of penitents already formed and actively meeting together. Thus the "spread of seriousness" and alarm at the sinful disorder of the traditional world tended to precede the creation of an emotional mass movement "under preaching." A further indication of the importance of order-disorder preoccupations for the spread of the new vision with its contrasted life style was the insistence on "works." Conversion could ultimately be validated among church members only by a radical reform of conduct. The Baptist church books reveal the close concern for the disciplinary supervision of such changes. . . .

A further mark of their radicalism, and without doubt the most significant aspect of the quest for a system of social control centered in the people, was the inclusion of slaves as "brothers" and "sisters" in their close community. When the Baptists sealed the slaves unto eternal life, leading them in white robes into the water and then back to receive the bread and wine, they were also laying upon them responsibility for godly conduct, demanding an internalization of strict Protestant Christian values and norms. They were seeking to create an orderly moral community where hitherto there had seemed to be none.

The slaves were members and therefore subject to church discipline. The incidence of excommunication of slaves, especially for the sin of adultery, points to the desire of the Baptists to introduce their own standards of conduct, including stable marital relationships, among slaves. A revealing indication of the perception of the problem in this area is found in the recurrent phrase that was sometimes given as the sole reason for excommunication: "walking disorderly." Discipline was also clearly directed toward inculcating a sense of duty in the slaves, who could be excommunicated for "disobedience and Aggrevation to [a] master."

The recurrent use of the words "order," "orderly," "disorderly" in the Baptist records reveals a preoccupation that lends further support to the hypothesis that concern for the establishment of a securer system of social control was a powerful impulse for the movement. "Is it orderly?" is the usual introduction to the queries concerning right conduct that were frequently brought forward for resolution at monthly meetings. . . .

When the Baptist movement is understood as a rejection of the style of life for which the gentry set the pattern and as a search for more powerful popular models of proper conduct, it can be seen why the ground on which the battle was mainly fought was not the estate or the great house, but the neighborhood, the farmstead, and the slave quarter. This was a contemporary perception, for it was generally charged that the Baptists were "continual fomenters of discord" who "not only divided good neighbours, but slaves and their masters; children and their parents ... wives and their husbands." The only reported complaint against the first preachers to be imprisoned was of "their running into private houses and making dissensions." The struggle for allegiance in the homesteads between a style of life modeled on that of the leisured gentry and that embodied in evangelicalism was intense. In humbler, more straitened circumstances a popular culture based on the code of honor and almost hedonist values was necessarily less securely established than among the more affluent gentry. Hence the anxious aggressiveness of popular anti–New Light feeling and action. . . .

Great popular movements are not quelled, however, by outfacing, nor are they stemmed by the ridicule, scorn, or scurrility of incomprehension. Moreover, they draw into themselves members of all sections of society. Although the social worlds most open to proselytizing by the Baptists were the neighborhoods and the slave quarters, there were converts from the great houses too. Some of the defectors, such as Samuel Harris, played a leading role in the movement. The squirearchy was disturbed by the realization that the contemptible sect was reaching among themselves. . . .

The intensity of the conflict for allegiance among the people and, increasingly, among the gentry, makes intelligible the growing frequency of violent clashes of the kind illustrated at the beginning of this article. The violence was, however, one-sided and self-defeating. The episode of April 1771 in which the parson brutally interfered with the devotions of the preacher, who was then horsewhipped by the sheriff, must have produced a shock of revulsion in many quarters. Those who engaged in such actions were not typical of either the Anglican clergy or the country gentlemen. The extreme responses of some, however, show the anxieties to which all were subject, and the excesses in question could only heighten the tension. . . .

FURTHER READING

Jon Butler, "Enthusiasm Described and Decried: The Great Awakening as Interpretive Fiction," *Journal of American History* 69 (1982), 305–325

C. C. Goen, *Revivalism and Separatism in New England, 1740–1800* (1962)

David D. Hall, *Worlds of Wonder, Days of Judgment: Popular Religious Belief in Early New England* (1989)

Alan Heimert, *Religion and the American Mind: From the Great Awakening to the Revolution* (1966)

Rhys Isaac, *The Transformation of Virginia, 1740–1790* (1982)

David S. Lovejoy, *Religious Enthusiasm in the New World: Heresy to Revolution* (1985)

Harry S. Stout, *The New England Soul: Preaching and Religious Culture in Colonial New England* (1986)

Patricia J. Tracy, *Jonathan Edwards, Pastor: Religion and Society in Eighteenth-Century Northampton* (1979)

Marilyn J. Westerkamp, *Triumph of the Laity: Scots-Irish Piety and the Great Awakening, 1625–1760* (1988)

CHAPTER

11

Mature Societies
in Colonial America

☙

American society changed dramatically in the middle decades of the eighteenth century, taking on characteristics that historians label as "mature." Native-born elites moved into leadership positions throughout the settlements in these years, and they developed relationships and roles suited to American conditions and demands. The colonial assemblies found sources of strength and ways of manipulating the imperial relationship.

Styles of life in the colonies achieved new standards. The wealthy appointed their newly elegant homes with imported fine furniture and china dishes. Whereas even the most successful seventeenth-century colonist had lived in a structure that was basically a large farmhouse, eighteenth-century elite homes began to be built around a central hall flanked by large rooms. The new house plan provided a setting for entertaining on a grand scale; at the same time it fostered a new emphasis on privacy in family life. Formerly guests walked through the front door directly into the living space; now family activities were hidden away, and only selected individuals were admitted to the living quarters.

Similar shifts occurred at all levels of society, as prices of imported English goods fell after 1740 and the volume of imports went up. Even families of modest means replaced wooden dishes with pottery and added chairs to their homes. Literacy grew as education was more widely available. The colonists attempted to keep in touch with European culture through personal libraries; Benjamin Franklin was involved in the creation of the first lending library in Philadelphia to widen access to books.

As urban areas grew, some historians have pointed to greater social differentiation, with a class of landless poor people emerging in the cities. On southern plantations slave forces were consolidated, and slave life became more regimented.

☙ D O C U M E N T S

Virginian Robert Beverley, whose description of public and private buildings in Virginia is the subject of the first document, wrote at the beginning of the eighteenth century, celebrating the new style of life in his colony and demonstrating the settlers' understanding of their own environment and its requirements. In the second excerpt colonist Hugh Jones describes Virginia's crops and the life of the slaves who tended them. In the third selection, passages from the diary of English-educated Virginian William Byrd of Westover, largely written in a secret code, show him beginning the day by reading Latin and Greek and often doing exercises (his "dance"). He usually ended his day by going out to the slave quarters and talking with "his people" (his slaves). In the fourth document the very different diary entries of tobacco planter Landon Carter for 1770 show how closely involved he was in the daily details of tending the crop and how deeply he relied on his slaves' knowledge. In the midst of this account, this slaveowner compares British attempts to tax the colonists to enslavement.

The excerpt in the fifth document from Benjamin Franklin's *Autobiography* describes his care as a young businessman to appear industrious, frugal, and business-like. Franklin gives a vivid impression of the shift taking place in households across the colonies to a higher standard of living, as his wife suddenly insists that he eat his porridge with a silver spoon from a china bowl. The final document, taken from John Adams's diary, records the future revolutionary and president's early days in the study of the law and his social insecurity among the elite members of the bar; he particularly resents the airs of fellow student Robert Treat Paine, who patronized him. The law profession was Adams's road to the status he so strongly desired.

Robert Beverley Describes Established Life in Virginia, 1705

There are two fine Publick Buildings in this Country, which are the most Magnificent of any in *America:* One of which is the College [of William and Mary] . . . , and the other the Capitol or State-House, as it was formerly call'd: That is, the House for Convention of the General Assembly, for the Setting of the General Court, for the Meeting of the Council, and for keeping of their several Offices.

Not far from this, is also built the publick Prison of the Country, which is a large and convenient Structure, with Partitions for the different Sexes, and distinct Rooms for Petty-Offenders. To this is also annexed a convenient Yard to Air the Criminals in, for preservation of their Life and Health, till the time of their Trial.

These are all erected at Middle-Plantation, now nam'd *Williamsburgh,* where Land is laid out for a new Town. The College, and Capitol are both built of Brick, and cover'd with Shingle.

The Private Buildings are of late very much improved; several Gentlemen there, having built themselves large Brick Houses of many Rooms on a Floor, and several Stories high, as also some Stone-Houses: but they don't covet to make them lofty, having extent enough of Ground to build upon; and now and then they are visited by high Winds, which wou'd incommode a towring Fabrick. They always contrive to have large Rooms, that they may be cool in Summer. Of late they have made their Stories much higher than formerly, and their Windows large, and sasht with Cristal Glass; and within they adorn their Apartments with rich Furniture.

All their Drudgeries of Cookery, Washing, Daries, etc. are perform'd in Offices detacht from the Dwelling-Houses, which by this means are kept more cool and Sweet.

Their Tobacco-Houses are all built of Wood, as open and airy as is consistent with keeping out the Rain; which sort of Building, is most convenient for the curing of their Tobacco.

Their common covering for Dwelling-Houses is Shingle, which is an Oblong Square of Cypress or Pine-Wood; but they cover their Tobacco-Houses with thin Clapboard; and tho' they have Slate enough in some particular parts of the Country, and as strong Clay as can be desired for making of Tile, yet they have very few tiled Houses; neither has any one yet thought it worth his while, to dig up the Slate, which will hardly be made use of, till the Carriage there becomes cheaper, and more common.

Hugh Jones on Agriculture and Slave Life in Virginia, 1724

The Negroes live in small cottages called quarters, in about six in a gang, under the direction of an overseer or bailiff; who takes care that they tend such land as the owner allots and orders, upon which they raise hogs and cattle, and plant Indian corn (or maize) and tobacco for the use of their master; out of which the overseer has a dividend (or share) in proportion to the number of hands including himself; this with several privileges is his salary, and is an ample recompence for his pains, and encouragement of his industrious care, as to the labour, health, and provision of the Negroes.

The Negroes are very numerous, some gentlemen having hundreds of them of all sorts, to whom they bring great profit; for the sake of which they are obliged to keep them well, and not overwork, starve, or famish them, besides other inducements to favour them; which is done in a great degree, to such especially that are laborious, careful, and honest; though indeed some masters, careless of their own interest or reputation, are too cruel and negligent.

The Negroes are not only encreased by fresh supplies from Africa and the West India Islands, but also are very prolifick among themselves; and they that are born there talk good English, and affect our language, habits, and customs; and though they be naturally of a barbarous and cruel temper, yet are they kept under by severe discipline upon occasion, and by good laws are prevented from running away, injuring the English, or neglecting their business.

Their work (or chimerical hard slavery) is not very laborious; their greatest hardship consisting in that they and their posterity are not at their own liberty or disposal, but are the property of their owners; and when they are free, they know not how to provide so well for themselves generally; neither did they live so plentifully nor (many of them) so easily in their own country, where they are made slaves to one another, or taken captive by their enemies.

The children belong to the master of the woman that bears them; and such as are born of a Negroe and an European are called Molattoes; but such as are born of an Indian and Negroe are called Mustees.

Their work is to take care of the stock, and plant corn, tobacco, fruits, etc. which is not harder than thrashing, hedging, or ditching; besides, though they are out in the violent heat, wherein they delight, yet in wet or cold weather there is little occasion for their working in the fields, in which few will let them be abroad, lest by this means they might get sick or die, which would prove a great loss to their owners, a good Negroe being sometimes worth three (nay four) score pounds sterling, if he be a tradesman; so that upon this (if upon no other account) they are obliged not to overwork them, but to cloath and feed them sufficiently, and take care of their health.

Several of them are taught to be sawyers, carpenters, smiths, coopers, etc. and though for the most part they be none of the aptest or nicest; yet they are by nature cut out for hard labour and fatigue, and will perform tolerably well; though they fall much short of an Indian, that has learned and seen the same things; and those Negroes make the best servants, that have been slaves in their own country; for they that have been kings and great men there are generally lazy, haughty, and obstinate; whereas the others are sharper, better humoured, and more laborious. . . .

As for timber they abound with excellent good; having about eight sorts of oak, several kinds of walnut-tree and hickory and pignut, pine, cedar, and cypress for shingles; which covering is lighter than tiles, and being nailed down, are not easily blown off in any tempest or gust.

The oak, etc. is of quick growth, consequently will not last so long as ours; though it has a good grain, and is freer from knots, and will last long enough for shipping, and ordinary uses.

When a tract of land is seated, they clear it by felling the trees about a yard from the ground, lest they should shoot again. What wood they have occasion for they carry off, and burn the rest, or let it lie and rot upon the ground.

The land between the logs and stumps they how up, planting tobacco there in the spring, inclosing it with a slight fence of cleft rails. This will last for tobacco some years, if the land be good; as it is where fine timber, or grape vines grow.

Land when tired is forced to bear tobacco by penning their cattle upon it; but cowpen tobacco tastes strong, and that planted in wet marshy land is called nonburning tobacco, which smoaks in the pipe like leather, unless it be of a good age.

When land is tired of tobacco, it will bear Indian corn, or English wheat, or any other European grain or seed, with wonderful increase.

Tobacco and Indian corn are planted in hills as hops, and secured by wormfences, which are made of rails supporting one another very firmly in a particular manner.

Tobacco requires a great deal of skill and trouble in the right management of it.

They raise the plants in beds, as we do cabbage plants; which they transplant and replant upon occasion after a shower of rain, which they call a season.

When it is grown up they top it, or nip off the head, succour it, or cut off the ground leaves, weed it, hill it; and when ripe, they cut it down about six or eight leaves on a stalk, which they carry into airy tobacco houses; after it is withered a little in the sun, there it is hung to dry on sticks, as paper at the paper-mills; when it is in proper case, (as they call it) and the air neither too moist, nor too dry, they strike it, or take it down, then cover it up in bulk, or a great heap, where it lies till they have leisure or occasion to stem it (that is pull the leaves from the stalk) or strip it (that is take out the great fibres) and tie it up in hands, or streight lay it; and so by degrees prize or press it with proper engines into great hogsheads, containing from about six to eleven hundred pounds; four of which hogsheads make a tun, by dimension, not by weight; then it is ready for sale or shipping.

There are two sorts of tobacco, viz. Oroonoko the stronger, and sweetscented the milder; the first with a sharper leaf like a fox's ear, and the other rounder and with finer fibres: but each of these are varied into several sorts, much as apples and pears are; and I have been informed by the Indian traders, that the inland Indians have sorts of tobacco much differing from any planted or used by the Europeans.

The Indian corn is planted in hills, and weeded much as Tobacco.

This grain is of great increase and most general use; for with this is made good bread, cakes, mush, and hommony for the Negroes, which with good pork and potatoes (red and white, very nice and different from ours) with other roots and pulse, are their general food.

Indian corn is the best food for cattle, hogs, sheep and horses; and the blades and tops are excellent fodder, when well cured, which is commonly used, though many raise good clover and oats; and some have planted sanfoin, etc.

In the marshes, and woods, and old fields is good range for stock in the spring, summer, and fall; and the hogs will run fat with certain roots of flags and reeds, which abounding in the marshes they root up and eat.

Besides, at the plantations are standard peach-trees, and apple-trees, planted out in orchards, on purpose almost for the hogs.

The peaches abound, and are of a delicious taste, and apple-trees are raised from the seeds very soon, which kind of kernel fruit needs no grafting, and is diversifyed into numberless sorts, and makes, with good management, an excellent cyder, not much inferior to that of Herefordshire, when kept to a good age; which is rarely done, the planters being good companions and guests whilst the cyder lasts. Here cherries thrive much better (I think) than in England; though the fruit-trees soon decay, yet they are soon raised to great perfection.

As for wool, I have had near as good as any near Leominster; and it might be much improved if the sheep were housed every night, and foddered and littered as in Urchinfield, where they have by such means the finest wool; but to do this, would be of little use, since it is contrary to the interest of Great Britain to allow them exportation of their woollen manufactures; and what little woollen is there made might be nearly had as cheap, and better from England.

As for provision, there is variety of excellent fish in great plenty easily taken; especially oysters, sheepheads, rocks, large trouts, crabs, drums, sturgeons, etc.

They have the same tame fowl as in England, only they propagate better; but these exceed in wild geese and ducks, cohoncks, blew-wings, teal, swans, and mallard.

Their beef and veal is small, sweet, and fat enough; their pork is famous, whole Virginia shoots being frequently barbacued in England; their bacon is excellent, the hams being scarce to be distinguished from those of Westphalia; but their mutton and lamb some folks don't like, though others extol it. Their butter is good and plentiful enough. Their venison in the lower parts of the country is not so plentiful as it has been, though there be enough and tolerably good; but in the frontier counties they abound with venison, wild turkies, etc. where the common people sometimes dress bears, whose flesh they say, is not to be well distinguished from good pork or bacon.

They pull the down of their living geese and wild and tame ducks, wherewith they make the softest and sweetest beds.

The houses stand sometimes two or three together; and in other places a quarter, half a mile, or a mile, or two, asunder, much as in the country in England.

Planter William Byrd's Diary
of a Planter's Month, 1740

1. I rose about 6, read Hebrew and Greek. I prayed and had coffee. I danced. The weather was cool and cloudy, the wind north. I wrote English and walked. My cold continued. I put things in order till dinner when I ate rice milk. After dinner came Doctor Mollet but had no news but a good stomach. After dinner we walked and played cards at night till 9. I prayed.

2. I rose about 6, read Hebrew but no Greek but wrote letters [to go] by the boat. I danced. The weather was cold and clear, the wind west. About 10 the Doctor went off and I wrote English and walked till dinner and ate roast beef. After dinner walked again. At night read English. Mrs. Byrd had the headache. I talked with my people, read English and prayed. My cold continued.

3. Rose about 6, read Hebrew and Greek. I prayed and had [pulse?]. I danced. The weather continued cold and clear, the wind west. I wrote several things, walked and read English till dinner when I ate roast turkey. After dinner we walked again. In the evening the people came with the wagon from Meherrin. I walked at night, talked with my people, read English and prayed. My cold continued. God save me.

4. I rose about 6, read Hebrew and Greek. I prayed and had coffee. I danced. The weather was cold and clear, the wind north. About 12 came John

William Byrd, "Diary for December 1740," in *Another Secret Diary of William Byrd of Westover*, ed. Maude H. Woodfin, trans. and coll. Marion Tinling. (Richmond, Virginia: The Dietz Press, Inc., 1942), 116–124. Reprinted by permission of Ms. Marion Tinling.

Stith and his wife, Mr. Pinkard and his wife, and Betty Stith, and dined. Captain Branch called but stayed not to dinner. I ate salt fish. After dinner it threatened rain so Mr. Pinkard and his wife stayed; the rest went. I prayed.

5. I rose about 6, read Hebrew and Greek. I prayed and had coffee. I danced. The weather was warm and cloudy, the wind north. I received letters from England from our friends, who were well, thank God. I walked and wrote English till dinner. Mrs. Stith's daughter and Mrs. Pinkard dined with us and I ate roast mutton. After dinner the company went away. I talked with my people and prayed.

6. I rose about 6, read Hebrew and Greek. I prayed and had tea. I danced. The weather was cold and wet, the wind northeast. It rained great part of the day. I wrote English till dinner when I ate rice milk. After dinner we talked because we could not walk. Nobody came from the Falls. At night I talked with my people, read English and prayed. My cold continued.

7. I rose about 6, read Hebrew and Greek. I prayed and had coffee. I danced. The weather was cold and clear, the wind northwest. I went not to church because it was cold. After church came no company but only Billy Hardyman. I ate roast beef. After dinner we talked and walked a little. Dr. Mollet came in the evening and stayed. I talked with my people and prayed.

8. I rose about 5 and prayed. I drank two dishes chocolate. The weather was cold and clear, the wind north. I recommended my family to the Almighty and about 8 went in the chariot as far as the lower church and then proceeded on horseback to Williamsburg, where we got about 3. I dined with the Commissary and ate roast mutton. After dinner we talked [of] all the news till 8, retired and prayed.

9. Rose about 6 and put my house in order. I prayed and breakfasted with the Commissary upon chocolate. Then went to the Governor's and saw Captain Lloyd and Mr. Stanton. About 12 went to the capitol, spoke to the [grand] jury, sat till 3, dined with Wetherburn, invited Captain Lloyd and other gentlemen, and ate roast venison. Sat till 7 and supped with the ladies at the Governor's; retired about 9 and prayed.

10. Rose about 6, prayed and had coffee. About 10 went to Colonel Grymes's and then returned to the Commissary's to council and kept Mr. Gooch in his place and refused the good King's orders; then dined with the Commissary and ate boiled pork. After dinner went to Lady Randolph's and then to Mr. Barradall's where I stayed with Colonel Robinson till 11; then went home and prayed.

11. I rose about 6, read only Greek. I appointed an overseer for Mount Folly. I prayed and had coffee. The weather was warm, the wind southwest. I went about 12 to Colonel Grymes's, who was gone; then to the coffeehouse, and then dined with Mr. Needler and ate hog's head. After dinner Dr. Mollet and I walked and in the evening I went to Lady Randolph's, played cards till 9, then went home and retired.

12. I rose about 6, prayed and had rice milk. The weather was cold and cloudy, the wind northeast. I rode to the new church and met my chariot and got home about 3 and found my family well, thank God. I ate salt fish. After

dinner I put things in order and walked. At night talked with my people and gave them cider, and prayed.

13. I rose about 6, read Hebrew and Greek. I prayed and had tea. I danced. The weather was cold and clear, the wind northwest. I wrote several things and walked till dinner, when I ate tripe. After dinner put things in order and walked. All well at the Falls, thank God. I talked with my people, sat an hour with my children, retired, read English, and prayed.

14. I rose about 6, read Hebrew and Greek. I prayed and had coffee. I danced. The weather began to be very cold, the wind north, so I went not to church but cleaned myself. Molly Stith came home to dine with us and I ate roast duck. After dinner drank tea, then walked a little in the garden. Molly Stith went home. At night talked with my people, read English, and prayed.

15. I rose about 6, read only Greek because I talked with Mr. Wood who came last night. I prayed and had tea. I danced. It was extremely cold, the wind northwest. We cut wood in the swamp. I persuaded Mr. Wood to go to Roanoke. I ate giblets for dinner. I had a letter from Daniel Custis that he was sick, and I answered it. At night I talked with Mr. Wood, spoke with my people and prayed.

16. I rose about 6, read Hebrew and Greek. I prayed and had hominy. I danced. The weather was cold and cloudy, the wind north, and snowed a little. Mr. Wood went away and I wrote several things till dinner when I ate salt fish. After dinner I put things in order but danced instead of walking because it was overcast. At night I talked with my people, read English and prayed. It rained first, then snowed much.

17. I rose about 6, read Hebrew and Greek. I prayed and had tea. I danced. The weather was cold with a snow, the wind northwest. My man Tom continued sick. I wrote English till one when Mr. Ned Randolph came, but brought no news. I ate roast pork. After dinner we talked till the evening, but could not look out, it was so cold. At night we played cards and supped till 11. I prayed.

18. I rose about 6 and read nothing. I prayed and had coffee. I danced. The weather was very cold, with snow and a cold wind at west. Mr. Randolph stayed and we played piquet all the morning till dinner when I ate roast goose. After dinner we talked of several matters till the evening when we played again till supper and I ate potato and milk. About 11 we retired and I prayed.

19. I rose about 6, read Hebrew and Greek. I prayed and had hominy. The weather continued very cold and clear, the wind northwest. However, Mr. Randolph went away and I wrote several things till dinner when I ate rice milk. After dinner it grew cloudy and threatened snow but it came not. I danced because I could not walk. At night talked with my people and prayed.

20. I rose about 6, read Hebrew and Greek. I prayed and had tea. I danced. The weather was cold and clear, the wind west and thawed a little. I wrote English and walked in the gallery till dinner when I ate sparerib. After dinner put several things in order. We lost one of the flats [seedling beds]. At night came Mr. [Ward]. I talked with my people and prayed. Dreamed my wife was drowned.

21. I rose about 6, but read nothing because talked with Mr. [Ward]. I prayed and had coffee. I danced. The weather continued cold and clear and froze extremely. I talked with Mr. [Ward] about my affairs above till 12, when he went away and I sent more people after my boat, God forgive me. I ate mutton for dinner. After dinner I danced because I could not walk, talked with my people, and prayed.

22. I rose about 6, read Hebrew and Greek. I prayed and had tea. I danced. The weather continued extremely cold, the wind still northwest. No news of my people; God preserve them. I read English. About one the people came, thank God, and brought the lost boat home. I examined my [cellars] and found them improved pretty well. I ate minced mutton. After dinner danced because I could not dance [*sic*]. I talked with my people and prayed.

23. I rose about 6, read Hebrew and Greek. I prayed and had hominy. The weather continued extremely cold; the wind blew hard at northwest. Two of my people brought down a beef in the night because it would not drive [*sic*]. I read English and walked in the gallery till dinner when I ate sausage and eggs. After dinner put things in order and danced because could not walk. At night talked with my people and prayed. It froze extremely hard.

24. I rose about 6, read Hebrew and Greek. I prayed and had tea. I danced. The weather was extra cold and clear, the wind still northwest and the river just frozen over. I wrote letters and walked in the gallery till dinner when I ate mutton steak. After dinner I put things in order and danced because I could not walk. At night L-s-n's son brought two turkeys, and some eggs and a goose came from Hanover. I talked with my people and prayed.

25. I rose about 6, read Hebrew and Greek. I prayed and had coffee. I danced. The weather was very cold and cloudy, the wind north and threatened more snow. Nobody went to church except my son because of the cold. I put myself in order. After church came two playfellows for my son, young Stith and Hardyman. I ate roast turkey. After dinner we talked and I danced. I talked with my people and prayed.

26. I rose about 6, read Hebrew and Greek. I prayed and had hominy. It snowed all last night and rained all day. God [preserve] us from a freeze. I gave G-r-n, Harry, and A-r-g-l a vomit for going off the plantation and staying all night, which did more good than whipping. I ate roast turkey. After dinner it held up and I talked with my people and prayed. I fell down [m-n-s].

27. I rose about 6, read Hebrew and Greek. I prayed and had tea. I danced. The weather was warmer, the wind southwest in the morning but came at noon again to northwest. I settled some accounts and read English till dinner when I ate roast goose. After dinner my son's visitors went home, notwithstanding the snow. I danced for want of walking. I talked with my people and ordered everything to be well fed.

28. I rose about 6, read Hebrew and Greek. I prayed and had coffee. I danced. It snowed again this morning a little, the wind north. I put myself in good repair and walked in the gallery. Tom fell and hurt his back for which he was bled and had a [s-r-q-r]. I ate broiled turkey for dinner and

then walked in the gallery. I talked with my people and prayed. Old B-s-n [*or* B-v-n] died; God save his soul.

29. I rose about 6, read Hebrew and Greek. I prayed and had tea. I danced. The weather was cold and cloudy, the wind southwest but thawed little. I read English and walked in the gallery till dinner when I ate salt fish and eggs. After dinner I danced because I could not walk. It was warmer and threatened rain but none came. I talked with my people and prayed. I slept not well.

30. I rose about 6, read Hebrew and Greek. I prayed and had tea. I danced. The weather was much warmer and cloudy, the wind west and threatened rain, but it came not, though it thawed all day. I read English till dinner when I ate roast turkey. After dinner I put things in order and danced because I could not walk. At night talked with my people, read English, and prayed.

31. I rose about 6, read Hebrew and Greek. I prayed and had tea. I danced. It continued to thaw, the wind northeast. I read English till dinner when I ate pork and peas. After dinner read English and danced because could not walk. I talked with my people and prayed. It snowed.

Planter Landon Carter on the Demands of Tobacco, 1770

29. Tuesday

Yesterday I rode by my fork plantation to Coll. Tayloe's and if anybody could have seen the least sign of those scuds of rain that happened on Friday morning, friday night, and the Sprinkling Saturday in the night we must have discovered it. But excepting in the plant patch there did not appear the least moisture so that little profess that George who was setting Corn there had left off upon account of the dryness of the earth and had got to weeding his field.

As we rode round we had the opportunity of discovering the Tobacco ground which Coll. Tayloe had planted on friday. On horseback we could not see above 3 plants in the whole 30,000. I sent Nassau in. He walked deep in the rows but could not see one alive and it was it seems the general complaint on Sunday with every body that had planted that the ground worm had cut off most of that which stood.

We have this morning just such another little sprinkling which promised so much that really I had inclined to have some hills cut off as my plants at the fork are fine and large but I had scarce given my orders when I found occasion by the ceasing of the rain to send to the overseer to keep on dunging till it should rain to some purpose. Indeed it is a difficult matter to act because,

Landon Carter, *The Diary of Colonel Landon Carter of Sabine Hall, 1752–1778*, ed. Jack Greene (Charlottesville: University Press of Virginia for Virginia Historical Society, 1965), 417–420. Reprinted by permission of The University Press of Virginia.

though planting without rain might be done very well and the plants in a manner so covered with earth that the worms could hardly cut them under ground, yet with wet earth the Cover would bake and injure the plant.

I find this business of dunging is a heavyer jobb than I would chuse it to be as the people yesterday were lazyer than common for what, the dung [was] not very far off. They seemed when I came home not to have done much.

Sam arrived from Mr. Edwards' with a particular account of Longwith's and Freshwater's Crop. Longwith does not tend but a little more than 10,000 Cornhills and not 20,000 Tobacco hills for 26 sharers and has not left for Freshwater 7,500 Tobacco hills per head at Blough point. But Freshwater himself has taken in 15,000 Corn hills a head so that from this we may discover the reason why we have made nothing for seven years there. Longwith had 3 shares which were profitable enough to him at the same time very indifferent for me considered in the real proportion and so I have written to that fellow very largely. It seems I have made Mr. Edwards my overlooker there very angry but I cannot help it for I will not starve and such management any longer there must bring me to it.

By accounts from all parts above and below very dry. The Assembly is sitting but only finishing the business left undone last session. Nothing said about the repeals of the Revenue Acts. The Association met and formed a Committee of 20 to amend that scheme but it seems they are so divided that at present there will be very little chance of agreeing to the amendments. Some of them are full as hearty as I thought they would be. Persons parading from no principle but only to make a show of Patriotism and Mr. T———— is at last found out to be the man I always took him, a noisy declaimer on nothing or next a kin to it he and Pendleton at the head of a party who were for meeting the Parliament half as they call this partial repeal of the acts so whilst we were inslaved by those that were not repealed we must go our half and give up that point.

Fine Language this, just as if there could be any half way between Slavery and freedom. Certainly one like of the former preserved must be the hold to which the [rest] of the chain might at any time be joined when the forging Smith's thought proper to add to it.

The rain, as I imagined it would do, left us almost as soon as a man could say John Smith Pease. I went down to see the hills cutting off and so little water had fallen that they were quite dry and dusty to a mere shell at top. However I have ordered there 18,000 to be planted this night in that dry dusty earth and covered over as I have done for 2 years past. The night moisture possibly will keep the plants alive as they are large and laid in full growth as to their roots till we can get a rain and I have observed that ground worm very seldom eats within the earth so that the covering them over will probable be a preservative against his ravages till the warmer weather shall put a period to his rising.

I have now the 2 Cow keepers, the sheep woman, 4 stout hands, sick, one lain in and Mary Ann in the Kitchin o[illegible] of my Crop gang at this very busy time.

30. Wednesday

Went to Mr. Ball's yesterday with Mr. Berkeley. A great prospect of rain but none as yet fallen which from the 6th of April 55 days including since the earth here has been blessed with any real moisture. It has mizzled, scudded, and sprinkled four times in the time once half an hour, once 15 minutes, once three minutes, and once perhaps 10 minutes, all of which did not even make moisture enough to hold out picking any thing of a plant patch. Nevertheless, having some very fine plants at the fork, I ordered Lawson yesterday to get about 15,000 of them ready drawn to plant between 5 and dark in the way I pursued last year, that is, open the hills with my hand put the plant with its roots at full liberty, press the earth close round upon those roots up to the level of the hill, then bend the plant to the sunrise and lay a handful of dry dust over it to the tips of the leaves.

But Lawson stranger like to the time such a work might be done in did not get above 8,000 plants drawn and planted in the place designed.

This day finish covering in my dung upon the hill. The whole ground replenished to beyond the valley going to the Mill and about 9 rows in the wattled ground for which we must contrive and scrape our stubbs another day.

Set the people this day to turning the rest of the hills in the last year's Cowpen ground by the gate below to compleat that piece in order to be planted every night in the same manner if no rain falls. I believe the natural moisture of the earth perpetually rising will keep the plant alive till we may have rain and the covering prevent the attacks of the ground worm who never eat below the earth. If so, the hastiness of others has not put them in any forwardness before me. Mr. Ball told me his people wormed over the day before the 30,000 he had planted and got 8 measured quarts of worms and yesterday he himself took 8 worms out of the same ground and five off from many hills.

Captain Quiney's boat brought my Goods, to wit, Billy Ball's box, A small cask of earthern ware for ditto No. 1. No. A cases for myself and 25 bags of salt, a Cheese, a speaking Trumpet, Some Seed, and a fan, and one last No. 1 R[obert] W[ormeley] C[arter].

It seems it took the fork gang all day yesterday setting the right hand corn field which is but one fourth of the ground they tend. The hemp wed out by Gardener Tom though very indifferently come up by means of the dry weather and I will fancy the badness of the seed for tutt was a Rascal in saving it. Lame Johnny has been 3 days weeding the flax and as he goes on will be three weeks but he says the young crab grass is coming much in it. We must take a day all hands to do this jobb at once.

We set in the Riverside Corn field tomorrow to hoe and set the corn if the ground [is] moistened.

31. Thursday

At last a mighty blizz of rain is come. It come on drop by drop from about dark last night so that we may reckon a full 30 days' dry weather in May and 24 in April.

I pursued my method of dry planting yesterday to the number of what my Overseer calls 15,000 but as he overreckoned the day before dry planting above 1,500 plants I have sent to have these counted.

My situation is such that, although I have more plants big enough, the ground I have cut off being of the stiffest land and quite mucky by the rain all night as I have no over abundance of plants I must run no chance of throwing them away in such a wet season.

Again as the hills I have turned is in the same stiff land it will evidently be making mortar of them to cut them of. Therefore the season must dry away more before I can venture upon that. Of course my hands can only go to setting Corn in my light fields till this season and its very moist effects shall abate. Then I must prepare a good stock of hills for dry planting or what moisture may happen and in particular turn all my hardest ground by which time I do suppose I shall have a great plenty of plants fit. But during this my river side corn field has all its lists to break up owing to the quantity I tend as well as the hardness of the Tobacco hills that I have turned and the vast heaps of dung I have buried. However I am in hopes the great breadth of the ridges which I hoed to plant Corn in will keep that from suffering or being in the least injured till those lists can be hoed and as the Fork are better than 3 parts done weeding I do imagine I shall have 6 of those hands at least to throw in and help out with this work very soon.

I receive this rain with prodigious pleasure. The earth dearly wanted it in all my cultivations as well as the old fields and every thing I hope will be benefited by it for my plant patches were all cleaned wed out.

Benjamin Franklin on How to Get On in Philadelphia (c. 1730–c. 1750), 1793

... I now opened a small stationer's shop. I had in it blanks of all kinds; the correctest that ever appeared among us. I was assisted in that by my friend Breintnal. I had also paper, parchment, chapmen's books, etc. One Whitemarsh, a compositor I had known in London, an excellent workman, now came to me, and worked with me constantly and diligently; and I took an apprentice, the son of Aquila Rose.

I began now gradually to pay off the debt I was under for the printing-house. In order to secure my credit and character as a tradesman, I took care not only to be in *reality* industrious and frugal, but to avoid the appearances to the contrary. I dressed plain, and was seen at no places of idle diversion. I never went out a fishing or shooting; a book indeed sometimes debauched me from my work, but that was seldom, was private, and gave no scandal; and, to show that I was not above my business, I sometimes brought home the paper I purchased at the stores, through the streets on a wheelbarrow. Thus being esteemed an industrious, thriving young man, and paying duly for what I bought, the merchants who imported stationery solicited my custom; others proposed supplying me with books, and I went on prosperously. In the meantime, Keimer's credit and business declining daily, he was at last forced to sell his printing-house, to satisfy his creditors. He went to Barbadoes, and there lived some years in very poor circumstances.

His apprentice, David Harry, whom I had instructed while I worked with him, set up in his place at Philadelphia, having bought his materials. I was at first apprehensive of a powerful rival in Harry, as his friends were very able, and had a good deal of interest. I therefore proposed a partnership to him, which he fortunately for me rejected with scorn. He was very proud, dressed like a gentleman, lived expensively, took much diversion and pleasure abroad, ran in debt, and neglected his business; upon which, all business left him; and, finding nothing to do, he followed Keimer to Barbadoes, taking the printing-house with him. There this apprentice employed his former master as a journeyman; they quarrelled often, and Harry went continually behind-hand, and at length was obliged to sell his types and return to country work in Pennsylvania. The person who bought them employed Keimer to use them, but a few years after he died. . . .

At the time I established myself in Pennsylvania, there was not a good bookseller's shop in any of the colonies to the southward of Boston. In New York and Philadelphia, the printers were indeed stationers; but they sold only paper, almanacs, ballads, and a few common school-books. Those who loved reading were obliged to send for their books from England; the members of the Junto had each a few. We had left the ale-house, where we first met, and hired a room to hold our club in. I proposed that we should all of us bring our books to that room, where they would not only be ready to consult in our conferences, but become a common benefit, each of us being at liberty to borrow such as he wished to read at home. This was accordingly done, and for some time contented us.

Finding the advantage of this little collection, I proposed to render the benefit from the books more common by commencing a public subscription library. I drew a sketch of the plan and rules that would be necessary, and got a skilful conveyancer, Mr. Charles Brockden, to put the whole in form of articles of agreement to be subscribed; by which each subscriber engaged to pay a certain sum down for the first purchase of the books, and an annual contribution for increasing them. So few were the readers at that time in Philadelphia, and the majority of us so poor, that I was not able with great industry to find more than fifty persons, mostly young tradesmen, willing to pay down for this purpose forty shillings each, and ten shillings per annum. With this little fund we began. The books were imported. The library was opened one day in the week for lending them to subscribers, on their promissory notes to pay double the value if not duly returned. The institution soon manifested its utility, was imitated by other towns, and in other provinces. The libraries were augmented by donations, reading became fashionable; and our people having no public amusements to divert their attention from study, became better acquainted with books, and in a few years were observed by strangers to be better instructed and more intelligent than people of the same rank generally are in other countries.

When we were about to sign the above-mentioned articles, which were to be binding on us, our heirs, etc., for fifty years, Mr. Brockden, the scrivener, said to us, "You are young men, but it is scarcely probable that any of you will live to see the expiration of the term fixed in the instrument." A number of us, however, are yet living; but the instrument was after a few years rendered null, by a charter that incorporated and gave perpetuity to the company.

The objections and reluctances I met with in soliciting the subscriptions made me soon feel the impropriety of presenting one's self as the proposer of any useful project that might be supposed to raise one's reputation in the smallest degree above that of one's neighbours, when one has need of their assistance to accomplish that project. I therefore put myself as much as I could out of sight, and stated it as a scheme of *a number of friends,* who had requested me to go about and propose it to such as they thought lovers of reading. In this way my affair went on more smoothly, and I ever after practised it on such occasions; and, from my frequent successes, can heartily recommend it. The present little sacrifice of your vanity will afterwards be amply repaid. If it remains a while uncertain to whom the merit belongs, some one more vain than yourself may be encouraged to claim it, and then even envy will be disposed to do you justice, by plucking those assumed feathers, and restoring them to their right owner.

This library afforded me the means of improvement by constant study, for which I set apart an hour or two each day, and thus repaired in some degree the loss of the learned education my father once intended for me. Reading was the only amusement I allowed myself. I spent no time in taverns, games, or frolics of any kind; and my industry in my business continued as indefatigable as it was necessary. I was indebted for my printing-house; I had a young family coming on to be educated, and I had two competitors to contend with for business who were established in the place before me. My circumstances, however, grew daily easier. My original habits of frugality continuing, and my father having, among his instructions to me when a boy, frequently repeated a proverb of Solomon, *"Seest thou a man diligent in his calling, he shall stand before kings, he shall not stand before mean men,"* I thence considered industry as a means of obtaining wealth and distinction, which encouraged me—though I did not think that I should ever literally *stand before kings,* which, however, has since happened; for I have stood before *five,* and even had the honour of sitting down with one, the King of Denmark, to dinner.

We have an English proverb that says, *"He that would thrive must ask his wife."* It was lucky for me that I had one as much disposed to industry and frugality as myself. She assisted me cheerfully in my business, folding and stitching pamphlets, tending shop, purchasing old linen rags for the paper-makers, etc. We kept no idle servants, our table was plain and simple, our furniture of the cheapest. For instance, my breakfast was for a long time bread and milk (no tea), and I ate it out of a two-penny earthen porringer, with a pewter spoon. But mark how luxury will enter families, and make a progress, in spite of principle; being called one morning to breakfast, I found it in a china bowl, with a spoon of silver! They had been bought for me without my knowledge by my wife, and had cost her the enormous sum of three and twenty shillings; for which she had no other excuse or apology to make but that she thought *her* husband deserved a silver spoon and china bowl as well as any of his neighbours. This was the first appearance of plate and china in our house; which afterwards, in a course of years, as our wealth increased, augmented gradually to several hundred pounds in value. . . .

John Adams on His Legal Education, 1758

Tuesday [24 October]

Rode to Boston. Arrived about $\frac{1}{2}$ after 10. Went into the Court House, and sett down by Mr. Paine att the Lawyers Table. I felt Shy, under Awe and concern, for Mr. Gridley, Mr. Prat, Mr. Otis, Mr. Kent, and Mr. Thatcher were all present and looked sour. I had no Acquaintance with any Body but Paine and Quincy and they took but little Notice. However I attended Court Steadily all Day, and at night, went to Consort with Samll. Quincy and Dr. Gardiner. There I saw the most Spacious and elegant Room, the gayest Company of Gentlemen and the finest Row of Ladies, that ever I saw. But the weather was so dull and I so disordered that I could not make one half the observations that I wanted to make.

Wednesday [25 October]

Went in the morning to Mr. Gridleys, and asked the favour of his Advice what Steps to take for an Introduction to the Practice of Law in this County. He answered "get sworn."

Ego. But in order to that, sir, as I have no Patron, in this County.

G. I will recommend you to the Court. Mark the Day the Court adjourns to in order to make up Judgments. Come to Town that Day, and in the mean Time I will speak to the Bar for the Bar must be consulted, because the Court always inquires, if it be with Consent of the Bar.

Then Mr. Gridley inquired what Method of Study I had pursued, what Latin Books I read, what Greek, what French. What I had read upon Rhetorick. Then he took his Common Place Book and gave me Ld. Hales Advice to a Student of the Common Law, and when I had read that, he gave me Ld. C[hief] J[ustice] Reeves Advice [to] his Nephew, in the Study of the common Law. Then He gave me a Letter from Dr. Dickins, Regius Professor of Law at the University of Cambridge, to him, pointing out a Method of Studying the civil Law. Then he turned to a Letter He wrote himself to Judge Lightfoot, Judge of the Admiralty in Rhode Island, directing to a Method of Studying the Admiralty Law. Then Mr. Gridley run a Comparison between the Business and studies of a Lawyer or Gentleman of the Bar, in England,

and that of one here. A Lawyer in this Country must study common Law and civil Law, and natural Law, and Admiralty Law, and must do the duty of a Counsellor, a Lawyer, an Attorney, a sollicitor, and even of a scrivener, so that the Difficulties of the Profession are much greater here than in England.

The Difficulties that attend the study may discourage some, but they never discouraged me. [Here is conscious superiority.]

I have a few Pieces of Advice to give you Mr. Adams. One is to pursue the Study of the Law rather than the Gain of it. Pursue the Gain of it enough to keep out of the Briars, but give your main Attention to the study of it.

The next is, not to marry early. For an early Marriage will obstruct your Improvement, and in the next Place, twill involve you in Expence.

Another Thing is not to keep much Company. For this application of a Man who aims to be a lawyer must be incessant. His Attention to his Books must be constant, which is inconsistent with keeping much Company.

In the study of Law the common Law be sure deserves your first and last Attention, and He has conquered all the Difficulties of this Law, who is Master of the Institutes. You must conquer the Institutes. The Road of Science is much easier, now, than it was when I sett out. I began with Co. Litt. and broke thro.

I asked his Advice about studying Greek. He answered it is a matter of meer Curiosity.—After this long and familiar Conversation we went to Court. Attended all Day and in the Evening I went to ask Mr. Thatchers Concurrence with the Bar. Drank Tea and spent the whole Evening, upon original sin, Origin of Evil, the Plan of the Universe, and at last, upon Law. He says He is sorry that he neglected to keep a common Place Book when he began to study Law, and he is half a mind to begin now. Thatcher thinks, this County is full.

Thursday [26 October]

Went in the morning to wait on Mr. Prat. He inquired if I had been sworn at Worcester? No. Have you a Letter from Mr. Putnam to the Court? No. It would have been most proper to have done one of them things first. When a young Gentleman goes from me into another County, I always write in his favour to the Court in that County, or if you had been sworn, there, you would have been intitled to be sworn here. But now, no Body in this County knows any Thing about you. So no Body can say any Thing in your favour, but by hearsay. I believe you have made a proper Proficiency in science, and that you will do very well from what I have heard, but that is only hearsay. [How different is this from Gridleys Treatment? Besides it is weak, for neither the Court nor the Bar will question the Veracity of Mr. Gridly and Mr. Prat, so that the only Uncertainty that can remain is whether Mr. Putnam was in Earnest, in the Account he gave of my Morals and Studies to them Gentleman, which cannot be removed by a Line from him, or by my being sworn at Worcester, or any other Way than by getting Mr. Putnam sworn.] After this, he asked me a few, short Questions about the Course of my studies which I answered, and then came off as full of Wrath as [I] was full of Gratitude when I left Gridley the morning before. Prat is infinitely harder of Access than Gridley. He is ill natured, and Gridley is good natured.—Attended Court all Day, and at night waited on Otis at his office where I conversed with him and he, with great Ease and familiarity, promised me to join the Bar in recommending me to the Court. Mr. Gridley lent me Van Muydens Compendiosa Institutionum Justiniani Tractatio in usum Collegiorum. Editio tertia prioribus Auctior et emendatior. Pax Artium Altrix.—After I have mastered this, I must read Hoppius's Commentary on Justinian. The Design of this Book is [to] explain the technical Terms of the civil Law, and to settle the Divisions and Distributions of the civil Law. By the Way this is the first Thing a student ought to aim at, viz. distinct Ideas under the terms and a clear apprehension of the Divisions and Distributions of the science. This is one of the principal Excellences of Hawkins's Pleas of the Crown, and it is the very End of this Book of Van Muyden's.

Let me remarke here on important neglect of the last Week. I omitted minuting the Names of the Cases at Trial in my Ivory Book, and I omitted to keep Pen, Ink and Paper at my Lodgings, in order to comitt to Writing, at Night, the Cases and Points of Law that were argued and adjudged in the Day.

Let me remember to mark in my Memorandum Book, the Names of the Cases, and the Terms and Points of Law that occur in each Case, to look these Terms and Points in the Books at Otis's, Prats or any other office, and to digest and write down the whole in the Evening at my Lodgings. This will be reaping some real Advantage, by my Attendance on the Courts, and, without this, the Observations that I may make will lie in total Confusion in my mind.

Friday, Saturday, Sunday, Monday [27–30 October]

All Spent in absolute Idleness, or what is worse, gallanting the Girls.

Tuesday [31 October]

Set down, and recollected my self, and read a little in Van Muyden, a little in naval Trade and Commerce.

Wednesday [1 November]

Read a little in Van Muyden, and a little in naval Trade and Commerce.

Thursday [2 November]

Rode as far as Smelt Brook. Breakfasted, made my fire and am now set down to Van Muyden in Earnest. His latin is easy, his deffinitions are pretty clear, and his Divisions of the subject, are judicious.

Sunday [5? November]

Drank Tea at Coll. Quincy's. He read to me a Letter Coll. Gouch wrote him in answer to his Questions, whether a Justices Court was a Court of Record? and then concluded, "So that Sammy was right, for he was all along of that Opinion. I have forgot what your Opinion was?" [This must be a Lye, or else Partiality and parental affection have blotted out the Remembrance that I first started to his son Sam and him too, the Doubt whether he had Jurisdiction as a Justice—and made him really imagine, what he wished had been true viz. that Samll. had started it. If he did remember he knew it was insult to me. But I bore it. Was forgetfulness, was Partiality, or was a cunning Design to try if I was not vain of being the Starter of the Doubt, the true Cause of his saying, He forgot what my Opinion was.]

Sam has the utmost Reason to be grateful to Mr. Pratt. He will have an opportunity 100 times better than Mr. Prat had of rising into the Practice and Reputation of the Law. I want to see and hear Sam at the Bar. I want to know how he will succeed. I am concerned for him. The Govr. likes Sam much better than Ned. He has seen or heard some of Neds freaks. This is a Partiality in favor of one Child and against another quite indecent in a father. Tis great Weakness to expose himself so before Strangers.

Monday [6? November]

Went to Town. Went to Mr. Gridleys office, but he had not returned to Town from Brookline. Went again. Not returned. Attended Court till after 12 and began to grow uneasy expecting that Quincy would be sworn and I have no Patron, when Mr. Gridly made his Appearance, and on sight of me, whispered to Mr. Prat, Dana, Kent, Thatcher &c. about me. Mr. Prat said no Body knew me. Yes, says Gridley, I have tried him, he is a very sensible Fellow.—At last He rose up and bowed to his right Hand and said "Mr. Quincy," when Quincy rose up, then bowed to me, "Mr. Adams," when I walked out. "May it please your Honours, I have 2 young Gentlemen Mr. Q. and Mr. Adams to present for the Oath of an Attorney. Of Mr. Q. it is sufficient for me to say he has lived 3 Years with Mr. Prat. Of Mr. Adams, as he is unknown to your Honours, It is necessary to say that he has lived between 2 and 3 Years with Mr. Put[nam] of Worcester, has a good Character from him, and all others who know him, and that he was with me the other day several Hours, and I take it he is qualified to study the Law by his scholarship and that he has made a very considerable, a very great Proficiency in the Principles of the Law, and therefore that the Clients Interest may be safely intrusted in his Hands. I therefore recommend him with the Consent of the Bar to your Honors for the Oath." Then Mr. Prat said 2 or 3 Words and the Clerk was ordered to swear us. After the Oath Mr. Gridley took me by the Hand, wished me much Joy and recommended me to the Bar. I shook Hands with the Bar, and received their Congratulations, and invited them over to Stones to drink some Punch. Where the most of us resorted, and had a very chearful [Chat?].

Tuesday, December 3 or 4 [5?]

Bob Paine is conceited and pretends to more Knowledge and Genius than he has. I have heard him say that he took more Pleasure in solving a Problem in Algebra than in a frolick. He told me the other day, that he was as curious after a minute and particular Knowledge of Mathematicks and Phylosophy, as I could be about the Laws of Antiquity. By his Boldness in Company, he makes himself a great many Enemies. His Aim in Company is to be admired, not to be beloved. He asked me what Duch Commentator I meant? I said Vinnius.—Vinnius, says he, (with a flash of real Envy, but pretended Contempt,) you cant understand one Page of Vinnius.—He must know that human Nature is disgusted with such incomplaisant Behaviour. Besides he has no Right to say that I dont understand every Word in Vinnius, or even in [...] for he knows nothing of me. For the future let me act the Part of a critical spy upon him, not that of an open unsuspicious friend.—Last Superiour Court at Worcester he dined in Company with Mr. Gridly, Mr. Trowbridge, and several others, at Mr. Putnams, and altho a modest attentive Behaviour would have best become him in such a Company, yet he tried to ingross the whole Conversation to himself. He did the same, in the Evening, when all the Judges of the Superiour Court with Mr. Winthrop, Sewall, &c. were present, and he did the same last Thanksgiving day, at Coll. Quincies, when Mr. Wibirt, Mr. Cranch &c. were present. This Impudence may sett the Million a Gape at him but will make all Persons of Sense despize him, or hate him. That evening at Put[nam]s, he called me, a Numbskull and a Blunder Buss before all the Superiour Judges. I was not present indeed, but such expressions were indecent and tended to give the Judges a low Opinion of me, as if I was despized by my Acquaintance. He is an impudent, ill-bred, conceited fellow. Yet he has Witt, sense, and Learning, and a great deal of Humour, and has Virtue and Piety except his fretful, peevish, Childish Complaints against the Disposition of Things. This Character is drawn with Resentment of his ungenerous Treatment of me, and Allowances must therefore be made, but these are unexaggerated facts.

Lambert setts up for a Witt and a Humourist. He is like a little nurley ill natured Horse that kicks at every Horse of his own size, but lears and shears off from every one that is larger. I should mind what I say before him for he [is] always watching for wry Words to make into a droll story to laugh at. He laughs at John Thayer, for saying, "Lambert, I am sorry [I] am your good Friend I am sorry. This will cost you between 2 and 3 hundred Pounds." And it was a silly, [... impertinent?], ignorant Speech. He laughs at Field for being nettled at his laughter. Field complained that he laughed at him. Lambert said, I will laugh when I please. If you carry me to the Rat hole I will laugh all the Way, and after I get there.—Such fellows are hated by all mankind, yet they rise and make a figure, and People dred them.

Altho men of bitter witt, are hated and feared, yet they are respected, by the World.

Quære, was there ever a Witt, who had much Humanity and Compassion, much Tenderness of Nature? Mr. Congreve was tender, extreamly tender of giving offence to any man. Dr. Arbuthnot was a[s] great a Wit and Humourist, yet he was tender, and prudent. Mr. Cranch has Witt, and is tender and [gentle?].

The other Night I happened to be at the Drs., with Ben. Veasey. He began to prate upon the Presumption of Philosophers in erecting Iron Rods to draw the Lightning from the Clouds. His Brains were in a ferment with strong Liquor and he railed, and foamed against those Points and the Presumption that erected them, in Language taken partly from Scripture and partly from the drunken Disputes of Tavern Philosophy, in as wild mad a manner as King Lear raves, against his Daughters Disobedience and Ingratitude, and against the meaness of the Storm in joining with his Daughter against him in Shakespears Lear. He talked of presuming upon God as Peter attempted to walk upon the Water, attempting to controul the Artilry of Heaven, an Execution that Mortal man cant Stay—the Elements of Heaven, fire, Heat, Rain, Wind, &c.

Let me search for the Clue, which Led great Shakespeare into the Labyrinth of mental Nature! Let me examine how men think. Shakespeare had never seen in real Life Persons under the Influence of all those Scenes of Pleasure and distress, which he has described in his Works, but he imagined how a Person of such a Character would behave in such Circumstances, by analogy from the Behaviour of others that were most like that Character in nearly similar Circumstances, which he had seen.

❧ E S S A Y S

In the essays that follow, historians Richard D. Brown of the University of Connecticut and Timothy H. Breen of Northwestern University explore the means by which men achieved a sense of identity and membership in eighteenth-century America. In the tobacco colonies and New England alike, coming of age involved acquiring the skills that made men effective. For the planters, that meant learning in detail to recapitulate the routines of previous generations. For the young New Englanders John Adams and Robert Treat Paine, it meant a Harvard education and apprenticeship in the law, a profession that took on new status in this period. In both situations these men developed a sense of fellowship, and rivalry, with those going through the same experiences at the same time. Finally, although their lives and routines differed dramatically, leaders in both regions learned through vivid experience the price and benefits of involvement in the British commercial and political system.

John Adams, Robert Treat Paine, and the Practice of Law

RICHARD D. BROWN

Before the Revolutionary era lawyers were few, confined to Boston, and they seldom held any public office. From the colony's founding and for a century thereafter, no practicing lawyer was ever elected to the General Court; and after one was elected in 1738, twenty years passed before an attorney was again elected. Even within the judiciary, where legal expertise might be most highly valued, trained lawyers were rarities. Colonial and provincial magistrates were usually drawn from the ranks of land-owning gentlemen and farmers and from among the merchant elite, men who were well-connected to their constituencies.

Lawyers, who had never been welcome in the Puritan colony, were widely viewed with suspicion. Indeed no occupation or profession was so generally mistrusted in colonial tradition as lawyers, who were frequently berated along with usurers as parasites who preyed on their neighbors and society at large. Their emergence as a small but significant professional group dates from the 1730s. Even after the expansion of commerce created jobs and legitimacy for the legal profession, it was widely seen as a necessary evil rather than a positive good. To the degree that lawyers gained prestige and recognition during the mid-18th century—and they did—their enhanced stature was not connected to any noticeable shift in the Yankee Puritan outlook, but was rather the result of the increasing Anglicization of the upper reaches of Massachusetts society through connections with royal government and English trade. During the Revolution most lawyers remained loyal to the Crown; and many abandoned republican Massachusetts in 1775–76.

Yet this exodus, particularly of senior Boston and Salem lawyers, in what one scholar calls "one of the strangest paradoxes of early American history," did not stigmatize the profession as a whole, and it was to lawyers that the public increasingly turned for leadership. Even though most prominent lawyers had come down on the Tory side, there were others, often younger men, who had established outstanding republican credentials in the 1760s—James Otis, Joseph Hawley, Oxenbridge Thatcher, Robert Treat Paine, and John Adams among them. Ever since the Stamp Act resistance in 1765, the Revolutionary movement had thrust lawyers into major political roles. Their rise from sufferance to prominence was already underway. . . .

Among the chief reasons people came to know and to support attorneys in politics was their unique placement, social and regional, in 18th-century Massachusetts communication networks. Learned and articulate, lawyers were also known to be informed about public affairs beyond parish and township boundaries. Moreover as politics based on paternalistic leadership faded, it was lawyers—more than clergymen, merchants, landed gentlemen, or yeomen—who were publicly on view as shrewd, knowledgeable agents and advocates. In light of the prevailing social ethos that idealized union and harmony, the ethos that normally guided clergymen and town officers alike, lawyers were exceptional because they were free to assert a new political role as public advocates. For them, engaging in conflict violated no cherished values; it was a routine, calculated exercise. Since controversy was their business, they came to appear as appropriate agents to defend community interests as the conflict with Britain grew.

Robert Treat Paine and John Adams were two lawyers who came to assume such roles. Their careers from the time they graduated from Harvard College in 1749 and 1755, respectively, until the Massachusetts General Court selected them to serve as delegates to the Continental Congress in 1774, illustrate how, as lawyers, these two brilliant young men came to emerge as central public figures in the oldest, largest, and most influential New England colony. In both cases their places as lawyers in the communication networks of the province and their towns and counties account substantially for their political prominence.

Though Paine and Adams both had kinfolk scattered through New England as a consequence of their ancestors' arrival during the Great Migration of the 1630s, neither built his career on the strength of powerful connections or family wealth. And while neither man began life poor, they were both self-made men who climbed by calculating their advancement and exploiting their opportunities. For both of them family support for a Harvard college education launched their journeys into the first rank of Massachusetts and national leadership. Yet how Paine and Adams came to Harvard, and how they achieved recognition and power were not foreordained. Law, for Robert Treat Paine, became a means for halting the downward slide of his family's fortunes, while for John Adams the law supplied a ladder upward from his respectable but modest origins. Their choice of law and their means of pursuing it reveal how the unique position of lawyers in provincial information networks enabled them to achieve legitimacy and recognition as political leaders in Massachusetts.

Robert Treat Paine was the son of a Harvard-trained clergyman, Thomas Paine, who resigned from his Weymouth pulpit in the 1730s to become a Boston merchant. By the time "Treat," as he was then called, was ready for college, at age fourteen, in 1745, his father's ventures were prospering. On paper, at least, Thomas Paine was worth tens of thousands of pounds: he owned ships, land, a Boston mansion, and a few domestic slaves. At Harvard, Treat's social status, which was enhanced by his father's college degree and wealth as well as his mother's descent from the 17th-century Connecticut Governor Robert Treat, placed him ninth among twenty-five new students. Had Thomas Paine's business continued to thrive it appears that Treat would also have become a merchant. But owing to the hazards of shipping during King George's war and post-war credit, Treat's father was deeply in debt by his senior year. Consequently Robert Treat Paine left Harvard in 1749 with the tastes and expectations of a rich man's son but without the means of satisfying them. He would have to make a career from scratch.

Before deciding what to do, he took the job that was open to any impecunious college graduate as a stopgap—that of schoolmaster in a remote country town, in this case Lunenburg, forty miles northwest of Boston. Being a schoolmaster in central Massachusetts was no career for an ambitious college graduate, and, predictably, Paine soon grew restless with the social isolation it entailed. Yet Paine's first reaction to his new role, his amused gratification at suddenly becoming a learned authority among country people who valued information highly, gives an inkling of his future as a lawyer-statesman. Simply by being learned and informed he acquired instant celebrity at Lunenburg. Boarding at the home of a militia officer he reported, "in the evning great numbers of the Neighbours (i.e. 5 or 6) resorted there for the benefit of Conversation; and seeing their Schoolmaster there and so lately come from Boston too, they Questioned me on subjects relating to Marketts State Politics &c many of which Subjects scarce ever before entertain'd my mind. To all these I gave very learned and elaborate Answers, and in Short when I did nott understand the Topic I follow'd that renown'd Practice of using Words and Expressions without meaning." Though he made fun of the bumpkins, he liked being plied with "*so many* Questions" and being called "a *Philosopher.*" He did not even mind his friends' raillery when they called him "the *Lunenburg Oracle,*" because the stature and authority that a learned, cosmopolitan gentleman enjoyed in the information-starved countryside was flattering to the eighteen-year-old Paine.

But as the months stretched on, Lunenburg was not so rewarding as to compensate for his isolation from his adoring sisters and his college friends. "I live here almost out of the world," he groaned; so he left in 1750 for a teaching post in Boston. From there he began to seek his fortune in what seemed the quickest way possible—trade. His first scheme was a voyage to the Carolinas, but he lost money on the cargo of tar he brought back and two further trips to North Carolina were no more profitable. Next he tried a venture to the Mediterranean, which proved more educational than lucrative. Before concluding that trade would not be the easy route to wealth that it had been for his father, he led a whaling expedition to Newfoundland, with equally disappointing results. Only then did he turn to law.

Although for the secular-minded Paine the decision in favor of law was pragmatic—his hobbies, clockmaking, mechanics, and physics were unrelated—it was an ideal choice. Highly articulate and fond of speaking in company, Paine was also an active reader and essayist according to current English tastes. As a lawyer he would enter a learned, liberal profession that had become lucrative in Boston by the mid-1750s and was only just beginning to penetrate the rest of the province. As he explained to his father, "I doubt not I shall get ahead. . . . If a new County be Created there must be some Lawyers and I don't doubt with diligent application to my studies I shall be qualified."

Paine began his studies in January 1755 with a relative, Abijah Willard, in Lancaster, Worcester County. He supported himself by keeping school and preaching in Shirley, where the pulpit was vacant. Though no scholar of religion, he found, as at Lunenburg, he could please the country people. They did not scorn his patched, shabby college gown, nor were they aware that in the half-dozen sermons he gave them he was exhausting his theological wisdom. His excursions as a preacher were welcome distractions from the dry business of studying law. As he confided to a sister, "my circumstances in Life obliges [me] to apply closer to my Secular Studies than my Inclination . . . I have no other prospects of Subsistence but the Labours of my Brain, and Necessity urges that my Gains should be speedy." In spite of his resolve, however, Paine took a vacation from his law studies in the summer and fall of 1755 to join New England's expedition against the French at Crown Point on Lake Champlain. Attracted by the adventure as well as the cash payment that service as a chaplain promised, Paine returned with enough money to live in Boston as an apprentice to a leading attorney, Benjamin Prat. After that there were no more detours, and Paine was admitted to the Suffolk County bar in 1757, qualifying as a barrister in the superior court a year later. Though law had begun as a respectable meal ticket for Robert Treat Paine, he found in it a calling that suited his temperament. In court, where he would have to communicate authoritatively with his superiors on the bench while also persuading yeoman and artisan jurors, his capacity for serious learning and his glib self-assurance would win respect.

For John Adams, whose family background and personality contrasted with Paine's, the destination was the same but the journey was different. Unlike Paine, Adams was a self-critical, utterly conscientious person who measured himself according to ideal ethical and professional standards that he could never satisfy. Though less self-confident than Paine, at bottom he was far more ambitious. Where Paine's objective was respectable wealth, Adams wanted more; and he embraced law as a learned discipline and a professional calling that held the promise of lasting fame.

When John Adams was born in 1735 he was already "destined . . . long before his birth to a public Education" by a father who was, though a shoemaker and farmer, "fond of reading" and an admirer of learning. Later, although Adams would speak of his parents' "Ignorance," he described his father as an ideal type of the successful yeoman who

> by his Industry and Enterprize soon became a Person of more Property and Consideration in the Town than his Patron had been. He became a Select Man, a Militia Officer and a Deacon in the Church. He was the honestest Man I ever knew. In Wisdom, Piety, Benevolence and Charity In proportion to his Education and Sphere of Life, I have never seen his Superior.

With such a father encouraging a career of learning and piety in the ministry, Adams' decision to practice law was the result of much soul-searching that saw him leaning to medicine and divinity before finally deciding. . . .

. . . Nevertheless Adams would become a lawyer. He agreed with the conventional Yankee criticisms that a lawyer "often foments more quarrels than he composes, and inriches himself at the expense of impoverishing others more honest and deserving than himself," but he would not be that kind of a parasitic lawyer. Observation of provincial politics had taught him that "Law is indeed an Avenue to the more important offices of the state," and it was just this sort of public recognition that he craved. He worried that his "Birth and fortune" permitted him "no hopes of Being useful that way," but he believed the goal itself was virtuous—"the happiness of human Society is an object worth the pursuit of any man."

Several months later, when Adams at last contracted to study law with James Putnam of Worcester, he was still of two minds. . . . So as to conquer his lingering doubts about the path he had chosen he resolved "never to commit any meanness or injustice in the Practice of Law." That he still harbored the "illiberal Prejudices" against lawyers that were part of his Massachusetts heritage was evident in the brave assertion he made to himself that "the Study and Practice of Law, I am sure does not dissolve the obligations of morality or of Religion." At bottom what Adams sought was the secular role that his own generation was to create, wherein he could not only become prosperous but also achieve fame through public service that was morally equivalent to the ministry.

When he dreamed of his future in the 1750s Adams himself understood such hopes were fanciful. The more experienced, socially sophisticated Paine seeing the law as a passport to prestige and prosperity for someone whose assets were his wits, grasped the current reality. So did a generation of students at Harvard and Yale who opted for the law instead of the ministry in unprecedented numbers from the mid-1740s to the early 1760s. Yet as it turned out, partly because of this influx of native, college-trained lawyers— many of whom were ministers' sons—the ideal of the legal profession changed. By the 1770s it was coming to approach Adams' earlier vision of public service. The New England college culture that the new generation brought with them to the profession combined the ideals of Roman honor and glory with a commitment to Christian virtue. From the perspective of the older and more worldly, London-trained and immigrant lawyers who had helped create the profession in Boston, this idealistic college culture seemed a naive affectation at best. According to lawyers who remained loyal to the Crown, this idealism was a fraud.

Naive and sincere or not, this culture nourished a communication network among recent graduates and formed a central motif in the early careers of lawyers like Paine and Adams. It influenced their personal development, their social behavior, and their understanding of their roles as lawyers in society. The young men who entered the legal profession in the 1750s and 1760s, while other friends prepared for medicine and the ministry, often remained in close touch, and in their letters and visits constantly sought to uphold the idealistic standards of learning, refinement, and virtue they had adopted at college. Whether they read law, medicine, or divinity, they also read Vergil and Cicero. Apprentice lawyers like Paine and Adams who were transcribing deeds and writs also copied the forms of prose and poetry of the most approved modern writers in the original essays and verse they wrote to amuse and impress each other. The consequences for the legal profession, for public life, and for regional communication patterns in Massachusetts, both among individuals and for communities, were far-reaching.

One dimension of college culture that Paine's and Adams' fellow alumni carried into their professional careers was the fraternal posture, with both the cooperative and competitive relationships fraternity embodies. Addressing each other as "Brother" long after college, they formed quasi-familial networks that, as the legal profession became formally organized, reinforced the clubby, guild-like aspirations of the bar. Simultaneously they competed with each other for stature according to the values they shared— learning, virtue, and the ability to perform in public, a talent that brought worldly success in terms of clients and reputation. This competition reshaped the model of the lawyer to include virtue and public service in place of cunning, and created an information network that in its province-wide collegiality resembled that of clergymen.

The content and values of college culture that were so much more re-warding emotionally than the details of common law and techniques of plead-ing were intertwined. Understanding nature through scientific study, for ex-ample, was learning about the Divine creation. Pondering the orations of Cicero—a favorite among this generation of lawyers—combined lessons in rhetoric with homilies on civic virtue. The object in keeping up one's learning was to maintain the identity so dearly acquired at college. Only by continuing to cultivate the studies and manners of the college man could they retain the elevated, cosmopolitan qualities that entitled any college graduate, whatever his family origin, to the rank of gentleman. For those like Paine and Adams whose careers placed them miles away from Cambridge and Boston, the ne-cessity for maintaining the college network was especially keen.

Had they all enjoyed the privilege of being Boston lawyers like the first two generations in the profession, their identities as cosmopolitan gentlemen would have been more secure. For in the first half of the 18th century, vir-tually all Massachusetts lawyers lived in Boston where they met together daily in coffeehouses and taverns as well as at court. Routinely mixing with the leading officials and merchants of the province, they easily remained part of a community of gentlemen, aloof from the uneducated "pettifoggers" with whom country lawyers had to practice and compete. Later, when Paine and Adams took up law, established Boston lawyers like Robert Auchmuty and Benjamin Prat were insulated from what Adams called the "tittle-tattle" of local conversation. For the lucky few who could, like Adams' classmate Jon-athan Sewall, pursue a Boston and a royal office-holding career in the 1750s and 1760s, it was much easier to retain a genteel identity than for the more numerous graduates who, like Paine and Adams, ended up in Taunton, Brain-tree, or farther afield. . . .

. . . Having eagerly incorporated college culture into his own world view, Adams would not and could not be merely a lawyer. Like his peers, he sought to be a cosmopolitan gentleman. Writing melodramatically to another lawyer friend, Adams avowed that without "the Aquisition of Knowledge . . . it would be a punishment to live." . . .

Classical, philosophical, and Christian learning was ultimately what de-fined a gentleman in provincial Massachusetts. And among college graduates, whatever their age, their learning supplied significant class consciousness. Col-lege stamped them as cosmopolitan gentlemen who, whether obscure or prom-inent, enjoyed access to a network of peers who rose to stations of importance. For lawyers no less than clergy, these connections supplied avenues of infor-mation and acquaintance beyond their profession as they traveled the court circuit and when, later on, they moved into the legislature. . . .

. . . Apprenticeship, which often meant moving into his mentor's home, as Adams did, included access to the master lawyer's social and professional circles, where making an impression was as much a part of one's apprentice-ship as mastering the law. Since religion, natural science, and history rivaled politics as topics of discussion, the legal reports and commentaries that were the apprentice's primary study were not sufficient. To be prepared for society they must also read as the gentry read, from a miscellany of current and classical authors.

Robert Treat Paine, with his cultivated Boston background and his wide-ranging experience in coastal and transatlantic trade and in the army, excelled in company. With a mixture of envy and irony Adams described him as a "universal Scholar, gay Companion, and accomplish'd Gentleman," after spending an evening with him at the home of a Worcester gentleman. . . .

Where only the local gentry were concerned, a college graduate might readily excel in company. But, when the superior court and its entourage made their circuit through the counties, the competition was keener and the stakes much higher for a future barrister. "Last Superior Court at Worcester," Adams noted that Paine "dined in Company with Mr. Gridly, Mr. Trowbridge, and several others, at Mr. Putnams, and altho a modest attentive Behavior would have best become him in such a Company, yet he tried to ingross the whole Conversation to himself. He did the same, in the Evening, when all the Judges of the Superiour Court with Mr. Winthrop, Sewall, &c were present." By now Paine, a newly admitted barrister, was capable of flying high in company. Though Adams regarded him as "impudent, ill-bread, [and] conceited," he conceded that Paine also possessed "Witt, sense, and Learning, and a great deal of Humour, and has Virtue and Piety." For Adams, who lacked Paine's vivacity and social self-confidence, the strategy for impressing his elders and betters would be less adventuresome and far more circumspect.

Impetuously, Adams had indeed begun by aiming "at Wit and Spirit, at making a shining Figure in gay Company." Though "in Company with Persons much superior to my self in Years and Place," like Paine he had "talked to shew my Learning." But lacking the panache to carry off such a performance, Adams retreated "to labour more for an inoffensive and aimiable . . . Character." His way of impressing leading lawyers and jurists would be solid and sedate—he would outdistance his peers by the depth and breadth of his legal scholarship. The civil law would be the key to his victory since, as he noted, "few of my Contemporary Beginners, in the Study of the Law, have the Resolution, to aim at much Knowledge in the Civil Law." When he had achieved some familiarity with Justinian and the commentaries of the Dutch scholar Vinnius, he believed he would "gain the Consideration and perhaps the favour of Mr. Gridley and Mr. Pratt." Adams, who formed this strategy after many visits in his mentor James Putnam's home, some on occasions when Gridley and Prat were part of the company, had read the clues accurately. When Adams called on Gridley to seek his patronage for admission to the Suffolk County bar, the senior barrister regarded as the most scholarly of Boston attorneys interviewed Adams at length. Adams then accompanied Gridley to court and observed its proceedings before calling on Oxenbridge Thatcher to seek his support. With Thatcher the conversation was indirect: "Drank Tea and spent the whole Evening, upon original sin, Origin of Evil, the Plan of the Universe, and at last, upon Law." This was the conversation of a New England gentleman that a Tidewater gentleman might see as cant. When the evening was over, Thatcher observed that Suffolk County was already "full" of lawyers, but he made no objection to Adams joining their number.

Two weeks later Adams' apprenticeship formally ended when Gridley introduced him to the court, announcing that Adams had

> a good Character from him [Putnam], and all others who know him, and that he was with me the other day several Hours, and I take it he is qualified to study the Law by his scholarship and that he has made a very considerable, a very great Proficiency in the Principles of the Law, and therefore that the Clients Interest may be safely intrusted in his Hands. I therefore recommend him.

When the formal ritual was completed, Adams sealed his entrance into this select fraternity in the customary way by inviting the members of the bar to a tavern "to drink some Punch." With that, Adams joined Paine as a practicing attorney. . . .

. . . When lawyers opened offices and entered practice, they needed clients immediately—people who would entrust their property interests to them, over-looking their youth and inexperience for the sake of their technical learning and verbal ability. As apprentices a Paine or an Adams strove to impress their betters in the profession and in society; as practicing attorneys it was also urgent to please the ordinary land-owning farmers and artisans of the coun-tryside and villages. Building one's reputation and visibility, acquiring prom-inence and respect, were the essentials for establishing a paying clientele.

In their frustration with these realities both Paine and Adams privately wished that family wealth and connections could have enabled them simply to step into a prosperous practice as did, they imagined, some of their better situated peers. Yet in the late 1750s when they began, like nearly all young lawyers they could not expect wealthy merchant clients or lucrative and pres-tigious government patronage. The fact was that men like Paine and Adams had seized law as an opportunity precisely because they lacked advantages of wealth and prominent patrons. Both were attracted to the prospect of earning a living in law by the realization that outside of Boston and Salem there were few trained, college-educated lawyers; and in some long-settled counties there were scarcely any even as late as the 1760s. By establishing practices in Taunton and Braintree, Paine and Adams selected locations where they could provide a new professional level of service. . . .

. . . In making his place and building his reputation, the fledgling lawyer needed to woo and impress a shifting array of people both above and below him in the social hierarchy. He needed to be capable of talking Latin or Yankee, and prepared to quote technical treatises and cite English case law, besides referring to popular writings like Watts and Doddridge and the alma-nac. At the same time, both for personal and professional reasons it was important to remain current in the belletristic and philosophical college culture of one's peers. That it was necessary to engage in several levels of commu-nication in order to build up a practice is evident from John Adams' beginning in Braintree. For him the town offered particular advantages, not only because "there had never been a Lawyer in any Country Part of the then County of Suffolk," but because he could save on expenses by living with his parents, who were eager to have him. Moreover, though Adams' talents as a lawyer were unknown locally, he was a native son, known to most of the inhabitants as the promising offspring of their respected North Parish deacon and select-man. Adams' family background would disarm suspicions that in another town might taint him with the generic mendacity associated with lawyers. But just being Deacon Adams' son was not enough, as he well knew. . . .

So Adams, who had just recently been immersing himself in Justinian to impress Jeremiah Gridley, now set his books aside and began to make the local rounds, finding to his dismay after spending months on Latin codes, that knowing the province law of Massachusetts was more pertinent than the civil law. Instead of an evening with fellow lawyers, an evening spent at the home of a militia officer "gave me Opportunity to display some knowledge of Law." A visit to a deacon's led to conversations on British politics, and on the way home to others on "Husbandry, and the Tittletattle of the Town." Pursuing local visibility, Adams made himself known "as a knowing as well as a familiar young fellow" to local officials who were opinion leaders, as well as to the ordinary men and women whose gossip, smiles, and frowns could make or break his reputation. To "speak and shake Hands," to inquire after wives and children, to listen respectfully to loquacious townsmen, and to "mix with the Croud in a Tavern, in the Meeting House or the Training field" were Adams' tasks. The objective was "to sett the Tongues of old and young Men and Women a prating in ones favour."

Until he gained a secure following and a busy practice, Adams pursued the path of pleasing those he saw as his inferiors in learning, ability and aspiration. One spring morning, for example, he accompanied his father to an auction of leases on town lands because of what he could learn about the process and the local people, as well as to "Spread" his reputation and "lift myself into Business." Afterwards he triumphantly reported, "I was consulted by 2 Men this afternoon, who would not have applied to me if I had not been at Vendue." As Adams' first cases came along, he worried over their disposition from concern at the appearance he would make. When he lost his first case before Major Crosby, the Braintree Justice of the Peace—involving damages when a farmer seized and impounded a neighbor's stray cow— Adams was acutely embarrassed. Because he had prepared a defective writ, he worried "it will be said I undertook the Case but was unable to manage it." The victor would "proclaim it," so the news would be "in the mouth of every Body . . . [and] An opinion will spread among the People, that I have not Cunning enough to cope with [the farmer] Lambert." His competitors like "Bob P[aine]" would "pick up this Story to laugh at." Though the case was trivial in itself and would never be published in a newspaper, it would cer-tainly make the rounds of the Braintree information network of households and taverns, and possibly spill beyond the town into the county as well. Har-vard College, book-learning, and the respect of the Boston bar could not erase this defeat.

This early setback was actually useful to Adams, since it convinced him to redouble his efforts to earn the respect of common property holders by mastering their everyday legal issues. Along the way some of Adams' college-bred airs were replaced by a solid respect for common farmers and what they could teach him. Encouraging polite conversation was a staple of contemporary English advice literature for would-be gentlemen like Adams: books were best for instruction about the past, travel was encouraged for learning about other lands, but it was said that conversation was the key to understanding people and society. In England, in Virginia, and in Massachusetts too, this prescription applied to the drawing room, tavern, and coach conversations of the well-bred—not the discourse of common farmers. But Adams, in the course of making himself familiar and visible, discovered he was learning both about his own society and the law of Massachusetts along the way. "You may get more," he observed, "by studying Town meeting, and Training Days, then you can by reading Justinian and all his voluminous and heavy Commentators." Questions put by his farmer clients "led me into Useful Thoughts and Inquiries," he noted, matters that his own studies omitted. Most surprising to Adams, common people could teach him much that he had not gleaned in Worcester at the polite dining tables of the Putnams and Chandlers or at the court sessions and tavern suppers that accompanied them. On some subjects he found "that as much knowledge in my Profession is to be acquired by Conversing with common People about the Division of Estates, Proceedings of Judge of Probate, Cases that they have heard as Jurors, Witnesses, Parties, as is to be acquired by Books." In cultivating the ordinary property holders of Suffolk County Adams not only achieved visibility, he acquired knowledge of common legal practices that made his professional training serviceable and effective.

The progress of Adams' reputation here was all based on local impressions and reports. On his second outing before Major Crosby, "a long obstinate Tryal . . . of the most litigious, vexatious suit," Adams was the victor. Next day "the story" was already spreading: "Salisbury told my Uncle and my Uncle told Coll. Quincy." The account circulating told how "saucy" Adams had been, and that the young lawyer had "whipped" Major Crosby by reminding the old Justice of the Peace that he was under oath not to advise either party but to "do Justice equally." Six months later, with more victories to his credit, Adams was confident when he again appeared before Crosby. Though he knew he was still making "Mistakes, and omissions," he also knew himself to be "more expert" each time. "I feel my own strength," Adams reported, "I see the complacent Countenances of the Crowd, and I see the respectful face of the Justice, and the fearful faces of Petty foggers." By his third year in practice Adams had come into his own as a legal force in his own community. Within only a few more years he would, like Paine, be a force in the county and province. Possessing a secure local reputation based on practical results, he could now turn his attention to winning the esteem of a more cosmopolitan audience whose legal business involved tens, hundreds, even thousands of pounds.

The precise nature of the reputations Adams and Paine developed are not readily known, but their general outlines can be reconstructed from their own behavior and their relationships with lawyers and other prominent people. From their early days in Boston when they were seeking admission to the bar, both were regarded as sufficiently promising to win swift admission to the legal fraternity. Indeed Paine, who began in Boston under the patronage of his mentor Benjamin Prat (himself a student of Jeremiah Gridley), was raised to the rank of barrister only a year after qualifying for practice. That he chose to settle in Taunton in 1761 was a measure of just how discouragingly competitive Boston was for young attorneys in a hurry to succeed. At the Bristol County seat, Taunton, as at Braintree and many other towns where commercial agriculture flourished, there was a sufficient volume of business to support a lawyer. Heretofore this business had been divided among many part-time, self-taught practitioners who, with a law manual or two, were as competent as local justices required. Called "pettifoggers" by members of the bar, these men possessed practices and reputations that were purely local. The arrival on the scene of a Paine or an Adams posed a dire threat to their business.

The turf battles that pitted learned, cosmopolitan newcomers against these local practitioners were crucial to the way that professional lawyers defined themselves by exploiting their information advantages as they cultivated the people. In order to build a successful practice, college-bred lawyers like Adams had to start by creating a local base in which they sharply and self-consciously differentiated themselves from the pettifoggers. Though the lawyers ultimately won this struggle, their opponents were not helpless in their efforts to stave off professional competition. Adams, the interloper, righteously denounced the "dirty and ridiculous Litigations [that] have been multiplied ... owing to the multiplicity of Petty foggers." To block him, Adams reported that one of these pettifoggers "set himself to work to destroy my Reputation." If Adams had not actively promoted his own reputation for accessibility and competence, his local base certainly would have been undermined.

Yet attorneys like Adams and Paine enjoyed advantages that pettifoggers—a motley array of farmers, traders, artisans, and tavern-keepers—however troublesome their local gossip-mongering, could not touch. College-bred lawyers possessed outside connections and superior training that brought victories at the county courts such as the Inferior Court of Common Pleas and at the Superior Court of Judicature. Traveling the court circuits, pleading together, contesting each other, arguing in court and conversing out of it, the professional lawyers developed an understanding of each other's abilities and characters. Competition notwithstanding, they felt a fraternal solidarity. . . .

Adams and Paine, who were very much part of this movement of professionalization, actively cultivated relationships with well-placed lawyers and judges through correspondence and socializing. Adams even joined his patron Gridley in founding a sodality or reading club of half-a-dozen lawyers who met periodically in Boston in the mid-1760s. It was for this group that Adams began the research that resulted in his *Dissertation Concerning the Canon and Feudal Law,* a work that appeared in installments in the *Boston Gazette* and later won an audience in England where it was printed as a pamphlet, and which ultimately led to Adams' election to the English Society for the Bill of Rights. Here was the reputation and recognition among the learned and prominent that Adams had long cherished.

Books were crucial to Adams' and Paine's self-images and to the reputations they sought to convey to the leading men of the province. In the
decades following their graduation from Harvard both men actively collected
libraries of hundreds of volumes. At Taunton and Braintree, where no one
else had a first-rate library, the incentive to have one's own collection was
keen for those who wished, as they did, to keep up with their peers in Boston.
Paine, who inherited the residue of his father's ministerial library, began with
a running start in religion and theology. Over the years, however, as Paine
became a gentleman of the law, he sold off some of his inherited holdings
in Latin, Greek, and Hebrew, and built a more secular, polite collection to
complement his law books. When he made a catalog of his library in 1768,
he held hundreds of titles including poetry, belles lettres, and political essays,
in addition to works in history, travel, natural philosophy, theology and law.
This same list shows that Paine routinely lent books out, mostly to friends
and relations living in the Taunton region, but including also clergymen, physicians, and other lawyers—including Jeremiah Gridley and his Taunton colleague Daniel Leonard. . . .

As with Paine, the goal of building a first-rate legal and political library
was part of Adams' ambition from his early days with Putnam and as
Gridley's protégé, a time when he had "suffered very much for Want of
Books." To fulfill this dream he must first be prosperous, so Adams recalled,
when "in the Years 1766 and 1767 my Business increased, as my Reputation
spread, I got Money and bought Books and Land." Though he began in the
usual way by making the rounds of Boston booksellers, Adams came to the
conclusion that he must have some more regular system to provide for his
needs in current publications. His solution was to establish a standing order
with the London booksellers and publishers E. and C. Dilly. In addition to
specific titles that he would request from time to time, they were to send him
"every Book and Pamphlet, of Reputation, upon the subjects of Law and
Government as soon as it comes out." Josiah Quincy, his younger colleague
with whom he had worked defending the British soldiers in the trial following
the Boston Massacre, already had such an arrangement, and Adams was ready
to spend up to £30 yearly—half a country clergyman's salary—so as to keep
himself and his collection current. Many years later Adams would be able to
boast that "by degrees I procured the best Library of Law in the State." For
Adams, clearly, the possession of his library was an embodiment of his faith
in the doctrine that knowledge is power. . . .

The style of public speaking that the new generation of lawyers like
Adams and Paine cultivated was direct and familiar rather than pedantic, but
it was also elevated above the common tavern or town-meeting harangue.
Indeed it might be likened to the evangelical style that George Whitefield had
popularized throughout the colonies during their youth. In addition, college
experience, and the practice of declaiming Cicero in English translation as a
private exercise, colored their sense of dramatic form as well as their appreciation of selfless patriotic appeals. Though Paine's prosecution of the soldiers
after the Boston Massacre resulted in somewhat lenient verdicts, his oral performance was a triumph. As a friend wrote, "you attracted closely the Atten-

tion of your Audience *Ciceronian like* & Increas'd your Fame." Though it
was Adams' misfortune to argue the unpopular side of the case, defending
the soldiers, the jury found him and his colleague Josiah Quincy persuasive,
so Adams and Quincy, as well as Paine, gained recognition from this public
service.

What was crucial, however, in creating the image of lawyers as public
servants was serving as advocates on the popular side of an issue as Paine
had done. "To have the Passions, Prejudices, and Interests of the whole Audience, in a Mans Favour," Adams recognized, "will convert plain, common
Sense, into profound Wisdom, nay wretched Doggerell into sublime Heroics."
Six months after the Boston Massacre trial ended, on July 4, 1771, Adams
had his day in the sun when, at a session of the superior court sitting in York
County, he successfully argued for a £10 penalty against customs officials for
taking an excessive fee. Though Adams believed his performance was just
average, he was congratulated effusively for "the Patriotick manner in which
you conducted that Cause," and he was assured that he had consequently
"obtained great Honour in this County." Indeed, as the case was ending, "a
Man came running down" from the courthouse exclaiming, "'That Mr. Adams
has been making the finest Speech I ever heard in my Life. He's equall to
the greatest orator that ever spoke in Greece or Rome.'" It was in the prosecution of such popular causes that the image of lawyers as public servants
rather than parasites took shape. Because of their strategic location in a legal
system built on advocacy, certain privileged, well-connected lawyers were
viewed as lackeys to tyranny, while others outside the shadow of government
patronage were seen as champions of liberty.

Heretofore, under ordinary circumstances, there had been no reason for
the legal profession to take on such public importance. In the past, clergymen
and magistrates had possessed a virtual monopoly on public address in a
society where their voices were respected as authoritative. Other than town-
meeting debates, New England had no tradition of public contention, certainly
not by learned, eloquent gentlemen publicly disputing secular issues. Public
controversy, when it arose, was carried on in the newspapers, in pamphlets,
and from the pulpit. Until now, courtroom argument had never been infused
with broad, patriotic themes designed to appeal to the many. This was a new
genre—analogous to New Light preaching—created by lawyers in a forum
especially adapted to their station and capacities. In 1761, when James Otis,
Jr., electrified young attorneys like Adams as he argued against Writs of Assistance before a tiny audience in the council chamber, he was inaugurating
a new form of public speaking and a new role for lawyers. Several years
later Patrick Henry's legendary courtroom declamation "Give me liberty, or
give me death" acted as a similar catalyst in Virginia. Henry, like Otis, like
Paine, like Adams, was paid by his clients to argue particular cases which
under the right circumstances could transform lawyers into professional advocates of the public interest. In contrast to magistrates and clergymen who
sought to preserve harmony—albeit on their own terms—quarrels, controversy,
argument, were the lawyers' meat and drink, advocacy their calling. . . .

Yet the fact that most lawyers, and particularly the mature Boston barristers, became loyalists demonstrates that it was not legal expertise or the profession of law as such that qualified a man for public service. Instead, lawyers became legitimate public officials because of the special niche they occupied in Massachusetts' multiple information networks, a place that enabled them to cement relationships with the people of their counties and with the Boston Whig elite. Serving as intermediaries between local communities and the cosmopolitan world of imperial politics, they were ideally situated to serve as spokesmen who could speak to and for their constituents. Simultaneously serving their own and the public interest, they redefined their occupation so that lawyers could be agents of public as well as private interests. . . .

The Symbolic World of the Tobacco Planter

TIMOTHY H. BREEN

Sometime late in the 1760s, Richard Henry Lee composed an essay entitled "That State of the Constitution of Virginea [*sic*]." Considering Lee's reputation as an outspoken defender of American liberties, one might assume that the document dealt primarily with British corruption and parliamentary oppression. In point of fact, however, Lee focused his attention upon other topics. After briefly describing the colony's political structure, he turned to "our staple" and explained how Virginians cultivated tobacco. Lee analyzed each step in the long agricultural routine—sowing, transplanting, weeding, topping, cutting, curing, and packing—for, in his opinion, it was important that people unfamiliar with this culture know exactly "how much labour is required on a Virginean estate & how poor the produce."

Lee's preoccupation with the production of tobacco would not have surprised his neighbors on Virginia's Northern Neck, men like Landon Carter and George Washington. After all, it is modern historians who insist upon treating these people as lawyers, as lawmakers, as political theorists, as almost anything in fact except as planters. This perspective has distorted our understanding of the world of the eighteenth-century Virginians. Tobacco touched nearly every aspect of their existence. It was a source of colonial prosperity, a medium for commercial transactions and payment of taxes, and a theme of decorative art, and the majority of the planters' waking hours were spent, as they would have said, in "making" a crop. Almost every surviving letter book from this period contains a description of tobacco production, and even Thomas Jefferson, who never distinguished himself as a planter, instructed a European correspondent in the mysteries of cultivating the Virginia staple.

However much the Virginians themselves wrote about tobacco, historians seldom show much interest either in its production or in its relation to the

"The Culture of Agriculture: The Symbolic World of the Tidewater Planter, 1760–1790" by T. H. Breen is abridged from *Saints & Revolutionaries, Essays on Early American History,* Edited by David D. Hall, John M. Murrin, and Thad W. Tate, by permission of the author, T. H. Breen, and W. W. Norton & Company, Inc. Copyright © 1984 by W. W. Norton & Company.

culture of the great Northern Neck families: the Carters, Corbins, Fitzhughs, Lees, and Taylors, to cite just a few of the more prominent names. The reasons for this oversight are clear. First, since many planters became revolutionaries, researchers have naturally emphasized the Virginians' grievances against the British imperial system and their thoughts about a new form of government.

But the members of this particular ruling group were unusual in a second way. Unlike other landed elites that Western historians have studied, this one actually directed the production of a staple crop. In other words, Virginia planters did not retire to metropolitan centers, divorcing themselves from the annual agricultural routine. And third, twentieth-century scholars find it difficult to comprehend the productive aspects of agrarian culture. In their analyses of preindustrial societies, they seize upon the familiar—the nuclear family or urban conflict, for example—while ignoring the daily activities of the great majority of the population. As a result of this bias, we possess substantial studies of colonial cities, urban artisans, and mob violence, but almost nothing perceptive about the work culture of the early American farmers. . . .

. . . As anthropologists have discovered, forms of cultivation influence the character of a people's culture. Analysis of agricultural activities in narrow economic terms, as simply a matter of counting bushels and bales, of calculating rates of growth, obscures the relation between crop and cultivator. Plants assume special significance for the grower, and over several generations the products of the fields become associated with a particular set of regional values, a pattern of land tenure, a system of labor, even a festive calendar. . . .

Colonial Virginians concentrated on tobacco. . . . On the eve of the American Revolution, the cultivation of tobacco gave both *shape* and *meaning* to planter culture. Indeed, in view of the centrality of a single staple in the colonists' lives, one can write confidently of a "tobacco mentality." . . .

On one level, the crop shaped general patterns of behavior. The plant possessed a special, even unique, set of physical characteristics that in turn influenced the planters' decisions about where to locate plantations and how to allocate time throughout the year. In other words, tobacco affected perceptions of time and space; and without doubt, the Virginia work routine—very different from that associated with sugar and coffee—contributed powerfully to the development of a tobacco mentality.

On a second level, however, tobacco gave meaning to routine planter activities. It was emblematic not only of a larger social order, its past, its future, its prospects in comparison with those of other societies, but also of the individual producers. The personal link between planter and tobacco is fundamental to the argument of this essay. The staple provided the Lees and Carters of eighteenth-century Virginia with a means to establish a public identity, a way to locate themselves within an intricate web of human relationships. The crop served as an index of one's worth and standing in a community of competitive, highly independent growers; quite literally, the quality of a man's tobacco was the measure of the man. Both aspects of the tobacco mentality— as shaper of everyday experience and as source of individual and corporate meaning—help to explain the intensity of the planters' commitment to the staple and to the customs that it spawned. . . .

Colonial Virginians acknowledged the profound impact that tobacco had had upon the development of their society. They were less certain, however, whether the results had been beneficial. A case in point was the planters' settlement pattern, a use of space that clearly set them apart from other colonial Americans. The earliest Virginians had carved out riverfront estates often located miles from the nearest neighbor. As time passed, colonists spread west and north along the waterways in search of fresh lands on which to establish their sons and daughters. Each generation faced the same problem; each behaved much as its predecessor had done. Crown officials complained that dispersed living discouraged urban development and invited military disaster, and while Virginians recognized the desirability of prosperous commercial centers—New England towns without Puritans—they refused to abandon their isolated plantations.

By the middle of the eighteenth century, dispersed settlement was accepted as an inevitable product of a particular type of agriculture. Tobacco may not in fact have caused dispersion—the planters might have maintained the fertility of their original tracts—but contemporary Virginians nevertheless blamed their staple for creating a dispersed population. . . .

The cultural implications of Virginia's dispersed settlement pattern were obvious. Social relations among the colony's great planters were less frequent, less spontaneous than were those enjoyed by wealthy towndwellers in other parts of America. The majority of the planter's life was spent on his plantation in the company of family, servants, and slaves. Some Virginians found this "solitary and unsociable" existence difficult to endure. Like William Fitzhugh, Virginia's most successful seventeenth-century planter, they relied on libraries to compensate for the absence of "Society that is good and ingenious." . . .

Other tobacco planters viewed their situation more positively. While admitting that their lives were slow-moving, even a bit dull, they bragged that physical isolation generated personal independence. The cultivation of tobacco transformed them into "Patriarchs," men who depended upon no one but "Providence." Landon Carter, for example, described Sabine Hall in 1759 as an "excellent little Fortress . . . built upon a Rock . . . of *Independence.*"

However cranky Carter may have appeared to contemporaries, his celebration of untrammeled individualism was not unusual in this colony. Visitors reported that an independent turn of mind was a central characteristic of planter society. . . .

The cultivation of tobacco also shaped the planters' sense of time, their perception of appropriate behavior at particular points throughout the year. . . .

As grown in eighteenth-century Virginia, tobacco placed major demands upon the planter throughout the year. There was no "dead season" when laborers turned their attentions to other pursuits. From the moment they put out the seed to the time that they loaded hogsheads on British ships, the workers were fully occupied in making a crop. Tobacco was not like wheat, a plant that farmers sowed and simply waited for to mature. The Virginia staple could never be taken for granted. It dictated a series of jobs, any one of which, if improperly performed, could jeopardize the entire venture. Each step in the process required personal skill, judgment, and luck. . . .

. . . Moreover, unless one understands exactly what was at stake at every point—the dangers, the requirements, and the critical, often subtle decisions made by planters throughout the year—one cannot fully comprehend the relation of culture to agriculture.

The production cycle for Northern Neck tobacco began in late December or early January. The commonly accepted date for planting seed in specially enriched beds was about twelve days after Christmas. The precise timing depended upon a number of variables, but according to one prosperous gentleman, "The best time for sowing the seed is as early after Christmas as the weather will permit." The small seedbeds, usually not larger than a quarter of an acre, were carefully manured. Some were even fertilized with wood ash. In either case, once the seed had been placed in the ground, the planter covered the entire bed with branches in order to protect the tobacco from possible frost damage. Knowledgeable producers prepared several different "plant-beds," frequently separated by considerable distances. This practice insured that the accidental destruction of one bed by cold, disease, or pests would not deprive the planter of an opportunity to make a good crop. But there were always risks. Prudent Virginians understood that the odds against a single plant's surviving to maturity were exceedingly high, and during this initial stage, "an experienced planter commonly takes care to have ten times as many plants as he can make use of."

The second phase of tobacco cultivation, transplanting seedlings from the beds to the main fields, occupied the full attention of the plantation labor force for several months. The work usually commenced in late April, but as in all stages of tobacco production, the exact timing depended in large part upon the planter's judgment. He alone decided whether the tiny plants were sufficiently developed to survive the operation. According to common wisdom, the tobacco leaves were supposed to be "as large as a dollar." Virginians looked for additional signs—the thickness of the young leaves, the general appearance of the plants—subtle indicators that one learned to recognize through long experience.

However skilled the planter may have been, transplanting was an anxious time for everyone. Chance played a central role in this procedure. Success required frequent rains, for soaking moisture loosened the soil and allowed the planter to pull up the seedlings without harming their roots. The work was difficult and unpleasant. Because no one could predict when the rains would fall, one had to take advantage of major storms, termed "seasons" by colonial Virginians. "When a good shower . . . happens at this period of the year," wrote one well-informed grower, "the planter hurries to the plant bed, disregarding the teeming element, which is doomed to wet his skin." Laborers rushed frantically from the beds to the fields where small tobacco hills had already been laid out. A seedling was dropped on "every hill . . . by the negro-children; the most skilful slaves then . . . planting them." Under perfect conditions, transplanting could be finished by late May, but in fact the job spilled over into June. William Tatham, an eighteenth-century Virginian who published a detailed description of tobacco cultivation, explained that the fields were seldom fully planted until "the *long season in May;* which (to make use of an Irishism) very frequently happens in June."

As the tobacco ripened over the summer, the planter and his slaves performed a number of tedious chores. The crop could not be ignored, not even for a week. Producers waged constant battle against weeds, and over the course of the growing season, each tobacco hill was hoed as many as three times. Since major planters like Landon Carter cultivated more than a hundred thousand plants, weeding obviously took a considerable amount of time. After eight to twelve leaves appeared on each plant—how many depended upon "the fertility of the earth"—the planter ordered his workers to begin topping. This operation, literally the removal of the top of the plant, prevented the tobacco from flowering. The goal was to channel the plant's energies into the leaves. No sooner had the topping been completed than the tobacco started putting out suckers, secondary shoots that had to be removed before they deprived the leaves of important nutrients. Throughout this period each plant received regular, individual attention; each task was done by hand.

The next step, cutting the tobacco, generated considerable tension on the plantations of the Northern Neck. It was well known that the operation took place sometime in September. The difficulty came in determining the exact day on which to start. As every planter understood, even a slight error in judgment could ruin the entire crop. An early frost, for example, was capable of destroying every plant that stood unprotected in the fields, and as the September days passed, the danger of frost increased. On the other hand, it was folly to cut tobacco that was not fully ripe. Immature leaves seldom cured properly. The decision to cut, therefore, tested the planter's competence.

And yet, notwithstanding the critical importance of this moment in the production cycle, Virginians offered no universal description of ripe tobacco. Each planter had to rely on his own judgment. He simply sensed when the tobacco was ready for cutting; it had the "right" appearance. According to Tatham, "The tobacco, when ripe, changes its colour, and looks greyish; the leaf feels thick, and if pressed between the finger and thumb will easily crack." He then added, "experience alone can enable a person to judge when tobacco is fully ripe." Richard Henry Lee, a man who possessed the necessary experience, advised growers to look for "spots appearing on the leaf." Other planters adopted different guidelines, a mixture of local custom and informed intuition, none of which guaranteed success.

Colonial Virginians did not refer to the September cutting as a harvest. Such a term would have suggested finality, the completion of the annual agricultural cycle. But for the tobacco planter, cutting led immediately to another arduous task, curing, and if he failed at this stage, it did not much matter how skillfully the transplanting or cutting had been performed. One English visitor who closely studied the cultivation of tobacco claimed that proper curing represented the planter's most difficult challenge, "and, for want of knowledge and care, there are every year many hogs-heads spoiled, and worth nothing." He insisted, in fact, that "the curing of tobacco is an art." Another man termed it "an art most difficult of attainment."

Again, the crucial factor was personal judgment. The cut tobacco was hung in special curing barns and dried until it seemed ready for packing. The trick was to produce a leaf neither too dry nor too moist. Excess moisture would almost certainly cause the tobacco to rot while being shipped. But leaves that were allowed to dry too long became brittle and sometimes turned to dust before reaching Great Britain.

Wise planters naturally tried to terminate the curing process at the moment that the tobacco became dry yet pliable, a time that Virginians called simply "case." This point, Tatham explained, "can only be judged of safely by long experience." The problem was that the condition of the tobacco could change from hour to hour, moving in and out of "case" depending upon the humidity. Wet days supposedly gave the cured tobacco leaves greater flexibility and thus made them easier to handle. "This condition," observed Tatham, "can only be distinguished by diligent attention, and frequent handling; for it often changes this quality with the change of the weather in a very short space of time." If the colony experienced a particularly rainy fall, however, the planter was sometimes forced to light fires in the curing barns. The heat assisted the drying process but could create other difficulties. As Jefferson reported, "great care is necessary as it [the tobacco] is very inflammable, and if it takes fire, the whole, with the house, consumes as quickly as straw would."

Successful curing did not mean that the tobacco was ready for market. Several complex operations still remained. When the leaves reached "case," workers quickly "stripped" them from the stalks on which they had hung in the barn. Those planters who obtained the highest returns for their tobacco also "stemmed" the leaves. This was a monotonous job. Slaves, both men and women, removed "the largest stem or fibres from the web of the leaf," leaving a handsome product that could be packed easily. The speed with which stemming was accomplished depended upon the slaves' "expertness." One had to learn the necessary skills, and "those unaccustomed to it find it difficult to stem a single plant." Regardless of the workers' training, these operations required considerable amounts of time, and during the autumn months it was not unusual for the slaves to labor long into the night over the individual leaves.

Only when these tasks had been completed could the planter order "prizing" to begin. Layer after layer of leaves was placed in hogsheads manufactured by plantation coopers. Men then pressed or "prized" the leaves until there was space for additional layers. This process was repeated until the hogshead weighed at least a thousand pounds. Sometimes the pressure on the tobacco cracked the staves, and the hogshead burst. No wonder that Tatham concluded that prizing "requires the combination of judgment and experience." These jobs—stripping, stemming, and prizing—continued throughout the fall. A prosperous Virginia planter, Richard Corbin, advised a plantation manager that with careful planning of the work routine, "the Tobacco will be all prised before Christmas, weigh well, and at least one hhd [hogshead] in Ten gained by finishing the Tobo thus early." But Corbin counseled perfection. Often the hogsheads were not ready for shipment to the public warehouses and inspection until well after the New Year.

Not until the following spring, a full fifteen months after the sowing of the tobacco seed, did the planter send loaded hogsheads to the European market. By that time, of course, another crop was in the ground, and he faced a new round of agricultural decisions. The schedule contained few slack periods, no time during which the grower could be completely free of anxieties about the state of his crop. . . .

This onerous production schedule affected eighteenth-century planter culture in several significant ways. First, the staple became the arbiter of time, of work and play. The tobacco calendar discouraged communal activities. It contained no clear culmination, no point at which the producer could relax and enjoy the fruits of his labor. Even cutting tobacco could not be termed a genuine harvest. It never generated autumn festivals, for curing followed hard upon cutting. One task was as important as the other. Recreational activities—cockfights and horse races, for example—had to be scheduled around the cultivation of tobacco, fit somehow into the established work routine. It is not surprising that after George Washington dropped the cultivation of tobacco for that of wheat, he discovered that he had more time for fox hunting, his favorite pastime. As one of his biographers explains, wheat altered the pace of Washington's life, for in this type of agriculture, "The ground was plowed; the grain was planted; after that, nothing need to be done or could be done, except keep livestock away, until harvest."

Second, the staple promoted social cohesion. This claim appears paradoxical, for how could a crop that restricted communal activities, that heightened the planter's autonomy, generate a sense of common identity and purpose? The answer lies in a shared work process. The production of tobacco provided highly individualistic planters with a body of common rules and assumptions that helped bind them together. As one labored in the fields, whatever the time of year, one knew that people on other plantations were engaged in the same agricultural routine. A planter did not actually have to see other men at work to know what they were doing.

This shared framework of labor experience made distant, often unrelated planters appear less alien than they would have had they been urban artisans or cultivators of other crops. The tobacco production schedule became a kind of secular litany, and at the drop of a hat, planters recited the steps necessary to transform seeds into marketable leaves. The fabric of rules tied an individual not only to his neighbors but also to his predecessors. Since time out of mind—or so it must have seemed—Virginians had followed the same calendar, and thus the very process of cultivating tobacco placed a man within a tradition as old as the colony itself. Predictably, one visitor discovered that "the planters never go out of the beaten road, but do just as their fathers did." Social cohesion was a product of common agricultural assumptions, shared symbols, and collective judgments. Indeed, it was out of these strands of tradition, rules, and judgment that the staple planters of tidewater Virginia created a distinct culture.

Because tobacco very powerfully shaped the patterns of everyday work experience, the plant acquired considerable symbolic importance. Indeed, its emblematic qualities were central to the development of a tobacco mentality. On one level, the dominant staple reflected the entire social order. It was synonymous with Virginia, and when one mentioned tobacco in the Anglo-Saxon world of the eighteenth century, one inevitably evoked images of wealthy planters, slave laborers, and great houses. On a second level, the crop came to represent the individuals who cultivated it. In itself tobacco was culturally neutral, but in the absence of an adequate circulating currency, it provided Virginians with a means to forge a public identity, a mechanism for placing people into a generally accepted hierarchy. In both cases, the *colonial* and the *individual,* tobacco was the measure of the people who produced it.

By the middle of the eighteenth century, Virginia society and the cultivation of tobacco were generally regarded as being synonymous. To be sure, the colonists grew other crops, such as corn, but these plants never shared tobacco's prominence. According to one Frenchman who visited Virginia in 1765, "the produce of the Soil is hemp, Indian Corn, flax, silk, Cotton and great quantity of wild grapes, but tobacco is *the* staple Commodity of virginia [*sic*]." The evidence in support of this observation was overwhelming. The leaf appeared to be ubiquitous. One encountered it growing on the small farms scattered along the colony's back roads, on the vast fields of the great riverfront plantations, on the wharves near the public warehouses. It dominated conversation in Williamsburg and Fredericksburg. No wonder an English traveler labeled tobacco "the grand staple of Virginia." Robert Beverley, a Tidewater planter who avoided extravagant language, called tobacco simply "our staple." . . .

The close identification with the crop also operated on a personal level. In colonial Virginia, tobacco provided a medium—a cultural ether—within which the planter negotiated a public reputation, a sense of self-worth as an agricultural producer. In part, the deep ties between the Virginia planter and the staple resulted from the peculiar characteristics of tobacco. As we have seen, its cultivation required personal attention; at every stage the planter made crucial judgments about the crop's development. . . . The Virginia planters naturally insisted on being present at every step of the process, and however boring life on the isolated plantations may have seemed, they seldom were in a position to become absentee owners. Growing tobacco was a personal challenge.

Of course, the planters recognized that their presence did not in itself guarantee success. Many aspects of tobacco cultivation were beyond their control. Regardless of his skills, the planter still had to reckon with luck, with chance factors like pests and weather that undermined the best-laid plans. Such "accidents," as Virginians sometimes called them, were an inescapable part of farming. . . .

In fact, however, Carter [the Virginia planter Landon Carter] and his contemporaries were unwilling to submit [to "accidents"]. Fatalism was foreign to their outlook. Instead, they believed in the existence of an agricultural *virtù,* a set of personal attributes that ultimately determined the quality of a man's crop. This sense of power—and, of course, responsibility—is the reason why colonial planters came to regard their tobacco as an extension of self. To be sure, "accidents" might ruin a crop or two, but over the long haul there was no explanation other than incompetence why an individual could not produce good tobacco. . . .

The highest praise one could bestow on a Virginia planter was to call him "crop master," a public recognition of agricultural excellence. Many aspired to this rank, but success proved elusive. . . .

Virginians quickly learned which planters possessed superior judgment, and at critical points in the production process, they turned to crop masters for advice. Cutting the tobacco was such a time. Writers like Tatham provided inexperienced planters with general descriptions of ripe leaves and changes in color and thickness, but books somehow never conveyed adequate information. In frustration, Tatham declared that ripening is "easier to understand than to express." "It is a point," he concluded, "on which I would not trust my own experience without consulting some able crop-master in the neighbourhood." . . .

Even the names given to the various kinds of tobacco testified to the close personal relation between the planter and his crop. People unfamiliar with the cultivation of this staple assumed that colonial Virginians grew only two varieties, Oronoko and sweet scented. While this information may have been technically correct, Virginians recognized finer distinctions. "Question a planter on the subject," one man explained, "and he will tell you that he cultivates such or such a kind: as, for example 'Colonel Carter's sort, John Cole's sort,' or some other leading crop master." . . .

The centrality of tobacco in the lives of these men spawned a curious system of social ranking, one strikingly different from that normally associated with modern industrial societies. The planter's self-esteem depended—in part, at least—upon the quality of his tobacco. This measure, of course, was highly subjective. It left him extraordinarily vulnerable to the opinion of other men. However excellent a person regarded his own crop as being, a sharp-eyed critic could always find flaws in it. Virginians worried about these negative judgments and . . . took them quite personally. Indeed, the planters seem to have cultivated tobacco as much to gain the respect of merchants and neighbors—in other words, of people with whom they maintained regular face-to-face contacts—as to please the anonymous chewers, smokers, and snuffers who ultimately purchased the staple in Europe. . . .

Not surprisingly, the price they received for their tobacco obsessed colonial planters. The sources of this preoccupation were cultural as well as economic. To be sure, men like Carter and Lee strove to maintain a favorable balance with the British merchant houses. They hated debt. Nevertheless, they were also concerned with the judgment of other planters. Price provided a reasonably unambiguous measure of the worth of a man's tobacco, its quality; and in this sense a high return validated a person's claim as crop master. Historians who described these Virginians solely as agricultural capitalists eager to maximize income miss a crucial aspect of the tobacco mentality. These planters competed in the market not only for pounds and pence but also for honor and reputation. . . .

Criticism of a man's tobacco, however tactfully phrased, set off a frenzy of self-examination. Whenever planters received a low price, for example, they assumed that somehow they must be at fault. Their reaction was almost reflective. The problem, they reasoned, must have been in production, in the management of the labor force—in other words, in themselves—and they usually accepted responsibility for the poor showing of their tobacco in the British market. . . .

In a sense, the planters were too caught up in an endless cycle of production, too blinded by the tobacco mentality, to become fully successful capitalists. They were trapped by the assumptions of a staple culture. There seems no other plausible explanation for their extraordinary naiveté about international market procedures. One experienced Virginia merchant complained that the planters held "wild & chimerical notions" about price-setting mechanisms. Indeed, men who exercised the closest scrutiny over cutting and curing seem to have been mystified about what happened to their tobacco once it left America. They speculated about factors of supply and demand, but about commercial practices that ate into their profits, they remained ignorant. In 1774, for example, Fitzhugh confessed to an English merchant with whom he had dealt for more than a decade, "I really do not understand your manner of keeping my Interest Act [Account]." . . .

Like Landon Carter, George Washington assumed that a man's reputation was only as good as the tobacco he grew. After the conclusion of the French and Indian War in Virginia (by late 1758 the war with France no longer threatened the colony's frontier), Washington returned to Mount Vernon determined to become a successful planter. At this point, in 1759, it did not occur to him to cultivate another staple. Virginians grew tobacco, and he saw no reason to doubt that he could make a quality leaf. In 1762 he offered an overseer a monetary incentive to bring in a better crop than normal because of the "well known intention of the said George Washington to have his tobacco made and managed in the best and neatest manner which in some manner lessens the quantity." To whom Washington's intentions were well known was not spelled out in this agreement, but he probably realized that his Northern Neck neighbors—the Lees, Fitzhughs, and Carters—kept a sharp watch over his progress as a planter.

The results humiliated Washington. He was a proud man, and no matter how diligently he worked the stubborn fields of Mount Vernon, he could not produce the kind of quality leaves that one saw on the plantations of the James, Rappahannock, and York rivers. In his own eyes, the crucial measure was price. However hard he tried, he still received lower returns than did his friends and neighbors. In bitter frustration, Washington wrote to an English merchant complaining, "I am at a loss to conceive the Reason why Mr. Wormeleys, and indeed some other Gentlemen's Tobaccos should sell at 12d last year and mine . . . only fetch $11\frac{1}{2}$." Washington knew that the results of his sales were no secret. These much publicly discussed prices provided an index to his skills as a producer, and it was with the conventions of Virginia culture in mind that he protested, "Certain I am no Person in Virginia takes more pains to make their Tobo. fine than I do and tis hard when I should not be well rewarded for it."

Hard indeed. Frustration turned to depression. In 1762 Washington wrote painfully of his own failure as a planter. "I confess," he scribbled, "it [tobacco cultivation] to be an Art beyond my skill, to succeed in making good Tobo. as I have used my utmost endeavours for that purpose this two or 3 years past; and am once again urged to express my surprise at finding that I do not partake of the best prices that are going." At this point in his life, Washington was a captive of the tobacco mentality. He could have turned aggressively to other crops in the early 1760s, but to have done so would have made him less a Virginian. It would have cut him off from the only source of public esteem other than soldiering that he had ever known.

Frustration eventually gave way to anger. Throughout his long military and political career, Washington's self-control impressed contemporaries. He sometimes seemed incapable of showing passion of any sort. But in September 1765 his pitiful tobacco sparked a remarkable outburst. He reminded an English correspondent, Robert Cary, that the price he had obtained for his tobacco was "worse than many of my Acquaintances upon this River, Potomack." The comments that he imagined men were whispering behind his back were too much for Washington to bear. "Can it be otherwise . . . a little mortifying than to find, that we, who raise none but Sweet-scented Tobacco, and endeavour I may venture to add, to be careful in the management of it . . . ," he asked rhetorically, "should meet with such unprofitable returns? Surely I may answer No!" These were words for Patrick Henry, not for the reserved Washington. He decided that if he could not excel at the planter's trade, not become a tobacco crop master, then he would shift his attention to a different plant. It is essential to recognize how the decision was made. He began with the traditional culture. For a decade he persisted. Washington was not drawn into the wheat market, because he carefully calculated that grain would bring increased profits. Rather, he was forced out of the tobacco market.

Virginians, then, were planters. However much political theory they had read, however familiar they were with the writings of John Locke or Francis Hutcheson, however much time they spent impressing one another in Williamsburg, they remained products of a regional agrarian culture. Tobacco shaped their society and defined their place within it. From the perspective of a cultural anthropologist, the plant possessed immense symbolic significance for the planters and their families. By the middle of the eighteenth century, this staple had been tightly woven into the fabric of the colonists' every-day life; it gave meaning to their experience. One would predict, therefore, that any alteration in the traditional relation between planter and tobacco would have far-reaching, even revolutionary, implications for the entire society. . . .

ᘛ *F U R T H E R   R E A D I N G*

Timothy H. Breen, *Tobacco Culture: The Mentality of the Great Tidewater Planters on the Eve of the Revolution* (1985)
Joy Day Buel and Richard Buel, Jr., *A Way of Duty: A Woman and Her Family in Revolutionary America* (1984)

Edward M. Cook, Jr., *The Fathers of the Towns: Leadership and Community Structure in Eighteenth-Century New England* (1976)

Jack P. Greene, *The Quest for Power: The Lower Houses of Assembly in the Southern Royal Colonies, 1689–1776* (1963)

Christine Leigh Heyrman, *Commerce and Culture: The Maritime Communities of Colonial Massachusetts, 1690–1750* (1984)

Allan Kulikoff, *Tobacco and Slaves: The Development of Southern Cultures in the Chesapeake, 1680–1800* (1986)

Gary B. Nash, *The Urban Crucible: Social Change, Political Consciousness, and the Origins of the American Revolution* (1979)

A. G. Roeber, *Faithful Magistrates and Republican Lawyers: Creators of Virginia Legal Culture, 1680–1810* (1981)

Carole Shammas, "Consumer Behavior in Colonial America," *Social Science History* 6 (1982), 67–86

———, *The Pre-industrial Consumer in England and America* (1990)

Settling the Backcountry

ॐ

The backcountry, which ran along the piedmont from Pennsylvania to Georgia, was progressively opened up as opportunities for owning land decreased in the settled areas to the east. Like all other regions settled later in the colonial period, the backcountry drew population from many sources in Europe and included Scots-Irish, Scottish Highlanders, French, and Germans. These colonists arrived in groups throughout the eighteenth century, building communities designed to sustain their own heritage in the new environment. Although the backcountry lay within the colonial patents of the established colonies, in many ways it was a region with a unity of its own. Settlers who landed at the port of Philadelphia flowed southward along the foothills, adding to populations moving directly west, and built chains of settlement.

Frontier regions always have had a special place in American folklore. The national myth has portrayed frontier settlers as men and women who, impatient with the constraints of life in the hierarchical East, struck out to find a place where they could live as individuals. Travelers through the backcountry in the eighteenth century depicted the colonists there as "white savages"—people who first chose to live outside society and then were further corrupted by dwelling in close proximity to the American natives. Diarists commented contemptuously on the "slovenly" look of their farms and on the disorderly nature of frontier life.

Recent scholars have reexamined both sides of this myth. The new picture portrays a far more settled society, which sought to replicate elements of the life of eastern communities as quickly as possible. Movements such as the separate Regulator campaigns of North Carolina and South Carolina fought the corruption of the eastern establishment and its neglect of the frontier's needs. Moreover, historians have revised the image of free land and free men on the frontier as they have concluded that much of the backcountry had been taken up by large landowners prior to mass immigration into the region, and that many frontier families lived as poor tenants on these estates.

ॐ D O C U M E N T S

The Anglican minister Charles Woodmason traveled as a missionary through the Carolina backcountry in the 1760s. His influential journal, excerpted in the first document, provided the definitive picture of the poor quality of life and religious decadence he saw on the frontier; he believed that the New Light preachers had done particular harm in the region. In the second document, dating from 1765, newly arrived governor William Tryon writes home to his uncle, Sewallis Shirley, about his impressions of the people and land of North Carolina, particularly the hard life of the frontier. Nonetheless, the backcountry attracted such groups as the Moravians, a pietistic sect organized in Germany in the 1720s under the leadership and patronage of Count Nicholas Zinzendorf. The Moravians previously had settled in Pennsylvania and Georgia, and in 1752 Bishop August Gottlieb Spangenberg traveled from Bethlehem in Pennsylvania to survey the prospective site in North Carolina. His evaluation, excerpted in the third document, shows the potential conflict between paternalistic plans developed in Europe and the demands of the environment. Other writers, such as the anonymous writer in the fourth selection of a preface to the travel account of naturalist John Bartram, advocated expansion of the colonies and castigated settlers for not seizing the initiative.

Olaudah Equiano wrote a classic narrative describing the experience of being enslaved in Africa and transported to sale and slavery in America in the mid-eighteenth century; in the fifth selection he vividly recounts his feelings as a young boy who had arrived in Virginia in 1757 at age twelve as he came to understand the full meaning of his enslavement. In the final reading Sir William Gooch, lieutenant governor of Virginia, writes to the Board of Trade in 1729 describing the danger of runaway slaves congregating in the western mountains and attacking frontier settlements.

The Reverend Charles Woodmason Views the Backcountry in the 1760s

... Saturday September 3) Rode down the Country on the West Side the Wateree River into the Fork between that and the Congaree River—This is out of my Bounds—But their having no Minister, and their falling (therefrom) continually from the Church to Anabaptism, inclin'd me to it—The People received me gladly and very kindly. Had on Sunday 4—a Company of about 150—Most of them of the Low Class—the principal Planters living on the Margin of these Rivers.

Baptiz'd 1 Negroe Man—2 Negroe Children—and 9 White Infants and married 1 Couple—The People thanked me in the most kind Manner for my Services—I had very pleasant Riding but my Horse suffered Greatly. The Mornings and Evenings now begin to be somewhat Cool, but the Mid day heat is almost intolerable—Many of these People walk 10 or 12 Miles with their Children in the burning Sun—Ought such to be without the Word of God, when so earnest, so desirous of hearing it and becoming Good Christians, and good Subjects! How lamentable to think, that the Legislature of this Province will make no Provision—so rich, so luxurious, polite a People! Yet they are deaf to all Solicitations, and look on the poor White People in a Meaner Light than their Black Slaves, and care less for them. Withal there is such a

Reprinted, by permission of the editor and the publisher, from *The Carolina Backcountry on the Eve of the Revolution: The Journal and Other Writings of Charles Woodmason, Anglican Itinerant,* edited by Richard J. Hooker. Published for the Institute of Early American History and Culture, Williamsburg, Virginia. © 1969 The University of North Carolina Press.

Republican Spirit still left, so much of the Old Leaven of Lord Shaftsbury and other the 1st principal Settlers still remains, that they seem not at all disposed to promote the Interest of the Church of England—Hence it is that above 30,000£ Sterling have lately been expended to bring over 5 or 6000 Ignorant, mean, worthless, beggarly Irish Presbyterians, the Scum of the Earth, and Refuse of Mankind, and this, solely to ballance the Emigrations of People from Virginia, who are all of the Established Church.—50 [miles]; [total] Miles 2846

It will require much Time and Pains to New Model and form the Carriage and Manners, as well as Morals of these wild Peoples—Among this Congregation not one had a Bible or Common Prayer—or could join a Person or hardly repeat the Creed or Lords Prayer—Yet all of 'em had been educated in the Principles of our Church. So that I am obliged to read the Whole Service, omitting such Parts, as are Repetitious, and retaining those that will make the different Services somewhat Uniform—Hence it is, that I can but seldom use the Litany, because they know not the Responses.

It would be (as I once observ'd before) a Great Novelty to a Londoner to see one of these Congregations—The Men with only a thin Shirt and pair of Breeches or Trousers on—barelegged and barefooted—The Women bareheaded, barelegged and barefoot with only a thin Shift and under Petticoat—Yet I cannot break [them?] of this—for the heat of the Weather admits not of any [but] thin Cloathing—I can hardly bear the Weight of my Whig and Gown, during Service. The Young Women have a most uncommon Practise, which I cannot break them off. They draw their Shift as tight as possible to the Body, and pin it close, to shew the roundness of their Breasts, and slender Waists (for they are generally finely shaped) and draw their Petticoat close to their Hips to shew the fineness of their Limbs—so that they might as well be in Puri Naturalibus—Indeed Nakedness is not censurable or indecent here, and they expose themselves often quite Naked, without Ceremony—Rubbing themselves and their Hair with Bears Oil and tying it up behind in a Bunch like the Indians—being hardly one degree removed from them—In few Years, I hope to bring about a Reformation, as I already have done in several Parts of the Country.— ...

Received Letters from England—One acquaints me with death of the Reverend Mr. Crallan, 10 days after his Embarking. This is the 13th or 14th of the Clergy dead or gone here within these 2 Years—This Gentleman grew insane before his departure. He was a Saint—An Angel in his Life and Manners—A most pious and devout Young Man, and yet he could not escape the Censure of these flighty, Proud, Illprincipled Carolin[i]ans. They are enough to make any Person run Mad—And they crack'd the Brain of one Young Man Mr. Amory the Year before. We have two now in the same Condition—And others, whose Situation is so uneasy, that Life is a Burden to them—I would not wish my worst Enemy to come to this Country (at least to this) Part of it to combat perpetually with Papists, Sectaries, Atheists and Infidels—who would rather see the Poor People remain Heathens and Ignorants, than to be brought over to the Church. Such Enemies to Christ and his Cross, are these vile Presbyterians. ...

But let us go on, and examine if in the General Corruption of Manners these New Lights have made any Reform in the Vice of Drunkenness? Truly, I wot not. There is not one Hogshead of Liquor less consum'd since their visiting us, or any Tavern shut up—So far from it, that there has been Great Increase of Both. Go to any Common Muster or Vendue, Will you not see the same Fighting, Brawling Gouging, Quarreling as ever? And this too among the Holy ones of our New Israel? Are Riots, Frolics, Races, Games, Cards, Dice, Dances, less frequent now than formerly? Are fewer persons to be seen in Taverns? or reeling or drunk on the Roads? And have any of the Godly Storekeepers given up their Licences, or refus'd to retail Poison? If this can be made appear, I will yield the Point. But if [it] can be made apparent that a much greater Quantity of Rum is now expended in private families than heretofore—That the greater Part of these religious Assemblies are calculated for private Entertainments, where each brings his Quota and which often terminates in Intemperance and Intoxication and both Sexes, Young and Old: That one half of those who resort to these Assemblies Go more for sake of Liquor, than Instruction, or Devotion. That if it be proven that Liquor has been top'd about even in their very Meeting Houses, and the Preachers refreshed with Good Things, and after the Farce ended Stuff'd and Cramm'd almost to bursting, then it must be granted that little or no Reform has been made among the Vulgar in Point of Intemperance save only among some few Persons in some Places where the Mode only is chang'd, and drinking in Public wav'd for the Indulgence of double the Consumption in Private.

The horrid Vice of Swearing has long been a reproach to the Back Inhabitants, and very justly—for few Countries on Earth can equal these Parts as to this greivous Sin. But has it ceas'd since the Admission of rambling Fanatics among us? I grant that it has with and among many, whom they have gain'd to their Sect. Yet still it too much prevails. But the Enormity of this Vice, when at the Highest, produc'd no Evils, Jarrs, disturbances Strifes, Contentions, Variance, Dissimulations, Envyings, Slanders, Backbitings and a thousand other Evils that now disturb both the Public Places and repose of Individuals. So that where they have cast out one Devil, Seven, and twice Seven others have enter'd In and possess the Man. For never was so much Lying, Calumny, Defamation, and all hellish Evils and vexations of this Sort that can spring from the Devil and his Angels, so brief so prevalent, so abounding as since the Arrival of these villanous Teachers, Who blast, blacken, Ruin, and destroy the Characters, Reputations, Credit and Fame of all Persons not linked with them to the Ruin of Society, the Peace of families, and the Settlement of the Country.

We will further enquire, if Lascivousness, or Wantoness, Adultery or Fornication [are] less common than formerly, before the Arrival of these *Holy* Persons? Are there fewer Bastards born? Are more Girls with their Virginity about them, Married, than were heretofore? The Parish Register will prove the Contrary: There are rather more Bastards, more Mullatoes born than before. Nor out of 100 Young Women that I marry in a Year have I seen, or is there seen, Six but what are with Child? And this as Common with the Germans on other Side the River, as among You on this Side: So that a

Minister is accounted as a Scandalous Person for even coming here to marry such People, and for baptizing their Bastard Children as the Law obliges Me to register All Parties who are Married, and all Children Born. This occasions such Numbers (especially of the Saints) to fly into the next Province, and up to the German Ministers and any where to get Married, to prevent their being register'd, as therefrom the Birth of their Children would be trac'd: And as for Adulteries, the present State of most Persons around 9/10 of whom now labour under a filthy Distemper (as is well known to all) puts that Matter out of all Dispute and shews that the Saints however outwardly Precise and Reserved are not one Whit more Chaste than formerly, and possibly are more privately Vicious.

And nothing more leads to this Than what they call their Love Feasts and Kiss of Charity. To which Feasts, celebrated at Night, much Liquor is privately carried, and deposited on the Roads, and in Bye Paths and Places. The Assignations made on Sundays at the Singing Clubs, are here realized. And it is no wonder that Things are as they are, when many Young Persons have 3. 4. 5. 6 Miles to walk home in the dark Night, with Convoy, thro' the Woods? Or staying perhaps all Night at some Cabbin (as on Sunday Nights) and sleeping together either doubly or promiscuously? Or a Girl being mounted behind a Person to be carried home, or any wheres. All this indeed contributes to multiply Subjects for the King in this frontier Country, and so is wink'd at by the Magistracy and Parochial Officers but at some time, gives great Occasion to the Enemies of Virtue, to triumph, for Religion to be scandalized and brought into Contempt; For all Devotion to be Ridicul'd, and in the Sequel, will prove the Entire banishment and End of all Religion—Confusion—Anarchy and ev'ry Evil Work will be the Consequence of such Lewdness and Immorality.

But certainly these Reformers have put some Stop to the many Thefts and Depradations so openly committed of late Years?—To answer this Question recourse must be had to the Magistrates and Courts of Justice, who are ready to declare, that since the Appearance of these New Lights, more Enormities of all Kinds have been committed—More Robberies Thefts, Murders, Plunderings, Burglaries and Villanies of ev'ry Kind, than ever before. And the Reason hereof, Is, That most of these Preaching fellows were most notorious Thieves, Jockeys, Gamblers, and what not in the Northern Provinces, and since their Reception and Success here have drawn Crowds of their old Acquaintances after them; So that the Country never was so full as at present of Gamesters Prostitutes, Filchers, Racers, Fidlers and all the refuse of Mankind. All which follow these Teachers, and under the Mask of Religion carry on many detestable Practises. In short, they have filled the Country with Idle and Vagrant Persons, who live by their Criminalities. For it is a Maxim with these Vermin of Religion, That a Person must first be a Sinner e're He can be a Saint. And I am bold to say, That the Commonality around, do not now make half the Crops nor are $\frac{1}{4}$ so Industrious, as 3 Years ago. Because half their Time is wasted in traveling about to this and that Lecture—and to hear this and that fine Man, So that they are often a Month absent from their families. . . .

For only draw a Comparison between them and Us, and let an Impartial Judge determine where *Offence* may chiefly be taken, At our Solemn, Grave, and Serious Sett Forms, or their Wild Extempore Jargon, nauseaus to any Chaste or refin'd Ear. There are so many Absurdities committed by them, as wou'd shock one of our *Cherokee* Savages; And was a Sensible Turk or Indian to view some of their Extravagancies it would quickly determine them against Christianity. Had any such been in their Assembly as last Sunday when they communicated, the Honest Heathens would have imagin'd themselves rather amidst a Gang of frantic Lunatics broke out of Bedlam, rather than among a Society of religious Christians, met to celebrate the most sacred and Solemn Ordinance of their Religion. Here, one Fellow mounted on a Bench with the Bread, and bawling, *See the Body of Christ,* Another with the Cup running around, and bellowing—*Who cleanses his Soul with the Blood of Christ,* and a thousand other Extravagancies—One on his knees in a Posture of Prayer—Others singing—some howling—These Ranting—Those Crying—Others dancing, Skipping, Laughing and rejoycing. Here two or 3 Women falling on their Backs, kicking up their Heels, exposing their Nakedness to all Bystanders and others sitting Pensive, in deep Melancholy lost in Abstraction, like Statues, quite insensible—and when rous'd by the Spectators from their pretended Reveries Transports, and indecent Postures and Actions declaring they knew nought of the Matter. That their Souls had taken flight to Heav'n, and they knew nothing of what they said or did. Spect[at]ors were highly shocked at such vile Abuse of sacred Ordinances! And indeed such a Scene was sufficient to make the vilest Sinner shudder. Their Teacher, so far from condemning, or reproving, them, call'd it, the Work of God, and returned Thanks for Actions deserving of the Pillory and Whipping Post. But that would not have been *New* to some of them. And if they can thus transgress all bounds of Decency Modesty, and Morality, in such an Open Public Manner, it is not hard to conceive what may pass at their Nocturnal Meetings, and Private Assemblies. Is there any thing like this in the Church of England to give Offence?

But another vile Matter that does and must give Offence to all Sober Minds Is, what they call their *Experiences;* It seems, that before a Person be dipp'd, He must give an Account of his Secret Calls, Conviction, Conversion, Repentance &c &c. Some of these Experiences have been so ludicrous and ridiculous that *Democritus* in Spite of himself must have burst with Laughter. Others, altogether as blasphemous Such as their Visions, Dreams, Revelations—and the like; Too many, and too horrid to be mention'd. Nothing in the *Alcoran* Nothing that can be found in all the Miracles of the Church of Rome, and all the Reveries of her Saints can be so absurd, or so Enthusiastic, as what has gravely been recited in that *Tabernacle* Yonder—To the Scandal of Religion and Insult of Common Sense. And to heighten the Farce, To see two or three fellows with fix'd Countenances and grave Looks, hearing all this Nonsense for Hours together, and making particular Enquiries, when, How, Where, in what Manner, these Miraculous Events happen'd—To see, I say, a Sett of Mongrels under Pretext of Religion, Sit, and hear for Hours together a String of Vile, cook'd up, Silly and Senseless Lyes, What they know to be Such, What they are Sensible has not the least foundation in Truth or Reason, and to encourage Persons in such Gross Inventions must grieve, must give great Offence to ev'ry one that has the Honour of Christianity at Heart.

Then again to see them Divide and Sub divide, Split into Parties—Rail at and excommunicate one another—Turn out of Meeting, and receive into another—And a Gang of them getting together and gabbing one after the other (and sometimes disputing against each other) on Abstruse Theological Question—Speculative Points—Abstracted Notions, and Scholastic Subtelties, such as the greatest Metaph[ys]icians and Learned Scholars never yet could define, or agree on—To hear Ignorant Wretches, who can not write—Who never read ten Pages in any Book, and can hardly read the Alphabett discussing such Knotty Points for the Edification of their Auditors, is a Scene so farcical, so highly humoursome as excels any Exhibition of Folly that has ever yet appear'd in the World, and consequently must give High offence to all Inteligent and rational Minds.

If any Thing offensive beyond all This to greive the Hearts and Minds of serious Christians presents it Self to view among them, it is their Mode of Baptism, to which Lascivous Persons of both Sexes resort, as to a Public Bath. I know not whether it would not be less offensive to Modesty for them to strip wholly into Buff at once, than to be dipp'd with those very thin Linen Drawers they are equipp'd in—Which when wet, so closely adheres to the Limbs, as exposes the Nudities equally as if none at All. If this be not Offensive and a greivous Insult on all Modesty and Decency among Civiliz'd People I know not what can be term'd so. Certainly a few chosen Witnesses of the Sex of the Party, and performance of the Ceremony in a Tent, or Cover'd Place, would be equally as *Edifying,* as Persons being stript and their Privities expos'd before a gaping Multitude who resort to these Big Meetings (as they are term'd) as they would to a Bear or Bullbaiting.

It must give Great Scandal and Offence to all Serious Minds thus to see the Solemn Ordinances of God become the Sport, Pastime and Derision of Men . . .

Governor William Tryon Assesses the Prospects for Life in the North Carolina Backcountry, 1765

The Calculation of the Inhabitants in this Province is one hundred and twenty Thousand White & Black, of which there is a great Majority of White People. The Negroes are very numerous I suppose five to one White Person in the Maritime Counties, but as you penetrate into the Country few Blacks are employed, merely for this Simple reason, that the poorer Settlers coming from the Northward Colonies sat themselves down in the back Counties where the

Governor William Tryon to his uncle, Sewallis Shirley, July 26, 1765, in William S. Powell, ed., "Tryon's 'Book' on North Carolina," *North Carolina Historical Review,* 34 (1957), 411. Reprinted with permission of North Carolina Division of Archives and History, Raleigh.

land is the best but who have not more than a sufficiency to erect a Log House for their families and procure a few Tools to get a little Corn into the ground. This Poverty prevents their purchasing of Slaves, and before they can get into Sufficient affluence to buy Negroes their own Children are often grown to an age to work in the Field. not but numbers of families in the back Counties have Slaves some from three to ten, Whereas in the Counties on the Sea Coast Planters have from fifty to 250 Slaves. A Plantation with Seventy Slaves on it, is esteemed a good property. When a man marries his Daughters he never talks of the fortune in Money but 20 30 or 40 Slaves is her Portion and possibly an agreement to deliver at stated Periods, a Certain Number of Tarr or Turpentine Barrels, which serves towards exonerating the charges of the Wedding which are not grievous here. . . .

Bishop August Gottlieb Spangenberg on Moravian Plans for the Settlement of Wachovia, 1752

. . . Nov. 11. From camp on the Catawba River, about forty miles above Andreas Lambert's place, according to the judgment of our hunters. [This sheet is marked "dem Jünger," that is, for the special consideration of Count Zinzendorf.] I am sitting in the tent thinking about your Patriarchal Plan for the settlement in North Carolina, and considering it in view of the local circumstances. First, there are the Indians. Our land lies in a region much frequented by the Catawbas and Cherokees, especially for hunting. The Senecas, too, come here almost every year, especially when they are at war with the Catawbas. The Indians in North Carolina behave quite differently from those in Pennsylvania. There no one fears an Indian, unless indeed he is drunk. Here the whites must needs fear them. If they come to a house and find the man away they are insolent, and the settler's wife must do whatever they bid. Sometimes they come in such large companies that a man who meets them is in real danger. Now and then a man can do as Andreas Lambert did:—A company of Senecas came on his land, injured his corn, killed his cattle, etc. Lambert called in his bear hounds, of which he has eight or nine, and with his dogs and his loaded gun drove the Indians from his place.

Every man living alone is in this danger, here in the forest. North Carolina has been at war with the Indians, and they have been defeated and have lost their lands. So not only the tribes that were directly concerned, but all the Indians are resentful and take every opportunity to show it. Indeed they have not only killed the cattle of the whites, but have murdered the settlers themselves when they had a chance.

There are other things to make life hard for those living *alone* and *for themselves.* For instance a woman is ill, has high fever,—where is the nurse, medicine, proper food? The wife of the nearest neighbor lives half a mile, perhaps several miles away, and she has her children, her cattle, her own household, to care for, and can give her only a couple of hours, or at most only one day or one night.

Another thing.—By the Patriarchal Plan I understand that each family would live alone, and work for its own support. What will happen to those who have not the necessary talents? How will it go with men and women brought up in our congregations, who I fear have little conception of the difficulties they will have to face? What will they do in circumstances where each must help himself as best he can? How bear the hard work necessary to success, when each must say with Jacob, "In the day the drought consumed me and the frost by night"?

To speak plainly:—Among fifty members brought up in our congregation, or who have lived with us some years, there is probably not one who could maintain himself alone in the forest. They have had no experience, and even those who have the intelligence do not know how.

I do not say this to throw difficulties in the way of your whole plan, on the contrary I consider it important, and believe the Lord through it will achieve His own ends, but I suggest consideration of the best method of attaining that end.

Perhaps it would be wise to settle six to ten families together, each in its own house, all working under a capable overseer; and after a time, if any wishes to settle on his own farm, as in Pennsylvania, then to try to arrange it for him.

But I desist. I know I may not have found the right solution of the problem; the Lord will show us how it may best be done. . . .

An Advocate of Expansion
to the Mississippi River, 1751

. . . Knowledge must precede a settlement, and when *Pensilvania* and *Virginia* shall have extended their habitations to the branches of the *Mississippi* that water these provinces, on the west side of the *Blue Mountains,* we may reasonably hope to insure a safe and easy communication with the most remote known parts of *North America,* and to secure the possession of a dominion unbounded by any present discoveries.

If this desirable prospect appear chimerical, because great and distant, it is at least true, that no obstacle can be pointed out, but what we may easily remove.

England already possesses an uninterrupted line of well-peopled provinces on the coast, successively begun within less than 150 years, she sees them every year augmented by an accession of subjects, excited by the desire of living under governments and laws formed on the most excellent model upon earth. In vain do we look for an equal prosperity among the plantations of other *European* nations because every power has transplanted its constitution with its people. This surprizing increase of people is a foundation that will bear a mighty superstructure, we need no other proof than in the wonderful growth of one of the provinces, (*Pensilvania* I mean) which tho' the youngest of all, yet being more particularly founded on the principles of moderation (*the first of all political Virtues*) and every way fam'd for the wisdom and lenity of its government, is become the admiration of those who compare it with any thing related by history, and the well-known refuge of———*the oppress'd and persecuted,* who chearfully abandon their native soil to purchase the inestimable blessings of liberty and peace.

The inhabitants of all these colonies have eminently deserved the character of industrious in agriculture and commerce. I could wish they had as well deserved that of *adventurous in inland discoveries,* in this they have been much outdone by *another Nation,* whose poverty of country and unsettled temper have prompted them to such views of extending their possessions, as our agriculture and commerce now make necessary for us to imitate....

Olaudah Equiano Recalls His Enslavement, 1750s

... I have already acquainted the reader with the time and place of my birth. My father, besides many slaves, had a numerous family, of which seven lived to grow up, including myself and sister, who was the only daughter. As I was the youngest of the sons, I became, of course, the greatest favorite with my mother, and was always with her; and she used to take particular pains to form my mind. I was trained up from my earliest years in the art of war: my daily exercise was shooting and throwing javelins, and my mother adorned me with emblems, after the manner of our greatest warriors. In this way I grew up till I had turned the age of eleven, when an end was put to my happiness in the following manner: Generally, when the grown people in the neighborhood were gone far in the fields to labor, the children assembled together in some of the neighboring premises to play; and commonly some of us used to get up a tree to look out for any assailant, or kidnapper, that might come upon us—for they sometimes took those opportunities of our parents' absence, to attack and carry off as many as they could seize. One day as I was watching at the top of a tree in our yard, I saw one of those people come into the yard of our next neighbor but one, to kidnap, there being many stout young people in it. Immediately on this I gave the alarm of the rogue, and he was surrounded by the stoutest of them, who entangled him with cords, so that he could not escape, till some of the grown people came and secured him. But, alas! ere long it was my fate to be thus attacked, and to be carried off, when none of the grown people were nigh. One day, when all our people were gone out to their works as usual, and only I and my dear sister were left to mind the house, two men and a woman got over our walls, and in a moment seized us both, and, without giving us time to cry out, or make resistance, they stopped our mouths, and ran off with us into the nearest wood. Here they tied our hands, and continued to carry us as far as they could, till night came on, when we reached a small house, where the robbers halted for refreshment, and spent the night. We were then unbound, but were unable to take any food; and, being quite overpowered by fatigue and grief, our only relief was some sleep, which allayed our misfortune for a short time. The next morning we left the house, and continued travelling all the day. For a long time we had kept the woods, but at last we came into a road which I believed I knew. I had now some hopes of being delivered;

for we had advanced but a little way before I discovered some people at a distance, on which I began to cry out for their assistance; but my cries had no other effect than to make them tie me faster and stop my mouth, and then they put me into a large sack. They also stopped my sister's mouth, and tied her hands; and in this manner we proceeded till we were out of sight of these people. When we went to rest the following night, they offered us some victuals, but we refused it; and the only comfort we had was in being in one another's arms all that night, and bathing each other with our tears. But alas! we were soon deprived of even the small comfort of weeping together. The next day proved a day of greater sorrow than I had yet experienced; for my sister and I were then separated, while we lay clasped in each other's arms. It was in vain that we besought them not to part us; she was torn from me, and immediately carried away, while I was left in a state of distraction not to be described. I cried and grieved continually; and for several days did not eat anything but what they forced into my mouth. . . .

. . . Thus I continued to travel, sometimes by land, sometimes by water, through different countries and various nations, till, at the end of six or seven months after I had been kidnapped, I arrived at the sea coast. It would be tedious and uninteresting to relate all the incidents which befell me during this journey, and which I have not yet forgotten; of the various hands I passed through, and the manners and customs of all the different people among whom I lived—I shall therefore only observe, that in all the places where I was, the soil was exceedingly rich; the pumpkins, eadas, plantains, yams, &c. &c., were in great abundance, and of incredible size. There were also vast quantities of different gums, though not used for any purpose, and everywhere a great deal of tobacco. The cotton even grew quite wild, and there was plenty of red-wood. I saw no mechanics whatever in all the way . . . The chief employment in all these countries was agriculture, and both the males and females, as with us, were brought up to it, and trained in the arts of war.

The first object which saluted my eyes when I arrived on the coast, was the sea, and a slave ship, which was then riding at anchor, and waiting for its cargo. These filled me with astonishment, which was soon converted into terror, when I was carried on board. I was immediately handled, and tossed up to see if I were sound, by some of the crew; and I was now persuaded that I had gotten into a world of bad spirits, and that they were going to kill me. Their complexions, too, differing so much from ours, their long hair, and the language they spoke (which was very different from any I had ever heard), united to confirm me in this belief. Indeed, such were the horrors of my views and fears at the moment, that, if ten thousand worlds had been my own, I would have freely parted with them all to have exchanged my condition with that of the meanest slave in my own country. When I looked round the ship too, and saw a large furnace of copper boiling, and a multitude of black people of every description chained together, every one of their countenances expressing dejection and sorrow, I no longer doubted of my fate; and, quite overpowered with horror and anguish, I fell motionless on the deck and fainted. When I recovered a little, I found some black people about me, who I believed were some of those who had brought me on board, and had been receiving their pay; they talked to me in order to cheer me, but all in vain. I asked them if we were not to be eaten by those white men with horrible looks, red faces, and long hair. They told me I was not, and one of the crew brought me a small portion of spirituous liquor in a wine glass; but, being afraid of him, I would not take it out of his hand. One of the blacks, therefore, took it from him and gave it to me, and I took a little down my palate, which, instead of reviving me, as they thought it would, threw me into the greatest consternation at the strange feeling it produced, having never tasted any such liquor before. Soon after this, the blacks who brought me on board went off, and left me abandoned to despair. . . .

At last, when the ship we were in, had got in all her cargo, they made ready with many fearful noises, and we were all put under deck, so that we could not see how they managed the vessel. But this disappointment was the least of my sorrow. The stench of the hold while we were on the coast was so intolerably loathsome, that it was dangerous to remain there for any time, and some of us had been permitted to stay on the deck for the fresh air; but now that the whole ship's cargo were confined together, it became absolutely pestilential. The closeness of the place, and the heat of the climate, added to the number in the ship, which was so crowded that each had scarcely room to turn himself, almost suffocated us. This produced copious perspirations, so that the air soon became unfit for respiration, from a variety of loathsome smells, and brought on a sickness among the slaves, of which many died— thus falling victims to the improvident avarice, as I may call it, of their pur- chasers. This wretched situation was again aggravated by the galling of the chains, now became insupportable, and the filth of the necessary tubs, into which the children often fell, and were almost suffocated. The shrieks of the women, and the groans of the dying, rendered the whole a scene of horror almost inconceivable. Happily perhaps, for myself, I was soon reduced so low here that it was thought necessary to keep me almost always on deck; and from my extreme youth I was not put in fetters. In this situation I expected every hour to share the fate of my companions, some of whom were almost daily brought upon deck at the point of death, which I began to hope would soon put an end to my miseries. Often did I think many of the inhabitants of the deep much more happy than myself. I envied them in the freedom they enjoyed, and as often wished I could change my condition for theirs. Every circumstance I met with, served only to render my state more painful, and heightened my apprehensions, and my opinion of the cruelty of the whites.

One day they had taken a number of fishes; and when they had killed and satisfied themselves with as many as they thought fit, to our astonishment who were on deck, rather than give any of them to us to eat, as we expected, they tossed the remaining fish into the sea again, although we begged and prayed for some as well as we could, but in vain; and some of my country- men, being pressed by hunger, took an opportunity, when they thought no one saw them, of trying to get a little privately; but they were discovered, and the attempt procured them some very severe floggings. One day, when we had a smooth sea and moderate wind, two of my wearied countrymen who were chained together (I was near them at the time), preferring death to such a life of misery, somehow made through the nettings and jumped into the sea; immediately, another quite dejected fellow, who, on account of his illness, was suffered to be out of irons, also followed their example; and I believe many more would very soon have done the same, if they had not been prevented by the ship's crew, who were instantly alarmed. Those of us that were the most active, were in a moment put down under the deck; and there was such a noise and confusion amongst the people of the ship as I never heard before, to stop her, and get the boat out to go after the slaves. However, two of the wretches were drowned, but they got the other, and afterwards flogged him unmercifully, for thus attempting to prefer death to slavery. In this manner we continued to undergo more hardships than I can now relate, hardships which are inseparable from this accursed trade. Many a time we were near suffocation from the want of fresh air, which we were often without for whole days together. This, and the stench of the necessary tubs, carried off many. . . .

. . . At last, we came in sight of the island of Barbadoes, at which the whites on board gave a great shout, and made many signs of joy to us. We did not know what to think of this; but as the vessel drew nearer, we plainly saw the harbor, and other ships of different kinds and sizes. . . .

We were not many days in the merchant's custody, before we were sold after their usual manner, which is this: On a signal given (as the beat of a drum), the buyers rush at once into the yard where the slaves are confined, and make choice of that parcel they like best. The noise and clamor with which this is attended, and the eagerness visible in the countenances of the buyers, serve not a little to increase the apprehension of terrified Africans, who may well be supposed to consider them as the ministers of that destruction to which they think themselves devoted. In this manner, without scruple, are relations and friends separated, most of them never to see each other again. I remember, in the vessel in which I was brought over, in the men's apartment, there were several brothers, who, in the sale, were sold in different lots; and it was very moving on this occasion, to see and hear their cries at parting. O, ye nominal Christians! might not an African ask you—Learned you this from your God, who says unto you, Do unto all men as you would men should do unto you? It is not enough that we are torn from our country and friends, to toil for your luxury and lust of gain? Must every tender feeling be likewise sacrificed to your avarice? Are the dearest friends and relations, now rendered more dear by their separation from their kindred, still to be parted from each other, and thus prevented from cheering the gloom of slavery, with the small comfort of being together, and mingling their sufferings and sorrows? Why are parents to lose their children, brothers their sisters, or husbands their wives? Surely, this is a new refinement in cruelty, which, while it has no advantage to atone for it, thus aggravates distress, and adds fresh horrors even to the wretchedness of slavery.

. . . I now totally lost the small remains of comfort I had enjoyed in conversing with my countrymen; the women too, who used to wash and take care of me were all gone different ways, and I never saw one of them afterwards.

I stayed in this island for a few days, I believe it could not be above a fortnight, when I, and some few more slaves, that were not saleable amongst the rest, from very much fretting, were shipped off in a sloop for North America. On the passage we were better treated than when we were coming from Africa, and we had plenty of rice and fat pork. We were landed up a river a good way from the sea, about Virginia county, where we saw few or none of our native Africans, and not one soul who could talk to me. I was a few weeks weeding grass and gathering stones in a plantation; and at last all my companions were distributed different ways, and only myself was left. I was now exceedingly miserable, and thought myself worse off than any of the rest of my companions, for they could talk to each other, but I had no person to speak to that I could understand. In this state, I was constantly grieving and pining, and wishing for death rather than anything else. While I was in this plantation, the gentleman, to whom I suppose the estate belonged, being unwell, I was one day sent for to his dwelling-house to fan him; when I came into the room where he was I was very much affrighted at some things I saw, and the more so as I had seen a black woman slave as I came through the house, who was cooking the dinner, and the poor creature was cruelly loaded with various kinds of iron machines; she had one particularly on her head, which locked her mouth so fast that she could scarcely speak; and could not eat nor drink. I was much astonished and shocked at this contrivance, which I afterwards learned was called the iron muzzle. Soon after I had a fan put in my hand, to fan the gentleman while he slept; and so I did indeed with great fear. While he was fast asleep I indulged myself a great deal in looking about the room, which to me appeared very fine and curious. The first object that engaged my attention was a watch which hung on the chimney, and was going. I was quite surprised at the noise it made, and was afraid it would tell the gentleman anything I might do amiss; and when I immediately after observed a picture hanging in the room, which appeared constantly to look at me, I was still more affrighted, having never seen such things as these before. At one time I thought it was something relative to magic; and not seeing it move, I thought it might be some way the whites had to keep their great men when they died, and offer them libations as we used to do our friendly spirits. In this state of anxiety I remained till my master awoke, when I was dismissed out of the room, to my no small satisfaction and relief; for I thought that these people were all made up of wonders. In this place I was called Jacob; but on board the *African Snow,* I was called Michael. I had been some time in this miserable, forlorn, and much dejected state, without having anyone to talk to, which made my life a burden, when the kind and unknown hand of the Creator (who in very deed leads the blind in a way they know not) now began to appear, to my comfort; for one day the captain of a merchant ship, called the *Industrious Bee,* came on some business to my master's house. This gentleman, whose name was Michael Henry Pascal, was a lieutenant in the royal navy, but now commanded this trading ship, which was somewhere in the confines of the county many miles off. While he was at my master's house, it happened that he saw me, and liked me so well that he made a purchase of me. I think I have often heard him say he gave thirty or forty pounds sterling for me; but I do not remember which. However, he meant me for a present to some of his friends in England: and as I was sent accordingly from the house of my then master (one Mr. Campbell) to the place where the ship lay. . . .

Report on a Runaway Slave Community in the Virginia Mountains, 1729

My Lords:

. . . Sometime after my Last a number of Negroes, about fifteen, belonging to a new Plantation on the head of James River formed a Design to withdraw from their Master and to fix themselves in the fastnesses of the neighbouring Mountains. They had found means to get into their possession some Arms & Ammunition, and they took along with them some Provisions, their Cloaths, bedding and working Tools; but the Gentleman to whom they belonged with a Party of Men made such diligent pursuit after them, that he soon found them out in their new Settlement, a very obscure place among the Mountains, where they had already begun to clear the ground, and obliged them after exchanging a shot or two by which one of the Slaves was wounded, to surrender and return back, and so prevented for this time a design which might have proved as dangerous to this Country, as is that of the Negroes in the Mountains of Jamaica to the Inhabitants of that Island. Tho' this attempt has happily been defeated, it ought nevertheless to awaken us into some effectual measures for preventing the like hereafter, it being certain that a very small number of Negroes once settled in those Parts, would very soon be encreas'd by the Accession of other Runaways and prove dangerous Neighbours to our frontier Inhabitants. To prevent this and many other Mischiefs I am training and exercising the Militia in the several counties as the best means to deter our Slaves from endeavouring to make their Escape, and to suppress them if they should.

❧ E S S A Y S

Philip D. Morgan, a historian at Florida State University, has analyzed slave life in the eighteenth century extensively. In the first essay he argues that, despite travelers' testimony, Virginia piedmont plantations acquired a large slave presence and came to resemble the pattern of the contemporary tidewater. Thus backcountry slaves had the same ability to form kin and neighborhood networks as those to the east and suffered the same problems of life on overseer-run plantations with absentee landlords. In the second essay Daniel B. Thorp of Virginia Polytechnic Institute and State University also takes up the question of how radically the backcountry differed from the earlier-settled East. In examining the Moravian settlements at Wachovia in the North Carolina piedmont, Thorp finds that the planters arrived with well-defined, idealistic plans for community structure and modes of agriculture but modified these blueprints, without losing their core, in the light of circumstances in the region. In the process the planters discovered that the agricultural and settlement practices appearing "slovenly" to outsiders were chosen because they seemed to make the best sense in the backcountry environment.

Slave Life in Virginia's Piedmont

PHILIP D. MORGAN

Slavery first expanded into the Virginia piedmont in the 1720s. The institution took root rapidly. By the middle of the eighteenth century—just about a generation after its introduction—forty thousand slaves, one-third of the colony's total, resided in the piedmont's rolling hills. Within a further generation, a remarkable transformation took place. The piedmont slave population almost trebled in size; Virginia emerged from the Revolutionary War with more slaves living beyond, than within, the fall line. The center of black life had shifted extraordinarily rapidly from tidewater to piedmont. . . .

Turning from the technicalities of population growth to its implications, we need to investigate the changing balance of Africans and creoles among the piedmont slave population. Two contrasting facts immediately command attention. First, although African immigration was not central to slave population growth in the piedmont, more Africans resided beyond the fall line than in tidewater in the late colonial era. In terms of the relative proportions of Africans and creoles, in other words, the late colonial piedmont did replicate to some degree an earlier tidewater experience. Even more notable, however, was the speed at which the piedmont slave population approximated the contemporary, rather than an earlier, tidewater pattern. Native-born slaves soon came to dominate the piedmont slave population, much as they did in contemporary tidewater. Once again, extension rather than replication seems the dominant story.

Still, in certain piedmont counties at particular times the adult population was heavily African. In Amelia County, which probably received more Africans than any other Chesapeake county in the forty years before Independence, about 60 percent of the adult slaves in 1755 were Africans. In 1782, although the proportion had dropped considerably, it still stood at around one-fifth. Even by the late 1760s and early 1770s, the demand for Africans was relatively brisk in certain piedmont counties. In July 1769 Richard Adams considered himself fortunate to have eighty slaves to sell on the upper James. Two years later, another James River merchant informed a correspondent who had proposed an "African Scheme" that "Negroes will always sell well here." As if to prove the point, in 1772 Paul Carrington bought fifty slaves at Bermuda Hundred in order to sell them to eager southside purchasers.

Once Africans reached the plantations, their presence was not always documented. An occasional name or ethnic designation in an inventory, as in

Philip Morgan, "Slave Life in Piedmont Virginia, 1720–1800," in Lois Green Carr, Philip Morgan, and Jean Russo, eds., *Colonial Chesapeake Society,* 433–484. Published for the Institute of Early American History and Culture, Williamsburg, Virginia. © 1989 The University of North Carolina Press.

Angola Jack, Ebo Sam, Malagawyou Bess, and Gambia James, often provides the only clue to an African identity. Somewhat more exceptional were the quarters of Mrs. Mayo and those of Philip Mayo of Goochland County. On the former estate, seven of seventeen tithables had African names (Jolloff, Quaw, Fatima, Congo, Cudjo, Shantee, and Cudjee), as did four of thirteen on the latter (Bussee, Jallapa, Jubah, and Abanah). Or it might take an unusual event for Africans to come to our notice. The deaths of "two new Negroes" in Goochland County in 1762 prompted the county court to order an inquest. In Prince Edward County, an African influence might explain the extraordinary action of Jacob, who when cornered by six whites, defended himself with "sharp pointed darts of a sufficient length and size to kill a man at a great distance." Or, even more indirectly, we might infer an African presence from place-names. Eighteenth-century Cumberland County, for instance, had its Angola and Guinea roads, its Little Guinea Neck, and its Great Guinea and Angola creeks.

The prominence of Africans among the piedmont runaway population, particularly in the earliest years, provides the most direct evidence of their widespread presence. The residences of two slave runaways captured in Louisa County in the mid-1740s could not be determined because neither spoke English. Presumably, it was the slave himself who gave his name to a capturer in Spotsylvania County in 1744: he called himself "Angola Tom." In the following year Sambo, Aaron, and Berwick ran away from their quarter in Orange County eight months after their arrival in the colony; two slaves imported from Senegambia ran away within a month of being brought to Hanover County; and in 1751 David ran from his quarter on Willis Creek in Albemarle County less than a month after arriving on the ship *Williamsburg* with 294 other Africans. These aliens in the piedmont, like their compatriots throughout the New World, took to flight to express their detestation of their new surroundings and situation.

Also typical of Africans throughout the New World, these piedmont immigrants formed strong attachments to fellow shipmates. The scow *Yanimarew* imported 240 Africans in the summer of 1770. One month after being purchased and taken to Amherst County, Charles ran away. Meanwhile, in Richmond three other African men, imported in the same slaver, fled their master. They apparently sought out the companionship of their former shipmates (perhaps Charles was among them), for their master reported "it is imagined that they were seen some time ago (along with three others of the same cargo) on Chickahominy, and it is supposed they are still lurking about the skirts of that swamp." A similar venture occurred the following year when a twenty-year-old man and a twelve-year-old girl, recently purchased by the same master from an African slaver, "went off with several others, being persuaded that they could find the way back to their own Country."

The presence of restive Africans may help account for the heavy concentration of "poisoning" cases that appeared in piedmont county courts in the second half of the eighteenth century. Of about 180 slaves tried for "poisoning" in colonial Virginia county courts, two-thirds resided in the piedmont.

Rarely can alleged poisoners be proven to have been Africans, but the high concentrations of such cases in counties where large numbers of Africans lived, together with information such as the African names of some alleged poisoners, make the connection plausible. Furthermore, an offhand remark by Edmund Pendleton, a resident of Caroline County (adjoining the piedmont), suggests such a connection in the contemporary mind. In 1777, when referring to the atrocities perpetrated by the British army, Pendleton exclaimed that they had descended to the "low, mean, petiful, skulking, perfidious, wicked Italian & African business of Poisoning."

Even though an African influence was noticeable in the late-eighteenth-century piedmont, it was a constantly dwindling one. The proportion of Africans in the piedmont slave population quickly assumed a profile similar to that of tidewater. In 1755 perhaps as many as one-third of adult slaves throughout the piedmont were Africans. By 1782, in spite of the importation of around 15,000 Africans, almost all of whom went to various piedmont counties, the proportion had dropped to about one in ten. Moreover, by the late colonial period, many Africans were longtime residents of the piedmont region and no longer easily distinguished from creoles. In 1777, Aberdeen, a thirty-five-year-old blacksmith, resided on the Falls Plantation in Chesterfield County. He "came into the country young," his master noted, and therefore spoke "very good English." In the same year, a Fauquier County African was described as "affect[ing] to pronounce the English language very fine, or rather to clip it." He could also read and write.

An African named Bacchus best personifies the speed with which these immigrants adjusted to their new surroundings. In the space of about three years in the early 1770s, Bacchus left a dizzying trail of crime across both tidewater and piedmont. In that time, he ran away at least four times, faced four separate criminal charges, was branded in the hand, heard himself pronounced guilty and sentenced to hang in two county courts, but evaded the hangman's noose on both occasions. In 1771 this "thick set, and well made," seventeen-year-old lad spoke "broken English," but two years later his proficiency had improved so that his master described his speech as only "somewhat broken." His assimilation was never total, however, for he retained his African name, Juba, while also employing the English names Jemmy and James. Nevertheless, he was sufficiently conversant with white ways to pass as a free black in Chesterfield County. In that capacity, it seems, Bacchus got wind of the Somerset Case (a famous legal decision of 1772 that was widely but erroneously perceived to outlaw slavery in England) and imagined he would be free if only he could get to that country. This was, according to his master, "a Notion now too prevalent among the Negroes." Indeed, Bacchus was thought to be in the company of another of his master's fugitives, a twenty-seven-year-old "very black" woman who had since passed herself as free, using the name Sukey Jones. That news of the Somerset Case had reached the ears of a humble African like Bacchus in piedmont Virginia, some three thousand miles away, speaks well of his initiative and resolve, but more particularly of his political education.

Piedmont Africans creolized quickly, one might conjecture, precisely because they came into contact with large numbers of accomplished and assimilated slaves. By the late colonial era, the African newcomer could regularly encounter slaves like painter Peter Brown, raised in Petersburg, who was "fond of Singing," or thirty-year-old Jacob from Louisa County, who could read and write, spoke "in the Scotch-Irish dialect, and in conversation frequently use[d] the words moreover and likewise," or twenty-eight-year-old Sam from Amelia County, a carpenter and cooper, who could "read print, pretends to a deal of religion, has been a good fiddler, and is acquainted with many parts of Virginia." If an African ran away in a group after midcentury, he usually accompanied creoles, not fellow Africans. Three men ran away from Archibald Cary's forge in Chesterfield County in 1766. One was a Virginia-born carpenter, another a Virginia-born foreman, and the third a Gold Coast native, now a fireman. Nine years later, two Africans who spoke only a rudimentary English ran away with a Jamaica-born black and a Virginian mulatto from their Prince Edward County quarter.

Masters must have been reduced to hoping that their African slaves would fail to emulate the examples set by their creoles. An incident involving a highly assimilated slave belonging to Peter Nunnery of Goochland County illustrates the problems with which masters had to contend. In 1747, Nunnery's runaway slave was thought to have stolen a horse's bell. He was pursued and eventually overtaken in Henrico County by three whites. When confronted, the slave at first denied the charge, then under some duress confessed to the theft, and finally promised to reveal the bell's hiding place. He first took the group to a pile of logs, pretended to search for the missing item, then "s[ai]d with a Laughter that he made [a] fool of them and that the Bell was not there." Not surprisingly, this charade angered his captors, who proceeded to beat him, whereupon the slave promised to reveal the true whereabouts of the bell. But he repeated the performance at a fodder stack. By now the whites were livid with rage and began cutting switches in order to whip the impudent black, but the slave attempted to convince them to follow him one more time to a hollow tree stump by the river's edge where all would be revealed. At this point, one of his captors declared that "he would . . . follow [the] son of a bitch no more for he could make a bell sooner," but the slave won his reprieve from the other two. On their way to the river, the bondman managed to slip away, get ahead of his captors, and jump into the river. When urged to come out, he began "laughing at [them and] Sunk in their sight & they saw him no more." If, as seems likely, this self-assured slave went to his death making a fool of whites, no doubt he would have wanted it no other way.

Creoles soon dominated slave life in the piedmont. Although almost all Africans who reached Virginia from midcentury onward made their home in the piedmont, their numbers were never large enough to put much of an African stamp on the emerging slave society. Piedmont Africans certainly resisted slavery in characteristic ways and seem to have been at the heart of the widespread resort to magic. More noticeable, however, is the speed at which they creolized, evident in everything from their acquisition of English language skills to their running away with native-born slaves. Creoles set the standard and tone of this regional society remarkably quickly.

Since the piedmont received many immigrants in the colonial era, the region's slaves did not find it easy to establish a measure of family life. In this sense, black life in the piedmont replicated an earlier phase of the tidewater slave experience. At the same time, there were important differences between the two experiences. Piedmont immigrants were primarily creoles, not Africans. Not surprisingly, therefore, the adult sex ratios among piedmont slaves rapidly approached equality. Taking the region as a whole, adult male slaves out-numbered females heavily during the first decade or so of piedmont settlement. But these imbalanced sex ratios were relatively short-lived. By the late 1730s and early 1740s, there were fewer than 120 men for every 100 slave women in the piedmont. More-skewed imbalances periodically reoccurred as waves of immigrants moved into the region, but the overall trend was a rapid downward one. By the late 1760s and 1770s there were almost as many women as men.

Even more striking is the proportion of children to be found in the pied-mont slave population. In part this can be attributed to the composition of both migration streams, since young slaves predominated among creole and African newcomers. In any case, from the first years of piedmont settlement, and for much of the colonial period, children outnumbered women by at least two to one.... In sum, the youthfulness of the piedmont slave population was striking.

The available measures of the fecundity of female slaves—such indicators as age at first birth, length of intervals between births, and completed family size—support and help account for this youthfulness. Some piedmont slave women were remarkably young when they conceived their first child. Lilly, a Jerdone slave, was not even fifteen when she first conceived. The average age of conception in the late colonial period was 18.2 years, dropping slightly to 17.7 years in the late eighteenth century. Piedmont slave mothers bore children regularly and rapidly—one every twenty-eight months on average, not taking into account early infant mortality. Finally, piedmont slave women probably lived longer than their tidewater counterparts. Robert Rose thought the death of his slave woman Judith sufficiently noteworthy to put in his diary because she was "the first Slave of Mine that has died in Albemarle." This was almost a decade after Rose first set up quarters there. Not surprisingly, therefore, completed family sizes were generally larger for piedmont, than for tidewater, slaves.

Truncated family structures inevitably characterized such a youthful im-migrant population. In the late 1750s Peyton Randolph, like many another tidewater planter, established a new plantation in the piedmont. He transferred a number of his young slaves to a quarter in what became Charlotte County, over a hundred miles away from his home plantation. No doubt these teen-agers and young adults left kin behind when they moved west. Moreover, the imbalance between men and women meant that large age differentials (of about ten years) separated spouses, when they were fortunate enough to marry.

Just over twenty years later, however, some of the children of the original immigrants had reached maturity and established families of their own. Nanny, for instance, certainly left kin behind when she came to the piedmont as a twenty-five-year-old mother of four children. But by 1784, at least two of her three daughters had given birth themselves and Nanny was a grandmother to four children, one of whom bore her name. Sarah, another Randolph slave, was about twenty years of age when she was moved to the piedmont and already the mother of three children, including twins; she gave birth to at least three more children in her new home. By 1784 two of her daughters had married and each had one child apiece. Nanny and Sarah were therefore matriarchs of rapidly growing slave clans.

Struggling to re-create a semblance of an ordered family life, Nanny, Sarah, and their fellow Randolph slaves were at least more fortunate than the slaves of Francis Willis, a planter who made his home in Gloucester County, but who had quarters in the piedmont. In 1766 Willis died and the majority of his slaves in Cumberland and Hanover counties were sold. Few piedmont planters could afford to purchase large lots of slaves. Indeed, most could buy no more than a single slave, so the sale scattered 101 slaves among sixty-one purchasers. Only occasionally can we be certain that families were separated (the couple Butcher Will and his wife Venus were sold with their "sucking child," also named Venus, but their two sons Sam and Lewis were sold separately). However, since three-quarters of the men were sold singly, while almost half of the women were sold with at least one child, it seems a fair assumption that these sales broke many husband-wife, not to mention parent-child, relationships.

A firsthand description of one slave sale is sufficiently interesting to be explored in depth. It took place in the winter of 1787 in Powhatan County, the very heart of the piedmont. Mr. Gay, a Powhatan resident, was apparently in deep debt, particularly to Robert Hare of Philadelphia, who employed the local planter Benjamin Harrison to look after his interests. Gay was forced to put up every one of his slaves, fifty-seven in all, for public auction at the Powhatan County Courthouse. Six slaves who were already mortgaged were immediately claimed. Of those remaining, twelve were not even "set up," owing to their advanced ages and general unsuitability. Their fate is unknown. The sale itself went slowly; as night fell, only twelve slaves had been purchased. In order to protect Mr. Hare's interest, Harrison bought the remaining twenty-seven slaves at £40 apiece. Harrison showed a measure of compassion by allowing his acquisitions to return to Gay that night in order to "collect their little effects together." However, within a few days, Harrison had sold six at £70 each, making a tidy profit. He then advertised his willingness to sell the others privately and set another date for a second public auction. Noting that his purchases had not been clothed that year, he proposed remedying the omission so that they might "sell better." He explained to Hare that "the plan of carrying them from Court to Court will not do at this season of the year for so many [are] small negroes." No mention was made of keeping families together; rather, business decisions ruled this, and presumably many another, slave sale.

The arbitrariness with which slave family members could be dispersed is revealed in a number of cases concerning a father's verbal gift of a slave to one of his children. In the early 1750s George Thompson of Goochland County gave a slave to his daughter Joyce "as soon as the said [slave] Girl was born." He told Joyce "to take care of her for that he had no more to do with the said Girl." In 1769 a lodger in the Cumberland County household of William Angela, Sr., remembered a conversation between Angela and his daughter Betty some fifteen years previous. The father promised to give his daughter a slave infant named Biddy, provided Betty take care of the child. His action was largely a response to the "grumblings" of his son Benjamin, who as overseer on his father's plantation objected to Biddy's mother "coming in to tend the negro child." In this way, Betty acquired her own slave, and a slave mother was deprived of the care of her own daughter.

Small holdings, constant sales and mortgages, and distribution of property among large numbers of heirs, not to mention the heartlessness displayed by men like Angela, must have exacerbated the chances of separation facing many piedmont slave families. An elderly couple, Tony and his wife, Phillis, were perhaps typical. Both had been born in Lancaster County around the 1720s, but were sold to a Culpeper master, who in turn sold them to an adjacent Fauquier County planter. With each sale, Tony and Phillis had been separated from progressively more of their "several children," so that almost a half-century later they had children "dispersed through Culpeper, Frederick and Augusta Counties." When they ran away in 1770, their master had trouble predicting their whereabouts, in part because they might be harbored by any one of their many progeny. Later in the century, when riding the Hanover circuit, the Methodist minister James Meacham was distraught to see a black couple's children torn from them because they were "legacy'd" to widely scattered heirs. "The crys of the poor Captive Woman . . . on her Taking leave of her children," were, in Meacham's opinion, "enough to move the heart of the most obdurate."

Yet many slaves like Tony and Phillis struggled to maintain kin ties; some, particularly those belonging to the larger planters, managed to create a remarkably robust family life. . . .

Larger planters could more readily afford to be respectful of slave kin ties. In 1776, when John Blair offered to exchange his slaves in Hanover County for Thomas Adams's land in Albemarle County, he acknowledged that the predominantly youthful character of his slaves "might not suit," but stressed that he "could not think of separating them from their mothers." Thirteen years later, in an action that must have been repeated on many a piedmont plantation, a slave named Frank "asked leave" of his master, Col. Francis Taylor of Orange County, to "have Miss M. Conway's Pat for a Wife." Taylor employed Frank as his messenger and errand runner, a valuable slave whose wishes ought to be respected if possible and who already traveled off the plantation. Thus Taylor "did not object," particularly when Frank told him that he "had the necessary consent." Frank must have anticipated his master's approval, because he had already set the time of the wedding for the following evening.

Some slaves—those who became Baptists in the late eighteenth century—were exposed most directly to white views on family morality. Indeed, the most common disciplinary offense brought against black Baptist church members involved a transgression of family norms—whether adultery, fornication, attempted rape, even in one case "attempting to bead with a white woman." At the same time, white Baptists at least recognized slave marriages. . . .

Slave families also took the initiative in naming their children. Two patterns are particularly noticeable. Naming after extended kin was perhaps the most common. . . . Only one slave family in many piedmont slave lists named a daughter after a mother.

Just as naming patterns indicate the emergence of strong nuclear families and extended kin among piedmont slaves, so do the actions of runaway slaves. By the late colonial period, more and more runaway slaves were attempting to reunite with separated spouses and parents; in some cases, kin networks were thought to be supporting the absentee. Sall, a twenty-five-year-old mulatto woman who ran away from an Amherst County quarter in 1774, was said to be "of a numerous Family of Mulattoes, formerly belonging to a Gentleman of the Name of Howard in York County . . . and where probably she may attempt to go again, or perhaps into Cumberland, or Amelia, where . . . many of her kindred live." Abraham, who ran away from his Chesterfield County master in 1777, was said to have "a Wife at a Quarter of the Hon. William Nelson's, Esq. in king William; several Relations at Mr. Claiborne's, in the same county; some at Mr. William Dandridge's and Mr. Sherwood Tinsley's, in Hanover County, at some of which Places," his master conjectured, "he is harboured." Cuthie from Mecklenburg County was supposed to have gone toward York County, where she had "several relations"; Sye from Chesterfield County was thought to be "lurking" in Gloucester County, where he had "many Relations." A wide range of "connections," as contemporary masters termed them, supported some piedmont runaways in the late colonial period.

By the end of the eighteenth century, the building and rebuilding of kin ties had produced dense social networks for some piedmont slaves, in both town and countryside. . . . In deepest Bedford County, in the southwestern part of the piedmont, an old couple belonging to Thomas Jefferson was surrounded by a bevy of grown children, in-laws, and grandchildren. The quarter was almost one extended family.

Although the obstacles placed in the way of family formation and maintenance were formidable, many piedmont slaves overcame them. It is impossible to say how many of the region's slaves enjoyed a measure of family life, but the surviving evidence, overrepresentative as it may be of the larger plantations, suggests a surprisingly high number, at least after midcentury. . . .

The development of a robust family life went hand in hand with the emergence of an Afro-American society in the piedmont. In part, this was a function of demographic and economic forces. . . . The increasing size of plantation units also created greater opportunities for piedmont slaves to develop a social life of their own. Generally speaking, within one or two decades after the formation of a piedmont county, a majority of its slaves resided on plantations with more than ten slaves. Indeed, by the early 1780s about 40 percent of slaves in most piedmont counties resided on plantations of more than twenty slaves. The rapidity with which plantation sizes in the piedmont caught up with—and, in some cases, surpassed—those in the tidewater is remarkable. Finally, by the 1780s at least, the density of the slave population in many piedmont counties approached tidewater levels, thereby facilitating contacts and communication among slaves.

Black actions, not just impersonal forces, made vital contributions to the development of an Afro-American society in the piedmont. A prime example of the black community ministering to its own needs is the widespread resort to magic, something that contemporary whites pejoratively labeled a propensity for poisoning. At any rate, the dispenser of medicines, charms, or poisons clearly was a person of influence within the slave community. Indeed, even whites recognized the power of such slaves. . . .

On the other hand, a large number of alleged poisonings appear to have been little more than one slave administering roots, powders, or charms to others. Court judgments reflect the harmlessness of many "poisoning" cases. . . . Some slaves used "poisons" as charms to influence their masters. Peg of Louisa County administered a substance procured from a slave man in the neighborhood "to keep peace in the family, and to make her Master kind to her." Sarah of Prince Edward County put black seeds "resembling Jaucestor seeds" into the peas she prepared for her white family "for the purpose of making her mistress love her."

Although the widespread resort to magic bound piedmont slaves together, the practice also reflected serious internal tensions within the slave community. In fact, many poisoning incidents that came before piedmont county courts were as much inwardly directed at blacks as outwardly targeted against whites. Intrablack conflict, perhaps stemming from frictions between different African ethnic groups or between Africans and creoles, or from the natural stresses to which all slave communities were subject, lay at the heart of many of these cases. . . .

Exciting much less controversy, slaves turned to black doctors, as well as black conjurers, though they may have made less of this distinction than did their masters. In 1752, William Dabney of Goochland County paid 11s. 3d. to John Bates "for the use of his negroe Doctor" among his slaves. Over two decades later, Charles Yates bought a slave in Culpeper County only to find that he had been long "distempered" and under the hands of "Negro Doctors" for years. Benjamin Harrison employed a slave doctor on his plantation, while a Chesterfield County master disapproved of his slave Sambo's doctoring. Black midwives often delivered slave women. Francis Taylor noted that "Granny Venus" attended at the delivery of his slave woman Milly. Blacks turned to other blacks for physical as well as psychological support.

The growth of intercounty and cooperative networks in the actions of slave runaways also provides evidence of an emergent cohesiveness within the black community. As the century proceeded, slaves ran away over greater distances and often remained at large for extensive periods. . . .

Cooperative actions were common in the committing of crimes. Just over 40 percent of the four hundred or more slaves prosecuted in a number of piedmont county courts committed their alleged crimes in groups of two or more persons. . . . [A] large proportion of the group crimes involved slaves belonging to separate masters. Indeed, this was true of 60 percent of the crimes committed by groups. Cross-plantation alliances were the norm. . . .

Whites also encouraged blacks to turn on one another. An unwritten but consistently pursued policy of divide and rule put considerable pressure on black cohesiveness. Sometimes slaves served as prosecution witnesses against other bondmen. In cooperative crimes, one slave might be induced to secure his freedom by incriminating his comrades. In Cumberland County in 1765, Toby was found guilty of hog stealing when his partner in crime, Charles, turned King's evidence. It later transpired that Charles had been "a false witness"; for his pains, he was nailed to a pillory for an hour by his ears, which were then cut off. Though the white community encouraged slaves to act as turncoats, they had to be reliable ones. Pecuniary incentives also induced divisiveness, as when slaves or free blacks secured rewards for capturing runaways or conveying them back to their masters. In these and other ways, whites encouraged divisions among slaves.

Another division among blacks arose from the simple fact that not all blacks were slaves. Apart from all the obvious and distinguishing advantages of freedom, skin color usually demarcated free blacks from slaves. Unlike the vast majority of slaves, most pre-Revolutionary free blacks were mulattoes. . . .

However, whatever their complexion, most free blacks were not far removed from slaves—either in station or residence. Most lived for a large part of their lives as bound servants, presumably alongside slaves. . . .

A small Afro-Indian community also emerged in the piedmont. Like the free black community, it lived in a twilight zone between slavery and freedom. Thus, a Cumberland County slave, a "Mulatto" named Jim, ran away from his master in 1772 seeking the "Right to his Freedom," as his master put it. His father "was an Indian of the Name of Cheshire," so his master guessed he would "call himself JAMES Cheshire or Chink." Another mulatto runaway slave, from Dinwiddie County, was thought to be joining his brother, who had been "several Times brought from among the Indians on Pamunkey River." A third mulatto slave, also from Dinwiddie, was said to be "of the Indian breed"; he sought his freedom from the General Court in 1773. Again, like free blacks, Afro-Indians lived in close proximity to slaves. In 1762 two quarters in Chesterfield County contained thirty "Negroes," fourteen mulattoes, and four Indians. Indians and blacks inevitably married one another. Patrick Rose of Amherst County assumed that his runaway slave Ben had joined his Indian wife, because "she sold off, and moved from her late Dwelling Place in Albemarle, a few Days before the Fellow ran away."

In sum, although serious divisions existed within the Afro-American community of the piedmont, a voluntary cohesiveness, not to mention the cohesion forced on blacks by white hostility, developed quickly. From the actions of runaways and rebels to the more mundane activities of black conjurers and doctors, the black community attempted to stand together. Not always successful, the black community appeared resilient in the face of formidable odds. There were always casualties, ranging from a slave like Ralph who, piqued at being given a mule to ride rather than a horse, beat "the poor Jack without mercy" until it died, to "old Caesar," who was charged with the attempted rape and buggery of a four-year-old white girl. Nobody escaped the effects of slavery no matter where they lived. But the pathology of slavery does not seem to have been any more developed in the piedmont than in the tidewater.

Black-white relations assumed a special character in the piedmont. Generally speaking, as plantation units increased in size throughout tidewater, more Afro-Americans lived on quarters beyond their masters' direct supervision. In the piedmont, however, a reverse trend was evident—at least in the short run. In the earliest years of a piedmont county, large numbers of slaves resided on quarters with overseers. In Amelia in 1740 at least a third of the county's slaves lived on units where masters were absent. In 1760 just over half of the slaves in recently created Loudoun County lived on quarters supervised by overseers. As more piedmont whites became slaveholders and as some tidewater masters transferred their residences into the piedmont, the proportion of slaves under the direct purview of a master increased. By the late 1770s, the vast majority of slaves in Amelia County, and other piedmont counties, resided on plantations with a resident master, although a significant minority occupied satellite quarters some distance from the home estate.

The more-distanced relationship with a master, which was a prominent feature of the slave experience particularly in the early piedmont, had obvious advantages. Some piedmont slaves no doubt enjoyed the relative autonomy inherent in absentee estates. Others may have valued the opportunities for traveling back and forth between piedmont quarter and tidewater home plantation, driving livestock, or taking crops to market....

Yet from the perspective of the slaves' material well-being, the drawbacks of a more-distanced relationship with masters probably outweighed the advantages. Many piedmont slaves depended on distant tidewater owners for supplies....

The poor opinion in which piedmont overseers were generally held was undoubtedly small compensation to the slaves for the cruelties they suffered, but at least it provided them with opportunities to redress grievances....

Piedmont slaves could ... occasionally exploit the tenuous position occupied by many a white overseer. Most piedmont overseers averaged only a year or two in the employ of a single planter. A particularly revealing incident occurred on one of Edward Ambler's piedmont quarters in 1770, with the hiring of a new overseer, John Smith. He immediately incurred the opposition of the fourteen adult slaves put under him. According to the plantation steward, the problem lay in the attitude of Smith's predecessor, Thomas Wingfield, who "was so good natured to the Negroes under him that he suffered them to Impose on him very much." In the last year of Wingfield's incumbency, the steward continued, "the Negroes were almost free." As a result, they were "very unwilling to give up the privileges they [had been] allowed." Indeed, "they seem," noted the steward, "to be determined to Maintain them" and tried to get Smith "turned off." The slaves prevailed on George, the oldest bondman on the plantation, to visit their master, thinking that "a complaint from him wou'd be listened to." Although Smith apparently had the backing of his superiors at this time, he was replaced the following year.

The example of Thomas Wingfield suggests that some overseers, only too well aware of the precariousness of their position, took the line of least resistance and sided with the slaves. . . .

By the late colonial era, many more piedmont slaves resided on plantations headed by masters and, particularly on the larger estates, became subject to a more patriarchal planter style. . . .

Patriarchs prided themselves on their responsiveness to the human, as well as the material, needs of their slaves. Erasmus Gill of Stirling Castle in Dinwiddie County allowed his slave Aggy and her youngest children to go to Petersburg because Aggy was "desirous of living with her Husband." Gill arranged for her eldest child, Page, to be "brought up by some genteel Lady to learn how to soe, and attend to other domestic duties" in a three-year apprenticeship "for good Cloaths &c. provided she is treated with tenderness." A Fredericksburg master permitted his "old & faithful family slave" Charles to "see for the last time" his "other old acquaintances" in Stafford County. Patriarchal benevolence was not confined to the tidewater gentry.

Indeed, as the eighteenth century proceeded, the rough edges of life in the interior were gradually smoothed away. Harsh sentences for slaves seem to have become less common over time. A good indication of the changing temper of the times comes from an anonymous letter to the *Virginia Gazette* in 1773. In it, a man known by the initials R. M. (almost undoubtedly Robert Munford of Amelia County) is said to have practiced barbaric cruelties upon his slaves, including the slaughter of at least fifty and the castration and dismemberment of a captured runaway. Presumably, the claims were exaggerated, but most notable is that one piedmonter would criticize the inhumanity of another. Whatever the reality, slavery was not *meant* to be barbaric any longer.

Smaller planters were, of course, less able to afford the liberality of their more prosperous neighbors. . . . And it is they who invariably stood in the dock when masters were accused of either killing or wounding one of their own slaves. In most of these cases, the gentlemen justices discharged their less affluent neighbors without further trial—confirming the gentry's magnanimity toward fellow whites. Humble yeomen, however, were often incorrigible. When Daniel McPherson, a veteran of the Royal Highland Company Regiment that had fought in Quebec, confronted a slave suspected of theft, he acted in the classic small slaveholder manner. Rather than resorting to the courts, he whipped the man. Later, the same slave was incautious enough to jeer at McPherson, using "scurrilous language" to boot. McPherson was on his schooner at the time, but waded into the water intent on beating the slave a second time. The two men fought in the river, oblivious to the larger dangers they faced, were swept away, and drowned. This sort of confrontation was a far cry from the patriarchal ideal.

Not all small planters were devoid of benevolent feelings. In July 1773 Toby, a slave belonging to James Wimbish of Halifax County, disappeared for over twelve years. When Wimbish discovered his bondman, he found that Toby had fought for his country in the Revolutionary War by enlisting in the 14th Virginia Regiment under a fictitious name. Upon his retirement, he had married a white woman, by whom he had several children. Wimbish, in his words, felt "compassion" toward his slave and "subscribed a considerable sum toward obtaining his freedom, which was effected by several Gentlemen who bore part of the loss." Even here, then, gentlemen aided a small planter. . . .

. . . [T]he piedmont was the center of the evangelical revival that swept Virginia in the late colonial era. In this respect, the piedmont was hardly replicating or extending a tidewater experience; it was leading the way. . . . However, the first sustained proselytization of slaves took place in neighboring Hanover County at midcentury, under the inspired leadership of the charismatic Presbyterian Samuel Davies. In 1751 Davies reported that one hundred slaves attended his services and that forty had been baptized in the previous three years. Four years later, the numbers had increased to three hundred and one hundred, respectively. His efforts then gained momentum, for in 1757 he claimed to have baptized one hundred and fifty black adults in the previous eighteen months and to have sixty black communicants in attendance. The influence of this revival radiated outward to other piedmont counties. Slaves who had been converted by Davies but transferred to Charlotte County proselytized other slaves in their new home.

What is perhaps most surprising about this Presbyterian success was its conservative and bookish nature. Davies and his disciples thought it part of their mission to teach the slaves to read. In the middle of the nineteenth century, one Virginian recalled seeing African slaves clasping the books given to them by their eminent preacher. Davies was also demanding of his converts. He acknowledged that he was "affraid of discouraging them . . . by imposing high Forms of Admission to Baptism," but equally he underlined his caution at not "swelling the number of proselites with only nominal Christians." He excluded many blacks from baptism because they thought it either a fashionable communal rite or, more ominously, a means to "be upon an Equality with their Masters." Davies strenuously opposed these misinterpretations of his message. Indeed, he reported that planters were impressed "by the visible Reformation wrought by his preaching among the Slaves, whose Sobriety and diligence excited their Curiosity."

Evangelical successes among the slaves gained impetus as less conservative groups—first the New Light Baptists and then the Methodists—began to make their influence felt. The New Lights established their first beachhead in Virginia in the southside. The earliest Baptist church records report small black memberships. In 1759 the Lunenburg County Anglican minister spoke of the "spectre of dissenters" hovering around him. He singled out for particular notice their opening up of the ministry to all, "whether he be a slave or a free Person." Piedmont slaves were certainly preaching. . . .

Indeed, Baptist slaves had to be independent, for masters openly scorned their slaves' religious sincerity. In 1767 a Buckingham County master referred to his slave woman "pretend[ing] much to the religion the Negroes of late have practised." Ten years later a Prince Edward County master described his mulatto runaway as "pretend[ing] to know something of religious matters, and misses no opportunity of holding forth on that subject." Slaves faced more than derision for their beliefs. In 1769 James Ireland noted that the "poor negroes have been stripped and subjected to stripes" in Culpeper County for listening to the Baptists. Nine years later, Cumberland County masters petitioned the governor to put a halt to their slaves' attendance at night meetings. They cited two reasons: first, the "fruits of disobedience and insolence to Masters," but even more significant, the slaves' "glorying in what they are taught to believe to be the persecution for Conscience's Sake."

In the 1770s the Methodists too began to make inroads in the piedmont, particularly in the southside. In June 1776, at a chapel near Petersburg, Methodist circuit rider Thomas Rankin had "a powerful meeting" with a large number of whites and blacks. "What was peculiarly affecting to him," he noted, were the blacks in the gallery, "almost every one of them upon their knees; some for themselves, and others for their distressed companions." In the following month, Rankin, now joined by Francis Asbury, attended a number of extremely emotional meetings in this area. On one occasion, Asbury had to stop a meeting "again and again, and beg of the people to compose themselves." In the congregation were "Hundreds of Negroes ... with tears streaming down their faces." ...

Why were the Baptists, Methodists, and to a lesser extent, Presbyterians so successful among piedmont slaves? Part of the reason lay in the evangelicals' emphasis on an untutored, spontaneous religious response. . . .

The musical and emotional responsiveness of slaves encouraged and impressed evangelical preachers. Samuel Davies spoke of the "torrent of sacred harmony" of which blacks were capable. "The Negroes above all the human species that ever I knew," he declared, "have an ear for Music, and a Kind of extatic delight in Psalmody." One evening in Mecklenburg County, the singing of blacks in a nearby cottage inspired James Meacham to pray with them. He was so moved as to feel that "Heaven was just then at hand." A month later, at another home, Meacham "awaked in raptures of Heaven by the sweet Echo of Singing in the Kitchen among the dear Black people (who my Soul loves)." Scarcely had he "ever heard anything to equal it upon earth." The "hollering" of slaves impressed John Kobler when on the Bedford circuit, while Thomas Morrell observed at Lanes Chapel near Petersburg that "the people in Virginia are fond of noisy meetings particularly the blacks." If the "noise" made by blacks appeared "too mechanical" to Morrell, he was nevertheless impressed by its "power." By mechanical, Morrell may have been suggesting a choreographed response, a characteristic feature of the Afro-American religious tradition.

The evangelicals' success among slaves also owed much to their initial willingness to adopt a radical stance toward the white opponents of black conversion. Until the 1700s many Baptist and Methodist preachers actively opposed slavery. . . .

Another indication of the radical stance of evangelicalism—at least in the context of late-eighteenth-century Chesapeake society—was the implicit or even explicit egalitarianism that characterized their disciplinary proceedings. Although evangelical church discipline certainly served to buttress the master's authority over his slave, disciplinary meetings rarely served to rubber-stamp a master's whim. In 1786 Tussekiah Baptist Church in Lunenburg County resolved to "deal" with black members just as with whites. At the Boar Swamp Baptist Church in Hanover County, five years later, a disciplinary action followed precisely this procedure: two women, one a slave and the other a free white, were together brought before the church, accused of adultery, and excommunicated. The Meherrin Baptist Church of Lunenburg County disciplined whites for their transgressions against slaves. Brother Charles Cook "acknowledged his sin in unlawfully burning one of his negroes." In another case, two blacks accused a white woman of "the sin of anger & unchristian language."

Who among the slaves responded to the evangelical message? Creoles were probably the most likely converts, but Africans were not to be discounted. Samuel Davies described his efforts to teach a forty-year-old African, "a very stupid lubberly Fellow in appearance and but [in]differently acquainted with our Language." Despairing of his own abilities, Davies was later amazed to find the slave succeeding on his own. Simply passing on further books to him, Davies discovered that his former pupil could "read English almost as intelligibly as he can speak it." . . .

Most significant of all, perhaps, is the occasional suggestion of a distinctive black religiosity, owing something no doubt to these African roots. . . .

Perhaps no better testimonial exists to some of the dominant themes of slave life in the piedmont than the prayer said to have been written by a slave in "the lower part of Virginia" in the year 1790 and recorded by the Quaker Joshua Evans. It speaks to the formidable odds slaves faced; to their resilience of spirit; to their familiarity with white ways; to their religious faith; and, above all, to their desire and hopes for freedom.

> Lord, if thou dost with equal eye,
> See all the sons of Adam rise,
> Why dost thou hide thy face from slaves,
> Confin'd by fate to serve such knaves?
> Stolen and sold in Africa,
> Transported to America,
> Like hogs and sheep in market sold,
> To stand the heat, and bear the cold,
>
> When will Jehovah hear our cries?
> When will the sun of freedom rise?
> When will a Moses for us stand,
> And free us all from Pharoah's hand?
> What tho' our skin be black as jet,
> Our hair be curl'd our noses flat,
> Must we for this, no freedom have
> until we find it in the grave?

Contentment, Lord, on me bestow,
While I remain a slave below,
And whilst I suffer grief and wrong;
May thy Salvation be my song.

Moravian Ideals and North Carolina Backcountry Realities

DANIEL B. THORP

In the United States the story of cultural contact and assimilation has largely been the story of a white, English, Protestant culture established during the seventeenth century affecting and being affected by subsequent waves of African, European, and Asian immigrants and their cultural impedimenta. Some of these non-English groups have entered the Anglo-American mainstream quickly and unobtrusively, while others have done so reluctantly and incompletely. It is to the latter group that historians and sociologists have generally assigned those members of the Moravian Church (Unity of the Brethren) who migrated from eastern Germany to America during the middle years of the eighteenth century and arrived in central North Carolina during the final years of the colonial period to establish a cluster of settlements known as Wachovia.

For two centuries historians have described these Moravian pioneers as xenophobes who regarded any change in their community, however minor or remote from Wachovia's theological underpinnings, as declension from the colony's initial perfection. In the 1760s Charles Woodmason labeled the Moravians "a Set of *Recabites* among the People of *Israel*—Forming a Distinc[t] Body, different in all things from All People". . . .

But such descriptions seriously distort the true nature of Moravian colonization and of the church's response to Anglo-American culture in North Carolina. Certainly the men who planned and supervised Wachovia's establishment wanted the colony to remain Moravian, but they also wanted it to survive. Consequently the Brethren distinguished between those ideas and practices that were fundamental to their Moravian identity and those that merely contributed to their worldly success. The former they guarded like zealots, but the latter they valued only as long as their usage contributed to the colony's success. The Moravians were quite willing to replace Old World ways with Anglo-American practices when the latter seemed better suited to Moravian goals. Woodmason . . . and the others not-withstanding, Wachovia's early history provides a clear example not of cultural protectionism but of what Terry G. Jordan describes as "partial assimilation." . . . Shortly after arriving in Carolina they [Moravians] demonstrated a willingness to abandon many external characteristics of their German heritage, but they jealously guarded their Moravian identity until the second quarter of the nineteenth century.

Daniel B. Thorp, "Assimilation in North Carolina's Moravian Community," *Journal of Southern History* LII (February 1986), 19–42. Copyright 1986 by the Southern Historical Association. Reprinted by permission of the Managing Editor; text abridged, footnotes deleted.

Two aspects of Wachovia's development that indicate the process of partial assimilation—village morphology and farming techniques—will be described here. The Moravians who established Wachovia arrived in North Carolina with the intention of setting up compact, German-style, agricultural villages because their leaders believed that such villages would contribute to the colony's success. Within a dozen years, however, many of those same leaders had decided that with slight modifications the settlement pattern of their Anglo-American neighbors would meet Moravian needs better and adopted it. Moreover, they realized that the often denigrated practices of Carolina farmers were actually much better suited to that colony's environment and demography than the improved methods emerging in Europe and gave up the latter for their neighbors' backward techniques. This partial assimilation of Anglo-American norms was not the result of any unconscious change in the Moravians' ultimate goal, as others have suggested; rather, it was a conscious change in the means by which they sought to achieve that goal.

The region of North Carolina into which the Moravians moved in 1753 was dominated by small family farms. This situation had long disturbed the English government, and the North Carolina assembly had tried to rectify it by legislating towns into existence. But the effort was something of a disappointment; a Moravian visitor, August Gottlieb Spangenberg, said of these communities in 1752, "they have neither houses nor inhabitants, are towns only by Act of Assembly." Europeans had been arriving in the Piedmont for two decades by the early 1750s, but the only towns in the region, Hillsboro and Salisbury, barely deserved the name. Hillsboro was established in the early 1750s and by 1764 had become, as William Few, one of its residents, recalled, "a small village, which contained thirty or forty inhabitants, with two or three small stores and two or three ordinary taverns . . . ." The legislature called Salisbury into being in 1753, though construction did not actually being until 1755. Later that year, when Governor Arthur Dobbs passed through, Salisbury consisted of a courthouse and seven or eight log houses.

The role of these settlements was, of course, much greater than their physical dimensions; they were central places performing important administrative, commercial, and social functions for the rapidly growing population around them. But the settlement pattern was predominantly rural. . . . Families on these farms lived quite distant from their neighbors and were often miles from the church or meeting house that was the only center the settlement had.

The Moravians, however, had no intention of living like their neighbors-to-be in Carolina. When in 1753 they purchased nearly 100,000 acres of land from John Carteret, Earl Granville and proprietor of the northern half of North Carolina, their plans for the tract demonstrated a clear determination to resist whatever it was in the southern environment that had continually frustrated English expectations of significant urban development in the region. The Brethren planned to resell two-thirds of the land to wealthy members or friends of the church to help cover the cost of settling the tract and on the remaining 30,000 acres to establish a refuge in which church members could live and worship in peace, free from the accusations and persecution they had encountered elsewhere during the preceding twenty years. At the center of the colony they intended to build an impressive octagonal city. In fact, if built as planned it would have been the largest city in eighteenth-century North Carolina. From this central location church elders would administer the society and economy of the entire Moravian colony. Plans for Wachovia also included the establishment of family farms, several communal farms operated by the church, and thirty-five "villages of the Lord"—compact agricultural villages scattered across the colony and occupied by members or friends of the church.

Moravian leaders seem to have had two major reasons for settling many of Wachovia's residents in villages. First, Wachovia was to be a *Moravian* colony. Not every resident of the colony had to be a member of the church, but Wachovia was to be a theocracy administered by the Moravian Church for the temporal benefit of the church and the spiritual benefit of its members. The accomplishment of that goal depended, in part, on the establishment of a colony in which compact settlement predominated, because the Unity was somewhat pessimistic about its members' ability to maintain their faith in the face of worldly temptation. Congregational elders, therefore, were supposed to watch their flocks carefully, and every member of the church was expected to keep an eye on his or her neighbors in an effort to prevent backsliding. If Wachovia's settlers scattered across the colony, it would be much more difficult to provide that sort of brotherly oversight. So the Unity wanted most of Wachovia's residents in either the central city or the "villages of the Lord." Moreover, compact settlement facilitated communal worship, an essential element in the eighteenth-century Moravian Church and the preferred forum in which to praise and thank the Lord for his role in salvation. While such worship was not impossible in a region of dispersed settlement, it was easier when members of the congregation lived close together.

Second, Wachovia's planners wanted the colony to succeed. By the 1750s most Europeans knew quite well that America was no Eden. It was an environment that was at best challenging and at worst fatal to newcomers. Among the elders who planned Wachovia there were certainly some, like the church's leader Nicholas Ludwig, Count von Zinzendorf, who underestimated the demands of colonization. But the founders also included Bishop August Spangenberg, who as a veteran of both the Moravians' abortive effort to settle in Georgia and their successful settlement in Pennsylvania, understood very well what was necessary for Wachovia's success. Thus, when Zinzendorf suggested early in the planning for Wachovia that some of its residents live on family farms, Spangenberg quickly pointed out the physical dangers inherent in that scheme—the chance of Indian attack and the inability of widely scattered settlers to help one another in emergencies. "What will happen," he asked,

> to those who have not the necessary talents? How will it go with men and women brought up in our congregations, who I fear have little conception of the difficulties they will have to face? What will they do in circumstances where each must help himself as best he can? How bear the hard work necessary to success, when each must say with Jacob, 'In the day the drought consumed me and the frost by night.'?
>
> To speak plainly:—Among fifty members brought up in our congregation,

or who have lived with us some years, there is probably not one who could maintain himself alone in the forest. They have had no experience, and even those who have the intelligence do not know how.

Spangenberg argued in favor of settling the colonists, at least initially, in groups of six to ten families so they could look after one another. Only after they had learned to cope with the unfamiliar environment would some be free to move out to family farms if they wanted.

In addition to these declared motives for establishing towns and villages in Wachovia, Moravian leaders were probably influenced by a powerful psychological motive as well—the hope of recreating many, if not all, aspects of the Old World societies from which they came. Cut off from the familiar environment, culture, and political and economic institutions of home, in strange and often hostile surroundings, colonists seized upon anything resembling their Old World as a reaffirmation of their membership in the core culture, proof that they were not slipping into the maw of savagery. This mimetic urge, no doubt, contributed to the Moravians' determination to avoid the dispersed pattern of settlement common in North Carolina. Most of the brothers and sisters in the Unity, and their leaders, came from a society in which nearly everyone lived in towns and villages. The need to demonstrate that they were still civilized undoubtedly inspired in them a determination to establish a similar pattern of settlement in North Carolina.

The result of these spiritual, temporal, and psychological factors was more than a simple desire to establish villages and a city in the Carolina backcountry. The Moravians also intended to model most of their new settlements on traditional plans found in their native Germany. The only exception was Wachovia's central city, later called Salem. Church leaders did not originally design that city according to any known German precedent. Instead, they chose a strikingly different plan adapted from the work of Vitruvius, the ancient Roman architect whose rediscovered writings were influential in seventeenth- and eighteenth-century Europe. But in building the "villages of the Lord," which were to occupy most of Wachovia's land, the elders did intend to follow German precedents. . . .

The Moravians . . . came from a region in which there was a long tradition of compact linear villages and open-field agriculture. One would therefore expect them to favor a similar pattern when they settled in North Carolina because it would offer them a familiar enclave in an unfamiliar environment. As Bishop Peter Böhler wrote in 1754, Unity officials hoped that the colonists would settle together "and have their woods and fences in common as it is in many villages in Europe."

The Moravians' first settlement in North Carolina, Bethabara, was not, however, the sort of community that church leaders envisioned for Wachovia, but only because it was unplanned and was supposed to last no more than a few years. Bethabara was begun in 1753 as a temporary settlement from which the Brethren would carry on construction of Wachovia's central city. Thus no one seems to have given any thought to its layout until it had grown into a flourishing village that refused to be temporary. Nor was the pattern of fields around Bethabara typical of that anticipated for villages in Wachovia. During Bethabara's early years the Unity established a communal economy. Orchards, gardens, and fields were all undivided tracts that the residents farmed together for the Unity in return for food, housing, clothing, and medical care for themselves and their children.

Not until 1759, when the church began its second settlement in Wachovia, did the Moravians consciously plan the sort of village with which they intended to dot the colony's landscape. By then a consensus had emerged that it was time to start building the thirty-five "villages of the Lord," and in May of that year the Provincial Synod for the United Brethren in America met in Lancaster, Pennsylvania, and directed August Spangenberg to go to North Carolina and establish "the first little village intended for Wachovia." The synod even supplied a name for the village, Bethania, which European leaders had sent to America via Bishop Peter Böhler—an indication that Count von Zinzendorf himself had probably authorized establishment of the village as a prototype for Wachovia's other "villages of the Lord." By June of that year Spangenberg was in Wachovia, and later that summer, as Bethania took shape, Spangenberg wrote an unknown correspondent describing what was becoming an almost perfect German street village. It already contained two rows of houses lining the main road and surrounded by orchard lots assigned to specific house lots. "All the remaining fields," the bishop explained, "will come later beyond these orchards and perhaps will be arranged in layers as is normal in Germany." . . .

The resulting pattern of landholding was quite like that found in eastern Germany and very unlike patterns found elsewhere in colonial North Corolina. First, the size of the holdings was extraordinarily small by North Carolina standards. . . . The median landholding among Bethania's residents was slightly over 22 acres, and no one held more than 33. In Germany such diminutive holdings were quite common. . . . But throughout backcountry North Carolina, the median estate was about 250 acres—more than ten times the median in Bethania.

Second, the disposition of the tracts in Bethania was radically different from the pattern usually found in North Carolina but was very similar to that common in eastern Germany. In colonial North Carolina, and the southern colonies in general, the great majority of farmers worked a single large piece of land. In Bethania, however, an individual's farm was invariably divided into a half-dozen tracts that were often widely separated from one another. . . . Moreover, residents of Bethania enjoyed communal rights to pasture land and a wood lot, as was common in the open-field systems of Germany. In Bethania, Wachovia's first planned village, the Moravians recreated the patterns of settlement and land distribution they had known in Germany.

The Brethren did not, however, replicate Bethania and fill their colony with German farming villages, in spite of their original intention to do so. In fact, when the church next established a settlement in Wachovia, Friedland in 1770, it forsook the compact German model altogether in favor of a more dispersed pattern similar to that common among Wachovia's Anglo-American neighbors. . . . The reason behind this shift from Bethania's compact settlement to the dispersed pattern of settlement in Friedland and from Bethania's agriculture on small tracts of land to Friedland's individual 200-acre holdings seems to have been the increasing difficulty the Unity faced in attracting settlers to Wachovia.

The Moravians had established Wachovia to provide a refuge in which church members would be able to live "without interfering with others & without being disturbed by them." Obviously, the accomplishment of that goal demanded that settlers be of acceptable quality; if not actually members of the Moravian Church, they had to be its friends and willing to live under its supervision in order to insure that the colony's Moravian population remained free from improper influences. But Wachovia's success also depended on the church's ability to provide an adequate number of colonists; there had to be enough settlers to make Wachovia as self-sufficient as possible and, thus, free it from the possibility that enemies of the church could undermine the colony by withholding supplies.

Throughout the colony's history the peopling of Wachovia demanded that the church pay close attention to both the quality and the number of its settlers. At first, there was no shortage of acceptable candidates for settlement in Wachovia because the Unity itself had the human and financial resources to provide them. By the late 1750s, however, the church could no longer afford to transport faithful but impoverished members from Europe to North Carolina. By 1764 migration to Wachovia had slowed to the point that Unity officials were afraid that unless they found an alternative source of colonists "this great Tract will not be settled . . . in fifty years." One such source was the general population of Britain's mainland colonies. That meant competing with other large landowners for the relatively small number of available tenants, and in that contest the Moravians quickly learned that replicas of European villages or estates seldom overcame the lure of individual farm ownership. This realization led the church to modify its settlement policy in ways that doomed the compact German village plan with which Wachovia's colonization had begun. This did not represent a change in basic Moravian goals or values, though; the Brethren still intended Wachovia to be a refuge for the benefit of the Moravian Church.

To attract additional settlers to Wachovia, the church began to issue advertisements describing the Moravian colony in glowing terms. "The land is very good," they declared, "has moderate water, pasture, arable land and woods." And they assured potential settlers that tracts were available near "mills, smiths, a store and craftsmen which one cannot do without in agriculture." The Moravians knew that land prices in colonies north of Carolina had risen in recent years and hoped that the lure of good land would increase the number of families interested in settling Wachovia. With an enlarged pool of applicants, the Unity would have a better chance of finding enough acceptable tenants to insure Wachovia's success. Those judged unfit to settle near the Brethren could be offered church-owned land outside Wachovia.

The Unity's campaign to attract new settlers was not confined to heralding the quality of Wachovia's land. It also included an increased willingness on the Moravians' part to sell rather than to rent their land and to convey it in larger parcels. . . . The decision to sell more church land was almost certainly the Unity's response to a preference among would-be settlers to own rather than rent their land. Frederic William Marschall, Wachovia's administrator, reported to his superiors that only the least enterprising people were willing to rent land, and the Moravians' financial records show that relatively few people moved to Wachovia as long as land there could only be leased. Evidently the church had realized by 1765 that the chance to own rather than rent land might attract to Wachovia the settlers it needed. When it became possible to buy Moravian land, there was a marked increase in the number of people from North Carolina, Maryland, Pennsylvania, and elsewhere seeking to settle in Wachovia.

The Moravians also decided during the early 1760s that they would have to offer larger tracts. . . .

The opportunity to buy individual lots large enough to farm profitably seems to have lured a sufficient number of settlers to Wachovia to warrant establishment of its next settlement, Friedland, which was begun in 1770. Friedland's first residents had originally emigrated from the Palatinate region of Germany to Broadbay (now Waldoboro), Maine, sometime before 1762. The Broadbay settlers had known Moravians in Germany, and in 1762 they welcomed the arrival of George Soelle, a Moravian missionary from Bethlehem, Pennsylvania. Soelle soon organized the community into a society, an association of Christians affiliated with the Moravian Church and served by a Moravian minister but whose members were not communicants of the church. Seven years later, in 1769, members of the Broadbay Society began moving to Wachovia at the invitation of the Reverend John Ettwein, formerly the acting executive in Wachovia and in 1769 a prominent leader of the Moravian community in Bethlehem.

From the Unity's point of view the Broadbay settlers were ideal candidates for admission to Wachovia. As members of a Moravian Society they had already shown their willingness to live in accordance with the rules of the Moravian Church, but as members of a society rather than a congregation they had no right to expect financial help from that church and would have to pay their own way to North Carolina. To the Broadbay families, Wachovia was inviting because the Unity could provide the land society members wanted with clear title to it. In Maine they had discovered that land they bought on arriving from Germany did not belong to the man from whom they bought it, and in searching for a place to move they wanted to be certain they could obtain clear title to whatever land they purchased. They had considered moving to an area near the Kennebec River in Maine but chose Wachovia instead, believing that in Wachovia they would be more likely to acquire both land and a legal deed. One year after the Broadbay families began arriving in Wachovia, nine 200-acre lots were laid out, and in early 1771 each family was allowed either to purchase a lot outright or to rent one with the option to buy it at any time during the next seven years. By mid-1771 at least seven families had purchased lots.

Those seven families were the nucleus of a community that soon expanded to include fourteen families, a meeting house, and a name—Friedland.

It did not, however, resemble the compact German villages that had inspired plans for Bethania. Rather, Friedland's design was an amalgamation of those villages and the looser settlements that Moravian colonists had found in North Carolina. . . .

. . . After the mid-1770s colonists arriving in Wachovia were free to settle on family farms unattached to any village. Bethania, therefore, remained an isolated example of the compact German pattern the Moravians had originally intended to use in settling Wachovia. But this shift from a compact village to a dispersed village to no village was not, as others have maintained, the result of a decline in the Moravians' commitment to their goals. Rather, it is an example of the church's willingness to adopt new methods in order to accomplish those goals. Wachovia required not only a population that accepted Moravian control but also one large enough to be self-sufficient. Success depended on maintaining a proper balance between the two. Church leaders quickly discovered that adherence to their original plan for the colony's villages might help to maintain the quality they wanted among settlers, but it would not attract them in numbers sufficient to guarantee Wachovia's success. The original plan was adequate only as long as Wachovia did not have to *attract* settlers, that is, as long as the Unity simply sent to North Carolina those people it deemed fit for the colony. When that became impossible and Wachovia had to compete with other settlements to attract colonists, the Unity then had to modify its plans. If the more popular, dispersed pattern of settlement denied the church one means of supervising Wachovia's residents, it had a variety of other mechanisms for controlling the population. An array of spiritual and secular authorities kept their eyes on every resident, and the power of those authorities to grant or withhold both religious and material comfort gave them a strong hold over the brothers and sisters. Moreover, by the mid-1770s the practical necessity for compact settlement declined. The Indian threat had been eliminated, and the decision to concentrate on attracting settlers experienced with American frontier life meant that close mutual support was less necessary than when the colony first began. So the elders felt it was safe to adopt different settlement patterns in order to make Wachovia more attractive.

The Moravians' assimilation of Anglo-American practices was not limited to village morphology, though. In addition to changing the way they settled their land, Moravian colonists in Wachovia also changed the way they farmed it. Earlier writers have described the Moravians as "advanced" agriculturalists who worked their land "intensively . . . and exhibited attitudes we should now characterize as 'conservationist'," while their neighbors employed extensive farming practices and raped the land with no concern for the needs of future generations. The surviving records indicate, however, that Moravian settlers abandoned some of their "advanced" practices in favor of their neighbors' "backward" techniques as soon as they discovered that the latter were better suited to the environment of Wachovia. Here again the Brethren demonstrated partial assimilation; they took from their neighbors those practices that made it easier to establish a successful Moravian colony and left the rest.

This is not to say that the Brethren were particularly advanced farmers when they came to North Carolina. In fact, few of them were farmers at all. Most members of the eighteenth-century Moravian Church were craftsmen or professionals. . . .

Moreover, those Brethren who were raised on farms had generally learned their craft in an agriculturally conservative region. During the eighteenth century English farmers led their European counterparts into an era of rapid change; new crops, new tools, and new techniques resulted in greatly increased yields on many English farms. Few of these improvements reached Germany, however, before the nineteenth century. Many Germans of the mid-eighteenth century still relied solely on the application of manure, the rotation of crops, and regular periods of fallow to maintain the fertility of their fields. Though the more innovative among them had begun cultivating clover, turnips, beans, and other crops on fallow land to revive the soil, there seem to have been few efforts to improve the quality of seed or crops in Germany. Throughout the region grain was still broadcast, then covered by harrowing, and harvested with a sickle. In the mid-eighteenth century German farming had changed remarkably little since the Middle Ages. . . .

There is little evidence that Moravian farmers were more aware than other Germans of advances in agricultural practices, though it does appear that August Spangenberg had learned something of the new scientific agriculture. He urged the Wachovia colonists to use oxen rather than horses as draft animals, on the grounds that "nearly all sensible economists are unanimous in maintaining that it is very thrifty to use carts drawn by oxen." Furthermore, when the colonists began raising grapes to produce wine, he directed them to use local rather than French vines because the former were better suited to the climate of North Carolina. The Brethren continued, however, to rely on regular periods of fallow, crop rotation, and manure application to maintain their fields, and there is no indication that they considered planting clover or applying lime. They continued to scatter their seed over lightly plowed fields, which they then harrowed, and to employ sickles in harvesting their grain crops.

Despite the lack of innovation in their own agricultural practices, the Moravians initially regarded North Carolina farmers as backward. In 1752 August Spangenberg led a party across North Carolina in search of land on which to establish the colony that became Wachovia. In a diary he kept during the journey Spangenberg noted with disdain the "farms of a North Carolina kind" on which "with the exception of corn . . . and hogs . . . the work is poorly done." Unfortunately, the peripatetic bishop seldom criticized specific practices of Carolina farmers. He was, however, particularly appalled by the treatment of cattle in North Carolina, and his diary contains several passages sharply critical of the many farmers who left their cows and horses to fend for themselves through the winter months. According to Spangenberg, these owners provided neither food nor shelter for their animals and demonstrated remarkable indifference to their fate. The prevailing attitude was, "if they live, they live," the bishop wrote. Spangenberg also criticized North Carolinians' animal husbandry on the grounds that it deprived them of manure, an indication that he disapproved of their reliance on the fertility of virgin soil to maintain crop yields.

It was essential to Wachovia's success that its settlers employ productive agricultural practices, and to Spangenberg, at least, that meant German rather than North Carolina techniques. Once the Moravians themselves began to farm Wachovia, however, they quickly adopted many of the same techniques that had so dismayed Spangenberg when he toured the province in 1752. The most fundamental change in Moravian farming was the nearly complete abandonment of efforts to preserve soil fertility. Like many others who settled on the southern frontier, the Brethren soon found that land there was so rich and labor so scarce that even rudimentary efforts at soil conservation were counterproductive. There are no indications that Moravian farmers in Wachovia made any attempt to manure their fields in the years before the American Revolution. Collecting and spreading manure required so much labor that with the same amount of work brothers could contribute more to the colony's productivity by clearing new fields. The age-old practice of letting fields lay fallow at regular intervals, which the Moravians seem to have used elsewhere, was equally unsuited to conditions in western Carolina. . . .

The Brethren also discovered that, in the Carolina climate, what Spangenberg had regarded as careless animal husbandry was actually a much more efficient allocation of resources than the labor-intensive methods common in northern Europe. The apparently limitless supply of fertile land in Wachovia removed the necessity of gathering manure to fertilize fields, which eliminated one of the principal reasons for penning livestock. Furthermore, except during especially harsh winters, the weather in North Carolina was mild enough to permit cattle and horses to winter safely in the bush. They seldom needed the weathertight German barns that required weeks of precious labor to erect. So, first impressions notwithstanding, Moravian farmers in Wachovia quickly followed their neighbors' example. They penned and fattened steers picked for slaughter and stabled their milch cows during the winter, but they left most of their livestock free to roam.

Moravian settlers brought with them to Wachovia a knowledge of traditional German agricultural practices, just as they brought a familiarity with traditional German village plans. And just as they modified their opinion of the settlement pattern most likely to produce a successful Moravian colony in North Carolina, they changed their opinion of the farming techniques best suited to the southern frontier. Moravian farmers had no particular interest in preserving German practices simply because they were German; they attached no spiritual or social significance to any particular agricultural techniques. Their priority was to find the particular allocation of resources that would best permit them "to clear land, plant corn, clear meadows, raise a good stock of cattle, build a mill, erect a smith shop, and [provide] the other essentials one needs" for successful colonization. They quickly discovered that in a region of abundant fertile land, mild winters, and a perennial shortage of labor the extensive farming of their Anglo-American neighbors was far more suitable to their circumstances than the more intensive techniques they had known in Germany. So almost immediately they began to accept some of their neighbors' practices. The Brethren did not, however, adopt North Carolina agricultural customs completely. Moravian assimilation was both partial and selective; they refused, for example, to raise as much corn as their neighbors did because they preferred the taste of wheat and realized greater profits from it. The Brethren adopted only those elements of Carolina farming that were more likely than their German equivalents to help them establish a successful Moravian colony.

In contrast to the historiographic tradition surrounding them, the Moravian founders of Wachovia did not object to every change that tended toward assimilation of Anglo-American patterns. Nor did they regard all such changes as detrimental. Members and leaders of the Unity recognized a distinction between the spiritual ends they sought, which were inviolate, and the temporal means they employed to achieve them, which were expendable. From the time they arrived in North Carolina, Moravian settlers demonstrated their willingness to modify many aspects of their heritage, such as village morphology and agricultural practices, if they thought that modifying these superficial characteristics would improve the chances of accomplishing their ultimate goal—the establishment of a successful, autonomous, Moravian community.

✌ F U R T H E R   R E A D I N G

Bernard Bailyn and Philip D. Morgan, eds., *Strangers Within the Realm: Cultural Margins of the First British Empire* (1991)

Richard R. Beeman, *The Evolution of the Southern Backcountry: A Case Study of Lunenburg County, Virginia, 1746–1832* (1984)

Carl Bridenbaugh, *Myths and Realities: Societies of the Colonial South* (1952)

Louis De Vorsey, "The Colonial Georgia Backcountry," in Edward J. Cashin, ed., *Colonial Augusta: "Key of the Indian Country"* (1986)

Rachel N. Klein, *Unification of a Slave State: The Lives of the Planters in the South Carolina Backcountry, 1760–1808* (1990)

Robert D. Mitchell, *Commercialism and Frontier: Perspectives on the Early Shenandoah Valley* (1977)

Gerald W. Mullin, *Flight and Rebellion: Slave Resistance in Eighteenth-Century Virginia* (1972)

Gregory H. Nobles, "Breaking into the Backcountry: New Approaches to the Early American Frontier," *William and Mary Quarterly,* 3d ser., 46 (1989), 641–670

CHAPTER
13

The Impact of the
European Wars for Empire
on America

✧

The massive influx of colonists into America in the mid-eighteenth century created pressure on colonial boundaries. Contained behind the barrier of the Appalachians, the colonists looked eagerly at the rich farmland of the Ohio Valley. Rank-and-file settlers hoped for land of their own, and colonial elites, having invested in vast tracts of land, sought to make fortunes from the new region.

The trans-Appalachian lands would not be settled without conflict. The Ohio Valley had become a gathering place for many Indians pushed westward by the land-hungry colonists. Here remnants of formerly populous tribes coalesced into new configurations and discovered the roots of a genuine pan-Indian consciousness. Leaders such as Neolin, the Delaware Prophet, called for Indians to abandon the trappings of European culture and resume the spiritual and material life of their ancestors. For the first time Indians were prepared to submerge their own rivalries in the common cause of resistance. They would ally themselves with colonial powers, playing off one against another to get the best terms but always keeping an eye on their own separate goals.

The third complicating feature was the French, who also claimed the region. French authorities had built a string of powerful forts to make good their claim. Both the young George Washington in 1754 and the English general William Braddock in 1755 were soundly defeated in attempts to evict the French. Thus began the American phase of the Seven Years' War, known in the colonies as the French and Indian War. For the first time in the long series of imperial wars between the two nations and their allies, the American mainland was a main theater of war. France looked very powerful in 1755, but the war ended in 1763 with the surrender of France's American territories to England, spelling the effective end of the Indians' playoff system.

❧ D O C U M E N T S

As traders and agents moved through the western territories, they reported the confused state of relations and the difficulty of gathering accurate information. The opening document, taken from the journal of Christopher Gist, agent for Virginia's Ohio Company, reveals the Indians' fear for their own future and their desire for a secure grant of land. Gist also shows the part that captives played in cross-cultural relationships. Similarly Swedish traveler Per Kalm writes in the second document of attempts to woo Indians to the English side. He also provides a valuable list of the items that Indians prized in trade. An Indian view of the influx of colonists is presented by the speech in the third document of Iroquois League sachem Canassatego to the Pennsylvania governor and his council.

The imperial wars were complicated because of difficult relations of the colonies with each other and with the regulars of the British Army. The regulars held the colonists in contempt and considered them unreliable, and the settlers rejected the swaggering demands of the officers. The report of South Carolina's 1740 St. Augustine expedition in the fourth document illustrates both the way in which colonial militias were viewed and the Indians' reasoning about their own participation in such conflicts. The fifth reading, Lord Loudoun's letter to the duke of Cumberland a year before the attack on Fort William Henry, shows the same attitudes at work.

These conflicts inevitably resulted in captives, many of whom later wrote of their experiences. The captivity narrative, of which Mary Rowlandson's account in the sixth document is the earliest, became a highly popular genre. (Rowlandson was captured in Lancaster, Massachusetts, where her husband was the minister.) The vivid images evoked by these narratives set their colonial readers' views of the Indians. They also have provided later readers with valuable information on Indian life and, although this was not their intention, have made it possible for us to understand the natives' view of events. In the final document, Captive John Williams, who, like Rowlandson, was eventually redeemed, describes being sent to live among the Roman Catholic French as a horror equaling that of captivity among the Indians.

Christopher Gist on Promises and Threats in Indian Diplomacy, 1751

... Tuesday 10   We hunted up and down these Creeks to examine the Land from the Mouths of Them, to the Place where We had crossed near the Heads of Them; in our Way to the Conhaway—They run near parallel at about 3 or 4 M Distance, for upwards of 30 M—The Land between Them all the Way is rich & level, chiefly Low Grounds & finely timbered with Walnuts, Locusts, Cherry Trees, & Sugar Trees

Wednesday 11   Set out E 18 M crossing three Creeks all good Land but hilly then S 16 M to our old Camp, where my Son had been frost-bitten After We had got to this Place in our old Tract, I did not keep any exact

Reprinted from *George Mercer Papers Relating to the Ohio Company of Virginia,* comp. and ed. Lois Mulkearn, 38–39, 101–104. Reprinted by permission of the University of Pittsburgh Press. © 1954 by University of Pittsburgh Press.

Account of Course and Distance, as I thought the River & Creeks sufficiently described by my Courses as I came down.

Thursday 12 I set out for Mohongaly crossed it upon a Raft of Logs from whence I made the best of my Way to Potomack—I did not keep exactly my old Tract but went more to the Eastward & found a much nearer Way Home; and am of Opinion the Company may have a tolerable good Road from Wills's Creek to the upper Fork of Mohongaly, from whence the River is navigable all the Way to the Ohio for large flat bottomed Boats—The Road will be a little to the Southward of West, and the Distance to the Fork of Mohongaly about 70 M—While I was at Mohongaly in my Return Home an Indian, who spoke good English, came to Me & said—That their Great Men the Beaver and Captain Oppamylucah (these are two Chiefs of the Delawares) desired to know where the Indian's Land lay, for that the French claimed all the Land on one Side the River Ohio & the English on the other Side; and that Oppamylucah asked Me the same Question when I was at his Camp in my Way down, to which I had made him no Answer—I very well remembered that Oppamylucah had asked Me such a Question, and that I was at a Loss to answer Him as I now also was: But after some Consideration my Friend said "I We are all one King's People and the different Colour of our Skins makes no Difference in the King's Subjects; You are his People as well as We, if you will take Land & pay the Kings Rights You will have the same Privileges as the White People have, and to hunt You have Liberty every where so that You dont kill the White Peoples Cattle & Hogs"—To this the Indian said, that I must stay at that Place two Days and then He would come & see Me again, He then went away, and at the two Days End returned as he promised, and looking very pleasant said He would stay with Me all Night, after He had been with Me some Time He said that the great Men bid Him tell Me I was very safe that I might come and live upon that River where I pleased—That I had answered Them very true for We were all one Kings People sure enough & for his Part he woud come to see Me at Wills's Creek in a Month. . . .

Tuesday . . . 25th This being Christmas Day I intended to read Prayers, but after inviting some of the white men they informed each other of my Intentions, and being of several different Perswasions, and few of them inclined to hear any good, they refused to come; But one Thomas Burney a Blacksmith who is settled there went about and talked to them and then several of them came, and Andrew Montour invited several of the well disposed Indians who came freely. By this time the morning was spent and I had given over all thoughts of them, but seeing them come to oblige all, and offend none, I stood up and said, Gentlemen I have no design or intention to give offence to any particular Sect or Religion, but as our King indulges us all in a liberty of conscience and hinders none of you in the exercise of your religious worships, so it would be unjust in you to endeavour to stop the Propagation of his. The Doctrine of Salvation, Faith and good works is what I only propose to treat of, as I find it extracted from the Homilies of the Church of England, which I then read to them in the best manner I could, and after

I had done the Interpreter told the Indians what I had read, and that it was the true Faith, which the great King and his Church recommended to his Children: The Indians seemed well pleased and came up to me and returned me their thanks and then invited me to live among them and gave me a name in their language. *Annosannoah.* the Interpreter told me this was the name of a good man that had formerly lived among them, and their King said that must be always my name, for which I returned them thanks but as to living among them, I excused myself by saying I did not know whether the Governor would give me leave, and if he did the French would come and carry me away, as they had done the English traders, to which they answered I might bring great guns and make a fort, that they had now left the French and were very desirous of being instructed in the principles of Christianity, that they liked me very well, and wanted me to marry them after the Christian manner, and baptize their Children; and then they said they would never desire to return to the French, or suffer them or their priests to come near them, more, for they loved the English, but had seen little religion among them; And some of their great men came and wanted me to baptize their children, for as I had read to them, and appeared to talk about religion, they took me to be a minister of the Gospel, upon which I desired Mr Montour the Interpreter to tell them, that no Minister could venture to baptize any Children, until those that were to be Sureties for them, were well instructed in the Faith themselves, and that was according to the great King's religion, in which he desired his Children should be instructed, and we dare not do it in any other way than was by Law established; but I hope if I could not be admitted to live among them, that the great King would send them proper Ministers to exercise that Office among them, at which they seemed well pleased and one of them went and brought me his Book, which was a kind of Almanack contrived for them by the French in which the days of the week were so marked that by moving a Pin every morning, they kept a pretty exact account of the time, to show me that he understood me and that he and his family always observed the Sabbath Day.

Wednesday ... 26th This day a woman who had been a long time a Prisoner and had deserted and been retaken and brought into the Town on Christmas Eve, was put to death in the following manner. They carried her without the Town and let her loose, and when she attempted to run away the persons appointed for that purpose pursued her, and struck her on the Ear, on the right side of the head, which beat her flat on her face on the Ground, they then struck her several times thro' the back with a Dart, to the heart, scalped her, and threw the scalp in the Air, and another cut off her head; there the dismal spectacle lay till the Evening and then Barney Curran desired leave to bury her which he and his Men and some of the Indians did just at dark.

Thursday ... December 27th 1750 to Thursday January 3d 1751. Nothing remarkable happened in the Town.

Friday ... 4th One Taafe an Indian Trader came to Town from near *Lake Erie* and informed us that the *Wiandots* had advised him to keep clear of the *Outawais* (a nation of Indians firmly attached to the French living near the lakes) and told him that the branches of the Lakes were claimed by the French; but that all the branches of the Ohio belonged to them and their brothers the English, and that the French had no business there, and that it was expected that the other part of the Wiandots would desert the French and come over to the English interest, and join their brethren on *Elk's eye creek* and build a strong Fort and town there.

Saturday ... 5th   The weather still continuing bad I stayed in the Town to recruit my horses and tho' corn was very dear among the Indians I was obliged to feed them well or run the risque of losing them as I had a great way to travel

Wednesday ... 9th   The wind southerly and the weather something warmer this day came into Town two traders from among the *Picqualinnees* (a tribe of the Tawightwis) and brought news that another English trader was also taken Prisoner by the French, and that three french Soldiers had deserted and come over to the English, and surrendered themselves to some of the Traders of the Pick town, and that the Indians would have put them to death, to revenge their taking our Traders, but as the French Indians had surrendered themselves to the English they would not let the Indians hurt them, but had ordered them to be sent under the care of three of our Traders, and delivered at this Town to George Croghan.

Thursday Jan. 10th   Wind still at South and warm.

Friday ... 11th   This day came into Town an Indian from near the Lakes and confirmed the news we had heard.

Saturday ... 12th   We sent away our People toward the lower Town intending to follow them the next morning and this evening we went into council in the Wiandot Kings house, the council had been put off a long time expecting some of their great men in, but few of them came, and this evening some of the king's council being a little disordered with liquor no business could be done, but we were desired to come next day.

Sunday ... 13th   No business done

Monday ... 14th   This day George Croghan by the assistance of Andrew Montour acquainted the king and council of this nation (by presenting them four strings of wampum) that the great King over the water their *Roggony* (Father) had sent under the care of the Governor of Virginia their brother a large present of goods, which were now landed safe in Virginia, and the Governor had sent me, to invite them to come and see him, and partake of their fathers charity, to all his children on the branches of Ohio.

In answer to which one of the Cheifs stood up and said, "That their king and all of them thanked their brother the Governor of Virginia for his care, and me for bringing them the news, but they could not give me an answer, until they had a full or general council of the several nations of Indians, which could not be till next spring, and so the king and council shaking hands with us, we took our leaves.

Tuesday ... 15th   We left *Muskingum* and went W. 5 m—to the *white womans creek* on which is a small town. This white woman was taken away from new England when she was not above ten years old by the French Indians. She is now upwards of fifty, and has an Indian husband, and several children, her name is Mary Harris; she still remembers they used to be very religious in new England, and wonders how the white men can be so wicked as she has seen them in these woods. . . .

Per Kalm on Indian Perceptions and Goals on the Frontier, 1750

. . . [I]t is to be observed that each English colony in North America is independent of the other, and that each has its own laws and coinage, and may be looked upon in several lights as a state by itself. Hence it happens that in time of war things go on very slowly and irregularly here; for not only the opinion of one province is sometimes directly opposite to that of another, but frequently the views of the governor and those of the assembly of the same province are quite different; so that it is easy to see that, while the people are quarrelling about the best and cheapest manner of carrying on the war, an enemy has it in his power to take one place after another. It has usually happened that while some provinces have been suffering from their enemies, the neighboring ones have been quiet and inactive, as if it did not in the least concern them. They have frequently taken up two or three years in considering whether or not they should give assistance to an oppressed sister colony, and sometimes they have expressly declared themselves against it. There are instances of provinces which were not only neutral in such circumstances, but which even carry on a great trade with the power which at that very time is attacking and laying waste some other provinces.

The French in Canada, who are but an unimportant body in comparison with the English in America, have by this position of affairs been able to obtain great advantages in times of war; for if we judge from the number and power of the English, it would seem very easy for them to get the better of the French in America.

It is however of great advantage to the crown of England that the North American colonies are near a country, under the government of the French, like Canada. There is reason to believe that the king never was earnest in his attempts to expel the French from their possessions there; though it might have been done with little difficulty. For the English colonies in this part of the world have increased so much in their number of inhabitants, and in their riches, that they almost vie with Old England. Now in order to keep up the authority and trade of their mother country and to answer several other purposes they are forbidden to establish new manufactures, which would turn to the disadvantage of the British commerce. They are not allowed to dig for any gold or silver, unless they send it to England immediately; they have not the liberty of trading with any parts that do not belong to the British dominion, excepting a few places; nor are foreigners allowed to trade with the English colonies of North America. These and some other restrictions occasion the inhabitants of the English colonies to grow less tender for their mother country. This coldness is kept up by the many foreigners such as Germans, Dutch and French, who live among the English and have no particular attachment to Old England. Add to this also that many people can never be contented with their possessions, though they be ever so large. They will always be desirous of getting more, and of enjoying the pleasure which arises from a change. Their extraordinary liberty and their luxury often lead them to unrestrained acts of selfish and arbitrary nature.

I have been told by Englishmen, and not only by such as were born in America but also by those who came from Europe, that the English colonies in North America, in the space of thirty or fifty years, would be able to form a state by themselves entirely independent of Old England. But as the whole country which lies along the seashore is unguarded, and on the land side is harassed by the French, these dangerous neighbors in times of war are sufficient to prevent the connection of the colonies with their mother country from being quite broken off. The English government has therefore sufficient reason to consider means of keeping the colonies in due submission. . . .

A Conference with the Indians

The governor of New York often confers at Albany with the Indians of the Five Nations, or the Iroquois, (Mohawks, Senekas, Cayugaws, Onondagoes, and Oneidas), especially when they intend either to make war upon, or to continue a war against the French. Sometimes, also, their deliberations turn upon their conversion to the Christian religion, and it appears by the answer of one of the Indian chiefs or sachems to Governor Hunter, at a conference in this town, that the English do not pay so much attention to a work of so much consequence as the French do, and that they do not send such able men to instruct the Indians, as they ought to do. For after Governor Hunter had presented these Indians, by order of Queen Anne, with many clothes and other presents, of which they were fond, he intended to convince them still more of her Majesty's good-will and care for them, by adding *that their good mother, the Queen, had not only generously provided them with fine clothes for their bodies, but likewise intended to adorn their souls by the preaching of the gospel; and that to this purpose some ministers should be sent to them to instruct them.* The governor had scarce ended, when one of the oldest sachems got up and answered *that in the name of all the Indians, he thanked their gracious good queen and mother for the fine clothes she had sent them; but that in regard to the ministers, they had already had some among them,* (who he likewise named) *who instead of preaching the holy gospel to them had taught them to drink to excess, to cheat, and to quarrel among themselves because in order to get furs they had brought brandy along with which they filled the Indians and deceived them.* He then entreated the governor to take from them these preachers, and a number of other Europeans who resided amongst them, for, before they came among them the Indians had been an honest, sober, and innocent people, but now most of them had become rogues. He pointed out that they formerly had the fear of God, but that they hardly believed his existence at present; that if he (the governor) would do them any favor, he should send two or three blacksmiths amongst them, to teach them to forge iron, in which they were inexperienced. The governor could not forbear laughing at this extraordinary speech. I think the words of St. Paul not wholly unapplicable on this occasion: For your sake the name of God is blasphemed amongst the heathens (Gentiles).

Indian Trade

The French in Canada carry on a great trade with the Indians; and though it was formerly the only trade of this extensive country, its inhabitants were considerably enriched by it. At present they have besides the Indian goods, several other articles which are exported. The Indians in this neighborhood who go hunting in winter like the other Indian nations, commonly bring their furs and skins to sell in the neighboring French towns; however, this is not sufficient. The Red Men who live at a greater distance never come to Canada at all; and lest they should bring their goods to the English, or the English go to them, the French are obliged to undertake journeys and purchase the Indian goods in the country of the natives. This trade is carried on chiefly at Montreal, and a great number of young and old men every year undertake long and troublesome voyages for that purpose, carrying with them such goods as they know the Indians like and want. It is not necessary to take money on such a journey, as the Indians do not value it; and indeed I think the French, who go on these journeys, scarcely ever take a sol or penny with them.

Goods Sold to the Natives

I will now enumerate the chief goods which the French carry with them for this trade, and which have a good sale among the Indians:

1. *Muskets, powder, shot,* and *balls.* The Europeans have taught the Indians in their neighborhood the use of firearms, and so they have laid aside their bows and arrows, which were formerly their only arms, and use muskets. If the Europeans should now refuse to supply the natives with muskets, they would starve to death, as almost all their food consists of the flesh of the animals which they hunt; or they would be irritated to such a degree as to attack the colonists. The savages have hitherto never tried to make muskets or similar firearms, and their great indolence does not even allow them to mend those muskets which they have. They leave this entirely to the settlers. When the Europeans came into North America they were very careful not to give the Indians any firearms. But in the wars between the French and English, each party gave their Indian allies firearms in order to weaken the force of the enemy. The French lay the blame upon the Dutch settlers in Albany, saying that the latter began in 1642 to give their Indians firearms, and taught the use of them in order to weaken the French. The inhabitants of Albany, on the contrary, assert that the French first introduced this custom, as they would have been too weak to resist the combined force of the Dutch and English in the colonies. Be this as it may, it is certain that the Indians buy muskets from the white men, and know at present better how to make use of

them than some of their teachers. It is likewise certain that the colonists gain considerably by their trade in muskets and ammunition.

2, a. *Pieces of white cloth,* or of a coarse uncut material. The Indians constantly wear such cloth, wrapping it round their bodies. Sometimes they hang it over their shoulders; in warm weather they fasten the pieces round the middle; and in cold weather they put them over the head. Both their men and women wear these pieces of cloth, which have commonly several blue or red stripes on the edge.

b. *Blue or red cloth.* Of this the Indian women make their skirts, which reach only to their knees. They generally choose the blue color.

c. *Shirts and shifts of linen.* As soon as an Indian, either man or woman, has put on a shirt, he (or she) never washes it or strips it off till it is entirely worn out.

d. *Pieces of cloth,* which they wrap round their legs instead of stockings, like the Russians.

3. *Hatchets, knives, scissors, needles,* and *flint.* These articles are now common among the Indians. They all get these tools from the Europeans, and consider the hatchets and knives much better than those which they formerly made of stone and bone. The stone hatchets of the ancient Indians are very rare in Canada.

4. *Kettles of copper or brass,* sometimes tinned on the inside. In these the Indians now boil all their meat, and they produce a very large demand for this ware. They formerly made use of earthen or wooden pots, into which they poured water, or whatever else they wanted to boil, and threw in red hot stones to make it boil. They do not want iron boilers because they cannot be easily carried on their continual journeys, and would not bear such falls and knocks as their kettles are subject to.

5. *Earrings* of different sizes, commonly of brass, and sometimes of tin. They are worn by both men and women, though the use of them is not general.

6. *Cinnabar.* With this they paint their face, shirt and several parts of the body. They formerly made use of a reddish earth, which is to be found in the country; but, as the Europeans brought them vermilion, they thought nothing was comparable to it in color. Many persons told me that they had heard their fathers mention that the first Frenchmen who came over here got a heap of furs from the Indians for three times as much cinnabar as would lie on the tip of a knife.

7. *Verdigris,* to paint their faces green. For the black color they make use of the soot off the bottom of their kettles, and daub the whole face with it.

8. *Looking glasses.* The Indians like these very much and use them chiefly when they wish to paint themselves. The men constantly carry their looking glasses with them on all their journeys; but the women do not. The men, upon the whole, are more fond of dressing than the women.

9. *Burning glasses.* These are excellent utensils in the opinion of the Indians because they serve to light the pipe without any trouble, which pleases an indolent Indian very much.

10. *Tobacco* is bought by the northern Indians, in whose country it will not grow. The southern Indians always plant as much of it as they want for their own consumption. Tobacco has a great sale among the northern Indians, and it has been observed that the further they live to the northward, the more tobacco they smoke.

11. *Wampum,* or as it is here called, *porcelaine.* It is made of a particular kind of shell and turned into little short cylindrical beads, and serves the Indians for money and ornament.

12. *Glass beads,* of a small size, white or other colors. The Indian women know how to fasten them in their ribbons, bags and clothes.

13. *Brass* and *steel wire,* for several kinds of work.

14. *Brandy,* which the Indians value above all other goods that can be brought them; nor have they anything, though ever so dear to them, which they would not give away for this liquor. But on account of the many irregularities which are caused by the use of brandy, the sale of it has been prohibited under severe penalties; however, they do not always pay implicit obedience to this order.

These are the chief goods which the French carry to the Indians and they do a good business among them. . . .

Canassatego's Speech, 1742

BRETHREN, the Governor and Council, and all present,

According to our Promise we now propose to return you an Answer to the several Things mentioned to us Yesterday, and shall beg Leave to speak to Publick Affairs first, tho' they were what you spoke to last. On this Head you Yesterday put us in Mind, first, "Of *William Penn's* early and constant Care to cultivate Friendship with all the *Indians;* of the Treaty we held with one of his Sons, about ten Years ago; and of the Necessity there is at this Time of keeping the Roads between us clear and free from all Obstructions." We are all very sensible of the kind Regard that good Man *William Penn* had for all the *Indians,* and cannot but be pleased to find that his Children have the same. We well remember the Treaty you mention held with his Son on his Arrival here, by which we confirmed our League of Friendship that is to last as long as the Sun and Moon endure: In Consequence of this, We, on our Part, shall preserve the Road free from all Incumbrances; in Confirmation whereof we lay down this String of Wampum.

You in the next Place said you would inlarge the Fire and make it burn brighter, which we are pleased to hear you mention; and assure you, we shall do the same, by adding to it more Fewel, that it may still flame out more strongly than ever: In the last Place, you were pleased to say that we are bound, by the strictest Leagues, to watch for each others Preservation; that we should hear with our Ears for you, and you hear with your Ears for us: This is equally agreeable to us; and we shall not fail to give you early Intelligence whenever any thing of Consequence comes to our Knowledge: And to encourage you to do the same, and to nourish in your Hearts what you have spoke to us with your Tongues, about the Renewal of our Amity and

Canassatego's speech in Carl Van Doren and Julian Boyd, eds., *Indian Treaties Printed* by Benjamin Franklin, 1736–1762. Reprinted by permission of the Historical Society of Pennsylvania.

the Brightening of the Chain of Friendship; we confirm what we have said with another Belt of Wampum.

BRETHREN, We received from the Proprietors, yesterday, some Goods in Consideration of our Release of the Lands on the West-Side of *Sasque-hannah,* It is true we have the full Quantity according to Agreement; but if the Proprietor had been here himself, we think, in Regard of our Numbers and Poverty, he would have made an Addition to them.—If the Goods were only to be divided amongst the *Indians* present, a single Person would have but a small Portion; but if you consider what Numbers are left behind, equally entitled with us to a Share, there will be extremely little. We therefore desire, if you have the Keys of the Proprietor's Chest, you will open it, and take out a little more for us.

We know our Lands are now become more valuable. The white People think we do not know their Value; but we are sensible that the Land is everlasting, and the few Goods we receive for it are soon worn out and gone. For the Future we will sell no Lands but when Brother *Onas* is in the Country; and we will know beforehand the Quantity of the Goods we are to receive. Besides, we are not well used with respect to the lands still unsold by us. Your People daily settle on these Lands, and spoil our Hunting.—We must insist on your Removing them, as you know they have no Right to settle to the Northward of *Kittochtinny-Hills.*—In particular, we renew our Complaints against some People who are settled at *Juniata,* a Branch of *Sasquahannah,* and all along the Banks of that River, as far as *Mahaniay*; and desire they may be forthwith made to go off the Land; for they do great Damage to our Cousins the *Delawares.*

We have further to observe, with respect to the Lands lying on the West Side of *Sasquahannah,* that tho' Brother *Onas* (meaning the Proprietor) has paid us for what his People possess, yet some Parts of that Country have been taken up by Persons whose Place of Residence is to the South of this Province, from whom we have never received any Consideration. This Affair was recommended to you by our Chiefs at our last Treaty; and you then, at our earnest Desire, promised to write a Letter to that Person who has the Authority over those People, and to procure us his Answer: As we have never heard from you on this Head, we want to know what you have done in it. If you have not done any thing, we now renew our Request, and desire you will inform the Person Whose People are seated on our Lands, that that Country belongs to us, in Right of Conquest; we having bought it with our Blood, and taken it from our Enemies in fair War; and we expect, as Owners of that Land, to receive such a Consideration for it as the Land is worth. We desire you will press him to send us a positive Answer: Let him say *Yes* or *No*: If he says Yes, we will treat with him; if No, we are able to do ourselves Justice; and we will do it, by going to take Payment ourselves.

It is customary with us to make a Present of Skins whenever we renew our Treaties. We are ashamed to offer our Brethren so few; but your Horses and Cows have eat the Grass our Deer Used to feed on. This has made them scarce, and will, we hope, plead in Excuse for our not bringing a larger Quantity: If we could have spared more we would have given more; but we are really poor; and desire you'll not consider the Quantity, but, few as they are, accept them in Testimony of our Regard.

Here they gave the Governor a Bundle of Skins.

A Report on Imperial Conflict in the South, 1740

. . . On the 28th, the General [James Oglethorpe], having marched all Night about Day Break being within five or six miles of Augustine, he came in Sight of five scattered Houses in some of which Smokes appeared. Thereupon, having caused the whole Body to halt at about a Quarter of a Mile's Distance, he ordered Lieut. Bryan with the six Voluntiers under him only to march up and attack those Houses. The Voluntiers obeyed, entered and searched every one of them; and having brought forth two Negroes Prisoners (some others escaping for Want of more Assistance) the General then advancing with the whole Party said, "Well, I see the Carolina Men have Courage but no Conduct." To which Lieut. Bryan replied, "Sir, the Conduct is yours." The Voluntiers would have burnt the Houses, but the General refused to permit them to do it, saying that they would serve for the Inhabitants that he should bring there. The two Negroes having confessed that they were Carolina Negroes (the one having run away from Mrs. Parker, and the other having been carried away by the Indians from Col. Gibbs) and they being, according to one of the Stipulations with the General, returnable to the Owners upon paying £5 Sterling per Head to the Captors, the Voluntiers offered either to pay him one Half the Salvage and keep them, or to receive one Half and give them up to him; but the General, claiming a Property in them, refused both, and took them to himself. It seems the General had also before at Diego taken away from those Voluntiers several Horses which they had caught to carry their Baggage. And although Cattle were very plenty yet it was with great Difficulty that they could, whilst they were there, obtain any fresh Provisions, being generally left to shift for themselves, though the General was frequently acquainted with it, who said that Diego Spinosa should be paid for all that were killed.

This Day the Party sent out of the Carolina Camp at Fort Diego the Day before returned without making the expected Discovery, and a fresh Party was sent down to the Palmeto Hut to assist in carrying up Provisions.

The same Day Col. Vander Dussen, in the Morning early, in the Camp at St. John's, struck most of the Tents which with a Quantity of Provisions &c. were put on board Boats, and sent away to the Palmeto Hut (Lacanela). He went himself with a Party of Men to see the same landed and returned again that Night.

On the 29th, at Day Break all the Tents in the Camp at St. John's were struck and every Thing put on board Boats to be sent to the Palmeto Hut. At the same Time another Part of the Carolina Regiment arrived there. In the Afternoon, Col. Vander Dussen having ordered to beat to Arms, marched all the Men to the Palmeto Hut from thence, leaving nothing at St. John's but the Transports with Provisions, Ammunition &c. Lieut. Col. Lejau had marched down to the Palmeto Hut from Fort Diego two hundred and fifty Men, who carried up thither most of the Provisions &c.

The General returned that Night late to Fort Diego with the Party which he carried from thence the 27th. The two Negroes, which had been taken, gave Information that the People of Augustine were in a starving Condition.

On the 30th, Col. Vander Dussen, leaving a small Party to guard the Provisions &c. remaining at the Palmeto Hut, marched from thence and came to the Camp at Fort Diego. There the Carolina Regiment (viz., so much of it as was then arrived), being ordered under Arms by the Colonel, was reviewed by the General. The Field Return was three hundred and seventy-eight Men besides Field Officers, Voluntiers and Cadets. In the Evening Ensign Mace with a Detachment of forty-two Men from both Regiments was sent to take Post on Augustine Point.

About this Time many of the Creek Indians (a fresh Party of which had joined the General at St. John's with Thomas Jones who, being of Indian Extract, was employed by him as a Linguist to the Creeks and Euchees and to head them) being tired with constant Fatigue, Day and Night, in ranging near three Weeks only backward and forward and disheartened that there was no Prospect of attacking Augustine, returned Home. It seems the General had ordered Jones to keep out constantly scouting around the Country with those Indians to watch the Enemy's Motions and to endeavour to take some Prisoners, but positively enjoined him not to permit the Indians to destroy any Houses. And Jones had often told the General that they would soon be tired with that Way of proceeding, for that they loved to go and do their Business at once and return Home again, to which the General had replied, If they have a mind to go Home, don't disturb them, let them go. The Cherokees also grew uneasy, and were disgusted because the General had shewed some Anger for their killing some Cattle at Diego and would not permit them to do it. Caesar, one of their Head Men, said, it was a strange Thing that they were permitted to kill the Spaniards but not their Cattle and threatened to carry all his Men Home. . . .

Lord Loudoun Views Imperial Conflict in the North, 1756

Albany, 29th August 1756.

Sir,

Enclosed I send Your Royal Highness, a Copy of a Letter I received from Major General Webb, with my Answer to it; I should not have done this, but that I thought it necessary, now on my outset, to make Your Royal Highness entirely Acquainted, with not only the things I do, but the manner of doing them.

The delays we meet with, in carrying on the Service, from every parts of this Country, are immense; they have assumed to themselves, what they call Rights and Priviledges, totaly unknown in the Mother Country, and are made use of, for no purpose, but to screen them, from giving any Aid, of any sort, for carrying on, the Service, and refusing us Quarters.

By the Mismanagement of the Commissary of the Transports, in Enlisting part of the Sailors in the Transports, and not employing them afterwards, and allowing the others to run away, I am now beginning to receive some of the Recruits for those two Regiments, and cannot for my heart, get up either Artillery or Ammunition, or hardly any thing, from thence. . . .

As to Quarters, this is the only Town has ever given any. . . . The Mayor is a Fool, and has made a great fortune by Supplying the French in Canada, which is now stopt since we come here, which provokes him; therefore I did not stop there, but sent for the Recorder, who is a Man of more sence, and told him the custom, in time of War, in all Countries, even in England itself, and the necessity there was, of Troops been lodged, and having all necessary things found for them here, in a Frontier Place; that I would in every thing, take the Civil Magistrate along with me, if they would Assist me; if they would not, I must follow the Custom of Armies, and help myself, for that I could not sit still, and see the Country undone, for the Obstinacy of a few Men: the Recorder did all he could, to change the Mayors Resolution, but to no Effect: So I have since that, Quartered the Men, by my own Quarter-Masters, and hitherto have billetted none, but where we had Billets from the Magistrates: On this occasion they have shut out several Officers, but have always made it up, till last Night, that another Cannadian Trader, threw an Officer's Baggage into the Street, and Barricaded the Door; and I sent a file of Men, and got the officer into Possession: my resolution is, if I find any more of this work, whenever I find a leading Man, shut out one of the People, to take the whole House for an Hospital, or a Store House, and let him Shift for himself. . . .

Since closing my Letter to Mr Fox, I have received a Letter from Mr Webb, Acquainting me, that his Party, sent out to bring Intelligence from Oswego, are returned; that they got as far as the Onondaga Indians, who assured them, that Oswego was burnt; that the french were gone off; that they had cut down a great many Trees on the River, above Oswego, before they went; that the ground at Oswego, lay cover'd with dead bodies, which raised such a Stench, they could smell it at a great distance; that they saved very few but Sailors, and a few Officers; that they said, that they were very much obliged to the English, for furnishing them with so many Cannon, to take their own Forts; that they hoped soon, to take Fort William Henry, and to be at Albany after that: but as those Onondago Indians, would not allow them to go on further, for fear as they said, of meeting with some parties of French Indians, who may be left behind; I by no means like this Intelligence. . . .

Affairs here, are in a very bad situation; Your Royal Highness knows what Troops I have; the New England Men, by all Accounts, frighten'd out of their Senses, at the name of a French Man, for those are not the Men they use to send out, but fellows hired by other Men who should have gone themselves; and the Forts much worse than we imagined; but those two things I shall be able to Inform you of, with Certainty, when Colonel Burton and Mr Montresor return, whom I hourly expect.

The Enemy I am afraid, are much stronger than You think, and all Accounts agree, that there is a Battalion of the Irish Brigade here; they Scattered Letters all round Oswego, this last Spring, promising great Rewards, to any Soldiers that would come over to them; which drew great numbers of the Irish Recruits, from the two Regiments there, which were mostly Roman Catholicks; And I will be far from venturing to assure You, that there are no Roman Catholicks in the other Regiments, tho' all possible care has been taken to prevent it, by Lieutenant Colonels Gage & Burton, and I find, most of the deserters from them, are Irish.

I have yet no returns, to the Circular Letters I writ, on the taking of Oswego: I hope they will fill up their New England Men, with better than they were first; but I must leave the Second Battalion of the *Royal Americans,* at least for some time, in Pensilvania; the first I think, I shall compleat immediately, and soon get here, if I can move any thing in this Country, which I think, if I had a little more leisure on my hands, I could do.

They will give you, not one Shilling, to carry on the War; they will give you no one thing, but for double the Money it ought to cost; that I cannot help Just now, but I hope a time will come, that with a little Sweet and a little Sower, they may be brought about.

I am, Sir, your Royal Highness most dutefull and obedient Servant

LOUDOUN

Albany, August 30th, 1756. I have just now received an Express from Sir William Johnson acquainting me that an old Indian is just arrived with him on whose Fidelity he can depend; who says the French are preparing at Oswego to attack the Great Carrying Place. That was what I suspected they would do, the Moment I saw the Onondago Indians would not let our Party proceed.

I have given Orders to send Mr. Webb 250 of the Highland Regiment, with Rogers Company of Rangers of 50. I send Buchanan of the Train with 12 of the Gunners and Orders repeated to send away all the useless things they have with them, such as Cannon dismounted, Shot for Guns at Oswego, and all the Atterail of Stores gone there. This is all the Supply I am able to give them.

I beg your Royal Highness will turn in your Mind what is to be done. I imagine it must end in an Expedition up the River St. Lawrence. Can you give us a Fleet to Support us? I will let you know, as soon as I can see how things will turn out, what Prospect of Success there may be.

Mary Rowlandson Describes Her Captivity Among the Indians, 1682

On the tenth of February 1675, Came the Indians with great numbers upon Lancaster: Their first coming was about Sun-rising; hearing the noise of some Guns, we looked out; several Houses were burning, and the Smoke ascending to Heaven. There were five persons taken in one house, the Father, and the

Mother and a sucking Child, they knockt on the head; the other two they took and carried away alive. Their were two others, who being out of their Garison upon some occasion were set upon; one was knockt on the head, the other escaped: Another their was who running along was shot and wounded, and fell down; he begged of them his life, promising them Money (as they told me) but they would not hearken to him but knockt him in head, and stript him naked, and split open his Bowels. Another seeing many of the Indians about his Barn, ventured and went out, but was quickly shot down. There were three others belonging to the same Garison who were killed; the Indians getting up upon the roof of the Barn, had advantage to shoot down upon them over their Fortification. Thus these murtherous wretches went on, burning, and destroying before them.

At length they came and beset our own house, and quickly it was the dolefullest day that ever mine eyes saw. The House stood upon the edg of a hill; some of the Indians got behind the hill, others into the Barn, and others behind any thing that could shelter them; from all which places they shot against the House, so that the Bullets seemed to fly like hail; and quickly they wounded one man among us, then another, and then a third, About two hours (according to my observation, in that amazing time) they had been about the house before they prevailed to fire it (which they did with Flax and Hemp, which they brought out of the Barn, and there being no defence about the House, only two Flankers at two opposite corners and one of them not finished) they fired it once and one ventured out and quenched it, but they quickly fired it again, and that took. Now is the dreadfull hour come, that I have often heard of (in time of War, as it was the case of others) but now mine eyes see it. Some in our house were fighting for their lives, others wallowing in their blood, the House on fire over our heads, and the bloody Heathen ready to knock us on the head, if we stirred out. Now might we hear Mothers and Children crying out for themselves, and one another, Lord, What shall we do? Then I took my Children (and one of my sisters, hers) to go forth and leave the house: but as soon as we came to the dore and appeared, the Indians shot so thick that the bulletts rattled against the House, as if one had taken an handfull of stones and threw them, so that we were fain to give back. We had six stout Dogs belonging to our Garrison, but none of them would stir, though another time, if any Indian had come to the door, they were ready to fly upon him and tear him down. The Lord hereby would make us the more to acknowledge his hand, and to see that our help is always in him. But out we must go, the fire increasing, and coming along behind us, roaring, and the Indians gaping before us with their Guns, Spears and Hatchets to devour us. No sooner were we out of the House, but my Brother in Law (being before wounded, in defending the house, in or near the throat) fell down dead, wherat the Indians scornfully shouted, and hallowed, and were presently upon him, stripping off his cloaths, the bulletts flying thick, one went through my side, and the same (as would seem) through the bowels and hand of my dear Child in my arms. One of my elder Sisters Children, named William, had then his Leg broken, which the Indians perceiving, they knockt him on head. Thus were we butchered by those merciless Heathen, standing amazed, with the blood running down to our heels. My eldest Sister being yet in the House, and seeing those wofull sights, and Infidels haling Mothers one way, and Children another, and some wallowing in their blood: and her elder Son telling her that her Son William was dead, and my self was wounded, she said, And, Lord, let me dy with them; which was no sooner said, but she was struck with a Bullet, and fell down dead over the threshold. I hope she is reaping the fruit of her good labours, being faithfull to the service of God in her place. In her younger years she lay under much trouble upon spiritual accounts, till it pleased God to make that precious Scripture take hold of her heart, 2 Cor. 12. 9. *And he said unto me, my Grace is sufficient for thee.* More than twenty years after I have heard her tell how sweet and comfortable that place was to her. But to return: The Indians laid hold of us, pulling me one way, and the Children another, and said, Come go along with us; I told them they would kill me: they answered, If I were willing to go along with them, they would not hurt me.

Oh the dolefull sight that now was to behold at this House! *Come, behold the works of the Lord, what dissolations he has made in the Earth.* Of thirty seven persons who were in this one House, none escaped either present death, or a bitter captivity, save only one, who might say as he, Job 1. 15, *And I only am escaped alone to tell the News.* There were twelve killed, some shot, some stab'd with their Spears, some knock'd down with their Hatchets. When we are in prosperity, Oh the little that we think of such dreadfull sights, and to see our dear Friends, and Relations ly bleeding out their heart-blood upon the ground. There was one who was chopt into the head with a Hatchet, and stript naked, and yet was crawling up and down. It is a solemn sight to see so many Christians lying in their blood, some here, and some there, like a company of Sheep torn by Wolves, All of them stript naked by a company of hell-hounds, roaring, singing, ranting and insulting, as if they would have torn our very hearts out; yet the Lord by his Almighty power preserved a number of us from death, for there were twenty-four of us taken alive and carried Captive.

I had often before this said, that if the Indians should come, I should chuse rather to be killed by them then taken alive but when it came to the tryal my mind changed; their glittering weapons so daunted my spirit, that I chose rather to go along with those (as I may say) ravenous Beasts, then that moment to end my dayes; and that I may the better declare what happened to me during that grievous Captivity, I shall particularly speak of the severall Removes we had up and down the Wilderness.

The First Remove

Now away we must go with those Barbarous Creatures, with our bodies wounded and bleeding, and our hearts no less than our bodies. About a mile we went that night, up upon a hill within sight of the Town, where they intended to lodge. There was hard by a vacant house (deserted by the English before, for fear of the Indians). I asked them whither I might not lodge in the house that night to which they answered, what will you love English men still? this was the dolefullest night that ever my eyes saw. Oh the roaring, and singing and danceing, and yelling of those black creatures in the night, which made the place a lively resemblance of hell. And as miserable was the wast that was there made, of Horses, Cattle, Sheep, Swine, Calves, Lambs, Roasting Pigs, and Fowl (which they had plundered in the Town) some roasting, some lying and burning, and some boyling to feed our merciless Enemies; who were joyful enough though we were disconsolate. To add to the dolefulness of the former day, and the dismalness of the present night: my thoughts ran upon my losses and sad bereaved condition. All was gone, my Husband gone (at least separated from me, he being in the Bay [Boston]. . . . I sat much alone with a poor wounded Child in my lap, which moaned night and day, having nothing to revive the body, or cheer the spirits of her, but in stead of that, sometimes one Indian would come and tell me one hour, that your Master will knock your Child in the head, and then a second, and then a third, your Master will quickly knock your Child in the head.

This was the comfort I had from them, miserable comforters are ye all, as he said. Thus nine dayes I sat upon my knees, with my Babe in my lap, till my flesh was raw again; my Child being even ready to depart this sorrowfull world, they bade me carry it out to another Wigwam (I suppose because they would not be troubled with such spectacles) Whither I went with a very heavy heart, and down I sat with the picture of death in my lap. About two houres in the night, my sweet Babe like a Lambe departed this life, on Feb. 18, 1675. It being about six yeares, and five months old. It was nine dayes from the first wounding, in this miserable condition, without any refreshing of one nature or other, except a little cold water. I cannot, but take notice, how at another time I could not bear to be in the room where any dead person was, but now the case is changed; I must and could ly down by my dead Babe, side by side all the night after. I have thought since of the wonderfull goodness of God to me, in preserving me in the use of my reason and senses, in that distressed time, that I did not use wicked and violent means to end my own miserable life. In the morning, when they understood that my child was dead they sent for me home to my Masters Wigwam: (by my Master in this writing, must be understood Quanopin, who was a Saggamore, and married King Phillips wives Sister; not that he first took me, but I was sold to him by another Narrhaganset Indian, who took me when first I came out of the Garison). I went to take up my dead child in my arms to carry it with me, but they bid me let it alone: there was no resisting, but goe I must and leave it. When I had been at my masters wigwam, I took the first opportunity I could get, to go look after my dead child: when I came I askt them what they had done with it? then they told me it was upon the hill: then they went and shewed me where it was, where I saw the ground was newly digged, and there they told me they had buried it: There I left that Child in the Wilderness, and must commit it, and my self also in this Wilderness-condition, to him who is above all. God having taken away this dear Child, I went to see my daughter Mary, who was at this same Indian Town, at a Wigwam not very far off, though we had little liberty or opportunity to see one another. She was about ten years old, and taken from the door at first by a Praying Ind and afterward sold for a gun. When I came in sight, she would fall a weeping; at which they were provoked, and would not let me come near her, but bade me be gone; which was a heart-cutting word to me. I had one Child dead, another in the Wilderness, I knew not where, the third they would not let me come near to: *Me* (as he said) *have ye bereaved of my Children, Joseph is not, and Simeon is not, and ye will take Benjamin also, all these things are against me.* I could not sit still in this condition, but kept walking from one place to another. And as I was going along, my heart was even overwhelm'd with the thoughts of my condition, and that I should have Children, and a Nation which I knew not ruled over them. Whereupon I earnestly entreated the Lord, that he would consider my low estate, and shew me a token for good, and if it were his blessed will, some sign and hope of some relief. And indeed quickly the Lord answered, in some measure, my poor prayers: for as I was going up and down mourning and lamenting my condition, my Son came to me, and asked me how I did; I had not seen him before, since the destruction of the Town, and I knew not where he was, till I was informed by himself, that he was amongst a smaller percel of Indians, whose place was about six miles off; with tears in his eyes, he asked me whether his Sister Sarah was dead; and told me he had seen his Sister Mary; and prayed me, that I would not be troubled in reference to himself. The occasion of his coming to see me at this time, was this: There was, as I said, about six miles from us, a smal Plantation of Indians, where it seems he had been during his Captivity: and at this time, there were some Forces of the Ind. gathered out of our company, and some also from them (among whom was my Sons master) to go to assault and burn Medfield: In this time of the absence of his master, his dame brought him to see me. I took this to be some gracious answer to my earnest and unfeigned desire. The next day, *viz.* to this, the Indians returned from Medfield, all the company, for those that belonged to the other small company, came through the Town that now we were at. But before they came to us, Oh! the outragious roaring and hooping that there was: They began their din about a mile before they came to us. By their noise and hooping they signified how many they had destroyed (which was at that time twenty three.) Those that were with us at home, were gathered together as soon as they heard the hooping, and every time that the other went over their number, these at home gave a shout, that the very Earth rung again: And thus they continued till those that had been upon the expedition were come up to the Sagamores Wigwam; and then, Oh, the hideous insulting and triumphing that there was over some Englishmens scalps that they had taken (as their manner is) and brought with them. I cannot but take notice of the wonderfull mercy of God to me in those afflictions, in sending me a Bible. One of the Indians that came from Medfield fight, had brought some plunder, came to me, and asked me, if I would have a Bible, he had got one in his Basket. I was glad of it, and asked him, whether he thought the Indians would let me read? he answered, yes: So I took the Bible, and in that melancholy time, it came into my mind to read first the 28. Chap. of Deut., which I did, and when I had read it, my dark heart wrought on this manner, That there was no mercy for me, that the blessings were gone, and the curses come in their room, and that I had lost my opportunity. But the Lord helped me still to go on reading till I came to Chap. 30 the seven first verses, where I found, There was mercy promised again, if we would return to him by repentance; and though we were scatered from one end of the Earth to the other, yet the Lord would gather us together, and turn all those curses upon our Enemies. I do not desire to live to forget this Scripture, and what comfort it was to me.

Now the Ind. began to talk of removing from this place, some one way, and some another. There were now besides my self nine English Captives in this place (all of them Children, except one Woman). I got an opportunity to go and take my leave of them; they being to go one way, and I another, I asked them whether they were earnest with God for deliverance, they told me, they did as they were able, and it was some comfort to me, that the Lord stirred up Children to look at him. The Woman *viz.* Goodwife Joslin told me, she should never see me again, and that she could find in her heart to run away; I wisht her not to run away by any means, for we were near thirty miles from any English Town, and she very big with Child, and had but one week to reckon; and another Child in her Arms, two years old, and bad Rivers there were to go over, and we were feeble, with our poor and course entertainment. I had my Bible with me, I pulled it out, and asked her whether she would read; we opened the Bible and lighted on Psal. 27, in which Psalm we especially took notice of that, *ver. ult., Wait on the Lord, Be of good courage, and he shall strengthen thine Heart, wait I say on the Lord.*

The Fourth Remove

And now I must part with that little Company I had. Here I parted from my Daughter Mary, (whom I never saw again till I saw her in Dorchester, returned from Captivity), and from four little Cousins and Neighbours, some of which I never saw afterward: the Lord only knows the end of them. Amongst them also was that poor Woman before mentioned, who came to a sad end, as some of the company told me in my travel: She having much grief upon her Spirit, about her miserable condition, being so near her time, she would be often asking the Indians to let her go home; they not being willing to that, and yet vexed with her importunity, gathered a great company together about her, and strip her naked, and set her in the midst of them; and when they had sung and danced about her (in their hellish manner) as long as they pleased, they knockt her on head, and the child in her arms with her: when they had done that, they made a fire and put them both into it, and told the other Children that were with them, that if they attempted to go home, they would serve them in like manner: The Children said, she did not shed one tear, but prayed all the while. But to return to my own Journey; we travelled about half a day or little more, and came to a desolate place in the Wilderness, where there were no Wigwams or Inhabitants before; we came about the middle of the afternoon to this place, cold and wet, and snowy, and hungry, and weary, and no refreshing, for man, but the cold ground to sit on, and our poor Indian cheer.

Heart-aking thoughts here I had about my poor Children, who were scattered up and down among the wild beasts of the forrest: My head was light and dissey (either through hunger or hard lodging, or trouble or altogether) my knees feeble, my body raw by sitting double night and day, that I cannot express to man the affliction that lay upon my Spirit, but the Lord helped me at that time to express it to himself. I opened my Bible to read, and the Lord brought that precious Scripture to me, Jer. 31. 16. *Thus saith the Lord, refrain thy voice from weeping, and thine eyes from tears, for thy work shall be rewarded, and they shall come again from the land of the Enemy.* This was a sweet Cordial to me, when I was ready to faint, many and many a time have I sat down, and weept sweetly over this Scripture. At this place we continued about four dayes.

The Fifth Remove

The occasion (as I thought) of their moving at this time, was, the English Army, it being near and following them: For they went, as if they had gone for their lives, for some considerable way, and then they made a stop, and chose some of their stoutest men, and sent them back to hold the English Army in play whilst the rest escaped: And then, like Jehu, they marched on furiously, with their old, and with their young: some carried their old decrepit mothers, some carried one, and some another. Four of them carried a great Indian upon a Bier; but going through a thick Wood with him, they were hindered, and could make no hast; whereupon they took him upon their backs, and carried him, one at a time, till they came to Bacquaug River. Upon a Friday, a little after noon we came to this River. When all the company was come up, and were gathered together, I thought to count the number of them, but they were so many, and being somewhat in motion, it was beyond my skil. In this travel, because of my wound, I was somewhat favoured in my load; I carried only my knitting work and two quarts of parched meal: Being very faint I asked my mistriss to give me one spoonfull of the meal, but she would not give me a taste. They quickly fell to cutting dry trees, to make Rafts to carry them over the river: and soon my turn came to go over: By the advantage of some brush which they had laid upon the Raft to sit upon, I did not wet my foot (which many of themselves at the other end were mid-leg deep) which cannot but be acknowledged as a favour of God to my weakned body, it being a very cold time. I was not before acquainted with such kind of doings or dangers. *When thou passeth through the waters I will be with thee, and through the Rivers they shall not overflow thee,* Isai. 43. 2. A certain number of us got over the River that night, but it was the night after the Sabbath before all the company was got over. On the Saturday they boyled an old Horses leg which they had got, and so we drank of the broth, as soon as they thought it was ready, and when it was almost all gone, they filled it up again.

The first week of my being among them, I hardly ate any thing; the second week, I found my stomach grow very faint for want of something; and yet it was very hard to get down their filthy trash: but the third week, though I could think how formerly my stomach would turn against this or that, and I could starve and dy before I could eat such things, yet they were sweet and savoury to my taste. I was at this time knitting a pair of white cotton stockins for my mistriss; and had not yet wrought upon a Sabbath day; when the Sabbath came they bade me go to work; I told them it was the Sabbath-day, and desired them to let me rest, and told them I would do as much more to morrow; to which they answered me, they would break my face. And here I cannot but take notice of the strange providence of God in preserving the heathen: They were many hundreds, old and young, some sick, and some lame, many had Papooses at their backs, the greatest number at this time with us, were Squaws, and they travelled with all they had, bag and baggage, and yet they got over this River aforesaid; and on Munday they set their Wigwams on fire, and away they went: On that very day came the English Army after them to this River, and saw the smoak of their Wigwams, and yet this River put a stop to them. God did not give them courage or activity to go over after us; we were not ready for so great a mercy as victory and deliverance; if we had been, God would have found out a way for the English to have passed this River, as well as for the Indians with their Squaws and Children, and all their Luggage. *Oh that my People had hearkened to me, and Israel had walked in my ways, I should soon have subdued their Enemies, and turned my hand against their Adversaries,* Psal. 81: 13. 14.

The Sixth Remove

On Munday (as I said) they set their Wigwams on fire, and went away. It was a cold morning, and before us there was a great Brook with ice on it; some waded through it, up to the knees and higher, but others went till they came to a Beaver-dam, and I amongst them, where through the good providence of God, I did not wet my foot. I went along that day mourning and lamenting, leaving farther my own Country, and travelling into the vast and howling Wilderness, and I understood something of Lot's Wife's Temptation, when she looked back: we came that day to a great Swamp, by the side of which we took up our lodging that night. When I came to the brow of the hil, that looked toward the Swamp, I thought we had been come to a great Indian Town (though there were none but our own Company) The Indians were as thick as the trees: it seemed as if there had been a thousand Hatchets going at once: if one looked before one, there was nothing but Indians, and behind one, nothing but Indians, and so on either hand, I my self in the midst, and no Christian soul near me, and yet how hath the Lord preserved me in safety? Oh the experience that I have had of the goodness of God, to me and mine!

The Seventh Remove

After a restless and hungry night there, we had a wearisome time of it the next day. The Swamp by which we lay, was, as it were, a deep Dungeon, and an exceeding high and steep hill before it. Before I got to the top of the hill, I thought my heart and legs, and all would have broken, and failed me. What through faintness, and soreness of body, it was a grievous day of travel to me. As we went along, I saw a place where English Cattle had been: that was comfort to me, such as it was: quickly after that we came to an English Path, which so took with me, that I thought I could have freely lyen down and dyed. That day, a little after noon, we came to Squaukheag, where the Indians quickly spread themselves over the deserted English Fields, gleaning what they could find; some pickt up ears of Wheat that were crickled down, some found ears of Indian Corn, some found Ground-nuts, and others sheaves of Wheat that were frozen together in the shock, and went to threshing of them out. My self got two ears of Indian Corn, and whilst I did but turn my back, one of them was stolen from me, which much troubled me. There came an Indian to them at that time, with a basket of Horse-liver. I asked him to give me a piece: What, sayes he, can you eat Horse-liver? I told him, I would try, if he would give a piece, which he did, and I laid it on the coals to rost; but before it was half ready they got half of it away from me, so that I was fain to take the rest and eat it as it was, with the blood about my mouth, and yet a savoury bit it was to me: *For to the hungry Soul every bitter thing is sweet.* A solemn sight methought it was, to see Fields of wheat and Indian Corn forsaken and spoiled: and the remainders of them to be food for our merciless Enemies. That night we had a mess of wheat for our Supper.

The Eight Remove

On the morrow morning we must go over the River, *i.e.* Connecticot, to meet with King Philip; two Cannoos full, they had carried over, the next Turn I my self was to go; but as my foot was upon the Cannoo to step in, there was a sudden out-cry among them, and I must step back; and instead of going over the River, I must go four or five miles up the River farther Northward. Some of the Indians ran one way, and some another. The cause of this rout was, as I thought, their espying some English Scouts, who were thereabout. In this travel up the River, about noon the Company made a stop, and sate down; some to eat, and others to rest them. As I sate amongst them, musing of things past, my Son Joseph unexpectedly came to me: we asked of each others welfare, bemoaning our dolefull condition, and the change that had come upon uss. We had Husband and Father, and Children, and Sisters, and Friends, and Relations, and House, and Home, and many Comforts of this Life: but now we may say, as Job, *Naked came I out of my Mothers Womb, and naked shall I return: The Lord gave, and the Lord hath taken away, Blessed be the Name of the Lord.* I asked him whither he would read; he told me, he earnestly desired it, I gave him my Bible, and he lighted upon that comfortable Scripture, Psal. 118. 17, 18. *I shall not dy but live, and declare the works of the Lord: the Lord hath chastened me sore, yet he hath not given me over to death.* Look here, Mother (says he) did you read this? And here I may take occasion to mention one principall ground of my setting forth these Lines: even as the Psalmist sayes, To declare the Works of the Lord, and his wonderfull Power in carrying us along, preserving us in the

Wilderness, while under the Enemies hand, and returning of us in safety again, And His goodness in bringing to my hand so many comfortable and suitable Scriptures in my distress. But to Return, We travelled on till night; and in the morning, we must go over the River to Philip's Crew. When I was in the Cannoo, I could not but be amazed at the numerous crew of Pagans that were on the Bank on the other side. When I came ashore, they gathered all about me, I sitting alone in the midst: I observed they asked one another questions, and laughed, and rejoyced over their Gains and Victories. Then my heart began to fail: and I fell a weeping which was the first time to my remembrance, that I wept before them. Although I had met with so much Affliction, and my heart was many times ready to break, yet could I not shed one tear in their sight: but rather had been all this while in a maze, and like one astonished: but now I may say as, Psal. 137. 1. *By the Rivers of Babylon, there we sate down: yea, we wept when we remembered Zion.* There one of them asked me, why I wept, I could hardly tell what to say: yet I answered, they would kill me: No, said he, none will hurt you. Then came one of them and gave me two spoon-fulls of Meal to comfort me, and another gave me half a pint of Pease; which was more worth than many Bushels at another time. Then I went to see King Philip, he bade me come in and sit down, and asked me whether I woold smoke it (a usual Complement nowadayes amongst Saints and Sinners) but this no way suited me. For though I had formerly used Tobacco, yet I had left it ever since I was first taken. It seems to be a Bait, the Devil layes to make men loose their precious time: I remember with shame, how formerly, when I had taken two or three pipes, I was presently ready for another, such a bewitching thing it is: But I thank God, he has now given me power over it; surely there are many who may be better imployed than to ly sucking a stinking Tobacco-pipe. . . .

John Williams on His Captivity
Among the French, 1707

. . . On the twenty-ninth of February, 1703,4, not long before break of day, the enemy came in like a flood upon us; our watch being unfaithful, an evil, whose awful effects, in a surprisal of our fort, should bespeak all watchmen to avoid, as they would not bring the charge of blood upon themselves. They came to my house in the beginning of the onset, and by their violent endeavours to break open doors and windows, with axes and hatchets, awaked me out of sleep; on which I leaped out of bed, and running toward the door, perceived the enemy making their entrance into the house. I called to awaken two soldiers, in the chamber; and returned toward my bed-side, for my arms. The enemy immediately brake into the room, I judge to the number of twenty, with painted faces, and hideous acclamations. I reached up my hands to the bed-tester, for my pistol, uttering a short petition to God, for everlasting mercies for me and mine, on the account of the merits of our glorified Redeemer; expecting a present passage through the valley of the shadow of death; saying in myself, as Isaiah xxxviii. 10, 11. *I said, in the cutting off my days, I shall go to the gates of the grave: I am deprived of the residue of my years. I said, I shall not see the Lord, even the Lord, in the land of the living: I shall behold man no more with the inhabitants of the world.* Taking down my pistol, I cocked it, and put it to the breast of the first Indian who came up; but my pistol missing fire, I was seized by three Indians, who disarmed me, and bound me naked, as I was in my shirt, and so I stood for near the space of an hour. Binding me, they told me they would carry me to Quebec. My pistol missing fire was an occasion of my life's being preserved; since which I have also found it profitable to be crossed in my own will. The judgment of God did not long slumber against one of the three which took me, who was a captain, for by sun-rising he received a mortal shot from my next neighbour's house; who opposed so great a number of French and Indians as three hundred, and yet were no more than seven men in an ungarrisoned house.

I cannot relate the distressing care I had for my dear wife, who had lain-in but a few weeks before, and for my poor children, family, and christian neighbours. The enemy fell to rifling the house, and entered in great numbers into every room of the house. I begged of God to remember mercy in the midst of judgment; that he would so far restrain their wrath, as to prevent their murdering of us; that we might have grace to glorify his name, whether in life or death; and, as I was able, committed our state to God. The enemies who entered the house were all of them Indians and Macquas, insulted over me a while, holding up hatchets over my head, threatening to burn all I had; but yet God, beyond expectation, made us in a great measure to be pitied; for though some were so cruel and barbarous as to take and carry to the door, two of my children, and murder them, as also a negro woman; yet they gave me liberty to put on my clothes, keeping me bound with a cord on one arm, till I put on my clothes to the other; and then changing my cord, they let me dress myself, and then pinioned me again: Gave liberty to my dear wife to dress herself, and our children. About sun an hour high, we were all carried out of the house, for a march, and saw many of the houses of my neighbours in flames, perceiving the whole fort, one house excepted, to be taken. Who can tell what sorrows pierced our souls, when we saw ourselves carried away from God's sanctuary, to go into a strange land, exposed to so many trials? The journey being at least three hundred miles we were to travel; the snow up to the knees, and we never inured to such hardships and fatigues; the place we were to be carried to, a popish country. Upon my parting from the town, they fired my house and barn. We were carried over the river, to the foot of the mountain, about a mile from my house, where we found a great number of our christian neighbours, men, women and children, to the number of an hundred, nineteen of whom were afterward murdered by the way, and two starved to death, near Cowafs, in a time of great scarcity or famine, the savages underwent there. When we came to the foot of the mountain, they took away our shoes, and gave us, in the room of them, Indian shoes, to prepare us for our travel. Whilst we were there, the English beat out a company, that remained in the town, and pursued them to the river, killing and wounding many of them; but the body of the army, being alarmed, they repulsed those few English that pursued them. . . .

After this, we went up the mountain, and saw the smoke of the fires in town, and beheld the awful desolations of Deerfield: And before we marched any farther, they killed a sucking child of the English. There were slain by the enemy, of the inhabitants of our town, to the number of thirty-eight, besides nine of the neighbouring towns. We travelled not far the first day; God made the heathen so to pity our children, that though they had several wounded persons of their own to carry upon their shoulders for thirty miles, before they came to the river, yet they carried our children, incapable of travelling, upon their shoulders, and in their arms. When we came to our lodging place, the first night, they dug away the snow, and made some wigwams, cut down some of the small branches of spruce trees to lie down on, and gave the prisoners somewhat to eat; but we had but little appetite. I was pinioned, and bound down that night, and so I was every night whilst I was with the army. . . .

. . . My youngest daughter, aged seven years, was carried all the journey, and looked after with a great deal of tenderness. My youngest son, aged four years, was wonderfully preserved from death; for though they that carried him, or drawed him on sleighs, were tired with their journey, yet their savage cruel tempers were so over-ruled by God, that they did not kill him; but in their pity, he was spared, and others would take care of him; so that four times on the journey he was thus preserved, till at last he arrived at Montreal, where a French gentlewoman, pitying the child, redeemed it out of the hands of the heathen. My son Samuel, and my eldest daughter, were pitied, so as to be drawn on sleighs, when unable to travel. And though they suffered very much through scarcity of food, and tedious journeys, they were carried through to Montreal. And my son Stephen, about eleven years of age, wonderfully preserved from death, in the famine whereof three English persons died, and after eight months brought into Chamblee. . . .

❧ E S S A Y S

The great wars for empire in the colonial period generated attitudes and stereotypes that survive even today. Contemporaries and earlier historians wrote of these conflicts as if they occurred exclusively between the empires. These commentators assumed the "savagery" of the Indians and the "civility" of the Europeans and colonists. More important, they saw the Indians, usually referred to as "French Indians" or "English Indians," not as having legitimate goals of their own but rather as tools of either side, and they perceived any deviation from that role as the innate treachery of the savage. Ian K. Steele, a historian at the University of Western Ontario, has examined a pivotal event in the creation of these myths, one used by two great nineteenth-century writers, historian Francis Parkman and novelist James Fenimore Cooper, as the foundation of important works. Steele has penetrated the stories to find the reality beneath. His account in the second essay can be compared to Francis Parkman's version of the same event in the opening selection.

The most terrifying prospect, one that colonists believed involved a fate worse than death, was capture by the Indians. Capture was terrible for men but unimaginably horrible in prospect for women. Popular captivity narratives provided a series of images that became the central truth about the Indians for men and women across the colonies. In the final essay James Axtell, William R. Kenan, Jr., Professor of Humanities and Professor of History at the College of William and Mary, realizing that (contrary to expectation) prisoners often became deeply attached to their adopted culture, examines these images using the captives' own accounts. In the process he uncovers the sound psychological reasoning behind many of the Indians' "barbarous" practices.

The Massacre at Fort William Henry: A Nineteenth-Century View

FRANCIS PARKMAN

... Fort William Henry [on Lake George, New York] was an irregular bastioned square, formed by embankments of gravel surmounted by a rampart of heavy logs, laid in tiers crossed one upon another, the interstices filled with earth. The lake protected it on the north, the marsh on the east, and ditches with *chevaux-de-frise* on the south and west. Seventeen cannon, great and small, besides several mortars and swivels, were mounted upon it; and a brave Scotch veteran, Lieutenant-Colonel Monro, of the thirty-fifth regiment, was in command.

General Webb lay fourteen miles distant at Fort Edward, with twenty-six hundred men, chiefly provincials. On the twenty-fifth of July [1757] he had made a visit to Fort William Henry, examined the place, given some orders, and returned on the twenty-ninth. He then wrote to the Governor of New York, telling him that the French were certainly coming, begging him to send up the militia, and saying: "I am determined to march to Fort William Henry with the whole army under my command as soon as I shall hear of the farther approach of the enemy." Instead of doing so he waited three days, and then sent up a detachment of two hundred regulars under Lieutenant-Colonel Young, and eight hundred Massachusetts men under Colonel Frye. This raised the force at the lake to two thousand and two hundred, including sailors and mechanics, and reduced that of Webb to sixteen hundred, besides half as many more distributed at Albany and the intervening forts. If, according to his spirited intention, he should go to the rescue of Monro, he must leave some of his troops behind him to protect the lower posts from a possible French inroad by way of South Bay. Thus his power of aiding Monro was slight, so rashly had Loudon, intent on Louisburg, left this frontier open to attack. The defect, however, was as much in Webb himself as in his resources. His conduct in the past year had raised doubts of his personal courage; and this was the moment for answering them. Great as was the disparity of numbers, the emergency would have justified an attempt to save Monro at any risk. That officer sent him a hasty note, written at nine o'clock on the morning of the third, telling him that the French were in sight on the lake; and, in the next night, three rangers came to Fort Edward, bringing another short note, dated at six in the evening, announcing that the firing had begun, and closing with the words: "I believe you will think it proper to send a reinforcement as soon as possible." Now, if ever, was the time to move, before the fort was invested and access cut off. But Webb lay quiet. . . .

. . . A brook ran down the ravine and entered the lake at a small cove protected from the fire of the fort by a point of land; and at this place, still called Artillery Cove, Montcalm prepared to debark his cannon and mortars.

Having made his preparations, he sent Fontbrune, one of his aides-de-camp, with a letter to Monro. "I owe it to humanity," he wrote, "to summon you to surrender. At present I can restrain the savages, and make them observe the terms of a capitulation, as I might not have power to do under other circumstances; and an obstinate defence on your part could only retard the capture of the place a few days, and endanger an unfortunate garrison which cannot be relieved, in consequence of the dispositions I have made. I demand a decisive answer within an hour." Monro replied that he and his soldiers would defend themselves to the last. While the flags of truce were flying, the Indians swarmed over the fields before the fort; and when they learned the result, an Abenaki chief shouted in broken French: "You won't surrender, eh! Fire away then, and fight your best; for if I catch you, you shall get no quarter." Monro emphasized his refusal by a general discharge of his cannon. . . .

The Indians were far from doing what was expected of them. Instead of scouting in the direction of Fort Edward to learn the movements of the enemy and prevent surprise, they loitered about the camp and in the trenches, or amused themselves by firing at the fort from behind stumps and logs. Some, in imitation of the French, dug little trenches for themselves, in which they wormed their way towards the rampart, and now and then picked off an artillery-man, not without loss on their own side. On the afternoon of the fifth, Montcalm invited them to a council, gave them belts of wampum, and mildly remonstrated with them. "Why expose yourselves without necessity? I grieve bitterly over the losses that you have met, for the least among you is precious to me. No doubt it is a good thing to annoy the English; but that is not the main point. You ought to inform me of everything the enemy is doing, and always keep parties on the road between the two forts." And he gently hinted that their place was not in his camp, but in that of Lévis, where missionaries were provided for such of them as were Christians, and food and ammunition for them all. They promised, with excellent docility, to do everything he wished, but added that there was something on their hearts. Being encouraged to relieve themselves of the burden, they complained that they had not been consulted as to the management of the siege, but were expected to obey orders like slaves. "We know more about fighting in the woods than you," said their orator; "ask our advice, and you will be the better for it."

Montcalm assured them that if they had been neglected, it was only through the hurry and confusion of the time; expressed high appreciation of their talents for bush-fighting, promised them ample satisfaction, and ended by telling them that in the morning they should hear the big guns. This greatly pleased them, for they were extremely impatient for the artillery to begin. About sunrise the battery of the left opened with eight heavy cannon and a mortar, joined, on the next morning, by the battery of the right, with eleven pieces more. The fort replied with spirit. The cannon thundered all day, and from a hundred peaks and crags the astonished wilderness roared back the sound. The Indians were delighted. They wanted to point the guns; and to humor them, they were now and then allowed to do so. Others lay behind logs and fallen trees, and yelled their satisfaction when they saw the splinters fly from the wooden rampart.

Day after day the weary roar of the distant cannonade fell on the ears of Webb in his camp at Fort Edward. "I have not yet received the least reinforcement," he writes to Loudon. . . .

He had already warned Monro to expect no help from him. At midnight of the fourth, Captain Bartman, his aide-de-camp, wrote: "The General has ordered me to acquaint you he does not think it prudent to attempt a junction or to assist you till reinforced by the militia of the colonies, for the immediate march of which repeated expresses have been sent." The letter then declared that the French were in complete possession of the road between the two forts, that a prisoner just brought in reported their force in men and cannon to be very great, and that, unless the militia came soon, Monro had better make what terms he could with the enemy.

The chance was small that this letter would reach its destination; and in fact the bearer was killed by La Corne's Indians, who, in stripping the body, found the hidden paper, and carried it to the General. Montcalm kept it several days. . . .

The position of the besieged was . . . deplorable. More than three hundred of them had been killed and wounded; small-pox was raging in the fort; the place was a focus of infection, and the casemates were crowded with the sick. A sortie from the entrenched camp and another from the fort had been repulsed with loss. All their large cannon and mortars had been burst, or disabled by shot; only seven small pieces were left fit for service; and the whole of Montcalm's thirty-one cannon and fifteen mortars and howitzers would soon open fire, while the walls were already breached, and an assault was imminent. Through the night of the eighth they fired briskly from all their remaining pieces. In the morning the officers held a council, and all agreed to surrender if honorable terms could be had. A white flag was raised, a drum was beat, and Lieutenant-Colonel Young, mounted on horseback, for a shot in the foot had disabled him from walking, went, followed by a few soldiers, to the tent of Montcalm.

It was agreed that the English troops should march out with the honors of war, and be escorted to Fort Edward by a detachment of French troops; that they should not serve for eighteen months; and that all French prisoners captured in America since the war began should be given up within three months. The stores, munitions, and artillery were to be the prize of the victors, except one field-piece, which the garrison were to retain in recognition of their brave defence.

Before signing the capitulation Montcalm called the Indian chiefs to council, and asked them to consent to the conditions, and promise to restrain their young warriors from any disorder. They approved everything and promised everything. The garrison then evacuated the fort, and marched to join their comrades in the entrenched camp, which was included in the surrender. No sooner were they gone than a crowd of Indians clambered through the embrasures in search of rum and plunder. All the sick men unable to leave their beds were instantly butchered. "I was witness of this spectacle," says the missionary Roubaud; "I saw one of these barbarians come out of the casemates with a human head in his hand, from which the blood ran in streams, and which he paraded as if he had got the finest prize in the world." There was little left to plunder; and the Indians, joined by the more lawless of the Canadians, turned their attention to the entrenched camp, where all the English were now collected.

The French guard stationed there could not or would not keep out the rabble. By the advice of Montcalm the English stove their rum-barrels; but the Indians were drunk already with homicidal rage, and the glitter of their vicious eyes told of the devil within. They roamed among the tents, intrusive, insolent, their visages besmirched with war-paint; grinning like fiends as they handled, in anticipation of the knife, the long hair of cowering women, of whom, as well as of children, there were many in the camp, all crazed with fright. Since the last war the New England border population had regarded Indians with a mixture of detestation and horror. Their mysterious warfare of ambush and surprise, their midnight onslaughts, their butcheries, their burnings, and all their nameless atrocities, had been for years the theme of fireside story; and the dread they excited was deepened by the distrust and dejection of the time. The confusion in the camp lasted through the afternoon. "The Indians," says Bougainville, "wanted to plunder the chests of the English; the latter resisted; and there was fear that serious disorder would ensue. The Marquis de Montcalm ran thither immediately, and used every means to restore tranquillity: prayers, threats, caresses, interposition of the officers and interpreters who have some influence over these savages." "We shall be but too happy if we can prevent a massacre. Detestable position! of which nobody who has not been in it can have any idea, and which makes victory itself a sorrow to the victors. The Marquis spared no efforts to prevent the rapacity of the savages and, I must say it, of certain persons associated with them, from resulting in something worse than plunder. At last, at nine o'clock in the evening, order seemed restored. The Marquis even induced the Indians to promise that, besides the escort agreed upon in the capitulation, two chiefs for each tribe should accompany the English on their way to Fort Edward." He also ordered La Corne and the other Canadian officers attached to the Indians to see that no violence took place. He might well have done more. In view of the disorders of the afternoon, it would not have been too much if he had ordered the whole body of regular troops, whom alone he could trust for the purpose, to hold themselves ready to move to the spot in case of outbreak, and shelter their defeated foes behind a hedge of bayonets.

Bougainville was not to see what ensued; for Montcalm now sent him to Montreal, as a special messenger to carry news of the victory. He embarked at ten o'clock. Returning daylight found him far down the lake; and as he looked on its still bosom flecked with mists, and its quiet mountains sleeping under the flush of dawn, there was nothing in the wild tranquillity of the scene to suggest the tragedy which even then was beginning on the shore he had left behind.

The English in their camp had passed a troubled night, agitated by strange rumors. In the morning something like a panic seized them; for they distrusted not the Indians only, but the Canadians. In their haste to be gone they got together at daybreak, before the escort of three hundred regulars had arrived. They had their muskets, but no ammunition; and few or none of the provincials had bayonets. Early as it was, the Indians were on the alert; and, indeed, since midnight great numbers of them had been prowling about the skirts of the camp, showing, says Colonel Frye, "more than usual malice in their looks." Seventeen wounded men of his regiment lay in huts, unable to join the march. In the preceding afternoon Miles Whitworth, the regimental surgeon, had passed them over to the care of a French surgeon, according to an agreement made at the time of the surrender; but, the Frenchman being absent, the other remained with them attending to their wants. The French surgeon had caused special sentinels to be posted for their protection. These were now removed, at the moment when they were needed most; upon which, about five o'clock in the morning, the Indians entered the huts, dragged out the inmates, and tomahawked and scalped them all, before the eyes of Whitworth, and in presence of La Corne and other Canadian officers, as well as of a French guard stationed within forty feet of the spot; and, declares the surgeon under oath, "none, either officer or soldier, protected the said wounded men." The opportune butchery relieved them of a troublesome burden.

A scene of plundering now began. The escort had by this time arrived, and Monro complained to the officers that the capitulation was broken; but got no other answer than advice to give up the baggage to the Indians in order to appease them. To this the English at length agreed; but it only increased the excitement of the mob. They demanded rum; and some of the soldiers, afraid to refuse, gave it to them from their canteens, thus adding fuel to the flame. When, after much difficulty, the column at last got out of the camp and began to move along the road that crossed the rough plain between the entrenchment and the forest, the Indians crowded upon them, impeded their march, snatched caps, coats, and weapons from men and officers, tomahawked those that resisted, and seizing upon shrieking women and children, dragged them off or murdered them on the spot. It is said that some of the interpreters secretly fomented the disorder. Suddenly there rose the screech of the war-whoop. At this signal of butchery, which was given by Abenaki Christians from the mission of the Penobscot, a mob of savages rushed upon the New Hampshire men at the rear of the column, and killed or dragged away eighty of them. A frightful tumult ensued, when Montcalm, Lévis, Bourlamaque, and many other French officers, who had hastened from their camp on the first news of disturbance, threw themselves among the Indians, and by promises and threats tried to allay their frenzy. "Kill me, but spare the English who are under my protection," exclaimed Montcalm. He took from one of them a young officer whom the savage had seized; upon which several other Indians immediately tomahawked their prisoners, lest they too should be taken from them.... Their broken column straggled forward in wild disorder, amid the din of whoops and shrieks, till they reached the French advance-guard, which consisted of Canadians; and here they demanded protection from the officers, who refused to give it, telling them that they must take to the woods and shift for themselves.... Jonathan Carver, a provincial volunteer, declares that, when the tumult was at its height, he saw officers of the French army walking about at a little distance and talking with seeming unconcern. Three or four Indians seized him, brandished their tomahawks over his head, and tore off most of his clothes, while he vainly claimed protection from a sentinel, who called him an English dog, and violently pushed him back among his tormentors. Two of them were dragging him towards the neighboring swamp, when an English officer, stripped of everything but his scarlet breeches, ran by. One of Carver's captors sprang upon him, but was thrown to the ground; whereupon the other went to the aid of his comrade and drove his tomahawk into the back of the Englishman. As Carver turned to run, an English boy, about twelve years old, clung to him and begged for help. They ran on together for a moment, when the boy was seized, dragged from his protector, and, as Carver judged by his shrieks, was murdered. He himself escaped to the forest, and after three days of famine reached Fort Edward.

The bonds of discipline seem for the time to have been completely broken; for while Montcalm and his chief officers used every effort to restore order, even at the risk of their lives, many other officers, chiefly of the militia, failed atrociously to do their duty. How many English were killed it is impossible to tell with exactness. Roubaud says that he saw forty or fifty corpses scattered about the field. Lévis says fifty; which does not include the sick and wounded before murdered in the camp and fort. It is certain that six or seven hundred persons were carried off, stripped, and otherwise maltreated. Montcalm succeeded in recovering more than four hundred of them in the course of the day; and many of the French officers did what they could to relieve their wants by buying back from their captors the clothing that had been torn from them. Many of the fugitives had taken refuge in the fort, whither Monro himself had gone to demand protection for his followers; and here Roubaud presently found a crowd of half-frenzied women, crying in anguish for husbands and children. All the refugees and redeemed prisoners were afterwards conducted to the entrenched camp, where food and shelter were provided for them and a strong guard set for their protection until the fifteenth, when they were sent under an escort to Fort Edward. Here cannon had been fired at intervals to guide those who had fled to the woods, whence they came dropping in from day to day, half dead with famine.

On the morning after the massacre the Indians decamped in a body and set out for Montreal, carrying with them their plunder and some two hundred prisoners, who, it is said, could not be got out of their hands. The soldiers were set to the work of demolishing the English fort; and the task occupied several days. The barracks were torn down, and the huge pine-logs of the rampart thrown into a heap. The dead bodies that filled the casemates were added to the mass, and fire was set to the whole. The mighty funeral pyre blazed all night. Then, on the sixteenth, the army reimbarked. The din of ten thousand combatants, the rage, the terror, the agony, were gone; and no living thing was left but the wolves that gathered from the mountains to feast upon the dead.

The "Massacre" at Fort William Henry: A Modern View

IAN K. STEELE

The compelling events of the brief existence of Fort William Henry . . . have simply demanded a careful retelling. The well-documented realities were much more subtle and revealing than James Fenimore Cooper's mythical classic *The Last of the Mohicans* (1826). The mixture of Indian, colonial, and European values produced cooperation, conflict, and confusion within the armies that fought for the Albany-Montreal corridor. The Battle of Lake George demonstrates the confusion accompanying the unprecedented commitment of European military resources to the persistent colonial rivalries on this frontier. The fort itself was an assertion of the European military presence on builders, garrisons, and enemies in this wilderness. The siege of 1757 displayed the uneasy, but effective, combination of Indian, colonial, and European warfare. The climactic "massacre at Fort William Henry" was a foreseeable collision of attitudes about prisoners of war, rather than the drunken or "homicidal" rage that has been depressingly popular as an explanation among historians.

The remembering of Fort William Henry has served a variety of purposes over the centuries. The conflict between European and colonial values and methods has been a favorite theme of historians seeking the roots of American and Canadian identity. The "massacre," which left more killed and missing than those at Deerfield or Lachine, became powerful in American folk memory, confirming attitudes toward American Indians that justified "removals" and wars. From this distance, the short and tragic story seems to have been part of the nineteenth century's "usable past." The twentieth century has, perhaps with humane intention, tended to forget Fort William Henry, or leave it to the "literature" of James Fenimore Cooper, Francis Parkman, or H.-R. Casgrain. What follows is a retelling based on new as well as familiar sources, an analysis of casualties and consequences, and an essay on the witnesses and the historians. This reopening of a sensitive subject is offered with the hope that readers will agree that understanding is preferable to forgetting. . . .

The sixteen men-of-war that sailed from Brest on May 3, 1755, were the French response to British initiatives for North America. . . . These three thousand *troupes de terre* were to be commanded by Maréchal de camp Jean-Armand, Baron de Dieskau. . . . Dieskau's instructions made it very clear that he was under the military orders of his fellow passenger on *L'Esperance* and now Governor-General of New France, Pierre-François de Rigaud de Vaudreuil de Cavagnal, Marquis de Vaudreuil. This fifty-eight-year-old Canadian soldier had established his reputation as tough, ruthless, and effective as governor of Louisiana. The fleet, which had a crossing of less than four weeks to Newfoundland waters, represented French determination to defend its version of the boundaries between empires in North America. . . .

Governor Vaudreuil was determined to take Fort William Henry in 1757 and made no secret of it. Throughout the winter, the English heard of the planned attack from Iroquois who had been to Montreal, from French soldiers taken prisoner, and from English prisoners who had escaped from Montreal. . . .

Vaudreuil's first major achievement of 1757 was the gathering of unprecedented numbers of Indian warriors for the campaign against Fort William Henry. His established belief in the military value of Indian warriors and their methods had been confirmed, during his first two years as governor of New France, by the major victories against Braddock and against the garrison at Fort Oswego. . . .

. . . Vaudreuil held a major conference at Montreal in December that brought Iroquois visitors from New York together with Caughnawaga, Nipissing, and Algonkin from the mission villages, some Potawatomi and Ottawa from Detroit and Michilimackinac, as well as a roster of Canadian guerrillas who interpreted for the Indians with whom they had raided. This meeting was to encourage recruiting for the Fort William Henry campaign, to impress the visiting Iroquois, and especially to warn the Mohawk, who had stayed away. The Ottawa and Potawatomi chanted their enthusiasm in a war song asking the French; "Father, we are famished; give us fresh meat; we wish to eat the English."

Recruiting in the *pays d'en haut* [upper Great Lakes] early in 1757 was phenomenal, more successful than Vaudreuil could have hoped. Some of the Ottawa and Potawatomi warriors who had been to Montreal in 1756 went home to recruit, encouraged by the commandants of the French trading posts of the upper lakes and by the recent victories. . . .

The only French influence over these visiting allies was exercised by Canadians with warrior reputations. . . .

The siege was to be a conventional European cannon duel, for which trenches were begun about seven hundred yards from the fort on the west side, shielded by wooden gabions filled with dirt, and fascines of bundled wood embedded in dirt from the trenching. The large cannon in Fort William Henry were directed toward disrupting construction of the battery and trenches, and the cannon of the fort's east curtain and bastions were helping to counter persistent Indian small-arms fire on the camp. Seven Indians were reported killed or wounded in the first day's action, and the English camp suffered about thirty casualties.

Montcalm's call to surrender, sent in under a flag of truce later in the day, was a mix of conventional military courtesy, warning, and threat. Montcalm correctly announced that he had superior forces and cannon, but neither had been seen in use as yet and Monro could not be sure of the claims. Montcalm emphasized that "I have it yet in my power to restrain the savages, and oblige them to observe a capitulation, as hitherto none of them has been killed, which will not be in my power in other circumstances." This offer showed his lack of awareness of Indian losses already sustained, and later became a helpful document for Montcalm, but it may also have represented an exaggerated belief in his own power over his Indian allies. Adam Williamson might have recalled that the message echoed one sent to the commander of the same fort less than five months earlier, before a siege which proved unsuccessful. Monro courteously dismissed the invitation, since he knew that a fortified garrison was expected to be able to hold off an attack by three times its number for a few days until reinforcements arrived. He reported the day's proceedings to Colonel Webb calmly, understating the losses of the first day, but concluding, "I make no doubt that you will soon send us a Reinforcement." . . .

The defenders in the fort could see the attackers at work, but lacked the men to oppose them with anything other than cannon and mortar fire. This slowed the French a little, but also caused the English concern when the first of their mortars exploded in the northwest bastion. Although there were no serious injuries and the mortar was promptly replaced by the only howitzer in the fort, this and the split muzzle of one of the 18-pounders were indicators of problems to come. Iron artillery suffered metal fatigue and was weakened as it heated, necessitating smaller charges of powder. To avoid explosion, it was recommended that iron cannon be allowed to cool after every twelve firings. Tearing the flammable roofs off the barracks, undertaken two days before any French cannon was fired, was also depressing.

The most severe fighting of this second day of the siege was around the entrenched English camp. Indian marksmen harassed those in the encampment constantly, despite some effective mortar fire from the fort and numerous sorties to force them back and protect the water supply. Monro did not hear from Webb, whose discouraging reply was captured and held by Montcalm, but that night Monro again wrote to his commander at Fort Edward. . . .

. . . On August 5, the third day of the siege, the fighting seemed much like that of the previous day for the English. The fort's gunners continued to bombard the new French trenches, driving back the La Sarre and Royal Roussillon regiments, which were protecting the trenches from a possible sortie. In this cannonading, both of the fort's 32-pounders burst and the last of the 18-pounders exploded, wounding several men. Those in the camp were able to replenish provisions and stores from the fort, but felt themselves under constant attack from the Indians. . . .

The Indians were becoming impatient with orders and saw themselves as having led in three days of fighting while waiting for Montcalm's cannon to fire. Many had left their positions to visit the French camp. Some adapted trenching to their own purposes much nearer the English camp, and others stalked the enemy from its own garden. . . .

Montcalm called a general council of the Indians to complain about their failure to stay at their posts and do systematic scouting. He objected to what he regarded as the foolishness of warriors exposing themselves unnecessarily, which had resulted in fifteen deaths. Montcalm offered belts and strings of wampum "to get them back again on the right path, to wipe out the past and to brighten the future with the light of good fortune." . . . Although pleased with the gifts and the news, the Amerindians also voiced their grievances with the conduct of the siege. The chiefs were not being informed of measures taken. Indian advice was not acted upon, without any explanation of why it was being ignored. They were not consulted on scouting arrangements, but "as though they were slaves, it was attempted to make them march without having consulted with their chiefs and agreed with them." Montcalm promised to do better, and the meeting ended amicably with the announcement that the cannon would begin firing the next day.

The fort announced the beginning of August 6 with two howitzer shells and a single heavy shot at 6:00 A.M., and it was answered by nine cannon and a mortar in the first battery of Montcalm's artillery. French artillerymen found the range quickly, and the French cheered when the flag in the fort was shot down. The symbolism immediately became deadly when a carpenter, attempting to repair the flagstaff, had his head shot entirely away by a subsequent shot. . . . When Monro wrote Webb later in the day, he pleaded for more artillery. Four cannon had burst during the preceding day, and the camp had been forced to send two of its remaining 12-pounders into the fort. . . .

After three hours of brisk firing, Montcalm called a halt in order to exploit his psychological advantage. Bougainville was sent forward with a flag of truce that was red, since the French flag had a white ground, and an escort of fifteen grenadiers. . . .

The truce had no overwhelming effect on the defenders, though it must have suggested that Montcalm was firmly in charge of his army. The Indians had made English desertion all but impossible throughout the siege. . . .

As Monro's hopes for reinforcement faded on the evening of August 8, Webb wrote his last letter to the embattled commander, a letter that was intercepted and never reached Fort William Henry. . . .

That evening, when Monro had no reason to hope for such a letter, he sent an engineer, probably Adam Williamson, to examine the state of the fort. The fort itself was intact, though both the northeast and northwest bastions had lost the top three feet of timbers and the casements had been somewhat damaged by exploding shells. The English artillery, ammunition, and other stores were nearly exhausted, "besides, the men had been without rest five nights, and were almost Stupified." The fort, designed by Captain William Eyre, had withstood three days of cannonading, exceeding the expectations of both the American doubters and the British military skeptics. The garrison of fort and camp had behaved better than Loudoun, Webb, or even Monro could have expected. Yet it was increasingly clear that the struggle was soon to end, one way or another. Monro called a council of war for the next morning.

Before dawn on August 9, the senior officers defending Fort William Henry met with their commander, as agreed the night before, to discuss capitulation. . . .

At a time when military honor was a cultivated art form, the terms of this surrender were most generous. . . . The prospect of feeding two thousand additional men was one deterrent; the other was the humanitarian consideration (or was it a subsequent deception to defend Montcalm's reputation?): "one could not have restrained the barbarity of the Indians, and it is never permitted to sacrifice humanity to what is only the shadow of glory." Consequently, the whole garrison was to march to Fort Edward the next morning, with drums beating, with colors flying, and with soldiers and officers retaining their arms and baggage. As a special mark of recognition for its "brave and honorable defense," the garrison could take one cannon in the procession, which was to be escorted by a detachment of French regulars and some of the officers and interpreters who fought with the Indians. In return, the defeated agreed not to bear arms against the French or their allies for eighteen months. It was also agreed that all French "officers, soldiers, Canadians, women, and Indians" taken prisoner in North America were to be returned to Fort Carillon within three months. The sick and wounded English who could not be transported to Fort Edward were to be in the care of Montcalm, and to be returned when well. Nothing more was demanded, except an officer as a hostage for the safe return of the French escort taking the column down the sixteen-mile road to Fort Edward.

Ultimately, terms derived from the latest European etiquette of war were only as meaningful as they were to an Ottawa or Potawatomi warrior. Indians were around the fort during the negotiations, calmly walking off with the few remaining horses they found there. . . . Montcalm decided to hold a general council of chiefs before signing the terms, even though this course admitted that the Indians were allies and not completely under his command. Accompanied by Young, Montcalm endeavored to explain the terms to those chiefs who assembled. He could not know how accurately, how completely, or with what editorial comments these terms were being translated for some sixteen hundred Indians of thirty-three tribes by eight interpreters, four missionaries, and a dozen Canadian irregulars who were listed as "Officers attached to the Indians" in the formal roster of the attacking army.

The assembled chiefs did not object to the terms and agreed to restrain their young warriors, but politeness may have been read as acquiescence. Even if these Indians discounted their own earlier rhetoric about eating and drinking enemies, they still claimed the right to pillage the fort and the entrenched camp after the English had left. Stores of war and provisions were, however, to be the property of the Canadian government, and the personal effects of the English officers and men were to be respected. The Indians were free to take what they thought fell between those categories.

At noon, a French detachment arrived at the gate of the fort, where a brief ceremony of transfer was held, and the 450 English duty soldiers marched off to their entrenched camp. At this point, a number of Indians ran in through the gate and gun embrasures in search of their promised booty. Members of the retreating garrison heard cries of "Murder" and "Help" from within the fort, where thirty sick and forty severely wounded had remained behind, some in the comparatively well-protected but isolated casements under the ramparts. Père Roubaud, who did not explain how a missionary came to be inside the fort so quickly, reported that a few of these unfortunate English were attacked and killed. . . . Indians watched with suspicion and derision as the English soldiers carried their belongings and as wagons hauled the officers' baggage. The French had some difficulty protecting the military stores and provisions from the Indians. There were complaints that the French took the best for themselves and that the Indians had been deceived by the surrender terms. One English officer heard an Indian chief "violently accuse the French general with being false and a liar to them, that he had promised them the plunder of the English, and they would have it." Anger would be intensified by the envy directed at those few warriors who had a trophy to prove they had been active in a great battle. The English, now gathered in the adjoining camp they had defended so well, gained no clear picture of what had happened in the fort, but could imagine.

Some Indians had already been inside the English entrenched camp before the capitulation was signed, and it is unlikely that they had been at Montcalm's council of chiefs or had heard the terms explained by them. At noon, Montcalm had posted a guard of two hundred French regulars inside the camp. Monro ordered the destruction of all liquor in the camp, but reports vary on how thoroughly and by what methods the liquor disappeared. That afternoon, English officers entertained their French counterparts with an impressive spread of delicacies, served with wine and beer. Indians were inside the camp throughout the afternoon, acquiring what they could and being considered troublesome and dishonorable thieves by both the English and the French. There was persistent difficulty about the English officers' baggage. European officers carried what any warrior would have regarded as an enormous amount of personal baggage. Some American officers, judging from their claimed losses, patronized the Albany clothiers in order to assert their status with multiple uniforms of velvets and silks in scarlet, blue, or green, topped with lace-trimmed beaver hats. Even warriors who exactly understood the terms of the surrender could presume that much legitimate booty was being unfairly protected as personal belongings. Some English officers offered money to Indians to leave their belongings alone. Other confrontations turned nasty, and Montcalm was called to settle matters. He used "entreaties, threats, flattery, conferences with chiefs, the intervention of officers and interpreters who have any authority with these barbarians." He left for his own camp about nine o'clock that night, after the Indians had been cleared from the camp. It was announced that the parolees would leave the camp at first light, but this display of French confidence masked well-founded fears.

Near midnight, an escort of two hundred French regulars picked from the La Reine and Languedoc regiments assembled quietly at the entrance to the camp. Monro, with Montcalm's prior approval, had ordered the march to Fort Edward that night in the hope that trouble with the Indians could be averted. In addition to his twenty-three hundred men pledged not to fight Frenchmen or their allies, including Indians, Monro was overseeing dozens of women, children, and other camp followers whose position had not been specified in the capitulation. It was one thing to trust French honor, but it was quite another to assume that all the Indians were aware of the terms, would not take them literally, and would not despise them, as their *coureurs de bois* translators may have encouraged them to do. Even without Indian anger, vengefulness, or inebriation, what could these soon-to-leave parolees expect from warriors who had spent weeks canoeing a thousand miles to fight for the martial trophies that were their only pay, were passports to manhood for some, and assurances of higher esteem for others.

The grenadiers led three companies of Monro's own Thirty-fifth Regiment out of the entrenchment, followed by the other three companies of the same regiment. The marching orders were suddenly countermanded because the Indians had noticed the preparations. . . .

The attempt to leave at midnight only added to the anger of the Indians. They could not fathom French behavior in wasting their victory and protecting their enemies from their allies. They resented the European conspiracy, which had defrauded them of their agreed share of the loot in the fort and now, apparently, plotted to trick them out of the timely search for spoils of war within the entrenchment as well. At the end of a very long day, Colonel Joseph Frye of the Massachusetts regiment noted, "All the Remainder of this night the Indians were in great numbers round our lines and seemed to shew more than usual malice in their looks which made us suspect they intended us mischief."

The long day for the English became an even longer night. They did not unpack the belongings they had gathered for the midnight departure and spent their sixth consecutive night with little sleep, this time without cover and presumably without liquor. Fears based on events and reports of the previous day were multiplied for many by the tales remembered from calmer campfires, or terrors that had been read in those captivity narratives popular in the British colonies. . . . Officers among the parolees were warned that the Indians would have to be gratified from the baggage, and "if any resistance was made by which a single Indian should be killed, it would not be in the power of Mr. De Montcalm to save a man from butchery." Fear was an easy victor over exhaustion.

As the eastern sky lightened to end that tense night, the English assembled by unit for the march, anxious to be gone, yet apprehensive. The Indians, who had stayed out of the English camp during the night by agreement reinforced by orders to the French pickets, were returning over the breastworks. Colonel Frye found them "in a worse temper (if possible) than last night, every one having a tomahawk, hatchet, or some instrument of death." After gaining few trophies at the surrender of the fort, and nearly being tricked out of everything portable by the attempted midnight departure, the few dozen Indians who came in first were more than "curious." Initially, demands again focused on the officers' baggage. . . . French officers with the escort advised the English to give up their packs, which was ordered.

As the British regulars began to move, increasing numbers of Indians became more insistent. In poignant conformity with the restrictions concerning loot, several Indians took away the horses that had been granted to pull the solitary brass cannon that symbolized the bravery of the British and the martial civility of the French. Captain Furnis of the Royal Artillery was with the regulars at the front of the intended column and reported that he and those near him gave up their packs. Indians not only were taking packs, but also began stripping officers and men of their clothing, swords, muskets, as well as drums, halberds, and fifes. The chance of conveying orders was fading amid the growing din, even if the terrified men had been able to obey. The regulars managed to assemble their line of march on the road outside the entrenchment. Those who still had their weapons were now ordered to carry them "clubbed." This demeaning gesture in European military etiquette was to avoid provoking the Indians by displaying bayonets, or provoking the French with any breach of parole. These regulars appear to have been flanked by most of the small French escort and would fare comparatively well in the ensuing violence.

Inside the encampment, the provincial troops suffered more. Miles Whitworth, a surgeon in Colonel Frye's Massachusetts militia regiment, later testified that he had remained with seventeen wounded men from his regiment, even after turning them over to the French surgeon the previous afternoon. The men were unable to join the march on the morning of August 10. The special night guard that the French had placed over the huts of the wounded was withdrawn without replacement as the English began to leave about 5:00 A.M. Indians entering the camp dragged the seventeen wounded out of their huts and immediately killed and scalped them in plain view of the horrified surgeon and soldiers of the colonial regiments. Whitworth testified that several Canadian officers, among whom he recognized St. Luc de la Corne, and French pickets posted nearby did nothing to help the wounded.

Meanwhile, other warriors were dragging Indians from the ranks of the American rangers and provincial regiments and forcing them over the breastworks. The English eyewitnesses, having seen what happened to the sick and wounded, presumed inaccurately that all these Indians would also be scalped or tortured in accordance with a military tradition that did not include immunity in return for promises not to fight for eighteen months. Blacks and mulattos among the English soldiers and camp followers were also hauled away. They, too, were treated better than the witnesses presumed. Both Indians and Europeans believed that blacks were property, and Montcalm's Indian allies therefore regarded them as loot. Although the Massachusetts regiment did not have women with it, witnesses from that group described violence against regular soldiers' wives and camp followers who were to be in the rear of the column. All these initial targets, the Indians, the blacks, the soldiers' families, and the wounded, suggest that someone conveyed the exact terms of the surrender to at least some of the Indian allies of the French, but did not, or could not, convey its spirit. As at Oswego, the wounded were Montcalm's personal charge, and their murder was read as his personal disgrace by one culture and as a minor matter by another. The initial burst of violence struck terror and produced clothes, watches, money, and arms, some of which were soon conveyed to the nearby Indian camp along with some of the first captives. . . .

Most of the English were out of the entrenchment when they were struck by the most ferocious of the attacks. Hundreds of warriors, on learning that scalps and prisoners had been taken in the entrenchment, emerged from their camps to look for their share. Someone began the dreaded war whoop that was an intertribal signal of attack. Warriors clambered over the deserted breastworks to join Indians already inside. Missionary Roubaud, who arrived minutes later, said of English stragglers still in their camp: "Woe to all those who brought up the rear, or to stragglers whom indisposition or any other cause separated however little from the troop. They were so many dead whose bodies very soon strewed the ground and covered the inclosure of the intrenchments."

Having dispatched those left behind, the warriors raced out of the entrenchment in pursuit of those gathered outside. Camp followers and the New Hampshire militia were hit first, since they were at the rear, but soon there were Indians around the whole English contingent. Families of the regulars, who had been in the garrison for months, were among the first to be attacked by warriors who were after the more prized soldiers beyond them.

The Massachusetts regiment, positioned near the rear of the column, provides our only witnesses of the actual slaughter. The colonel, reporting to his House of Representatives, remembered that no sooner were the troops out of the entrenchment "than the savages fell upon the rear, killing and scalping." Ensign John Maylem remembered the "hell whoop" followed by death everywhere for men, women, and children. Maylem wrote his account as a long poem dated seven months later. He mentioned "The harmless Babe (torn from its Mother's Arm and dash'd, impetuous, on the Wave-worn Cliff!)," already a common feature of New England captivity narratives for nearly a century. Another Massachusetts officer claimed that as the English were leaving the entrenchment, French soldiers taunted them with what the Indians were going to do to them, and the column became disorderly. At that, "the Indians pursued tearing the Children from their Mothers Bosoms and their mothers from their Husbands, then Singling out the men and Carrying them in the woods and killing a great many whom we saw lying on the road side." Jonathan Carver, a volunteer in the same regiment, remembered that, after the war whoop, the Indians began killing indiscriminately. Lamenting the impossibility of describing the "horrid scene," Carver wrote that "men, women, and children were dispatched in the most wanton and cruel manner, and immediately scalped. Many of these savages drank the blood of their victims, as it flowed warm from the fatal wound." . . .

At the first attack on the rear of the column, a halt was called and eventually obeyed by the Massachusetts regiment. Their colonel reported that, once the men knew what was happening farther back in the column, they pressed forward again in confusion. With some standards missing, a din of screams and whoops, and units mashing together, the provincial regiment disintegrated. The colonel admitted in a private letter that the attack drove his men "into Disorder, Render'd it impossible to Rally." He held some remnant of his regiment together until it reached the Canadian advance guard, less than a mile down the road from his place in the assembled column. These French refused him protection and urged him to take to the woods, which he did.

... Indians, who preferred the more individual style of combat and valued prisoners more than scalps at the end of a campaign, now gave chase.

What is clear from all the sources, and especially from Roubaud, is that the indiscriminate killing lasted for only a very short time. If all sixteen hundred warriors had attacked the column with hatchets for as little as sixty seconds, the results would have been very few survivors, since there are no indications of significant resistance by people who had been effectively disarmed. The change from slaughter to a gigantic scramble for prisoners was, according to Roubaud, due to the "patience" of the English. As he had noted earlier in describing the taking of prisoners among the survivors of the Parker expedition, Roubaud saw the Indians as wanting to take prisoners if it was safe to do so. Those leaving the Fort William Henry encampment were without functional weapons and aware of the terms of their parole, and some were husbands and fathers unable either to flee or to fight.

As the Indians began taking prisoners, the first senior French officers arrived from Lévis' camp, led by the Chevalier himself. Lévis put some spirit into the escort and scurried around attempting to protect the English, with the result that some of the escort were injured by Indians. Montcalm also came running from his camp nearly a mile away, accompanied by several of his officers. According to Roubaud, Montcalm tried exhortations, threats, and promises and finally resorted to force. He grabbed a nephew of Lieutenant Colonel Young from an Indian. In saving the youth, Montcalm sentenced several other prisoners to immediate death. Some captors, who saw what the angry Montcalm did, now chose to take a scalp rather than give up a prisoner. Montcalm did not stop the "massacre"; nor did he stop the taking of prisoners. He arrived after the killing had ended and did not have the military resources with him to intimidate the Indians. He demonstrated outrage, courage, and determination to remedy the situation, and he proceeded to recover prisoners by various means. Foremost among these was to call on the officers attached to the Indians, the missionaries, and the interpreters to negotiate with individual Indians for the recovery of prisoners. . . .

Almost all the Indians left quickly on August 10. Their campaign was terminated because they had the prisoners they had come for, and they intended to take them home in triumph. . . .

Those English soldiers who escaped completely at Fort William Henry ran to Fort Edward. The regulars of the Thirty-fifth and Royal American regiments, who had headed the column, lost their possessions and coats to the Indians or abandoned them in flight. . . .

The paroled garrison had been expected at Fort Edward. A runner had arrived about 7:00 P.M. on August 9 with word of the surrender, and its terms had been conveyed by two French officers who deserted and were brought in to General Webb on the morning of August 10. Webb had arranged for an escort of five hundred men to meet what was presumed to be a protected column, "but at 7 o'clock we saw about 30 of our People coming running down the Hill out of the woods along the Road that comes from William Henry, mostly stript to their Shirts and Breeches, and many without Shirts." . . .

... Senior officers were noticeably absent among these early arrivals, and there were only three commissioned officers, none ranking above captain, and a few color sergeants.

The first reports, by winded and frightened men who had just raced sixteen miles, were truer than seemed likely from their variety. The regulars near the front of the column had been stripped of most of their belongings and outer clothes, and had witnessed the killing of the wounded. Others from farther back in the line reported the treatment of blacks, mulattos, and Indians in the English column. Still others told of the slaughter of women and children. . . . Some of [the] regiment . . . were incorporating the presumptions of well-known captivity narratives into their account of the horror they had seen. As the refugees straggled in over the next few days, aided by a cannon fired at two-hour intervals, it became clear that only about ten out of more than eighty women had managed to reach Fort Edward, and that the refugees numbered only about six hundred. It was not unreasonable for men who had fled what they thought was a furious massacre by well over a thousand warriors to presume that some seventeen hundred people had been either killed or taken prisoner.

Men who had made the unsoldierly flight from Fort William Henry also had vital personal reasons why they could not minimize their ordeal. Just one month before, a colonial private in the Royal Americans had been shot there for desertion. On a single day of harsh discipline at Fort Edward, two more Royal Americans were to be "Shot by a Platoon of ye Companys they belong too" for desertion, and three men of the New York regiment received six hundred lashes apiece. The lashing was then suspended, but the three would soon receive the other four hundred of the thousand lashes that were their exemplary punishment for desertion. . . .

These appalling first accounts spread a great fear through the northern American colonies. Arrival of the refugees led a Massachusetts sergeant at Fort Edward to declare, "This & Yesterday are ye Two Most Sorrowful Day[s] that Ever were Known to N England." . . .

When the New York papers resumed publication, their conflicting reports included a major story printed by government order. This was the most extensive newspaper version of the slaughter, offered in the most graphic prose. "Indian blood hounds" were said to have killed and scalped many officers and men, and killed or captured the blacks and Indians. "The throats of most, if not all the women, were cut, their bellies ript open, their bowels torn out and thrown upon the faces of their dead and dying bodies: and, it is said, that all their women were murdered in one way or another." The gruesome details gathered, invented, or improved on by this "authority" included the view that all the children had been taken by the heels and had their brains dashed out against stones or trees. Readers were reminded of the murder of the wounded in Braddock's army and in the defeated garrison at Oswego, and were told that the survivors of Parker's expedition were not likely to be spared. Nor were readers to forget the innocent who were daily killed and captured along the frontier. The tirade ended by urging that no French prisoners be taken, no capitulations negotiated, and no quarter asked. Every armed man was to sell his life as dearly as he could. This panicked version of the Fort William Henry tragedy survived in American legend. . . .

On Sunday evening, August 14, 1757, a party of about thirty men, carrying a red flag of truce, approached Fort Edward. The detachment was led by Lieutenant Savornin of the La Sarre regiment and included Joseph Marin *fils,* several Indians, and Lieutenant Hamilton of George Monro's Thirty-fifth Regiment, who was carrying letters from Montcalm for Colonel Webb and Lord Loudoun. Montcalm's letters were to arrange for the return of English "officers and prisoners," who had received protection from the French after the incident at Fort William Henry.

In accordance with Montcalm's proposal, about five hundred of the missing soldiers, wives, servants, and sutlers were escorted halfway to Fort Edward the next day by an ample party of four hundred French grenadiers and Canadian volunteers. Monro was on horseback, the wounded Lieutenant Colonel John Young was on a stretcher, and Ezekiel Stevens of Derryfield, New Hampshire, was among those wearing French bandages on his head. He had survived being "tomahawked" and very thoroughly scalped, and wore a hat for the rest of his long life. The procession marched down the road, which was still littered with gruesome evidence of the tragedy. They could not be sure how many had died there. . . .

Montcalm had assured Webb, Loudoun, and the French court that the Indians were to be stopped at Montreal and the rest of their prisoners recovered and returned by way of Louisbourg and Halifax. Montcalm had promised that all the men taken from the Fort William Henry garrison would be returned. . . . All of this was easier said by Montcalm than done by Vaudreuil.

Most of the far-west Indians arrived back at Montreal with their prisoners by August 15, the same day Montcalm's army finished burning Fort William Henry and escorting the five hundred rescued English to Fort Edward. After pitching camp on the green outside Montreal that afternoon, some of the warriors killed, cooked, and ate one of their prisoners within full view of the others as well as the horrified townsmen. This killing, apparently without elaborate preliminary torture, was similar to the earlier fate of three soldiers. . . . In the earlier instance, it is possible that the killing had been done in ignorance of the price that prisoners could fetch in Montreal. This later killing may have been an expensive and deliberate act of defiance, meant to mock and exploit the sensitivities of the French and to initiate negotiations. . . .

Governor Vaudreuil wisely ignored Montcalm's absurd suggestion that the Indians be imprisoned for insubordination. Instead, he scolded the Indians for violating the terms of the capitulation, and then offered them two barrels of brandy per prisoner. The offer was flatly refused. Abbé Picquet recorded an Indian's logical response: "I make war for plunder, scalps, and prisoners. You are satisfied with a fort, and you let your enemy and mine live. I do not want to keep such bad meat for tomorrow. When I kill it, it can no longer attack me." In the course of the next two weeks, Vaudreuil negotiated the release of what he claimed were nearly all the prisoners brought to Montreal, each at an estimated cost to the king of France of 130 livres in goods and thirty bottles of brandy. . . .

For most of the 2308 men who surrendered, and as many as 148 family and camp followers, the "massacre" was the fright of their lives. The only persons reported to have been wounded there were Ezekiel Stevens and two of the French escort. Although all the survivors had reason to believe that the casualties were much higher, 268 soldiers (11.6 percent) did not return. Those soldiers and civilians killed in the "massacre at Fort William Henry" numbered at least 69 (2.8 percent), but could not possibly have exceeded 185 (7.5 percent) people.

The White Indians of Colonial America

JAMES AXTELL

The English, like their French rivals, began their colonizing ventures in North America with a sincere interest in converting the Indians to Christianity and civilization. Nearly all the colonial charters granted by the English monarchs in the seventeenth century assigned the wish to extend the Christian Church and to redeem savage souls as a principal, if not *the* principal, motive for colonization. This desire was grounded in a set of complementary beliefs about "savagism" and "civilization." First, the English held that the Indians, however benighted, were capable of conversion. "It is not the nature of men," they believed, "but the education of men, which make them barbarous and uncivill." Moreover, the English were confident that the Indians would want to be converted once they were exposed to the superior quality of English life. . . .

The second article of the English faith followed from their fundamental belief in the superiority of civilization, namely, that no civilized person in possession of his faculties or free from undue restraint would choose to become an Indian. "For, easy and unconstrained as the savage life is," wrote the Reverend William Smith of Philadelphia, "certainly it could never be put in competition with the blessings of improved life and the light of religion, by any persons who have had the happiness of enjoying, and the capacity of discerning, them."

And yet, by the close of the colonial period, very few if any Indians had been transformed into civilized Englishmen. Most of the Indians who were educated by the English—some contemporaries thought *all* of them—returned to Indian society at the first opportunity to resume their Indian identities. On the other hand, large numbers of Englishmen had chosen to become Indians— by running away from colonial society to join Indian society, by not trying to escape after being captured, or by electing to remain with their Indian

James Axtell, "The White Indians of Colonial America," *William and Mary Quarterly,* 3d ser. XXXII (1975), 17–44. Copyright © 1975 by James Axtell. Reprinted with permission of the author.

captors when treaties of peace periodically afforded them the opportunity to return home.

Perhaps the first colonist to recognize the disparity between the English dream and the American reality was Cadwallader Colden, surveyor-general and member of the king's council of New York. In his *History of the Five Indian Nations of Canada,* published in London in 1747, Colden described the Albany peace treaty between the French and the Iroquois in 1699, when "few of [the French captives] could be persuaded to return" to Canada. Lest his readers attribute this unusual behavior to "the Hardships they had endured in their own Country, under a tyrannical Government and a barren Soil," he quickly added that "the *English* had as much Difficulty to persuade the People, that had been taken Prisoners by the *French Indians,* to leave the *Indian* Manner of living, though no People enjoy more Liberty, and live in greater Plenty, than the common Inhabitants of *New-York* do." Colden, clearly amazed, elaborated:

> No Arguments, no Intreaties, nor Tears of their Friends and Relations, could persuade many of them to leave their new *Indian* Friends and Acquaintance[s]; several of them that were by the Caressings of their Relations persuaded to come Home, in a little Time grew tired of our Manner of living, and run away again to the *Indians,* and ended their Days with them. On the other Hand, *Indian* Children have been carefully educated among the *English,* cloathed and taught, yet, I think, there is not one Instance, that any of these, after they had Liberty to go among their own People, and were come to Age, would remain with the *English,* but returned to their own Nations, and became as fond of the *Indian* Manner of Life as those that knew nothing of a civilized Manner of living. What I now tell of Christian Prisoners among *Indians* [he concluded his history], relates not only to what happened at the Conclusion of this War, but has been found true on many other Occasions.

Colden was not alone. Six years later Benjamin Franklin wondered how it was that

> When an Indian Child has been brought up among us, taught our language and habituated to our Customs, yet if he goes to see his relations and make one Indian Ramble with them, there is no perswading him ever to return. [But] when white persons of either sex have been taken prisoners young by the Indians, and lived a while among them, tho' ransomed by their Friends, and treated with all imaginable tenderness to prevail with them to stay among the English, yet in a Short time they become disgusted with our manner of life, and the care and pains that are necessary to support it, and take the first good Opportunity of escaping again into the Woods, from whence there is no reclaiming them.

In short, "thousands of Europeans are Indians," as Hector de Crèvecoeur put it, "and we have no examples of even one of those Aborigines having from choice become Europeans!"

The English captives who foiled their countrymen's civilized assumptions by becoming Indians differed little from the general colonial population when they were captured. They were ordinary men, women, and children of yeoman stock, Protestants by faith, a variety of nationalities by birth, English by law,

different from their countrymen only in their willingness to risk personal insecurity for the economic opportunities of the frontier. There was no discernible characteristic or pattern of characteristics that differentiated them from
their captive neighbors who eventually rejected Indian life—with one exception. Most of the colonists captured by the Indians and adopted into Indian
families were children of both sexes and young women, often the mothers of
the captive children. They were, as one captivity narrative observed, the "weak
and defenceless."

The pattern of taking women and children for adoption was consistent
throughout the colonial period, but during the first century and one-half of
Indian-white conflict, primarily in New England, it coexisted with a larger
pattern of captivity that included all white colonists, men as well as women
and children. The Canadian Indians who raided New England tended to take
captives more for their ransom value than for adoption. When Mrs. James
Johnson gave birth to a daughter on the trail to Canada, for example, her
captor looked into her makeshift lean-to and "clapped his hands with joy,
crying two monies for me, two monies for me." Although the New England
legislatures occasionally tried to forbid the use of public moneys for "the
Ransoming of Captives," thereby prolonging the Indians' "diabolical kidnapping mode of warfare," ransoms were constantly paid from both public and
private funds. These payments became larger as inflation and the Indians'
savvy increased. . . .

When the long peace in the Middle Atlantic colonies collapsed in 1753,
the Indians of Pennsylvania, southern New York, and the Ohio country had
no Quebec or Montreal in which to sell their human chattels to compassionate
French families or anxious English relatives. For this and other reasons they
captured English settlers largely to replace members of their own families
who had died, often from English musketballs or imported diseases. Consequently, women and children—the "weak and defenceless"—were the prime
targets of Indian raids.

According to the pattern of warfare in the Pennsylvania theater, the Indians usually stopped at a French fort with their prisoners before proceeding
to their own villages. A young French soldier captured by the English reported
that at Fort Duquesne there were "a great number of English Prisoners," the
older of whom "they are constantly sending . . . away to Montreal" as prisoners of war, "but that the Indians keep many of the Prisoners amongst them,
chiefly young People whom they adopt and bring up in their own way." . . .

The Indians obviously chose their captives carefully so as to maximize
the chances of acculturating them to Indian life. To judge by the results, their
methods were hard to fault. Even when the English held the upper hand
militarily, they were often embarrassed by the Indians' educational power. On
November 12, 1764, at his camp on the Muskingum, [Col. Henry] Bouquet
lectured the Shawnees who had not delivered all their captives: "As you are
now going to Collect all our *Flesh,* and *Blood,* . . . I desire that you will use
them with Tenderness, and look upon them as Brothers, and no longer as
Captives." The utter gratuitousness of his remark was reflected—no doubt
purposely—in the Shawnee speech when the Indians delivered their captives

the following spring at Fort Pitt. "Father—Here is your *Flesh,* and *Blood* .. . they have been all tied to us by Adoption, although we now deliver them up to you. We will always look upon them as Relations, whenever the *Great Spirit* is pleased that we may visit them ... Father—we have taken as much Care of these Prisoners, as if they were [our] own Flesh, and blood; they are become unacquainted with your Customs, and manners, and therefore, Father we request you will use them tender, and kindly, which will be a means of inducing them to live contentedly with you."

The Indians spoke the truth and the English knew it. Three days after his speech to the Shawnees, Bouquet had advised Lt.-Gov. Francis Fauquier of Virginia that the returning captives "ought to be treated by their Relations with Tenderness and Humanity, till Time and Reason make them forget their unnatural Attachments, but unless they are closely watch'd," he admitted, "they will certainly return to the Barbarians." And indeed they would have, for during a half-century of conflict captives had been returned who, like many of the Ohio prisoners, responded only to Indian names, spoke only Indian dialects, felt comfortable only in Indian clothes, and in general regarded their white saviors as barbarians and their deliverance as captivity. Had they not been compelled to return to English society by militarily enforced peace treaties, the ranks of the white Indians would have been greatly enlarged.

From the moment the Indians surrendered their English prisoners, the colonists faced a series of difficult problems. The first was the problem of getting the prisoners to remain with the English. When Bouquet sent the first group of restored captives to Fort Pitt, he ordered his officers there that "they are to be closely watched and well Secured" because "most of them, particularly those who have been a long time among the Indians, will take the first Opportunity to run away." The young children especially were "so completely savage that they were brought to the camp tied hand and foot." Fourteen-year-old John McCullough, who had lived with the Indians for "eight years, four months, and sixteen days" (by his parents' reckoning), had his legs tied "under the horses belly" and his arms tied behind his back with his father's garters, but to no avail. He escaped under the cover of night and returned to his Indian family for a year before he was finally carried to Fort Pitt under "strong guard." "Having been accustomed to look upon the Indians as the only connexions they had, having been tenderly treated by them, and speaking their language," explained the Reverend William Smith, the historian of Bouquet's expedition, "it is no wonder that [the children] considered their new state in the light of a captivity, and parted from the savages with tears."

Children were not the only reluctant freedmen. "Several women eloped in the night, and ran off to join their Indian friends." Among them undoubtedly were some of the English women who had married Indian men and borne them children, and then had been forced by the English victory either to return with their mixed-blood children to a country of strangers, full of prejudice against Indians, or to risk escaping under English guns to their husbands and adopted culture. For Bouquet had "reduced the Shawanese and Delawares etc. to the most Humiliating Terms of Peace," boasted Gen. Thomas Gage. "He has Obliged them to deliver up even their Own Children born of white women." But even the victorious soldier could understand the dilemma into which these women had been pushed. When Bouquet was informed that the English wife of an Indian chief had eloped in the night with her husband and children, he "requested that no pursuit should be made, as she was happier with her Chief than she would be if restored to her home."

Although most of the returned captives did not try to escape, the emotional torment caused by the separation from their adopted families deeply impressed the colonists. The Indians "delivered up their beloved captives with the utmost reluctance; shed torrents of tears over them, recommending them to the care and protection of the commanding officer." One young woman "cryed and roared when asked to come and begged to Stay a little longer." "Some, who could not make their escape, clung to their savage acquaintance at parting, and continued many days in bitter lamentations, even refusing sustenance." Children "cried as if they should die when they were presented to us." With only small exaggeration an observer on the Muskingum could report that "every captive left the Indians with regret."

Another problem encountered by the English was the difficulty of communicating with the returned captives, a great many of whom had replaced their knowledge of English with an Algonquian or Iroquoian dialect and their baptismal names with Indian or hybrid ones. This immediately raised another problem—that of restoring the captives to their relatives. Sir William Johnson, the superintendent of Indian affairs, "thought it best to advertise them [in the newspapers] immediately, but I believe it will be verry difficult to find the Freinds of some of them, as they are ignorant of their own Names, or former places of abode, nay cant speak a word of any language but Indian." The only recourse the English had in such instances was to describe them "more particularly . . . as to their features, Complexion etc. That by the Publication of Such descriptions their Relations, parents or friends may hereafter know and Claim them."

But if several colonial observers were right, a description of the captives' physiognomy was of little help after they had been with the Indians for any length of time. Peter Kalm's foreign eye found it difficult to distinguish European captives from their captors, "except by their color, which is somewhat whiter than that of the Indians," but many colonists could see little or no difference. . . .

The final English problem was perhaps the most embarrassing in its manifestations, and certainly was so in its implications. For many Indians who had adopted white captives, the return of their "own Flesh, and Blood" to the English was unendurable. At the earliest opportunity, after bitter memories of the wars had faded on both sides, they journeyed through the English settlements to visit their estranged children, just as the Shawnee speaker had promised Bouquet they would. Jonathan Hoyt's Indian father visited him so often in Deerfield, sometimes bringing his captive sister, that Hoyt had to petition the Massachusetts General Court for reimbursement for their support. In 1760 Sir William Johnson reported that a Canadian Indian "has been since down to Schenectady to visit one Newkirk of that place, who was some years a Prisoner in his house, and sent home about a year ago with this Indians Sister, who came with her Brother now purely to see Said Newkirk whom she calls her Son and is verry fond of."

Obviously the feelings were mutual. Elizabeth Gilbert, adopted at the age of twelve, "always retained an affection toward John Huston, her Indian father (as she called him), for she remembered his kindness to her when in captivity." . . . The bond of affection that had grown in the Indian villages was clearly not an attachment that the English could dismiss as "unnatural."

Children who had been raised by Indian parents from infancy could be excused perhaps for their unwillingness to return, but the adults who displayed a similar reluctance, especially the women who had married Indian men and borne them children, drew another reaction. "For the honour of humanity," wrote William Smith, "we would suppose those persons to have been of the lowest rank, either bred up in ignorance and distressing penury, or who had lived so long with the Indians as to forget all their former connections. For, easy and unconstrained as the savage life is, certainly it could never be put in competition with the blessings of improved life and the light of religion, by any persons who have had the happiness of enjoying, and the capacity of discerning, them." If Smith was struck by the contrast between the visible impact of Indian education and his own cultural assumptions, he never said so.

To find a satisfactory explanation for the extraordinary drawing power of Indian culture, we should begin where the colonists themselves first came under its sway—on the trail to Indian country. For although the Indians were known for their patience, they wasted no time in beginning the educational process that would transform their hostile or fearful white captives into affectionate Indian relatives.

Perhaps the first transaction after the Indians had selected their prisoners and hurried them into cover was to replace their hard-heeled shoes with the footwear of the forest—moccasins. These were universally approved by the prisoners, who admitted that they traveled with "abundant more ease" than before. And on more than one occasion the knee-deep snows of northern New England forced the Indians to make snowshoes for their prisoners in order to maintain their pace of twenty-five to thirty miles a day. Such an introduction to the superby adapted technology of the Indians alone would not convert the English, but it was a beginning.

The lack of substantial food supplies forced the captives to accommodate their stomachs as best they could to Indian trail fare, which ranged from nuts, berries, roots, and parched corn to beaver guts, horseflank, and semi-raw venison and moose, eaten without the customary English accompaniments of bread or salt. When there was nothing to eat, the Indians would "gird up their loins with a string," a technique that at least one captive found "very useful" when applied to himself. Although their food was often "unsavory" and in short supply, the Indians always shared it equally with the captives, who, being hungry, "relished [it] very well." . . .

. . . Many redeemed prisoners made a point of insisting that, although they had been completely powerless in captivity, the Indians had never affronted them sexually. Thomas Ridout testified that "during the whole of the time I was with the Indians I never once witnessed an indecent or improper action amongst any of the Indians, whether young or old." Even William Smith admitted that "from very enquiry that has been made, it appears—that no woman thus saved is preserved from base motives, or need fear the violation of her honour." If there had been the least exception, we can be sure that this champion of civilization would have made the most of it.

One reason for the Indians' lack of sexual interest in their female captives was perhaps aesthetic, for the New England Indians, at least, esteemed black the color of beauty. A more fundamental reason derived from the main purpose of taking captives, which was to secure new members for their families and clans. Under the Indians' strong incest taboos, no warrior would attempt to violate his future sister or cousin. "Were he to indulge himself with a captive taken in war, and much more were he to offer violence in order to gratify his lust, he would incur indelible disgrace." Indeed, the taboo seems to have extended to the whole tribe. . . .

Captive testimony also chipped away at the stereotype of the Indians' cruelty. When Mrs. Isabella M'Coy was taken from Epsom, New Hampshire, in 1747, her neighbors later remembered that "she did indeed find the journey [to Canada] fatiguing, and her fare scanty and precarious. But in her treatment from the Indians, she experienced a very agreeable disappointment. The kindness she received from them was far greater than she had expected from those who were so often distinguished for their cruelties." More frequent still was recognition of the Indians' kindness to children. . . .

When the returning war parties approached the first Indian village, the educational process took on a new complexion. As one captive explained, "whenever the warriors return from an excursion against an enemy, their return to the tribe or village must be designated by war-like ceremonial; the captives or spoils, which may happen to crown their valor, must be conducted in a triumphant form, and decorated to every possible advantage." Accordingly, the cheek, chin, and forehead of every captive were painted with traditional dashes of vermilion mixed with bear's grease. Belts of wampum were hung around their necks, Indian clothes were substituted for English, and the men and boys had their hair plucked or shaved in Indian fashion. The physical transformation was so effective, said a twenty-six-year-old soldier, "that I began to think I was an Indian." Younger captives were less aware of the small distance between role-playing and real acceptance of the Indian lifestyle. When her captor dressed Frances Slocum, not yet five years old, in "beautiful wampum beads," she remembered at the end of a long and happy life as an Indian that he "made me look, as I thought, very fine. I was much pleased with the beautiful wampum."

The prisoners were then introduced to a "new school" of song and dance. "Little did we expect," remarked an English woman, "that the accomplishment of dancing would ever be taught us, by the savages. But the war dance must now be held; and every prisoner that could move must take its awkward steps. The figure consisted of circular motion round the fire; each sang his own music, and the best dancer was the one most violent in motion." To prepare for the event each captive had rehearsed a short Indian song on the trail. Mrs. Johnson recalled many years later that her song was "danna witchee natchepung; my son's was nar wiscumpton." Nehemiah How could not master the Indian pronunciation, so he was allowed to sing in English "I don't know where I go." In view of the Indians' strong sense of ceremonial propriety, it is small wonder that one captive thought that they "Seem[e]d to be Very much a mind I Should git it perfect."

Upon entering the village the Indians let forth with some distinctive music of their own. "When we came near the main Body of the Enemy," wrote Thomas Brown, a captive soldier from Fort William Henry, "the *Indians* made a Live-Shout, as they call it when they bring in a Prisoner alive (different from the Shout they make when they bring in Scalps, which they call a Dead-Shout)." According to another soldier, "their Voices are so sharp, shrill, loud and deep, that when they join together after one has made his Cry, it makes a most dreadful and horrible Noise, that stupifies the very Senses," a noise that naturally frightened many captives until they learned that it was not their death knell.

They had good reason to think that their end was near when the whole village turned out to form a gauntlet from the entrance to the center of the village and their captors ordered them to run through it. With ax handles, tomahawks, hoop poles, clubs, and switches the Indians flogged the racing captives as if to beat the whiteness out of them. In most villages, significantly, "it was only the more elderly People both Male and Female wh[ic]h rece[iv]ed this Useage—the young prisoners of Both Sexes Escaped without it" or were rescued from any serious harm by one or more villagers, perhaps indicating the Indian perception of the captives' various educability. When ten-year-old John Brickell was knocked down by the blows of his Seneca captors, "a very big Indian came up, and threw the company off me, and took me by the arm, and led me along through the lines with such rapidity that I scarcely touched the ground, and was not once struck after he took me." . . .

If the first rite tried to beat the whiteness out of the captives, the second tried to wash it out. James Smith's experience was typical.

> The old chief, holding me by the hand, made a long speech, very loud, and when he had done he handed me to three squaws, who led me by the hand down the bank into the river until the water was up to our middle. The squaws then made signs to me to plunge myself into the water, but I did not understand them. I thought that the result of the council was that I should be drowned, and that these young ladies were to be the executioners. They all laid violent hold of me, and I for some time opposed them with all my might, which occasioned loud laughter by the multitude that were on the bank of the river. At length one of the squaws made out to speak a little English (for I believe they began to be afraid of me) and said, "No hurt you." On this I gave myself up to their ladyships, who were as good as their word; for though they plunged me under water and washed and rubbed me severely, yet I could not say they hurt me much.

More than one captive had to receive similar assurance, but their worst fears were being laid to rest.

Symbolically purged of their whiteness by their Indian baptism, the initiates were dressed in new Indian clothes and decorated with feathers, jewelry, and paint. Then, with great solemnity, the village gathered around the council fire, where after a "profound silence" one of the chiefs spoke. Even a hostile captive, Zadock Steele, had to admit that although he could not understand the language spoken, he could "plainly discover a great share of native eloquence." ...

A more charitable account was given by James Smith, who through an interpreter was addressed in the following words:

> My son, you are now flesh of our flesh and bone of our bone. By the ceremony that was performed this day, every drop of white blood was washed out of your veins. You are taken into the Caughnewaga [French Mohawk] nation and initiated into a war-like tribe. You are adopted into a great family and now received with great seriousness and solemnity in the room and place of a great man. After what has passed this day you are now one of us by an old strong law and custom. My son, you have now nothing to fear. We are now under the same obligations to love, support and defend you that we are to love and to defend one another. Therefore you are to consider yourself as one of our people.

"At this time," admitted the eighteen-year-old Smith, "I did not believe this fine speech, especially that of the white blood being washed out of me; but since that time I have found that there was much sincerity in said speech; for from that day I never knew them to make any distinction between me and themselves in any respect whatever until I left them ... we all shared one fate." It is a chord that sounds through nearly every captvity narrative: "They treated me ... in every way as one of themselves."

When the adoption ceremony had ended, the captive was taken to the wigwam of his new family, who greeted him with a "most dismal howling, crying bitterly, and wringing their hands in all agonies of grief for a deceased relative." "The higher in favour the adopted Prisoners [were] to be placed, the greater Lamentation [was] made over them." After a threnodic memorial to the lost member, which may have "added to the Terror of the Captives," who "imagined it to be no other than a Prelude to inevitable Destruction," the mood suddenly shifted. "I never saw ... such hug[g]ing and kissing from the women and crying for joy," exclaimed one young recipient. Then an interpreter introduced each member of the new family— in one case "from brother to seventh cousins"—and "they came to me one after another," said another captive, "and shook me by the hand, in token that they considered me to stand in the same relationship to them as the one in whose stead I was placed."

Most young captives assumed the places of Indian sons and daughters, but occasionally the match was not exact. Mary Jemison replaced a brother who had been killed in "Washington's war," while twenty-six-year-old Titus King assumed the unlikely role of a grandfather. Although their sex and age may not always have corresponded, the adopted captives succeeded to all the deceased's rights and obligations—the same dignities, honors, and often the same names. ...

When the prisoners had been introduced to all their new relatives and neighbors, the Indians proceeded to shower them with gifts. . . .

Treatment such as this—and it was almost universal—left an indelible mark on every captive, whether or not they eventually returned to English society. Although captives like Mrs. Johnson found their adoption an "unnatural situation," they had to defend the humanity of the practice. "Those who have profited by refinement and education," she argued, "ought to abate part of the prejudice, which prompts them to look with an eye of censure on this untutored race . . . Do they ever adopt an enemy," she asked, "and salute him by the tender name of brother?" It is not difficult to imagine what effect such feelings must have had in younger people less habituated to English culture, especially those who had lost their own parents.

The formalities, purgations, and initiations were now completed. Only one thing remained for the Indians: by their daily example and instruction to "make an Indian of you," as the Delawares told John Brickell. This required a steady union of two things: the willingness and gratitude of the captives, and the consistent love and trust of the Indians. By the extraordinary ceremonies through which they had passed, most captives had had their worst fears allayed. From a state of apprehension or even terror they had suddenly emerged with their persons intact and a solemn invitation to begin a new life, as full of love, challenge, and satisfaction as any they had knwon. For "when [the Indians] once determine to give life, they give every thing with it, which, in their apprehension, belongs to it." The sudden release from anxiety into a realm of affirmative possibility must have disposed many captives to accept the Indian way of life.

According to the adopted colonists who recounted the stories of their new lives, Indian life was more than capable of claiming their respect and allegiance, even if they eventually returned to English society. The first indication that the Indians were serious in their professions of equality came when the adopted captives were given freedom of movement within and without the Indian villages. Naturally, the degree of freedom and its timing depended on the captive's willingness to enter into the spirit of Indian life. . . .

The presence of other white prisoners complicated the trust relationship somewhat. Captives who were previously known to each other, especially from the same family, were not always allowed to converse "much together, as [the Indians] imagined they would remember their former Situation, and become less contented with their present Manner of Life." Benjamin Peart, for example, was allowed the frequent company of "Two white Men who had been taken Prisoners, the one from Susquehanna, the other from Minisinks, both in Pennsylvania," even though he was a Pennsylvanian himself. But when he met his captive wife and infant son by chance at Fort Niagara, the Indians "separated them again the same Day, and took [his] Wife about Four Miles Distance." . . .

Once the captives had earned the basic trust of their Indian families, nothing in Indian life was denied them. When they reached the appropriate age, the Indians offered to find them suitable marriage partners. Understandably, some of the older captives balked at this, sensing that it was calculated to bind them with marital ties to a culture they were otherwise hesitant to accept. . . .

. . . [T]he weight of evidence suggests that marriage was not compulsory for the captives, and common sense tells us that any form of compulsion would have defeated the Indians' purpose in trying to persuade the captives to adopt their way of life. . . .

The captives' social equality was also demonstrated by their being asked to share in the affairs of war and peace, matters of supreme importance to Indian society. When the Senecas who had adopted Thomas Peart decided to "make a War Excursion," they asked him to go with them. But since he was in no mood—and no physical condition—to play the Indian, "he determinately refused them, and was therefore left at Home with the Family." The young Englishman who became Old White Chief was far more eager to defend his new culture, but his origins somewhat limited his military activity. "When I grew to manhood," he recalled, "I went with them [his Iroquois kinsmen] on the warpath against the white settlers, lest by some unlucky accident I might be recognized and claimed by former friends." . . .

Just after Thomas Ridout was captured on the Ohio, he was surprised to meet an English-speaking "white man, about twenty-two years of age, who had been taken prisoner when a lad and had been adopted, and now was a chief among the Shawanese." He need not have been surprised, for there were many more like him. John Tarbell, the man who visited his Groton relatives in Indian dress, was not only "one of the wealthiest" of the Caughnawagas but "the eldest chief and chief speaker of the tribe." Timothy Rice, formerly of Westborough, Massachusetts, was also made one of the clan chiefs at Caughnawaga, partly by inheritance from his Indian father but largely for "his own Super[io]r Talents" and "war-like Spirit for which he was much celebrated." . . .

. . . In public office as in every sphere of Indian life, the English captives found that the color of their skin was unimportant; only their talent and their inclination of heart mattered.

Understandably, neither their skill nor their loyalty was left to chance. From the moment the captives, especially the young ones, came under their charge, the Indians made a concerted effort to inculcate in them Indian habits of mind and body. If the captives could be taught to think, act, and react like Indians, they would effectively cease to be English and would assume an Indian identity. This was the Indians' goal, toward which they bent every effort in the weeks and months that followed their formal adoption of the white captives.

The educational character of Indian society was recognized by even the most inveterately English captives. Titus King, a twenty-six-year-old New England soldier, spent a year with the Canadian Indians at St. Francis trying—unsuccessfully—to undo their education of "Eight or ten young [English] Children." What "an awfull School this [is] for Children," he wrote. "When We See how Quick they will Fall in with the Indians ways, nothing Seems to be more takeing in Six months time they Forsake Father and mother Forgit thir own Land Refuess to Speak there own toungue and Seemin[g]ly be Holley Swollowed up with the Indians." ...

The final and most difficult step in the captives' transition from English to Indian was to acquire the ability to think as Indians, to share unconsciously the values, beliefs, and standards of Indian culture. From an English perspective, this should have been nearly an impossible task for civilized people because they perceived Indian culture as immoral and irreligious and totally antithetical to the civilized life they had known, however briefly. "Certainly," William Smith assumed, "it could never be put in competition with the blessings of improved life and the light of religion." But many captives soon discovered that the English had no monopoly on virtue and that in many ways the Indians were morally superior to the English, more Christian than the Christians. . . .

. . . To the acute discomfort of the colonists, more than one captive maintained that the Indians were a "far more moral race than the whites."

❧ F U R T H E R   R E A D I N G

Fred Anderson, *A People's Army: Massachusetts Soldiers and Society in the Seven Years' War* (1984)

James Axtell, *The Invasion Within: The Contest of Cultures in Colonial North America* (1985)

Francis Jennings, *Empire of Fortune: Crowns, Colonies and Tribes in the Seven Years War in America* (1988)

Richard R. Johnson, *Adjustment to Empire: The New England Colonies, 1675–1715* (1981)

Michael Kammen, *Empire and Interest: The American Colonies and the Politics of Mercantilism* (1970)

Alison Olson, "The Board of Trade and London-American Interest Groups in the Eighteenth Century," *Journal of Imperial and Commonwealth History* 8 (1980), 33–50

CHAPTER

14

The Sum of the

Colonial Experience

๛

John Winthrop told the passengers on the Arbella *bound for Massachusetts Bay in
1630 that their enterprise would be "as a city set on a hill," a beacon for Europe.
Ever since Winthrop uttered those words, historians have debated the issue of American exceptionalism. Is American culture unique? How much does it reflect the successful transplantation of Old World attitudes and practices? What was the impact
of the American environment, especially the leveling effects of the wide availability
of land, on ideas developed in Europe, where land was scarce and labor abundant?
How important was the importation into America of such a great variety of ethnic
and religious allegiances? Did they all melt into a new mixture, or do their separate attempts to maintain their own ways constitute the real story? Finally, what
role did slavery, the most unequal of institutions, play?*

*In 1831–1832 the liberal French aristocrat Alexis de Tocqueville toured the
young nation and wrote a portrait of this new phenomenon, the American. His account depicted Americans as restless, energetic, and obsessed with equality. In 1893
historian Frederick Jackson Turner penned one of the most influential essays in
American history, arguing that America was indeed unique and that the constant
repetition of the frontier experience as the line of settlement moved west had shaped
the nation's character. Turner concluded that inherited patterns and inherited status
alike broke down on the frontier. As society was reconstructed after this breakdown,
it took a new form: egalitarian, optimistic, anti-intellectual, and destructive of the
environment. Both of these influential portraits argued that the colonization of
America had indeed produced a new, modern way of life.*

*Historians have debated this issue ever since. In one form or another, these
questions, or assumptions about them, underlie many of the essays in this collection.*

๛ D O C U M E N T S

Letters and diaries from the colonial period demonstrate an abiding interest in the
defining characteristics of American culture and of their sources. Contemporaries
often wrote to refute the charge that they had become less cultured or civilized than

their European counterparts, and travelers scrutinized the communities through which they passed for signs of change. Bostonian Sarah Kemble Knight kept a journal, excerpted in the first document, of her trip to New York in 1704; in it she recorded the diversity she found. Dr. Alexander Hamilton of Maryland traveled northward in 1744. His trip put him in close contact with people of all sorts, sometimes in the same bed at an inn. In the second selection he gives a particularly acute picture of the ways in which wealth had come to supply some of the place of inherited gentility in American society. At the conclusion of his journey, he, too, commented on the variety he had seen. In the third document Pelatiah Webster, who sailed from Philadelphia to Charleston, South Carolina, in 1765, comments on this very different scene with great curiosity. The journal of Janet Schaw, who voyaged from Scotland to Wilmington, North Carolina, in 1774, differs from the others, as she ridicules the social pretensions of the locals. The fourth document features her description of a Wilmington version of the Boston Tea Party.

Many observers were skeptical that the disparate American provinces ever could submerge their differences and unite. It was Benjamin Franklin who first proposed, in 1754, that the colonies should adopt a formal union. The setting for Franklin's proposal was Albany, New York, where delegates of nine of the thirteen colonies had come together to meet with representatives of the Iroquois League. Franklin's Albany Plan of Union rounds out the documentary selections.

Sarah Kemble Knight on Dutch and English in New York, 1704

The City of New York is a pleasant, well compacted place, situated on a Commodious River which is a fine harbour for shipping. The Buildings Brick Generally, very stately and high, though not altogether like ours in Boston. The Bricks in some of the Houses are of divers Colours and laid in Checkers, being glazed look very agreeable. The inside of them are neat to admiration, the wooden work, for only the walls are plastered, and the Sumers [main beam] and Girt [girder] are planed and kept very white scourr'd as so is all the partitions if made of Boards. The fire places have no Jambs (as ours have) But the Backs run flush with the walls, and the Hearth is of Tiles and is as far out into the Room at the Ends as before the fire, which is Generally Five foot in the Low'r rooms, and the piece over where the mantle tree should be is made as ours with Joiners' work, and as I suppose is fasten'd to iron rods inside. The House where the Vendue was, had Chimney Corners like ours, and they and the hearths were laid with the finest tile that I ever see, and the stair cases laid all with white tile which is ever clean, and so are the walls of the Kitchen which had a Brick floor. They were making Great preparations to Receive their Governor, Lord Cornbury from the Jerseys, and for that End raised the militia to Guard him on shore to the fort.

They are Generally of the Church of England and have a New England Gentleman for their minister, and a very fine church set out with all Customary requisites. There are also a Dutch and Divers Conventicles as they call

---

Some of the spelling in this document has been modernized.

them, viz. Baptist, Quakers, &c. They are not strict in keeping the Sabbath as in Boston and other places where I had been, But seem to deal with great exactness as far as I see or Deal with. They are sociable to one another and Courteous and Civil to strangers and fare well in their houses. The English go very fashionable in their dress. But the Dutch, especially the middling sort, differ from our women, in their habit go loose, wear French muches which are like a Cap and a head band in one, leaving their ears bare, which are set out with Jewels of a large size and many in number. And their fingers hoop't with Rings, some with large stones in them of many Colours as were their pendants in their ears, which You should see very old women wear as well as Young.

They have Vendues very frequently and make their Earnings very well by them, for they treat with good Liquor Liberally, and the Customers Drink as Liberally and Generally pay for't as well, by paying for that which they Bid up Briskly for, after the sack has gone plentifully about, tho' sometimes good penny worths are got there. Their Diversions in the Winter is Riding Sleighs about three or four Miles out of Town, where they have Houses of entertainment at a place called the Bowery, and some go to friends' Houses who handsomely treat them. . . .

. . . [A]fter about a fortnight's stay there I left New-York with no Little regret, and Thursday, Dec. 21, set out for New Haven with my Kinsman Trowbridge, and the man that waited on me about one afternoon, and about three come to half-way house about ten miles out of town, where we Baited and went forward, and about 5 come to Spitting Devil, Else Kings bridge, where they pay three pence for passing over with a horse, which the man that keeps the Gate set up at the end of the Bridge receives.

We hoped to reach the french town and Lodge there that night, but unhappily lost our way about four miles short, and being overtaken by a great storm of wind and snow which set full in our faces about dark, we were very uneasy. But meeting one Gardner who lived in a Cottage thereabout, offered us his fire to set by, having but one poor Bed, and his wife not well, &c. or he would go to a House with us, where he thought we might be better accommodated—thither we went, But a surly old she Creature, not worthy the name of woman, who would hardly let us go into her Door, though the weather was so stormy none but she would have turned out a Dog. But her son whose name was gallop, who lived Just by Invited us to his house and shewed me two pair of stairs, viz. one up the loft and the other up the Bed, which was as hard as it was high, and warmed it with a hot stone at the feet. I lay very uncomfortably, insomuch that I was so very cold and sick I was forced to call them up to give me something to warm me. They had nothing but milk in the house, which they Boiled, and to make it better sweetened with molasses, which I not knowing or thinking oft till it was down and coming up again which it did in so plentiful a manner that my host was soon paid double for his portion, and that in specie. But I believe it did me service in Clearing my stomach. So after this sick and weary night at East Chester, (a very miserable poor place,) the weather being now fair, Friday the 22d Dec. we set out for New Rochell, where being come we had good

Entertainment and Recruited ourselves very well. This is a very pretty place well compact, and good handsome houses, Clean, good and passable Roads, and situated on a Navigable River, abundance of land well fined and Cleared all along as we passed, which caused in me a Love to the place, which I could have been content to live in it. Here we Rid over a Bridge made of one entire stone of such a Breadth that a cart might pass with safety, and to spare—it lay over a passage cut through a Rock to convey water to a mill not far off. Here are three fine Taverns within call of each other, very good provision for Travelers. . . .

Dr. Alexander Hamilton Surveys the Variety
of Pennsylvania, 1744

. . . The lower ferry of Susquehanna, which I crossed, is above a mile broad. It is kept by a little old man whom I found att vittles with his wife and family upon a homely dish of fish without any kind of sauce. They desired me to eat, but I told them I had no stomach. They had no cloth upon the table, and their mess was in a dirty, deep, wooden dish which they evacuated with their hands, cramming down skins, scales, and all. They used neither knife, fork, spoon, plate, or napkin because, I suppose, they had none to use. I looked upon this as a picture of that primitive simplicity practiced by our forefathers long before the mechanic arts had supplyed them with instruments for the luxury and elegance of life. I drank some of their syder, which was very good, and crossed the ferry in company with a certain Scots-Irish man by name Thomas Quiet. The land about Susquehanna is pritty high and woody, and the channell of the river rockey.

Mr. Quiet rid a little scrub bay mare which he said was sick and ailing and could not carry him, and therefor he 'lighted every half mile and ran a couple of miles att a footman's pace to spell the poor beast (as he termed it). He informed me he lived att Monocosy and had been out three weeks in quest of his creatures (horses), four of which had strayed from his plantation. I condoled his loss and asked him what his mare's distemper was, resolving to prescribe for her, but all that I could gett out of him was that the poor silly beast had choaked herself in eating her oats; so I told him that if she was choaked, she was past my art to recover.

This fellow, I observed, had a particular down hanging look which made me suspect he was one of our New Light biggots. I guessed right, for he introduced a discourse concerning Whitfield and inlarged pritty much and with some warmth upon the doctrines of that apostle, speaking much in his praise. I took upon me, in a ludicrous manner, to impungn some of his doctrines, which, by degrees, put Mr. Quiet in a passion. He told me flatly that I was damnd without redemption. I replyed that I thought his name and behaviour were very incongruous and desired him to change it with all speed, for it was very impropper that such an angry, turbulent mortall as he should be called by the name of Thomas Quiet.

Principio Iron Works—North East

In the height of this fool's passion, I overtook one Mr. B[axte]r, a proprietor in the iron works there, and, after mutual salutation, the topic of discourse turned from religious controversy to politicks; so putting on a little faster, we left this inflammed bigot and his sick mare behind. This gentleman accompanied me to North East and gave me directions as to the road.

Elk Ferry

I crossed Elk Ferry att 3 in the afternoon. One of the ferry men, a young fellow, plyed his tongue much faster than his oar. He characterized some of the chief dwellers in the neighbourhood, particularly some young merchants, my countrymen, for whom he had had the honour to stand pimp in their amours. He let me know that he understood some scraps of Latin and repeated a few hexameter lines out of Lilly's Grammar. He told me of a clever fellow of his name who had composed a book for which he would give all the money he was master of to have the pleasure of reading it. I asked him who this name sake of his was. He replied it was one Terence, and, to be sure, he must have been an arch dog, for he never knew one of the name but he was remarkable for his parts.

Bohemia

Thus entertained, I got over the ferry and rid to Bohemia, and calling att the mannor house there, I found no body att home. I met here a reverend parson who was somewhat inquisitive as to where I came from and the news, but I was not very communicative. I understood afterwards it was Parson W[y]e.

Bohemia Ferry

I crossed Bohemia Ferry and lodged att the ferry house. The landlord's name I cannot remember, but he seemed to be a man of tollerable parts for one in his station. Our conversation run chiefly upon religion. He gave me a short account of the spirit of enthusiasm that had lately possessed the inhabitants of the forrests there and informed me that it had been a common practise for companys of 20 or 30 hair brained fanaticks to ride thro' the woods singing of psalms. I went to bed att 9 att night; my landlord, his wife, daughters, and I lay all in one room.

Saturday, June 2d. In the morning there was a clear sky over head but a foggy horizon and the wind att south, which presaging heat, I set out very early.

Sassafrax Ferry

I took the road to Newtown upon Chester River, crossed Sassafrax Ferry att 7 o'clock in the morning, where I found a great concourse of people att a fair. The roads here are exceeding good and even, but dusty in the summer and deep in the winter season. The day proved very hot. I encountered no company, and I went three or four miles out of my way.

Newtown

I reached Newtown att 12 o'clock and put up att Dougherty's, a publick house there. I was scarce arrived when I met severall of my acquaintance. I dined with Dr. Anderson and spent the rest of the day in a sauntering manner. The northeren post arrived att night. I read the papers but found nothing of consequence in them; so after some comicall chat with my landlord, I went to bed att eleven o'clock att night.

Sunday, June 3d. I stayed all this day att Newtown and breakfasted with Th. Clay, where I met with one W———b, a man of the law, to appearance a civil, good natured man but set up for a kind of connoiseur in many things. I went to visit some friends and dined att the taverne where I was entertaind by the tricks of a female baboon in the yard. This lady had more attendants and hangers on att her levee than the best person (of quality as I may say) in town. She was very fond of the compliments and company of the men and boys but expressed in her gestures an utter aversion att women and girls, especially negroes of that sex—the lady herself being of a black complexion; yet she did not att all affect her country women.

Att night I was treated by Captain Binning of Boston with a bowl of lemmon punch. He gave me letters for his relations att Boston. Whiele we put about the bowl, a deal of comicall discourse pass'd in which the landlord, a man of a particular talent att telling comic storys, bore the chief part.

Monday, June 4th. The morning being clear and somewhat cool, I got up before 5 a'clock and soon mounted horse. I had a solitary route to Bohemia and went very much out of my way by being too particular and nice in observing directions.

Sassafrax and Bohemia Ferries

I reached Mr. Alexander's house on the mannor att 12 o'clock. There I stayed and dined and drank tea with Miss C[ours]ey. After some talk and laugh, I took my leave att 5 a'clock designing 12 miles farther to one Vanbibber's that keeps a house upon the Newcastle road, but instead of going there, I went out of my way and lay att one Hollingsworth's att the head of Elk.

Head of Elk

There is a great marsh upon the left hand of his house, which I passed in the night, thro the middle of which runs Elk. The multitude of fire flys glittering in the dark upon the surface of this marshe makes it appear like a great plain scattered over with spangles.

In this part of the country I found they chiefly cultivated British grain, as wheat, barley, and oats. They raise, too, a great deal of flax, and in every house here the women have two or three spinning wheels a going. The roads up this way are tollerably levell but, in some places, stonny. After a light supper I went to bed att 10 a'clock.

Pensylvania—Newcastle

Tuesday, June 5th. I took horse a little after 5 in the morning, and after a solitary ride thro stonny, unequall road, where the country people stared att me like sheep when I enquired of them the way, I arrived att Newcastle upon Delaware att 9 a'clock in the morning and baited my horses att one Curtis's att the Sign of the Indian King, a good house of entertainment.

This town stands upon stonny ground just upon the water, there being from thence a large prospect eastward towards the Bay of Delaware and the province of the Jerseys. The houses are chiefly brick, built after the Dutch modell, the town having been originally founded and inhabited by the Dutch when it belonged to New York government. It consists chiefly of one great street which makes an elbow att right angles. A great many of the houses are old and crazy. There is in the town two publick buildings, viz., a court house and church.

Att Curtis's I met company going to Philadelphia and was pleased att it, being my self an utter stranger to the roads. This company consisted of three men: Thomas Howard, Timothy Smith, and William Morison. I treated them with some lemmon punch and desired the favour of their company. They readily granted my request and stayed some time for me till I had eat breakfast. Smith, in his hat and coat, had the appearance of a Quaker, but his discourse was purged of thee's and thou's tho his delivery seemed to be solemn and slow paced. Howard was a talkative man, abounding with words and profuse in compliments which were generally blunt and came out in an awkward manner. He bestowed much panegyrick upon his own behaviour and conduct.

Morison (who, I understood, had been att the Land Office in Annapolis enquiring about a title he had to some land in Maryland) was a very rough spun, forward, clownish blade, much addicted to swearing, att the same time desirous to pass for a gentleman; notwithstanding which ambition, the conscientiousness of his naturall boorishness obliged him frequently to frame ill tim'd apologys for his misbehaviour, which he termed frankness and freeness. It was often, "Damn me, gentlemen, excuse me; I am a plain, honest fellow; all is right down plain dealing, by God." He was much affronted with the landlady att Curtis's who, seeing him in a greasy jacket and breeches and a dirty worsted cap, and withall a heavy, forward, clownish air and behaviour, I suppose took him for some ploughman or carman and so presented him with some scraps of cold veal for breakfast, he having declared that he could not drink "your damnd washy tea." As soon as he saw his mess he swore, "Damn him, if it wa'n't out of respect to the gentleman in company," (meaning me) he would throw her cold scraps out at the window and break her table all to pieces should it cost him 100 pounds for dammages. Then taking off his worsted night cap, he pulled a linnen one out of his pocket and clapping it upon his head, "Now," says he, "I'm upon the borders of Pensylvania and must look like a gentleman; 'tother was good enough for Maryland, and damn my blood if ever I come into that rascally province again if I don't procure a leather jacket that I may be in a trim to box the saucy jacks there and not run the hazard of tearing my coat." This showed, by the bye, that he payed more regard to his coat than his person, a remarkable instance of modesty and self denyall.

He then made a transition to politicks and damnd the late Sr. R[obert] W[alpole] for a rascall. We asked him his reasons for cursing Sr. R[obert], but he would give us no other but this, that he was certainly informed by some very good gentlemen, who understood the thing right well, that the said Sr. R[obert] was a damnd rogue. And att the conclusion of each rodomontade, he told us that tho he seemed to be but a plain, homely fellow, yet he would have us know that he was able to afford better than many that went finer: he had good linnen in his bags, a pair of silver buckles, silver clasps, and gold sleeve buttons, two Holland shirts, and some neat night caps; and that his little woman att home drank tea twice a day; and he himself lived very well and expected to live better so soon as that old Rogue B———t dyed and he could secure a title to his land.

The chief topic of conversation among these three Pensylvanian dons upon the road was the insignificancy of the neighbouring province of Maryland when compared to that of Pensylvania. They laid out all the advantages of the latter which their bungling judgement could suggest and displayed all the imperfections and dissadvantages of the first. They inlarged upon the immorality, drunkeness, rudeness and immoderate swearing so much practised in Maryland and added that no such vices were to be found in Pensylvania. I heard this and contradicted it not, because I knew that the first part of the proposition was pritty true. They next fell upon the goodness of the soil as far more productive of pasturage and grain. I was silent here likewise, because the first proposition was true, but as to the other relating to grain, I doubted the truth of it. But what appeared most comical in their criticisms was their making a merit of the stonnyness of the roads. "One may ride," says Howard, "50 miles in Maryland and not see as many stones upon the roads as in 50 paces of road in Pennsylvania." This I knew to be false, but as I thought there was no advantage in stonny roads, I even let them take the honour of it to themselves and did not contradict them.

Att Newcastle I heard news of Mr. H[asel]l, my intended fellow traveller. They told me he was att Willmington upon Cristin River. . . .

Philadelphia

The country round the city of Philadelphia is level and pleasant, having a prospect of the large river of Delaware and the province of East Jersey upon the other side. You have an agreeable view of this river for most of the way betwixt Philadelphia and Newcastle. The plan or platform of the city lyes betwixt the two rivers of Delaware and Skuylkill, the streets being laid out in rectangular squares which makes a regular, uniform plan, but upon that account, altogether destitute of variety.

Att my entering the city, I observed the regularity of the streets, but att the same time the majority of the houses mean and low and much decayed, the streets in generall not paved, very dirty, and obstructed with rubbish and lumber, but their frequent building excuses that. The State House, Assembly House, the great church in Second Street, and Whitefield's church are good buildings.

I observed severall comicall, grotesque phizzes in the inn wher[e] I put up which would have afforded variety of hints for a painter of Hogarth's turn. They talked there upon all subjects—politicks, religion, and trade—some tollerably well, but most of them ignorantly. I discovered two or three chaps very inquisitive, asking my boy who I was, whence come, and whether bound.

I was shaved by a little, finicall, hump backd old barber who kept dancing round me and talking all the time of the operation and yet did his job lightly and to a hair. He abounded in compliments and was a very civil fellow in his way. He told me he had been a journyman to the business for 40 odd years, notwithstanding which, he understood how to trim gentlemen as well (thank God) as the best masters and dispaired not of preferment before he dyed.

I delivered my letters, went to dine with Collector Alexander, and visited severall people in town. In the afternoon I went to the coffee house where I was introduced by Dr. Thomas Bond to severall gentlemen of the place, where the ceremony of shaking of hands, an old custom peculiar to the English, was performed with great gravity and the usuall compliments. I took private lodgings att Mrs. Cume's in Chestnut Street.

Thursday, June 7th. I remarked one instance of industry as soon as I got up and looked out att my chamber window, and that was the shops open att 5 in the morning. I breakfasted with Mrs. Cume and dined by invitation with Dr. Thomas Bond where, after some talk upon physicall matters, he showed me some pritty good anatomical preparations of the muscles and blood vessels injected with wax.

After dinner Mr. V[ena]bles, a Barbadian gentleman, came in who, when we casually had mentioned the free masons, began to rail bitterly against that society as an impudent, assuming, and vain caball pretending to be wiser than all mankind besides, an *imperium in imperio,* and therefor justly to be discouraged and suppressed as they had lately been in some foreign countrys. Tho I am no free mason myself, I could not agree with this gentleman, for I abhorr all tyrannicall and arbitrary notions. I believe the free masons to be an innocent and harmless society that have in their constitution nothing mysterious or beyond the verge of common human understanding, and their secret, which has made such a noise, I imagine is just no secret att all.

In the evening att the coffee house, I met Mr. H[asel]l, and enquiring how he did and how he had fared on his way, he replied as to health he was pritty well, but he had almost been devoured with buggs and other vermin and had met with mean, low company which had made him very uneasy. He added that he had heard good news from Barbadoes concerning his friends there—from one, who he imagined called himself Captain Scrotum, a strange name indeed, but this gentleman had always some comicall turn in his discourse. I parted with him and went to the tavern with Mr. Currie and some Scots gen[t]lemen where we spent the night agreeably and went home sober att eleven a'clock.

Friday, June 8. I read Montaign's Essay in the forenoon which is a strange medley of subjects and particularly entertaining.

I dined att a taveren with a very mixed company of different nations and religions. There were Scots, English, Dutch, Germans, and Irish; there were Roman Catholicks, Church men, Presbyterians, Quakers, Newlightmen, Methodists, Seventh day men, Moravians, Anabaptists, and one Jew. The whole company consisted of 25 planted round an oblong table in a great hall well stoked with flys. The company divided into comittees in conversation; the prevailing topick was politicks and conjectures of a French war. A knott of Quakers there talked only about selling of flower and the low price it bore. The[y] touched a little upon religion, and high words arose among some of the sectaries, but their blood was not hot enough to quarrell, or, to speak in the canting phraze, their zeal wanted fervency. A gentleman that sat next me proposed a number of questions concerning Maryland, understanding I had come from thence. In my replys I was reserved, pretending to know little of the matter as being a person whose business did not lye in the way of history and politicks.

In the afternoon I went to see some ships that lay in the river. Among the rest were three vessels a fitting out for privateers—a ship, a sloop, and a schooner. The ship was a large vessel, very high and full rigged; one Capt. Mackey intended to command her upon the cruise. Att 6 a'clock I went to the coffee house and drank a dish of coffee with Mr. H[asel]l.

After staying there an hour or two, I was introduced by Dr. Phineas Bond into the Governour's Club, a society of gentlemen that met at a taveren every night and converse on various subjects. The Governour gives them his presence once a week, which is generally upon Wednesday, so that I did not see him there. Our conversation was entertaining; the subject was the English poets and some of the foreign writers, particularly Cervantes, author of Don Quixot, whom we loaded with elogiums due to his character. Att eleven a'clock I left this club and went to my lodging.

Saturday, June 9th. This morning there fell a light rain which proved very refreshing, the weather having been very hot and dry for severall days. The heat in this city is excessive, the sun's rays being reflected with such power from the brick houses and from the street pavement which is brick. The people commonly use awnings of painted cloth or duck over their shop doors and windows and, att sun set, throw buckets full of water upon the pavement which gives a sensible cool. They are stocked with plenty of excellent water in this city, there being a pump att almost every 50 paces distance. There are a great number of balconies to their houses where sometimes the men sit in a cool habit and smoke.

The market in this city is perhaps the largest in North-America. It is kept twice a week upon Wednesdays and Saturdays. The street where it stands, called Market Street, is large and spacious, composed of the best houses in the city. . . .

Annapolis

I arrived att Annapolis att two o'clock afternoon and so ended my peri-grinations.

In these my northeren travells I compassed my design in obtaining a better state of health, which was the purpose of my journey. I found but little dif-ference in the manners and character of the people in the different provinces I passed thro', but as to constitutions and complexions, air and government, I found some variety. Their forms of government in the northeren provinces I look upon to be much better and happier than ours, which is a poor, sickly, convulsed state. Their air and living to the northward is likewise much pre-ferable, and the people of a more gygantick size and make. Att Albany, in-deed, they are intirely Dutch and have a method of living something differing from the English.

In this itineration I compleated, by land and water together, a course of 1624 miles. The northeren parts I found in generall much better settled than the southeren. As to politeness and humanity, they are much alike except in the great towns where the inhabitants are more civilized, espe-cially att Boston.

Pelatiah Webster Describes the Uniqueness of Charleston, 1765

May 1765

. . . MONDAY 27.   Spent in viewing the town. It contains abt. 1,000 houses, with inhabitants, 5,000 whites and 20,000 blacks; has 8 houses for religious worship, viz. St. Philip's and St. Michael's, Church of England, large stone buildings with porticos with large pillars and steeples. St. Michael's has a good ring of bells. 1 Scotch presbyterian church; 1 independent, called the New England Meeting; 1 Dutch church, and two Baptist meetings, and one French church: these 3 last very small.

The Statehouse is a heavy building of abt. 120 by 40 feet. The council chamber is about 40 feet square, decorated with many heavy pillars and much carvings, rather superb than elegant. The assembly room is of the same di-mensions; but much plainer work. 'Tis convenient enough. There are sundry publick offices kept in small apartments below; there are two flights of stairs, one leading to the council chamber, the other to the assembly room. Below stairs is a court house where the courts of common pleas and pleas of the crown are kept, but is yet unfinished.

The streets of this city run N. and S., and E. and W., intersecting each other at right angles; they are not paved except the footways within the posts, abt. 6 feet wide, which are paved with brick in the principal streets.

There are large fortifications here but mostly unfinished and ruinous. There is a pretty fort on James Island called Johnson's Fort which commands the entrance of the harbour, and a great number of breastworks and cannon all round the town with a fosse much filled up. There are also mounds thrown up and ditches round the back part of the town but all ruinous and nearly useless.

The town stands on a neck of land formed by the two rivers, Ashley on the S. and Cowper on the north, fronting the bay abt. 9 miles within the bar. The two rivers are not more than a mile apart at several miles north of the town, and the only considerable road which leads from the city is up the neck and called The Path and at six or seven miles from the town it forks and runs into the various parts of the country.

The laborious business is here chiefly done by black slaves of which there are great multitudes. The climate is very warm. The chief produce is rice and indigo. The manufacture of hemp is set afoot and like to succeed very well. They have considerable lumber and naval stores. They export annually 100,000 barrels of rice and 60,000 lbs indigo (rice worth on average 6 shillings per ct. i.e. 30/- per bbl., indigo from 3/- to 3/6 per lb.), with considerable pine boards, tar, turpentine, hemp, staves, etc.; have very few mechanic arts of any sort, and very great quantities of mechanic utensils are imported from England and the northward colonies.

They have no considerable seminaries of learning, but many youth of quality go to London for an education. The people are vastly affable and polite, quite free from pride, and a stranger may make himself very easy with them.

The whites in this province are computed at abt. 20,000 and the blacks at 4 times that number. The English settlements extend two or three hundred miles into the country westward into the Cherokee and Catawba's country, and those distant westward parts of the province are settled by great numbers of people that travel from the northward for lands from the back parts of Pensylvania, Maryland and Virginia, and consist mostly of Dutch and Irish families. The pine sandy plains extend two hundred miles westward before any mountains rise, nor is there a mill or any other water works to be found in all that space.

There is a little wheat raised in this province, but poor in quality, nor will it produce more than two thirds of the price of the northward flour which is the principal supply of bread. Few apples grow here, all the cyder used here is imported. There are a few vessels built here, and are all planked with pitch pine plank, and the crooked timbers are live oak, (a wood of great firmness and great durableness) and the beams, keels, and all other strait timbers are of pitch pine. 'Tis said that a ship well built here will last thirty years.

There is a pretty well chosen library in town purchased by private subscriptions of a number of gentlemen, by the name of the Charlestown Library Society.

The most active season of the year is from December to May by which time most of their crops of rice and indigo are brought to town and shipped off, so that during the great heat of the succeeding summer months the merchants in town have little to do. There are but few country seats near the town, and many people move to considerable distances up into the country to spend the summer and avoid the intense heats and confined air of the town: the winds generally blowing during the summer months from the south and S. W., from off the hot sands of Florida and Georgia, are much warmer than the Westindia breezes which come in from the sea.

Dined this day with Mr. Thomas Shirley, a very polite English gent., residing here in very genteel fashion; is an ingenuous ready man; was bread a merchant, has travelled much, understands several modern languages; passed the afternoon agreably with him.

TUESDAY 28.   Still viewing the town with some attention. Dined with Mr. William Glen, a reputable merchant in the town who deals largely in the London trade; in the afternoon took an airing into the country with him in his chair several miles; the road is level and sandy and would be very hot were it not shaded by fine avenues of large trees growing close by each side of the road and shading it.

WEDSDAY 29.   Still sauntring abt. town as much as the great heats will permit. Dined with Mr. Tho. Smith, a reputable merchant in this town and in very fine business; is an agreable sensible kind man; passed my time with him very pleasantly several hours.

THURSD. 30.   Dined this day with Mr. John Poaug, a Scotch merchant in this city, a very genteel polite man.

FRID. 31.   Dined with Reverend Robt. Smith, rector of St. Philips's in this city, an English gent., educated at University of Cambridge, a very sociable and polite clergyman.

June 1765.

SAT. 1.   Rode into the country seven miles with Mr. Tho. Laughton Smith to the country seat of Col. Benjn. Smith. Dined there. Spent the afternoon very pleasantly; the Col. is a gent. of abt. 50, cheerful, easy, and generous, has a great fortune and declines business, having turned over his mercantile affairs into the hands of his son Tho.

SUND. 2.   Attended divine service at St. Michael's. Dined at Mr. Torrans's on the bay, a reputable merchant, with Col. Howard and sundry European gent. Mr. Torrans is a sensible man and deals largely as a merchant in partnership with Mr. Poaug 'fore mentioned.

MONDAY, 3.   Dined this day with Mr. Thomas Liston, a reputable merchant born here; is a man of great openess and politeness, of generous sentiments and very genteel behaviour; passed the afternoon very agreably in his sumer house with him and Mr. Lindo, a noted Jew, inspector of indigo here.

TUESD. 4.   The militia all appeared under arms, abt. 800, and the guns at all the forts were fired, it being the king's birthday. The artillery co. made a good appearance and performed their exercises and firings very well. The militia were not so well trained and exercised, but made a pretty good and handsome appearance. N. B. The militia and artillery of Charlestown are said to consist of 1,300 men in the whole list from 16 to 60 years old. Dined with Mr. Wm. Glen afore mentioned.

WEDS. 5.   Rode out to Mr. George Marshal's country seat 3 miles from town on Ashley River. Dined there; viewed his plantation; saw his rice and indigo growing in the field, and his Negroes howing it. The rice grows much like rye but somewhat finer and paler. The indigo is a dark colored weed growing on a clumsy stalk which branches much and bears single leaves somewhat like buckwheat and abt. as high. I viewed also his vats for steeping, beating and lyming his indigo, the trough for pressing it, conveniences for drying, etc., in short the whole process, but it not being the season for making it, I could not have an opportunity of seeing the process performed.

Mr. Marshal is a Scotch gentleman of great humanity and courtesy. . . .

Now I have left Charlestown an agreable and polite place in which I was used very genteelly and contracted much acquaintance for the time I staid here. The heats are much too severe, the water bad, the soil sandy, the timber too much evergreen; but with all these disadvantages, 'tis a flourishing place, capable of vast improvement; will have I fear some uncomfortable bands of banditti on its frontiers soon, it's distance from proper authority having already drawn there great numbers of very idle dissolute people who begin to be very troublesome. . . .

Janet Schaw on Her Visit
to Wilmington, North Carolina, 1774

I have been in town a few days, and have had an opportunity to make some little observations on the manners of a people so new to me. The ball . . . was intended as a civility, therefore I will not criticize it, and tho' I have not the same reason to spare the company, yet I will not fatigue you with a description, which however lively or just, would at best resemble a Dutch picture, where the injudicious choice of the subject destroys the merit of the painting. Let it suffice to say that a ball we had, where were dresses, dancing and ceremonies laughable enough, but there was no object on which my own ridicule fixed equal to myself and the figure I made, dressed out in all my British airs with a high head and a hoop and trudging thro' the unpaved streets in embroidered shoes by the light of a lanthorn carried by a black wench half naked. No chair, no carriage—good leather shoes need none. The ridicule was the silk shoes in such a place. I have however gained some most amiable and agreeable acquaintances amongst the Ladies; many of whom would make a figure in any part of the world, and I will not fail to cultivate their esteem, as they appear worthy of mine.

Janet Schaw, *Journal of a Lady of Quality,* ed. Evangeline Walker Andrews and Charles Mclean Andrews (New Haven: Yale, 1923), 153–156. Copyright © 1923 by Yale University Press.

I am sorry to say, however, that I have met with few of the men who are natives of the country ... and as their natural ferocity is now inflamed by the fury of an ignorant zeal, they are of that sort of figure, that I cannot look at them without connecting the idea of tar and feather. Tho' they have fine women and such as might inspire any man with sentiments that do honour to humanity, yet they know no such nice distinctions, and in this at least are real patriots. As the population of the country is all the view they have in what they call love, and tho' they often honour their black wenches with their attention, I sincerely believe they are excited to that crime by no other desire or motive but that of adding to the number of their slaves.

The difference between the men and the women surprised me, but a sensible man, who has long resided here, in some degrees accounted for it. In the infancy of this province, said he, many families from Britain came over, and of these the wives and daughters were people of education. The mothers took the care of the girls, they were train'd up under them, and not only instructed in the family duties necessary to the sex, but in those accomplishments and genteel manners that are still so visible amongst them, and this descended from Mother to daughter. As the father found the labours of his boys necessary to him, he led them therefore to the woods, and taught the sturdy lad to glory in the stroke he could give with his Ax, in the trees he felled, and the deer he shot; to conjure the wolfe, the bear and the Alligator; and to guard his habitation from Indian inroads was most justly his pride, and he had reason to boast of it. But a few generations this way lost every art or science, which their fathers might have brought out, and tho' necessity no longer prescribed these severe occupations, custom has established it as still necessary for the men to spend their time abroad in the fields; and to be a good marksman is the highest ambition of the youth, while to those enervated by age or infirmity drinking grog remained a last consolation.

The Ladies have burnt their tea in a solemn procession, but they had delayed however till the sacrifice was not very considerable, as I do not think any one offered above a quarter of a pound. The people in town live decently, and tho' their houses are not spacious, they are in general very commodious and well furnished. All the Merchants of any note are British and Irish, and many of them very genteel people. They all disapprove of the present proceedings. Many of them intend quitting the country as fast as their affairs will permit them, but are yet uncertain what steps to take. This town lies low, but is not disagreeable. There is at each end of it an ascent, which is dignified with the title of the hills; on them are some very good houses and there almost all my acquaintances are. They have very good Physicians, the best of whom is a Scotchman, at whose house I have seen many of the first planters. I do not wish however to be much in their company, for, as you know, my tongue is not always under my command; I fear I might say something to give offence, in which case I would not fail to have the most shocking retort at least, if it went no further. . . .

The Albany Plan of Union, 1754

PLAN OF A PROPOSED UNION *of the Several Colonies of Massachusetts Bay, New Hampshire, Connecticut, Rhode Island, New York, New Jerseys, Pensylvania, Maryland, Virginia, North Carolina, and South-Carolina; for their mutual defence and Security, and for extending the British Settlements in North America.*

That Humble Application be made for an Act of the Parliament of Great Britain, by Virtue of which one General Government may be formed in America, including all the said Colonies, within and under which Government each Colony may retain its present constitution, except in the particulars wherein a Change may be directed by the said Act as hereafter follows.

That the said General Government be administred by a President General, to be appointed and supported by the Crown

And a Grand Council to be Chosen by the Representatives of the People of the Several Colonies, met in their respective Assemblies

That within   Months after the passing of such Act, The house of Representatives in the Several Assemblies that happen to be sitting within that time, or that shall be specially for that purpose Convened, may and shall choose Members for the Grand Council, in the following Proportions; that is to say.

Massachusetts Bay	7
New Hampshire	2
Connecticutt	5
Rhode Island	2
New York	4
New Jerseys	3
Pensylvania	6
Maryland	4
Virginia	7
North Carolina	4
South Carolina	4
	48

Who shall meet for the first time at the City of Philadelphia in Pensylvania, being called by the President General as soon as conveniently may be after his Appointment.

That there shall be a new Election of Members for the Grand Council every Three Years; and on the Death or Resignation of any Member, his place shall be Supplyed by a new Choice at the next Sitting of the Assembly of the Colony he represented.

That after the first Three Years when the Proportion of Money arising out of each Colony to the General Treasury can be known the Number of Members to be chosen for each Colony shall from time to time in all ensuing Elections be regulated by that Proportion (Yet so as that the Number to be chosen by any one Province, be not more than Seven nor less than two.)

That the Grand Council shall meet once in every Year, and oftner if Occasion require, at such time and place as they, shall adjourn to, at the last preceeding Meeting, or as they shall be called to meet at by the President General on any Emergency, he having first obtained in writing the consent of Seven of the Members to such Call, and sent due and timely notice to the whole.

That the Grand Council have power to chuse their Speaker and shall neither be desolved, prorogued, nor continue sitting longer than Six weeks at one time, without their own consent or the Special Command of the Crown.

That the Members of the Grand Council shall be allowed for their Service Ten Shillings Sterling p Diem during their Sessions, and Journey to and from the place of Meeting; Twenty Miles to be reckoned a Days Journey.

That the Assent of the President General be requisite to all Acts of the Grand Council; and that it be his Office and Duty to cause them to be carried into Execution.

That the President General with the Advice of the Grand Council, hold or direct all Indian Treaties in which the General Interest or Wellfare of the Colonies may be concerned, and make peace or declare War with Indian Nations.

That they make such Laws as they Judge Necessary for regulating all Indian Trade.

That they make all Purchases from Indians for the Crown, of Lands now not within the Bounds of particular Colonies, or that shall not be within their Bounds when some of them are reduced to more Convenient Dimensions.

That they make new Settlements on such purchases, by granting Lands in the Kings Name reserving a quit Rent to the Crown for the use of the General Treasury.

That they make Laws for regulating and Governing such new Settlements, till the Crown shall think fitt to form them into particular Governments.

That they raise and pay Soldiers, and Build Forts for the defence, of any of the Colonies, and Equip Vessells of Force to guard the Coasts and protect the Trade on the Ocean, Lakes or Great Rivers: But they shall not Impress Men, in any Colony without the consent of its Legislature—That for these purposes they have power to make Laws and lay and leavy such general Duties, Imposts or Taxes as to them shall appear most equal and just, Considering the Ability and other Circumstances of the Inhabitants in the several Colonies and such as may be collected with the least Inconvenience to the People, rather discourging Luxury, than loading Industry with unnecessary Burthens.

That they may appoint a General Treasurer, and a particular Treasurer in each Government when necessary, and from time to time may order the sums in the Treasuries of each Government into the General Treasury, or draw on them for Special Payments as they find most convenient. Yet no money to issue but by joint orders of the President General and Grand Council, Except where sums have been appropriated to particular purposes, and the President General is previously impowered by an act to draw for such sums.

That the General accounts shall be yearly settled and reported to the several Assembly's.

That a Quorum of the Grand Council impowered to act with the President General, do consist of Twenty five members among whom, there shall be one or more from a Majority of the Colonies;

That the Laws made by them for the purposes aforesaid shall not be repugnant, but as near as may be agreeable to the Laws of England, and shall be transmitted to the King in Council for approbation as soon as may be, after their passing, and if not disapproved within Three Years after presentation to remain in Force.

That in case of the Death of the President General, the Speaker of the Grand Council for the time being shall succeed and be vested with the same powers and Authorities to continue until the Kings Pleasure be known.

That all Military Commission Officers whether for Land or Sea Service to act under this General Constitution shall be nominated by the president General; but the approbation of the Grand Council is to be obtained before they receive their Commissions. And all Civil officers are to be nominated by the Grand Council, and to receive the president Generals approbation before they officiate: But in Case of a vacancy by Death or removal of any officer Civil or Military under this Constitution, The Governor of the Province in which such vacancy happens, may appoint till the pleasure of the President General and Grand Council, can be known. That the Particular Military as well as Civil Establishments in each Colony remain in their present State this General Constitution notwithstanding; and that on sudden Emergencies, any Colony may defend itself, and lay the accounts of Expence thence arisen before the president General and Grand Council, who may allow and order payment of the same, as far as they judge such accounts just and reasonable.

After Debate on the foregoing Plan

RESOLVED

That the Commissioners from the Several Governments, be desired to lay the same before their Respective Constituents for their Consideration, and that the Secretary to this Board transmit a Copy thereof with this vote thereon, to the Governor of each of the Colonies which have not sent their Commissioners to this Congress.

His Honour proposed to the Board, that agreeable to their Resolutions of the 24 June they would now consider, the Expediency of Building Forts in the Indian Country. It was determined that considering the present wavering Disposition of the Sennecas, it was expedient that a Fort should be Built in their Country at a place called Irondequat or Tierondequat. Ordered

That a Committee be appointed to consider what further Forts may be necessary in the Country of the Six Nations, and that each Colony name a Member for this Committee.

ORDERED

That Mr Chambers and Mr Peters be a Committee to revise the Minutes settled and agreed to by this Board.

Adjourned till to Morrow Morning at 9 aClock.

❧ E S S A Y S

Historians Jack P. Greene of the University of California, Irvine, and David Hackett Fischer of Brandeis University each have written a major synthesis answering the questions posed at the beginning of this chapter: What is the sum of the colonial experience? Can we speak of "American culture" in the decades before the Revolution? Their answers differ profoundly.

Historians traditionally have identified New England, with its tradition of self-governing, small farming communities, as the core of American culture. Professor Greene demonstrates in the first essay that New England in fact was the one section that least participated in the shared colonial development. All the regions, although very different in their origins and despite continuing differences, converged into a common American pattern by the close of the colonial period.

Professor Fischer, on the other hand, presents evidence that the mainland colonies comprised four major regions, each settled by a particular group of people from a specific culture area in Europe. So distinct were these cultures, Fischer maintains, that traces of them survive even today. He concludes that the close of the colonial period saw not one but four colonial cultures.

Convergence and the Creation of a Colonial Culture

JACK P. GREENE

... If, as observed Samuel Williams, whose *History of Vermont,* published in 1794, was one of the first systematic attempts to analyze the main features of the emerging American society, a "similarity of situation and conditions" had gradually pushed the colonies toward a similitude of society and values, more specifically, toward "that natural, easy, independent situation, and spirit, in which the body of the [free] people were found, when the American war came on," still a second major influence—inheritance operating in the form of growing metropolitanization or anglicization—was important in helping to erode differences among the colonies. If this development was partly the result of efforts by metropolitan authorities to bring the colonies under closer political and economic control, it was also attributable to an ever more intense involvement between metropolis and colonies in virtually all spheres of life. Together with an increasing volume of contacts among individuals and the

Jack Greene, "Convergence: Development of an American Society, 1720–1780." Excerpts from chapter 8 of *Pursuits of Happiness* (Chapel Hill: University of North Carolina Press for The Institute of Early American History and Culture, 1988). Reprinted by permission of The University of North Carolina Press.

improved communications that accompanied them, this growing involvement drew the colonies more and more into the ambit of British life as the eighteenth century advanced and thereby tied them ever more closely to metropolitan culture.

As the ties with the metropolis thus tightened and became more robust, the pull of metropolitan culture grew, and the standards of the metropolis increasingly came to be the primary model for colonial behavior, the one certain measure of cultural achievement for these provincial societies at the outermost peripheries of the British world. Throughout the colonies, and especially among the emergent elites, there was a self-conscious effort to anglicize colonial life through the deliberate imitation of metropolitan institutions, values, and culture. Thus, before the mid-1770s, British-Americans thought of themselves primarily as Britons, albeit Britons overseas. Contrary to the dominant opinion among earlier historians, colonial comparisons of the colonies with Britain rarely came out in favor of the colonies. The central cultural impulse among the colonists was not to identify and find ways to express and to celebrate what was distinctively American about themselves and their societies but, insofar as possible, to eliminate those distinctions so that they might—with more credibility—think of themselves and their societies—and be thought of by people in Britain itself—as demonstrably British.

Among the several colonial regions, of course, there remained significant differences.... [T]he relatively greater affluence derived by the southern and West Indian colonies from staple agriculture had enabled them to purchase many more black slaves, to devote more time both to the pursuit of the good life and to politics and the law, to cultivate metropolitan cultural models more assiduously, to rely more heavily upon metropolitan cultural institutions rather than to develop their own, and to be more self-indulgent and less industrious. By contrast, New England still was considerably more religious, had much lower levels of wealth concentration, and, along with the Middle Colonies, was more heavily urbanized. The Middle Colonies were perhaps the least settled socially, were certainly more heterogeneous in the religious and ethnic composition of their free populations, and may have had the most highly developed social and commercial infrastructures. During the late eighteenth century, however, these differences were largely ones of degree.

Not even the presence of so many slaves in the southern and island colonies, certainly the most conspicuous difference between them and New England, was yet a crucial distinguishing feature among the colonies. In general, there was a steady diminution in the ratio of black slaves to the free population from the most southern to the most northern colonies. As late as 1770, however, slavery was still an expanding, not a contracting, institution in every one of the island and continental colonies except New Hampshire and Nova Scotia. New York, Rhode Island, New Jersey, and Pennsylvania all had populations with a higher proportion of slaves than did the Chesapeake as late as 1700 to 1710 during the early stages of that region's large-scale transition to a slave labor system, and no colony had acted to try to ban slavery, which would be legal in Britain itself for another sixty years. Slavery was everywhere an integral and accepted component of British American culture, and limitations of space were almost certainly more important than ratios of slaves to free people in contributing to the beginnings of a cultural rift between the island and continental colonies after 1750. Given the strong convergence of cultural development in colonial British America by the 1740s and 1750s, it is by no means preposterous to suggest that all of the colonies, including Massachusetts and Connecticut, would have used slavery as extensively as did the southern and West Indian colonies had they had the resources and the incentives to do so.

As between 1660 and 1760 each of the regions of colonial British America became both more creole and more metropolitan, as they increasingly assimilated to a common American social and behavioral pattern and to British cultural models, they became more and more alike, and this powerful social convergence resulted in the emergence and articulation of a common cultural pattern that, though present to some degree throughout the British American world, was especially evident among the continental colonies. If the central features of this pattern were most powerfully manifest at the center of British North America, in the Chesapeake and Middle Colonies, they were also present to a conspicuous degree in the peripheries, in the Lower South and New England. This pattern can be discussed under three rubrics: growth, differentiation, and values.

     ... [T]he growth of the colonies was genuinely impressive, and in each colonial region demographic growth was particularly dramatic. ... Once a solid base had been established ... in the Chesapeake and New England during the last half of the seventeenth century, population grew at a rapid rate, ranging between 200 and 300 percent every half-century. ... This growth resulted from both immigration and natural increase. Perhaps as many as one out of five new whites were immigrants; a much higher proportion of new blacks, especially in the islands, derived from slave imports. By far the largest source of this vigorous demographic rise on the continent, however, was natural increase. This increase was primarily the result of three factors: declining mortality, younger ages at marriage of from four to five years for women than in Europe, and a bountiful food supply and high nutrition that already by the 1750s had operated to make male residents of the continental colonies three to three and one-half inches taller than their British counterparts. Natural growth was, however, lower in cities and in coastal areas of the Chesapeake and Lower South, where, as in the West Indies, mortality was significantly higher. Nevertheless, in overall population trends, the mortality differential between northern and southern colonies may have been at least partly offset by a more plentiful food and protein supply in the South, one indication of which was that the average height of militiamen during the Revolution increased from North to South. The special demographic vigor demonstrated by the continental colonies was no doubt also stimulated by the continuing availability of land and the high levels of economic opportunity to meet the demands of both the growing population and an expanding overseas commerce. ...

     The psychology of expansiveness implied by the demographic performance of the populations of colonial British America, especially on the continent, was also reflected in the extent of territorial expansion and the mobility of the population. At the conclusion of Queen Anne's War in 1713, the continental settlers were still clustered in a series of noncontiguous nuclei close to the Atlantic seaboard. There were two large centers of settlement, one in the Chesapeake and another covering the coastal regions of eastern and southern New England and reaching up the Connecticut River valley. Two smaller concentrations of population fanned out from Philadelphia and New York, and there were isolated groups of settlement on the central Maine coast, in the upper Connecticut River valley in what is now southeastern Vermont, around Albany on the Hudson River, on the upper Delaware River in the vicinity of Easton, Pennsylvania, on the lower Delaware, at three widely dispersed points in Tidewater North Carolina, and at Charleston and Port Royal in South Carolina.

During the next fifty years, population spilled out in all possible directions from these nuclei until by the 1760s and 1770s there was one long continuum of settlement stretching from Georgia to Maine and reaching inland for more than 150 miles, and new nuclei were building in East and West Florida and Nova Scotia. This rapid spread of settlement was one sign of the high levels of geographical mobility among settlers in all regions on the continent. Although southerners were somewhat more mobile than New Englanders, no region had a persistence rate much above 60 percent during the third quarter of the eighteenth century, and farmers everywhere showed an especially strong propensity to move. Residents from New York north tended to move longer distances north into upper New York and New England; those from Pennsylvania south tended to move west and south into the broad upland areas between the seacoast and the Appalachian Mountains.

But the most striking evidence of growth lies in the economic realm. . . . [T]he economic performance of every region over time was impressive. Growth seems not to have been especially rapid before 1740, but every available indicator—numbers of slaves, rising levels of personal wealth, volume of agricultural production, amount of exports, value of imports from Britain, quantities shipped in the coastal trade—suggests extraordinary growth thereafter. McCusker and Menard estimate that the gross national product (GNP) multiplied about twenty-five times between 1650 and 1770, increasing at an annual average rate of 2.7 percent for British America as a whole and 3.2 percent for British North America. This increase, they posit, may have represented a real per capita growth rate of 0.6 percent, which was twice that of Britain and was "sufficient to double income" over that period. By the time of the American Revolution, this vigorous economic growth had produced a standard of living that may have been "the highest achieved for the great bulk of the [free] population in any country up to that time." . . . The sources of this remarkable prosperity lay in a combination of the demands for food and other commodities on the part of the burgeoning population and in growing overseas markets for colonial products. Though the proportion of income gained through exports declined over time, it was still substantial in 1770. . . . The value of exports per capita and per free white resident increased from North to South, reflecting the greater per capita wealth of the free white populations of those regions. . . . Both import and export figures reflect the development of a considerable coastwise trade among the colonies. Though all four regions participated in this trade, it was dominated by New England and the Middle Colonies, and it marked the early stages in the articulation of an integrated "American" economy through which products from all regions were widely distributed for domestic consumption on a continental scale.

As McCusker and Menard have remarked, these figures "describe a strong, flexible, and diverse economy . . . able to operate without a considerable metropolitan subsidy," at least in peace time. In stark contrast to the situation during the first generations of settlement, none of these continental regions relied heavily on foreign investment. Rather, they "accumulated most of their capital on their own" through the productivity of their inhabitants, savings, and capital improvements, developments that were also reflected in the emergence of a resident and highly skilled commercial sector. The impressive performance of the economies of every one of these regions in turn probably also heralded, to one degree or another, increased specialization of production and a consequent lowering of production costs; improvements in transportation and a resulting decline in distribution costs; advances in human capital, including rising technical expertise; improvements in economic organization; and at least some technological advances such as occurred in shipbuilding and shipping.

This impressive demographic, territorial, and economic growth supported an increasingly complex society with an ever larger range, more dense distribution, and more deeply established agglomeration of social institutions. These included families and kinship groups; neighborhoods and hamlets; stores and artisanal establishments; local judicial and administrative institutions; churches; transportation facilities, including roads, bridges, ferries, and a few canals; and a variety of cultural institutions, including schools, libraries, clubs, and other social organizations. Although many of these institutions were well represented in the countryside, others, including especially commercial and artisanal establishments and cultural institutions, were most fully developed in the towns.

The extensive spread of population and the continuing rustication process it represented meant that as the eighteenth century proceeded, a declining proportion of the population lived in towns. Yet substantial urbanization occurred in all of the older settled areas, especially after 1720. Boston was the largest colonial town into the 1740s, when its population leveled off to between fifteen and sixteen thousand, where it remained for the rest of the colonial period. At some point between 1745 and 1760, the populations of both Philadelphia and New York passed that of Boston. By 1775 the population of Philadelphia was perhaps as high as forty thousand, that of New York twenty-five thousand. Also by 1775, Charleston and Newport had populations ranging between nine and twelve thousand; Baltimore and Norfolk, both of which had developed primarily after 1750 in the Chesapeake, traditionally the least urbanized area of continental America, had around six thousand; a dozen towns—New Haven, Norwich, New London, Salem, Lancaster, Hartford, Middletown, Portsmouth, Marblehead, Providence, Albany, Annapolis, and Savannah—had between three and five thousand; and perhaps as many as fifty other places had between five hundred and three thousand people. . . .

The increasingly complex occupational structure of the towns, a trend that was also evident, if to a much less impressive extent, in the countryside, was one powerful indication of the results of the steady process of social differentiation that had been occurring in all the major regions of colonial British America during the century after 1660. For instance, the resident commercial sector of the population had developed during these years into an increasingly complex group ranging from petty retailers, peddlers, and hawkers at the lowest level up through primary traders composed mostly of country storekeepers and urban retailers, to secondary traders or wholesalers who collected local products from and distributed finished goods to retailers, to tertiary traders or large merchants who presided over the overseas trade and offered more and more sophisticated financial and insurance services to the commercial economy. A similar development can be followed with regard to the professions, including the ministry, medicine, and the law. . . .

The process of social differentiation can also be observed in the development of a much more sharply articulated social structure. To be sure, even at the end of the colonial period, the emerging social hierarchies in the several regions of colonial British America were all much less finely developed and more open than in metropolitan Britain. Nowhere was there anything remotely resembling a legally privileged aristocracy. Indeed, colonial society was not yet divided into well-defined social classes but consisted of two broad and not always discrete social categories, independents and dependents. *Independents* were those with sufficient property in land, tools, or personal goods to make them theoretically free from external control by any other person; *dependents* were those whose wills, in Sir William Blackstone's phrase, were subject to the control of the people on whom they depended.

By contemporary standards, the independent proportion of the population was very large. At the top of this category, the most successful planters, merchants, landlords, and lawyers were, by the 1720s and 1730s in the oldest colonies and by the 1740s and 1750s in the newer ones, a self-conscious and conspicuous elite that, though consisting of no more than two to three percent of colonial families, was distinguished from the rest of society by its substantially greater wealth and affluent and refined lifestyles. Manifest in their clothing, consumption patterns, housing, modes of transportation, education, cosmopolitan outlook, prominence in both public office and the emerging cultural infrastructures, and cultivation of the traditional values of the British rural and urban gentries, including liberality, civility, and stewardship, the superior social status of these developing elites was also evident in the large number of dependents their members could command and by the passive deference usually accorded them by other independent members of society. Yet this largely self-made group, as Richard Hofstadter has remarked, had "only a slender sense of the personal prerogative, the code of honor, or the grand extravagance" usually associated with its equivalents in Europe. Rather, it exhibited "the disciplined ethic of work, the individual assertiveness, the progressive outlook ... and the calculating and materialistic way of life" associated with the burgeoning middle classes of contemporary Britain....

Certainly in the 1760s and 1770s, as earlier, the most impressive aspect of the free population of Britain's American colonies was the extraordinarily large number of families of independent middling status, which was proportionately substantially more numerous than in any other contemporary Western society. Situated immediately below the elite and, like their counterparts in England, sharing, in many cases, the values and the orientations of those just above them, this vast and increasingly differentiated body of yeoman farmers, artisans, smaller traders, and lesser professionals included the great bulk of independent people in the colonies. In every region of continental colonial British America, their sheer numbers meant that the emerging American society would be "a preponderantly middle-class world" in which "the simpler agencies of the middle class" would be "in strong evidence: the little churches of the dissenting sects, the taverns ... the societies for [social and] self-improvement and 'philosophical' inquiry, the increasingly eclectic little colleges, the contumacious newspapers, the county court houses and town halls, the how-to-do books, the *Poor Richard's Almanack*."

In the developing American social schema, agricultural tenants and people employed with contracts in the service, industrial, and commercial sectors constituted an ambiguous intermediate group who, though they in many cases enjoyed sufficient resources in the form of their own skills and property to function and be regarded by the rest of society as independent people, were at least technically dependent on their landlords or employers. But such people formed only a small part of the social category of dependents. Because they were defined in the early modern British world as extensions of their husbands and fathers' legal and social personalities, wives and children together were certainly the largest groups of dependents in colonial America. At least within the confines of the free population, however, most, if not the vast majority, of women and children were members of families whose male head was independent. As a consequence, they assumed his independent social status.

When colonial Americans referred to *social* dependents, they were talking largely about people who fell into one or the other of three groups of laborers, all of whom were employed to provide a substantial amount of the extraordinary effort required to produce the food and the vendible commodities necessary to sustain this rapidly expanding and still highly exploitive society: free laborers, servants, and slaves. Although much of the labor in the farm colonies, especially in New England, where the pace of economic development was slower and the labor requirements much lower, had been supplied by family members, the demand for labor ... was a persistent problem in the land- and resource-rich but labor-poor colonies from New York south to Barbados. Over time, first in New England and then in the Chesapeake and Middle Colonies, an expanding pool of free laborers, mostly younger men and women just getting started in life, slowly developed into a significant, if notoriously expensive, component of the labor market. By the mid-eighteenth century, male laborers in this category may have constituted as much as 10

percent of the adult male population of large towns and an even larger percentage of the inhabitants of smaller towns and long-established rural districts.

From the Middle Colonies south, however, servitude, which was also present in New England, especially before 1720, had almost certainly been a more
important means of supplying the demand for labor beyond what could be
provided by family members, and the predominant form of servant labor was
provided through indentured servitude, a new institution developed in the first
half of the seventeenth century to meet the heavy labor requirements of the
West Indian and Chesapeake colonies. Servitude was a transitional status that
enabled people to secure passage to the colonies in return for selling their
labor for a set period of time, at the end of which they hoped to move into
a position from which they could acquire land and an independent status.
With the substitution of blacks for whites as plantation laborers, beginning in
the West Indies and extending to the continent during the closing decades of
the seventeenth century, servitude changed from an institution that supplied
primarily unskilled labor to one that furnished considerable amounts of skilled
labor, albeit by the mid-eighteenth century throughout the colonies slaves were
more and more being trained to perform skilled tasks formerly assigned to
servants. Notwithstanding these changes in the institution and use of white
servitude, however, the demand for unskilled servant labor remained high in
all regions of continental British America except New England. The especially
high demand for such labor in the Chesapeake and Middle Colonies was
evidenced by the eagerness with which buyers snapped up as many as forty
to fifty thousand largely young, male, and minimally skilled convicts transported from Britain between 1718 and 1775.

Life was no picnic for servants, who had traditionally been and still in
the mid-eighteenth century were often worked hard, but servitude at least held
out an eventual promise of freedom and independence for the more ambitious
and fortunate of those who survived their terms; the same could not be said
for slaves.... [B]lacks—of whom all except perhaps 1 to 2 percent were
slaves—constituted the largest single category of the dependent population,
over a third of the population of colonial British America as a whole and
more than 20 percent in the continental colonies in 1760. These substantial
numbers remind us of the extraordinary extent to which the growth and prosperity of the emerging society of free colonial British America as well as the
high incidence of independent individuals who lived there were achieved as
a result of slave labor, of the forced emigration from their widely dispersed
homelands of thousands of people of African descent and their systematic
subjugation to an intrinsically harsh and virtually inescapable labor regime
based on racial discrimination and enforced by the full power of the law....

In the Chesapeake, the first and oldest center of slavery on the continent,
slaves, both those who lived on large plantations and the majority who resided
on smaller units, mostly lived under the direct management of white families,
were thoroughly subjected to the assimilative pressures of white paternalism,
enjoyed relatively little autonomy, and had very few opportunities to obtain
freedom. Having already acquired a more balanced sex ratio and a creole
majority by the mid-eighteenth century, Chesapeake blacks early achieved a

more stable family life; the proportion of new Africans, most of whom ended up on smaller units in newer areas, declined steadily; differences within the black population diminished more quickly; blacks developed no distinctive language and managed to retain relatively few African cultural survivals; and an Afro-American culture "evolved parallel with Anglo-American culture and with considerable congruence."

Slavery in the Lower South contrasted markedly with that in the Chesapeake. There, profitable staple agriculture developed later; the concentration of slaves on larger units with a minimum of white supervision and the widespread use of the task system tended to limit the effects of white paternalist ideology, to give blacks more autonomy in their daily lives, and to enable them, like West Indian slaves, to play a major role in the internal marketing system; Africans continued to be imported in substantial numbers throughout the eighteenth century; and a higher incidence of interracial sexual liaisons created the conditions for the appearance of at least a small black and mulatto free population. In such conditions, "the transformation of Africans into Afro-Americans . . . was a slow halting process that left most black people alienated from white society and fully equipped to establish their own distinctive culture," one that in language, patterns of familial descent, and work practices "incorporated more of West African culture into their new lives than any other black peoples on mainland North America."

Although there were outposts of the plantation system in the northern colonies, in the iron plantations of the Middle Colonies, and in the large stock-farming operations in the Narragansett country of Rhode Island, most blacks in the northern colonies tended to live and work either as agricultural workers on small units of production in the countryside or in small numbers as domestics, hired laborers, teamsters, and dock and maritime workers in towns. Indeed, as [Ira] Berlin has remarked, the importance of slaves "to the growth of Northern cities increased during the eighteenth century" as urban slavery "moved steadily away from the household to the docks, warehouses and shops." A steady rise in the "importance of slaves to the work force" in the northern colonies after 1730 led to considerable importations directly from Africa, particularly into Rhode Island and the Middle Colonies, throughout the middle decades of the eighteenth century. This development enabled blacks to draw upon and to "remain acutely conscious of their African inheritance" at the same time that their emerging Afro-American culture was being increasingly "integrated into the larger Euro-American one."

Notwithstanding the importance of these substantial differences among the slave systems of continental British North America, however, it is important to an understanding of the character of the emerging society and culture of British North America to emphasize certain basic similarities among them. No region displayed a manifest reluctance to employ slaves before the 1760s and 1770s. If only those colonies from New York south "had fairly elaborate slave codes," they all still "sanctioned slaveholding on the eve of the American Revolution" and "had at least the rudiments of a statutory law of slavery or race" that "defined slavery as a lifetime condition," made slave status "hereditable through the mother," identified it racially with people of African descent, defined slaves as property, and established a system of "racial etiquette" designed to maintain a clear and permanent distinction between the free white inhabitants and their black slaves. Everywhere, this well-established system of racial slavery was thus based on "the permanent, violent domination of natally alienated and generally dishonored persons" defined primarily on the basis of color and without "social existence" outside the persons of their free owners. Along with the continuing importance of the institution of servitude, the powerful presence, wide diffusion, and—except in Nova Scotia and New Hampshire—expanding use of slavery in the 1760s and 1770s throughout colonial British America provides a vivid reminder of just how fundamentally exploitive that society was.

If the emerging society of late colonial British America was at once expansive, mobile, prosperous, increasingly more differentiated, and exploitive of its least fortunate members, it fulfilled many of the most sanguine hopes of the first settlers. . . .

Notwithstanding the "serene rustic image of self-sufficient communities" invoked by some historians to characterize colonial British America, no group of colonists, as Carole Shammas has shown, were "commercial primitives" in the sense that they were entirely cut off from the secular market society of this broader Atlantic commercial world. Very few households had the resources necessary to be self-sufficient and therefore had both to supplement "homegrown products with textiles, flour, butter, and meat bought from tradesmen, peddlars, and neighboring producers" and to function in an environment in which the prices that were almost always "attached to their labor and goods" were invariably "affected by regional, continental, and international markets." Even in the most isolated areas of colonial New England, Shammas has found, colonial Americans "fully participate[d] in" this emerging commercial world. . . . Indeed, the social depth and extent of British-American involvement in this consumer revolution provided a remarkable testimony to the breadth of economic well-being among colonists in all regions: the top two-thirds of the population participated in it, whereas only the top quarter did so in Britain.

In this emerging secular and commercial culture, the central orientation of people in the littoral became the achievement of personal independence, a state in which a man and his family and broader dependents could live "at ease" rather than in anxiety, in contentment rather than in want, in respectability rather than in meanness, and, perhaps most important, in freedom from the will and control of other men. On the eastern side of the Atlantic, in Britain and in Ireland, and in the confined spaces of the small Atlantic and Caribbean island colonies, the proportion of independent men in the total male population was small. But in the continental colonies, the opportunity to acquire land, an independent trade, or both was so wide as to put the achievement of independence within the grasp of most able-bodied, active, and enterprising free men. The prospect for "a very comfortable and independent subsistence" held out by promotional writers, land developers, and government authorities contributed throughout the colonial era to act as a powerful magnet in attracting settlers to new colonies and newly opening areas.

Moreover, although the achievement of genuine affluence and a gentle status was confined to a relatively small number of people, as it was in contemporary Britain, the comparatively widespread realization of independence by people whose beginnings were modest, a realization achieved mostly by the disciplined application of industry to the mastery of the soil, contributed to an equally broad diffusion of an expansive sense of self-worth throughout the independent, mostly landowning adult male population....

In this situation, the achievement and peaceful enjoyment of personal independence, the objective that had initially drawn so many of both the first settlers and later immigrants to the colonies, continued to be the most visible and powerful imperative in the emerging American culture, the principal aspiration and animating drive in the lives of colonists in all regions. The most popular cultural image in eighteenth-century British America was the biblical image of the independent farmer sitting contentedly and safely under his own shade trees in front of his own home in full view of his fields, his flocks, and his dependents, including slaves if he had them. This was precisely the image Thomas Jefferson evoked in the Declaration of Independence when he included among the inalienable rights of man not merely life and liberty but also the "pursuit of happiness."...

... [T]he people who created and perpetuated the new societies of colonial British America sought not merely personal independence as individuals and the welfare of their families but also the social goal of improved societies that would both guarantee the independence they hoped to achieve and enable them to enjoy its fruits. Indeed, demands and aspirations for improvement were nearly as prominent among settlers in these new societies as were those for independence and affluence.

Ubiquitous in the economic writers of early modern Britain, the language of improvement as it took shape in Britain primarily referred to schemes, devices, or projects through which the economic position of the nation might be advanced, the estates or fortunes of individuals might be bettered, or existing resources might be made more productive.... In the new and relatively undeveloped societies of colonial British America, ... the term *improvement* acquired a much wider meaning: it was used to describe a state of society that was far removed from the savagery associated with the native Indians. An *improved* society was one defined by a series of positive and negative juxtapositions. Not wild, barbaric, irregular, rustic, or crude, it was settled, cultivated, civilized, orderly, developed, and polite. The primary model for an improved society was the emerging and more settled, orderly, and coherent society of contemporary Britain. For new frontier settlements within the colonies, it was the older occupied areas along the seacoast. With re-creation and not innovation as their aim, colonial British Americans generally aspired to a fully developed market society with credit, commercial agriculture, slavery, and a rapid circulation of money and goods. They wanted a settled and hierarchical social structure with social distinctions ranging from the genteel down to the vulgar. In particular, they wanted a social structure that would enable successful independent and affluent people, in conformity with the long-standing traditions of Western civilization (and probably all other highly developed civilizations), to exploit dependent people. They desired authoritative, if not very obtrusive, political institutions that could facilitate their socioeconomic and cultural development and would be presided over by people whose very success in the private realm testified to their merit and capacity and gave them a legitimate claim to political leadership. They wanted vital traditional social institutions that would contribute to and stand as visible symbols of their improvement, including churches, schools, and towns. . . .

By the 1730s and 1740s in older colonies and by the 1740s and 1750s in the newer ones, both provincial and, except in the most recently settled areas, local politics were dominated by coherent, effective, acknowledged, and authoritative political elites with considerable social and economic power, extensive political experience, confidence in their capacity to govern, and—what crucially distinguished them from their European counterparts—broad public support. Second, they had viable governing institutions at both the local and provincial levels most of which were becoming more and more assimilated to those in metropolitan Britain, vigorous traditions of internal self-government, and extensive experience in coping with the socioeconomic and other problems peculiar to their own societies. Third, even though political participation was limited to white, independent, adult males, their political systems were almost certainly more inclusive and more responsive to public opinion than those of any other societies in the world at that time, and they were becoming more and more capable of permitting the resolution of conflict, absorbing new and diverse groups, and, as their recent histories had so amply attested, providing political stability in periods of rapid demographic, economic, and territorial expansion.

If the several colonial polities were becoming more expert, they were also becoming far more settled. By the mid-eighteenth century, levels of collective violence and civil disorder were ordinarily low, few colonies had outstanding issues that deeply divided the polity, society routinely accepted existing institutional and leadership structures, relations among the several branches and levels of government had been thoroughly regularized, rates of turnover among elected officials were low, changes in leadership followed an orderly process through regular constitutional channels without serious disruption of the polity, and factional and party strife was either being routinized or reduced to levels at which it was not dysfunctional within the political system. As was manifest in declining turnover among elected representatives to the colonial assemblies in most colonies, the electorate increasingly exhibited a passive and uncoerced deference toward the governing elite. With their attentions firmly concentrated on their own individual and family goals in the private realm, the vast bulk of the electorate seems, in ordinary times, to have had little interest in taking an active role in public life. Together, these developments brought a new stability and regularity to colonial political life in the three or four decades before 1760.

Notwithstanding these developments, the public realm everywhere remained small. Citizens expected little from government . . . . Indeed, possessing limited powers, colonial governments necessarily exerted only weak authority and were heavily dependent upon public opinion, which sharply limited the scope for action among political leaders. Government in these always potentially highly participatory polities was necessarily consensual. Always open to challenge from dissatisfied elements among the free population, the several polities of late colonial British America invariably contained a latent potential for widespread popular mobilization.

If many of the features of these emerging American political systems revealed a growing capacity for accommodation among increasingly differentiated and complex social populations within the several colonial polities, the same can be said for developments in other areas of cultural life. The societies of all regions of colonial British America remained predominantly English. But the substantial immigration of non-English groups after 1713 and, notwithstanding the strong predisposition of people from many of these groups to settle in communities of their own kind, the consequent intermingling of peoples of diverse cultural and national backgrounds and competing religious persuasions slowly edged people toward a habit of compromise and an enhanced capacity for the toleration and acceptance of ethnic, cultural, and religious diversity. At the same time, the overwhelming cultural preoccupation with the pursuit of individual and family happiness in the socioeconomic area seems everywhere to have weakened the impulse to try to enforce a coercive religious uniformity. . . .

Among the several colonial regions, there remained significant differences. At least on the continent, however, these regions were becoming increasingly alike during the generations immediately preceding the American Revolution. Over that period, a common developmental process produced a slow but powerful cultural and social convergence that mitigated the sharp variations that had distinguished the several regions of colonial British America from one another during the early generations of settlement. Out of this steady process of convergence emerged the beginnings of an American cultural order that was waiting to be defined during and immediately after the era of the American Revolution. . . .

Divergence in Four Colonial Cultures

DAVID HACKETT FISCHER

Exodus: The Four Great Migrations, 1629–1750

After 1629 the major folk movements began to occur. . . . [T]he first wave (1629–40) was an exodus of English Puritans who came mainly from the eastern counties and planted in Massachusetts a very special culture with unique patterns of speech and architecture, distinctive ideas about marriage

David Hackett Fischer, "Four British Folkways in America: The Origin and Persistence of Regional Culture in the United States," conclusion of *Albion's Seed* (New York: Oxford, 1989), excerpts from 785–788, 793–796, 803–820. Reprinted by permission of Oxford University Press.

and the family, nucleated settlements, congregational churches, town meetings, and a tradition of ordered liberty.

The second wave brought to Virginia a different set of English folkways, mainly from a broad belt of territory that extended from Kent and Devon north to Northamptonshire and Warwickshire. This culture was characterized by scattered settlements, extreme hierarchies of rank, strong oligarchies, Anglican churches, a highly developed sense of honor and an idea of hegemonic liberty.

The third wave (ca. 1675–1715) was the Friends' migration, which carried yet another culture from England's North Midlands to the Delaware Valley. It was founded on a Christian idea of spiritual equality, a work ethic of unusual intensity, a suspicion of social hierarchy, and an austerity which Max Weber called "worldly asceticism." It also preserved many elements of North Midland speech, architecture, dress and food ways. Most important, it deliberately created a pluralistic system of reciprocal liberty in the Delaware Valley.

The fourth great migration (1717–75) came to the backcountry from the borderlands of North Britain—an area which included the Scottish lowlands, the north of Ireland and England's six northern counties. These emigrants were of different ethnic stocks, but shared a common border culture which was unique in its speech, architecture, family ways and child-rearing customs. Its material culture was marked by extreme inequalities of condition, and its public life was dominated by a distinctive ideal of natural liberty.

Each of these four folk cultures in early America had a distinctive character which was closer to its popular reputation than to many academic "reinterpretations" in the twentieth century. The people in Puritan Massachusetts were in fact highly puritanical. They were not traditional peasants, modern capitalists, village communists, modern individualists, Renaissance humanists, Victorian moralists, neo-Freudian narcissists or prototypical professors of English literature. They were a people of their time and place who had an exceptionally strong sense of themselves, and a soaring spiritual purpose which has been lost beneath many layers of revisionist scholarship.

The first gentlemen of Virginia were truly cavaliers. They were not the pasteboard protagonists of Victorian fiction, or the celluloid heroes of *Gone with the Wind*. But neither were they self-made bourgeois capitalists, modern agro-businessmen, upwardly mobile yeomen or "plain folk." Most were younger sons of proud armigerous families with strong Royalist politics, a devout Anglican faith, decided rural prejudices, entrenched manorial ideals, exalted notions of their own honor and at least the rudiments of an Aristotelian education. The majority of Virginia's white population were indentured servants, landless tenants and poor whites—a degraded rural proletariat who had no hope of rising to the top of their society. Not a single ex-servant or son of a servant became a member of Virginia's House of Burgesses during the late seventeenth century. The mythical figures of Virginia cavaliers and poor whites were solidly founded in historical fact.

The culture of the Delaware Valley was dominated by British Quakers and German Pietists whose Christian beliefs had a special moral character.

Here again, their culture has been distorted by historical revisionists who have variously "reinterpreted" them as utopian cranks, manipulative materialists, secular pluralists and the "first modern Americans." The modernity of the Delaware Valley has been much exaggerated, and the primitive Christian roots of William Penn's "holy experiment" have too often been forgotten.

The backsettlers also possessed a strong and vibrant culture which also has been much misunderstood. They were not ancient Celts, or wild Scotch-Irish savages, or innocent children of nature. Neither were they rootless pluralists, incipient entrepreneurs, agents of the Edinburgh enlightenment or heralds of the New South. The majority, no matter whether northern Irish, lowland Scots or North Country English, shared a culture of high integrity which had been tempered in fire of the British borderlands. The more we learn by empirical research about these four cultures of British America, the more distinctive they appear from one another, and the closer to historical "myths" which they inspired.

British Origins: The Regional Factor

The origins of these cultures were highly complex, involving differences of British region, religion, rank, and generation, as well as of the American environment, and the process of migration. Let us briefly examine each of these determinants, beginning with British regions—not because this factor was more important than any other, but because it has been less clearly understood. . . .

Four historical regions in seventeenth-century Britain were specially important to this inquiry. The first of them lay in the east of England, and included the three peninsulae of East Anglia itself, eastern Lincolnshire and the northeastern fringe of Kent. The boundary of this territory ran through the old counties of Rutland, Huntingdon and Hertford. In the seventeenth century, this area was commonly called the "East" or "eastern England." With the addition of Kent it corresponded roughly to the area of the "Eastern Association" which supported Parliament in the English Civil War. This region produced approximately 60 percent of emigrants to Massachusetts.

A second historical region, which sent many sons to Virginia, was a broad belt of territory through the south of England, extending from Kent to Devon, and north as far as Warwick. It encompassed the ancient kingdom of Wessex and its Mercian protectorates—the realm of Alfred and Aethelred. This area had the least articulated sense of regional identity because it believed itself to be the heartland of the country—in Henry James's phrase, "midmost England, unmitigated England." Nevertheless, it had a cultural existence which was defined by its history, in ways that made it distinct from East Anglia, the North Country and the Celtic cultures of Wales and Cornwall to the west. Roughly 60 percent of Virginia gentlemen and servants came from this region.

A third historical region lay in the North Midlands of England. It included a broad belt of territory from Cheshire and Derbyshire north through Lancashire and the West Riding of Yorkshire to southern Cumbria. This area was called "the North Country" in the seventeenth century. Thus a Quaker named

John Crock wrote, "I was born in the North Country." Another wrote that "he heard of a people in the North of England, who preferred the light. . . ." And a third described Quakerism as "glad tidings brought out of the north." This area was the source of approximately 60 percent of the Quaker population which settled in the Delaware Valley.

The fourth historical region was an area which included the English counties of Westmorland, Cumberland, Northumberland, Durham, and the North Riding of Yorkshire, together with the southern counties of Scotland. As early as the fifteenth century this region was called the "border," or "borders," and its inhabitants called themselves "borderers." These people of Scotland and northern England, together with their transplanted cousins in Ulster, were very mixed in their ethnicity, but they shared a common culture which was shaped by the history of their region. More than 60 percent of settlers in the American backcountry were immigrants or the children of immigrants from northern Ireland, the lowlands of Scotland, and the six northern counties of England. . . .

British Origins: The Religious Factor

Of all the determinants which shaped the cultural character of British America, the most powerful was religion. During the seventeenth century, the English-speaking people were deeply divided by the great questions of the Protestant Reformation. These divisions in turn created a broad spectrum of English denominations in the New World.

The "right wing" of the British Reformation was the party of Anglican Episcopacy which favored an inclusive national church, a hierarchy of priests, compulsory church taxes and a union of church and crown. Its worship centered on liturgy and ritual, its theology became increasingly Arminian in the seventeenth century, and its creed was defined by the Book of Common Prayer. This denomination was specially strong in the south and west of England. It was destined to dominate Virginia for more than a century.

Next to the Episcopalians on Britain's spectrum of religious belief were Presbyterians. They also favored a broad national church, but one which was ruled by strong synods of ministers and elders rather than by bishops and priests. The theology of Presbyterianism was Calvinist; its worship centered on preaching and conversion. The Presbyterians were numerous in Northern Britain, where they made much use of evangelical field meetings and prayer meetings. They became very strong in the American backcountry.

Near the center were Congregationalists, who defined their position as the "middle way." Their church government was a mixed confederacy of independent congregations and weak synods. Their theology took a middle ground between Arminianism (which tended toward rationalism and free will) and Antinomianism (the dominion of the spirit). Their formal beliefs were defined by the Synod of Dort (1618–19) in the five points of Calvinism (total depravity, limited atonement, unconditional election, irresistible grace and the final perseverance of the saints)—a Christian creed of extreme austerity. This group was strong in the eastern counties of England. It founded the colonies of Massachusetts and Connecticut.

To the left of the Congregationalists were the Separatists, who believed in the autonomy of each congregation, and wished to separate themselves from the corruption of an unreformed national church. Their theology was broadly Calvinist, and their classical text was Robert Browne's *Reformation without Tarrying for Any* (1583). This denomination included the *Mayflower* Pilgrims who founded Plymouth Colony.

Farther left were various sects of Anabaptists, many of whom subscribed to the five points of Calvinism, but added a "sixth principle" that baptism should be restricted to regenerate Christians. Their theology stressed the working of the Holy Spirit more than the teaching of divine law. Their church was a fellowship in which worship was a sharing of the spirit of Grace. Most Baptists also believed in the separation of church and state, primarily to preserve the church from spiritual pollution. They founded the colony of Rhode Island.

Beyond the Baptists were the Quakers, who believed that Jesus died not merely for a chosen few but for everyone, and that a Holy Spirit called the Inner Light dwelled within all people. Their beliefs rose from the teachings of George Fox and received their classic statement in Robert Barclay's *Apology for the True Christian Religion*. Quakers rejected the legitimacy of established churches, ordained clergy and formal liturgy. Their meetings for worship centered upon the movement of the spirit. This denomination first appeared in the North Midlands of England. It founded the colonies of West Jersey, Pennsylvania and Delaware.

Because religion touched so many parts of life in the era of the reformation, these denominational divisions created deep cultural differences which have survived in American regions long after their original purposes have been lost.

British Origins: The Factor of Generations

The four migrations came not only from different regions, ranks and religions, but also from different generations. The key concept here is that of an *historical* generation—not a demographic cohort but a cultural group whose identity is formed by great events. In the turbulence of the twentieth century, for example, everyone recognizes the "generation of the Great Depression," the "generation of World War II," and the "generation of the '60s." Seventeenth-century England had similar historical generations, which were defined by the same events that set the major folk migrations in motion.

Each of these migrations created a culture which preserved something of the moment when it was born. The Puritans settled Massachusetts within a period of eleven years from 1629 to 1640—an epoch in English history which is remembered by Whig historians as the "eleven years' tyranny." This was the time when Charles I tried to rule without a Parliament and Archbishop William Laud attempted to purge the Anglican Church of Puritans. The great constitutional and religious issues of this epoch were carried to the Puritan colonies and became central to the culture of New

England—persisting as intellectual obsessions long after they had been forgotten in the mother country.

A large part of Virginia's migration of cavaliers and indentured servants occurred between 1649 and 1660, an unstable era of English history called the interregnum. In this period of disorder the dominant elite was an oligarchy of English Puritans, and their victims included a group of defeated Royalists, some of whom carried to Virginia a culture which was defined not merely by their rank and party but also by their generation—in its fascination with constitutional questions, its obsession with honor, and its contempt for the arts of peace. The culture of America's tidewater south was to retain these characteristics long after England had moved beyond them.

The Friends' migration to the Delaware Valley happened mainly in the years from 1675 to 1689. This was part of an historical epoch which began with the Restoration, and continued through the reigns of Charles II (1660–85) and his Catholic brother James II (1685–88). In this period of English history, the great questions were about how people of different beliefs could live in peace together. That question was central to the cultural history of the Delaware colonies, and remained so for many years.

Another period of English history followed the Glorious Revolution of 1688, when a pattern of political stability formed "as suddenly as water becomes ice," in historian J. H. Plumb's words. The government of England passed firmly into the hands of an oligarchy of country gentlemen. This solution created new problems which concerned the relationship between England's governing elite and others—in particular, the people of Ireland, Scotland, America, the London mob and the rural poor. Violent conflicts set in motion yet another wave of emigration which brought to America the great question of whether the rights of English gentlemen belonged to other people. These issues took root in the American interior, where they survive even to our own time. All four folk cultures of Anglo-America preserved the dominant themes in English history during the years when they began.

American Development: The Environment

British culture was not the only determinant of regional differences. The American environment also played an important role—not by "breaking down" or "dissolving" European culture (as the frontier thesis suggested) but by more complex material pressures which modified European cultures in some respects and reinforced them in others.

In New England, the Puritans selected a rigorous environment which was well suited to their purposes. The climate (colder and more changeable than today) proved exceptionally healthy to Europeans, but high mortality among African immigrants reinforced a Puritan ambivalence toward the growth of slavery. The configuration of New England's coastline and the distribution of soil resources in small pockets of alluvial fertility encouraged town settlement. The Indians of Massachusetts Bay had been nearly destroyed by disease before the Puritans arrived; conflicts remained at a comparatively low level for nearly fifty years except during the Pequot War.

The Virginians encountered a very different environment. The Chesapeake Bay, with its 6,500 miles of tidal shoreline, its hundreds of rivers and creeks, and its abundance of good soil, encouraged scattered settlement and plantation agriculture. The climate (about the same as today) produced bountiful staple crops. But the Chesapeake estuary was unhealthy, and European death rates were twice as high as in New England. Africans had lower mortality rates than in the northern colonies, and slavery developed rapidly from the late seventeenth century. The large Indian population of the Powhatan Confederacy strongly resisted English settlement, with much bloody fighting.

The Delaware Valley offered yet a third set of environmental conditions. This area proved more salubrious than the Chesapeake, but less so than Massachusetts. Its climate was mild and its soil endowment was the richest of the eastern colonies, producing crop yields above all other coastal regions for three centuries. An abundance of mineral resources and a fall line only a few miles from the sea supported rapid industrial development. The Delaware Indians were not warlike in the early years of settlement. Altogether this environment was perfectly suited to the purposes of the Quakers, as they well knew when they chose to settle there. For many years it supported their "holy experiment" in prosperity and peace.

The southern backcountry was a densely forested highland region of enormous proportions. Markets were distant and travel difficult, but the abundance of land and water encouraged the rapid growth of family farming and herding. The climate was comparatively mild and healthy. The Indians were numerous and very hostile to European settlement. The backcountry became a cockpit of international rivalry, and was ravaged by major wars in every generation from 1689 to 1815. The climate, resources and dangers of this American environment were well matched to the culture of the British borderlands. . . .

American Development: Immigration and Race

. . . British America's voluntary migration encouraged religious diversity rather than uniformity. It also allowed like-minded colonists of various sects to settle together and to transplant their own folkways to the New World.

Immigration also promoted regional development in another way. For many years, the American colonies effectively became their own gatekeepers. They were able to control the process of immigration themselves, and did so in very different ways.

The Puritan colonies stubbornly enforced a policy of strict exclusion despite imperial opposition. The homogeneity of New England's population was not an historical accident; it arose from the religious purposes and social values of a regional culture.

The founders of Pennsylvania had very different ideas about immigration. William Penn and the Quaker elite of the colony made a special effort to attract European Protestants whose values were compatible with their own. English Quakers, German Pietists and Swiss Anabaptists all believed deeply in the doctrine of the inner light, religious freedom, the ethic of work and the evil of violence. The immigration policy of the Quakers expanded the community of Christian values beyond the boundaries of their own sect, and deliberately encouraged a diversity of national stocks in the Delaware Valley.

The rulers of Virginia adopted still a third immigration policy. Puritans and Quakers were not welcome; many were banished or driven out. But the Virginians actively recruited a servile underclass to support their manorial ideal, first by bringing in large numbers of English servants, and then by importing African slaves. Their object was not merely to solve a problem of labor scarcity (which might have been done in many other ways) but to do so in a manner consistent with their hierarchical values.

The backsettlers were not able to control immigration to the southern highlands in any formal way. But local neighborhoods had other methods of deciding who would go or stay. The old folk custom of "hating out" was used when necessary. The prevailing cultural climate also had a similar effect; in the late eighteenth and early nineteenth century, for example, Quakers and Congregationalists left the southern backcountry, moving north to a more congenial cultural environment.

Local control of immigration thus tended to reinforce cultural differences between regions. Even as most parts of British America became more diverse during the eighteenth century, they did so in very different ways, according to purposes and values of their founders.

One effect of immigration was to change the racial composition of the four major regions of British America. African slaves were imported to every colony, but in very different proportions. In many parts of New England blacks were never more than 1 percent of the population before 1760; in some southern coastal counties, blacks were more than a majority by that date.

To understand the relationship between race and regional culture in British America, one must study carefully the timing and sequence of historical change. An important and neglected fact about race slavery in British America is that it developed very slowly. Africans did not begin to arrive in large numbers until the late seventeenth century. The presence of blacks did not begin to have a major cultural impact on British America until the late seventeenth and early eighteenth century. Then, the impact was profound. The problem of race relations moved rapidly to the center of cultural history in the plantation colonies. African folkways also began to transform the language and culture of Europeans, and the "peculiar institution" of slavery created new folkways of its own. . . .

The Expansion of Four Regional Cultures

By the year 1770 the four folk cultures had taken firm root in British America. All expanded rapidly. Emigrants from Massachusetts founded colonies with similar cultures in Connecticut, New Hampshire, southern Maine, eastern Vermont, Long Island, East Jersey, upstate New York and northern Ohio. The culture of tidewater Virginia expanded into southern Maryland, southern Delaware, coastal North Carolina and west beyond the mountains to parts of Kentucky. The folkways of the Delaware Valley spread through West Jersey, eastern Pennsylvania, parts of northeastern Maryland and central Ohio. After 1740 the borderers of North Britain rapidly occupied the Appalachian highlands from Pennsylvania to Georgia, and moved west to the Mississippi.

The people of these four cultures shared many traits in common. Nearly all spoke the English language, lived by British laws, and cherished their ancestral liberties. Most dwelled in nuclear households, and had broadly similar patterns of marital fertility. Their prevailing religion was Christian and Protestant. Their lands were privately owned according to peculiar British ideas of property which were adopted throughout much of the United States. But in other ways these four British cultures were very different from one another. The more we learn empirically about them, the less similar they appear to be. . . .

Other Colonial Cultures

The four major cultures did not embrace all of British America. Other cultural areas also existed. Some were of considerable size, though smaller than the major regions. The largest of these other cultures was New Netherland, which occupied much of the Hudson Valley. In 1700 Dutch burghers and boers were two-thirds of the population in Dutchess and Ulster counties, three-quarters in Orange County, five-sixths in Kings County and nine-tenths in Albany. They also colonized part of East Jersey, where as late as 1790 they were 75 percent of the population in Bergen County, and 80 percent in Somerset County.

This was a very conservative culture. Its old-fashioned Dutch dialect survived even into the mid-nineteenth century. Its architecture remained distinctive for broad barns, hay barracks, stepgabled town houses, and low, narrow farmhouses with half doors. Settlement patterns retained a special character, with homes built in distinctive irregular clusters around a reformed church. Rates of internal migration were exceptionally low, and Dutch households had a different demographic profile from those of English neighbors, with fewer children and more slaves. In 1738, most Dutch families in King's County were slave-owners.

This culture developed its own special ways of dealing with other ethnic groups. It combined formal toleration, social distance and inequality in high degree. The result was an ethnic pluralism that became more atomistic than in the Delaware Valley and more hierarchical than in New England. The peculiar texture of life in New York City today still preserves qualities which existed in seventeenth-century New Amsterdam—and Old Amsterdam as well.

The culture of New Netherland did not expand far beyond its original boundaries. Its population remained small. In 1664, only 7,000 Dutch settlers (and 3,000 non-Dutch) were living in New Netherland. By 1790 only about 98,000 people of Dutch descent were living in the United States—less than one-tenth the population of New England, and a small fraction of the other major regional populations.

Another distinctive colonial culture developed on the coast of South Carolina. Some of its founding families came from the West Indies; others were

French Huguenots, and more than a few were emigrants from tidewater Virginia. Three-quarters of the low-country population in 1790 were slaves who came mostly from the Congo basin and the coast of Angola. These groups rapidly developed their own unique customs and institutions, which were closer to the Caribbean colonies than to the Chesapeake. Speech ways were heavily influenced by the "Gullah" (Angola) dialect of the black majority. Building ways were a unique amalgam of Caribbean, French, African and English elements. Patterns of settlement were marked by the highest level of urbanization in colonial America: nearly 25 percent of low-country whites lived in Charleston. The wealth of its white families was the greatest in the colonies (£450 in 1740), and highly concentrated in a few hands. The annual rhythm of life was regulated by a pattern of transhumance that did not exist in other mainland colonies. This area became a distinct cultural region, but it never developed into a major cultural hearth. As late as 1790 less than 29,000 whites lived in the South Carolina low country, compared with more than 300,000 whites in eastern Virginia and 450,000 in the southern back settlements (of whom 112,000 were in the South Carolina upcountry alone).

Yet another colonial culture developed in North Carolina's Cape Fear Valley, where Highland Scots began to arrive circa 1732. Many followed after the '45 Rebellion, and by 1776 their numbers were nearly as large as the white population in the South Carolina low country. Other ethnic groups also settled in the Cape Fear Valley, but so dominant were highlanders that Gaelic came to be spoken in this region even by people who were not Scots. There is a story of a newly arrived Highland lady who heard two men speaking in Gaelic:

> Assuming by their speech that they must inevitably be fellow Highlanders, she came nearer, only to discover that their skin was black. Then she knew that her worst foreboding about the climate of the South was not unfounded and cried in horror, "A Dhia nan fras, am fas sinn vile mar sin?" (O God of mercy, are we all going to turn black like that?)

Even in the twentieth century, the Cape Fear people sent to Scotland for ministers who were required to wear the kilt, play the pipes, and preach in Gaelic. . . .

Rhythms of Regional Development

Every regional culture had its own history, which unfolded in its own way. But all of them passed through a similar sequence of stages which created a powerful rhythm in colonial history. The first stage was the transit of culture from Britain to America, in which individual actors played decisive roles. In Massachusetts, for example, Puritan leaders such as John Winthrop and John Cotton shaped the future of their region when they decided to bring the charter of the Massachusetts Bay Company to the New World, to define church membership in a rigorous way, to create a standard model for town government, and to block the growth of a Puritan aristocracy in New England. In Virginia, Sir William Berkeley made many critical decisions when he recruited a colonial elite, encouraged the growth of slavery, drove out Puritans and Quakers, and discouraged schools and printing. In Pennsylvania, William Penn's decisions transformed the history of a region—in the design of local institutions, the recruitment of German immigrants, and the content of libertarian laws. In the southern highlands the backcountry "ascendancy" played a seminal role. All of these cultural leaders gave a direction to regional development.

The second stage was a cultural crisis of great intensity. It always began as an internal conflict among immigrant elites who supported the founding purposes of their colony, but disagreed on issues of authority, order, and individual autonomy. In Massachusetts, the crisis came with the Separatist challenge of Roger Williams (1635–36) and the Antinomian Crisis of Anne Hutchinson (1638–39). In Virginia, the critical period was that of Bacon's Rebellion (1676) and the violent repression that followed (1676–77). Pennsylvania's crisis occurred in the 1690s, when William Penn briefly lost control of the colony (1692–94) and the Quaker colonists were deeply divided by the "Keithian schism" (1692). The critical time in the back settlements was the Regulation (1768–70). In each case a new clarity was brought to regional cultures by these events.

These crises were followed by a period of cultural consolidation which occurred in Massachusetts during the 1640s, in Virginia during the 1680s, in Pennsylvania during the early decades of the eighteenth century, and in the backcountry during the late eighteenth century. In every case, the dominant culture of each region was hardened into institutions which survived for many years. In Massachusetts, for example, courts, churches, towns, schools, and militia all were given their definitive shape in laws which were passed within the span of a few years, mostly in the period from 1636 to 1648. Something similar happened in most other colonies at comparable stages in their development.

This period of consolidation was followed by a complex and protracted process of cultural devolution. In New England, that trend occurred in the half-century from 1650 to 1700, when Puritans became Yankees. It happened in Virginia from 1690 to 1750, when Royalists became Whigs. It took place in the Delaware Valley during the transition from the second to the third stage of Quakerism, and the development of a more inward-looking faith in an increasingly pluralistic society. In the backcountry, it happened as backsettlers evolved into frontiersmen. In every instance, founding purposes were lost, but institutions were preserved and regional identities were given new life.

FURTHER READING

Charles M. Andrews, *The Colonial Period of American History,* 4 vols. (1934–1938)
Bernard Bailyn, *Voyagers to the West: A Passage in the Peopling of America on the Eve of the Revolution* (1986)

———— and Philip D. Morgan, *Strangers Within the Realm: Cultural Margins of the First British Empire* (1991)

Angus Calder, *Revolutionary Empire: The Rise of the English-Speaking Empires from the Fifteenth Century to the 1780s* (1981)

Jack P. Greene and J. R. Pole, eds., *Colonial British America: Essays in the New History of the Early Modern Era* (1984)

John J. McCusker and Russell R. Menard, *The Economy of British America, 1607–1789* (1985)